COLD WAR STATESMEN CONFRONT THE BOMB

Cold War Statesmen Confront the Bomb

Nuclear Diplomacy since 1945

EDITED BY

John Lewis Gaddis
Philip H. Gordon
Ernest R. May

AND

Jonathan Rosenberg

OXFORD

UNIVERSITY PRESS

OXFORD

UNIVERSITY PRESS

Great Clarendon Street, Oxford OX2 6DP

Oxford University Press is a department of the University of Oxford.
It furthers the University's objective of excellence in research, scholarship,
and education by publishing worldwide in

Oxford New York

Athens Auckland Bangkok Bogotá Buenos Aires Calcutta
Cape Town Chennai Dar es Salaam Delhi Florence Hong Kong Istanbul
Karachi Kuala Lumpur Madrid Melbourne Mexico City Mumbai
Nairobi Paris São Paulo Singapore Taipei Tokyo Toronto Warsaw

with associated companies in Berlin Ibadan

Oxford is a registered trade mark of Oxford University Press
in the UK and in certain other countries

Published in the United States
by Oxford University Press Inc., New York

British Library Cataloguing in Publication Data

Cold War statesmen confront the bomb: nuclear diplomacy since 1945 /
edited by John Lewis Gaddis . . . [et al.].
Includes bibliographical references and index.
1. Nuclear arms control. 2. Cold War. 3. United States—Foreign
relations—Soviet Union 4. Soviet Union—Foreign relations—United
States I. Gaddis, John Lewis.
JZ5665.C65 1999 327.47073'09045—dc21 98-49340
ISBN 0-19-829468-9

1 3 5 7 9 10 8 6 4 2

Typeset by Hope Services (Abingdon) Ltd.
Printed in Great Britain
on acid-free paper by
Bookcraft Ltd.,
Midsomer Norton, Somerset

CONTENTS

ACKNOWLEDGEMENTS

The editors and contributors gratefully acknowledge the assistance of the Nuclear History Program, which supported the initial research upon which these essays are based, and the Contemporary History Institute at Ohio University, where they were first presented. We would also like to thank Helga Haack of the International Institute for Strategic Studies and Michael Spirtas of US CREST for their help in preparing the essays for publication, as well as Dominic Byatt and Amanda Watkins at the Oxford University Press.

John Lewis Gaddis
Philip H. Gordon
Ernest R. May
Jonathan Rosenberg

NOTES ON THE CONTRIBUTORS

S. David Broscious received a Ph.D. in History from Ohio University.

Andrew P. N. Erdmann is completing a Ph.D. in History from Harvard University and is currently a Peace Scholar, United States Institute of Peace.

John Lewis Gaddis is Robert Lovett Professor of History at Yale University. He is the author of several books on the Cold War, including most recently *We Now Know: Rethinking Cold War History*.

Philip H. Gordon is a Director of European Affairs at the National Security Council in Washington, DC. He has previously held teaching and research posts at the International Institute for Strategic Studies in London and the Johns Hopkins University School of Advanced International Studies in Washington, DC. His previous books include *A Certain Idea of France: French Security Policy and the Gaulist Legacy*. The views expressed in this chapter are the author's own and do not necessarily reflect those of the US government.

Hope M. Harrison is Assistant Professor of Government and Law at Lafayette College, Easton, Pennsylvania. She has held research posts at the Kennan Institute for Advanced Russian Studies, the Woodrow Wilson International Center for Scholars, Washington, DC, and the Norwegian Nobel Institute, Oslo, Norway.

Ernest R. May is Charles Warren Professor of American History at Harvard University. He is the author of numerous publications including *The Making of the Monroe Doctrine* and, most recently, *The Kennedy Tapes: Inside the White House during the Cuban Missile Crisis* and *Rethinking International Relations*.

Annette Messemer was a visiting student at the Fletcher School of Law and Diplomacy at Tufts University from 1990 to 1992.

John Mueller is Professor of Political Science and Film Studies, Director, Dance Film Archive; and Director, Watson Center for the Study of International Peace and Cooperation, at the University of Rochester. His books include *Retreat from Doomsday: The Obsolescence of Major War*.

Philip Nash teaches History at Raymond Walters College of the University of Cincinnati. He is also author of *The Other Missiles of October: Eisenhower, Kennedy, and the Jupiters, 1957–63*.

Jonathan Rosenberg received a Ph.D. in History from Harvard University. He is currently Assistant Professor of History at Florida Atlantic University and is completing a study of the relationship between world affairs and the US civil rights movement in the twentieth century, to be published by Princeton University Press.

Neal Rosendorf is a Ph.D. candidate in History at Harvard University.

Shu Guang Zhang is Professor of History of US Foreign Relations at the University of Maryland. He has written two books, *Deterrence and Strategic Culture, Chinese–American Confrontations 1949–58,* and *Mao's Military Romanticism, China and the Korean War.*

Vladislav M. Zubok is a visiting fellow at the National Security Archive, a non-government centre and library of declassified documents at George Washington University, and is co-author of the prize-winning book *Inside the Kremlin's Cold War.*

1

Introduction

ERNEST R. MAY

PRESIDENT Harry S. Truman is remembered, among many other things, for being the first—and so far the only—political leader to use nuclear weapons. Whether Truman had weighed the pros and cons or simply did not intervene to halt long-contemplated operations has been debated for decades. Whatever the case, after US aircraft dropped atomic bombs on Hiroshima and Nagasaki, Truman did order that the single remaining bomb not be used against a third Japanese city. In a diary note on a cabinet meeting held the day after the Nagasaki bombing, Secretary of Commerce Henry A. Wallace wrote that Truman 'said the thought of wiping out another 100,000 people was too horrible. He didn't like the idea of killing, as he said, "all those kids".'[1]

In his first major policy speech after the Japanese surrender, Truman said:

The discovery of the means of releasing atomic energy . . . may some day prove to be more revolutionary in the development of human society than the invention of the wheel, the use of metals, or the steam or internal combustion engine. Never in history has society been confronted with a power so full of potential danger and at the same time so full of promise for the future of man and for the peace of the world.[2]

Winston Churchill, who was Britain's Prime Minister until just before Hiroshima and Nagasaki, had had a hand in the highly secret atomic weapons programme from its inception, five years before Hiroshima. He was thus far ahead of Truman, who had not been told of the programme until April 1945, when the death of Franklin Roosevelt made him President instead of Vice-President. Yet Churchill's expression of awe matched Truman's. When told of the immense yield of the test bomb exploded at Alamogordo, New Mexico, a month before Hiroshima, Churchill said, 'This atomic bomb is the Second Coming in wrath.'[3] Nine years later, after the far more powerful hydrogen bomb had been proof-tested, Churchill said in his last great speech in the House of Commons:

A curious paradox has emerged. Let me put it simply. After a certain point has been passed, it may be said, the worse things get the better. The broad effect of the latest developments is to spread almost indefinitely and at least to a vast extent the area of mortal danger. . . . Here again we see the value of deterrents, immune against surprise and well understood by all persons on both sides—I repeat on both sides—who have the power to control events. . . .

Then it may well be that we shall, by a process of sublime irony, have reached a stage in this story where safety will be the sturdy child of terror, and survival the twin brother of annihilation.[4]

Soviet dictator Joseph Stalin at first minimized the atomic bomb. 'Atomic bombs are meant to frighten those with weak nerves,' he declared, 'but they cannot decide the fate of wars since atomic bombs are quite insufficient for that.'[5] Though Churchill and Roosevelt had kept the bomb programme secret from him, Stalin had learned of it from his scientists and his spies. Even while straining to fight the Germans and even though assuming that a workable atomic bomb was years off, Stalin committed scarce resources to an atomic bomb project of his own. After Hiroshima, he committed huge new resources to a panic effort to develop a bomb, even though, at the time, he saw desperate need for those resources for post-war reconstruction and security. Once this effort succeeded, Stalin voiced respect for the bomb's potential, even if never awe comparable to Truman's or Churchill's. He is recorded as expressing satisfaction with the Soviet nuclear test of 1949 by observing: 'If we had been late with the atomic bomb by a year or year and a half, then we perhaps would have had it "tested" on ourselves.'[6]

Countless others voiced comparable wonderment. The cultural historian Paul Boyer has shown how, after Hiroshima, poets and writers in the United States struggled to express their sense of the dawn of an entirely new and terrifying age. Hermann Hagedorn, who had written adoring biographies of Theodore Roosevelt and of Roosevelt's fellow 'Rough Rider', General Leonard Wood, penned a despairing epic poem, entitled 'The Bomb That Fell on America', saying that the Hiroshima and Nagasaki bombs

Erased no church, vaporized no public building . . . did not dissolve their bodies,
But it dissolved something important to the greatest of them, and the least.
What it dissolved were their links with the past and with the future.
It made the earth, that seemed so solid, Main Street, that seemed so well-paved, a kind
  of vast jelly, quivering and dividing underfoot.[7]

The historian of science Spencer Weart has assembled evidence of how nuclear fission and thermonuclear fusion, the keys to the atomic and hydrogen bombs, became subjects around which men and women rewove ancient myths of alchemy and witchcraft, doom and deliverance. For millions upon millions, the symbols of the atomic age were the giant ants of the 1954 movie, 'Them!', or the monsters that gave titles to movies such as 'Godzilla' and 'The Beast from 20,000 Fathoms'. Weart writes:

the new radioactive horrors were descendants of the clay golem and the alchemist's chaotic mass. Therefore, they may well have had the same terrifying meaning: violation of forbidden secrets punished by loss of true life and feeling, a takeover by the most inhuman and bestial parts of oneself, a wrong turning in the attempt at rebirth.[8]

The phrase 'nuclear revolution' became commonplace.

In his arresting book, *Retreat from Doomsday*, the political scientist John Mueller questions whether, in international relations, nuclear weapons actually had revolutionary effects.[9] In his view, the British publicist Norman Angell had it basically right when he wrote in *The Great Illusion* that industrial, technological, and institutional evolution had rendered large-scale war obsolete.[10] Angell's timing was bad. His book came out just prior to the outbreak of World War I. But his logic, Mueller thinks, was sound. The awful destructiveness of World War I simply proved his point. Absent the historical accident of Hitler, Mueller also contends, there would have been no World War II. For developed countries, Mueller argues, large-scale war had already become a barbarous anachronism akin to duelling and slavery. Nuclear weapons had little to do with this change; they were, in Mueller's words, 'essentially irrelevant'.

The essays in this volume bring together evidence of how ten Cold War statesmen thought about nuclear weapons, especially at moments when they had to contemplate setting in motion chains of events that might present them with a clear choice of using or not using such weapons. The essays deal not only with Truman, Churchill, and Stalin but with Truman's immediate successors: Dwight D. Eisenhower and John F. Kennedy; Stalin's successor, Nikita Khrushchev; Eisenhower's Secretary of State, John Foster Dulles; and three leaders of other nations: France's Charles de Gaulle, Germany's Konrad Adenauer, and China's Mao Zedong.

These essays aim to promote debate about John Mueller's thesis. They do not pretend to test his propositions in any remotely scientific way. There are logical grounds for questioning whether historical evidence can ever be used to test propositions about statecraft.[11] In any event, Mueller is sensible enough not to pretend that his propositions lend themselves to empirical verification or falsification. He simply puts forward a line of reasoning which has some internal coherence and which gains some plausibility with each additional year of what John Lewis Gaddis has labelled the 'long peace'—the half-century and more after World War II marked by no armed conflict among major powers.[12] The question for a reader of this book is whether evidence regarding ten key statesmen of the first decade or two of that era seems to match Mueller's line of reasoning or to match better the more conventional reasoning captured in the phrase, 'nuclear revolution' (and in political scientist Elspeth Rostow's remark that the atomic bomb should have received the Nobel Peace Prize[13])—that dread of nuclear war, not of war *per se*, transformed the calculus that had governed inter-state or international relations ever since states and nations came into being.

As the reader will discern, these Cold War statesmen appeared to think that nuclear weapons were revolutionary in character. They invoked the awful power of these weapons as a reason either for caution on their own part or for expecting caution on the part of others. But Mueller can rejoin that this was rationalization, explaining choices that would have been the same, absent nuclear weapons, and that could have been equally well rationalized by reference to Passchendaele or the Blitz or Stalingrad or Dresden or the fire-bombing of Tokyo.

A reader's conclusion as to whether nuclear weapons really mattered or were 'essentially irrelevant' will probably turn less on the particulars in these essays than on pre-existing presumptions. The editors and authors doubt that anyone who starts this book inclined to agree with Mueller will put it down convinced that Mueller was wrong. We are even more doubtful that any reader initially disposed to question Mueller's arguments will come to our final pages concluding that, after all, Mueller was right. What the book does do is to present evidence challenging readers to examine more closely their own reasoning about the role and effects of nuclear weapons during the first twenty years of the Cold War.

This introduction suggests some questions that readers may want to put to themselves as they try to figure out how these essays on disparate individuals connect with one another and how the accumulating evidence bears on the central question of the role of nuclear weapons in the 'long peace.' Asking the same questions about each of the ten statesmen may help readers not only to frame their own conclusions more precisely but also possibly to note and probe inconsistencies in their own thinking or in that of the editors and authors. The first questions relate simply to categorization of data about these men. The second set of questions concerns suppositions about how the individuals' opinions took form and changed or did not change. The third and final set relate to historical causation—whether and to what extent individual beliefs concerning nuclear weapons could have influenced decisions or events.

Anything more than a sketchy summary of the range of possible opinions regarding nuclear weapons would be useless. The literature analysing alternative nuclear strategies is as abundant as—and rather resembles—literature on transubstantiation. Moreover, much of this literature is genuinely scientific in the sense that it has progressively generated new research programmes subject at least to logical truth tests if not to tests by experimentation.[14] All that is necessary here is a rudimentary catalogue of views that might have been held or voiced by these ten statesmen regarding the potential usability or non-usability of nuclear weapons.

At one extreme, the words or implied words of any one of these statesmen can be taken as asserting that nuclear weapons were simply new weapons of war. In an 'as-told-to' autobiography, General Curtis E. LeMay, the architect of America's Strategic Air Command, asked why it was any worse 'to kill people with a nuclear bomb than to kill people by busting their heads with rocks'.[15]

At the other extreme, the statesman can be understood to say or imply that nuclear weapons were unusable in any circumstances. This appears to have been the private view of Kennedy's successor, Lyndon Johnson. As presidential scholar Richard Neustadt recalls, Johnson claimed to have had a recurrent dream. In the dream, he would wake up in the night, pick up his red telephone, and say, 'Secretary of Defense, you there? Joint Chiefs, you there? CinCSAC, you there? This is your Pres-i-dent. I've been tossing and turning, and I've decided that we've got to hit the Russians with all our A-bombs and H-bombs. So I'm putting my thumb on the button. I'm mashing it down.' Johnson would then stop and say, 'And do you know what they say to me? They say, "F*** you, Mr. Pres-i-dent".'[16] In a characteristic way, Johnson was saying that no statesman would order, and no rational public servants would execute, a nuclear strike.

As the reader will see, all the statesmen treated in this book displayed ambivalence with regard to nuclear weapons and nuclear war. At one time or another, each spoke or wrote of nuclear weapons as weapons that might actually be used and yet, at some other time, spoke of nuclear war as impossible or unthinkable.

Konrad Adenauer is the one figure in the book who controlled no nuclear arsenal. He was also arguably the one whose country was most sure to be destroyed if nuclear war actually occurred. This makes it not surprising that, in a 1953 speech, he approached the stance later taken by Lyndon Johnson. 'Ultimately', he said, 'the development of the bomb will destroy war itself.'[17] But, four years later, Adenauer made another speech in which he noted that there were big nuclear weapons and small—or tactical—nuclear weapons. Adenauer said: 'Tactical atomic weapons are basically nothing but the further development of artillery. . . . They are after all practically normal weapons.'[18] (At the time—1957—the smallest tactical nuclear warhead had explosive power approximately one-quarter that of the Hiroshima bomb. Many had warheads several times as powerful as either the Hiroshima or the Nagasaki bomb.[19])

Eisenhower seemed equally self-contradictory. Late in his presidency, he would fume at proposals for new nuclear weapons, saying that nuclear war was 'preposterous'. He said that nuclear war would obliterate the Northern Hemisphere. But he had begun his presidency by insisting that his advisers consider use of nuclear weapons to end the stalemated war in Korea, and in March 1955, during the first crisis focused on the Chinese offshore islands, Quemoy and Matsu, he answered a press conference question by saying of nuclear weapons: 'I can see no reason why they shouldn't be used just exactly as you would use a bullet.'[20]

The extremes—the positions of LeMay and Lyndon Johnson and those of Adenauer and Eisenhower in the statements just quoted—fit comfortably with John Mueller's argument. If nuclear weapons are thought to be indistinguishable from other weapons, then they cannot be credited with any peculiar role in preventing war. If the destructiveness of some nuclear weapons is the key to their role as deterrents, then the 'long peace' seems due to fear of the destructiveness of war, not necessarily to nuclear weapons as such. If, on the other hand, nuclear weapons are thought to be totally unusable, then, again, their existence cannot provide the major explanation for there being no large-scale war. To borrow Denis Healey's phrase, it requires at least a 'microscopic belief' that nuclear weapons might be used to invest them with deterrent effects.

Hence, when reviewing the opinions of these ten statesmen, readers may want to note where their opinions seem to lie, at any given moment, on a spectrum of positions between those of LeMay and Lyndon Johnson. It may even be useful if the reader keeps in mind the crude diagram which appears as Figure 1, for only opinions that can be placed somewhere inside the semicircle A–B–C imply belief that nuclear weapons are, in and of themselves, deterrents to any move toward war. Opinions anywhere around the fringe outside that semicircle can be interpreted as implying that nuclear weapons do not have such centrality in the statesman's thinking.

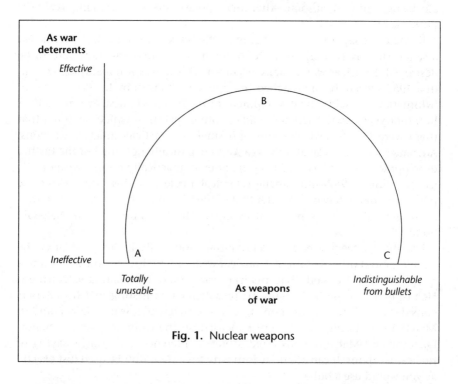

Fig. 1. Nuclear weapons

About the literal interpretation of any statesman's words, readers should be in rough agreement. There is not much ambiguity in the description of nuclear weapons as susceptible to being 'used just exactly as you would use a bullet' or of nuclear war as 'preposterous'. As to whether a statesman really meant what he said, there can be a good deal of argument. The chapters on Adenauer and Eisenhower go into some detail about the circumstances surrounding the utterances quoted above. Readers may easily conclude that Adenauer, Eisenhower, or others were not necessarily expressing their actual beliefs but were speaking with an eye to effects on particular audiences at particular moments. Even when Eisenhower urged his inner circle to consider using nuclear weapons in Korea, he can be viewed as intending only to force consideration of the possibility. Inwardly, he may have been resolved not to use nuclear weapons because he viewed them as different in kind from other weapons.

Here, also, the reader must take into account, at least in a rudimentary way, some of that logic-chopping that makes nuclear strategy resemble the more esoteric branches of theology. For the essence of nuclear deterrence was to establish some degree of credibility for an inherently incredible threat. And one way of creating such an illusion was to talk about escalation from one level of conflict to another. The reader is challenged therefore not only to note what these statesmen said but to look underneath their words to try to detect whether, at any given moment, they seem actually to have thought nuclear war sufficiently possible and sufficiently frightful so that the prospect weighed heavily on their policy choices.

This brings us to the second set of questions, the purpose of which is to highlight changes that may have taken place over time (or not taken place) in how these statesmen thought about nuclear weapons. Mueller's thesis supposes collective long-term learning. His time-scale is Darwinian. It took many generations for civilizations to develop norms against duelling and slavery and, in his view, large-scale war. The nuclear revolution thesis supposes shorter-term learning—that the shock of Hiroshima or, if not that, of the first thermonuclear tests produced the effect which both theses seek to explain—the half-century of the 'long peace'. So a reader who wants to think hard about these competing theses may wish to note how, in differing ways, the sketches of these ten statesmen answer the following questions:

(1) Before the advent of nuclear or thermonuclear weapons, was the statesman disposed to view war as natural, perhaps inevitable, in international relations, or was he already disposed to regard war as obsolete?

(2) If any pattern appears in his statements as to the usability or non-usability of nuclear weapons, does this pattern seem correlated to accumulating knowledge about these weapons, and, if so, how and why?

That these questions are not easy to answer can be demonstrated by reference again to Adenauer and Eisenhower. Both men had long careers in public life prior to Hiroshima. Both had made contradictory statements about war well before nuclear weapons existed. And their later contradictory statements about nuclear weapons ran in different directions. In Eisenhower's case, the trend seems to support a hypothesis that, the more a statesman knew about nuclear weapons, the more he was likely to be war-averse. Between Eisenhower's saying that nuclear weapons were like bullets and his condemning nuclear war as 'preposterous' occurred a great deal of learning, especially about the potentialities of thermonuclear weapons. Adenauer, on the other hand, asserted that nuclear weapons had abolished war at a time when he still

knew little or nothing about the weapons. By the later date, when he characterized them as 'normal' weapons, he knew at least a little about their characteristics, and he had been forced to read in great detail about a NATO exercise,
code-named 'Carte Blanche', in which a hypothetical campaign to defend
Germany with tactical nuclear weapons had ended with the entire country
depopulated and desolate.[21] This evidence seems to support the exactly opposite hypothesis that, the more a statesman knew about nuclear weapons, the
less likely he was to distinguish between nuclear war and non-nuclear war.

When trying to make sense of such evidence, readers should take account of
their own presuppositions. Since antiquity, differing theories have been
advanced to explain how humans go from thinking one thing to thinking
something different—how, in other words, they learn. One theory, going back
at least to Plato, supposes learning to involve primarily reaching into one's
own mental resources. In Plato's *Meno*, Socrates questions an ignoramus and
elicits from him all the principles of plane geometry. 'Searching and learning
are, as a whole, recollection,' he concludes. At the opposite extreme is the
theory that learning derives almost entirely from experience, with the mind
starting as essentially a blank slate. In his *Essay on Human Understanding*, John
Locke posed the question, 'How comes [the mind] to be furnished?' and goes
on: 'To this I answer, in one word, from experience. In that all our knowledge
is founded.'

All usable theories have fallen somewhere between these two extremes. The
Meno could not have continued with Socrates drawing from his interlocutor
the soundings in the Piraeus or the actual processes by which Alcibiades
gained and lost power in Athens, and Locke had to acknowledge both that
some experience was 'about the internal operations of our minds' and that the
mind had inborn faculties of 'judgement'. Nevertheless, Plato and Locke symbolize the alternatives of stressing deduction or induction as the primary
processes of learning.

Of efforts to articulate an intermediate positon, the most closely reasoned is
that of Immanuel Kant. In effect, Kant argued that, while humans learn from
experience, they understand only experience that fits into categories already
in their minds. The categories, to be sure, can become more differentiated and
even change as experience accumulates. But the mind can never absorb any
experience that it is not already prepared to absorb.

While these summaries do a good deal less than justice to any of these
thinkers, especially to Kant, they may suffice to remind readers of alternative
premises that they themselves may bring to examining evidence of how the
opinions of these ten statesmen appeared to evolve.

In this volume, the essay on Churchill dwells on his long experience of and
fascination with war. Those on Eisenhower and de Gaulle highlight their backgrounds as professional soldiers, while those on Stalin, Khrushchev, and Mao
tell of their participation in revolutions and civil wars as well as in World War
II. The essays on Truman, Adenauer, and Kennedy note their comparatively
limited experience of military decision-making in the pre-nuclear era. For a

neo-Platonist, who tends to think that an individual's character, convictions, and inclinations are substantially determined by genes and early conditioning, these backgrounds may seem to hold the keys to understanding positions adopted by these men later in life.

The essays on these statesmen also tell a good deal about the immediate circumstances surrounding their statements and actions when in office during the nuclear era. Someone with premises nearer to Locke's may attach more importance to these circumstances than to any data about the statesmen's earlier lives. A reader more persuaded by Kant than by either Plato or Locke may make the effort to consider both background and circumstances. In these essays, one sees Truman, Eisenhower, Kennedy, Stalin, Khrushchev, de Gaulle, and Adenauer all involved in crises over Berlin which put flatly before their noses a prospect of having to choose between seeming to beat a cowardly retreat or standing fast at the risk of possibly suicidal war. Looking at these crises, a neo-Kantian might try to divine what 'war' and 'nuclear weapons' had come to mean as schemata in the minds of the individual statesmen and equally what they seemed to be calculating at a given moment.[22]

A reader may find it rewarding to attend to the consistency or inconsistency of her own or his own readings of these essays. Someone who concludes that pre-nuclear experience provides a key to understanding Churchill but not to understanding Truman, for example, may want to reflect on why this should seem so. Quite possibly, the answer lies in the particular balance of theories to which the reader is attached, and there is no inconsistency. The answer could also be, however, that the reader needs to work out more carefully just what she or he believes about how experience affects thinking.

The third and last set of questions worth noting in this introduction have to do with the reader's presuppositions regarding determinacy in history. Here, the difference between the Mueller thesis and nuclear revolution thesis is narrow, not wide. Mueller sees beliefs and actions of individuals as important factors in history. While he contends that the effective abolition of large-scale war was inevitable, he sees this as occurring because humans gradually came to change the beliefs on which they acted. In his view, World War I occurred because not enough statesmen had yet come around to the new way of thinking, and World War II came about because one erratic but charismatic individual—Hitler—insisted on one last test of the old thinking. Writers hypothesizing a nuclear revolution also ascribe high importance to the beliefs and actions of individuals. They differ from Mueller only in taking it to be Hiroshima or some related set of events that caused changes in beliefs and actions.

Some readers, however, may be less inclined than either Mueller or writers of the nuclear revolution persuasion to ascribe the 'long peace' to actions by national leaders actuated by beliefs in their individual minds. No book or article published in the USSR could have ever implied that individual actors had such power over events. Someone writing in the Marxist-Leninist canon can allow for accidents. In his autobiography, Leon Trotsky conceded that his illness in the autumn of 1923 had something to do with Stalin's successful rise to power and that this had been something which no one could have foreseen.[23] But no orthodox Marxist-Leninist could explain a chain of events such as 'the long peace' except in terms of basic economic and social forces. Even texts accused in retrospect of feeding a 'cult of personality' for Stalin or Mao ascribed to their heroes only superior scientific understanding of predetermined currents in history.

Hardly anyone not subject to Soviet-style censorship has ever reconstructed history in such completely mechanistic fashion. Large numbers of scholars and others not subject to serious censorship, however, have taken the view that extended sequences of events are best interpreted as products of forces over which individual political leaders have relatively little control. Though leaders may think they make choices, this line of reasoning runs, they are actually at the mercy either of some social equivalent of natural law or of a pervasive ideology. Among political scientists who specialize in international relations, there are dogmatic neo-realists who presume that statesmen almost always maximize state power. Among historians, there are dogmatic neo-Marxists who regard all or most statesmen as simply ventriloquists' dummies for power élites.

As one can crudely identify alternative theories of learning with Plato, Locke, or Kant, so, without reaching for such extremes, one can identify alternative theories of historical causation with Roman or Greek schools of historiography—Plutarch perhaps representative of writers for whom history was essentially biography, Thucydides of writers who took human history to be fated. Another pairing might be Thomas Carlyle, as author of *The Hero in History*, and Marx or Engels as sophisticated forerunners of their mostly doctrinaire disciplines. More recent exemplars of these two ways of thinking are the philosopher Sir Karl Popper on the one hand and the historian E. H. Carr on the other, and Popper and Carr seem better reference points here because both lived into, and commented on, the Cold War.

In various works, particularly his two-volume *The Open Society and its Enemies*, Popper expounded the thesis that history should be understood as a record of the exercise of free will. Thus, in Popper's view, Russia became Bolshevik, then Leninist, then Stalinist because certain Russians who believed in historical determinism chose to seize power and other Russians acquiesced. Indeed, he credits Lenin with having had the practical wisdom to recognize that Marxist determinism was 'astonishingly naïve' and to adapt to circumstances.[24]

Carr, most compactly in his little book, *What Is History?*, protested dicta such as Popper's. He acknowledged that the surface of history was often shaped by contingency. He insisted, however, that broad currents had to be explained by forces beyond accident and choice. In his ten-volume history of the Soviet Union up to 1929, Carr allowed chance to kill Lenin at 53 and bring to power Stalin rather than Trotsky or Bukharin or someone else. But Carr portrayed the Bolshevik revolution and the policies of Lenin and Stalin as products of basic conditions in Russia and as virtually inevitable, no matter who had seized or held the helm.

Just as readers may mine more ore from these essays by asking whether their own evaluations of the importance of background versus immediate circumstances remain consistent, so they may profit also from attending to the question of whether, from essay to essay, they hold consistent views regarding the degree to which these statesmen had or did not have genuine freedom of choice. In both domains, inconsistency may be better than consistency. Someone inclined to think that Eisenhower and Khrushchev had little freedom of choice in the Berlin crisis of 1958, but that Kennedy and Khrushchev did make crucial choices in the Cuban missile crisis of 1962, can probably learn a great deal both by puzzling as to why this might seem so to anyone and why in particular it seems so to her or to him.

The 'long peace' after World War II is an immensely important subject of study. Agreed-upon conclusions as to why events ran as they did after 1945 are likely to serve as axioms guiding efforts to avoid war and preserve peace in decades to come. It is crucial that we develop these conclusions with more care than has been characteristic in the past in the fabrication of axioms for statecraft (as the axioms after World War I counselling 'appeasement' and those after World War II counselling 'non-appeasement'.[25]) It thus can be of much more than academic consequence whether we come generally to believe that the 'long peace' was due to statesmen's dread of nuclear war or, as Mueller contends, to a secular trend making any large-scale war seem irrational or to other factors, including perhaps ones wholly outside the minds of élites.

It is because conclusions about the causes of the 'long peace' can have large consequences that we open this book by imploring readers not only to think hard about the evidence arrayed here but also to ask themselves why they interpret the evidence as they do. The examples cited parenthetically in the preceding paragraph should be cautionary. Axioms counselling 'appeasement' and then 'non-appeasement' fixed themselves in minds that did not pause very long over the question of whether their attractiveness derived from their internal logic, tested against an array of evidence from experience, or from preconceptions into which these axioms comfortably snuggled. We think the reader who will learn most from these essays is one who approaches them in a self-questioning frame of mind.

PART I

Superpowers

2

Longing for International Control, Banking on American Superiority: Harry S. Truman's Approach to Nuclear Weapons

S. DAVID BROSCIOUS[1]

IN late August 1945 Harry Truman confronted one of the less onerous tasks bequeathed to him by his predecessor—redesigning the presidential seal and flag. Apparently, as a point of protocol, Franklin Roosevelt had been irritated by the fact that five-star generals possessed one more star on their shoulders than did the existing presidential emblem.[2] Consequently, he ordered a new design. Unfinished at the time of Roosevelt's death, the project fell into Truman's lap. The new emblem presented to Truman on 26 August contained two basic alterations. First, to placate Roosevelt, the old four-star pattern was replaced by one displaying forty-eight stars encircling the traditional eagle. Second, to symbolize the end of World War II, the eagle's head was rotated from right to left, thus casting the bird's gaze away from the arrows in its left talon and toward the olive branch in its right. According to Clark Clifford, Truman liked the modifications but suggested one change of his own: 'he wanted to have lightning emanating from the arrowheads in the left claw of the eagle as a "symbolic reference to the tremendous importance of the atomic bomb".' Although Clifford was able to convince the president that such an addition would mar the aesthetic quality of the seal, he contends that Truman's idea 'told more than [the president] publicly acknowledged about the impact the bomb had had on his thinking'.[3]

Clifford's story substantiates what is commonly assumed—that the advent of the atomic bomb powerfully affected Harry Truman. Yet the anecdote reveals precious little about how the atomic bomb shaped Truman's thinking. Historians of the Truman administration have not fared much better in this regard. The precise boundaries of the bomb's influence on Truman's intellectual framework and, consequently, on his diplomacy, remain uncharted.[4] Furthermore, no effort has been made to establish the relationship between

Truman's thinking about the atomic bomb and his pre-August 1945 attitudes toward international politics and statecraft. One result of this neglect has been an unsettling reliance by historians on bold quotes which leap forth from sundry presidential remarks. Furthermore, scholars have underrated the more general role of personality and individual learning in explaining why nuclear weapons have not become instruments of great-power war, and how nuclear weapons have contributed to the apparent obsolescence of great-power warfare.[5] This essay seeks to document Truman's thought regarding the bomb (and nuclear energy more broadly) in order to gain a more exact understanding of how Harry Truman confronted the responsibilities of power in the nuclear age.

Truman, The Bomb, and Civilization

As a senator, Truman had almost stumbled upon the Manhattan Project while serving as chairman of the Congressional Committee to Investigate the National Defense Program,[6] and James F. Byrnes had talked to him about it in general terms shortly after Truman became president on 12 April 1945.[7] Truman's first substantive exposure, however, came during a 25 April meeting with Secretary of War Henry L. Stimson and General Leslie Groves, director of the Manhattan Project.[8] During the course of that conversation, Stimson raised the following points about the atomic bomb: (1) within four months the United States would in all probability possess a weapon capable of destroying a city with one blow; (2) while the United States would retain a monopoly of this new weapon 'for some years', that position could not be maintained indefinitely; (3) in the distant future adversaries would be able to employ this weapon in a surprise attack 'suddenly and with devastating power'; (4) with this weapon 'modern civilization might be completely destroyed'; (5) 'the control of this weapon . . . would involve such thorough rights of inspection and internal controls as we have never heretofore contemplated'; (6) American leadership in atomic weapons development imparted a moral responsibility to prevent any atomic disaster from befalling civilization; and, (7) if atomic energy was properly used, the United States might create a situation 'in which the peace of the world and our civilization can be saved'.[9] Undoubtedly this was a lot to absorb for a president who had been in office less than two weeks.[10]

The first person Truman saw after Stimson and Groves left his office that day was J. Leonard Reinsch, a radio-station director serving in the White House temporarily as the new president's speech coach. 'I have just gotten some important information,' the president told Reinsch, 'I am going to make a decision which no man in history has ever had to make. . . . I'll make the decision but it is terrifying to think about what I will have to decide.'[11] This comment suggests that Truman fully understood the gravity of Stimson's briefing and was so startled by it that he felt compelled to unload its burden, however cryptically, upon a man who was neither a close adviser nor a personal friend.

Writing about the meeting shortly after leaving the White House, Truman recalled: 'Stimson said very gravely that he didn't know whether we could or should use the bomb because he was afraid that it was so powerful that it could end up destroying the whole world. I felt the same fear as he and Groves continued to talk about it.'[12]

Despite this concern, Truman told Reinsch that he would 'make the decision' on whether or not to use the atomic bomb in prosecuting the war. Yet the tenor of his declaration suggests that he believed there was no decision to make—if the new weapon worked, it would be used.[13] Thus, on the day that the Interim Committee presented its recommendations to the president regarding the employment of the atomic bomb against Japan, Truman told Byrnes that 'he had given thought to the problem and, while reluctant to use this weapon, saw no way of avoiding it'.[14] During a radio broadcast three days after the bombing of Hiroshima, the president proclaimed flatly that 'having found the bomb we used it'.[15] In his memoirs, however, Truman described the decision to use the bomb in more forceful terms: 'Let there be no mistake about it. I regarded the bomb as a military weapon and never had any doubt that it should be used.'[16]

Concluding the war was indeed, as McGeorge Bundy argues, Truman's 'first and principal business'.[17] Through its devastating impact, policy-makers anticipated, the new weapon would expedite victory and save lives by compelling Japan's surrender without recourse to an invasion of the Japanese home islands. John Newhouse contends that another influence on the decision to use the bomb may have been the price tag of the Manhattan Project— roughly $2 billion. Had the bomb worked but not been used, the Truman administration might have confronted an outraged Congress and public.[18] Finally, Truman's desire to continue Roosevelt's policies and projects—one of which, of course, was the atomic bomb—may also have influenced his decision to employ the new weapon against Japan. In short, the pressures pushing the new president to use the atomic bomb were indeed great, making Truman appear (as described by Groves) 'like a little boy on a toboggan', careening downhill, filled simultaneously with great excitement and great trepidation.[19]

Truman's claim that the atomic bomb was just another military weapon was, in all probability, an *ex post facto* attempt to invest himself with more authority than he actually felt at the time. Certainly his initial reaction upon learning about the Manhattan Project suggests this. More importantly, however, Truman's statements and policies during the remainder of his presidency make it clear that he did not view atomic weapons as merely another tool of war. When Atomic Energy Commissioner Thomas E. Murray registered concern in January 1953 over Truman's public statement that 'atomic weapons [were] in a moral category separate from so-called conventional weapons and perhaps separate from biological and chemical methods of warfare', the president informed Murray that the atomic bomb was, in fact, 'far worse than gas and biological warfare because it affects the civilian population and murders them by the wholesale'.[20]

Truman's response to the successful testing of the atomic bomb on 16 July 1945, moreover, clearly signals the depth of his understanding that atomic weapons were extraordinary. Writing in his diary on that day, the president remarked, 'I hope for some sort of peace—but I fear that machines are ahead of morals by some centuries and when morals catch up, perhaps there'll be no reason for any of it. I hope not. But we are only termites on a planet and maybe when we bore too deeply into the planet there'll be a reckoning—who knows?'[21] Here Truman articulated the same fear he had felt during the 25 April meeting with Stimson and Groves. But he also went much further, expressing a concern that technology was outpacing morality. Implicitly, the president raised the possibility that morality would have to be updated to keep pace with technological change. This point became explicit in Truman's first major address on the domestic and international dimensions of atomic energy, delivered to Congress on 3 October 1945:

The discovery of the means of releasing atomic energy began a new era in the history of civilization. The scientific and industrial knowledge on which this discovery rests does not relate merely to another weapon. It may some day prove to be more revolutionary in the development of human society than the invention of the wheel, the use of metals, or the steam or internal combustion engine. Never in history has society been confronted with a power so full of potential danger and at the same time so full of promise for the future of man and for the peace of the world.

Toward the end of the speech, Truman suggested that 'in international relations as in domestic affairs, the release of atomic energy constitutes a force too revolutionary to consider in the framework of old ideas.'[22] Less than a year later, in a markedly more sombre spirit, the president confided to his diary that 'the human animal and his emotions change not much from age to age. He must change now or he faces absolute and complete destruction and maybe the insect age or an atmosphereless planet will succeed him.'[23]

With the phrase, 'never in history has society been confronted with a power so full of potential danger and at the same time so full of promise for the future of man and for the peace of the world,' Truman laid bare the central tenet of his thinking with respect to atomic energy. It was a conviction to which he held firmly throughout his tenure in 'the great white jail'.[24] Five years later, for example, Truman sounded the same stark duality in his State of the Union address: 'The human race has reached a turning point. Man has opened the secrets of nature and mastered new powers. If he uses them wisely, he can reach new heights of civilization. If he uses them foolishly, they may destroy him.'[25]

The heights Truman had in mind were the peaceful applications of atomic energy. Although the course of events left Truman little time to focus on these possibilities,[26] he did elaborate his views on them in June 1952, during the keel-laying ceremony of the *Nautilus*, the world's first nuclear-powered submarine.[27] The first atomic explosion at Alamogordo, the president told the audience, was a terrible moment, and it was a wonderful moment, too, for mankind. It was a terrible moment because it heralded a new weapon of war, a new weapon of destruction more nearly absolute than anything ever known to man before. It was a wonderful moment because it opened up for all men enormous possibilities of peaceful progress, of industrial development and economic growth and better lives for human beings everywhere. . . . This vessel is the forerunner of atomic-powered merchant ships and airplanes, of atomic powerplants producing electricity for factories, farms, and homes.

In his peroration, Truman insisted that 'with the tools of modern science—of which the most marvelous can be this new thing, atomic energy—and with the ancient moral truths of religion and philosophy, mankind can build a world in which poverty, hunger, and war are banished once and for all. This is the vision we should keep before us.'[28]

In the *Nautilus* address, Truman also noted the paradox that 'most of our progress toward the peaceful application of atomic energy has come under the pressure of military necessity'.[29] 'It is a matter of practical necessity in the kind of world in which we live today that we gave priority to security,' he observed in his memoirs, published several years later, 'but I have always had the profound hope that atomic energy would one day serve its rightful purpose—the benefit of all mankind.'[30] Truman, thus, simultaneously embraced an image of the kind of world that could be and an image of 'the kind of world in which we live today'. Whereas the former held forth the hope of eradicating human want and war, the latter embodied a fear of apocalyptic catastrophe. Both images served as bases for presidential action.[31]

Before turning to Truman's policies on nuclear energy, however, it is important to clarify his views concerning general war in the atomic age, the use of nuclear weapons, and the relationship between his hope and his fear. Addressing the issue of war in his final State of the Union address, Truman proclaimed:

We have entered the atomic age, and war has undergone a technological change which makes it a very different thing from what it used to be. War today between the Soviet empire and the free nations might dig the grave not only of our Stalinist opponents, but of our own society, our world as well as theirs. . . . The war of the future would be one in which man could . . . destroy the very structure of a civilization that has been slowly and painfully built up through hundreds of generations. Such a war is not a possible policy for rational men.[32]

Such sentiments might amount to nothing more than the morosely grandiloquent ruminations of a man about to vacate the White House and worried about his place in history ('I prevented the destruction of the world during my watch'). But in fact, Truman was issuing a warning, and not for the first time. On 7 October 1945, in apparently spontaneous remarks, Truman announced that 'we can't stand another global war. We can't ever have another war, unless it is total war, and that means the end of our civilization as we know it. We are not going to do that.'[33] Seven months later Truman reiterated the point. 'Civilization cannot survive an atomic war,' the president told an audience at Fordham University, 'Nothing would be left but a world reduced to rubble.'[34]

Given this outlook on the consequences of war in the nuclear age, it should hardly be surprising that Truman viewed the use of nuclear weapons with great solemnity. In May 1948, Chairman of the Atomic Energy Commission David E. Lilienthal briefed the president on the results of a recent series of atomic tests conducted on Eniwetok Atoll. Referring to the bombings of Hiroshima and Nagasaki, Truman replied, 'I gave the order for the others, and I don't want to have to do that again, ever. What I hope you [Lilienthal and the AEC] will work hard at is the peaceful things about it, not the destructive. But until we are sure about peace, there's nothing else to do.'[35] Early in 1949, he talked with Lilienthal about a recent book which argued that nuclear weapons were ordinary weapons. According to Lilienthal, Truman retorted, 'But this isn't just another weapon . . . not just another bomb. People make a mistake about that when they talk that way.' Later in the conversation, the president grimly promised, 'Dave, we will never use it again if we can possibly help it.'[36]

Truman's comment clearly indicates that, while hesitant to employ nuclear weapons, he was by no means prepared to rule out such a course of action. During the 1948 Berlin crisis, for example, Truman told Secretary of Defense James Forrestal that 'he prayed he would never have to make such a decision again, but if it became necessary, no one need have a misgiving but [that] he would do so'.[37] Although the president refused to specify under what conditions he would be willing to use nuclear weapons—much to the frustration of Forrestal and other military planners—it is clear that Truman seriously entertained the possibility of employing them as an instrument of war. Thus, on the one hand, Truman envisaged nuclear weapons as the gateway to Armageddon. On the other hand, he reluctantly granted that under certain, unspecified conditions, they might have to be used despite their promise of destruction.

How did Truman resolve this apparent contradiction? The United States knew, he declared unambiguously in his 1953 State of the Union address, that 'war [in the nuclear age] is not a possible policy for rational men. We know this, but we dare not assume that others would not yield to the temptation science is now placing in their hands.'[38] Truman hoped that atomic energy would be used for the benefit of all humanity, but he also feared that nuclear weapons could destroy humanity. His strategy for realizing his hope and containing his fear first appeared in his 3 October 1945 address to Congress. 'The hope of civilization', the president informed assembled legislators,

lies in international arrangements looking, if possible, to the renunciation of the use and development of the atomic bomb, and directing and encouraging the use of atomic energy and all future scientific information toward peaceful and humanitarian ends. The difficulties in working out such arrangements are great. The alternative to overcoming these difficulties, however, may be a desperate armament race which might well end in disaster.[39]

In this spirit, the president wrote former Georgian governor Chase Osborn in December 1945, that the 'control of atomic energy is one of the gravest problems that faces civilization today'.[40] This was a message Truman reiterated time and again during his presidency.[41] After leaving the White House, Truman summarized his thoughts and feelings in the following fashion: 'Ever since Hiroshima I had never stopped thinking about the frightful implications of the atomic bomb. We knew that this revolutionary scientific creation could destroy civilization unless put under control and placed at the service of mankind.'[42] International control, thus, was Truman's answer to the central dilemma posed by atomic energy—the simultaneous hope and fear inspired by this revolutionary force.

Yet, Truman did not rely on international control alone. Realizing that this was a tall order, he also developed a fall-back position: 'I was firmly committed to the proposition that, as long as international agreement for the control of atomic energy could not be reached, our country had to be ahead of any possible competitor. It was my belief that, as long as we had the lead in atomic developments, that great force would help us keep the peace.'[43] This was not a belief Truman came to only after efforts to achieve international agreement had failed. As early as 9 August 1945, three days after the bombing of Hiroshima, Truman told a radio audience that 'the atomic bomb is too dangerous to be loose in a lawless world. . . . We must constitute ourselves trustees of this new force—to prevent its misuse, and to turn it into channels of service to mankind. It is an awful responsibility that has come to us.'[44] If an international arrangement could not secure for humanity the benefits of atomic energy and act as a bulwark against nuclear cataclysm, Truman believed, then the United States—through its nuclear monopoly and latter superiority—would at least secure the peace by exploiting the bomb's advantage as a deterrent to aggression and to the dangers now inherent in general war.

There are two points worth noting about Truman's two-track approach to atomic energy.[45] The first is the relative speed with which it evolved. Within three months of the bombings of Hiroshima and Nagasaki, Truman had roughed out all the major elements of his thinking about atomic energy. The second is that Truman maintained this basic framework throughout his presidency. Of course, the emphasis given to each track changed over time, but the structure of his thought remained constant—either nuclear energy had to be placed under international control or the United States had to retain its nuclear advantage.

Truman's Approach to Foreign Affairs—Prior to Hiroshima

To a considerable extent, Truman's approach to atomic energy resembled his attitudes toward foreign affairs prior to the advent of the atomic bomb—a framework that Melvyn P. Leffler labels 'pragmatic internationalism'.[46] Wilson D. Miscamble makes a similar point, contending that Truman's thinking about foreign affairs prior to becoming president combined idealistic and realistic tendencies in such a manner that he 'hoped that men could be rein-vigorated in the cause of peace but if that failed he believed one should be mil-itarily prepared for all possibilities'.[47]

According to Alonzo L. Hamby, Truman's internationalism revolved around 'the belief that the United States should exercise vigorous leadership in post-war world affairs and work for the betterment of mankind'.[48] Truman's com-mitment to this principle revealed itself most dramatically in his support for the Moral Rearmament programme during the late 1930s. Led by Frank N. D. Buchman, Moral Rearmament sought to achieve international harmony through a global reawakening of traditional Christian morality.[49] Participat-ing in a world-wide radio programme produced by Moral Rearmament in October 1939, Senator Truman proclaimed:

The battle is for a new world—a world of peace and love. We have been gratified to see this Nationwide response in America to the challenge of moral rearmament. In every walk of life, our citizens are awakening to those Christian virtues of honesty, purity, unselfishness, and love which form the bedrock of national character, and which enlist the citizens of a democracy in constructive national service. . . . The essential condition of any lasting world peace is a new spirit among nations. Without such a new spirit no general settlement will be possible. With it there might be achieved a realistic reorder-ing of world affairs which would endure. . . . I believe that the future of civilization must largely depend upon the success of moral rearmament.[50]

Although Truman's commitment to Moral Rearmament quickly waned after he was warned in 1944 that the movement contained pro-Fascist and anti-Semitic strains,[51] he remained dedicated to the idea of universal peace and brotherhood.

Truman also served as the 'guiding spirit' of the B^2H^2 resolution, introduced in the Senate in March 1943,[52] which called on the United States to support the formation of a permanent international organization empowered 'to pro-vide for the assembly and maintenance of a United Nations military force and to suppress by immediate use of such force any future attempt at military aggression by any nation'.[53] When the Chairman of the Senate Foreign Relations Committee, Tom Connally, attempted to substitute a far weaker resolution, Truman joined a group of ardent internationalists (dubbed the 'willful fourteen') to propose a series of amendments to Connally's resolution that revived the spirit and tone of B^2H^2.[54] Although Connally's resolution ulti-mately passed, Truman's ghost sponsorship of the B^2H^2 resolution and subse-quent membership in the 'willful fourteen' demonstrate his commitment to internationalism.

Yet another indication of Truman's internationalism manifested itself in his co-sponsorship of a March 1944 resolution calling on the president to convene a conference of the United Nations to consider measures and institutions designed to facilitate post-war international economic co-operation, which was 'essential, not only to winning the war but equally to the establishment and maintenance of an enduring peace'.[55] In short, prior to becoming presi-dent, Truman believed that only international moral, political and economic co-operation would yield what he once had imagined would be 'a golden age of health, peace, and prosperity',[56] in which the central concern of all nations would be the betterment of mankind.

Yet, Truman's yearning for an international 'golden age' did not blind him to the prevalence of armed conflict among nations. Convinced that not all nations shared his goal of establishing international harmony, Truman strongly advocated military preparedness during the late 1930s and early 1940s, so that peaceful nations would be able to defend themselves against aggression.[57] Speaking before a conference of the American Legion in March 1938, he affirmed his 'hope that we shall never have to fight again . . . [but] the best way to keep from it is to be adequately prepared for all contingencies'.[58] A month later, appearing at a meeting of Young Democrats in Bolivar, Missouri, Truman expressed the same theme, stating that 'I am for peace now and forevermore, but I'm not fool enough to believe that in a world full of thugs we can have peace if we can't whip the thugs. Our Navy and our properly trained land forces are the best guarantee we have for peace.'[59]

What were the sources of Truman's pragmatic internationalism? His service as an artilleryman during World War I stands out as the single most important event that shaped his subsequent idealism. Truman's World War I experience intermingled with his Victorian sense of history as progress, with the result that he warmly embraced President Woodrow Wilson's vision of permanent international harmony grounded in a League of Nations.[60] Retrospectively, Truman recalled having been so stirred by Wilson's war messages that he felt like 'Galahad after the Grail' as he ventured forth to battle the Kaiser's Germany.[61] Truman's later conviction that World War II might have been prevented had only the United States joined the League of Nations in 1919 only reinforced his commitment to internationalism.[62] At a deeper level, Truman's internationalism stemmed from what J. Phillipp Rosenberg describes as Truman's basic sense of honesty and 'duty to his fellow man'.[63] With respect to foreign affairs, this belief system inclined Truman to hope that nations could rely on one another to better all mankind.

But World War I also heightened Truman's realism, his sense of the importance of power in a dangerous, anarchic world. Part of the lesson Truman derived from America's rejection of the League of Nations was that the United States had evaded its responsibilities as a great nation by refusing to throw its might behind the one force that could forestall future aggression.[64] More fundamentally, his faith in human progress coexisted with a belief that human nature was flawed and that, consequently, the course of progress would be neither straight nor easy. In contrast to someone like Frankin Roosevelt, who revelled in subtlety, David McCullough argues that Truman was 'inclined to see things in far simpler terms, as [either] right or wrong'.[65] Nations either worked toward greater international harmony or embarked on aggression. In Truman's mind 'there were good men and there proved to be bad men', Clark Clifford once recalled, 'and, by God, he was going to see to it that the men in white hats prevailed and [that] the men in the black hats did not prevail.'[66] To accomplish this, of course, the white hats required the power to thwart the black hats whenever they rode into town.

Truman wrote to his wife in September 1947 that 'all we can do is go ahead working for peace—and keep our powder dry.'[67] Although written during his presidency and within the context of the Cold War, this unadorned line captures the simultaneity of Truman's idealism and realism. It also underscores the point that his basic foreign policy beliefs did not change with the advent of nuclear energy.[68] In a very real sense, Truman simply absorbed nuclear energy into a pre-existing pattern of thought that housed both idealistic and realistic elements—if international co-operation could not harness the danger and promise of nuclear energy, the United States would have to rely on nuclear superiority to deter aggression or to prevail in war should deterrence fail. There was, however, one distinction: peace had become much dearer in the nuclear era because the costs of war had increased so dramatically. As Truman forthrightly stated in his memoirs, 'the destruction of Hiroshima and Nagasaki was lesson enough for me. The world could not afford to risk war with atomic weapons.'[69]

Groping for an Atomic Diplomacy

Despite initial hopes that nuclear weapons would yield diplomatic dividends, Harry Truman and his advisers never worked out a precise strategy for exploiting their new-found leverage.[70] Certainly, Truman's early 'atomic diplomacy' reflected what Robert Messer describes as the president's 'groping confusion'—his tendency early in his administration to oscillate 'in his views and actions, depending on the circumstances and advice of the moment'.[71] Consider, for instance, the manner in which Truman told Stalin about the American atomic bomb during the Potsdam conference. Although no definitive account of their conversation exists, one thing is clear—Truman mentioned the new weapon in only the most elliptical and evasive terms. Truman's presentation (or lack thereof), according to Messer, reflected a compromise between the conflicting advice of Byrnes (who was now Secretary of State) and Henry Stimson. Byrnes adamantly argued that the United States should make no disclosure about the bomb until after it had been employed against Japan, in order to maximize its shock value and, hence, its leverage in dealing with an increasingly difficult Soviet ally. Stimson, however, worried that such an approach would only exacerbate Soviet suspicion of the United States and thus limit prospects for post-war co-operation. The Secretary of War, therefore, pushed for some form of limited disclosure to Stalin.[72] Unable or unwilling to make a clear choice, Truman opted for a sort of middle ground—that is, to inform Stalin about the bomb without really saying anything conclusive.[73] The result, as Truman recounted in his memoirs, was that he 'casually mentioned to Stalin that [the United States] had a new weapon of unusual destructive force'.[74]

Any hope that the American bomb might secure diplomatic advantage evaporated at the London Council of Foreign Ministers meeting (4 September–8

October 1945) when Soviet Foreign Minister V. M. Molotov truculently dismissed the importance of America's new weapon. Curiously, Byrnes and Truman had failed to consider that, just as they were attempting to gain leverage from the bomb, the Soviets might seek to minimize such leverage.[75] In the wake of the London Conference, only three months into the nuclear era, the Truman administration abandoned the notion that the atomic bomb could be used to extract diplomatic concessions from Moscow.[76] Indeed, responding to Budget Director Harold D. Smith's suggestion in October 1945 that he had 'an atomic bomb up [his] sleeve', Truman said, 'yes, but I am not sure it can ever be used.'[77] By this time, the American government was already attempting to realize Truman's hope for the international control of atomic energy.

International Control of Atomic Energy

Unlike Truman, Assistant Secretary of State Dean Acheson 'knew nothing about an atomic weapon until the bombs were exploded over Hiroshima and Nagasaki'.[78] Like Truman, however, Acheson was taken aback by these events. On the night Hiroshima was bombed, he wrote that 'if we can't work out some sort of organization of great powers, we shall be gone geese for fair.'[79] Like Truman, he immediately envisaged the spectre of untold, future disaster and sensed the need for some form of international control of atomic energy. Yet for Acheson, the key to controlling this revolutionary force centred on the great powers, not on bringing morals into alignment with technology. As he stated in a 25 September 1945 memo to Truman, 'the real issues [surrounding atomic energy] involve the methods and conditions which should govern interchange of scientific knowledge and the international controls which should be sought to prevent a race toward mutual destruction.' One of the critical premises underwriting this conclusion was Acheson's conviction that 'the United Nations cannot function in this field without agreement between the United States, the United Kingdom, and the U.S.S.R. This agreement, if it is to be reached, should be attempted directly and not with the added complication of fifty or more other countries being involved at the start.'[80]

In advancing this position, Acheson was reiterating his support for an argument Stimson had put forward in an 11 September memo to Truman and during a 21 September Cabinet meeting devoted largely to atomic energy.[81] On both occasions, the Secretary of War advocated proceeding with talks on international control among the great powers before going to the fledgling United Nations. According to David McLellan, Acheson was simply displaying his desire 'to root American foreign policy in the possibilities that were inherent in human nature and in the nation-state system'.[82] Effective international control, in Acheson's view, required building on national rather than supranational foundations.

The importance of Acheson's (and Stimson's) position is that Truman based his 3 October address to Congress in part on Acheson's 25 September memorandum.[83] The president stated that discussion of the international problem [of atomic energy] cannot be safely delayed until the United Nations Organization is functioning and in a position adequately to deal with it. I therefore propose to initiate discussions, first with our associates in this discovery, Great Britain and Canada, and then with other nations, in an effort to effect agreement on the conditions under which cooperation might replace rivalry in the field of atomic power.[84]

While starting down the path laid out by Stimson and Acheson, Truman took his first steps tentatively. Thus, he did not call for immediate talks with the Soviet Union.[85] In part, the president's reluctance to commit fully to a great-power approach stemmed from his wariness of Moscow's intentions. It also reflected, however, his intense concern with guarding the secret of the bomb, not just from the Soviets but from the entire world.[86]

Privately, Truman expressed greater reservations about the Stimson–Acheson approach to international control. In a letter to his wife, written the day after what the president described as a 'stormy Cabinet meeting discussing the atomic bomb', Truman observed that Stimson and his supporters had been 'arguing for free interchange of scientific knowledge'. Simply put, this was a course the president strongly opposed in the absence of an effective international control regime.[87] Indeed, on 18 September, Truman had told Joseph Davies:

When we get down to cases, is any one of the Big Powers—are we, going to give up these [atomic] locks and bolts which are necessary to protect our house . . . against possible outlaw attack . . . until experience and good judgement say that the community is sufficiently stable and decent, and the police force sufficiently reliable to do the job for us[?] Clearly, we are not. Nor are the Soviets. Nor is any country if it can help itself.[88]

It should hardly come as a surprise, then, that Truman proved unwilling to follow Stimson and Acheson down the path of great-power co-operation regarding international control.

On 15 November 1945, at the conclusion of a conference with British Prime Minister Clement Attlee and Canadian Prime Minister William Mackenzie King, Truman publicly committed the United States to the goal of working for international control through the new United Nations, rather than through direct negotiations with the Soviet Union. The three heads of state proposed the early establishment of a special UN commission to consider 'the most effective means of entirely eliminating the use of atomic energy for destructive purposes and promoting its widest use for industrial and humanitarian purposes'.[89]

After Byrnes had secured Soviet acceptance of a United Nations Atomic Energy Commission at the Moscow Council of Foreign Ministers meeting (12–29 December 1945), Truman needed an official position on the international control of atomic energy. Consequently, on 7 January 1946, Byrnes announced that he was forming a special committee to study the issue. Ironically, the chairman of this committee was Under-Secretary of State Acheson.[90] Acheson, in turn, appointed a five-man board of consultants to work full-time on the problem.[91] The result, the Acheson–Lilienthal report, was submitted to Byrnes on 17 March 1946. The report called for the phased creation of an international Atomic Development Authority (ADA) to maintain a monopoly of control over 'all intrinsically dangerous operations in the field' of atomic energy.[92] Largely the brain-child of J. Robert Oppenheimer, the Acheson-Lilienthal report boldly called for establishing a supranational entity designed to control the destructive aspects of nuclear energy while facilitating the development of its benefits.

The most remarkable feature of the report was its assumption that individual nations, acting on the principle of self-help, would counter any violation of the proposed ADA monopoly.[93] As described by Acheson in a 23 April 1946 radio interview:

The authority's dangerous production plants, stockpiles, and other installations will be strategically distributed geographically. You can see what would happen, then, if a nation bent on atomic war should seize the international plants within its borders. Such a course would be a clear danger signal to the world. Other nations would have atomic plants within their own borders so that they would not be at a disadvantage. If a nation did seize the Authority's installations that were located within its territory, it would still take at least a year or more to produce bombs. Therefore, the plan can provide by this dispersion of installations a great measure of security against surprise attack.[94]

Although not without shortcomings, the Acheson–Lilienthal report offered a truly imaginative approach for realizing the hope and containing the fear spawned by atomic energy. In Acheson's estimation the report was 'a brilliant and profound document'.[95] By basing a supranational solution (effective international control of atomic energy) to a supranational problem (the prospect of civilization's destruction) on core national principles (self-help), the plan proposed the outlines of a mechanism that could have fostered a transition to a new approach to international relations in the area where such a transformation was almost universally regarded as critical.

The Acheson–Lilienthal report seemed to answer Truman's call for transcending the 'framework of old ideas'. Truman, however, failed to heed his own summons. On the day the Acheson committee submitted its conclusions to the Secretary of State, Truman and Byrnes publicly announced that Bernard Baruch would represent the United States at the United Nations Atomic Energy Commission. Although selected primarily in order to garner Congressional support for the work of the UNAEC, Baruch insisted on imposing his personal imprint on Washington's international control proposal. While accepting most of the Acheson–Lilienthal report, Baruch was determined to include provisions for the swift and sure punishment of, and a suspension of the Security Council veto with respect to, violations of any final agreement.[96] The debate came to a head on 7 June 1946, when the matter was presented to Truman and the president decided in favour of the so-called Baruch Plan.[97]

Why did Truman approve Baruch's strategy? According to Bundy, 'Truman's decision came easily' because he agreed with Baruch on the veto and punishment issues:[98] recall, for instance, Truman's remark to Davies back in September 1945.[99] When he pictured effective international control in his mind, the president imagined a kind of 'police force'. The Baruch Plan was committed to making this a reality. The Acheson–Lilienthal approach, in contrast, did not seem to offer the same ironclad guarantee.[100] Although written in reference to the 19 June 1946 Soviet counter-proposal on international control, Truman may also have had the Acheson–Lilienthal report in the back of his mind when he suggested that

if we accepted the Russian position, we would be deprived of everything except their promise to agree to controls. Then, if the Russians should launch an atomic armament race, our present advantage and security gained by our discovery and initiative would be wiped out. As I wrote to Baruch on July 10 [1946], 'We should not under any circumstances throw away our gun until we are sure the rest of the world can't arm against us.'[101]

Truman, in short, would accept nothing less than investing a supranational body with prerogatives traditionally prevalent only within nations—namely, police power. Escalating tensions within the American–Soviet relationship during the spring of 1946 only reinforced Truman's wariness of Soviet intentions and his reluctance to throw away his nuclear 'gun' in the absence of an ironclad international control regime.[102]

When confronted with the key policy decision concerning his desire for international control of nuclear energy, therefore, Truman settled the issue based on his fear (his drive to contain the destructive capacity of nuclear energy), rather than on his hope that nuclear energy would benefit humanity. Baruch unveiled his plan before the world on 14 June 1946,[103] and as Bundy states, 'within weeks the plan, as a real possibility, was gravely ill, and in less than six months it was dead.'[104] Indeed, as Acheson wrote in June 1947, 'although we have not lost hope of achieving an international control regime and intend to continue the effort in the [UN] AEC as long as we can, I, personally, and most other observers are much discouraged by present prospects.'[105]

Yet singular or even primary responsibility for the failure of these international control efforts does not rest solely with Harry Truman. The Acheson–Lilienthal plan was not without its flaws, nor was the Soviet Union particularly forthcoming in its own approach to international control. The point, rather, is that Truman allowed his hope to succumb to his fear too quickly and too easily. Truman's insistence on the international equivalent of a police force came at the expense of the promising idea contained in the Acheson–Lilienthal report. While no one can criticize Truman's prudence—as a head of state he was, after all, responsible for his nation's security—he can be indicted for an unwillingness to move beyond 'the framework of old ideas', something that he himself claimed was necessary to confront the revolutionary force of nuclear energy.

Civilian versus Military Control of Nuclear Energy

With respect to the control of America's nuclear energy programme and, more critically, its nuclear weapons, Truman's attitude was relatively straightforward: 'Because of the power and world significance of atomic energy, I was convinced that it had to be placed under civilian control.'[106] If one believed, as Truman did, that nuclear weapons were not ordinary weapons and that such weapons should not be used again except under the most dire conditions, then it made perfect sense for the nation's nuclear stockpile to rest in the hands of civilians directly responsible to the president. During the 1948 Berlin crisis, after denying Secretary of Defense James Forrestal's request to transfer custody of the nation's nuclear weapons from civilian to military control, Truman commented that he did not want to have 'some dashing lieutenant-colonel decide when would be a proper time to drop [a nuclear weapon]'.[107]

Initially, however, Truman did not rush to support the concept of civilian control. During the fall of 1945, as the nation debated who should take over the Manhattan Project and steer America's nuclear energy programme into the future, Truman tentatively endorsed the May–Johnson bill, which called for military control of the country's nuclear energy programme. Relatively quickly, however, Truman reversed himself. On 30 November 1945, he indicated that he thought that 'the May–Johnson bill should be amended to provide for civilian supremacy'. At the same time the president stressed the importance of civilian control to Senator Brien McMahon, Chairman of the Senate's Special Committee on Atomic Energy.[108] McMahon responded by formulating a competing bill that passed into law as the Atomic Energy Act on 1 August 1946. Under its provisions, the government would retain a complete monopoly in the field of nuclear energy, a presidentially appointed Atomic Energy Commission would oversee the nation's nuclear energy programme and control its nuclear weapons stockpile, and presidential authorization would be required for the transfer of nuclear weapons to the military and for the actual use of such weapons.

It is difficult to explain why Truman vacillated on the issue of civilian control during the fall of 1945. Responding to a question, posed during an 18 October press conference, about whether he was content with the May–Johnson bill, the president replied, 'I think it is satisfactory. I don't know, because I haven't studied it carefully. When it comes up here for me to sign it, I will make up my mind on what I shall do with it.'[109] Whether Truman was testing the waters for public reaction to the May–Johnson bill or simply telling the truth is hard to determine. What is clear, however, is that Truman quickly came to the conclusion that the dangers inherent in nuclear war were too great to allow control over the nation's nuclear programme to slip too far from his grasp.

Yet the enactment of the Atomic Energy Act was not to be Truman's last battle in the war over civilian–military control. Less than two years later, the military again attempted to grab the 'lightning' from the president and the

AEC. According to Steven Rearden, the military's dilemma with respect to civilian control of the nuclear stockpile was that it hindered 'acquiring the technical expertise . . . [necessary] to perform handling and maintenance functions'. This, in turn, 'jeopardized military preparedness'. Having been informed of these concerns in late 1947, the AEC responded on 1 March 1948 with a report that 'proposed a joint AEC–military training programme to prepare the armed forces for surveillance and inspection duties'.[110] Unsatisfied and hinting at the military establishment's true agenda, military planners pushed the issue further—to the point of securing a presidential meeting, scheduled for 21 July 1948.

In Forrestal's words, 'the subject of the meeting was the presentation of a formal request of the National Military Establishment for an executive order from the President turning custody of the atomic bomb to the Military Establishment.' After both the military and the AEC presented their views,[111] Forrestal records, 'the president made the observation that the responsibility for the use of the bomb was his and that was the responsibility he proposed to keep. He said he would reserve decision.'[112] Two days later, Truman rejected the request. According to Lilienthal, the president explained that

I don't think we ought to use this thing [the atomic bomb] unless we absolutely have to. It is a terrible thing to order the use of something . . . that is so terribly destructive, destructive beyond anything we have ever had. You have got to understand that this isn't a military weapon. . . . It is used to wipe out women and children and unarmed people, and not for military uses. So we have got to treat this differently from rifles and cannon and ordinary things like that. . . . You have got to understand that I have got to think about the effect of such a thing on international relations. This is no time to be juggling an atom bomb around.[113]

The time, of course, was the height of the Berlin crisis. In a 23 July letter to his wife, Truman wrote after a hectic week: 'to cap it all off, Forrestal comes with all his help and reads me a letter suggesting I order all atomic bombs turned over to the army. Now wouldn't that be a nice peace gesture?' The president went on to characterize his Secretary of Defense's appeal as a 'blunder'.[114]

After this, there was no other concerted challenge by the military to civilian supremacy over the nation's nuclear energy programme. There were, however, three developments that chipped away at civilian pre-eminence. In July 1950, shortly after the Korean War broke out, the Joint Chiefs of Staff asked for the authority to store the non-nuclear components of nuclear weapons overseas. The following month, the JCS requested the additional authority to store these components aboard aircraft carriers. Truman approved both petitions.[115] Finally, on 10 September 1952, Truman signed a statement of agreed concepts regarding nuclear weapons. The product of the president's Special Committee of the National Security Council for Atomic Energy (SCNSCAE), the statement called for the following: the SCNSCAE to be the president's principal source of advice on nuclear energy matters; specific presidential authorization for the use of nuclear weapons; Department of Defense custodial responsibility for nuclear weapons stored overseas and for those in the United States necessary to ensure operational readiness; AEC custodial responsibility for all other nuclear weapons; the Defense Department's provision of security for all nuclear weapons storage sites; and AEC access to all nuclear weapons in Defense Department custody.[116] Understanding why Truman, as a firm proponent of civilian control of nuclear energy, agreed to these encroachments on the AEC's turf requires an examination of nuclear warfare policy during the Truman administration.

Nuclear Warfare Policy

'Nuclear warfare policy' under Truman was, in fact, something of a contradiction in terms. As David Rosenberg notes, through 1948 Truman's initiatives in the field of atomic energy focused almost exclusively on the international control and domestic custody of nuclear energy. Even after beginning to address the problem of nuclear strategy, Rosenberg adds, Truman's 'legacy was one of ambiguity'.[117] Yet, however enigmatic Truman's nuclear warfare policy was, it accurately reflected a dilemma in the president's own mind—how to reconcile a belief that nuclear weapons, in the absence of international control, were at once a gateway to Armageddon and a deterrent to aggression.

Truman rarely immersed himself in the details of nuclear strategy.[118] Yet in early May 1948, when briefed on a war plan code-named HALFMOON, he did intervene.[119] Uncomfortable with the plan's emphasis on a nuclear air offensive to counter Soviet aggression, the president ordered the Joint Chiefs to devise an alternate plan relying exclusively on conventional weapons. Although drafting of the substitute plan was abandoned during the Berlin crisis, the president's intercession did spark a process which helped delineate American nuclear war strategy.[120] On 19 May in response to the president's request, Army Secretary Kenneth Royall asked the National Security Council to review nuclear strategy. From Royall's perspective, it appeared

necessary, in order to insure a clear understanding on the part of all agencies responsible for various aspects of United States security, that a high level decision be taken as to the intention of the United States to employ atomic weapons in [the] event of war. While the Department of the Army has been conducting its war planning on the basis that atomic weapons would be used, I believe there is some doubt that such [an] employment is a firm United States Government policy.[121]

The outcome of Royall's appeal was NSC 30, the Truman administration's basic policy statement regarding nuclear warfare.

On 16 September 1948, the National Security Council considered NSC 30 and approved only two paragraphs of the document:

It is recognized that, in the event of hostilities, the National Military Establishment must be ready to utilize promptly and effectively all appropriate means available, including atomic weapons, in the interest of national security and must therefore plan accordingly.

> The decision as to the employment of atomic weapons in the event of war is to be made by the Chief Executive when he considers such [a] decision to be required.[122]

In short, American policy-makers decided that US policy should be to leave the question of nuclear use with the president, not to attempt to pinpoint the conditions under which such use would become necessary, and yet, to ask the military to be ready to use nuclear weapons if and when the president so ordered. This rather loose construction endured as the foundation of American nuclear strategy throughout the remainder of the Truman administration.[123]

Nor should this be surprising. After all, Truman perceived nuclear weapons as both a doorway and a deterrent to civilization's annihilation. Perhaps more unexpected was Truman's unwillingness to delineate when, or under what conditions, he would employ nuclear weapons. Admittedly, the issue was not an easy one. In the wake of the failed US–UN 'final' offensive in Korea during the winter of 1950–1, the United States considered whether to expand the war to encompass the People's Republic of China and, potentially, the Soviet Union. Truman recalled framing the issue in the following terms:

There was no doubt that we had reached a point where grave decisions had to be made. If we chose to extend the war to China, we had to expect retaliation. Peiping and Moscow were allies, ideologically as well as by treaty. If we began to attack Communist China, we had to anticipate Russian intervention. Of course we wanted no war on any scale. But neither did we or the world want Communist slavery. And the question now was whether we had actually reached the point where this slavery had so threatened us that we had to move to the destruction of cities and the killing of women and children.[124]

In this instance, Truman decided that the point of launching a nuclear war had not arrived. Yet the criteria for escalating to atomic warfare remained vague. One wonders what, in Truman's mind, would have constituted the point at which 'Communist slavery' would appear so threatening as to necessitate the use of nuclear weapons. 'I believe that we are in a position where we will never have to make [the decision to use nuclear weapons] again,' Truman told a group of new Democratic Congressmen in April 1949, 'but if it has to be made for the welfare of the United States, and the democracies of the world are at stake, I wouldn't hesitate to make it again. I hope and pray that will never be necessary.'[125] Beyond these rather nebulous parameters Truman refused to commit himself.[126]

Truman's reluctance to define more precisely his strategy or criteria for using nuclear weapons reflects a cognitive condition that psychologists Irving L. Janis and Leon Mann refer to as defensive avoidance, which they define as 'a means of coping with the painful stresses of decision-making'. More specifically, it represents a particular form of defensive avoidance known as procrastination, a stress-releasing safety valve that functions by simply postponing or delaying a decision.[127] Recall that Truman's nuclear strategy, such as it was, rested on contradictory propositions. On the one hand, the president sincerely felt that a war involving nuclear weapons carried the distinct possibility of destroying not just the United States but all civilization. On the other hand, he was equally convinced that nuclear weapons constituted a critical component in the democratic world's defences against its enemies. The structure of Truman's thought, thus, led him to the paradoxical and hence cognitively stressful possibility of risking the annihilation of the United States and the democratic world (indeed, all civilization) in order to defend them. The president resolved this dilemma by means of cognitive procrastination—he simply refused to delineate the conditions that would warrant assuming the risk. Truman, in short, defused his intellectual predicament by declining to confront it.[128]

The Question of Escalation: Korea 1950–1

The Korean conflict was the one occasion during Truman's presidency when the threat of general war seemed palpable and policy-makers seriously considered whether the United States should, or even could, commit itself to a general war. During late 1950 and early 1951—as the United States confronted first the onslaught of the People's Republic of China's massive intervention and then the possibility of pushing the retreating North Koreans and Chinese forces back across the 38th parallel—the Truman administration questioned whether or not the United States should expand the war to the Chinese mainland. On 11 September 1950, prior to the Chinese intervention, Truman had approved NSC 81/1, which concluded that 'it would not be in our national interest . . . nor presumably would other friendly members of the United Nations regard it as being in their interest, to take action in Korea which would involve a substantial risk of general war.'[129] American policy-makers believed that enlarging the field of military operations to include the People's Republic of China carried a significant risk of general war, primarily because of the Sino-Soviet treaty of alliance signed in February 1950. According to Rosemary Foot, the only time American policy-makers considered it likely that the Soviet Union would invoke its alliance with the People's Republic and directly enter the conflict was the period between the Chinese intervention and the spring of 1951.[130]

On 16 May 1951, the National Security Council concluded, in NSC 48/5, that the United States should 'seek to avoid precipitating a general war with the USSR . . . to deter further Soviet aggression, and to form the basis for fighting a global war should this prove unavoidable'. With respect to Korea, the paper called for avoiding 'the extension of hostilities in Korea into a general war with the Soviet Union, and seek to avoid the extension beyond Korea of hostilities with Communist China, particularly without the support of our major allies'. NSC 48/5 did, however, stipulate that plans be readied in case an expansion of the war became necessary.[131] In December, NSC 118/3 reasserted the desire to avoid transforming the limited action in Korea into a general war. Yet it also laid out courses of action intended to expand the conflict should the ongoing armistice talks 'clearly fail'.[132]

What is clear from the foregoing is that American policy-makers consistently sought to keep the Korean conflict limited. Truman later asserted that 'every decision I made in connection with the Korean conflict had this one aim in mind: to prevent a third world war and the terrible destruction it would bring to the civilized world.'[133] His words suggest that the spectre of nuclear war certainly exerted some influence on his decision not to expand the conflict. Reformulating Truman's concern, Melvyn Leffler contends that American policy-makers refused to expand hostilities in Korea because they feared precipitating 'an escalatory cycle they could not control'.[134]

There were, however, other factors involved. Foot concludes that the United States decided against expanding the conflict in favour of pursuing a settlement based on the *status quo ante bellum* because of uncertainty surrounding the Soviet Union's likely response, 'lack of allied support for an expanded war, and American political and military weaknesses'.[135] Her evaluation parallels the reasons Truman listed in a May 1951 speech before a Civil Defense Conference. 'I have refused to extend the area of the conflict in the Far East, under the circumstances which now prevail,' the president declared,

and I am going to tell you exactly why. I have refused on military grounds. [Expanding the war] would not lead to a quick and easy solution of the Korean conflict. . . . Furthermore, a deep involvement on our part in a war in China . . . would have critical military consequences in Europe. [Additionally, America's allies] do not believe that we should take the initiative to widen the conflict. . . . If the United States were to widen the conflict, we might well have to go it alone. [Finally,] we will not take any action which might place upon us the responsibility of initiating a general war—a third world war. . . . Remember this, if we do have another world war, it will be an atomic war. . . . I do not want to be responsible for bringing that about.[136]

Clearly, for Truman, fear of nuclear war figured into his calculation to keep the Korean conflict limited.

Was that fear the decisive factor for the president? Probably not. Even if the United States could have somehow guaranteed itself control over the escalatory process, the low state of American military preparedness in late 1950 and early 1951 indicates that the United States would have been extremely hard pressed to wage a global war. Additionally, NSC 81/1 asserted that 'it would not be in our national interest to take action in Korea which did not have the support of the great majority of the United Nations, even if, in our judgement, such action did not involve a substantial risk of general war.'[137]

Several considerations, therefore, led to the decision to avoid extending the war. Any one of the factors mentioned—the conventional military dimension, alliance politics, or fear of a general (nuclear) war—could have led American policy-makers away from a course of expansion. What must not be overlooked, however, is the simple fact that, for Harry Truman, the fear of nuclear war was an important element in his decision not to expand a limited war into a general war. While this conclusion does not add a great deal of strength to the contention that nuclear weapons account for the long peace of the post-war period, it does weaken the argument that nuclear weapons have played a negligible role in the world's extended respite from general war.[138]

The Decision to Develop the Hydrogen Bomb

McGeorge Bundy describes the decision to develop the hydrogen or thermonuclear bomb as the 'second great step of the nuclear age', ranking in importance only behind Roosevelt's October 1941 decision to explore the feasibility of the atomic bomb. From Bundy's perspective, the decision meant that 'for the human race there was no turning back'.[139] David Rosenberg shares Bundy's assessment. In his estimation, Truman's decision to proceed with the hydrogen bomb 'held considerable historical importance because it publicly confirmed the United States' commitment to a strategic arms race with the Soviet Union'.[140] In fact, it was a decision Truman found very easy to make.

Having been prompted by the nuclear scientific community to consider the feasibility of building a hydrogen bomb during the fall of 1949, the Atomic Energy Commission announced its verdict on the matter on 9 November.[141] Commissioners Lilienthal, Sumner T. Pike, and Henry D. Smyth recommended against development of the so-called 'Super'. Commissioners Lewis Strauss and Gordon E. Dean, in contrast, advocated using the current opportunity 'to reopen with the [Soviet Union] . . . consideration of satisfactory international control of weapons of mass destruction. If that fails, . . . then proceed, if the Defense Establishment concurs, with the development [of the Super], and announce this fact publicly.' Given their deep division on the issue and their belief that the decision was too important to be left to the AEC, the Commissioners 'considered it [their] duty to lay the problem before [the president]'.[142]

Truman assigned the issue to his Special Committee of the National Security Council for Atomic Energy, composed of Lilienthal, Secretary of State Acheson, and Secretary of Defense Louis Johnson. Although the Special Committee met formally only a few times, the Committee members wrestled with whether to proceed with the hydrogen bomb between November 1949 and January 1950. On 31 January, they presented their conclusions to Truman. They recommended that the president: (1) 'direct the Atomic Energy Commission to proceed to determine the technical feasibility of a thermonuclear weapon'; (2) 'direct the Secretary of State and the Secretary of Defense to undertake a reexamination of [US] objectives in peace and war and of the effect of these objectives on our strategic plans, in light of the probable fission bomb capability and possible thermonuclear bomb capability of the Soviet Union'; and (3) 'indicate publicly the intention of this Government to continue work to determine the feasibility of a thermonuclear weapon'.[143]

When the Special Committee met with Truman, however, he asked one simple question: 'Can the Russians do it?' Assured by the assembled advisers that they could and that there was not much time, the president said, 'In that case, we have no choice. We'll go ahead.'[144] According to Lilienthal, Truman also said that 'he had always believed that we should never use these weapons and that our whole purpose was peace; that he didn't believe we would ever use them but we had to go on and make them because of the way the Russians were behaving; we had no other course.'[145] In his memoirs, Truman asserted that 'by the fall of 1949, development of the "super"—the thermonuclear or hydrogen—bomb had progressed to the point where we were almost ready to put our theories into practice. I believed that anything that would assure us the lead in the field of atomic energy development for defense had to be tried out.'[146]

Truman's maximum position had been an international control regime that could harvest the benefits of nuclear energy for humanity while also preventing a nuclear war. His minimum position was reliance on American nuclear superiority as the principal deterrent to nuclear war. Truman's decision to proceed with the development of the hydrogen bomb indicated his willingness to settle for his fall-back position. During a meeting in July 1949, Truman summarized this attitude when he declared, 'As you know we have made every effort to obtain international control of atomic energy. We have failed to get that control—due to the . . . contrariness of the Soviets. I am of the opinion we'll never obtain international control. Since we can't obtain international control we must be strongest in atomic weapons.'[147] Consequently, when Truman had to determine whether to build a weapon that scientists at the time estimated would possess from 20 to 100 times the explosive power of the atomic bomb, it proved to be an easy decision for him to make.[148]

Michael Mandelbaum contends that 'the magnitude and speed of the change in human destructive capacity embodied in nuclear weapons' produced a revolution in warfare.[149] From a material or environmental standpoint, it is extremely difficult to dispute this claim. But the search for evidence of a nuclear revolution must not rest with material factors alone. Indeed, it is arguable that revolutions of any kind do not and cannot occur unless historical actors themselves perceive and respond to drastic alterations within their environment. In this sense, Harry Truman's confrontation with nuclear energy is peculiarly instructive. Truman did perceive the revolutionary nature of nuclear energy. Recall, for instance, that as early as 3 October 1945, the president informed Congress of his conviction that 'the release of atomic energy constitutes a force too revolutionary to consider in the framework of old ideas'.[150] Yet, it is equally clear that Truman never responded to the nuclear revolution by stepping outside his own framework of old ideas. In fact, the structure of the president's foreign policy beliefs was not modified at all with the advent of nuclear weapons. He continued to embrace the dualism of hoping and working for a better world, while recognizing and responding to international realities. In other words, he was hoping and working for the promotion of humanity's interests while also trying to assure American interests.

Truman, it seems, failed to close the gap between the environmental conditions wrought by the nuclear revolution and his attitudes toward those conditions. Consequently, he manifested no evidence of what Joseph S. Nye, Jr. refers to as 'nuclear learning'—that is, the assimilation of knowledge about nuclear energy into one's existing beliefs in such a way that those beliefs are altered.[151] Whether one judges Truman harshly or kindly on this point largely depends upon how one views history. For those who stress the importance of environmental factors, Truman appears as a rather retrograde figure who was either unable or unwilling to confront the nuclear age. For those who emphasize the significance of human perceptions and actions, Truman's record calls into question the very existence of a nuclear revolution. History, however, is dominated by neither environment nor actor, but rather by their intermingling.[152] Nor does there exist only a single environmental reality within which actors operate.[153] Truman embraced the idea of a nuclear revolution. Yet he also remained convinced that, despite this revolution, other environmental factors still held force—namely, international anarchy, aggression and the need to defend against aggression.[154] In short, there existed within Truman's mind a clash between the imperatives of the nuclear age and of the anarchic international system within which the nuclear revolution unfolded.

What was the legacy of this struggle for the mind of Harry Truman? While hoping that an international regime of some sort could eliminate the prospect of nuclear war and foster the peaceful use of the atom, he was also ready and willing to rely on America's lead in the field of nuclear energy to contain the horrors inherent in nuclear war. In a very real sense, however, Truman short-changed his hope. By demanding firm assurances that no nation could pick up a nuclear 'gun' before he was willing to put down his own 'gun', he exceeded the limits of what was possible at the time.[155] How could one reasonably expect the Soviet Union to accede to such terms? In this, Truman was blinded by his own faith in America's virtue.[156] He failed to see that other nations did not (and, under anarchic international conditions, could not afford to) share his conviction that the United States would disarm once an international control regime was in place. Truman asked other nations to take a leap of faith that he himself was unwilling to make.[157]

As the Cold War gathered momentum, Truman rejected his forward position in favour of his fall-back stance with respect to nuclear energy. As Soviet–American relations buckled under ideological, international systemic, and policy pressures, Truman increasingly viewed the Soviets as the principal 'thugs' of the world.[158] Once he concluded that co-operation with the Soviet Union lay outside the realm of possibility, continuing to push in the direction of international control was, from his vantage point, foolish and dangerous.[159] The United States had to guarantee the free world's safety against Soviet aggression and nuclear war. That guarantee, in turn, rested in large measure on the deterrent value Truman saw in nuclear superiority.

Ironically, Truman's appreciation of nuclear energy as a revolutionary force actually eliminated any concern he might have had over the phenomenal increase in the hydrogen bomb's destructive power. If containing the threat of nuclear war required American nuclear superiority, the qualitative dimensions of that superiority became irrelevant to Truman. While this may appear irresponsible, two points are worth remembering. First, one of Truman's fundamental duties as president was to ensure the nation's security.[160] Of course, it can be argued that relying on a deterrent which—by Truman's own admission—threatened to destroy both the United States and its enemies was hardly a responsible approach to fulfilling this duty. This, however, raises the second point. Truman firmly believed that American nuclear pre-eminence would forestall civilization's destruction because no nation would risk engaging in a general war from a position of relative inferiority, and because the United States itself would use nuclear weapons only *in extremis*. If Truman is to be faulted in this context, it should be for failing to delineate clearly the conditions, no matter how extreme, under which he thought that it would become necessary for the United States to use nuclear weapons.

Although internally consistent, Truman's logic contained two flaws. First, nations do start wars from positions of strategic inferiority. Truman, as a student of history, should have been sensitive to the fact that Japan initiated war with the United States in 1941 precisely because of its tenuous strategic position.[161] Second, power imbalances tend to make weaker parties insecure, leading them to try to enhance their power capabilities. Of course, such efforts appear threatening to the stronger parties and they, in turn, respond by augmenting their power resources. Power imbalances, in short, tend to produce a negative feedback system of insecurity.[162]

This closed-loop dynamic locked Truman into his fall-back position. Having defined the Soviet Union as a non-co-operative partner and as a threat, the president accepted the need for American nuclear superiority in order to deter Soviet aggression and prevent nuclear war. Yet this commitment could only increase the Soviet Union's own sense of insecurity and its perception of the United States as a threat. Any compensatory action Moscow took, in turn, merely heightened Truman's allegiance to American nuclear superiority. This feedback system made it extremely difficult to return to the track of containing the destructive aspects and unlocking the beneficial aspects of nuclear energy by means of international control. It also made any nuclear learning by Harry Truman that much more unlikely.

In the end, the structure of Truman's thought regarding nuclear energy ensnared not only himself, but his nation as well. This was a trap from which the United States would not even begin to free itself for at least two and one half decades, when the Nixon administration adopted the doctrine of nuclear sufficiency (as opposed to superiority).[163] It is a snare from which the nation has yet to escape completely. If Truman is to be criticized for any aspect of his approach to nuclear energy, it should be for unwittingly setting and springing this trap.

3

Stalin and the Nuclear Age

VLADISLAV M. ZUBOK[1]

THE most powerful dictator of the century, Joseph Stalin had many incarnations: a member of the first Bolshevik government and a fierce Commissar during the Civil War; the ruthless builder of the Soviet state and Soviet industry; the butcher of millions of potential 'traitors'; the commander-in-chief during World War II; the high priest of 'scientific communism'; an actor playing a 'wise statesman' *vis-à-vis* Western counterparts; and a suspicious tyrant to his subordinates.

The 'nuclear Stalin' was another of these many facets. For seven years after World War II had ended, Stalin presided over the creation of a military-industrial complex that allowed his successors to achieve strategic parity with the United States in the most hectic and expensive arms race in human history. He died just five months after the test of the first American multi-megaton device and only five months before the explosion of the first Soviet transportable thermonuclear bomb.

Extraordinary secrecy has surrounded Soviet nuclear history in the past, and only recently has documentary evidence begun to emerge. Since 1991, veterans of the Soviet nuclear complex, among them academician Yuli Khariton, have been permitted to speak and write publicly.[2] David Holloway, in his important book, presented for the first time a political and scientific history of the early Soviet atomic programme, setting it in the broad context of the arms race and international relations. Articles and documentary publications by others also benefit from the new evidence.[3] Finally, leading authorities and official historians of the first Russian nuclear laboratory and the atomic ministry have published well-documented books on the creation of the first Soviet atomic bomb.[4] Still, the documents that illuminate Stalin's views on the issues of war and peace in the nuclear age are extremely rare, and most of the evidence on Stalin's role is indirect.

This chapter examines how 'nuclear education', i.e., the process of learning to live with the bomb, affected Stalin's views on international security and his foreign policy. Among the questions asked are the following: Did Stalin perceive the revolutionary implications of the bomb for world politics and security? How and to what extent did the bomb affect his post-war plans? Did the

US atomic monopoly help reduce Stalin's geopolitical ambitions? Were any meaningful agreements possible with Stalin on the international control of atomic weapons? Would Soviet nuclear policies have been different in any significant way without Stalin?

In this chapter, I will first explain Stalin's vision of security for the Soviet Union at the end of World War II. Then, I will focus on Stalin's reaction to the American atomic project before and after the bombing of Hiroshima and Nagasaki, and address the question of why it took him so long to decide on making a bomb of his own. Then I provide a brief estimate of Stalin's reaction to America's 'atomic diplomacy' and plans for international control of atomic energy. In conclusion, I will examine Stalin's estimates of the prospects for war in the atomic age, and the impact those estimates had on Soviet foreign conduct.

Stalin's Statesmanship and the Atomic Issue by 1945

World War II was a cataclysmic event for the peoples of the Soviet Union and for Stalin himself. Soviet society was exhausted and longed for peace and co-operation with the Allies. But the police state built by Stalin in the previous decade had proved its enormous potential in the crucible of the war; Stalin's entire political career seemed vindicated. As Stalin looked into the future, his views on international security remained rooted in the past.

For Stalin, who considered himself a politician of the Marxist-Leninist school and Lenin's best student, there was never a sharp distinction between war and peace. Peace inevitably breeds new wars, as profound forces of economic development generate imperialist expansion. The transition from war to peace, with its secret agreements and spheres of influence, was as crucial as the military planning of victory. Stalin's vision of security never envisaged the possibility of preventing war (imperialists would unleash it anyway). Instead, it was reducible to two assumptions: prepare for war at *all* times, and, if war breaks out among other powers, try, through means of diplomacy, to get the best deal without direct and costly involvement. So Stalin's thinking, in military and diplomatic terms, was one of ruthless *realpolitik*.

Stalin believed he alone could combine the preparations for war with a diplomacy of peace. His dismal failure to predict the outbreak of war on 22 June 1941 must have made him even obsessed with fear of losing in a future transition to peace. Just months after Hitler's attack, Stalin already sought to set the terms of a future peace settlement. At first his main partner was Great Britain, which, in Stalin's estimate, could emerge from the war as a second great European power. During the visit of Anthony Eden to Moscow in December 1941, the Soviet leader formulated requirements about the post-war settlement: legitimization of the new Soviet borders, which included the territories annexed during the Soviet–Nazi Pact of 1939–41.[5]

After the battle of Stalingrad was over, Stalin began to devote more time to post-war plans and ordered the creation of several special commissions: one of them, by Maxim Litvinov, was 'on preparation of peace treaties and a post-war settlement' and another, under Ivan Maisky, on post-war reparations. A memorandum from Maisky to Molotov, sent in January 1944, gives a glimpse of the Soviet world-view. In the document, which Molotov brought to the attention of Stalin, Voroshilov, Mikoian, and Beria, Maisky wrote: 'Our specific goal in the construction of a post-war world would be creation of such a situation, during which the security of the USSR and preservation of peace, at least in Europe and Asia, would be assured for a durable term.' This 'durable term' would allow sufficient time for:

(a) the USSR to become so powerful that it would not have to worry about any hostile strategy in Europe and Asia. Moreover, that no single power or combination of powers in Europe or in Asia would even think about nurturing such an intention.

(b) Europe, at least for continental Europe, to become socialist, thereby excluding the very possibility of generating war in this part of the world.

Leaving Maisky's dreams of socialist Europe aside, this document pointed to Stalin's core expectation: absolute Soviet predominance in Eurasia.[6]

Maisky saw—and that is the most remarkable feature of the document—no major and immediate threats to Soviet security from any power, including the United States, after the war. He described the United States as 'a country of the highly dynamic imperialism which would energetically seek to expand in various parts of the world—America and Asia, in Australia and Africa.' Yet, he believed that American expansion would be mainly a headache for Great Britain with its sprawling colonial empire. Unless a series of 'proletarian revolutions' flared up in Europe, US–Soviet relations would not have any ground for collision, particularly in Europe. Concerns about US strategic military power are strikingly absent from Maisky's calculations. 'If Germany can be maintained in the state of dismemberment and weakness', he wrote, then 'there would be only one mighty land power in Europe—the USSR, and only one mighty sea power—Great Britain.' He then observed:

Of course, the United States is not a mighty land power in our understanding of this word, and it will hardly ever become one. In this way it has much in common with Great Britain. Of course, two oceans lie between the USSR and the US, which make our country *relatively invulnerable even for American aviation (at least, during the first post-war period.* [author's emphasis]

Maisky warned the Soviet leadership that if 'in some more distant future', US–Soviet relations would sour, 'America could then create many serious complications for the USSR': for example, promoting 'the resurgence of Germany and Japan'.[7]

Maisky's analysis (and Litvinov's), with its emphasis on the perspectives of post-war co-operation, was a common orientation among the Soviet leadership during the war, although Stalin looked at those perspectives with a great deal of realism and suspicion.[8] He expected the Western allies to strike a separate peace with Germany.[9] He also suspected that they would try to prevent the Soviet Union from using its position of strength after the war. A number of Western secret plans, including the development of new weapons like radar, attempts to prevent Soviet access to world supplies of oil and uranium, and others, fed Stalin's suspicions. By May 1942, Stalin knew that the Americans were spending enormous resources on the development of the atom bomb. He wanted to know more. On 14 June 1942, Pavel M. Fitin, the head of the NKVD intelligence, contacted the intelligence stations in New York, London, and Berlin:

Reportedly the White House has decided to allocate a large sum to a secret atomic bomb development project. Relevant research and development is already in progress in Great Britain and Germany. In view of the above, please take whatever measures you think fit to obtain information on:

- the theoretical and practical aspects of the atomic bomb projects, on the design of the atomic bomb, nuclear fuel components, and the trigger mechanism;
- various methods of uranium isotope separation, with emphasis on the preferable ones;
- trans-uranium elements, neutron physics, and nuclear physics;
- the likely changes in the future policies of the USA, Britain, and Germany in connection with the development of the atomic bomb;
- which government departments have been made responsible for co-ordinating the atomic bomb development efforts, where this work is being done, and under whose leadership.[10]

The decision to upgrade dramatically atomic espionage must have been reported to Stalin and approved by him. The point about 'likely changes in future policies' under the impact of atomic weapons follows up on the instructions which Stalin personally gave in late summer 1941 (in Fitin's presence) to Vassily Zarubin, a new Soviet chief of station in New York. Stalin welcomed any information that would 'hasten the defeat of Fascist Germany and uncover secret plans of the Allies with regard to post-war settlement'.[11]

For some time Stalin did not react to this information. Only after Stalingrad did the concern that Hitler could also get the bomb persuad him on 11 February 1943 to authorize scientific-technical work on the utilization of atomic energy. Many years later, Sergei V. Kaftanov, the co-ordinator of the Scientific Technical Council at the State Defence Committee, recalled his arguments at that moment: 'I said: of course, there is a risk. We are risking a dozen, perhaps even a hundred million roubles . . . If we do not take this risk, we are risking to lose more: we can find ourselves disarmed in the face of the enemy, possessing atomic weapons. Stalin paced back and forth and said: "It has to be done".'[12] The 1943 episode shows that Stalin was alerted to the enormous potential of having the bomb and the great risk in not having it. But then he seemed to 'forget' about the bomb for more than two years.

Among top state officials and future managers of the project, few realized until 1945 that the atom could be split.[13] According to Khariton, in 1942 'it was difficult to expect a positive reaction to the proposals [to start building the bomb immediately] which to many looked as fantasies.'[14] In April 1943,

Georgi Flerov, a young physicist, sent a letter to Stalin urging him to begin building the bomb. Arguing with many sceptics, Flerov wrote: 'The only thing that makes the uranium projects so fantastic is their too far-reaching perspectives in case of a successful solution to the task . . . A real revolution will take place in military science.'[15] We do not know if Stalin read the letter. But could the man who mistrusted his intelligence, have had any faith in scientists?[16]

Like his bitter opponent Hitler, Stalin simply could not afford a full-scale atomic project during the world war: only the United States could take a two-billion dollar risk at that time. When fear of the German bomb faded, his interest in the atomic project receded in favour of the much more urgent everyday problems of pushing the still formidable forces of the Wehrmacht back to Berlin. Besides, Stalin had good reasons to think of the Manhattan Project as a costly long shot.

Interesting confirmation of Stalin's thinking comes from the meeting between Stalin and Averell Harriman on 8 August 1945. Harriman said it was 'a good thing we had invented this and not the Germans'. Among American policy-makers 'no one even dared think it would be a success. It was only a few days before the President told Stalin about it in Berlin that we had learned definitely that it would work successfully.' Stalin replied that 'Soviet scientists said that it was a very difficult problem to work out.' He told Harriman that both Hitler and England 'had gotten nowhere with this research, although they had excellent physicists'. When Harriman answered that the Americans had pooled their knowledge with the British since 1941 and had built 'enormous installations to conduct the experiments to achieve final results', Stalin knowingly said 'it had been very expensive'.[17] By the moment of Hiroshima, Stalin was no less informed than Harriman on what it took to become an atomic power. But before America created the bomb, the cost and risks seemed forbiddingly high.

The Soviet intelligence community, according to the memoirs of Pavel Sudoplatov, expected that Western powers would have to accept the Soviet Union as a world partner, recognize its sphere of influence in Eastern Europe and even make more concessions if the Soviet Union would join the war against Japan. 'But we did not foresee, despite the detailed evidence on the completion of works on the atomic bomb', that the Americans would use it against Japan. On 28 February 1945 Vladimir Merkulov, head of the MGB, reported to Beria: 'No time-frame of any certainty is available for the production of the first bomb, since research or design work has not yet been completed. It is suggested that the production of such a bomb will require one year at least and five years at the most.'[18] But there is no evidence that Stalin tried to 'outrace' the Americans. He did not expect that the bomb would have a great impact on the final stage of the war and the first months of peace.

In May 1942, when Stalin was on the brink, he cabled to Molotov and Maisky on Eden's proposal for a Soviet-British treaty: 'It does not cover the issue of the security of borders, yet perhaps it is not so bad, for our hands won't be tied. The issue on borders, or rather on the security guarantees for our borders will be decided by force . . .'[19] In February–May 1945, after the Soviet army demonstrated so convincingly its superiority both over the Wehrmacht and Western armies (overcoming their discomfiture in the Ardennes), Stalin must have felt like an omnipotent Caesar. Molotov, who was his closest and only collaborator on post-war foreign policy, later admitted that by the end of the war Stalin's head 'got swelled'.[20]

The camaraderie among the 'Big Three' at the Yalta Conference did not dispel entirely Stalin's suspicions, but it boosted the claims that after the war the United States 'would be interested at least in the neutrality of the USSR, in order to fulfil their imperialist plans'.[21] The prospect of beneficial, even profitable relations with Washington made Stalin refrain from overly crude demonstrations of his power. He also disbanded the Comintern and told European communists to forget about 'proletarian revolutions' and to co-operate with the Western allies. He even made temporary concessions on Poland to break up a US–British alignment against the Soviet Union on this issue. Nevertheless, while hoping for partnership, he remained a cynical isolationist: he used every 'quiet' means and pushed his subordinates to secure Soviet post-war gains before the war ended.

Stalin Enters the Nuclear Race

The test in Alamogordo on 16 July 1945, followed just seven weeks later by the destruction of two Japanese cities, was a blow to Stalin's calculations. In fact, it was not until that time that Stalin learned from his intelligence that he was dealing, contrary to earlier reports, not with the equivalent of '2,000 to 10,000 tons of conventional explosives, but with a much more powerful weapon'.[22] Even on 10 July when Soviet intelligence passed information from Klaus Fuchs ('Charles') and Bruno Pontecorvo ('Mlad') to Beria that the first test was expected to take place soon, there was no mention of the actual yield.[23] In short, not only did the bomb become a reality in July 1945 (rather than in February 1946 or later), but it was twice as powerful as the highest estimate!

This error was significant for Soviet security. Stalin planned the Berlin operation and a blitzkrieg against the Japanese army in Manchuria as the final actions of the war to leave the whole world convinced of Soviet invincibility. From now on the USA had the ability to destroy Soviet cities from bases in Europe and the Middle East. Now, the image of the undefeatable land armies of the USSR was counterbalanced by the image of the armadas of 'Superfortresses' with atomic bombs. Stalin said to Harriman that the bomb 'would mean the end of war and aggressors'. The American ambassador added that 'it could have great importance for peaceful purposes'. 'Unquestionably', muttered Stalin. But he knew that the correlation of forces itself, was shattered.[24]

At Potsdam, Stalin told Truman that he hoped the USA would make 'good use of it [the bomb] against the Japanese'. Yet, he seemed to think that Japan was about to surrender anyway; the bombing just gave them 'a pretext'. The veterans of both the Soviet atomic project and intelligence recall, that 'the

Soviet government interpreted [the bombing] as atomic blackmail against the USSR, as a threat to unleash a new, even more terrible and devastating war.'[25] Soviet nuclear scientists agreed with Stalin that the American atomic monopoly was a terrible danger for Soviet security.

Some historians believe that until Hiroshima, Stalin did not appreciate the significance of the bomb. Thomas B. Cochran and Robert Standish Norris argue that Stalin and Beria 'in particular' may not have comprehended the significance of the Trinity test.[26] The main argument in favour of this supposition is that Stalin did not sanction the crash atomic programme immediately after Truman's announcement: he did so only on 20 August, two weeks after Hiroshima, and more than a month after Trinity, when the Special Committee was created under Beria's supervision with the task of creating a new atomic industry and building the bomb as soon as possible.

This interpretation, in my view, is based on a misunderstanding of the character and content of Stalin's choices at that time. Hiroshima made a big impression on Stalin,[27] but already at Potsdam, he must have appreciated the significance of the bomb (and his own miscalculation). According to Georgi Zhukov, Stalin said at Potsdam: 'I should talk to Kurchatov about the acceleration of our works.'[28] It is doubtful that Stalin at that juncture spoke to Kurchatov or realized what 'the acceleration' meant in reality. It took him some time to turn his full attention from the talks with the West to the atomic problem and to think through the requirements—economic and scientific—that the development of the atomic industry entailed.

We now know that it meant an unprecedented set of decisions, on the highest political level, that would alter drastically the relations between Stalin's police state and the scientific community, produce a quantum leap in the organizational and technological sophistication of many sectors of the Soviet economy, and ultimately create a modern Soviet military-industrial complex. In practical terms, it meant finding ways to excavate hundreds of thousands of tons of uranium ore in the Soviet Union, East Germany, Czechoslovakia, Poland, and Bulgaria, to build huge uranium-processing plants and nuclear reactors in the remote corners of the country (at times inside granite mountains), to accumulate 'pure' graphite, to build nuclear reactors, plutonium 'factories', and a complex concerned with the actual design, development, and assembly of atomic weapons. A Russian researcher believes that 14.5 billion roubles were spent in 1947–9 on the project. It must have cost much more than the Manhattan Project *in absolute figures*, not to mention as a percentage of gross national income.[29] In the Soviet Union of 1945, bled white after the war, only Stalin could have undertaken an operation of such magnitude. And it should come as no surprise that he needed some time before making up his mind.

The anti-intellectualism of Stalin's regime made this task even harder. Before the emergence of the atomic problem, the role of scientific advice in the Soviet power structure was minimal. Stalin preferred engineers, designers, industrialists, whose language he learned to speak.[30] Even the most distinguished senior Soviet scientists, Abram Ioffe, Piotr Kapitsa, Nikolai Semyonov (most importantly, members of the GKO's Scientific-Technical Council) failed to persuade Stalin to declare the atomic project—and the fundamental science related to it—a state priority.[31] The head of the pilot project of 1943, Igor Kurchatov, young and not even a member of the Academy, did not meet Stalin until January 1945. After Trinity and Hiroshima, Kurchatov and other nuclear physicists suddenly discovered that everyone wanted to see them in the halls of power.[32]

In the weeks after Potsdam, Stalin was looking for an optimal organization that would be able to achieve the task of building the bomb amid the post-war poverty and destruction. Lavrenty Beria, head of the NKVD and member of the State Defence Committee, became a natural candidate: a ruthless henchman and a formidable organizer, who understood the implications of modern technology and science.[33] On 29 September 1944, Kurchatov, frustrated and looking for a powerful ally, wrote to Beria, asking him 'to give instructions about such an organization of works that would correspond to the potential and significance of our Great State in world culture'.[34] In February 1945, Beria helped transfer young physicists from the Red Army for the atomic project. Initially, Stalin wanted to place all atomic affairs in the hands of the NKVD, since it was present in production units throughout the country, was in charge of railroads, highways, radio, and other communications, and, with Gulag labour, was itself the largest sector of the Soviet economy.[35]

But after discussions with a number of senior officials, including Beria and Boris Vannikov, a minister of war munitions and supply, Stalin decided that the atomic project must have special status. It 'must remain under control of the Central Committee and must work in strict secrecy', Stalin told Vannikov. 'The committee must be invested with extraordinary powers. This business must be undertaken by the whole party. [Georgy] Malenkov is a secretary of the CC, he will plug in the local party organizations.'[36] This decision, as Yuli Khariton commented many years later, converted the project into a 'business of exceptional, first-priority state importance'.[37] A decree of 20 August created a Special Committee at the State Defence Committee, consisting of Beria (chairman), Kurchatov, the Nobel Prize-winning physicist Piotr L. Kapitsa, head of the Party Secretariat Georgi M. Malenkov, head of the State Planning Commission Nikolai A. Voznesensky, Minister of Armaments Boris L. Vannikov, and two deputy ministers of the NKVD, Avraami P. Zaveniagin and Viktor A. Makhnev. The other structures included the Scientific Technical Committee on atomic energy and the First Main Directorate (in Russian: PGU) of the Sovnarkom (then Council of Ministers).[38] This organizational model served as a prototype for the creation of the rocket, strategic aircraft, and air-defence industries.

Beria and his deputies were given *carte blanche* to enrol the best scientists, engineers, organizers, and industrialists from other branches of the economy to take any facilities and resources they needed. The State Bank opened a special unlimited credit line; the Gosplan created a First Directorate to supply the project with everything without delay. 'The work then developed on a grandiose scale. Mind-boggling things!' recalled Efim Slavsky, a future head of the atomic complex.[39] On 18 October Beria received a report from the head of NKVD Merkulov, with a blueprint (from Fuchs) of the plutonium bomb of the Trinity-Nagasaki type.[40] By the end of 1945, all was in place for the rapid development of the bomb.

Stalin liked to monitor all armaments projects, sometimes to the smallest detail. But nuclear physics was well beyond his understanding, so he left the day-to-day management and logistics of the project in the hands of Beria and Kurchatov. Soon, however, the first strains became visible among the members of the Scientific-Technical Council. Kapitsa, the independently minded physicist who had worked in the Rutherford Laboratory at Cambridge in the 1930s, openly rebelled against Beria's dictatorship inside the project. Appealing to Stalin as 'a scholar and thinker' in his letters, Kapitsa invited him to become a leader of this unfolding grandiose, scientific-technical revolution.[41] For him, building the bomb, while important, was not a goal in itself. He argued against copying the American device, and suggested, instead, a two-year research programme.[42]

On 18 December Kapitsa sent Molotov a draft of his article on the world scientific situation 'in connection with questions of atomic energy'. To see atomic energy only as a means of destruction was as trivial and absurd as to regard electricity primarily as a source of energy for the electric chair. The article criticized secrecy in atomic works. On 2 January 1946, the physicist sent another letter to Stalin, opposing the imitation of the American bomb. 'It is necessary to realize our creative power and capabilities . . . We must find our own way of building the bomb, and the jet-engine . . .'[43]

Another great scientist conveyed his opinion on the significance of the nuclear age to Stalin on 8 November. Beria reported on an interview that an NKVD agent Yakov Terletsky had conducted with the world-famous Danish physicist Niels Bohr about the American atomic project.[44] Bohr revealed no secrets, but did send to the Soviet leadership the same message he had tried in vain to convey to the US and British leaders. When Terletsky asked if there was a real possibility of protection from atomic bombs. Bohr answered:

I am positive that there is no real method of protection from atomic bombs . . . The introduction of jets, you understand, and a combination of these two discoveries makes the task of fighting the atomic bomb hopeless.

Bohr also said that only international co-operation, the exchange of scientific discoveries, and the internationalization of scientific achievements 'can lead to the elimination of war, hence to the elimination of the very necessity of using the atomic bomb'. He said that all scientists 'without exception' who had worked on the atomic bomb, 'are indignant that great scientific discoveries fall into the hands of a group of politicians'. Bohr concluded his message with a prediction:

One should keep in mind that atomic energy, open as it is, cannot belong to one nation because any country which does not have it now can very quickly find out this secret independently. What then? Either the victory of common sense or a devastating war resembling the end of mankind.

Bohr was a friend of Kapitsa's (whose letter helped Terletsky meet the Danish physicist). They both felt resentment at the prospect of seeing fundamental science exploited by a 'group of politicians'.

Stalin definitely heard this message and his response was quick and clear. Kapitsa was allowed to resign from the atomic project. On 25 January 1946, in the presence of Molotov and Beria, he received Igor Kurchatov in his Kremlin office and spoke with him for two hours. According to Kurchatov's notes, Stalin never smiled and the conversation was serious in tone. Stalin was obviously suspicious of Kapitsa and other Soviet senior physicists (Ioffe and Sergei Vavilov, President of the Soviet Academy of Science) as invisible opponents. 'What are they up to?' he asked suspiciously. 'Do they work for or against the Motherland?'

While defining the atomic project as a patriotic deed, Stalin promised to raise the role of science and the status of leading scientists. He let Kurchatov know that he recognized the longer-term potential of the nuclear revolution. 'Regarding the views on the future development of the works,' Kurchatov jotted down, 'Com. Stalin said that one should not engage in small-scale work, but it is necessary to conduct them on a broad front, on a Russian scale, and that in this respect all possible help will be provided.' But above all he wanted the bomb. 'The work should be done quickly,' he said, and 'along the main lines.'[45] This meeting set the terms of a concordat between the Soviet leadership and the top scientific community for decades to come.

Stalin apparently understood that the copy of the American 'Fat Man' was just the first stage of work 'on a Russian scale.' In fact, Kurchatov's team moved along parallel tracks, developing an original Soviet device, although, when it came to the decision to test, they preferred the 'Fat Man' as a proven model. From the beginning, Stalin seemed to aim not simply to end the American monopoly, but to turn the Soviet Union into a nuclear superpower second to none.

In the shortest time 'a new branch of science and technology—the atomic one' emerged from nowhere.[46] Nuclear physics, an underfunded and arcane discipline, rapidly became a darling of the state, a giant that dominated the field of Soviet science.[47] The organization of the project, with only minor revisions, survived Stalin, and developed successfully for half a century (in the 1980s the number of people with 'nuclear clearance', according to CIA estimates, reached 900,000[48]). The First Main Directorate reported directly to the Politburo, and, in addition, Beria and other PGU leaders reported personally to Stalin. The unique status of the atomic complex continued to exist after the first Soviet atomic test on 29 August 1949.

The remarkable thrust of Stalin's atomic programme became clear as it began to produce ideas and products based on original research, not on data from atomic espionage. The second bomb, which fell into this category and was much smaller than the American version, was tested on a tower in September and dropped from a bomber in October of 1951.⁴⁹ The initiative to create a Soviet hydrogen bomb, independently from Fuchs's reports about the British–American effort, dates back to a special report of the group of young nuclear physicists (including I. Gurevich, Ya. Zeldovich, I. Pomeranchuk, and Yu. Khariton) to the government in early 1946.⁵⁰ And in 1948, Beria created another special research group, headed by Igor E. Tamm (which included Andrei Sakharov and Vitaly Ginzburg), which in 1948 produced the ideas implemented in August 1953 in the first thermonuclear bomb. Unlike Truman, Stalin never had to 'decide' about entering the thermonuclear stage of the race: the implicit authorization was given to Kurchatov shortly after World War II ended.

Stalin engaged in the nuclear race with the United States as he had done with other great projects in his life: with thorough preparation, concentration of all resources, and determination to prevail against high odds. After overcoming the setback of Hiroshima, he surpassed the contemporary Western leaders in grasping the new requirements for organization and technology dictated by the nuclear age. While the US president enjoyed the American monopoly and relaxed in confidence that the Soviet Union would not repeat the American technological miracle for many years, Stalin created in just three years a gigantic new complex capable of competing with the United States, a country of virtually unlimited technological and economic resources.

Stalin's Atomic Diplomacy

Russia's position as the 'underdog' in world affairs, dominated by the United States, shaped Stalin's public and diplomatic response to the four long years of the American atomic monopoly. Among Stalin's priorities in his post-war diplomacy was to minimize America's atomic trump-card. He considered the Potsdam conference the first success in his counter-strategy.⁵¹ As Molotov recalled many years later, 'Truman in Potsdam decided to surprise us . . . I believe he wanted to beat us on the head [with this news].' But, according to Molotov, Stalin 'understood that they [the Americans] still were not in a position to unleash a war. They possessed only one or two bombs, and they detonated them after all above Hiroshima and Nagasaki, and nothing was left. But even if they had more, it could not play any role then.'⁵² Another witness, Georgi Zhukov, recalled that Molotov in Potsdam commented about the Americans: 'They are raising the ante.' 'Let them,' answered Stalin, grinning.⁵³

Stalin kept his dignified pose throughout the conference, but in fact, he was already playing the game of strategic deception that he would play for the rest of his life. The essence of it was spelled out by Litvinov in his letter to Molotov on 8 December 1945. Commenting on a TASS report that Henry Wallace had quoted his opinion that the Nagasaki bomb would be the last one, and that the United States now wanted peace, Litvinov wrote: 'All this is a sheer fraud, since I have never spoken to any Americans and foreigners in general about the Atomic Bomb. I have always believed and believe now that, since any talks about the Atomic Bomb cannot produce positive results for us, the most beneficial stand for us is to pay complete indifference to this topic, to avoid speaking or writing about it, until we are asked.'[54]

After the death of Roosevelt and the electoral defeat of Churchill ('the devil you know'), Stalin had to deal with people who were unfamiliar with the wartime understandings and commitments: Harry Truman and James Byrnes in Washington, Clement Attlee and Ernest Bevin in Britain. After Potsdam, Stalin told Chinese Foreign Minister T. V. Soong that Truman impressed one as an honest man, but Byrnes was 'a clever man', who 'played a big role'. The Soviet Embassy in Washington long regarded Byrnes as an opponent of the 'Roosevelt line' (of partnership between the USSR and the United States), seeing him as a mouthpiece of a 'reactionary grouping' of Southern Democrats. After Potsdam, Stalin suspected Byrnes of intending to use the US atomic monopoly for imposing American terms on the post-war settlement and thereby forcing the Soviet Union 'to respect' the Yalta agreements in a way Stalin never intended to do, particularly in Eastern Europe. He was piqued when Truman rejected his proposal to give the Soviets a role in the occupation of Hokkaido and the conclusion of the armistice with the Japanese government.

The first opportunity to teach the Americans a lesson presented itself at the London meeting of foreign ministers in late August and September. In the middle of the conference, Stalin instructed Molotov, who came to the session, to show 'resolute determination' to oppose Byrnes's pressure to change the regimes in Bulgaria and Rumania, which had been approved by Moscow. 'The failure of the conference,' Stalin cabled, 'would mean the failure of Byrnes, and it should not upset us too much.' Molotov counter-attacked across the board: he resisted the US position on procedural questions; he asked to give to the USSR 'a mandate' to rule over Palestine, Libya, and Cyrenaica; he turned down any compromises on Rumania and Bulgaria; he explicitly ignored the US atomic monopoly and the nuclear question at large. After the failure of the session, Molotov explained his actions to Soviet ambassadors in the following words: 'We had to make sure in the long-term perspective, that the first session of the CFM would bring about failure to certain American and British circles attempting, for the first time since the end of the war, to unleash a diplomatic attack on the conquests of the Soviet Union abroad that had been achieved during the war.'[55]

Stalin's move was a success. Byrnes, dismayed by the deadlock at the CFM session, decided to recognize future Soviet predominance in South-eastern Europe. Averell Harriman rushed to Gagra, where Stalin spent his long post-war vacation, to negotiate a compromise. Stalin played the gracious host, and made some concessions to the Americans by recognizing their exclusive right of occupation in Japan and making some minor concessions on the political set-up in Rumania and Bulgaria.

But from Stalin's viewpoint, the American failure to use the bomb as an instrument of international pressure did not mean the end of 'atomic diplomacy'. He believed that an equally important goal of the Americans would be the creation of pseudo-international mechanisms that would prolong the existence of the American monopoly and legitimize sanctions against the Soviet atomic programme. From Donald MacLean and Kim Philby, Stalin was informed that, initially, the Labour Prime Minister Clement Attlee supported the idea of sharing the atomic secret among the former 'Big Three' to help build trust. But pressed by Churchill and Ernest Bevin, Attlee made an about-face and, on 5 November 1945, told the members of his Cabinet that the American atomic monopoly should be preserved as a means of containing possible aggression.[56]

In late November, after the US–British–Canadian declaration calling for the creation of a United Nations Commission on Atomic Affairs, the Soviet ambassador in Washington cabled to Moscow that this was a plot designed to weaken the Soviet position in the UN and 'to somewhat ameliorate the aggressive character of the Anglo-Saxon alliance of "atomic powers"'.[57] By early December 1945, it had become clear that, despite the idealistic motivations of some American officials, among them David Lilienthal and Dean Acheson, the Americans were not prepared to sacrifice their power for the sake of an international arms control organization.[58] The Truman administration decided to keep the atomic secret from the USSR, to use the United Nations and other means of public diplomacy to legitimize America's atomic monopoly, and to prohibit the Soviets from achieving atomic status.

At the CFM meeting in Moscow, however, Stalin feigned ignorance of these aims. When Molotov, probably revealing the defiant stand in the Kremlin towards the bomb, began to taunt James B. Conant, one of the leaders of the Manhattan Project, Stalin cut him short. He congratulated Conant and the American atomic scientists. The bomb was 'too serious a matter to joke about', he said, and 'we must work together to see that this great invention is used for peaceful ends.' Charles Bohlen, present at the meeting, decided that 'from that moment on the Soviets gave the atomic bomb the serious consideration it deserved.'[59] In fact, as later researchers suspected, the episode was 'a little farce'.[60]

Stalin was ready to thwart the Baruch Plan long before it was announced. On 19 June 1946, Andrei Gromyko, a Soviet representative in the United Nations, reacted to it with a prepared proposal to 'ban the bomb', that was designed to win popularity among religious and intellectual groups in Europe and North America. At first, the 'Gromyko Plan' was a modest success, and the Soviet-inspired world-wide campaign created some problems for Washington. But it soon lost its effectiveness.

From the viewpoint of Soviet diplomats in the field, a continuation of the propaganda battle around international atomic control would increasingly push the Soviets into a position of weakness and defence. The weakest point was the Soviet refusal to accept international on-site inspections. Stalin and Molotov knew that American experts came to the conclusion that no inspection could give certain knowledge of non-proliferation. Some Soviet experts suggested taking the next step in the propaganda game: they wrote to Molotov that one should accept the controls but couple them with counter-proposals unacceptable to the American side.[61] Skobeltsyn wrote to Beria, Molotov, Vyshinsky, and Dekanozov, proposing to allow American visits to Soviet plants.[62] But Stalin could never agree to such proposals: the risk was too great that the Americans might accept, in order to learn more about Soviet uranium reserves and production.[63]

Against this background, Stalin watched the American preparations for and later the first series of atomic tests in peacetime, at the Bikini atoll in July 1946. The Truman Administration decided to invite Soviet observers in order to signal to the Soviet government America's intention to treat atomic weapons as a matter of global responsibility.[64] Yet, when Molotov received in February 1946 an offer to send observers to Bikini, the Kremlin viewed it as another attempt at atomic intimidation of the USSR, and the veterans of the Soviet atomic project believe this even today.

One of the spontaneous reactions to the Bikini test came from a Soviet observer (and the MGB officer) S. P. Alexandrov, who told American journalists upon his arrival in San Francisco from the test-site that it would not take long for the Soviet Union to produce its own bomb. The resulting publication in the press attracted the attention of Vladimir Dekanozov, Beria's man and deputy Minister of Foreign Affairs. He consulted with both bosses and concluded that the Soviets should not disclaim this statement. But he suggested to Molotov and Beria that Professor Alexandrov should be instructed to refrain, from now on, from giving any interviews without a proper sanction. Molotov concurred.[65]

Then Stalin himself decided to comment on Bikini. In September 1946, he released to the international media his 'interview' with American journalist Alexander Werth. One particular sentence read: 'Atomic bombs are meant to frighten those with weak nerves, but they cannot decide the fate of wars since atomic bombs are quite insufficient for that.'[66]

Other episodes revealed growing tensions behind Moscow's feigned confidence. On 29 October 1946, well before the Soviet atomic project began to show results, Molotov, in a speech at the UN General Assembly, went much further. He taunted 'some arrogant and shortsighted' politicians who relied on the atomic monopoly. He also said that the American atomic bombs could be countered by 'atomic bombs and something else on another side'. Many years later, Molotov claimed he did it on his own initiative 'so that our people would feel more or less self-confident'. 'Stalin then told me: "Boy, you're tough!" We still did not have anything at that time, and I was aware of it.' But Stalin used this bravado 'to end all talk of our weakness'.[67]

By that time, there were rumours in the Soviet Union about 'our weapon of a colossal power'.[68] Stalin and Molotov played up to them. Later, Nikita Khrushchev made bragging about Soviet missiles a part of strategic deception.

Often this policy is seen as a function of Khrushchev's personality, and it is significant that Stalin, despite his cautious nature, did not refrain from dabbling with it when he believed Soviet strategic weakness necessitated it.

Was Stalin Deterred by the Bomb?

If somebody had asked Stalin after Hiroshima in 1945 and again at the end of his life in late 1952, whether he believed the bomb would affect the likelihood of war in the future, he might have given two different answers. In 1945, he would probably have said that the US atomic monopoly encouraged America's drive for world hegemony and made the prospects of war more likely. In early 1950, after the first Soviet test, he was ready to say that after the first test of the Soviet bomb, the correlation of forces shifted again in favour of the forces of socialism and peace.

It seems that at no point after the surrender of Germany and Japan in 1945 had Stalin stopped worrying about a future war. The terrible experience of World War II was fresh enough to convince Soviet leaders (and in effect all other world leaders) that in the atomic age big wars had become 'obsolescent'. Expectation of an even more terrible and protracted war was part and parcel of Stalin's vision of international politics; it was both a conviction and a tool for domestic mobilization and control. In his speech in February 1946, Stalin invoked the image of a future war between two imperialist blocs to call for the acceleration of Soviet economic recovery and programmes of rearmament.[69] But Stalin did not expect a war any time soon. And, contrary to some allegations, he did not fan a war scare for post-war mobilization and repression.[70]

There seemed to be another linkage in Stalin's mind between the duration of peace and the atomic bomb. Namely, the longer the American atomic monopoly lasted, the more realistic US plans 'of world domination' would appear, and therefore, the greater the chance of confrontation. Liquidation of the US atomic monopoly would allow Stalin to extend the period of war preparations; but even Stalin did not know for how long.

Stalin's public stand, designed to deceive US policy-makers and the world public, continues to confuse historians who want to know how much Stalin feared pre-emptive war and, therefore, to what extent the US nuclear 'deterrent' really forced him to change his plans and to be even more cautious in his policies. Yet, most recent revelations suggest that Stalin thought the probability of nuclear war in 1946 and even into 1947 was very low. Often he behaved assertively in the international arena precisely because he felt the need to snub the 'atomic diplomacy' of Truman and Byrnes and compensate for the impression of Soviet economic and technological weakness.

In his memoirs, Truman claimed that the atomic monopoly first helped to deter Stalin from aggressive plans in Iran, and even compelled him to withdraw Soviet troops from Northern Azerbaijan in March 1946. In fact, as archival research demonstrates, Soviet withdrawal had nothing to do with

America's 'atomic diplomacy'. The Stalin government was satisfied with the status quo in Iran and only wanted to ensure Soviet control over oil-fields in the northern part of the country (in part to keep the British oil companies out). On the strategic side, Stalin wanted to prevent a US-British alignment over Iran and felt that the continued presence of troops there could trigger this development.[71]

Since the first glimpse of America's 'atomic diplomacy', Stalin assessed it from two angles: its psychological, symbolic effect; and its real back-up (the stockpile and dynamics of the production of atomic weapons). According to Molotov, even in Potsdam, Stalin knew from intelligence that the whole American stockpile by the end of the war consisted of 'one or two bombs'. On 19 September 1945, after Hiroshima and Nagasaki, Fuchs reported to the Soviets that the United States produced one hundred kilograms of uranium-235 and twenty kilograms of plutonium per month. These figures, recalled a veteran of Soviet atomic espionage, 'allowed Soviet scientists to define how many bombs the United States could produce annually'. Until the 1950s the United States had no capacity for an atomic blitzkrieg.[72]

Also, the Soviets moderated their early estimates of the atomic bomb: despite its monstrous destructive force, it was still not an 'absolute weapon'. Those estimates were paralleled by Western studies (and Soviet intelligence had this kind of information from Fuchs, who analysed the effects of the Hiroshima and Nagasaki bombings for Los Alamos). The research on the effects of atomic explosions revealed that, with good civil defence and shelters, a single atomic bomb could not destroy a medium-size agglomeration of military industries. After an initial euphoric moment, Western military and intelligence experts concluded that even a series of atomic bombardments would not decide the outcome of a future war. They even regarded it as comparable to the 'conventional' carpet bombing of Dresden, Hamburg, and Tokyo.

The Bikini tests in July 1946, while forcing Stalin to intensify his atomic counter-diplomacy, tended to confirm these conclusions. Soviet observers of the Bikini test reported to the leadership that the results of the test turned out to be 'less significant in comparison with what had been expected here'. They noticed that the shock-wave could not sink ships located near ground zero.[73]

In the same spirit, two months later a group of Soviet military officers, who obtained US permission to visit Hiroshima on the first anniversary of the atomic bombardment, reported to Moscow that the first estimates about the awesome power of the bomb turned out to be exaggerated. If troops and the civilian population had stayed in shelters, the report concluded, they would have survived the blast and the impact. The report dismissed the danger of radiation as a very short-term factor.[74] This mood contrasted with the first reaction noticed by the British ambassador in Moscow, Archibald Clark Kerr, who noted that with the advent of the bomb 'the three hundred divisions [of the Red Army] were shorn of much of their value'.[75] The divisions still mattered, at least until the production of atomic bombs achieved a mass scale.

Soviet military contingency planning for Central Europe remained purely defensive, as well, at the end of 1946—a good sign that Stalin and his General Staff did not believe a war in Europe was in the making, and thus did not foresee the need for any pre-emptive or counter-offensive actions on their part.[76] At the same time, as the Cold War was clearly intensifying and as the Soviet atomic project developed, Stalin and various officials down the line of command could not completely discount American atomic capabilities. The discussion by the US Joint Chiefs of contingency plans to use atomic weapons against the USSR must have leaked to the Kremlin.

Besides an aerial attack, the Soviets contemplated the possibility of enemy agents smuggling atomic charges into Soviet cities. On 5 October 1946, a Soviet expert in the UN Atomic Energy Commission warned the leadership of the possibility of an 'anonymous atomic war' against the USSR and proposed to mobilize the MGB-MVD forces to 'establish more stringent custom-police control over the luggage of foreigners'. He also proposed to check with Geiger counters 'the areas of special risk to this kind of anonymous war, considering the current international situation and a possible country-aggressor'.[77] After the Soviet test in 1949, the US intelligence community warned its leadership about the same threats from the Soviet side, in almost exactly the same words.[78]

As for Stalin, he took these threats seriously. He was concerned that if the Americans learned about the Soviet 'crash' programme to build the bomb, they might overreact and deliver a strike against its installations. In 1946, upon learning from Beria and Kurchatov that the first atomic reactor had become operational on 25 December 1946, Stalin warned that it was of the utmost importance that foreign intelligence must not learn about this. According to Slavsky, for a while this news remained a closely guarded secret from anyone inside the project, except for a tiny circle.[79]

From early 1948 until the first Soviet test, Stalin faced several contradictory pressures. On the one hand, the Soviet atomic project was developing apace. But simultaneously, as the tensions of the Cold War grew, Stalin had to reckon with the possibility that the United States might be tempted to nip the Soviet atomic capability in the bud. Unfortunately, the evidence on Stalin's policies during this period is even more slender than for the previous one. The US atomic monopoly could not prevent Stalin from imposing a blockade on West Berlin, just as American intelligence expected him to do. And it was not the American atomic threats, but the spectacular success of the Western airlift to Berlin, along with the painful economic counter-blockade of the Soviet zone of Germany, that led Stalin to retreat in April 1949. Stalin was careful at all times not to provide the United States with a *casus belli*, but this may have been caused as well by other reasons: economic and general unpreparedness of the Soviet Union for a war against the United States, the willingness to wait until Chinese communists would complete their victory in the Far East, etc.

The CIA experts believed in November 1948 that 'the state of the Soviet economy currently acts as a deterrent on the implementation of Soviet aggressive designs'.[80]

It is also easy to see that during this period the time factor and the uncertainty linked to it acquired supreme importance for Stalin. Who would outrace whom? How would the Americans, with their plans of preparation for war (and from 1947 on Stalin assessed Western intentions only in these terms), react when they learned of Soviet rearmament programmes, particularly the atomic one? He pressed for early results: initially the test of the plutonium bomb was scheduled before January 1948 and of the uranium—before June 1948. But after a setback with the reactor and other problems, the tests were postponed till March–December 1949. Even in the spring of 1949 the production level of metallic plutonium was still far from critical. Many problems were being resolved on the march, and only the experts could guess whether success was near. Sometimes Beria could not be sure that Kurchatov was not duping them. The rumour was that an alternative team was assigned to replace Kurchatov, Khariton, and others, had the bomb failed to explode.[81]

Stalin concealed his inner tension, but at this point it must have been high. According to Kurchatov, at the meeting on the eve of the test, Stalin himself said: 'The atomic bomb must be made by all means.' At another meeting with the project leaders, after the test, Stalin said: 'If we had been late with the atomic bomb by a year or year and a half, then we perhaps would have gotten it "tested" against ourselves.'[82]

It is still hard to document the evolution of Stalin's perception of the bomb's power. It seems that he understood both its destructive power and its terrible psychological impact that exceeded the power of armour, aviation, and artillery taken together. One episode with Beria is suggestive of Stalin's attitudes. During the preparations for the first atomic test in Semipalatinsk, Khazakhstan, Beria suddenly became incensed. He screamed: 'I will tell you myself!' Then he started to talk nonsense. It gradually became clear from his monologue that he wanted everything at the test site to be totally destroyed in order to provide the maximum terror.'[83]

Stalin was eager to learn every detail about the first test, especially how the visual effects there compared to the Bikini tests.[84] The documentary about the explosion that Stalin watched showed that all construction and military equipment within the range of three to five kilometers was destroyed, and that animals were killed or badly burnt. Stalin seemed satisfied, but was far from euphoric. He ordered an acceleration in production of the existing model, which was an improved, compact, and transportable type.[85]

The Kremlin leader wanted to keep the first test of the Soviet atomic bomb a secret. When, prior to the test, he met with the atomic scientists, he asked Yuli Khariton, the scientific director of an atomic laboratory (Arzamas-16), if two less powerful bombs could be made from the plutonium that was available, 'so that one bomb could remain in reserve'. He must have been thinking about the situation of four years before, when the Americans found themselves without atomic bombs after Hiroshima and Nagasaki and he had learned about it. Now the Soviets found themselves in a similar situation, but Stalin did not want to delay the test. He simply preferred to delay the announcement until he could have one or two bombs in his stockpile.[86] Only on 25 September, three weeks after the United States disclosed the Soviet test, did Stalin allow TASS to make an official announcement about the end of the American monopoly.

In Stalin's view, the Soviet test in August 1949 delayed the prospect of war which otherwise could have happened in 1950–1 (Stalin had spoken of 'a year or a year and a half'). It has also been argued in the West that Stalin's arrogance after the atomic test can explain the origins of the Korean War. As recent archival research indicates, the fervent nationalism of Kim Il Sung, the Machiavellian relations between Stalin and Mao Zedong, and the US policy of excluding Korea from its 'defense perimeter' all played a part in this affair.[87] Stalin cabled to Mao on 14 May 1950, that 'in the light of the changed international situation, we agree with the proposal of the Koreans to get down to reunification.'[88]

There is no hard evidence that the end of the American atomic monopoly contributed to this conclusion. After all, Stalin did not speak about the 'correlation of forces'. However, his miscalculation in authorizing Kim's attack against South Korea might plausibly be linked to the Soviet atomic test. The fact that the Americans failed to pre-empt it and at the same time left their Chinese Nationalist allies in the lurch must have relieved temporarily his worst fears. In January 1950, just at the moment when Stalin signalled to Kim his willingness to help with 'reunification', the Truman Administration announced its intention to build a thermonuclear bomb. From Stalin's viewpoint, it must have looked as if the United States was not yet ready for a war—at least for several years.

Another episode shows that Stalin might indeed have thought so. Stalin's reaction to the unexpected US intervention and then the destruction of the North Korean armed forces was, as always, extremely cautious: he was, as before, determined to avoid a direct clash with the Americans and for a moment even refused to provide the Chinese People's Liberation Army with extensive air cover from Soviet territory. In the presence of colleagues from the Presidium, he admitted he would rather let the Americans reach the Soviet border in Korea than risk a premature war.[89] At the same time, when he pushed Mao Zedong to send Chinese armies to Korea, he argued: 'The USA, as the Korean events showed, is not ready at present for a big war.' Of course, he admitted, the Americans:

could still be drawn into a big war out of considerations of prestige, which, in turn, would drag China into the war, and along with this draw into the war the USSR, which is bound with China by the Mutual Assistance Pact. Should we fear this? In my opinion, we should not . . . If the war is inevitable, then let it be waged now, and not in a few years, when Japanese militarism will be restored as an ally of the USA.[90]

The Korean War did not escalate into World War III, and Stalin's words must have sounded prophetic to Mao. But what would happen when the United States was equipped to win a big war? In 1950, the Soviet Union still could not strike the United States, ten thousand miles away. American B-36 bombers could not reach Soviet nuclear installations, but the next version, the B-47, could reach most corners of Stalin's empire.[91] In early 1950 he created a Third Chief Directorate of the Council of Ministers, which was ordered to design a defence of Moscow in the event of an aerial nuclear attack. According to one of the participants, Stalin was concerned that even a few American bombers with atomic bombs could destroy Moscow. He said that Allied aviation was able to delete Dresden from the map even without atomic weapons. 'And today they have more planes, a sufficient number of atomic bombs, and they are nestled practically next to our door. So we should have a totally different type of air-defence, which would be capable, even under a massive attack, of not allowing through even a single aircraft.' The final design envisaged two rings of radar and missile bases around the Soviet capital. In 1952–3, the enormously expensive and hectic construction began.[92]

It is unclear when and how Soviet intelligence contributed to Stalin's concern that a surprise attack might destroy basic Soviet centres, communications, and industries. After the declassification of some Pentagon contingency plans for an aerial attack on the Soviet Union (Dropshot, Offtackle, etc.), several Soviet sources indicated that they had been well-known to the Soviet leadership from the moment of their conception. Some of the National Intelligence Estimates, prepared by the CIA, reached Stalin's desk, and in the fall of 1951 at least several NIEs dealt with the consequences of a US air strike against the USSR. It is important to understand: America planned to drop atomic bombs on the Soviet Union to defend Western Europe. But Stalin saw those plans as a threat to destroy him in a surprise attack, just as Hitler had sought to do.[93]

Gradually, as the Korean War stabilized along the thirty-eighth parallel, it became clear how significant was the American superiority in air power: even without atomic bombs, the Americans inflicted horrendous casualties and destruction in Korea. Stalin searched for the means to cope with this threat. He ordered the Main Operational Directorate, the planning heart of the Soviet General Staff, to prepare for the deployment of superior Soviet tank forces in Central Europe. According to his doctrine of retaliation, a powerful force of armoured divisions would occupy the territory of NATO allies all the way to the English Channel and the Atlantic coast of Europe. According to Marshall Sergei Akhromeyev, Stalin believed that this armoured threat would counter the American nuclear threat. The General Staff veterans recall another of Stalin's instructions: American pilots must reckon with the possibility that by the time they return from their missions, their airfields will have been taken over by Soviet tanks. It was a crude bluff since Americans had stationed their strategic aviation as far away as the North African coast.[94]

Stalin also ordered sabotage operations against American forward-based air-fields, in case of war. A Special Bureau Number One for Diversions and Intelligence of the MGB planned through 1948–53 to cause serious damage to the enemy.[95] Many of these actions may now seem to be bizarre bluffs, but this is less the case if one reads the now declassified CIA estimates of Soviet war capabilities. The thrust of those estimates after August 1949 was that there was a very remote chance that Soviet atomic weapons would be used against the United States. Even if Stalin did not obtain these estimates through espionage, his actions were consistent with the logic of deterrence, given that he hoped to create as much uncertainty as possible for a potential atomic aggressor.

During the Korean War, the Soviet military based their plans on the belief that the war with the 'imperialists' would be waged only with conventional weapons. 'The use of atomic weapons by them was considered problematic, and hence of little probability,' says the most recent study by Soviet military historians. 'The proposition, that the United States would not use nuclear weapons in the nearest future, was borne out by the experience of the Korean war (1950–3).'[96]

In the last months of his life, the 'small' Committee of Information, one of the Soviet bureaus of intelligence analysis, reported to Stalin in a similar mes-sage, that US military leaders are not convinced in practicality of using the atomic bomb in Korea. They are afraid that, if the use of atomic weapons does not ensure real preponderance for the United States, that would deal a final blow to US prestige. Besides, in this case, in their opinion, the existing US stockpile of atomic weapons would considerably lose its importance as a means of intimidation.[97]

How did Stalin react to this information? Was he as recklessly complacent as was his military about the possibility of nuclear escalation in the Korean War? The memoirs of Nikita Khrushchev portray Stalin as an old man, increas-ingly obsessed with insecurity and the expectation that war might break out any day. Yet, the old dictator had another motivation as well. Stalin remained 'an old curmudgeon' till his last breath—walking on the razor's edge of con-frontation, probably deciding to lead 'this last and decisive battle' of his life to a victorious conclusion. The hasty unanimity with which, after Stalin's death, his successors began to put out the Korean conflagration—motivated by their fear of possible escalation—speaks volumes about the real fear and tension that the nuclear-charged confrontation began to evoke inside the Kremlin.

We will never know how Stalin would have reacted to the appearance of the 'superbomb' and whether, had he lived longer, he would have concluded that thermonuclear weapons would lead to the obsolescence of major war. But we should hardly complain about it. The start of a new and more dangerous phase of the nuclear age coincided almost perfectly with the changing of the guard in the Kremlin.

In conclusion, Stalin understood the military and political significance of atomic weapons and directed all available resources to obtaining this weapon, as soon as he could do so after the end of World War II. His record in preparing the Soviet Union for the eventuality of an atomic war is impressive. But in all other respects, Stalin remained largely a statesman operating on the premises and experience of the pre-nuclear age. For him the emergence of atomic weapons made the prospect of a future war more terrifying, but no less likely.

He spent the rest of his life and the enormous resources of the Soviet Union preparing his country for war. Initially, he was cautious and reasonably pragmatic, and did not grasp the opportunity for expansion or aggression. In most cases, e.g. Iran and Germany, his objectives were limited and defensive. He expected to prevent a US–British alignment, to use the breathing space of peace for restoration of the Soviet economy and for military rearmament. Only after the victory of the Chinese communists did he break this rule and authorize aggression on a limited scale on the Korean peninsula.

America's atomic monopoly did not play a substantial role in deterring Stalin in the first phase of the Cold War. He knew that the US atomic arsenal was not sufficient to destroy the Soviet Union. Stalin was determined to defend his spheres of influence and to dispel any sign of possible Soviet weakness in the face of America's atomic sabre-rattling. At the same time, he was firmly convinced—along with most of his ministers and scientists—that only a similar force could deter the United States from using its atomic weapons again. And he was also concerned that, if the Americans learned about the Soviet crash programme, they might attempt to destroy it.

In about 1949 Stalin became particularly concerned about the possibility of an American atomic aerial attack. The period of maximum tension came at about the time of the first Soviet test. After the test was successful, he must have concluded that the United States would not be ready for a confrontation with the Soviet Union for several years to come. However, this led Stalin to a gross miscalculation about American intentions, when he, 'in the light of the changed international situation', sanctioned North Korean aggression in June 1950.

How should we understand the 'nuclear Stalin' among the dictator's many facets? Stalin, a genius of state terror, power-broking and war diplomacy, was different from statesmen in the democratic countries, but his outlook on world politics was consistent with the *realpolitik* of the pre-nuclear age. He had as much inclination as some of his 'liberal' Western counterparts to regard nuclear power as a means of augmenting military power and—in larger terms—the power of the state. One can even say there was a generic way in which both democratically elected politicians and post-revolutionary dictators reacted to this unprecedented technological breakthrough in military affairs.

Still, there are three obvious distinctions between Stalin and his Western contemporaries in the way he approached the start of the nuclear age. First, the ideological element in Stalin viewed war as a great opportunity for the social and political transformation of the world, despite the huge human and economic toll that it exacted. For Stalin, the peace after World War II was merely a transition period before the start of another war. However, he wanted to delay this war until the USSR had built up its strength. From this perspective he took Hiroshima not as the last episode of World War II but as the first salvo in a new confrontation. The atomic monopoly in his eyes could mean American domination in the non-communist world. Since Stalin also viewed the world as split into 'socialist' and 'capitalist' spheres of influence, this could mean that the next great war would occur not between the 'imperialist' powers, but between the United States and the Soviet Union.

Second, as a suspicious dictator, Stalin never trusted America's good intentions. He did not take seriously the opportunity to avoid the arms race or to establish international control over atomic energy. He believed the Truman Administration not only intended to deny the Soviet Union the fruits of victory through 'atomic diplomacy', but he also regarded the Bikini tests as a clear case of America's 'atomic blackmail'. His response to this was assertive, sometimes bordering on provocative behaviour, with the aim of teaching America a lesson. In a sense, Stalin's suspicions proved to be contagious—as the Cold War became rapidly militarized and driven by mutual fears and suspicions.

Third, for Stalin the author of the modern police state, the nuclear age became a further powerful justification for turning the Soviet Union into a super-secret 'black-box', and for continuing to rely on extraordinary wartime policies of mobilization and production. He was determined to build the bomb in complete secrecy, regardless of the cost in human and material resources. In the process, he created a totally new military-industrial complex and sought to end the strategic invulnerability of the United States. Without Stalin's will, it is doubtful that a task of this magnitude could have been achieved by a war-weary Soviet Union.

4

John Foster Dulles' Nuclear Schizophrenia

NEAL ROSENDORF

RECENT studies of John Foster Dulles have made much of his 'complex amalgam' of seemingly contradictory characteristics[1]; he was at his most inconsistent over the issue of nuclear weapons. Dulles registered strong disapproval, on moral grounds, of the atomic bombing of Japan and warned at the time of the dangerous precedent the USA was setting in using nuclear weapons. He expressed on many occasions his profound anxiety about this weapon which could literally destroy humanity. Several times he suggested international controls of one sort or another on nuclear energy. Indeed, late in 1945 one of Dulles' colleagues at the Council on Foreign Relations asserted disapprovingly to then-Under Secretary of State Dean Acheson that Dulles held a 'pacifist ivory tower bias'.[2]

Yet, for some years Dulles was an ardent proponent of massive retaliation, which threatened a possible thermonuclear strike in response to conventional aggression. Dulles strove to break down the 'false distinction' between the A-bomb and conventional weapons which was working, he believed, to the Soviets' military and propaganda advantage. He counselled the use of nuclear weapons more than once. Dulles eventually moved away from massive retaliation toward a flexible response approach, partly because he recognized that huge thermonuclear bombs would always be perceived as terror weapons and thus serve the USSR's purposes, partly because they did not offer a credible deterrent against anything other than an all-out Soviet strike that was becoming ever less likely, partly because these bombs truly could destroy the human race. However, integral to his proposed flexible arsenal were small, 'clean' nuclear weapons as a cost-effective, usable deterrent against low-level provocation that would keep down the risk of escalation if employed.

This examination will incidentally address political scientist John Mueller's counterfactually-based assertion that 'while nuclear weapons may have substantially influenced political rhetoric, public discourse, and defense budgets and planning, it is not at all clear that they have had a significant impact on the history of world affairs since World War II.'[3] However, rather than explicitly test Mueller's thesis,[4] I want to focus on John Foster Dulles' oscillating thinking about the bomb—to put it somewhat melodramatically, Dulles' 'nuclear schizophrenia'.

John Foster Dulles never developed a coherent attitude or policy toward nuclear weapons, as we shall see. This chapter does not purport definitively to answer the question of why Dulles experienced swings back and forth between anxiety over the atomic bomb's terrible potential for destruction and eagerness to use the bomb as a diplomatic, and occasionally military, club; 'why' is a metaphysical black hole down which too many historians have already disappeared.

None the less, there is one possible partial explanation. From as early as 1939 (prior to the outbreak of World War II), when he wrote *War, Peace and Change*, through the earliest years of the Cold War, Dulles espoused the belief that it was much too risky to rely on large-scale armament as a deterrent to war.[5] Recognizing the unprecedented destructive power of the atomic bomb, Dulles called for international control of atomic energy.[6] He viewed the Soviet Union as 'dynamic' and atheistic but believed that the Soviets recognized the unique danger which nuclear weapons posed to humanity;[7] moreover, given the USSR's defensive military tradition and the Communist Party's reliance on subversion, at which they were practised, it was unlikely, in Dulles' opinion, that the Soviets would attempt to launch an invasion against the nuclear-armed West.[8]

However, the invasion of South Korea by its communist northern neighbour caused Dulles to adopt a very different view of the Soviets. He now saw the USSR as recklessly adventuristic, undeterred by 'moral principles backed by potential might'; henceforth, the USA would have to rely on 'military strength-in-being'.[9] In adopting this position, Dulles evidently re-evaluated a position he had dismissed eleven years earlier. Dulles noted in *War, Peace and Change*, 'It is sometimes argued that large armament is the best peace policy. Of course, individual states may from time to time be so circumstanced that their particular peaceful future can best be assured by armament . . . It cannot be denied that the argument for armaments has some plausibility.' At the time Dulles had concluded that 'it is, however, unsafe to place our hope of peace upon the terrifying influences of vast armament. The consequences of being wrong are too appalling.'[10] But now, judging from his shift to support for nuclear deterrence, the USA was in Dulles' estimation an 'individual state . . . so circumstanced' that it required atomic weapons to assure its 'particular peaceful future'.

Additionally, US reliance on nuclear weapons dovetailed with another Dulles axiom articulated in 1939 which he had never abandoned. He wrote at the time that 'armament on the modern scale involves great unproductive expenditure. Raw materials and labor are required to be diverted from the production of consumer goods. No nation can arm on the scale now current without appreciably lowering the national standards of living. This in turn accentuates internal difficulties.'[11] Nuclear weapons, while not by any means cheap, were much less expensive than the conventional armaments and manpower in which the communist bloc held a clear lead. Dulles, like the President under whom he would serve as Secretary of State, always perceived economic vitality as integral to America's strategic power; he opposed any attempt to match the USSR soldier for soldier, weapon for weapon.

Obviously, Dulles' use of the pragmatic economic-vitality argument in the nuclear era was at ethical loggerheads with his pre-war espousal of the same position—in 1939 he had tied his criticism of diverting industry, raw materials, and manpower to armaments to his general opposition to deterrence based on a huge military machine; with his post-Korean invasion change of heart, Dulles was making a utilitarian argument in support of a deterrence policy which threatened massive nuclear retaliation against non-nuclear aggression.[12] It would not be too hyperbolic to say that Dulles' use of the economic-vitality argument in support of American reliance on nuclear deterrence amounted to a perversion of his earlier, anti-deterrence motivated position.

It is evident that there existed, beneath the very real contradictions, a certain tortured constancy to Dulles' thinking about nuclear weapons. Dulles would never abandon his early anxiety about the atomic bomb's potential to destroy the human race or his support for some sort of international controls—even as he continued to press for the integration of cost-effective, 'usable' tactical nuclear weapons into the US arsenal. Clearly, historians need to examine more closely than they have *War*, *Peace and Change* and his other relevant pre-Korean invasion writings and correspondence in order to broaden their understanding of Dulles' subsequent attitudes toward the bomb.

In light of John Foster Dulles' later reputation as a trigger-happy nuclear warrior, the certitude and the speed with which he expressed his initial horrified reaction to the atomic bomb is noteworthy. The *Enola Gay* dropped its payload over Hiroshima on 6 August 1945. The next day Dulles, who was then the chairman of the Federal Council of Churches' Commission on a Just and Durable Peace, co-authored a telegram to the Council's president, Bishop G. Bromley Oxnam, in which he expressed his grave reservations about this new superweapon:

We are considering possible issuance tomorrow or next day of interfaith statement on atomic bombing presumably signed by yourself . . . Would suggest statement somewhat as follows[:] 'the atomic bomb places mankind in deadly peril. Only defense against [it] lies in moral integrity and sense of responsibility of those who control it. If new power in hands of men is to be used responsibly, its initial use must set sound precedent. Therefore, we urge Allied governments give Japanese nation adequate opportunity reconsider terms of surrender before further devastation by atomic bomb visited on upon the people of Japan.

We further urge as soon as practicable control of this cosmic power be placed under international supervision at service of peace and human welfare. Atomic energy must serve whole family of nations, or mankind will perish.[13]

Dulles immediately set about fashioning a comprehensive statement in which he went considerably further in expressing his anxiety over the atomic bomb and his deep misgivings over its use by the United States.

As Dulles wrote, the USA dropped a second A-bomb, this time on Nagasaki. Two days later, on 10 August, Dulles and Oxnam jointly issued the statement to the press. Remarkably, given its contents, its public nature, and the later, controversially hawkish development of Dulles' thinking about nuclear weapons, this statement has been given scant notice by historians.[14] One cannot hope to understand the degree to which Dulles' views oscillated without taking into account his seminal declaration on the issue. For this reason, it is necessary to redress the historiographic oversight and examine the Dulles–Oxnam press release in some detail.

Dulles wrote that Americans could be proud that 'under their auspices a scientific miracle has been performed'. He warned, however, that while humanity had discovered 'incalculable new energy which can work for a fuller, better life for all', this same power 'might also make this planet uninhabitable'. The only defence against the latter fate was America's self-restraint and sense of responsibility. Dulles asserted that the United Nations had to be rapidly developed: 'The world,' he declared, 'has overnight become desperately dependent on international controls and on the mutual trust upon which they rest.'

In the most strongly worded segment of the statement, Dulles cautioned that the example the USA set in employing the atomic bomb against Japan would profoundly affect the future:

One choice open to us is immediately to wreak upon our enemy mass destruction such as men have never before imagined. That will inevitably obliterate men and women, young and aged, innocent and guilty alike because they are part of a nation which has attacked us and whose conduct has stirred our deep wrath. *If we, as a professedly Christian nation, feel morally free to use atomic energy in that way, men elsewhere will accept that verdict. Atomic weapons will be looked upon as a normal part of the arsenal of war and the stage will be set for the sudden and final destruction of mankind.* (emphasis added)

Dulles called for 'at least a temporary suspension or alteration' of the atomic bombing campaign so that the Japanese might have an opportunity to 'give the Japanese people adequate opportunity to react to the new situation' and surrender. He noted that such munificence would require the United States to exercise great self-restraint. 'However,' Dulles wrote, 'our supremacy is now so overwhelming that such restraint would be taken everywhere as evidence, not of weakness, but of moral and physical greatness.'[15]

President Harry S. Truman's response to the Dulles–Oxnam statement is not known.[16] However, Dulles believed for some time that his declaration had been instrumental in bringing about a cessation of the atomic bombing campaign. He wrote to an associate on the Federal Council of Churches that 'I think we can feel better for having called upon our government to exercise [moral restraint] with reference to this extremely dangerous new weapon, and there has, I gather, been at least some suspension, which even though temporary may improve the moral stature of our nation in the world.'[17] Several days after issuing the statement, Dulles wrote an editorial piece for the Dallas Morning News in which he further underlined his anxieties about the devastating new weapon and his hope that it would be placed under international control; it also starkly documents Dulles' perception that the atomic bomb was a unique addition to the global order. This article, like the Dulles–Oxnam statement, is dramatic when compared to Dulles' later image but little (if at all) noted by historians; it too warrants close examination.

'As we move from war to peace,' Dulles wrote, 'we feel little jubilation and much concern. For the atomic bomb proves, what [sic] we feared, that the next major war will be a thousand-fold more disastrous than the worst war we have yet known. We feel uncertain that the United Nations will be able to prevent that war and keep the peace.' Dulles stated that this uncertainty was justified— while great wars customarily have brought in their wake sincere peace efforts, they have always failed. The present effort would fail as well unless the USA handled the problem more intelligently and realistically than ever before. 'Fortunately,' he continued, 'we are off to a good start. The San Francisco Charter makes a new and hopeful approach to the problem of keeping peace . . .' Dulles once again stressed the importance of placing nuclear energy under international control.[18]

Dulles, it is clear, viewed nuclear weapons from the outset as a military and diplomatic watershed. As he thought through the strategic implications of the atomic bomb, he became increasingly concerned about how the Soviets in particular might make use of the new weapon. He wrote to a friend in December 1945, 'The development of the atomic bomb has certainly changed the situation from what it was.' Nuclear weapons, Dulles claimed, enormously increased the power of initiative. The Soviet Union's leaders were 'dynamic' and 'atheistic', unrestrained by the satiation and morality which inhibited the 'static' West. Dulles noted that Soviet Foreign Minister Vyacheslav Molotov had indicated in a recent speech that he believed the West's 'rather tough position' at the Council of Foreign Ministers meeting in London was due to the American monopoly of the atomic bomb. Dulles asserted that 'of course, any use of the atomic bomb against Russia never entered our minds'. He noted darkly, 'the fact, however, that it entered Molotov's mind indicates what might have been the case had their position been reversed.'[19]

None the less, despite the Soviets' discomfiting predilections, Dulles did 'not think that anything cataclysmic is going to happen for some years'.[20] He continued to warn about the atomic bomb's revolutionary impact on world affairs and to call for international controls. In early 1946 Dulles observed that 'when war comes, nations avail themselves of any weapon which they think will make the difference between victory and defeat.' Any international agreement forswearing the use of nuclear weapons would surely fail, as had all similar preceding agreements. 'It can be taken as absolutely certain,' he declared, 'that, in the event of a another major war, the parties will, if they can, use atomic energy, any agreement to the contrary notwithstanding.' The United Nations could not be a law-making body while there was no global consensus as to what constituted justice. But the UN could help advance the process of building trust between nations, and the USA could help the UN by subjecting its atomic knowledge, through the General Assembly, 'to the dictates of the same world opinion that we would invoke in favor of the other post-war settlements'. Dulles had 'no idea what the Assembly would recommend and it is not of primary importance'. What was most important, wrote Dulles, 'is that we accept a procedure which shows that we really mean it when we say that we are merely a trustee of atomic power'.[21]

The Soviet Union did not accept the Baruch Plan for the international control of atomic energy, which the USA proffered later in 1946. Despite his disappointment, Dulles continued to advocate such a programme. He had not changed his views by March of 1948, although he was becoming frustrated by the USSR's unwillingness to sign on to the plan he envisaged. Speaking in Toronto, he offered that 'it may be possible to have world government with respect to some particular matters, even before it is possible to have world government generally. That is possible because there are some matters as to which there is already a large measure of world-wide agreement. One of these matters is the control of atomic energy . . .' Dulles declared that the Atomic Energy Commission had 'developed a program on which there could be substantial unanimity except for the Soviet Union'. Dulles moderated his criticism of the Soviets with the optimistic opinion that 'even here the difference appears as a difference of procedure and not of substance'. He admonished the USSR for 'wrangling about procedure' for over two years while 'knowledge about how to use—and misuse—atomic energy also grows in different parts of the world'. Dulles observed that 'this year—1948—may be the last during which any single country will have any effective monopoly of the knowledge of how to use atomic energy.' Dulles, giving vent to his fundamental distrust of the 'dynamic', 'atheistic' Soviet dictatorship, warned that international rule over nuclear energy should be put into effect before 'atomic "know how" can be a menace in the hands of men who believe that their ends justify even means of violence'.[22]

The Berlin blockade further darkened Dulles' already pessimistic view of the Soviets. Dulles was no doubt alarmed by Stalin's destabilizing scheme, which apparently ran the risk of provoking US nuclear retaliation.[23] He ruefully cautioned President Truman in October 1948 that 'the American people would execute you if you did not use the bomb in the event of war'.[24] Still, Dulles remained convinced that the Soviet Union did not want war. He made his opinion clear in an interview in July 1949: 'That doesn't mean they will constantly recede—that you can do anything you want with them. They will accept a war if they think you are forcing it on them—but, in my opinion, Soviet policy prefers not to rely on war as a means of achieving its ends.' When asked to what extent the possession by the USA of the atomic bomb acted as a factor in deterring the USSR, he replied, 'I don't think it is a decisive factor—

although that's only a guess.'[25] The Communist Party, Dulles claimed, 'depends for its effectiveness on the subversive war, the infiltration, the attempt to overthrow existing institutions because of their weaknesses.' Outright military aggression would undermine essential propaganda efforts to portray the USSR 'as peace-loving and desirous of bringing to the people peace and prosperity'.[26]

And then the Soviets detonated an A-bomb. Dulles had been among those who expected the Soviets to develop a nuclear weapon by 1949, so he was not shocked by the event. In *War or Peace*, published in 1950, Dulles reiterated his belief that the USSR was not inclined to go to war. He declared once again that 'Soviet Communism is a doctrine which, theoretically, could gain world-wide acceptance without military conquest.' However, the Soviet Union, by ending the United States' monopoly on atomic energy, had 'radically altered the strategic situation to its own advantage'. America's ability to launch a nuclear attack against the Soviet Union 'is now largely neutralized by the ability of the Soviet to deliver atomic bombs in the United States and Western Europe. Perhaps the position is more than neutralized, for our economy may be more vulnerable than that of the Soviet Union to atomic attack.' Dulles recognized that possession of the bomb 'greatly increases the area within which the Soviet Communist leaders and the leaders of local Communist parties can exert terroristic threats'.[27]

Still, Dulles warned that the USA must not allow itself to be carried away by allowing parochial political or military factors to determine foreign policy. The Western Europeans, he asserted, were uncomfortable with guarantees of an American atomic attack to be unleashed on the USSR after the Soviets had already conquered them. He noted his support for the Military Assistance Program, which was designed to aid the Western European powers develop a co-ordinated defence of the Continent. Dulles was concerned as well about America's long-standing image in the eyes of the world 'as a peace-loving nation'. If the United States were to seem militaristic, then the USSR, which despite its violently subversive tactics was successfully waging a 'peace offensive', would be handed a propaganda victory at America's expense. While 'it would be folly to risk the safety of the nation upon the accuracy of what, at best, are educated guesses' about the USSR's military predilections, America's 'moral authority' was its most valuable asset in the Cold War. Dulles asserted that the military must remain firmly subordinated to civilian decision-makers. The military's advice, valuable though it was, had to be weighed, Dulles stated, 'by those who believe that war is not inevitable that we can and must have peace, and that it may be necessary to take some chances for peace'.[28] But within a short time Dulles would adopt a very different view.

The communist invasion of South Korea on 25 June 1950, shocked Dulles, who had in fact visited Seoul just a week earlier.[29] The Soviets, it seemed, were in fact ready to go to war for expansionistic purposes. A month after the outbreak of hostilities, Dulles wrote that the United States had to shift its approach to Soviet expansionism from the 'preventive phase' to the 'phase of opposition'. He precipitately abandoned his recent advocacy of American reliance primarily on 'moral authority': 'Since international Communism may not be deterred by moral principles backed by potential might,' Dulles proclaimed, 'we must back these principles with military strength-in-being, and do so quickly.'[30] The entry of the Peoples' Republic of China into the Korean War in October 1950 would only have intensified Dulles' genuine fear that the communist world was quite capable of fielding armies in the cause of expansion.

Dulles had decisively changed his thinking on nuclear weapons. But his present bellicose attitude did not so much supplant his earlier perspective as graft the new upon the old. As a result, his pronouncements both public and private would be contradictory virtually from one to the next; worried appraisals of atomic weaponry's potential for world destruction alternated with cold-blooded reckonings of the contributions reliance on nuclear deterrence made to America's fiscal health. These oscillations in perspective reflected Dulles' burgeoning nuclear schizophrenia.

Dulles' most famous pre-Eisenhower administration policy statement betrayed no bifurcated patterns of thinking. 'A Policy of Boldness', published in *Life* magazine in May 1952, displayed a more aggressive version of the new-found bellicosity that Dulles had evinced in his 1951 statement.[31] Although he again reiterated his usual assertion that the USSR would in all likelihood not go to war—which, in retrospect, seems a disingenuous portrayal of his opinion at that point—Dulles declared that there was only one correct response to the communist military threat: '*that is for the free world to develop the will and organize the means to retaliate instantly against open aggression by Red armies, so that, if it occurred anywhere, we could and would strike back where it hurts, by means of our choosing*' (emphasis in original text). The point, however, was not to wage general war, but to prevent its outbreak. 'If that catastrophe occurs,' Dulles claimed, 'it will be because we have allowed these new and awesome forces to become the ordinary killing tools of the soldier when, in the hands of statesmen, they could serve as effective political weapons in defense of the peace.'[32]

With this statement Dulles explicitly embraced the argument he had rejected thirteen years earlier in *War, Peace, and Change*. 'Of course,' Dulles had written in his first book, 'individual states may from time to time be so circumstanced that their particular peaceful future can best be assured by armament.' He had dismissed this idea at the time, declaring that 'with such individual cases we are not here concerned, for what we are considering is a world system designed to eliminate force as the mechanism of organic evolution . . . It is . . . unsafe to place our hope of peace upon the terrifying influences of vast armament. The consequences of being wrong are too appalling.'[33] Now, however, the United States faced a nuclearized, expansionistic USSR that had seemingly demonstrated its bellicosity in Korea. America was in Dulles' opinion 'so circumstanced' and hence completely justified in wielding the atomic bomb for its very survival.

'A Policy of Boldness' resurrected another argument from *War, Peace, and Change* that Dulles had always espoused—but now the ethical cant was profoundly different. He wrote in 1939 that 'armament on the modern scale involves great unproductive expenditure. Raw material and labor are required to be diverted from the production of consumer goods. No nation can arm on the scale now current without appreciably lowering the national standards of living. This in turn accentuates internal difficulties.'[34] Dulles recognized the economic compatibility between this perspective and nuclear weapons—the fact that atomic bombs were appreciably less expensive than equivalent conventional firepower—well before 1952. He evidently felt uneasy over the amorality of this dovetailed argument, as he raised the topic only obliquely in the pre-Korean invasion *War or Peace*.[35]

The North Korean attack removed such reservations. Dulles had been reading and virtually memorizing Stalin's *Problems of Leninism*, in which he discerned a Soviet plan to bankrupt the West by subjecting it to a debilitatingly expensive conventional arms race. Now that the USSR had thrown down the gauntlet, Dulles could assert openly—and apparently in good conscience—'In June 1950 we responded hastily to the North Korean attack upon the republic of Korea, and we then plunged into a vast armament program for ourselves and for our Western allies . . . Ours are treadmill policies which, at best, might perhaps keep us in the same place until we drop exhausted.' The solution, of course, was 'atomic energy, coupled with strategic air and sea power, [which] provides the community of free nations with vast new possibilities of organizing a community power to stop open aggression before it starts and reduce, to the vanishing point, the risk of general war.'[36]

Republican candidate for president General Dwight D. Eisenhower was discomfited by Dulles' advocacy of 'a community punishing force known to be ready and resolute to retaliate, in the event of any armed aggression, with weapons of its choosing against targets of its choosing at times of its choosing'.[37] Eisenhower wrote Dulles, 'we must be successful in developing collective security measures for the free world—measures that will encourage each of these countries to develop its own economic and spiritual strength. Exclusive reliance upon a mere power of retaliation is not a complete answer to the broad Soviet threat.'[38] However, despite his evident uneasiness with Dulles' emphasis on a policy of nuclear retaliation against even conventional aggression, Eisenhower chose him to serve as his Secretary of State.

Almost immediately the new administration took up the question of exactly how to employ nuclear weapons to advance US policy goals. Eisenhower had promised during his campaign to extricate the United States from the draining and inconclusive Korean War. Peace talks had been going on between the USA and the PRC for years to no avail; the Chinese kept throwing up roadblocks, at least partly on the assumption that the USA would tire of the domestically unpopular conflict. In February 1953, at an extraordinary National Security Council meeting, Eisenhower sounded out his new cabinet on the subject of nuclear weapons policy and seemed to advocate the military use of nuclear weapons to break the stalemate.[39] Reviewing a report from the field that a large-scale communist attack seemed imminent, Eisenhower 'expressed the view that we should consider the use of tactical atomic weapons on the Kaesong area, which provided a good target for this type of weapon. In any case, the President added, we could not go on the way we are indefinitely.' Secretary Dulles raised the 'moral problem and the inhibitions on the use of the A-bomb, and Soviet success in setting atomic weapons apart from all other weapons as being in a special category'. Dulles had spent years arguing this very point, but now, with the battle lines unequivocally drawn and nuclear deterrence firmly embraced, he declared that 'it was his opinion that we should try to break down this false distinction'.[40]

Dulles here articulated the basis of a policy tack he would pursue for the balance of his tenure: enhance deterrence's credibility by making nuclear weapons appear usable, even against conventional challenges. When it became apparent that large, 'dirty' (radioactively speaking) nuclear devices were a credible deterrent only against an attack with similar devices, Dulles would champion small, clean, atomic weapons.

In an NSC meeting a week later, Dulles drove home his position on using nuclear weapons to promote America's defence inexpensively. Eisenhower stated at one point that the United States was 'trying to build redoubts throughout the free world, to be manned so far as possible by indigenous armed forces . . . Briefly summarized,' said the President, 'he meant, "Get outposts established and get our own people home".' Dulles inquired whether this meant that the USA should proceed slowly with its atomic programme, with defence predicated in the main on American or indigenous conventional forces. The President replied that the United States 'cannot depend solely, or perhaps even primarily, on atomic bombs' if Europe was considered America's first line of defence, and he was 'emphatically concerned with the buildup of Europe's defenses'. The Chairman of the Joint Chiefs of Staff believed that the USA had to develop both its conventional and atomic capabilities. Dulles replied that 'this might be reasonable enough, but where would the money come from? It might be impossible to do both.'[41] Dulles had apparently abandoned morality, and even personal anxiety, in favour of economic expediency.

Several months later, however, he revealed that he still possessed his long-established sense of dread over nuclear weapons. The Soviets detonated a thermonuclear device in August 1953, matching the American H-bomb success of a year earlier, which may have reminded Dulles just how grave was the threat he had so often warned about in the past. Speaking before the United Nations General Assembly in November, Dulles expressed his apprehension in terms that harkened back to the mid-1940s, long before he had given up on the USSR and embraced nuclear deterrence. '. . . Physical scientists,' he solemnly declared, 'have now found the means which, if they were developed, can wipe life off the surface of the planet.' Dulles continued, warning that

These words that I speak are words that can be taken literally. The destructive power inherent in matter must be controlled by the idealism of the spirit and the wisdom of the mind. They alone stand between us and a lifeless planet. There are plenty of problems in this world. . . . But there is no problem which compares with this central, universal problem of saving the human race from extinction.[42]

Dulles spoke as well in support of international control. While he was keenly aware of the propaganda necessity of depicting America as reasonable and the Soviets as obstructionist, his rhetoric here as well closely resembled his pre-Korea position. Dulles stated that the nations had so far been unsuccessful in developing the institutions for international control. 'Therefore, some of the nations have developed their own community measures to deter aggression and to give protection to moral values that they cherish.' (Once again, Dulles presented the United States and its allies as special cases, 'so circumstanced' by Soviet bellicosity that they were justified in relying on nuclear deterrence—his oscillations never ceased.) The crucial missing element, said Dulles, was trust among the concerned nations.

But trust alone could not accomplish the job; verifiability was crucial: We have faith that the time may come—it might come quickly and suddenly—when political leaders would be prepared to put into effect international agreements limiting armaments. When that moment comes, the nations should be able to seize it. That moment—we must not let it escape. Perhaps it could never be recaptured. But to seize the moment requires that the technical analysis of the problem should before then have been advanced.

Dulles insisted that any proposals meet one fundamental test: there had to be 'effective safeguards to ensure the compliance of all nations and to give adequate warning of possible evasions or violations . . .'[43] Dulles may have been cynically playing for propaganda points on the Soviets' well-known acute aversion to any kind of inspection. But his basic statement of support for internationalized control of nuclear energy was consistent with both his earlier, pre-Korea pronouncements and future ruminations on the subject. In a May 1954 NSC meeting Dulles raised the idea of a moratorium on nuclear testing provided tests recently completed had given the USA a clear qualitative edge over the USSR and, more to the point, that it could be satisfactorily monitored. (Dulles eventually rescinded the idea).[44]

Two years later he would again propose international nuclear energy controls, this time evidently in earnest. In a private conversation with Eisenhower, Dulles asserted 'that atomic power was too vast a power to be left for the military use of any one country'; hence, it should be 'internationalized for security purposes'; if the USSR would be willing to relinquish its veto, the United Nations Security Council would assume control 'so as to universalize the capacity of atomic thermonuclear weapons to deter aggression'.[45] Dulles' original thinking on nuclear weapons would continue to co-exist awkwardly with his more recently adopted hawkish posture.

Several months after giving his UN speech, Dulles revealed the degree to which he had embraced a bellicose attitude toward nuclear weapons. During a December 1953 NSC meeting, just days before Eisenhower was to give his famous 'atoms for peace' speech (which Dulles felt uncomfortable with because of its 'public diplomacy' approach[46]), he went beyond advocating the efficacy of nuclear deterrence—he advocated the actual use of atomic weapons. A truce had been signed in July 1953 which ended hostilities in Korea. However, negotiations for a final settlement became bogged down, and by December the Eisenhower administration was uneasily considering the possibility that the Chinese might be planning a large-scale resumption of hostilities. JCS Chairman Admiral Arthur Radford proposed that if the Chinese attacked, the USA would respond with nuclear counter-attacks against their positions in Korea, Manchuria, and North China which would 'defeat the Chinese Communists in Korea and make them incapable of aggression there or anywhere else in the Far East for a very considerable time'. Dulles observed in turn that Radford's plan contemplated general war against both the PRC and the USSR. He believed that 'there were grave disadvantages to a course of action such as this' and offered the State Department's more modest counter-proposal, 'which would be less likely to involve the Soviet Union in the war': 'the State Department felt that the first of such courses of action amounted to a full atomic strike in Korea itself. The second involved the bombing of troop concentrations in and near the area of Korea.' Dulles envisaged 'the prosecution of a war which would produce a victory *in* Korea'[47] (emphasis in original text). Of course, no Communist Chinese attack occurred, a peace agreement was worked out, and Korea settled into an uneasy stability; moreover, even if hostilities had resumed, it is unclear whether Eisenhower would have authorized the use of nuclear weapons to repel the Chinese.[48] Still, in advocating the use—as opposed to the brandishing—of the A-bomb should the Chinese attack, Dulles was going beyond using nuclear weapons to deter 'open aggression before it starts and reduce, to the vanishing point, the risk of general war'.[49]

A month later, Dulles delivered his infamous 'massive retaliation' speech to the Council on Foreign Relations. He declared that local defences had to be reinforced by 'massive retaliatory power' (privately he minimized the utility of local defences[50]). 'The way to deter aggression,' maintained Dulles, 'is for the free community to be willing and able to respond vigorously at places and with means of its own choosing.' Dulles believed, as did Eisenhower, that the tacit threat of nuclear force had persuaded China to abandon its negotiating intransigence over the Korean conflict and conclude a disengagement agreement. He asserted that 'in Korea this administration effected a major transformation. The fighting has been stopped on honorable terms. That was possible because the aggressor, already thrown back to and behind his place of beginning, was faced with the possibility that the fighting might, to his own great peril, soon spread beyond the limits and methods which he had selected.' In retrospect, it is likely that Stalin's death and the general loosening of tensions his passing engendered was the crucial factor in causing the Chinese to soften their bargaining position. But Dulles' faith in the singular deterrent and coercive power of nuclear weapons was significantly enhanced.[51]

Dulles made clear his faith in a question and answer session which followed the delivery of his CFR speech. He commented on Walter Lippmann's assertion that the Soviet nuclear arsenal had rendered collective security obsolete and unworkable: 'I do not accept that view at all, and in fact I adopt quite the contrary view that the existence of this terrific weapon makes more essential than ever before that the collective security concept should be adhered to.' Dulles told his audience to imagine an international system in which the USA did not possess retaliatory power to cancel out that of the Soviets. The USSR, run by 'a group of people who have no moral inhibitions . . . [to whom] power is something to be used . . . to crush out liberty and extend their type of dictatorship all over the world', could 'come to a certain country—let us call it country X—and threaten an immediate nuclear attack if Soviet demands were not met. The only bulwark against such blackmail is just one thing alone and that is that it is known that the United States has the capacity to retaliate massively and therefore they do not dare to do that.'[52]

Dulles continued to reiterate this policy line, in similarly hyperbolic terms, over the next several months. At a NATO meeting in Paris in April 1954, Dulles clarified the US position regarding atomic and hydrogen weapons. He noted once again that 'the free world would have great difficulty in matching the non-atomic military strength of the Soviet bloc man for man. Such an effort would impose critical strains upon the economic, social, and fiscal orders of many of the free nations and expose them to serious instability and unrest within their own borders.' Having made his economic argument, he turned to the Soviet threat and the necessary Western counterpoise: 'it is indispensable that the free world possess and maintain a capacity for instant and formidable retaliation . . . Without that, the free world might be totally dominated by the power possessed by the Soviet rulers, a power the use of which is not inhibited by any moral considerations. Such power, in such hands, is restrained only by a fear of retaliation . . .' Dulles pressed his case for breaking down the 'false distinction', claiming that 'without the availability for use of atomic weapons, the security of all NATO forces in Europe would be in grave danger in the event of a surprise Soviet attack . . . it should be our agreed policy, in the case of (either general war or local) war, to use atomic weapons as conventional weapons against the assets of the military whenever and wherever it would be of advantage to do so, taking account of all relevant factors'[53] (parentheses in original).

But the inconsistencies in Dulles' perspective could crop up in the midst of his most overblown oratory. In the course of the NATO presentation, he stated that the Western retaliatory capacity had to exist 'until the day may come when the awful possibilities of massive destruction can be done away with by effective international control of atomic energy with suitable safeguards'.[54] While this statement can be interpreted as a sop by Dulles to US allies who were uneasy about massive retaliation, it is consistent with the sentiments Dulles had been expressing intermittently since 1945. During a public speech earlier the same month, after delivering his boilerplate warning that 'the rulers of the Soviet bloc are not inhibited by any moral considerations . . . they have no compunctions at all about mass destruction' and that only the USA nuclear deterrent stood in their way, Dulles reverted momentarily back to his mid-1940s rhetoric and described nuclear war as 'the last desperate catastrophe'.[55] This despite Dulles' desire to break down the 'false distinction' between nuclear and conventional weapons that was aiding the Soviet propaganda position.

Just as the first Quemoy-Matsu crisis was breaking out in September 1954, Clare Booth Luce wrote Dulles a memorandum on foreign policy in which she suggested that the USA pre-emptively launch a nuclear attack against the PRC to 'liberate' the mainland. A politic Dulles responded to Luce that the liberation of China 'by war using nuclear weapons, is a matter which deserves and receives very careful consideration. But to take the initiative in precipitating atomic war involves the greatest consequences in terms of our world-wide relations. It is not clear that on balance we would win.'[56] In fact, although he framed his reply diplomatically in deference to Luce's political and public opinion clout, Dulles could not have conceived of such a strategy, if for no other reason than that unilateral US nuclear action would probably destroy the Western Alliance; he was acutely sensitive to the Allies' anxieties about US nuclear policy.[57] Expediency would have been strengthened by Dulles' deep-rooted aversion to precipitating all-out global war. His response amounted to an utter rejection of Luce's proposal; he may very well have regarded her idea as crackpot.

Dulles evaluated US national security policy in late 1954: 'The increased destructiveness of nuclear weapons and the approach of effective atomic parity,' he asserted, 'are creating a situation in which general war would threaten the destruction of Western civilization and of the Soviet regime, and in which national objectives could not be attained through a general war, even if a military victory were won.'[58] He counselled, among other things, that the USA should maintain 'flexible military capabilities' to enhance the credibility of its deterrent but avoid provocative actions, although Dulles' idea of flexibility meant smaller, 'cleaner' nuclear weapons, as he would later explicitly state.[59] For Dulles, at least some of the time, the trick to avoiding the risk of a world-ending thermonuclear exchange was to develop nuclear weapons small enough which, if used, could not reasonably provoke the Soviets into unleashing Armageddon. Moreover, the Soviets were not to be apprised of this flexible approach. A reporter asked Dulles in December 1954 whether a US 'strategic atomic attack would only be used in retaliation for the same thing'; Dulles replied 'that he preferred not to answer that question because he thought it would serve a greater use outside of this room than in it'.[60] America's official posture remained that the Soviets might expect a full-scale thermonuclear attack in response to non-nuclear aggression.

During the Quemoy-Matsu crisis, Dulles stepped up his campaign to break down the 'false distinction' between nuclear and conventional weapons in order to keep credible the threat of massive retaliation. He declared during a press conference in December 1954 that current US 'policies will gradually include the use of atomic weapons as conventional weapons for tactical purposes'. Dulles went on to draw a sharp distinction between the tactical and strategic uses of weapons:

That distinction is not peculiar to atomic weapons. The same distinction existed during the last war when there came the question as to whether or not to carry out the bombing of the German cities. The question of whether or not you use weapons of any kind for massive retaliation and mass destruction is a question which poses itself in any war.

As I say, it is not distinctive to the use of atomic weapons which are merely weapons which have greater destructive capabilities than the weapons that were known before then. There has been a progressive increase throughout history of the destructive capacity of weapons. That always brings with it these problems as to whether you use them for tactical purposes or for so-called strategic purposes.[61]

Encountering friction over this policy tack, Dulles attempted to backtrack slightly. In February 1955 he professed that 'the question of just when the war justifies the use of these more powerful weapons is something which doesn't lend itself to very accurate preview. In the main, if there is only a small activity, it would not be necessary to use atomic weapons.' However, Dulles then qualified this remark, noting once again that atomic weapons were being treated to a great extent as conventional weapons. 'It does not seem to make much sense,' he said, if you have one bomb—one artillery shot—which will do the business, but use a hundred others which are most costly and the result is just the same.'[62]

Dulles continued during the offshore island crisis to blur the distinction between nuclear and conventional weapons. While speaking with reporters in March 1955, he claimed that although the former were 'weapons of relatively small dimensions with considerably more explosive power than is contained in the conventional weapons . . . they are weapons of precision'. Dulles then added a singularly disquieting thought: 'I imagine that if the United States became engaged in a major military activity anywhere in the world that those weapons would come into use because, as I say, they are more and more becoming conventional and replacing what used to be called conventional weapons.'[63] Robert Bowie, the head of the State Department's Policy Planning Staff, was suspicious that Dulles was receiving faulty information from JCS Chairman Radford and commissioned a CIA report estimating the number of civilian deaths should the USA attack military targets near Quemoy and Matsu with nuclear weapons; the number the CIA arrived at was well into the millions.[64] However, Dulles would continue, in both classified and public forums, to push the idea that nuclear weapons could be used conventionally.

In the months following Dulles' policy assessment and his problematic statements on nuclear policy, the idea came up within the Eisenhower administration of using an upcoming Four-Power summit meeting to make a dramatic arms control proposition. Eventually, the idea became focused down into the Open Skies proposal. Dulles was sceptical about using a highly public forum such as a summit conference to engage in serious negotiations; he felt quite justifiably that such venues placed pressures on the participants to show significant results, which in turn increased the likelihood of a Western negotiating slip and a policy of appeasement.[65] However, Dulles gave the subject of arms control renewed attention. He struck a sceptical note in a private memorandum to Eisenhower in late June 1955, warning that 'the greater military potential of the United States . . . gives the United States its maximum bargaining power and this is a power that should not be cheaply relinquished.' He counselled at this point, 'It is suggested that while any present plan could and should hold out the promise of future agreed stabilization and/or reduction of armament . . . there should not be any effort to agree on any overall plan until first a measure of inspection has been tried out and found to be workable.'[66]

But this did not mean that Dulles was unequivocally opposed to arms limitation under any circumstances. In an NSC meeting the next day he pursued a line of reasoning which recalled his 1948 opinion that 'it may be possible to have world government with respect to some matters, even before it is possible to have world government generally. That is possible because there are some matters as to which there is already a large measure of world-wide agreement. One of these matters is the control of atomic energy.' This is not to say that Dulles believed that the US and the USSR held similar views concerning how to control the risk of thermonuclear war; but the superpowers did concur that nuclear weapons threatened the end of the world, and this fundamental concurrence could leave open the possibility of some arms control agreement that would lessen the global threat and be advantageous to the USA.[67] He stated firmly that he disagreed with the Defense Department's contention 'that major change in the attitude and policies of the Soviet Union was an absolute precondition precedent to any acceptable plan for arms limitation'.

Dulles pronounced that the issue of arms control 'was of tremendous importance for the entire future of the United States'. The USA had to make some positive gesture; otherwise it would lose the support of its allies and the right to use bases in their countries. Moreover, Dulles said, 'he believed that the Soviets genuinely wanted some reduction in the armaments burden in order to be able to deal more effectively with their severe internal problems. Accordingly, the Soviet Union might be prepared to make concessions.' Dulles proposed that the USA reverse the Soviet strategy of calling for a disarmament plan first and a solution to the inspection problem afterward. By studying the problem of supervision and policing before formulating the plan to be policed, 'we would have world opinion on our side rather than the Russian side.'[68]

After the Geneva Conference, Dulles reviewed the disarmament talks in another NSC meeting and declared that although Eisenhower's proposal on an exchange of blueprints and mutual aerial reconnaissance was dramatic, 'it was also a serious means of initiating' an arms control programme. He further 'stated his belief that no state would initiate nuclear war unless it was certain that it would not be destroyed by a nuclear retaliatory blow. He said the President's plan could prevent nuclear war by making a surprise attack impossible.' Dulles expressed his support for transparency on both sides, contending that the number of planes necessary for reconnaissance to be effective might be relatively low. He said that he had made this point in rebutting an argument against Open Skies advanced by Senate Majority Leader William Knowland, who envisaged 'hundreds of Soviet planes over the United States dropping nuclear bombs simultaneously during their "peaceful" reconnaissance'.[69] But Dulles' position on arms control was not nearly as concrete as his statements here indicated. Within months he would display the extent of his mental turmoil.

The venue for this display was a lengthy memorandum on nuclear policy which Dulles submitted to Eisenhower in late January 1956. He wrote that 'current trends with respect to nuclear weapons, unless counteracted, could become seriously unfavorable to the United States' and listed the hazards which lay ahead. 'The United States may be physically endangered,' Dulles warned, noting worriedly that 'the Soviet Union is developing a capacity to devastate the United States by sudden attack. The Soviet destructive power . . . may, in a few years, become so great that it could, at a single stroke, virtually obliterate our industrial power and gravely impair our ability to retaliate, so that retaliatory capacity would lose much of its deterrent influence.' Additionally, America's world strategy, based on allies in Europe and Asia holding the forward positions while the USA wielded the bomb, might suffer as repugnance to the use of nuclear weapons grew to the point that these allies would retreat from collective defence.

America's moral leadership, Dulles continued, was endangered as well because of the world's 'growing, and not unreasonable fear that nuclear weapons are expanding at such a pace as to endanger human life on this planet, or at least vast segments of that life'. Despite the initial positive reception of the 'atoms for peace' and Open Skies proposals, it had become apparent that 'the United States has no broad plan for nuclear disarmament' even if those proposals were accepted; the Soviets had moved into the resulting 'vacuum' with its own sweeping proposals, causing the 'great masses to feel that at least the Russians *want* to end the thermonuclear danger while we are represented as stalling and trying to think up good reasons for perpetuating the danger and making it even greater'. America's moral leadership in the world might be stolen away by 'those whose creed denies moral principles'.

After setting forth this grim picture, Dulles began his gyrations. He declared that 'Soviet promises are utterly undependable' and expounded his oft-expressed conviction that the communist leaders were amoral and would both break promises and ruthlessly use superior power if they gained it. Furthermore, there were neither 'dependable controls for totally eliminating nuclear weapons' nor an 'international organization which can be dependably entrusted with the task of enforcing peace and deterring war'. Only nuclear weapons, he asserted, 'provide the United States with the needed worldwide power at bearable cost'. Therefore, while the US should keep up intensive efforts to find a workable disarmament programme, it had to recognize that disarmament measures alone could not reverse the current nuclear situation. Suggesting that the solution lay in the political, rather than the technical, realm, Dulles effectively reversed himself. He evoked the anxious rhetoric of his early post-war admonitions with the assertion that 'the stakes are too great to allow, or seem to allow, admitted obstacles to preclude moving toward such international controls of nuclear power as will provide the human race with insurance against its self-destruction.'

Dulles recommended, in conclusion, a programme which resuscitated his pre-1950 calls for international controls: 'Nuclear power which now approaches the power of annihilation should not be the weapons tool of individual nations.' He proposed prohibiting individual nations from possessing nuclear weapons, or even conventional weapons in excessive amounts. The UN should be remade into an effective peace-keeping agency by removing the veto from the Security Council and then providing it with 'sufficient atomic weapons . . . as to overbalance any atomic or other weapons as might be surreptitiously retained by any nation'.[70] How Dulles reconciled this legalistic approach, dependent on binding international treaty, is both unclear and indicative of the clash between Dulles' thinking from the immediate post-war period and the more recent attitudes which had been grafted onto it.

Eisenhower expressed to Dulles his belief that effective inspection could work.[71] Dulles, clearly impressed by the President's opinion, stated publicly that dependable inspection procedures were an achievable prerequisite to disarmament. Speaking before the Senate Subcommittee on Disarmament, he declared forcefully and in terms that explicitly echoed *War, Peace, and Change*,

The destructive power of modern weapons is such that a major war with these weapons would inevitably destroy a great part of the human race. So much is this realized that, so far as major war is concerned, there is developing a situation of mutual deterrence. But it would be reckless to assume that this is a permanently reliable preventive of war. Events could happen which would lead, perhaps by successive stages, to the use of these awesome weapons. The human race, if it desires to survive, must find a way to free itself of this constant menace of destruction which could come about even through mistake or miscalculation.[72]

Dulles stated that the United States advocated as a first step to disarmament an inspection system 'so thoroughgoing and comprehensive that it will exclude for practical purposes a sudden surprise attack of devastating magnitude and give substantial advance notice of any preparation for such an attack'. If conditions could be created so that the superpowers no longer feared a crippling surprise attack, 'then potential power can to some extent replace actual force in being, and that would open the way to some substantial limitation of armament'.[73]

But Dulles could not hold fast to this viewpoint. In July 1956 he sought to dampen hopes of speedily finding a workable solution to the arms control question, telling a reporter that while there was 'a growing realization throughout the world that some limitation of armament is becoming more and more imperative in view of the increasingly destructive character of modern armaments . . . I am not sure that any great progress has yet been made in finding agreed technical ways of assuring that disarmament would be upon a dependable and controlled basis.'[74]

Dulles revealed considerably greater doubt in May 1957 while reviewing a draft of a speech Eisenhower was to deliver. Dulles felt that a passage of the speech wrongly omitted any reference to the possibility of an arms limitation agreement, but his objections were based on the unpalatability, not the inaccuracy, of pessimism: 'It presupposes that this thing must go on indefinitely until there is a real peace with the Soviet Union' which would involve the settlement of outstanding political questions. Although Dulles had stated in 1955 that he did not believe fundamental change in the Soviet Union was a prerequisite to concluding any arms control agreement with the USSR, he now felt 'that is probably the case'. Looking over the rest of the text, Dulles added that another passage did not represent the Administration's official line separating reduction of arms from the elimination of world tensions. 'In theory,' he posited, '[reduction of global tensions] could at least be achieved by a limitation of armament agreement.' However, Dulles did not at this point view the theory as realistic. The draft of the speech claimed 'there is only one hope, etc. That is probably right but we don't want to say there is only one hope. That indicates our disarmament efforts are hopeless and that we are not going at it with any sincerity.'[75] But judging from Dulles' most recent stated viewpoint, this seemed to be precisely the case.

Dulles welded together his conflicting sentiments in a July 1957 broadcast address. He spoke, on the one hand, in pre-Korean invasion terms: 'Already large nuclear weapons are so plentiful that their use in general war could threaten life anywhere on the globe. And as matters are going the time will come when the pettiest and most irresponsible dictator could get hold of weapons with which to threaten immense harm.' Dulles announced to the nation that the US government believed that 'it can be made difficult if not impossible for any nation to launch a massive surprise attack'. However, he warned, 'It is not practicable to assure the abolition of nuclear weapons . . . Therefore, we must make our plans on the assumption that the nations which now have nuclear weapons would use them in war.' Dulles maintained that until the United States saw 'convincing proof' that the USSR was serious about arms control, 'our safety primarily depends on having the best weapons, large and small, that we can develop.' This meant continued nuclear testing, 'which makes it possible to develop even smaller weapons and to insure that larger weapons will have less radioactive fallout . . . In such ways it can be insured that nuclear weapons if they had to be used could be confined more closely to distinct military objectives.'[76]

The CIA report ordered by Robert Bowie in 1955 had evidently not convinced Dulles that there was no such thing as a precise nuclear weapon. His fear of a thermonuclear Armageddon, it is clear from the extant documents, was profound. His by now deeply ingrained distrust of the Soviet Union, however, seemed to push Dulles away from embracing wholeheartedly a hypothetical arms control programme (although he never abandoned the idea outright), with its risks and intangibles, but rather to look to small, low-radioactivity nuclear weapons—which were themselves hypothetical—in the belief that they would accomplish Dulles' twin goals of pulling America back from the brink and not expending huge sums on a conventional force substantial enough credibly to deter the Soviet conventional threat. He thus defended, in March 1957, the Eisenhower administration's extreme reluctance to declare a moratorium on nuclear testing:

I would say that if we had not had the last tests, we would be in ignorance—the whole world would have been in ignorance, I think, of the nuclear possibilities, which are extremely important, of having nuclear explosions without any appreciable fallout . . . Which indicates the testing is not in itself always a bad thing, because it develops the possibility of clean weapons, which had not been known, heretofore.[77]

Dulles claimed that the testing then underway was 'not designed . . . to demonstrate the capacity to build bigger bombs', of which the USA already had an ample number. 'The whole problem,' he said, 'is to develop the capacity to have smaller weapons with more tactical power and with less fallout, so they become more distinctly a military weapon than a mass-destruction weapon.'[78]

Dulles reiterated this position when he addressed the Armed Forces Policy Council 'Secretaries Conference' in Quantico, Virginia, in June of 1957. The growth of Soviet nuclear capabilities, Dulles said, had diminished the efficacy of America's threat of an all-out nuclear attack as a deterrent against 'local ['small-scale' was crossed out in the draft] attack'. To supplement the American retaliatory capability, the USA had to devise a strategy and maintain flexible military force which would convince the USSR that the Western Allies had the means effectively to counter local aggression. Moreover, the USA had to persuade the Allies that such attacks could be met 'without necessarily inviting all-out nuclear war' and to work simultaneously to decrease the risk of these local conflicts, which still might escalate into general war. The cornerstone of this flexible approach would be an enlarged stockpile of small-yield nuclear weapons; these would, among their other benefits, diminish 'political difficulties in the US use of nuclear weapons'.[79]

Dulles and Eisenhower received encouragement in this line of thinking from AEC Chairman Strauss and some influential scientists. Strauss told the assembled NSC in mid-June 1957 that, in light of continuing Soviet propaganda efforts to portray nuclear weapons as indiscriminate, it was 'essential that public opinion come to understand that the United States does possess tactical nuclear weapons, and that they can be used in military operations without causing indiscriminate devastation'. Thus reassured about the efficacy of tactical atomic weapons, Dulles advised the NSC, which was considering plans to cut its overseas forces because of a domestic budgetary crunch, 'to keep working on our objective of convincing all our allies to depend more on the deterrent capacity of our nuclear retaliatory capability, and less on local defenses'. Rather than rush redeployment of American forces, said Dulles, with the new tactical nuclear weapons Strauss had described, the USA 'might be able to maintain defenses in foreign areas at minimal cost'.[80]

Several prominent physicists, including Edward Teller, Ernest Orlando Lawrence, and Mark Mills, told Eisenhower that 'we now believe that we know how to make virtually clean weapons, not only in the megaton range but all the way down to small kiloton weapons.' Refinement of the technology would take some time and effort, but if the USA were to not develop these weapons and convert over existing arsenals, 'then—if the "dirty" weapons should be used in war—our failure would truly be a "crime against humanity"'. (They subsequently assured Eisenhower that, after clean weapons had been developed, 'it is possible to put "additive materials" with them to produce radioactive fall-out if desired.') They warned the President that the USA was capable of holding tests without fear of detection from more than 100 miles away—which meant that the USSR probably had the same ability.[81] Reports such as those by Strauss and the physicists reinforced Dulles' post-Korean invasion hawkish attitudes, although the oscillations still did not stop.

The Gaither report's recommendation that the USA embark on a large-scale fallout shelter-building programme spurred Dulles to grope, for one serendipitous moment, toward the strategy that would become the superpowers' *modus vivendi* for the second half of the Cold War. Dulles was discomfited by the possible effects of a shelter programme on both public opinion and the conduct of US diplomacy. 'If it were possible by a wave of the hand to create shelters,' he said, 'we would be better off with them than without them.' But a building programme would gravely affect Americans' psyches: the US had 'been operating on the theory that the best war preventive was a retaliatory capability in cooperation with our allies . . . it was difficult to combine a strong offense and a strong defense. Burrowing into the ground would inevitably have a bad effect on our offensive mood and capability.' Moreover, such a programme would 'bring home to the people our lack of faith in our capability to deter war' and would make America's policy formulators, who were dependent on voter support, less bold.[82]

AEC Chairman Lewis Strauss followed up Dulles' statement with a rumination on a shelter programme's destabilizing effect on deterrence—might not the Soviets be moved to attack pre-emptively on the eve of completion of a truly effective shelter programme? Dulles pondered Strauss' idea and raised one of his own near the conclusion of the meeting: 'perhaps the United States and the USSR should conclude a disarmament agreement under which neither would build shelters.' Dulles, in suggesting that stability and security might best be preserved by allowing a degree of vulnerability on both sides of the superpower confrontation, had hit upon the fundamental principle of Mutual Assured Destruction, which would become the cornerstone of US strategic policy under a future president, Richard Nixon, who as Eisenhower's vice-president was present at this NSC meeting.[83]

Part of the reason for Dulles' moderation in the face of exhortations to militancy by Lewis Strauss and scientists such as Edward Teller may have been his growing realization that a shift in Soviet policy under Khrushchev was underway. He had noted earlier that the USSR might be serious about arms control negotiations because the Kremlin wished to concentrate on the country's internal problems.[84] Now Dulles stated, in an NSC meeting in March 1958, that while it was true that the USSR had achieved greater global influence than it had a decade earlier, 'this is primarily due to the fact that the behavior of the Soviet Union was better now than it had been then. In its attempts to control the destinies of other countries, it is much more sophisticated and subtle.' The USSR, insisted Dulles, no longer dared to force its control on other countries 'by direct and forceful action, but feels obliged to use more subtle approaches'. Commenting on a suggestion that the USA should attempt to undermine the Soviets' new-found influence, he asserted that 'not only can we not prevent this improvement in the behaviour of the Soviet Union, it was a question whether we wanted to prevent this improvement.' While the Kremlin's intentions were still nefarious, their behaviour, at least, had improved, 'and ultimately the Soviets may become more civilized'.[85]

Dulles evinced a growing confidence that arms control inspection and detection could be effective and displayed flexibility about the means of implementing such a programme. When physicist Hans Bethe contended in early April 1958 that the USA had the right to more monitoring posts in the USSR than would the Soviets in the USA because of the Soviet Union's much greater size, Dulles replied that if the Soviets wanted to cover satisfactorily the entire Western Hemisphere they would insist on a very large number of posts. 'In our concern over what we may feel we require from the Soviet Union in the way of checkpoints on its territory,' Dulles said, 'we must not overlook the demands that would be made by the USSR for stations in the Free World.'[86]

Additionally, Dulles believed, it would be a mistake for the USA to push for overflights of the Sino-Soviet area, as it would greatly complicate efforts to obtain an agreement on a verifiable testing halt. He felt that 'it would be much harder to induce the Soviet Union to agree to overflights than it would to induce the Soviets to permit the stationing of trained personnel on the ground at fixed posts in the Soviet Union.' Most significantly, in terms of Dulles' evolving perspective on arms control—and, by extension, deterrence in general—was his embryonic perception of the workability of 'sufficiency': 'it was the Secretary's view that the consequences of the detection of a clandestine test were so serious that they themselves constituted a very considerable deterrent.' In his view, an inspection system that could guarantee even a 50 per cent chance of detecting a secret nuclear test 'would be sufficient to deter the Soviets from attempting to evade an agreement to cease nuclear testing'.[87]

Despite his increasing moderation, however, Dulles continued his attempts to square the circle and make nuclear weapons useful as something other than a Sword of Damocles suspended over the entire world. While claiming that the Administration's first choice was to eliminate nuclear weapons, if this could not be achieved the best alternative was to 'develop the weapons so that they can be effectively used as a defensive weapon without a mass destruction of humanity'. He considered, during a news conference at the beginning of April 1958, the damage such weapons would inflict and summed up his perception of the crucial difference between the 'old' and 'new' nuclear warhead techno-logy:

Now I don't say that they will ever be a very nice thing to be hit by. But it wasn't very nice to be hit by all the bombing that hit Berlin, or by the fire bombs that were dropped on Tokyo. But there is a difference between a weapon which will destroy on impact a very considerable area, and a weapon which through fall-out will destroy or impair human life through areas of a thousand miles or more in diameter.

Dulles assured the gathered reporters that the Administration had 'decided that we could not, in fairness to our responsibilities to the American people, perhaps to humanity, desist in a program, which we believe to be sound, merely for propaganda purposes'.[88]

To be sure, Dulles' statement was larded with propaganda value; but it reflected, in somewhat hyperbolic terms, Dulles' own thinking on the uses of tactical nuclear weapons. Multi-megaton thermonuclear weapons had ren-dered war untenable and constrained American diplomacy; with 'clean' atomic weapons, war could once again be credibly threatened, thus restoring to the USA its most potent coercive instrument. But the key to developing these new-generation weapons was continued testing, and Dulles was per-suaded by a group of disarmament 'wise men' in late April 1958 that such test-ing would only marginally enhance US technology while advancing to a greater extent the Soviet programme.[89] Within a month, Dulles had again reversed himself.

Within days he reversed himself once more. He predicted, during a meeting of the NSC in early May, that within three years the populations of America's Western European allies would split from their governments' support for the US policy of massive retaliation, which would pose a great threat to the alliance system. As a result, Dulles insisted, it was urgent for the United States 'to develop the tactical defensive capabilities inherent in small "clean" nuclear weapons, so that we can devise a new strategic concept which will serve to maintain our allies and our security position in Western Europe'. The massive nuclear deterrent, he claimed, had just about run its course as the principal ele-ment in the US arsenal; the USA had to be in a position to 'fight defensive wars which do not involve the total defeat of the enemy'.[90] But no workable for-mula for utilizing tactical nuclear weapons was developed; during the second Quemoy-Matsu crisis, a frustrated Dulles complained to the Chairman of the JCS, 'There was no use having a lot of stuff and never being able to use it.'[91] Dulles, until the day he died, never found a practical use for the 'stuff'.

The advent of atomic weapons clearly caused John Foster Dulles to alter his extant views about America's ability to threaten the use of, or actually employ, its vast military might. He considered them revolutionary, holding out as they did the threat of humanity's destruction. Thus, Dulles as a case study casts doubt on John Mueller's thesis concerning the irrelevance of nuclear weapons in the post-war period. However, it is also evident that Dulles' views on nuclear weapons were an intensification, an adaptation, and, to an extent, a perversion of perspectives he had developed in the pre-World War II period. He had believed in 1939 that reliance on deterrence for a nation's safety was too risky, given the destructiveness of modern arms. None the less, the world had fought World War II and survived, albeit in a somewhat bruised state. Compared to the new atomic weapons, conventional arms seemed much less destructive and threatening than they once had; Dulles transferred his anxiety about global carnage to this exponentially more lethal technology, and along with it his ardour for international control.

This essay makes the case that Dulles' initial legalistic, moralistic thinking on nuclear weapons clashed sharply with the more bellicose, pessimistic, amoral perspectives he developed in the wake of the Korean invasion; the result was an unwieldy grafting together of the two which contributed significantly to Dulles' public and private policy oscillations. However, the foregoing thesis does not provide a complete explanation for Dulles' repeated changes of heart; nor does it demonstrate definitively Dulles' impact on Eisenhower's decision-making and thus the significance of his oscillations. An element critical to the filling in of these analytical gaps which is missing, for reasons of space, from this study is an examination of the interaction between Dulles and Eisenhower and the degree to which they influenced each other's thinking.

The archival record reveals an ongoing intellectual cross-fertilization process between the President and his Secretary of State, although both men were cognizant that the final decision-making authority, and the concomitant onus of responsibility, rested solely with Eisenhower. It is probable that at least some of Dulles' swings were attributable to his periodic deference to the President's opinion. The opposite side of the coin is the question of the degree to which Dulles influenced decision-making. The Eisenhower administration's policy toward nuclear weapons was notably disjointed: although the President obviously abhorred nuclear weapons, only two, abortive, arms control proposals were produced on his watch; meanwhile the threat of nuclear retaliation against conventional attack remained the cornerstone of American Cold War strategy. There is reason to believe that there was a cause-and-effect relationship between Dulles' gyrations and the Eisenhower administration's contradictory nuclear policies. But no conclusions about the impact of the Eisenhower–Dulles relationship on final policy can be addressed here; that subject requires its own study.

Even more baffling for its ultimate insolubility is the 'more than a hint of relish', to use McGeorge Bundy's phrase,[92] which Dulles, as Secretary of State, displayed while brandishing atomic threats or, more generally, the seeming ease with which ethics and expediency mingled in this self-styled Christian moralist's nuclear policy thinking. Without knowing the unknowable 'Why?'—it would take an historian who is both a clairvoyant and a medium to supply the answer—we can never fully comprehend the process that led John Foster Dulles to become a 'nuclear schizophrenic'. Perhaps, for want of a more rational, mensurable explanation, the ethical consistency which John Foster Dulles so clearly lacked is a rigour and luxury reserved for intellectuals and clerics, not for diplomats—no matter how ecclesiastically minded they might be.

5

'War No Longer Has Any Logic Whatever': Dwight D. Eisenhower and the Thermonuclear Revolution

ANDREW P. N. ERDMANN[1]

OMMON sense tells us that nuclear weapons *must* have had some impact on the Cold War because of their immense destructive power. When the United States possessed a nuclear monopoly and later clear strategic superiority, its enemies *must* have been scared and, therefore, extra cautious when America rattled its nuclear sabre. Once nuclear parity was achieved, then both sides *had* to be scared and, therefore, extra cautious all the time.

But every age has at least one Bishop Berkeley who questions the dicta of common sense. The nuclear age has been no different. First came the 'nuclear revisionists' who interpreted the nuclear age as a story 'mostly about the limited value of these [nuclear] weapons', both militarily and diplomatically, in order to buttress their policy recommendations.[2] The revisionists accepted that the superpowers' nuclear arsenals instilled mutual restraint, but questioned whether the transient American superiority of the early Cold War had been significant. The critique of common sense then moved beyond mere revisionism to what can be labelled 'nuclear nihilism', a position occupied by Professor John Mueller's thesis of nuclear weapons' 'essential irrelevance' for international stability. While their destructive potential is indisputably horrific, according to this analysis, nuclear weapons merely provided an 'extra insurance' to deterring major war during the Cold War. The effective deterrents were instead the images of a large conventional conflict on the scale of the two world wars, and, restraining the Soviet Union and its allies—the 'Detroit Deterrent'—the belief that the United States industrial capacity would enable it to triumph in any such war of attrition.[3]

For a variety of reasons, an investigation of Dwight D. Eisenhower's assessment of the nuclear weapons' impact on international relations promises to help us evaluate these challenges to our nuclear common sense. Although dissimilar in many respects, both the revisionists and nihilists perceive the nuclear era as an age defined more by continuity than by change. By adopting such synchronic perspectives, however, their interpretations fail to confront the importance of the fact that, as Jerome Kahan noted over twenty years ago, 'it was not until the mid-1950s that the features of the modern strategic nuclear era emerged with sufficient clarity to exert a significant effect on American defence and diplomacy'. These features were defined by the acquisition by both the United States and the Soviet Union of the technological means to 'gain a credible military capability to launch large-scale nuclear strikes from [their] own territory against the other side's homeland'—namely, sizeable arsenals of atomic and thermonuclear weapons combined with intercontinental delivery systems.[4] Furthermore, it was not until Eisenhower's presidency that American nuclear strategy and foreign policy were truly integrated at a high policy level.[5]

Neglect of this strategic transformation in turn leads the revisionists and nihilists alike to overlook the implications of this evolving context for the viability of the Detroit Deterrent. As an asymmetrical deterrent favouring the United States, the Detroit Deterrent's logic suggests that Americans would have had a relative advantage in international bargaining with the Soviets. Perhaps the perception of the United States' ability to win a conventional war could have emboldened American leaders, whether or not it induced caution in their adversaries. By repudiating the notion that strategic superiority was ever a meaningful concept in the nuclear age, however, the revisionists neglect the existence of the Detroit Deterrent; thus, they never confront the possible significance of its waning. On the other hand, while giving considerable attention to what deterrents restrained the behaviour of the Soviet Union and its ally the People's Republic of China (PRC) during the 1950s, Mueller devotes fewer than fifteen sentences to American crisis behaviour during the Eisenhower years. Blinkered by his synchronic perspective, he treats the Detroit Deterrent as a constant; therefore, like the revisionists, he fails to investigate whether its plausibility shifted with the strategic balance and, if so, the implications of such a shift for American behaviour.

The years of Eisenhower's presidency provide an effective historical laboratory because they were punctuated by numerous international crises. Over half of all nuclear crises occurred while Eisenhower was president.[6] As the 'nexus between peace and war', crises are a grey region where planning and declaratory policy fade into operational concerns and, thus, where belief reveals itself through action.[7] This coincidence, when combined with the aforementioned transformation of the strategic environment during these years, provides a unique context for analysing nuclear weapons' impact on American international conduct.

Lastly, the impact of nuclear weapons upon Eisenhower's understanding of international affairs merits investigation in its own right. Eisenhower was one of a handful of statesmen who both had acquired a sophisticated strategic appreciation of international conflict before 1945 and then held positions of responsibility in the age of thermonuclear weapons. Hence, the analysis of how Eisenhower coped with this transition should contribute to our understanding of the broader question of 'learning' in the domain of foreign policy.[8]

Tracing the development of Eisenhower's vision of the relationship between nuclear weapons and American national security policy, therefore, promises to shed at least one ray of light onto the murky subject of nuclear weapons' relevance or 'essential irrelevance' for international systemic stability. The 'total war' outlook Eisenhower acquired in the aftermath of World War I and how he then accommodated it to the demands of the Cold War up to 1952 will first be presented. Then the focus shifts to how these beliefs evolved and informed his decision-making as president. For ease of presentation and analysis, President Eisenhower's perception of nuclear weapons and his actual crisis decision-making is traced through three phases. During the first phase, from his inauguration in January 1953 through 1955, Eisenhower attempted to integrate nuclear weapons as the pre-eminent component of American national security policy, while leading the United States through the first three nuclear crises of his administration: the resolution of the Korean War, the Indo-China crisis of 1953–4, and the Quemoy-Matsu crisis of 1954–5. He did not initiate nuclear signalling in any crisis during the second phase, between the end of 1955 and early 1958, but he confronted the troubling implications of the superpowers' rapidly expanding thermonuclear potential. Finally, the third phase, which begins with Eisenhower's decision to intervene in Lebanon in 1958 and concludes with the end of his second term, encompasses both his decision-making in the Lebanon, second Quemoy-Matsu, and the Berlin Deadline crises, and his reflections on the changes wrought by thermonuclear weapons on the nature of warfare. By the time of his famous farewell address on 17 January 1961, Eisenhower's understanding of 'victory', 'defence', and the dynamics of escalation had been dramatically transformed by the realities of the thermonuclear age.

From World War I to the Nuclear Age, 1911–52

Without question Dwight D. Eisenhower is the man most experienced with national security affairs elected to the American presidency in the twentieth century. From his admission to the United States Military Academy at West Point in 1911 to his resignation as Supreme Allied Commander, Europe (SACEUR) over four decades later, his strategic vision steadily broadened and became more sophisticated. He brought to the White House a set of firmly held convictions about the relationship between military force and national policy. The origins and development of this intellectual framework are thus a prerequisite for comprehending Eisenhower's efforts as president to come to grips with the implications of the nuclear age.[9]

Although his name is forever linked in the public mind with D-Day and the defeat of Germany in World War II, World War I remained into the 1950s the foundation of Eisenhower's understanding of warfare. This is not because

Eisenhower personally experienced the horrors of combat on the Western Front along with his West Point classmates—because he did not. Rather, World War I profoundly influenced his development because it provided the reference point to which Eisenhower constantly referred as he came of age as a military professional.

Eisenhower's military career hardly began with promise. Like many others he attended West Point not out of any martial ardour, but to receive a free education. While he imbibed the values of 'Duty, Honor, Country', West Point with its formulaic, rote instruction failed to inspire Cadet Eisenhower intellectually. Graduating sixty-first in a class of 164 with a reputation as a prankster, the Commandant of Cadets recommended that Second-Lieutenant Eisenhower 'should be assigned to [an] organization under [a] strict commanding officer'—scarcely a ringing endorsement.[10] Nevertheless, Eisenhower excelled as a junior officer in a variety of assignments within the United States. Indeed, during World War I, he was so effective training recruits that his superiors would not release him for duty in France until it was too late to see action. In 1921, having just been rejected by the Infantry School at Fort Leavenworth, his career had apparently stalled.

At this point Eisenhower's career took a turn for the better, a change that ultimately transformed his appreciation of military affairs. General Fox Conner had been impressed by Eisenhower's innovative work on tank tactics at Camp Meade.[11] Conner, who had served during the Great War as General Pershing's operations chief and was respected as one of the Army's finest intellects, decided to take the young Eisenhower under his wing. Upon Conner's personal request Eisenhower was assigned to be his adjutant in Panama.[12] Beginning in January 1922 in the inhospitable tropical conditions of Camp Gaillard, Panama, Eisenhower's intellectual outlook changed fundamentally. Through directed readings followed by hours of probing discussion, Conner awakened in Eisenhower a lifelong interest in military thought and history. Never pedantic, Conner forced Eisenhower to consider history from the perspective of the participants—repeatedly asking him what he would have done differently if he had been in command. They also reviewed the experiences of the recent World War intensively, wargaming the battles themselves to refine their understanding of the problems of command in modern war. Struggling through Clausewitz's *On War* three times under Conner's guidance, Eisenhower also acquired a philosophical framework for relating military force to state policy.[13] Lastly, Conner instilled in Eisenhower a sense of immediate purpose. The Treaty of Versailles would lead to another war, Conner admonished, and the USA had to prepare to wage it in Europe in conjunction with its allies Britain and France. Eisenhower's lifelong commitment to military preparedness 'seeped' into him during these discussions with Conner.[14] In retrospect, Eisenhower considered his time with Conner 'a sort of graduate school in military affairs and the humanities'.[15]

He had acquired a pragmatic, reflective, and logical mind, one distinguished by its ability to formulate rapidly and succinctly an 'estimate of the situation' which encompassed the potential interactions between one's own actions and those of one's opponent. The power of this intellect with its capacity to relate methodically means to objectives then blossomed at the Command and General Staff School at Fort Leavenworth. In 1926 Eisenhower graduated first in his class of 275, an accomplishment that he attributed to his education in Conner's 'graduate school'.[16]

Following his success at Leavenworth, Eisenhower received a series of ever more important assignments between 1927 and 1935, including the Army War College, the Office of the Assistant Secretary of War, and finally personal assistant to the Chief of Staff of the Army, General Douglas MacArthur. With each assignment his strategic perspective continued to expand and mature. And with each assignment a particular conception of the 'lessons' from World War I increasingly shaped his vision of modern warfare.

For Eisenhower the war of the future would be a 'total' war like the Great War, one dominated by the mass mobilization of the competing societies' resources. The faculty of the Army War College—many of them veterans of the Great War—drummed this basic point into the heads of Eisenhower and his classmates. 'War today involves the whole nation', they emphasized.[17] Most fundamental, military power is ultimately the reflection of a nation's industrial mobilization potential. 'Our economic power, if protected, is the greatest single factor in the world's war-making ability,' future Commandant of the War College William D. Connor stressed in his introductory lecture to the Class of 1928; 'the full use of our vast economic advantage is a most important item in war planning, for it is the only thing we have of world importance'.[18]

Hearing such words, many officers merely nodded reflexively without pondering their significance. Eisenhower did not. Starting with his course work at the Army War College and continuing until he left with MacArthur for detached service in the Philippines in September 1935, he became one of the country's leading experts on industrial mobilization. Not only was he among the handful of officers who graduated from both the Army War College and the new Army Industrial College, he served on the faculty at the latter institution as well.[19] While working in the Office of the Assistant Secretary of War, Eisenhower played an instrumental role in formulating the Industrial Mobilization Plans of 1930 and 1933.[20] In the course of developing these plans he met and then worked with Bernard Baruch, the chairman of the wartime War Industries Board (WIB) and civilian 'godfather' of mobilization planning during the interwar period. Under Baruch's guidance, Eisenhower studied the WIB experience and became a firm convert to Baruch's creed that victory in a future war would depend ultimately upon economic mobilization, a mobilization that would require the government to take control of the nation's economy.[21] Equally important, through experiences like serving as the assistant executive secretary to the congressional War Policies Commission and drafting major reviews of military policy for Chief of Staff MacArthur, Eisenhower learned first-hand the politics of military policy within the War Department and the Congress.[22] Looking back after World War II, Eisenhower recalled that these experiences had forced him 'to examine world-wide military matters and to study concretely such subjects as the mobilization and composition of armies, the role of air forces and navies in war, tendencies toward mechanization, and the acute dependence of all elements on military life upon the industrial capacity of the nation. . . . The years devoted to work of this kind opened up to me an almost new world.'[23]

The unique set of experiences with Conner, Baruch, and MacArthur thus provided the conceptual framework with which Eisenhower analysed the approach of World War II. As the 1930s progressed, Eisenhower became increasingly convinced that war and then American participation were inevitable. Like World War I, the next war would pit competing societies against each other. The mobilization of America's vast industrial potential would be the key to victory.[24]

World War II reaffirmed the core elements of this network of beliefs that Eisenhower had embraced in the 1920s and early 1930s. In the months immediately following Pearl Harbor, Eisenhower stood at the centre of the strategic storm raging in Washington. Working for Chief of Staff George C. Marshall first as the deputy chief of the War Plans Division for the Far East and the Pacific and then as chief of the newly constituted Operations Division, he quickly emerged as one of the primary architects of the global strategy that guided the USA through World War II: American industrial might would supply the Allies, most especially the USSR, and keep them in the war; defeat of Germany through an invasion of North-western Europe as soon as practicable (which would also relieve pressure on the USSR) would be the highest priority objective; and, in the Pacific Theatre, allied forces would undertake a holding action and then counter-offensive.[25] He then achieved fame by bringing these plans to fruition as Supreme Commander of the invasion at Normandy and the subsequent defeat of Germany in Western Europe. This triumph confirmed his belief that success on the battlefield depends upon the close co-ordination of all combat arms—ground, air, and naval—in a single operation. Contemplating the material resources at his command as the war ended, Eisenhower could have no doubt that American industrial supremacy decisively influenced the course of the war.[26]

Between 1945 and 1952 Eisenhower's attention shifted from waging war to constructing a peacetime defence establishment. As Army Chief of Staff, President of Columbia University, acting Chairman of the Joint Chiefs of Staff (JCS), and, finally, the first SACEUR, he confronted the two most salient strategic developments of this period, the onset of the Cold War and the invention of nuclear weapons.[27]

Within two years of the end of World War II, the Cold War confrontation with the Soviet Union provided the defining focus for Eisenhower's national security planning. Based upon his personal contacts with Soviet military leaders and Joseph Stalin, he initially hoped—probably naïvely—that continued co-operation among the wartime allies would preserve the peace.[28] As relations with the former ally deteriorated, however, Eisenhower found himself in

1946 supervising the first contingency plans to counter a Soviet invasion of Western Europe.[29] The following year he could agree without hesitation with State Department Counselor Charles Bohlen's assessment that 'there are, in short, two worlds instead of one' and that the United States had to rally its European allies for the impending 'major political showdown' with the Soviet Union.[30] With the memories of the crusade against Hitler still fresh, Eisenhower swiftly made the transition to interpreting the conflict with the Soviet Union as the latest chapter in the long, historic struggle between liberty and tyranny. Thus, when he stepped down as Chief of Staff in 1948 to assume the presidency of Columbia University, Eisenhower conceived of the Cold War as essentially an ideological struggle between two competing 'ways of life'.[31]

He did not, however, consider the Soviet leaders reckless fanatics blinded by ideological fervour. Rather he judged them to be rational despots whose first priority remained the preservation of their own personal power. Given the unmistakable contrast between the USSR's own immense task of recovery from the ravages inflicted by Hitler's legions and the United States' massive and undamaged industrial base, the Soviet leaders would not intentionally embark upon a military confrontation with the West. Adopting the perspective of the Soviet adversaries as he had learned to do under Fox Conner's guidance, Eisenhower thus concluded that they would be deterred as long as the United States protected its industrial superiority, the Detroit Deterrent.[32]

Military force remained an essential component of the nation's strategy within this Cold War framework. For the words of the diplomat to have impact, they had to be backed by the potential for military deeds. The demands of deterrence also naturally required military force.[33] But, if deterrence should fail, the United States and its allies needed a defence establishment that could promise ultimate victory. Eisenhower did not relish the prospect of a future war. He never possessed a boyish enthusiasm for battlefield glories like his friend George Patton. Instead this Supreme Commander viscerally abhorred war, condemning it into his old age as the height of human folly. Having walked the landing beaches of North Africa, Sicily, and Normandy littered with dead and debris and then forced himself to see firsthand the naked, emaciated corpses stacked in the concentration camp at Gotha, Eisenhower had no illusions about a future war.[34] He consistently stressed that another world war would bring unspeakable horrors, perhaps worse than those of World War II. None the less, he accepted that until the Cold War was transcended, the United States needed to accept the real possibility of war.[35]

Eisenhower determined, therefore, that the fundamental strategic dilemma confronting the United States lay in striking the proper balance between military preparedness and the American 'way of life'. Unlike previous wartime emergencies, the Cold War's nature dictated that the United States needed to be prepared to wage it for an indefinite period of time. It would take decades before the Soviet tyranny would finally weaken from within. But if these prolonged expenditures for national security ever became so large as to force the government either to regulate the economy or undermine the economic vitality of the nation, then the defence establishment would be self-defeating. 'Military preparation', Eisenhower emphasized, 'must not mean national bankruptcy.'[36] Consequently, well before his campaign for the presidency Eisenhower had concluded that the Cold War struggle ultimately hinged upon the economic strength of the nation: first, because this economic strength provided the great deterrent; second, because it furnished the life-blood of the American system.[37]

Eisenhower's initial appreciation of nuclear weapons developed concurrently with the formulation of his Cold War strategic outlook. When he first learned at the Potsdam Conference in July 1945 of the successful test of an atomic device, Eisenhower instinctively wished that the United States would not use the 'horrible' weapon.[38] But as with the onset of the Cold War itself, he grimly accepted nuclear weapons as an inescapable and significant element in post-war defence planning. He displayed his ambivalent acceptance of this reality in the summer of 1946. On the one hand, he labelled the atomic bomb a 'hellish contrivance' and stated that the world would be a better place if nuclear weapons could be abolished. On the other, he endorsed the first peacetime nuclear tests at Bikini, designed to acquire more information on nuclear weapons' military potential, and advised his old friend Bernard Baruch, now US representative to the UN atomic energy negotiations, that the US should accept no international plan limiting its development of atomic weapons without the strictest verification and enforcement provisions.[39] Despite this initial ambivalence—and despite the distractions of demobilization, congressional hearings, and interservice struggles for prestige and power in the new defence establishment—Eisenhower became one of the best informed men in the government on the progress of the nuclear arsenal and the war plans for its use.[40]

Although nuclear weapons did not change the basic nature of warfare by either making all other weapons irrelevant or the use of force to achieve meaningful political objectives impossible, Eisenhower concluded, they had irrevocably transformed the requirements for American national security. Intimately familiar with the United States' extremely limited nuclear capabilities as well as numerous confidential analyses that concluded this arsenal would not be the decisive factor in a war in the foreseeable future, Eisenhower emphatically rejected the notion that nuclear weapons were a war-winning 'absolute weapon'.[41] Indeed, the cloak of secrecy shrouded the American nuclear programme so completely in the first years of the Cold War that military planners found themselves in the absurd position of not knowing the size of the nuclear stockpile or even if the use of these weapons would be authorized in wartime.[42] He took special pleasure, therefore, in ridiculing the notion that the age of 'Buck Rogers' or 'push-button' warfare had arrived—often citing Admiral Chester Nimitz's quip that all the US had was the button.[43] While not viewing it as an 'absolute weapon', Eisenhower did consider the atomic bomb a 'revolutionary' development, one that ushered in a 'new era of war-fare' and 'swept away' many 'old concepts of war'. The dramatic tone of this appraisal, however, should not obscure how Eisenhower specifically inter-preted this 'revolution'. The starting point of his reasoning remained his con-ception of 'total war' ultimately decided by industrial mobilization. The decisive element in a global war had been and remained the US industrial base. Until 1945 the United States could rely upon allies abroad and its geographic isolation to insure sufficient time for a mobilization of the American war machine. However, the development of long-range bombers and nuclear weapons meant a prospective enemy might be technologically capable of striking at the American homeland at the outset of hostilities for the first time in the nation's history. This possibility necessitated a revolution in American strategic policy. Thus, Eisenhower considered nuclear weapons part of a 'rev-olutionary' trend, since they helped remove forever the considerations of time and space that had previously provided the first line of US defence. Into the future the United States would need to deploy in peacetime an unprecedented level of forces-in-being in forward bases to deter or, if necessary, blunt a future surprise attack.[44] Accordingly, in 1947 Eisenhower took the lead with the JCS in proposing that future strategic planning assume the use of atomic weapons.[45]

While seving as acting Chairman of the JCS in early 1949, Eisenhower syn-thesized these different strands of thought into a coherent strategic concept, one which ultimately provided the foundation for the 1949 emergency war plan OFFTACKLE. In the period of rapid demobilization and extremely tight defence budgets following World War II, atomic weapons offered the only affordable basis for American defence of Western Europe. Even if the American public were willing to pay more for the peacetime defence establishment, Eisenhower felt that the USA could not maintain legions around the globe suf-ficient to deter the Soviets without threatening to undermine the American 'way of life'. OFFTACKLE, therefore, assumed that an initial nuclear strategic bombing campaign against the Soviet Union would not be decisive, but would help slow a Soviet invasion of Western Europe. A foothold on the continent might then be preserved which would allow in turn, *à la* World War II, an American mobilization and counter-offensive.[46] Imagining future war in terms of these two phases, Eisenhower stressed priority for strategic air power, increased production of nuclear weapons, and continued preparation for industrial mobilization.[47]

Eisenhower then carried this set of ideas to Europe when he served as NATO's first SACEUR. Ultimately, he hoped, the European allies would develop sufficient forces to mount a predominantly conventional defence of Western Europe. However, in 1951 and 1952 with the conventional balance greatly in favour of the Soviets, nuclear weapons alone offered prospects for a plausible 'forward defence' in central Europe. Eisenhower fought for the inte-gration of these weapons into NATO defence plans. Again, he denied that nuclear weapons alone would be decisive; instead they would provide the means to buy the time necessary for the mobilization of European reserves and American industrial potential. That force—the industrial might of the United States—remained ultimately the 'great deterrent'.[48]

When elected President of the United States on 4 November 1952, Eisenhower had wrestled with the implications of nuclear weapons for over seven years.[49] He considered these new weapons 'revolutionary', but in a restricted sense. They had not made another major war inconceivable, nor meaningful victory unimaginable. Rather, they were 'revolutionary' because they contributed to the elimination of the advantages of time and geographic isolation from US strategic planning. Eisenhower continued to have faith that the United States, with proper preparation, could preserve the decisive advantage afforded by its mobilization base and thus its deterrent. And the strength of the American economy and deterrent would in turn encourage psychological confidence in other nations resisting communist aggression.[50] But if a war with the USSR should come, he believed that after the initial assault had been contained, the US and its allies would triumph on the battlefield through a combination of air, naval, and land operations. In sum, Eisenhower approached his inauguration with a world war strategic mind-set, modestly revised to suit the nuclear Cold War.

One week after his election, Eisenhower's brief golfing vacation was interrupted for an unusual meeting in the manager's office at the Augusta National Golf Club. There Roy B. Snapp, the secretary of the Atomic Energy Commission (AEC), briefed Eisenhower on the latest developments in the American nuclear programme. Snapp handed the president-elect a Top Secret memorandum from AEC Chairman Gordon E. Dean. Dean's memorandum explained that on 31 October the AEC had successfully exploded 'Mike', the world's first thermonuclear device, at the Enewetok Atoll in the Pacific. The blast was estimated to be equivalent to over 10 million tons of TNT (10 megatons) or, in terms that were perhaps slightly more conceivable to the general, five hundred times more powerful than the Hiroshima bomb. Dean laconically stated that the island base for the test was now 'missing', replaced by an 'underwater crater some 1,500 yards in diameter'. Assimilating the news, the president-elect noted that, while he favoured scientific research, he did not feel that there was any reason 'for us to build enough destructive power to destroy everything'. Then on 19 November 1952 Eisenhower met the Commissioners of the AEC for a full briefing on the state of the nation's nuclear programme. Nuclear weapons were becoming cheaper and easier to manufacture and a thermonuclear weapon would be available in about one year.[51] Eisenhower now knew that he would be the first president to confront the thermonuclear age.

Confidence in Confrontation, January 1953–December 1955

At the end of his first day as President, Dwight D. Eisenhower pondered the experience. It did not seem especially novel. 'Plenty of worries and difficult problems. But such has been my portion for a long time—the result is that this just seems (today) like a continuation of all I've been doing since July 1941—even before that.'[52] Just as the stress of being responsible for significant decisions was familiar, so too were many of the issues before him. Nowhere was this more true than in the domain of national security policy. The decisions he made as president naturally reflected the intellectual outlook and set of firmly embedded assumptions that he had acquired during his long career as a military professional.

Throughout his eight years as president, Dwight D. Eisenhower based his New Look national security policy upon the conception of the Cold War struggle that he had formulated in the late 1940s. He consistently rejected that there was some specific 'danger date' whose arrival would tip the balance of power irrevocably in favour of the Soviet Union. Likewise, as demonstrated by his emphatic rejection of the campaign rhetoric of 'roll back' during Operation Solarium's discussion of the future of American national security policy in 1953, Eisenhower's waging of the Cold War would not include provocative operations to destabilize the Soviet Union and its allied regimes in Eastern Europe. Instead, he still envisaged the Cold War as a long-term trial, one that the American people and economy had to be prepared to wage indefinitely. In this struggle between two competing ideological systems, Eisenhower sincerely believed that the incredible defence build-up outlined originally in the Truman administration's NSC 68 in 1950 could not be sustained without eventually subverting the principles of a free-market economy, thus, transforming the country into a 'garrison state'. Since significant reductions in domestic government operations were not politically feasible, the only alternative was a new, more economical defence posture.[53]

Nuclear weapons seemed to provide the Eisenhower administration with the solution to its dilemma of fiscal constraints at home and extensive commitments abroad. As the AEC Commissioners had informed Eisenhower in November 1952, the United States was entering the age of nuclear plenty because of Truman's prior decisions to increase nuclear material production.[54] Based on his past experiences, Eisenhower concluded that a strong deterrent to communist aggression could be maintained and American conventional forces reduced through an increased reliance on the striking power of Strategic Air Command (SAC) and on tactical nuclear weapons.

Although Eisenhower continued to believe that the Soviet Union would not deliberately initiate a war with the United States, war might come by miscalculation. If so, he argued that the United States would prosecute the war employing all of its nuclear power. He now articulated more clearly than before his image of a general war with the Soviet Union. It was far from sanguine. He feared, as he told the National Security Council (NSC) in March 1954, that 'if a third world war were to begin with an enemy atomic attack on the United States, this country would itself be required to accept a totalitarian regime'.[55] At other times, he emphasized that because of the Soviets' growing strategic arsenal, Americans had a right to be frightened for the first time in their history.[56]

Yet, despite more public statements to the contrary, Eisenhower insisted in secret policy deliberations that 'victory' remained a coherent concept and that the United States could 'win' a general war with the Soviet Union.[57] While discussing NSC 5410, entitled 'US Objectives in the Event of General War With the Soviet Bloc', in March 1954, Eisenhower forcefully argued that 'everything in any future war with the Soviet bloc would have to be subordinated to winning that war'. Capturing his resolute approach to the possibility of waging nuclear war 'the President turned to paragraph 1 of the draft report, which read: "To achieve victory which will ensure the survival of the United States as a free nation and the continuation of its free institutions in the post-war period." This, said the President, he would change by putting a period after "victory" and deleting the rest of the paragraph, if not the rest of the paper.'[58] Eisenhower could not imagine how the United States would cope with, let alone exploit, the type of victory achieved in a nuclear war, but he still predicated policy on the pursuit of 'victory'.[59] 'Victory' remained not destruction alone, but the ability to destroy the enemy's will and war potential, while preserving one's own.[60]

These views were in accord with the prevailing understanding embodied in American strategic estimates in the early 1950s, namely that even a single surprise attack by either side would not resolve an atomic war.[61] The United States would never provoke war, but in event of a Soviet surprise attack Eisenhower believed that the USA should retaliate with all the power at its command: 'our only chance in a third world war against the Soviet Union would be to paralyse the enemy at the outset of the war.'[62] He hinted at possible pre-emptive action: SAC should strike 'in case of alert of actual attack'.[63] While conceding that it was a 'brutal' point of view, Eisenhower said that the only criterion should be 'just how much such a war plan would hurt the enemy'.[64] 'The matter of the morality of the use of these [atomic] weapons was of no significance.'[65] The first priority was to 'blunt the enemy's initial threat'. After an initial strategic bombing campaign of perhaps thirty days, a war of attrition would begin. There could be no major reinforcement of Europe in the first stages of the war since maintaining law and order domestically would be the 'big Army job'. Europe, however, would not be overrun because American strategic nuclear strikes would stall the Soviets' momentum. Most importantly, Eisenhower 'thought the essential was to save, through the initial period of hostilities, the ability of the U.S. to outproduce the rest of the world'. In sum, as it had since the late 1940s, his vision of a general war with the Soviet Union consisted of two phases: 'phase one would be the aversion of disaster; in phase two we would go on to win the war.'[66]

Eisenhower's confidence in US capability to emerge from such a war as the 'battered victor' derived from his foundational belief that, in a war of attrition, the US industrial base, once mobilized, would ensure victory.[67] Accordingly, Eisenhower supported in principle the idea of the complete abolition of atomic weapons precisely because it would be to the United States' military advantage. As he explained in June 1954, 'he was certain that with its great resources the United States would surely be able to whip the Soviet Union in any kind of war that had been fought in the past or any other kind of war than an atomic war.'[68] Though he doubted whether any such agreement could be negotiated, he would 'gladly' have gone back 'to the kind of warfare which was waged in 1941 if in 1945 the A-bomb had proved impossible to make'.[69] None the less, in April 1953 Eisenhower could still cogently invoke the lessons of World War II to rebut Senator Stuart Symington's criticism that the New Look's proposed reductions in defence expenditures would leave the United States vulnerable to a decisive atomic attack:

We pulverized Germany but their actual rate of production was as big at the end as at the beginning. It's amazing what people can do under pressure. The idea that our economy will be paralyzed is a figment of Stuart Symington's imagination.[70]

Contemplating the possibility of 'a 12–year mobilization program to achieve final victory' in a general war could scarcely have encouraged Eisenhower to seek a fight; yet he remained convinced that 'we can never be defeated so long as our relative superiority in production capacity is sustained.'[71]

This conviction, in turn, gave Eisenhower supreme confidence in the American deterrent's effectiveness. The student of Fox Conner, a skilled poker- as well as bridge-player, prided himself on his ability to step into other people's shoes to predict their potential behaviour.[72] Just as he had since the late 1940s, he concluded that the Soviet leaders would be cautious because they knew as he did that they could achieve nothing by war except an eventual American victory. Eisenhower's faith in the Detroit Deterrent reinforced his belief that the United States could use force in localized crises without fearing escalation to general war. This belief evidenced itself in the crises of 1953–5 in Korea, Indo-China, and the offshore islands, where Eisenhower threatened the use of force, both conventional and nuclear, to convey American resolve in a traditional manner.

In the case of Korea, both Eisenhower and his Secretary of State John Foster Dulles later attributed the successful resolution of the armistice talks to nuclear threats.[73] (Most recent scholarship questions this conclusion, emphasizing instead the death of Joseph Stalin for the later progress in the armistice negotiations.)[74] Their warnings, however, were rather ambiguous and equivocal.[75] The administration delivered a panoply of threats but specified only willingness to escalate the Korean conflict if an armistice agreement were not forthcoming. These threats were communicated through public declarations, secret diplomatic channels, and by military gesture. Publicly, for example, Eisenhower spoke of impressing the Chinese by 'deeds—*executed under circumstances of our own choosing*' and met with General Douglas MacArthur, perhaps the foremost advocate of expanding the war into China.[76] Eisenhower then used his State of the Union Address on 2 February 1953 to announce that the Seventh Fleet would no longer shield the coast of the People's Republic from attacks by Chiang Kai-shek's Nationalist forces based on Formosa.[77] Militarily, the air campaign against North Korea was escalated to unprecedented levels, including attacks on the North Korean irrigation system and its hydro-electric plants along the Yalu River.[78] Though he may have been overstating the truth, Dulles told the European allies later that year that the United States 'had already sent the means to the [Korean] theater for delivering atomic weapons. This became known to the Chinese through their good intelligence sources and in fact we were not unwilling that they should find out.'[79] Finally, at the truce talks themselves, meetings between the American Ambassador to the Soviet Union, Charles Bohlen, and Soviet Foreign Minster Vyacheslav Molotov, and at Dulles' talks with Prime Minister Nehru of India, the United States subtly signalled that it would escalate the war if the armistice talks broke down.[80] Dulles' language to Nehru indicates how thickly veiled the nuclear threat was, for he said only 'that if the armistice negotiations collapsed, the United States would probably make stronger rather than a lesser military exertion, and that this might well extend the area of the conflict'.[81]

Similar ambiguous threats were employed later to respond to the deteriorating French position in their war against the communist Vietminh in Indo-China. Twice before the debacle at Dienbienphu, Dulles made public declarations specifically designed to deter open Chinese intervention in Indo-China. On 2 September 1953, Dulles warned, 'there is a risk that, as in Korea, Red China may send its own army into Indo-China. The Chinese Communist regime should realize that such a second aggression could not occur without grave consequences which might not be confined to Indo-China.'[82] Those key phrases of this 2 September speech emphasizing the 'grave consequences which might not be confined to Indochina', were repeated again moments after the immortal words 'local defences must be reinforced by the further deterrent of massive retaliatory power' left Dulles' lips on 12 January 1954.[83] There can be little doubt that this speech before the Council on Foreign Relations, which quickly became known as the 'Massive Retaliation' speech, was 'pointedly warning China' not to intervene overtly in the conflict.[84]

While attempting to deter a Chinese Communist invasion of the Nationalist offshore island outposts, most notably Quemoy and Matsu, Eisenhower again threatened use of force.[85] These islands served as Nationalist bases for raids against the mainland and as symbols of Chiang Kai-shek's aspiration to return there permanently. Their loss, so the argument ran, could be a telling blow to Nationalist morale or even presage a Communist invasion of Formosa itself. Though the Mutual Defence Treaty signed with Chiang in December 1954 explicitly guaranteed only the security of Formosa and the Pescadores, it contained a clause indicating that it would 'be applicable to such other territories as may be determined by mutual agreement'.[86] By January 1955, Eisenhower had concluded that the possibility of the Chinese Communists miscalculating American resolve required more forceful signals of American resolve. Eisenhower sought a congressional resolution authorizing him to use armed force to protect Formosa, the Pescadores, and whatever other territories that might be essential for their defence—implying, of course, Quemoy and

Matsu.[87] In presenting the Formosa Resolution to Congress, Eisenhower emphasized that 'the United States must remove any doubt regarding our readiness to fight . . . and to engage in whatever operations may be required to carry out that purpose.'[88] Eisenhower subsequently stressed the nuclear facet of the phrase 'whatever operations . . . required'. He ordered the chairman of the Atomic Energy Commission to announce publicly that the current round of nuclear test explosions, Operation Teapot, was designed to evaluate low-yield weapons intended for battlefield use.[89] Eisenhower further underscored this theme by encouraging Dulles' public declarations that American forces in Asia were equipped 'with new and powerful weapons of precision which can utterly destroy military targets without endangering unrelated civilian centers', and that the United States was willing to use them against the PRC.[90] Eisenhower reaffirmed the implications of Dulles' statements, responding to a request at his 16 March 1955 press conference to comment on them with, 'in any combat where these things [i.e. nuclear weapons] can be used on strictly military targets and for strictly military purposes, I can see no reason why they shouldn't be used just exactly as you would use a bullet or anything else. . . . yes, of course they would be used.'[91]

While this litany of threats is perhaps the best-known facet of his early diplomatic tactics, Eisenhower also contemplated the use of force in all three crises. In the case of Korea, where American forces were already bogged down in a stalemate, Eisenhower promoted the escalation of the war, especially if the current round of armistice negotiations failed. When informed in February 1953 of the Communists' use of the 'Kaesong Sanctuary' as logistical base for a potential offensive, the President suggested that the United States consider using 'tactical atomic weapons on the Kaesong area, which provided a good target for this type of weapon'.[92] A few weeks later, as the minutes of the 31 March 1953 NSC meeting record, Eisenhower again 'raised the question of the use of atomic weapons in the Korean war. Admittedly, he said, there were not many good tactical targets, but he felt it would be worth the cost if, through the use of atomic weapons, we could (1) achieve a substantial victory over the Communist forces and (2) get to the line at the waist of Korea.' While acknowledging that the opinions of the world, especially of our European allies, needed to be considered, he and Dulles agreed that 'somehow or other the tabu [sic] which surrounds the use of atomic weapons would have to be destroyed'.[93] As military contingency planning proceeded, Eisenhower continued inquiring about possible targets for nuclear weapons in Korea. Though his military advisers stressed the dearth of acceptable tactical targets, the president adamantly insisted that he 'had reached the point of being convinced that we have got to consider the atomic bomb as simply another weapon in our arsenal'.[94]

Although some have argued that Eisenhower was averse to using nuclear weapons in Korea but wanted to be sure that the possibility had been discussed, his eagerness to suggest targets for their use and his insistence that the 'tabu' be destroyed seem more plausibly to support Richard Betts' conclusion that 'the principal division between the president and his military advisors . . . was on the *range* of nuclear options, with the president favoring a wider variety including battlefield use, and many of the solders inclined to reserve the weapons for the contingency of expanding the war to Chinese territory.'[95] The evidence that Eisenhower was not bluffing is compelling. On 19 May 1953, the JCS reported to Secretary of Defense Wilson their opinion regarding NSC 147, the document outlining the military options in Korea. The JCS advocated the expansion of the war into Manchuria, 'including extensive strategical and tactical use of atomic bombs'.[96] The next day the president accepted this recommendation 'as a general guide' for a new offensive, tentatively scheduled for May 1954.[97] Then on 22 May 1953 the JCS informed General Mark Clark, the commander of United Nations forces in Korea, that, if the final allied proposal were rejected, the armistice talks would be terminated, the sanctuary zones in North Korea voided, and tactical operations in preparation for the May 1954 offensive begun.[98] In later discussions of possible responses to a violation of the armistice, moreover, Eisenhower did not shy away from the nuclear option. In a January 1954 NSC meeting, for example, while emphasizing that he would maintain final authority over nuclear weapons and that they would only be used to counter a 'major Communist attack', Eisenhower insisted that 'the commander in the field to be told to be as ready as promptly as possible to use atomic weapons when the decision had been made'.[99]

During the Indo-China crisis of 1954 Eisenhower demonstrated again that his confidence in American power enabled him to consider his options unconstrained by concerns of a potential Soviet reaction. Since his country had just emerged from protracted engagement in Korea and he had no desire to fight for French colonialism, Eisenhower was understandably reluctant to deploy American forces from the outset. At an early NSC meeting to discuss the deteriorating situation in Indo-China, the president emphasized 'with great vehemence' his conviction that 'there is just no sense in even talking about United States forces replacing the French in Indochina'.[100] Furthermore, he did not encourage exploration of a nuclear option for Indo-China and there is no evidence that any such plans were considered seriously.[101] Eisenhower did, however, consider limited military intervention, primarily with air and naval forces. The plan for a massive single conventional air strike, code-named Operation Vulture, was unenthusiastically received by both Eisenhower and Dulles, partly because it was not accompanied by a French guarantee for substantive change in their political policies in Indo-China.[102] As it became clear that the entire French position might collapse, Eisenhower agreed to American intervention if four stringent conditions could be fulfilled: 'the Associated States would have to request assistance, the United Nations would have to approve, other nations would have to participate in an intervention and Congress would have to sanction it'.[103] In a later meeting of Dulles, Chairman of the JCS Admiral Arthur Radford, and congressional leaders, the congressmen insisted upon guarantees that Britain and other allies would participate before passing any resolutions granting the president even limited discretionary powers.[104] With the British unwilling to make such a commitment, this stipulation merely reinforced the president's earlier decision against unilateral intervention. In a post-mortem to the crisis, however, Eisenhower stressed that the United States did not intervene because 'the other nations had been unwilling to join us', not because he opposed intervention in principle or feared escalation.[105]

Eisenhower's decision-making during the first offshore island crisis confirms that he was not squeamish about employing military force, even without the support of key allies. At the beginning of the crisis in September 1954, both he and Secretary of State Dulles initially resisted accepting the JCS argument that the loss of the islands might be a fatal blow to Chinese Nationalist morale, which, in turn could lead to the loss of Formosa itself. They hoped that a peaceful resolution to the crisis, perhaps under the auspices of the United Nations, would relieve them of what Dulles appropriately described as 'a horrible dilemma'.[106] By January 1955, however, both accepted that the islands had taken on a symbolic significance incommensurate with their real military value. When the Chinese Communists threatened invasion of the Tachen Islands, two hundred miles to the north of Formosa, the time of decision was at hand. At the NSC meeting on 21 January 1955, Eisenhower decided that, if its help were requested, the United States would help evacuate the Tachens, but not reinforce them; that Quemoy and Matsu would be defended if attacks on these islands presaged an invasion of Formosa or the Pescadores; and, finally, that a congressional resolution, ultimately the Formosa Resolution, should be sought.[107] Though the terms of the Formosa Resolution were ambiguous concerning a commitment to defend Quemoy and Matsu, on 31 January the United States Ambassador on Formosa was ordered to reassure Chiang privately that the United States would defend the islands. For this commitment, Chiang agreed to evacuate the Tachens.[108]

By the middle of March 1955, both Dulles and Eisenhower determined that the United States would probably use tactical nuclear weapons to defend the islands. While hoping that the provision of more material assistance to the Nationalists might eliminate the need for an American intervention, they both grimly accepted that atomic weapons remained the last resort.[109] In the light of these decisions, the United States' posturing was intended to prepare the American people for the real possibility of nuclear strikes against the PRC as much as to deter an escalation to this awful end.[110]

Ironically, Eisenhower then displayed a willingness to risk escalation in order to convince Chiang to remove the immediate cause of the crisis. In late April, Eisenhower sent Admiral Radford and Assistant Secretary of State for Far Eastern Affairs Walter S. Robertson as his envoys to Chiang, hoping to persuade him to decrease the symbolic importance of Quemoy and Matsu by reducing their garrisons. They were also to inform Chiang that the United States was withdrawing its secret pledge of 31 January to defend Quemoy and Matsu. The American emissaries, however, presented a new quid pro quo which had been formulated earlier by Dulles and Eisenhower: evacuate the islands and the United States would effectively institute a blockade between Formosa and the mainland. This suggestion was made in full cognizance of its potential to provoke war with the PRC. Luckily, Chiang rejected this offer and, shortly thereafter, the Chinese Communists suspended their pressure on the islands.[111]

Even though Eisenhower contemplated the use of force in all three crises, he was hardly looking for a fight. Indeed, he demonstrated considerable flexibility in achieving his aims. As previously mentioned, Eisenhower's conditions for American intervention in Indo-China demonstrated that he was indeed not 'just an adventurer like Genghis Khan'.[112] In the case of Korea, concessions were forthcoming from both sides in the final months of negotiations.[113] Furthermore, while Chiang Kai-shek was supposedly unleashed by the removal of the Seventh Fleet, privately the US Ambassador in Formosa asked for and received oral assurances that Nationalist forces would not undertake any major operations against the mainland without prior American permission. Later, a shipment of aircraft to Formosa was delayed until this promise was confirmed in writing.[114] Similarly, with the signing of the Mutual Defence Treaty in December 1954, Chiang promised again that the Nationalists would not attack the mainland without American consent.[115] Earlier in the crisis, moreover, Eisenhower ignored the public outrage, including calls for military action, following the announcement that thirteen Americans shot down over China during the Korean War had been sentenced to lengthy prison terms for espionage.[116]

Though prudently restrained in some respects, Eisenhower still accepted a considerable measure of risk during these crises. Admittedly, he had sound economic, political, and alliance reasons for restraining the use of American force.[117] Except in the case of Indo-China, however, these concerns did not fundamentally constrain his policies. Eisenhower could seriously contemplate forceful action because he remained confident that the Soviets would not hazard the escalation of a local conflict to general war in the face of the United States' overall military superiority. In all three crises, intelligence estimates continued to reaffirm the two assumptions buttressing this confidence: first, that the United States still possessed real strategic superiority and that the Soviets could not yet strike a crippling blow to the country; second, that the Soviet Union would not initiate general war as long as the American application of force did not directly threaten Soviet vital interests, such as the survival of the Communist regime in China.[118] Eisenhower also did not underestimate 'the sanity of the Chinese Communists' in this regard.[119] Even when the risks of war seemed most intense during the first offshore island crisis, Eisenhower, inwardly optimistic, confided to this diary that 'I believe hostilities are not so imminent as is indicated by the forebodings of a number of my associates. . . . I have so often been through these periods of strain that I have become accustomed to the fact that most of the calamities that we anticipate really never occur.'[120]

Eisenhower never belittled Soviet power, however. When discussing the escalation of the Korean War, he admitted his 'one great anxiety . . . with respect to this proposal was the possibility of attacks by the Soviet Air Force on the almost defenceless centers of Japan'. This factor was 'always in the back of his mind'. This admission, though, was followed by his assertion that the 'quicker the operation was mounted, the less danger of Soviet intervention'.[121] But even after the Soviets exploded a thermonuclear device in August 1953, American assessments of Soviet capacity to inflict damage on the United States through the end of 1955 were not appreciably affected.[122] In November 1954 the JCS went so far as to 'guarantee' that 'in a limited or a full-scale war, the outcome for the United States, prior to Soviet achievement of atomic plenty, would be successful'.[123]

The JCS's qualification 'prior to Soviet achievement of atomic plenty' was crucial. From the time Eisenhower assumed the presidency, American estimates had consistently reported that the United States' decisive strategic superiority was a transitory phenomenon. Even though the United States was expected 'to maintain relative numerical and qualitative superiority in nuclear weapons and the means of their delivery' through the decade, sometime between 1956 and 1960 the Soviets would approach 'the absolute atomic capability of inflicting critical damage upon the U.S.'. 'Mutual deterrence' might then develop.[124] Perhaps, fearing mutual destruction, 'each side would be strongly inhibited from deliberately initiating general war or taking action which it regarded as materially increasing the risk of general war.'[125] However, such estimates were of future potentialities not current realities; they did not, therefore, undermine Eisenhower's early self-assurance.

When he looked into the future, though, Eisenhower acknowledged that the face of war would change. He had helped initiate this transition by accepting many of the recommendations of the Technological Capabilities Panel report of 1955, measures including increasing the dispersal of SAC bombers to minimize the risks of a disarming first strike, developing the U-2 reconnaissance aircraft, and granting 'highest priority' status to the nation's intercontinental ballistic missile (ICBM) effort.[126] The possibility of the latter development, thermonuclear-tipped missiles flying thousands of miles to hit their targets in minutes, was especially mind-boggling. He thought that the country needed some of these missiles 'as a threat and a deterrent', but 'not 1000 or more'. Anything more, he concluded, would mean that 'the nature of conflict has gotten beyond man'.[127] Eisenhower sensed that he was perhaps peering across a boundary into a novel epoch in the history of warfare.

In the final week of October 1955, Director of Central Intelligence Allen Dulles emphasized that one of the 'basic questions' remaining unanswered about the Soviet nuclear programme was 'whether the USSR will have megaton weapons for use by 1958'.[128] Less than one month later, the question was answered. On 22 November a Tu-16 bomber climbed into the skies above the Semipalatinsk test site on the steppes of Kazakhstan and released its payload. Seconds later a 1.6 megaton blast scorched the earth.[129] There would be no

easy escape for Eisenhower. He confronted an adversary armed with thermonuclear weapons. The future was coming.

Crossing the Divide, January 1956–June 1958

During his first three years in office, while he acknowledged the potential horrors of another world war, Eisenhower demonstrated in secret deliberations
that for him nuclear war was neither unthinkable nor unwinnable. The projections of the USSR's future nuclear potential remained just that, projections.
In his diary on 11 January 1956 Eisenhower categorically rejected 'the theory
of a thirty to sixty day war' because it 'has nothing to back it up'. Perhaps 'a
mutual destruction of terrifying proportions' might occur, but he thought
'this would not in itself necessarily end the war'. The general felt that warfare's
fundamental nature had not changed since the time of Scipio: 'Wars are conducted by the will of a population and that will can be at times a most stub-
born and practically unconquerable element. In ancient times the final siege
of Carthage is an example—in modern times the 1940 bombing of Britain and
the 1943–44–45 bombing of Germany are others.'[130] The following day, while
forcefully defending the nation's stockpiling programme, Eisenhower lectured
the members of the NSC about the nature of 'thermonuclear war' in words
right out of his diary: those who thought 'a future thermonuclear war would
be won or lost in a period of thirty days were crazy'. He cited various
'wiseacres' in the past who argued that wars would end quickly because
nations could not endure the burden. 'In point of fact,' the student of military
history reminded his audience, 'this had not been the case in the first and
second World Wars, and would certainly not be the case in any future
thermonuclear war.'[131]

Just eleven days later Eisenhower received a briefing by the Net Evaluation
Subcommittee on two prospective scenarios for a war on 1 July 1958.[132] The
first envisaged only a few hours of warning, the second assumed a month. The
summary graphically depicted for the president the implications of the
Soviets' thermonuclear arsenal. The results stunned the president. Eisenhower
confessed that he 'doubted that the human mind was capable of meeting and
dealing with the kind of problems that would be created by such an exchange
of blows'.[133] In the first case the federal government was 'wiped out' and the
country experienced 'practically total economic collapse'. The image of the
destruction was 'appalling'. Even though the Soviets would suffer roughly
three times the damage of the United States, American casualties were 'enormous', approaching 65 per cent of the population. 'It would literally be a business of digging ourselves out of the ashes, starting again.' Perhaps more
shocking, in the second case which assumed the Soviets concentrated on
American air bases, 'there was no significant difference in the losses we would
take'. And there seemed to be little the USA could do to minimize the damage
from such a strike, since 'the limiting factor on the damage inflicted was not
so much our own defensive arrangements as the limitations on the Soviet

stockpile of atomic weapons in the year '58.'[134] He concluded that in the future both sides would avoid taking actions which threatened escalation to war and, therefore, that the 'prospect of strategic thermonuclear war' would serve as the primary deterrent.[135]

Once thermonuclear weapons pushed casualty estimates from a first strike from millions to tens of millions, the effects of war became 'almost impossible to conceive of'.[136] When considered in these terms, Eisenhower could no longer view a superpower war in the same class as World War II, let alone the Punic Wars. While the NSC discussed disarmament policy in February 1956, for instance, Eisenhower insisted that 'if we could somehow eliminate the H-weapon, the world would be better off. He feared some of our thinking overlooked a transcendent consideration, namely, that nobody can win a thermonuclear war.'[137] The defining question of warfare, he concluded, was no longer how much damage could be inflicted on the enemy, but rather 'what is left of either country after the first 72 hours?'[138] In a letter to his friend Richard Simon, Eisenhower explained how this transformation in the basic logic of warfare was pushing humanity across a historic divide.

we are rapidly getting to the point that no war can be *won*. War implies a contest; when you get to the point that contest is no longer involved and the outlook comes close to destruction of the enemy and suicide for ourselves—an outlook that neither side can ignore—then arguments as to the exact amount of available strength as compared to somebody else's are no longer the vital issues. . . . But I repeat that [arms'] usefulness becomes concentrated more and more in their characteristics as deterrents than in instruments with which to obtain victory over opponents as in 1945. In this regard, today we are further separated from the end of World War II than the beginning of the century was separated from the beginning of the sixteenth century.[139]

In sum, thermonuclear weapons made war 'preposterous'.[140]

Eisenhower's vision of a future war reflected the uncertainties inherent in this time of transition. He remained convinced that after a nuclear attack martial law would be necessary for 'two decades at a minimum. Because the job of picking up the burned and broken and destroyed pieces.'[141] The preparation of proclamations for the 'Control of Alien Enemies' and for 'Suspending the privilege of the writ of habeas corpus . . .' for the president's review testify to the earnestness of these fears.[142] Technologically, the deterrent's nature was in flux. Eisenhower still believed in the deterrent power of SAC and carrier-based air power, but he recognized that the developing missile technology would soon alter the deterrent's structure.[143] When considering the matter of the redeployment of forces abroad, however, he seemed like a man living simultaneously in two different epochs. He insisted that plans for redeployment of major forces to Europe after a nuclear strike were impracticable, and, in another context, argued that creating stockpiles in Australia might be wise since they 'would have been very helpful to the United States in 1941'.[144] Epitomizing the conceptual incongruities of this period, Eisenhower once told the JCS that, although there might not be any winners in a thermonuclear war, 'we don't want to lose any worse than we have to'.[145]

Perhaps the most significant transformation in Eisenhower's understanding of the role of military force in international relations appears at first glance to be merely muddled semantics. President Eisenhower's initial reaction to the Security Resources Panel report 'Deterrence and Survival in the Nuclear Age' (more widely know as the 'Gaither Committee' report) exemplifies this profound change.[146] Submitted within weeks of the launch of Sputnik, the report's conclusion that the changing security environment demanded tremendous new defence expenditures presented Eisenhower the opportunity to offer his assessment of the nation's defence requirements in the missile age:

> The President said all military strength is of course relative to what a possible adversary has. He did, however, feel that we are getting close to absolutes when the ability exists to inflict 50% casualties on an enemy. In those circumstances there is in reality no defence except to retaliate. . . . he felt that maximum massive retaliation remains the crux of our defence. He was inclined to think that what we put into defence measures should be put into the security of our striking force.[147]

The idea that there is 'no defense except to retaliate' is incoherent as long as any traditional sense of defence is retained. It can only be meaningful if 'defence' has become synonymous with 'deter'.[148]

This semantic shift also highlights the beginnings of Eisenhower's rejection of his core belief that an 'aversion of disaster' phase, after which the United States would mobilize its vast industrial resources to defeat the enemy, would exist in nuclear war as it had in world wars. The logic of this conceptual change led Eisenhower to order estimates of how to paralyse the Soviet nation, not just its military forces, in the event of war.[149] Combining these elements, the equation of 'defence' with 'deterrence', the emphasis on defending retaliatory forces and not population or industry, and his interest in alternative targeting mixes, suggests that by early 1958 Eisenhower was haltingly moving toward the consideration of a secure, counter-value targeted, minimum deterrent posture.

Although Eisenhower had rejected the concept of 'victory' and begun to contemplate alternative deterrent force postures, his assumptions about escalatory dynamics remained essentially unchanged. Eisenhower continued to see a sharp dichotomy between local or peripheral wars and general war. Even though the sensibilities of 'world opinion' needed to be taken into account, he did not doubt that tactical nuclear weapons would be used in local wars.[150] Wars on the periphery—in Asia, for instance—could probably be contained by a resolute application of force, he reasoned, because 'the tactical use of atomic weapons against military targets would be no more likely to trigger off a big war than the use of [conventional] twenty-ton "block-busters".' On the other hand, the terms 'general war' and 'war between the US and U.S.S.R'. were still interchangeable since in Eisenhower's 'opinion it was fatuous to think that the U.S. and the U.S.S.R. would be locked into a life and death struggle without using [nuclear] weapons'.[151]

For many within the Eisenhower administration, however, the validity of these assumptions was increasingly suspect, especially in light of the formal acceptance of 'relative nuclear parity' with the Soviet Union for the first time in 1958.[152] What political scientists would subsequently label the 'stability-instability paradox' most concerned Special Assistant for National Security Affairs Robert Cutler. If a condition of mutual deterrence in strategic weapons exists, he argued, the Soviets might 'nibble their way into the fabric of the Free World by small aggressions'. In other words, stability at the strategic nuclear level might tempt the Soviets to pursue provocative behaviour at lower levels of conflict.[153] Both Dulles and Eisenhower vigorously rejected this interpretation. Dulles, for instance, argued that the Soviets were no more prone to take such risks than the United States.[154] The secretary of state, however, voiced forcefully his increasing reservations about the continued credibility of the American extended deterrent. He emphasized that the European allies were beginning to doubt the United States' willingness to employ massive retaliation to defend Europe. For Dulles, 'the massive nuclear deterrent was running its course as the principal element in our military arsenal.'[155]

Such reasoning bewildered Eisenhower. For him, it simply defied common sense. Again he rejected the implications of the 'stability–instability paradox'. Marking the beginnings of a shift in his opinions on escalatory dynamics, however, he argued that mutual deterrence would not provide an 'umbrella' under which small wars could be waged, but rather a 'lightning rod' which would tend to make global war more likely. It was simply absurd to imagine that a 'nice, sweet, World War II type of war' could occur in the context of a Soviet–NATO confrontation. 'What possibility was there', he asked, 'that facing 175 Soviet divisions, well armed both with conventional and nuclear weapons, that our six divisions together with the NATO divisions could oppose such a vast force in a limited war in Europe with the Soviets?'[156]

Many proposed augmenting the United States' capacity to wage limited, conventional wars even in the NATO theatre as the solution to this dilemma. This option was immediately foreclosed for the president. He considered the scenario of a war between the superpowers in Europe remaining limited below the strategic nuclear threshold simply a theoretical construction, something that could never occur in reality. Judging that the superpowers possessed the ability to 'destroy the other side completely', Eisenhower concluded that 'there was already in the world all the deterrent power that could be used'.[157] And his assessment of the Cold War's character remained unchanged. His mantra was familiar. The struggle would have to be waged for decades until the Soviet Union was reformed from within. The Soviets understood the ramifications of war and, therefore, were not looking to initiate a general war. To prevent the United States from becoming a 'garrison state', defence expenditures had to be controlled. But in the aftermath of the psychological shock of Sputnik, some response was needed to assuage the concerns of the public as well as to contain partisan political attacks. Eisenhower consistently fought against proposals for 'crash' programmes of any sort, though. Instead he begrudgingly accepted modest increases in the defence budget aimed at accelerating missile developments and deployments and protecting the SAC deterrent force from a disarming first strike—while calling for moderation and decrying 'hysteria' the entire way.[158] The primary audiences for these measures remained the American public and the European allies, not the Soviets. As the president candidly admitted to his secretary of defence when they discussed the post-Sputnik defence appropriations, 'he thought that about two-thirds of the supplementary funds are more to stabilize public opinion than to meet the real need for acceleration'.[159] If anything, therefore, as the world entered the missile age, Eisenhower was convinced more than ever before that American defence had to be based on the nuclear deterrent.[160]

Nostalgia and Doubt, July 1958–January 1961

In the years after his first nuclear crises, Eisenhower acknowledged that the strategic context was changing in a fundamental manner. He accepted intellectually and then viscerally that the Soviets' thermonuclear potential had transformed warfare's nature, and, consequently, was generating a condition of mutual deterrence. Confronting three more crises in rapid succession in 1958, Eisenhower demonstrated how far he had come since 1955.

On the surface his performance during the Lebanon intervention of July 1958 harkened back to an earlier era of nuclear diplomacy, to a time of confidence in the American deterrent's capacity to contain escalation. In the summer of 1958, a leftist military coup against the pro-Western Iraqi regime provided Lebanese President Camille Chamoun the excuse for which he had been waiting, to request American intervention to contain civil strife in his own country. Before the American intervention began, General Nathan Twining, Radford's successor as chairman of the JCS, informed the president of the JCS's opinion that the alert status of SAC should be increased. Twining agreed with their proposal except for the forward deployment of refuelling tankers because such movements could not be concealed and, thus, 'could well occasion a good deal of alarm'. Eisenhower, however, thought that such a signal might be beneficial and so ordered the dispersal of some of these units.[161] Although Dulles and Eisenhower exploited the menacing image of Soviet expansionism to justify the intervention in Lebanon to the Cabinet and congressional leaders alike, they saw the immediate threat in Lebanon as indigenous political instability which Nasser perhaps encouraged but did not create. When deciding to intervene, therefore, Eisenhower did not seriously consider the possibility of Soviet interference.[162] In essence, he knew that the deployment of SAC probably had nothing to deter.

Eisenhower's signalling during the second offshore islands crisis appeared reminiscent of his during the first. When a new crisis flared up in August 1958, two additional carriers reinforced the US Seventh Fleet, American naval forces were authorized to escort Nationalist supply convoys to within three miles of the islands, and SAC's base on Guam increased its alert status.[163] Eisenhower backed these deployments publicly, noting that 'it would be highly hazardous for anyone to assume that if the Chinese Communists were to attempt to change this situation by attacking and seeking to conquer these islands that this act could be considered or held to a "limited operation".'[164] He also suggested to Dulles that the secretary of state imply in a press conference that the United States would have to respond to an all-out attack on the islands.[165] But the confidence reflected in this firm policy sprung from intelligence reports that consistently concluded throughout the crisis that PRC force deployments revealed no intention to invade the islands.[166]

Despite the public façade of 1955 and sound reasons for confidence, Eisenhower expressed real concern that the Soviet Union might intervene to support its Chinese ally and insisted that the United States 'define fixed limits to the action' to prevent this escalation.[167] He did agree that tactical nuclear weapons might have to be used in the unlikely contingency of an invasion. Nevertheless, citing concerns of world opinion and fear of retaliation against Formosa, he expressly held this option in reserve. His response to military action would be measured and gradual.[168] This apprehension about the possibility of escalation helps explain departures from the precedent of 1955. Whereas in the previous crisis Eisenhower had delegated authority to the local naval commander to respond defensively to Chinese air attacks, including authorizing strikes against mainland airfields, in 1958 he insisted that any air attack against such targets could be ordered only upon his approval.[169] Likewise, while Eisenhower had offered Chiang a provocative American blockade of the coast between Formosa and the mainland in exchange for his abandonment of the islands in 1955, three and a half years later, he was willing to gamble only an offer of 'amphibious lift to Chiang so that he could take advantage of any weakening on the continent'.[170]

Shortly after the second crisis in the Taiwan Straits wound down, Eisenhower confronted the most serious crisis of his presidency, one over Berlin. Acutely conscious that the Western military position in Berlin was 'wholly illogical', Eisenhower altered his conduct accordingly.[171] He had always feared a crisis over Berlin.[172] His fears were realized early in November 1958 when Nikita Khrushchev initiated the Berlin Deadline crisis by intimating that the Soviet Union was preparing to turn control over access routes to Berlin to the East German government, a regime not recognized by the NATO allies. Harassment of an American convoy from Berlin followed shortly thereafter.[173] Then on 27 November the Soviet Union sent identical notes to the three other occupying powers of Berlin proposing negotiations on the city's status as a 'free city' and threatening to transfer responsibility for its access routes to the East Germans on 27 May 1959 unless 'a sound basis for the solution of the questions connected with the change in Berlin's situation' were achieved.[174] Eisenhower's initial 'instinct . . . was to make a very simple statement to the effect that if the Russians wanted war over the Berlin issue, they can have it'.[175] Once his tendency for hot temper and rhetorical outburst subsided, Eisenhower oversaw contingency planning and employed diplomatic signalling representing a subtle but significant departure from previous practice.

Throughout the crisis Eisenhower tried to convince the American public that the renewed tensions over Berlin should not be considered a 'crisis', but that they were simply part of the long-term struggle between the East and West. The Soviets did not want war; they were bluffing.[176] Privately, though, he was less confident. American estimates from the onset of the crisis concluded that the Soviets, though not seeking an armed showdown, were able and willing to implement the threat to transfer their administrative duties.[177] Indeed, US intelligence argued that if anyone's position looked like a bluff, it was the West's: 'Khrushchev is probably not convinced that the Western Powers will resort to local military action, and he will remain most difficult to convince that they will risk general war, over the transfer of access control.'[178] Adopting the Soviets' vantage point, Eisenhower had to admit that if he were Russian 'he could see flaws in the US position'.[179]

To check partisan criticism of his measured response to the crisis, Eisenhower accepted Vice-President Richard Nixon's proposal for a meeting with the leadership of Congress. Such a conference would allow the legislators to express their opinions while giving the president the opportunity to explain the 'general tack and general posture that the United States desires to present to the world'.[180] In two meetings on 6 March 1959, Eisenhower offered the congressmen a gloss on his approach to the Berlin situation. He opposed mobilization because it would derail the economy, thus raising the 'garrison state' spectre. His basic philosophy was to negotiate if possible, but he would never commit appeasement. He assured the legislative leaders that he was willing to 'push [the United States'] whole stack of chips into the pot' if the time came. This meant 'general war'. Representative Carl Vinson for one left convinced of 'the futility of considering limited action in the Berlin crisis' by Eisenhower's decisive generalities.[181]

Despite the impression conveyed by such talk for political consumption of pushing in stacks of chips, the secret contingency plans Eisenhower had already begun formulating reveal that he was prepared to play quite a few hands before going for broke. Following the detention of the American convoy at the Soviet checkpoint on 14 November 1958, the SACEUR, General Lauris Norstad, requested authorization to dispatch a second convoy to test Soviet intentions and then to use 'the minimum force necessary' to extricate the American personnel if protests did not work. Eisenhower refused this request.[182] A month later Eisenhower expressed dissatisfaction with the existing contingency plans covering the possibility of the closing of Berlin's routes to the West. The entire situation was a 'can of worms'. While considering the vague notion of a 'token force', he sought a plan that would both sustain a unified allied front and convey to the Soviets the seriousness of the situation without backing them into a corner.[183] Then on 29 January 1959, in the face of more belligerent advice from within his administration to the contrary, Eisenhower decided that US policy would eschew rapid escalation if the crisis came to a head.[184] He determined that the United States would not accept the transfer of Soviet responsibilities to East German officials, including the stamping of documents and the inspection of cargoes.[185] Desiring to be 'logical and moderate' in approach, though, he rejected outright the JCS proposal for sending a division down the autobahn. Instead, the president approved a much less provocative two-step plan of response to a Soviet attempt or announcement to substitute East German for Soviet officials. In step one, 'a scout car or some other vehicle with a capacity for shooting' would accompany the next trucks bound for Berlin. These vehicles would attempt the transit, but would desist if they encountered any physical obstructions and 'in no event would the armament be used unless [they] were fired upon'. Step two entailed an attempt to 'mobilize world opinion against the Soviet Union', further diplomatic sanctions such as the possible withdrawal of ambassadors, and, finally, military preparations including the evacuation of dependants. Only after these steps failed would Eisenhower consider additional military options. Modification of the Soviet 'ultimatum' would also be sought at the upcoming Foreign Ministers' meeting scheduled for April.[186] With refinements, such as the determination to reinforce the first convoy with cameras and possibly members of the press, the decisions of 29 January established the framework for subsequent contingency planning.[187] During the following months the national security bureaucracy explored a wide range of options to play for time and contain the escalation of the crisis should Khrushchev implement his initial threat.[188] None the less, fundamental questions such as the specific character of the military preparations after encountering obstructions on the road to Berlin and whether the United States was willing in the last resort, with or without allies, to escalate the conflict to general war remained unanswered within the government.[189]

While such questions could remain unanswered, Eisenhower calmly directed the development of a policy that balanced the need for firmness with the ability to draw out the issue in order to give the Soviets sufficient time to reconsider any escalatory action.[190] Even though answering these questions could be postponed, posing them placed strains on Eisenhower that he could not always conceal. After one session of reviewing the Berlin situation, he exclaimed 'you might as well go out and shoot everyone you see and then shoot yourself'.[191] Such a characterization of the decisions confronting him was not far-fetched: he admitted during the crisis that he feared tens of millions of immediate fatalities in the United States if the situation escalated to nuclear war.[192]

The pressures of preserving the allied rights in Berlin in this strategic context also eventually manifested themselves in Eisenhower's diplomatic signalling. Initially, through joint communiqués issued by the Federal Republic of Germany and the three Western occupying powers and then under the auspices of the North Atlantic Council, the Western allies expressed willingness to negotiate, but commitment to maintain their responsibilities in Berlin.[193] Eisenhower reiterated these views in discussions with Anastas Mikoyan, one of Khrushchev's deputies, in private talks in January 1959.[194] He authorized 'quiet preparatory and precautionary measures' that would be noticed by

Soviet intelligence but not the American public, such as building up check-points and increasing the military police escort between them. He rejected, though, such options as a congressional resolution on the issue or a general mobilization.[195]

In a series of public statements in March 1959 Eisenhower departed from these more subtle tactics in trying to convince the Soviets of American resolve. In a 4 March press conference he deliberately evaded a question concerning Secretary of Defense McElroy's previous intimations that the United States would consider a strategic first strike, arguing that any answer would 'create more misapprehension than . . . understanding'.[196] Apparently he then became convinced that the best way to deter the Soviets from provocative action was for him to communicate more directly that an armed confrontation would escalate to the nuclear level.[197] Consequently, at another press conference a week later Eisenhower was not so circumspect. Again facing a succession of questions concerning Berlin, the president began with the unequivocal statement that 'we are certainly not going to fight a ground war in Europe'. Would the United States use nuclear weapons to defend Berlin? After emphasizing that the allies would maintain their rights, Eisenhower responded, 'I don't know how you could free anything with nuclear weapons.' When pressed on the potentially inadequate size of American conventional forces in Europe to cope with a confrontation with the Soviets, he replied, 'You have got to go to other means.' The final question cut to the heart of the matter. Was there an option between nuclear war and acquiescence if the Soviets 'really started trouble over Berlin'? After elaborating on the theme that nuclear weapons could not 'free anything', Eisenhower answered:

I think we might as well understand this—might as well all of us understand this: I didn't say that nuclear war is a complete impossibility. I said it couldn't as I know free anything. Destruction is not a good police force. . . .

And, I must say, to use that kind of a nuclear war as a general thing looks to me to be a self-defeating thing for all of us. After all, with that kind of release of nuclear explosions around this world, of the numbers of hundreds, I don't know what it would do to the world and particularly to the Northern Hemisphere; and I don't think anybody else does.

But I know it would be quite serious.

He concluded the conference by emphasizing that 'we are never going to back up on our rights and responsibilities'.[198] He then reiterated these themes in a television and radio report to the nation on the Berlin situation, arguing that 'global conflict under modern conditions could mean the destruction of civilization. The Soviet rulers, themselves, are well aware of this fact.'[199]

These comments mark a fundamental transformation in Eisenhower's approach to crisis nuclear diplomacy. In previous crises, when manipulating fears of escalation, either by force deployments or by statements such as 'I can see no reason why they shouldn't be used just exactly as you would use a bullet', his threats implied a confidence that force, including nuclear weapons, could be used to the United States' advantage. In other words, Eisenhower's deterrence tactics were to make threats that could be implemented rationally. By openly stressing that nuclear war would be 'a self-defeating thing for all of us' in the midst of the Berlin crisis, however, Eisenhower did not threaten rational retaliation; rather, he invoked the image of irrational, uncontrolled escalation to a mutually destructive denouement.[200]

The Berlin issue continued to trouble Eisenhower even after tensions decreased following Khrushchev's denial that there had ever been an 'ultimatum' regarding Berlin's status. Military contingency planning continued, but with key decisions not made. The president still did not know how the United States would respond if the Soviets restricted access to the city to one road or cut its trade. While Chancellor Konrad Adenauer stressed that the juridical position of the allies be preserved, Eisenhower felt 'that we might end up preserving our juridical position while losing Berlin'.[201] And again, four months later, he expressed these same doubts, noting that 'neither De Gaulle nor Adenauer will face up to the question of what we should do in the face of possible East German impediments'. He then pointedly admitted that he 'was not sure that the U.S. government had completely faced up to the situation'.[202] Such doubts of the United States' ability to protect its rights in Berlin stand in marked contrast to Eisenhower's stance before the crisis, when he insisted without qualification that Western European security, and thus American security, hinged on the preservation of Berlin's status.[203] In the aftermath of the Berlin Deadline crisis, his confidence in the United States' ability to prevail diplomatically in a future crisis was clearly shaken.

While reconsidering the American commitment to Berlin, Eisenhower's vision of thermonuclear war continued to crystallize. The man who had previously ridiculed the concept of the 'thirty to sixty day war', accepted during the Berlin crisis that a '30-hour war' was possible. After both sides were obliterated in a matter of hours, the deadly effects of radiation would persist for years—truly throwing salt on the ground where modern Carthages once stood. Confronting estimates that some regions might be uninhabitable for three decades after an attack, he admitted mobilization planning was useless. So that planning could continue, he argued the assumptions of damage should be altered.[204] When contemplating large numbers of thermonuclear weapons, Eisenhower privately confessed 'the discussion loses all meaning since we would really be destroying civilization'.[205]

Estimates of nuclear destruction confirmed that the United States would never again be the arsenal of democracy. The president admonished those 'who were thinking in World War II terms' on such issues.[206] In a nuclear war, even an extra forty-two divisions would be irrelevant.[207] The 'antiquated concept' of mobilizing reserves to create 'a great overseas army' was a 'fantasy'.[208] Since 'general war had become restricted almost entirely to a nuclear battle', Eisenhower even questioned whether the military needed mobile forces to cope with foreseeable general war contingencies.[209] As his previous hopes for a recovery after a nuclear attack waned, he rejected in practice his prior insistence that the United States possess the 'residual power and capacity for quick recovery'.[210] He could not conceive of stockpiling enough material to allow the resumption of industrial activity after an attack. Perhaps, he pondered, 'we would all be nomads'. He doubted whether the stockpile would survive a nuclear attack and thought that, even if it did, it would be irrelevant since the nation's transportation infrastructure would be destroyed. The president sanctioned the stockpiling of medicine, but not raw materials and semi-manufactured items.[211] After over twenty-five years of commitment, Eisenhower repudiated his faith in the primacy of American mobilization capacity in the face of thermonuclear weapons' destructive power.

Eisenhower, however, never fully reconciled his conclusion that 'war no longer has any logic whatever' with targeting policy.[212] He painfully faced a central dilemma of the nuclear age, namely harmonizing the terrifying reality of what a nuclear war would entail with specific military plans to mitigate the holocaust should deterrence fail. He never wholly succeeded. When he contemplated a failure of deterrence, a rapid, perhaps pre-emptive counter-force strike to minimize the damage inflicted upon the United States and its allies seemed to be the least bad of the range of horrific measures. For instance, during the creation of the first Single Integrated Operations Plan (SIOP), which was intended to integrate the targeting of all American strategic forces, Eisenhower seemed to support counter-force oriented targeting, at least for the first strike.[213] His predelegation of launch authority to certain commanders in the field likewise implies a 'warfighting' orientation.[214] But in other contexts, the president advocated reliance on the submarine-based Polaris missile (whose inaccuracy precluded counter-force targeting), sceptically assessed the Air Force's ability to destroy mobile ICBMs by noting that 'the age of aircraft for actual use over enemy territory is fast coming to a close', and repeatedly emphasized his conviction that urban populations would be the primary targets in the next war.[215] And when Eisenhower reviewed the completed SIOP in the final weeks of his administration, he was horrified by its wanton destructiveness that far outstripped any rational policy objective. He insisted that 'we've got to get this thing right down to the deterrence'.[216] Compared to the confidence he placed in pre-emption when he still believed that a two-phase war and 'victory' were viable options, the change in his outlook is evident.[217]

His ever-strengthening belief that 'all we really have that is meaningful is a deterrent' enabled him to sacrifice consistency on the issue of targeting.[218] While others questioned the credibility of massive retaliation in the age of mutual deterrence, Eisenhower pressed for an even greater reliance on the nuclear deterrent.[219] The equation of 'defence' with 'deterrence' was crucial for his case. Once again, claims such as 'our real defense against their Polaris is our diversified, dependable deterrent' were incoherent when contemplating waging war in traditional terms.[220] This faith in the strategic nuclear deterrent helps explain further hints of a nascent conception of minimum deterrence in Eisenhower's advocacy of a strategic striking force of a few hundred missiles.[221] On one level, therefore, Eisenhower could neglect arcane matters such as specific targeting mixes because he believed that 'our guiding principle should be to let the USSR know that we have the power to destroy the Soviet Union if the latter attacks us'. 'If they knew their country would be destroyed,' he reasoned, 'the Soviet leaders would not dare attack.'[222]

Eisenhower retrenched his commitment to the strategic deterrent for more than just his traditional fiscal concerns. In the wake of the Berlin crisis and his acknowledgement that mutual deterrence was developing, Eisenhower's assumptions about escalatory dynamics were transformed. As he had since the beginning of his administration, Eisenhower consistently rejected the possibility that a European war could ever be limited to conventional weapons.[223] However, despite his earlier faith that conflicts on the periphery could be contained and that tactical nuclear weapons could serve as 'bullets', he now emphasized that 'these small, limited wars might readily develop into general war'.[224] Toward the end of his presidency, he no longer cited the advantages of tactical nuclear weapons when arguing against increasing conventional war capabilities. Instead, he stressed this shift in escalation dynamics because 'it was becoming increasingly dangerous to assume that limited wars could occur without triggering general war'. He admitted that 'his conviction in this matter was growing stronger all the time as he heard more and more discussion of nuclear capabilities'. With his faith that the Soviet leaders shared this realization, Eisenhower judged that the power of the superpowers' strategic nuclear arsenals would deter provocative actions well down the so-called escalatory ladder. Repeating his familiar refrain, he therefore concluded that 'all other military matters must remain secondary to the overriding importance of deterrence'.[225]

As his presidency drew to a close, Eisenhower felt nostalgia for the time before nuclear weapons, a time when the United States had no reason to fear the Soviet Union.[226] At times, thoughts of thermonuclear weapons' power to destroy civilization preoccupied him. Once, after listening to the president's laments about the nuclear menace, Chairman of the AEC John McCone attempted to hearten Eisenhower by noting that man had always sought the means to destroy his fellow man; it was not unique to the past decade. The only difference from the past, McCone continued, is just that our weapons are more destructive. Eisenhower acknowledged this point, but then countered by emphasizing that 'there is a distinct difference now between the present and the past in so far as in past wars there had always been a victor—now there would be none as all parties engaged in the war and a large segment of humanity not engaged would be destroyed.'[227]

The Significance of Crossing the Divide

Dwight D. Eisenhower crossed the thermonuclear divide during his presidency. Throughout his eight years in office, Eisenhower drew upon his professional military experience, and the self-confidence it afforded him, to formulate his own understanding of nuclear weapons' place in American national security policy. Although his belief that nuclear weapons were morally no different from any other weapon did not waver, his view of their efficacy as tools of statecraft and warfare evolved considerably. Beginning as early as 1956, in secret policy deliberations Eisenhower admitted that no matter how much more damage the United States could inflict relatively upon the Soviet Union, the absolute power of the Soviets' burgeoning thermonuclear arsenal diminished his confidence that he could control both crisis escalation and the actual use of these weapons. The spectre of an apocalypse haunted him when he considered the death and devastation these weapons could wreak in a matter of hours with their blast, fire, and poisonous radioactive fallout. He struggled to devise a strategy to cope with this new world, a world where major war no longer had logic. Contemplating a war in the missile age, the general who knew first-hand the forces of 'friction' and the 'fog of war' never truly accepted that a pre-emptive strategy offered a realistic escape from the threat of nuclear destruction.[228] Frustrated, in his final months as president, Eisenhower longed for a nuclear-free world.[229] His conviction that the United States would become a 'garrison state' under the burden of prolonged defence expenditures, however, only reinforced his belief that the strategic nuclear deterrent had to provide the mainstay of the United States' military policy. When he left office, therefore, Eisenhower simultaneously clung to nuclear weapons tighter than ever, while trying to push them away.

Eisenhower's changing assessment of the viability of the Detroit Deterrent highlights the transformation of his understanding of warfare's nature. During his first three years as president, Eisenhower did indeed rely on the Detroit Deterrent. The 'lessons' of World War I, which he had learned over two decades before as an expert in industrial mobilization planning and his World War II experience reaffirmed, led him to conclude that America's industrial capacity gave it the power to defeat the Soviet Union in a protracted war, even one involving nuclear weapons. He reasoned, therefore, that the Soviet leadership would not up the ante in a crisis because the knowledge that 'if they go to war, they're going to end up losing everything they have' has a tendency 'to make people conservative'.[230] In other words, military superiority—traditionally conceived—provided deterrence. By 1956, however, the combination of thermonuclear weapons and growing Soviet intercontinental delivery capabilities—first bombers and then ICBMs—made the Detroit Deterrent obsolete in Eisenhower's mind. He explicitly abandoned every single assumption embodied in the concept that, in John Mueller's words, America could do 'what it did after 1941' by 'mobilizing with deliberate speed, putting the economy on wartime footing, and wearing the enemy down in a protracted conventional major war of attrition massively supplied from its unapproachable rear base.'[231] The Detroit Deterrent no longer existed. Taking its place was the deterrent of mutual devastation. Thereafter, when he confronted the possibility of 'losing everything', Eisenhower became more conservative.

When the United States could still prevail in a general war, Eisenhower thought he could resolutely apply force in localized conflicts with little risk of

escalation by the Soviet Union.[232] When confronting the power of thermonuclear weapons, Eisenhower rejected this assumption. His re-evaluation of
tactical nuclear weapons, from considering them as just like 'block-busters' to
viewing them as provocative agents of escalation, exemplifies this renunciation.

The shift in Eisenhower's nuclear signalling tactics, moreover, suggests the
subtle influence of the thermonuclear revolution on diplomatic bargaining.
By invoking the image of thermonuclear war as 'a self-defeating thing' during
the Berlin crisis Eisenhower was not signalling a willingness to employ force
as a sensible instrument of American policy as he had in previous crises.
Rather, he was issuing what Thomas Schelling has described as 'the threat that
leaves something to chance'.[233] In the crises of 1953–5, he had tried to create
uncertainty in the minds of others, suggesting that he would be in complete
control of his own decisions. In the Berlin Deadline crisis, he was warning that
actions by others might take matters out of his control.

For Eisenhower it was thermonuclear weapons' destructive potential, not
the image of a protracted conventional war, that destroyed the 'logic' of war.
Thermonuclear weapons made any notion of 'victory' incoherent. Meaningful
defence could then only be deterrence. Facing this new setting, Eisenhower
reassessed the dynamics of international relations and altered his behaviour
accordingly. By the end of his presidency, therefore, superpower relations
had begun to operate according to a new logic, the logic of the thermonuclear
revolution.

6

Bear *Any* Burden? John F. Kennedy and Nuclear Weapons

PHILIP NASH[1]

O N 7 December 1962, in an address he gave at Los Alamos, New Mexico, President John F. Kennedy asked how the United States had successfully led the struggle to contain the 'Communist empire'. He answered by citing not only the United States Strategic Air Force,' but also its 'sons and brothers in Viet-Nam and Thailand and all around the globe'.[2] The President's oblique reference to nuclear weapons, before an audience that derived its livelihood from nuclear weapons design, typified his claims that he had reduced the country's reliance on them. But had he done so in reality? What were Kennedy's views on nuclear weapons? What role did those weapons actually play in his foreign policy? This chapter will attempt to answer these questions.

Two caveats about evidence are in order, though. While we 'bastards' may always be there with our 'pencils out',[3] we do not have much evidence regarding official discussion of nuclear weapons policy in the Kennedy administration. Does this mean that policy-makers simply did not discuss the weapons? Or did they raise the subject, but keep no record? Or did they take notes which have yet to become available? It is also difficult to come to grips with Kennedy's own views on nuclear weapons. He kept no significant diary, his early death denied us a memoir, and a great deal of relevant material from his presidency remains secret. Scholars will continue to depend heavily, therefore, at least into the near future, on published sources and the fallible memories of JFK's advisers, who are highly accessible and actively involved in shaping the history they helped make in the first place.[4] These qualifications mean that any conclusions about Kennedy and nuclear weapons must be tentative. This does not mean, however, that such a study is premature; an interim account is valuable if only because most of the relevant documents will not be available for years and because the recent secondary literature could use synthesis.

Pre-Presidential Years

As the nuclear age dawned in early August 1945, 28-year-old war veteran John Kennedy returned to the United States from a European journey. There is no record of his immediate reaction to the advent of atomic weapons,[5] but both before and after that event, and particularly during his thirteen years as Congressman, Senator, and presidential candidate, Kennedy developed some general views that would remain fairly consistent and help shape the role nuclear weapons were to play in his foreign policy after he entered the White House.[6]

The first source for Kennedy's attitudes is the undergraduate thesis he wrote at Harvard and then published in revised form as *Why England Slept* (1940). In concluding this analysis of Great Britain's defence policy in the 1930s, Kennedy drew a lesson for his own country: the United States must maintain a strong military to support its diplomacy and prevent war, especially when it confronted a totalitarian power. Although a product of the pre-nuclear era, this emphasis on military preparedness and 'negotiation from strength' would run like a thread through Kennedy's utterances on national security long after 1945.[7]

During his three terms in Congress (1947–53), Kennedy established himself as an internationalist who defined 'military preparedness' in broad terms. In 1947, he quickly announced his support for the Truman Doctrine, arguing that it had long been a 'cornerstone' of US policy to prevent the domination of Europe or Asia by any single power, and 'the atomic bomb and guided missile has [sic] not yet weakened that cornerstone'.[8] When the Soviet Union acquired its own atomic bomb in 1949, however, Kennedy did acknowledge US vulnerability: warning of an 'atomic Pearl Harbor', he called for greater civil defence efforts (and thereby foreshadowed his actions as President in 1961). Most important, Kennedy consistently supported greater spending on conventional ground and air forces,[9] and it is striking that he did this at least in part because he had begun, at an early date, to fear US overreliance on nuclear weapons. As early as May 1950, Kennedy inserted into the *Congressional Record* the report of a Harvard-MIT study group on US defence strategy that expressed this concern. 'Our present overwhelming commitment to atomic weapons and strategic bombardment,' Kennedy commented, 'may leave us no alternative in case of war except the initiation of an atomic war to which, in the long run, we may ourselves be more vulnerable.' This was one of his first direct references to the nuclear issue and the report may have been the basis for his opinion.[10] Although Kennedy was merely recognizing the work of others, here nevertheless was a clear rejection of 'massive retaliation' several years before that term entered the political lexicon.[11] Kennedy's criticism was all the more noteworthy, moreover, because it appeared while a fellow-Democrat occupied the White House, and thus lacked any partisan motivation.

It is thus entirely possible that Kennedy had already settled upon this stance by 1953, when plenty of partisan reinforcement appeared. That year, the 35-year-old Kennedy continued his swift political ascent by joining the US Senate, while Republican Dwight Eisenhower entered the White House and announced his 'New Look' policy, with its relatively heavy reliance on nuclear weapons. When Eisenhower's Secretary of State John Foster Dulles delivered his famous massive retaliation speech in January 1954, Kennedy responded quickly, fine-tuning his earlier critique by referring to the colonial war then reaching a climax in Indo-China: 'We must ask how the new Dulles' policy . . . will fare in these areas of guerrilla warfare. At what point would the threat of atomic weapons be used . . .?' 'Of what use would nuclear weapons be,' he asked, 'in opposing a Communist advance which rested not upon military invasion but upon local insurrection and political deterioration?'[12] Indeed, Kennedy argued a bit later, massive retaliation would actually encourage the Communists to advance 'through those techniques which they deemed not sufficiently offensive to induce us to risk atomic warfare'.[13] Kennedy made this fundamental critique of the New Look repeatedly at the time and would stand firmly by it thereafter.

It would be incorrect to imply, however, that nuclear weapons preoccupied Kennedy during his early Senate years. Through mid-1957, he devoted most of his attention to other issues such as foreign aid and Algeria. An article he published in *Foreign Affairs* in October 1957, the major foreign policy statement of his pre-presidential years, scarcely mentioned nuclear weapons.[14]

The launch of *Sputnik* and Kennedy's growing presidential aspirations changed all that. Kennedy had warned of the United States falling behind in the missile field as early as February 1956,[15] but the apparent smashing success of the Soviet intercontinental ballistic missile (ICBM) programme in 1957 brought nuclear weapons to the top of Kennedy's agenda. Almost immediately, he began attacking the Republican administration for allowing the alleged inferiority to develop and called for compensatory measures. He still did not lose sight, however, of the larger context in which he placed ICBMs. While continuing his calls for a greater conventional capability, he also stressed the importance of foreign aid as well as education and economic strength at home. He even warned against overemphasis of the missile question, which might divert attention from 'other avenues of Soviet advance'. Yet perhaps most important, Kennedy began advocating intensified efforts toward arms control, which, true to the thrust of *Why England Slept*, he continued to believe diverse military strength would safely allow.[16]

Over the next three years, Kennedy elaborated on these themes as he prepared and then kicked off his presidential campaign. He found support for his positions in the work of nuclear strategists such as Albert Wohlstetter[17] and retired generals such as James Gavin and Maxwell Taylor. Taylor's book, *The Uncertain Trumpet* (1959), proposed to replace massive retaliation with what he called 'flexible response'. Like its predecessor, flexible response was a deterrent strategy. But the difference was that it entailed 'a capability to react across the entire spectrum of possible challenge, for coping with anything from general atomic war to infiltrations and aggressions such as threaten Laos and Berlin.'

Taylor's book dovetailed neatly with and, in Kennedy's words, 'helped to shape' his views.[18]

It also became clear during this last pre-presidential period that Kennedy subscribed to the notion of a 'nuclear revolution': the idea that atomic weapons had decisively altered the nature of war. 'Until 1945 major wars could be won by adhering to the principles of Napoleon . . .,' he wrote just before the 1960 election. 'The atom has changed war, as it will change the world.'[19] In addition, he seemed to place little faith in the notion of limited nuclear war, or in tactical nuclear weapons, which he thought 'suffer from much the same handicaps as large atomic weapons'. The United States did need to stockpile these weapons to deter the Soviets from using them, but 'inevitably' their use would lead to 'larger and larger nuclear armaments on both sides, until the world-wide holocaust has begun'.[20] There might be distinct steps along the spectrum of conventional force, but once one side crossed the 'nuclear firebreak', Kennedy had no confidence that similar steps would exist.

The central issue for Kennedy, however, remained the Soviets' alleged lead in ICBMs, the 'missile gap',[21] which threatened to undermine US diplomacy and offer the Kremlin 'a new shortcut to world domination'. The Soviets' 'missile power will be a shield from behind which they will slowly, but surely, advance', he claimed, by means that included 'Sputnik diplomacy, limited brush-fire wars . . ., and the vicious blackmail of our allies'. In addition, Kennedy appears to have believed that the greater the gap, the more belligerent the USSR would become. 'Minimum deterrence', the strategy by which even an inferior nuclear force can deter effectively, might not work against 'the leaders of a totalitarian state'. Soviet nuclear superiority, therefore, had to be prevented at all costs, and indeed, in his more hawkish speeches, Kennedy suggested that *US* superiority—in all realms, nuclear as well as others—was an essential objective.[22]

To help remedy the situation, Kennedy proposed reducing the vulnerability of US strategic forces by increasing the airborne alert capability of the Strategic Air Command (SAC); accelerating the development and production of the Minuteman ICBM and Polaris submarine-launched ballistic missile (SLBM); and acquiring the larger and more mobile conventional forces envisaged under the doctrine of flexible response, which would yield alternatives besides 'retreat and nuclear warfare'.[23]

But for Kennedy, closing the missile gap would not merely prevent Sputnik diplomacy—Soviet intimidation based on its missile strength—while bolstering that of the West; it would also provide a sturdy basis for arms control. He repeatedly used Churchill's quotation, 'We arm to parley.' He saw the 'catastrophic arms race' as producing deadly atmospheric pollution, runaway nuclear proliferation, and ultimately, global annihilation; in face of this, the Eisenhower administration's disarmament efforts were half-hearted, disorganized, and inadequate. Thus the Senator called for far more serious measures in this field; a continuation of the nuclear test moratorium then in progress;

and a formal, comprehensive, verifiable test ban.[24] There is little evidence as to Kennedy's ultimate goal, and he himself probably gave it little thought, but at one point he did seem to endorse 'total nuclear disarmament'.[25]

In short, Kennedy's attack on Eisenhower came from two directions at once: the President was doing too little for defence, especially in the missile field, but also too little for arms control. This one-two punch was certainly clever politically, for it offered the broadest possible appeal. And yet Kennedy, true to his earlier views, saw no contradiction between the two approaches: only military strength permitted arms control, but both were essential to security.

Kennedy was often vague or even contradictory about the missile gap. Was it current or future? Was it one of overall military strength, or just ICBMs? Was it a problem of real military-diplomatic salience, or merely one of 'prestige' or perceptions? He chose to believe the most dire assessments of the strategic balance and disregard the rest. He failed to place ICBMs within the context of the overall US strategic deterrent, an exercise from which the United States would have emerged in much better shape. There is also some reason to question the extent to which Kennedy believed in the gap in the first place.[26]

But the fuzziness and domestic political aspects of Kennedy's arguments about the missile gap do not call into question the sincerity of the broader views he had come to hold, with great consistency, on nuclear weapons. He believed in a nuclear force that was survivable and strong, if not superior; in relying on that force not only to provide security and to support diplomacy, but also as a basis for meaningful arms control; in placing that force within the context of equally strong conventional forces; and, in turn, in embedding all military force within a foreign policy of diverse resources, from alliances to foreign aid.[27] These elements would characterize his nuclear policies as President.

Theory: Flexible Response

In January 1961, the Senator became President and the policy outsider now found himself policy-maker. Yet most of his views on nuclear weapons survived the transition remarkably unchanged. To the extent that Kennedy the President had a conceptual framework for the role of nuclear weapons in foreign policy, his strategy began as and would remain flexible response. By definition, this strategy meant a role for nuclear weapons in US foreign policy that was less than it had been under Eisenhower.[28]

Kennedy by no means neglected nuclear weapons while in office. Like massive retaliation, flexible response relied on nuclear weapons. The difference between the two was stark, but *relative*. Thus, Kennedy quickly embarked on the large strategic buildup he had advocated as a presidential hopeful. Prominent among Kennedy's first major defence decisions were the promised acceleration and expansion of the Polaris and Minuteman missile programmes. These and subsequent decisions under Kennedy generated a force of 1,840 strategic nuclear missiles, a 68 per cent increase over the 1,096 foreseen by Eisenhower's last defence budget. Overall, the number of strategic nuclear weapons in the US arsenal grew from 3,012 in April 1961 to 5,007 by July 1964—a 66 per cent increase, although much of this was 'in the pipeline' before January 1961.[29]

Despite this expansion, however, in theory Kennedy sought to avoid having to rely on nuclear weapons as much as Eisenhower had. In keeping with flexible response, his administration placed more emphasis on developing both greater conventional capabilities—especially airlift, sealift, and tactical air forces—and unconventional capabilities, most notably the Special Forces ('Green Berets'). Kennedy intended these forces to give him, as he continued to put it, alternatives besides 'humiliation' or 'all-out nuclear action'.[30] With such innovations as the Alliance for Progress and the Arms Control and Disarmament Agency, moreover, Kennedy showed that he was prepared to rely more heavily than Eisenhower had on foreign aid and arms control.

Kennedy's growing abhorrence of nuclear weapons probably reinforced his determination to become less dependent on them. In numerous public statements throughout his tenure, Kennedy stressed the unfathomable devastation that a nuclear war would bring. This he did even in late 1963, a time when superpower tensions had relaxed markedly. He felt it necessary to mention the '300 million Americans, Russians, and Europeans' who could be 'wiped out by a nuclear exchange' and to wonder if the survivors could 'endure the fire, poison, chaos, and catastrophe'.[31] Privately, the President displayed even greater concern. In 1961, after a briefing on the effects of nuclear weapons, Kennedy remarked to Dean Rusk: 'And we call ourselves the human race.' Later on, in a personal letter, he expressed his view that the 'prospect of a nuclear exchange is so terrible that I conceive that it would be preferable to be among the dead than among the quick'. A rumour even went around the Pentagon that the President, when touring a SAC base, had turned pale when shown a 20-megaton bomb. 'Why do we need one of these?' he supposedly asked.[32]

The New Frontiersmen continued to promote flexible response in large part, however, because they believed that the Soviet threat was assuming precisely the form they had claimed it would in their critique of Eisenhower's national security policy. In an address delivered just two weeks before Kennedy's inauguration, Soviet premier Nikita Khrushchev declared his country's support for 'wars of national liberation' in the Third World.[33] Deeply, indeed excessively impressed by the speech, the President circulated it and an accompanying analysis among his top appointees with instructions to 'read, mark, learn and inwardly digest'.[34] And, while over the next three years the Soviets would challenge the United States directly in Berlin and Cuba, persistent indirect Soviet involvement in such places as Laos, Vietnam, and the Congo led the administration to stick with the basic reasoning behind flexible response.[35]

Adherence to this doctrine appears time and again in the fundamental documents of the Kennedy national security policy.[36] The first formal manifestation of the Kennedy policy was the secret 'Acheson Report' on NATO submitted in March 1961. Produced under the guidance of former Secretary of State Dean Acheson and accepted by Kennedy as official US policy,[37] it contained a detailed endorsement of flexible response for the European theatre. 'First priority should be given,' it recommended, 'to preparing for the more likely contingencies, i.e. those short of nuclear or massive non-nuclear attack.'[38]

The commitment to flexible response, however, appears even more explicitly in the administration's 'Basic National Security Policy' paper (BNSP). Kennedy's Secretary of Defense Robert McNamara initially saw value in revising the last of Eisenhower's BNSPs (NSC 5906/1), and work on a new version began in spring 1961 under the co-ordination of Assistant Secretary of Defense Paul Nitze, who ran the Office of International Security Affairs (ISA). An early draft affirmed flexible response in ringing terms, emphasizing the importance of non-nuclear forces, especially for opposing large-scale aggression, but also saw the need for a variety of nuclear options should nuclear war break out.[39]

The first of two subsequent draft BNSPs was issued in March 1962 by the State Department's Policy Planning Council. The product of a collaborative effort by high-ranking officials, it called for 'an ability and readiness to use force' both to 'deter and deal with' all forms of communist aggression and pressure, from 'direct nuclear assault' to limited incursions and psychological coercion. The 'special imperatives of a nuclear-missile age', in addition, necessitated a policy that would minimize the likelihood that nuclear weapons would ever have to be used. The huge US losses expected in a nuclear exchange demanded means of 'limiting civil damage', 'non-nuclear defence alternatives', tactical and strategic nuclear forces 'both as deterrent and for combat', and arms control.[40]

In the spring of 1963, according to Nitze, several areas of disagreement over BNSP lingered between its civilian drafters and the JCS, and McNamara refused to resolve them because by now 'he didn't believe there was anything to be gained by the formulation of such a document'.[41] McNamara was merely expressing, however, what for some time had been the attitude toward BNSP at the very top: President Kennedy never approved any BNSP as formal policy, despite continuing support for it in some quarters. The main reason for this was his desire to avoid having any such formal statement tie his hands.[42] Thus a profound attachment to flexibility dictated both the substance and the form of Kennedy's foreign policy-making. The result was that BNSP—periodically revised, but never approved—accurately *reflected* the administration's thought about the role of nuclear weapons in foreign policy, but did not *guide* the way the administration would rely on them in the real world.

Shifts did occur in declared nuclear strategy—the well-known 'education of Robert McNamara'.[43] And the President was not always completely steadfast in his commitment to flexible response. According to the minutes of a top-level meeting in December 1962, he 'wondered whether, absent the problem of Berlin, there would really be a need for large-scale conventional forces' along the Iron Curtain because 'after all, any incursion across this line would in fact lead promptly to nuclear warfare, and for that reason the nuclear deterrent would be effective'.[44] This remarkable lapse notwithstanding, the theoretical role of nuclear weapons in US foreign policy as spelled out in flexible response remained virtually unchanged through the end of Kennedy's presidency. In a speech surveying foreign affairs he was to have delivered the day he died, Kennedy sounded the same themes he had all along. 'Overwhelming nuclear strength cannot stop a guerrilla war,' the address read. The successful outcome of the recent international crises had been based on a 'strength composed of many different elements, ranging from the most massive deterrents to the most subtle influences'. By assigning roughly equal emphasis to these various elements—from strategic and tactical nuclear weapons, to conventional forces, on to reliance on allies and propaganda—Kennedy to the end affirmed a doctrine that sought to reduce the role of nuclear weapons in national security policy.[45]

Practice: Flexible Restraint

It is obviously impossible, on the one hand, to compare how Kennedy *thought* about nuclear weapons with how he *used* nuclear weapons because he never *did* use them—nor did he even come close to doing so deliberately. On the other hand, one can gauge the extent to which he 'relied' on nuclear weapons—that is, their *considered* or *threatened* use—in the major international crises he faced. Quite simply, in the three crises Kennedy himself considered most grave[46]—Laos, Berlin, and Cuba—there is remarkably *little* evidence of reliance, to any significant extent, on nuclear weapons.

This is not a judgement of what *effect* US nuclear weapons had in terms of achieving US objectives or influencing Soviet behaviour; that is a separate issue beyond the scope of this essay. But from the standpoint of official *intent*, it is difficult to escape the conclusion that Kennedy largely succeeded in translating his stated goal—the relative denuclearization of US foreign policy—into practice.

The Nuclear Buildup

One might fairly ask: What about Kennedy's nuclear buildup, the daunting backdrop against which the major US–Soviet crises unfolded? Its effect on the Soviets was probably substantial, helping to provoke, to enlarge, or to confirm the need for their own corresponding buildup, depending upon whether they initiated theirs in 1960 or 1961.[47] Kennedy deserves criticism for his inattention to what effect his programmes might have on Soviet policy. Nor was his administration oblivious to the diplomatic implications of enhanced strategic might—or of preserved strategic superiority. Awareness of such implications, after all, is consistent with Kennedy's basic pre-presidential beliefs discussed earlier. It is intriguing, for example, that Secretary McNamara testified before Congress in April 1961 that a markedly reduced estimate of Soviet missile strength would have 'some but not much' effect on the administration's buildup.[48] Some administration officials periodically expressed their desire to maintain US strategic superiority, in the context of flexible response, of course, because that was the surest way to deter Soviet aggression.[49] Yet the desire for superiority was only one, and not the central, motivation behind the force expansion.

First, traditional worst-case thinking clearly played a role in Kennedy's buildup, irrespective of the missile gap, which gradually faded in 1961 as improved US intelligence techniques revealed how tiny the Soviet ICBM force really was. Despite the debunking of the gap, there was no guarantee that another, genuine gap might not develop. 'Since we could not be certain of Soviet intentions, since we could not be sure that they would not undertake a massive build-up,' McNamara later wrote, 'we had to insure against such an eventuality by undertaking a major build-up of our own . . .'[50] Second, domestic pressure for a buildup from both Congress and the military was formidable, or certainly perceived as such, and had an obvious impact. As Kennedy admitted in early 1962, 'we would probably be safe with less,' but the Congressional demand for 'more nuclear weapons is pretty strong. I don't think such sentiment can be rationally defended, but there it is.'[51] Third, there were the needs created by innovations in nuclear strategy, notably the concepts of 'counterforce' and 'damage limitation', which helped propel the buildup. Moreover, other considerations exerted at least some marginal influence on the Kennedy force levels, such as the President's persistent belief in the idea, however problematic, of negotiation from strength; the difficulty of disavowing his missile gap rhetoric during the 1960 campaign; and perhaps even the lure of job-creation in the US economy.[52]

It is important to note that Kennedy at several points exhibited restraint and undertook measures to 'stabilize' the arms race even as he accelerated its pace. These include his hesitancy in ordering the resumption of US nuclear testing after Khrushchev did so in 1961; the vigour with which he sought the limited test ban achieved two years later (a comprehensive ban remained his goal throughout the effort[53]); his success in improving the invulnerability and command and control of US strategic forces (that is, the buildup was as much *qualitative* as quantitative); as part of this, the placement of electronic locks on US strategic weapons to prevent unauthorized use—technology the administration then deliberately leaked to the Soviets; stepped-up tacit co-operation with the USSR in the form of a reconnaissance satellite regime; and instalment of the Moscow–Washington 'Hot Line' in 1963.[54] Kennedy's buildup, in short, does make him an 'arms racer', one who contributed mightily to the situation of nuclear 'overkill' that made the Cold War so terrifying.[55] He was careless (especially about Soviet reactions), at times alarmist, unnecessarily hasty, arbitrary as to precise force levels, and perhaps overly impressed by domestic pressure. Yet he was by no means an unmitigated arms racer; he was also an early 'arms stabilizer'. Nor, most importantly, was he primarily interested in building up in order to establish US superiority. And, to the extent that he was, he intended that superiority to deter the Soviets, not to 'compel' or coerce them.

Laos

The best way to judge the extent of Kennedy's 'reliance' on the expanded nuclear arsenal, however, is to examine the major superpower crises he faced. The first was the potential 'fall' of Laos to the Communist Pathet Lao in 1961 and 1962. In spring 1961, as Kennedy considered dispatching US troops to forestall a Pathet Lao victory, the JCS sought permission to use nuclear weapons should the Chinese meet a US intervention with one of their own. If the United States went into Laos, Army Chief of Staff George Decker argued, it 'should go in to win, and that means Hanoi, China, and maybe even using nuclear bombs'.[56] The JCS were not keen on sending troops into Laos, but if ordered to do so, they did not want to be hampered by limits on the size of the ground forces committed or on how high they could climb the escalation ladder if necessary.

Civilian officials also mentioned the use of nuclear weapons as a remote possibility. A joint State–Defense draft contingency plan of early May recommended that if the cease-fire talks then underway broke down and the Pathet Lao resumed its offensive, then forces of the Southeast Asia Treaty Organization (SEATO), including US troops, should intervene. Chinese counter-intervention, would raise the question of 'whether to attack targets in South China and whether to initiate use of nuclear weapons'.[57]

But the administration probed the possibilities with considerable caution. The State Department recommended that SEATO ground forces introduced into Laos 'have no mission or objective of approaching or menacing the frontier area between Laos, North Viet-Nam, and Communist China'.[58] The clear intent was to avoid provoking Chinese or North Vietnamese intervention, which might in turn risk escalation to a major, perhaps nuclear, conflict. Kennedy himself worried about what would happen if the United States used nuclear weapons in Laos. He asked, according to Ted Sorensen, 'where would it stop, how many other Communist movements would we have to attack, what kind of world would it be?'[59]

Most important was Kennedy's actual policy. He ended up agreeing to pursue a negotiated settlement in Geneva. He does not appear to have come close to sending troops into Laos in 1961, probably in part because such a decision might have led to nuclear use. While he refused at a meeting in late April to rule out US intervention, he and his advisers felt it best to avoid risking a wider conflagration. His main military move instead was to deploy the Seventh Fleet to the South China Sea; this he backed up with threats to the Soviets and Chinese that the United States would intervene with ground troops if necessary.[60] This strategy appeared to work, and if anything, the first Laos crisis reinforced Kennedy's belief in flexible response. Toward the end of May, when he commented that 'nuclear weapons cannot prevent subversion', he apparently had Laos in mind.[61]

The crisis resumed when the Pathet Lao broke the cease-fire and attacked the US-backed royalist forces in May 1962. Again the Joint Chiefs, joined at one point by McNamara, opposed the insertion of only limited forces into Laos; if force were to be employed, it would have to be on a large scale. 'What the United States would do if the Chinese Communists intervened [in that case] was not spelled out,' Roger Hilsman writes, 'but the general impression was that the recommendation would be to retaliate on the mainland with nuclear weapons.'[62]

Kennedy did order the nuclear-armed Seventh Fleet to the Gulf of Siam, but then rashly passed the buck to his subordinates when he reconsidered the order. 'You and Mac Bundy talk it over between you,' he told Hilsman, 'and *you and he decide whether to stop the Fleet or send the Fleet,* and let me know what you decide!!!'[63] This *de facto* delegation of authority to 'relatively minor officials' outside 'the military chain of command', Stephen Pelz argues, provokes 'disturbing questions about the possible misuse of such power in the nuclear age', particularly in times of crisis.[64] Still, the episode represents nuclear carelessness, not deliberate reliance on nuclear weapons for coercion or deterrence in a crisis—a crime of omission, not commission.

Moreover, although Kennedy ended up sending several thousand troops in addition to the Seventh Fleet, they went only into neighbouring Thailand, not Laos itself. And while this constituted a more drastic application of force than in the previous year, it seems to have been accompanied by even less talk of nuclear weapons, Hilsman's account notwithstanding. Indeed, at a meeting soon after the crisis had passed, top officials discussed military contingencies in some detail without even broaching the subject of nuclear weapons.[65]

Berlin

Berlin, in Khrushchev's words, 'the testicles of the West',[66] was the object of a far more serious crisis in the summer of 1961. At the Vienna Summit in June, Khrushchev had warned Kennedy that unless the German question was solved within six months, he would sign a separate peace treaty with East Germany, in effect forcing NATO to choose between the abandonment of West Berlin and war with the USSR. Kennedy was determined to uphold the western commitment to Berlin.[67] But how would he go about it? His policy overall was neither as cautious nor as reckless as it could have been; nuclear weapons played some role in its formulation and execution. Yet Kennedy and his top advisers never seriously considered nuclear use, and while they made nuclear threats, they relied more heavily on non-nuclear actions.

After rejecting a recommendation that he declare a national emergency, Kennedy announced the US response in a major address on 25 July. He did draw attention to the accelerated buildup he had launched earlier, which made an emphasis on nuclear weapons in this speech unnecessary. But in his words, 'even more importantly', Kennedy outlined a military programme that would facilitate a reliance on flexible response—a programme primarily conventional, not nuclear. His major requests were for the addition of personnel and non-nuclear weapons, a tripling of draft calls, and the activation of reserve units. Perhaps most significantly, these military preparations were part of a larger strategy outlined in the address that also encompassed negotiations.[68] At no point in the crisis were talks with Moscow ruled out; even in the tense days immediately following the construction of the Berlin Wall, Kennedy argued for a vigorous pursuit of negotiations.[69]

The 25 July address was powerful, perhaps even alarmist, but it reflected Kennedy's genuine fear of war over Berlin. US policy was built not 'on the assumption that the president might *choose* to launch a nuclear attack', the most careful study notes, but 'that a nuclear war was something that might well *happen.*'[70] This would help explain why civil defence and increased conventional force contributions by NATO allies, rather than more provocative actions, were the focus of Kennedy's reaction when the Wall went up on 13 August.[71]

Because nuclear war might happen, officials did consider how they would use nuclear weapons should it come to that. Bundy wrote Kennedy that the existing nuclear warplan, SIOP-62, seemed 'dangerously rigid' and if left unchanged 'may leave you very little choice as to how you face the moment of thermonuclear truth'. Kennedy might therefore want to discuss SIOP revision with McNamara.[72] Mid-level civilian officials spent some time planning a pre-emptive nuclear strike on the Soviet Union and even a possible 'nuclear warning shot'. Kennedy's opinion of these plans is unknown, but top advisers such as McNamara, Sorensen, and Nitze rejected them, and the President almost certainly did as well.[73]

Kennedy did approve NSAM 109, on 23 October. It outlined four phases of NATO response to an interruption of access to Berlin: first diplomacy, then mobilization, followed by conventional military action, and ultimately nuclear use—pure flexible response. Kennedy's thoughts on the nuclear phase four are again difficult to ascertain[74]—that is, apart from the fact that he approved the larger document, which suggests that he could at least conceive of exhausting the options under flexible response and waging nuclear war in defence of Berlin.[75] However, this was only on paper, after the crisis had eased considerably, and in any case it was nothing new; Kennedy had always been aware of his responsibilities and how, even under the terms of flexible response, those always included the possible use of nuclear weapons in war. It may also be that the contingency planning in NSAM 109 was partly meant for Soviet consumption—via the deliberate use of espionage channels—which might have qualified it as a threat of sorts, but not so much an official commitment to the document's recommendations.[76]

As is true regarding Laos, Kennedy deserves criticism for his careless delegation of authority. He unleashed in Berlin the bellicose General Lucius Clay, who as local commander took it upon himself to provoke the only direct US–Soviet armoured face-off in history. This could have led to combat and thence, conceivably, to nuclear war. Yet here too, Kennedy also circumvented Clay and worked behind the scenes with the Soviets to defuse the stand-off.[77]

Kennedy did, through advisers such as Nitze, McNamara, and Robert Kennedy, issue nuclear threats.[78] But he delivered his clearest public message on nuclear weapons in a most delicate manner. Encouraged by changing intelligence estimates, the President decided to debunk the missile gap once and for all in order to stop Khrushchev's nuclear sabre-rattling and also to reassure NATO allies and the American public. He carefully chose McNamara's deputy Roswell Gilpatric for the job—someone sufficiently high-ranking to make the statement credible, but minor enough to avoid having the Soviets perceive it as a threat.[79] With this and similar announcements, the administration was unambiguously declaring US strategic superiority, but not, significantly, the country's ability to fight a nuclear war and bear its costs.[80] Gilpatric's speech, furthermore, placed this declaration alongside others regarding the conventional buildup and efforts to strengthen US allies.[81]

Such actions, when viewed together with the steps he outlined on 25 July, suggest that on balance Kennedy was reluctant to brandish the increasingly evident US nuclear superiority. Indeed, he declined to make it the focal point of his Berlin policy. Rather, he placed greater emphasis on the non-nuclear facets of flexible response, augmenting US conventional forces and trying to persuade the NATO allies to do the same. He also repeatedly sought, publicly and privately, a negotiated settlement (despite the admittedly dim prospects for results). The President's caution, while it could have been greater, is nevertheless not what one might expect from a leader enjoying clear nuclear superiority.

Cuba

The third and most dangerous crisis was the one over missiles in Cuba in October 1962. Here Kennedy and his advisers on the famous 'ExCom' relied somewhat, but surprisingly little, on nuclear weapons. As with Berlin but even more so, they exhibited a cautiousness that contrasted sharply with the towering and by then openly confirmed US nuclear advantage.[82]

On the one hand, Kennedy threatened nuclear war once during the crisis, and he abandoned flexible response in so doing. Although veterans did tend later, with some justification, to view the crisis as having been a successful implementation of that doctrine, flexible response in fact gave way to massive retaliation redux. It was US policy, Kennedy announced in his carefully crafted television address announcing the presence of Soviet missiles in Cuba, 'to regard any nuclear missile launched from Cuba . . . as an attack by the Soviet Union on the United States, *requiring a full retaliatory response upon the Soviet Union*'.[83] As Fred Kaplan has pointed out, when the chips were down, flexible response doctrine does not appear to have mattered all that much. 'To the extent that nuclear weapons entered into the discussion at all,' he argues, 'their image hardly matched that associated with theories of controlled and limited options.'[84] Kennedy in this instance was tempted to reach first for his crude nuclear cudgel, not his refined multiple-level strategy.

Apart from Kennedy's speech, though, it is questionable how much the New Frontiersmen *deliberately* relied on nuclear weapons in the crisis. There is very little evidence—among evidence that is quite good—indicating the ExCom's conscious use of nuclear weapons for deterrence or 'compellence'. Top officials were virtually silent on the overall nuclear balance, JCS Chair Maxwell Taylor being apparently the only one to invoke US superiority. 'We have the strategic advantage in our general war capabilities,' he wrote to McNamara on 26 October. 'This is no time to run scared.' Ten days earlier, and more subtly, McNamara himself had recommended a SAC alert as a means of 'trying to deter' a 'Soviet military response' to the US air attack on Cuba then under consideration.[85] Such evidentiary fragments cannot be dismissed; they suggest that ExCom members at points did see some use in nuclear weapons, or were at least vaguely aware of US superiority and escalation dominance. They also give reason at least to qualify claims that the strategic balance played no role at all in the Cuban crisis.[86]

Still, far more impressive is the *lack* of references to nuclear weapons during the crisis. One might argue that the truly daunting US superiority spoke for itself, thus eliminating any need for official comment. The virtual absence of public references to nuclear weapons, under this theory, may have been deliberate. But this explanation fails to account for the near-total dearth of private references to nuclear capabilities one would expect if the ExCom had been mindful of or encouraged by US superiority. In fact, one of the few private remarks, by Kennedy himself, contradicts Taylor's. 'What difference does it make?' he asked about the Cuban deployment. 'They've got enough to blow us up already.' At the peak of the crisis on 27 October moreover, the President clearly feared that an armed clash would escalate uncontrollably.[87] Such bits of positive evidence hint that the US nuclear edge counted for little in the President's mind. But more important is the negative evidence supporting the same conclusion: although the jury is out until all the documents emerge, the almost complete silence about US superiority among Kennedy administration officials in their conversations with one another suggests that it was not particularly important to them.

Finally, there are numerous indications of US restraint during the crisis. Kennedy can be legitimately criticized for maintaining a double standard (objecting to Soviet missiles in Cuba while maintaining similar Jupiter missiles in Turkey), for acting out of political rather than security motives, or for choosing public confrontation over private diplomacy. US actions were neither 'brilliantly controlled' nor 'matchlessly calibrated',[88] not by a long shot. But given his determination to secure removal of the Soviet missiles, Kennedy's policy was fairly cautious. Perhaps this should come as no surprise, for his fear of escalation stemmed from his underlying fear that the crisis would lead to nuclear war. 'It isn't the first step that concerns me,' his brother quoted him as saying, 'but both sides escalating to the fourth and fifth step— and we don't go to the sixth because there is no one around to do so.'[89] Again, the direct evidence is sparse, but it seems plausible that this concern produced cautious behaviour, as seen in:

1. Kennedy's selection of the naval blockade over an air strike.[90]
2. Less evidence of planning for the use of nuclear weapons than in the Berlin crisis the previous year.
3. The willingness of several on ExCom, most notably Kennedy himself on 26–7 October, to consider trading the Jupiters in Turkey for the Soviet missiles in Cuba.[91]
   And on 27 October in particular:
4. The US concessions—the *secret* but *explicit* Jupiter missile deal and the pledge not to invade Cuba—that helped solve the crisis.
5. Robert Kennedy's approach to Soviet Ambassador Anatoly Dobrynin, which both sides understood as *not* including an ultimatum.[92]
6. The existence, within ExCom, of little support for an air strike, and some discussion of alternatives, such as tightening the blockade.[93]

To end the crisis, in short, Kennedy certainly made greater use of carrots, and less use of sticks, than earlier accounts of the crisis maintained. This fact, coupled with the ExCom's virtual silence on the strategic balance, suggests that in the crisis Kennedy was neither emboldened by nor deliberately relied upon the huge US superiority. It is difficult to support such assertions as, '[Kennedy] *used* America's overwhelming superiority to force Nikita Khrushchev to back down.'[94] Indeed, reflecting privately on the crisis three months later, Kennedy drew as the 'major lesson' not the importance of nuclear superiority, but rather of both sides having 'sufficient time to consider alternative courses of action'.[95]

Nuclear Weapons in Other Contexts
Outside of US–Soviet relations and the three specific crises outlined above, nuclear weapons played an even smaller role in Kennedy administration diplomacy. There is no evidence of threatened or considered use, for instance, in the Congo crisis, in Africa more generally, or elsewhere.

Nuclear weapons did, however, play a sizeable political role in US foreign relations. Because Kennedy's policy was intended, as Rostow put it, 'to bind up the northern half of the Free World more closely',[96] the President saw the weapons as tools useful for solidifying the Atlantic alliance. This is most evident in US attempts to establish the Multilateral Force (MLF), but also in the 1961 decision to proceed with the deployment of the obsolete Jupiters in Turkey, to appease the Turks and to avoid appearing weak to the USSR.[97] Conversely, nuclear weapons could produce political fissures in Washington's relationships, notably with Great Britain in the Skybolt affair of late 1962, but also with Japan and Canada.[98]

But nuclear weapons never constituted the sole nor even the primary focus of alliance and bilateral ties. Apart from State Department Atlanticists, the administration never enthusiastically pushed the MLF; from the beginning Kennedy attached a host of conditions to the project's development, and it remained only one element in his 'Grand Design' for Europe. Of equal or greater importance were his efforts to promote European integration, to reduce tariffs, and to persuade the major NATO allies to beef up their conventional military forces.[99]

To the extent that nuclear weapons figured in regional policies, it was with respect to non-proliferation. This was especially true in the Middle East, but also in Latin America, which during the missile crisis the administration considered establishing as a nuclear-free zone. Nuclear proliferation was Kennedy's main justification for the limited nuclear test ban, which in turn was the centrepiece of his foreign policy in 1963.[100]

China

Kennedy's greatest proliferation worry was the People's Republic of China. The President, according to Rostow, considered that nation's foreseeable entrance into the nuclear club 'as likely to be . . . the most significant and worst event of the 1960's'. Along with many other US policy-makers, he ascribed to the PRC a relative indifference to human life that suggested it could not be deterred as easily as the Soviet Union had been.[101] So great was his consternation that, according to the best study, his administration 'not only seriously discussed but actively pursued the possibility of joint military action *with the Soviets*' to destroy Chairman Mao's atomic bomb-production complex. Bundy discounts this as 'talk, not serious planning or real intent'. But even if only 'talk' it remains striking testimony to the depth of White House fears.[102]

In contrast to its flirtation with an aggressive non-proliferation policy aimed at China, the administration was more restrained during the Taiwan Straits mini-crisis of 1962. During spring and summer of that year, Nationalist leader Chiang Kai-shek stepped up his long-delayed preparations to invade the mainland. Washington refused, however, to support or encourage Chiang's plans.[103] Certainly Kennedy faced a far less serious confrontation in this sense than Eisenhower had in 1954–5 and 1958. But again, it is noteworthy that the Kennedy administration, while enjoying absolute strategic superiority over the pre-nuclear People's Republic, still laboured to prevent Chiang from touching off a more dangerous crisis.

Vietnam

To the immediate south, Vietnam was one of Kennedy's most serious foreign policy problems, especially in the fall of 1961, when the collapse of the US client regime in Saigon seemed imminent and some advisers proposed that Kennedy send in thousands of US troops. In the case of Vietnam, however, there is again virtually no evidence that top policy-makers even considered, much less threatened, the use of nuclear weapons.[104]

As with Laos, the JCS did leave open for consideration whether such weapons would be used against the Chinese should they intervene in the wake of a SEATO deployment to South Vietnam.[105] And on the civilian side, Nitze's deputy William Bundy wrote McNamara in early November that 'one possible omission' from a draft memo for the President was 'the issue of nuclear weapons as part of a punitive action'.[106] Shortly thereafter, Bundy outlined 'Scenario Z', the last of three 'bad scenarios':

Moscow comes to the aid of Hanoi and Peiping, supplying all necessary equipment (including a limited supply of air-deliverable nuclear weapons to retaliate in kind *against US use*) so that the outcome is a stalemate in which great destruction is wreaked on the whole area.[107]

This suggests that officials could conceive of an extreme contingency in which they would use nuclear weapons against the Soviets and Chinese in connection with Vietnam; it may also suggest that they could imagine a nuclear exchange remaining confined to a particular region. But Bundy acknowledged that scenarios 'X [US sits out, Saigon collapses] *and* Z are clearly nightmares', adding that the 'chances of the Soviets bringing about Z do not appear great in the short run'.[108]

Even such tentative ruminations as these do not appear to have taken place more widely or at higher levels. In fact, the report of the Taylor–Rostow mission, which recommended the large-scale dispatch of troops, discussed only contingencies that officials would 'hope to meet without the use of nuclear weapons' and recommended an expansion of reserve forces 'to cover action' only 'up to the nuclear threshold'.[109] The military undoubtedly had mildewed contingency plans that provided for nuclear use, and talk of using nuclear weapons in Vietnam certainly became more serious later as US involvement deepened under Lyndon Johnson. But under Kennedy, high-level policy on Vietnam resembled that regarding other regions: it seems to have allowed no significant role for nuclear weapons.

Interpretive Issues

To complete this review of Kennedy's attitude toward nuclear weapons, several larger interpretive issues remain to be addressed.

Nuclear Learning?

First is the issue of 'nuclear learning'.[110] Kennedy is a poor 'test case' in this regard if only because his public career lay entirely in the post-Hiroshima era. We thus have no way of reasonably supposing what his policies might have been had nuclear weapons never been invented. Nor did Kennedy have the time other leaders did for nuclear learning while in office, nor the opportunity to reflect upon his nuclear experiences in retirement. What relevant pre-nuclear views he had, primarily those spelled out in *Why England Slept*, he retained. He remained convinced that military strength—perhaps superiority, but certainly parity—was absolutely essential for successful diplomacy. Nuclear weapons do not appear, at any point, to have altered that fundamental (if broad) belief. And yet, he did view 1945 as a watershed; nuclear weapons had radically altered the nature of war, making its avoidance incomparably more vital than before. In this sense, both before and during his presidency,

Kennedy shared with most other leaders the agonizing dilemmas of an anarchic international system in a nuclear age.

It is difficult to argue that Kennedy became more cautious while in office, again because the 'database', the amount of time available for his views to evolve, was too limited. Although the missile crisis was clearly a sobering experience for Kennedy, too much is often made of his conciliatory American University speech eight months later.[111] No evidence exists, on the other hand, that he became *less* cautious. Kennedy remained remarkably consistent, and if nuclear learning occurred in his case, it did so as a result of his becoming President: after entering the White House, Kennedy exhibited a much keener awareness of what a nuclear war would be like than he had before. His public and private statements repeatedly reveal a profound concern over the nuclear threat and nuclear arms race, despite his own real contributions to that race. We can only speculate as to the reasons for this change: top-secret briefings on war plans and the effects of nuclear weapons probably played a role; he must have reflected inwardly on the awesome responsibility and power he held as President; and the crises he experienced no doubt helped stimulate such reflections. It is also reasonable to conclude that Kennedy's heightened concern, if only indirectly, restricted the role of nuclear weapons in his foreign policy.

The Relevance of Nuclear Weapons

What about the relevance of nuclear weapons to Kennedy? John Mueller minimizes that relevance, seeing Kennedy as fitting within a larger trend in which war was becoming less likely because *conventional* military operations alone would have been so devastating. The idea that Kennedy and Khrushchev 'would have glibly allowed' the Cuban missile crisis 'to escalate if all they had to worry about was a repetition of World War I or II is', he argues, 'singularly unconvincing'.[112] But did the existence of nuclear weapons in 1962 make escalation more likely, less likely, or have no effect at all? Is it not most probable that nuclear weapons made escalation less likely, that they *reinforced* Kennedy's existing restraint? Even the woefully inferior Soviet nuclear arsenal made Kennedy *additionally* reluctant to risk war, quite apart from a reluctance that admittedly stemmed from the prospect of conventional war.[113]

Neither this nor Mueller's view can be unequivocally confirmed by the evidence; the memos include no 'smoking guns'—historians are seldom so lucky. But if nuclear weapons were irrelevant to Kennedy, then why, when speculating about the use of nuclear weapons over Laos, did he worry about 'what kind of world it would be' afterwards? Why, in connection with Berlin, did the President discuss the 'risk of killing a million Americans' or 'destroying this country'? Why, after the Cuban missile crisis, did he comment that putting 'the *nuclear* equation' into the Cold War made it 'such a dangerous time', or that 'a *nuclear* exchange . . . would be a defeat for both sides'? And why did he say that 'there is not going to be any winner of the next war', that a nuclear war 'would not be like any war in history'?[114]

The answer would appear to be that nuclear weapons were in fact quite relevant to Kennedy. The above and many other similar examples suggest that
nuclear weapons had a significant impact on how Kennedy thought about war
and the use of force: he conceived of nuclear war as being substantially if not
radically different from, and worse than, conventional war. No evidence suggests that he ever took the prospect of a conventional war lightly. But Kennedy
was clearly struck by the havoc nuclear weapons would wreak if used. This
made him take war *even more* seriously and made him fear 'escalation' *even
more* deeply than he would have otherwise. Surely that renders nuclear
weapons 'relevant' to him.[115]

Kennedy and the Strategic Balance

But there is more to the *nature* of that 'relevance'. He certainly would have
considered nuclear weapons relevant if adversaries possessed superior numbers of them; Soviet strategic superiority would threaten nothing less than the
nation's survival, he argued, and therefore could never be tolerated.[116] But
enemy superiority was not the only worry. As we have seen, Kennedy believed
that the very existence of a Communist Chinese bomb would markedly affect
that state's behaviour, to the great detriment of the United States. In 1961
Kennedy privately remarked, according to a journalist's notes, that 'the
Chinese Communists are bound to get nuclear weapons in time, and from that
moment on they will dominate Southeast Asia'.[117] Here it is interesting to
note not only Kennedy's apparent belief that nuclear weapons would endow
Beijing with a capability it lacked otherwise, but also that the *relative numbers*
of such weapons did not appear to matter, that an assured US superiority over
an infant Chinese stockpile would provide no deterrent. To be sure, this suggests that Kennedy held certain views of the Chinese themselves. But it also
suggests that he thought that nuclear weapons were relevant, particularly to
the Chinese, and yet that numbers would not necessarily affect that relevance.

These views are entirely consistent with what appears to have been
Kennedy's attitude toward the meaning of *US* nuclear superiority. Although he
continued to consider both Soviet superiority and any Chinese capability
unacceptable, Kennedy while in office failed with few exceptions to exploit or
even to see much utility in the US nuclear advantage. Several of his advisers
placed great faith in the importance and uses of such superiority, and Kennedy
bears final responsibility for the nuclear threats they occasionally issued in
their official capacity. As the 1961 Gilpatric speech demonstrates, moreover,
Kennedy did see several reasons to put an end to Soviet nuclear sabre-rattling;
public declarations of US superiority were obviously the best, if not the only,
means of attaining that reasonable goal.[118] He was certainly attuned to the
indirect political implications of the strategic balance, and to the role it played
in the *perceptions* of allies, the Soviets, and the American public.

But beyond that, his comments and crisis behaviour suggest that he had
come to see US superiority as unusable, that the Soviet force, despite its inferiority, had cancelled out that of the United States. It is thus difficult to escape

the conclusion that John Kennedy represents minimum deterrence in action, and indeed, that he stuck with such an attitude despite intelligence indicating an ever-growing US advantage. Early on, in April 1961, ex-President Eisenhower noted Kennedy's view that 'the two great powers have now neutralized each other in atomic weapons and inventories'. And then in October of that year—on the eve of the Gilpatric address, when indisputable intelligence confirming the huge *US* lead was crossing his desk—Kennedy commented that 'we no longer have an overwhelming military advantage'.[119] Or consider again his remark a year later, during the missile crisis: 'They've got enough to blow us up already.' Indeed, if while in office Kennedy did change his opinion of the importance of US nuclear superiority in response to changing estimates of the strategic balance—as the missile gap disappeared, only to be replaced by another, monstrous gap in Washington's favour—then the 'pencil-wielding bastards' have failed to detect it. Moreover, if US nuclear superiority ended up having a significant *effect* on the Soviet Union, in the missile crisis or elsewhere, Kennedy does not seem to have been particularly impressed or to have changed his views as a result.

JFK and Nuclear Weapons

Nuclear weapons were thus relevant to Kennedy because their existence made him fearful and cautious, not because he believed US nuclear weapons or US nuclear superiority were actively useful. Nuclear weapons made a difference to him, but not in the way they did to other leaders, or even to others in his administration. The several 'hawks' who worked for him were far more impressed with the utility of nuclear weapons and the importance of the strategic balance than he was. Formally, Kennedy never went beyond almost ritually assigning nuclear weapons equal weight among other sources of force and influence. And in practice, Kennedy reduced their relative role in his foreign policy.

That overall policy was by no means flawless, nor even very successful, when one compares its results to its objectives. The means for achieving those objectives, flexible response, reduced US reliance on nuclear weapons; but these means misfired as well. If success in the 1962 missile crisis was the New Frontier's pride and joy, then surely the Vietnam débâcle represents its evil twin. Just as flexible response was a broad national security strategy, so should any ultimate assessment judge that strategy in its entirety.[120]

Nor, in his handling of nuclear weapons, was Kennedy a model of restraint; his administration did issue nuclear threats. Moreover, his nuclear buildup, despite flexible response, the demise of the missile gap, and his success at staving off demands for an even larger arsenal, was still excessive. It cost a great deal of money, increased the destruction a nuclear war could cause, and needlessly stoked the arms race.

Still, as Kennedy would have put it, 'in the final analysis', he exhibited a considerable caution, a quality that emerges as his nuclear policy's most prominent characteristic. A great deal of evidence remains inaccessible; when released, it may require a reappraisal of this assessment. But for now, Kennedy's reliance on non-nuclear 'assets' overshadowed his reliance on nuclear weapons, just as his nuclear restraint eclipsed any nuclear recklessness.

This is not surprising in view of the national security strategy Kennedy chose and the concerns about nuclear weapons he had. But it is surprising in light of the profound alarm with which Kennedy and most Americans— rightly or wrongly—viewed the Soviet threat; the frequency and intensity of the international crises Kennedy faced; and the widely acknowledged, enormous superiority of the US nuclear arsenal. The extent to which Kennedy hyped the threat, helped bring on the crises, and worsened the overkill must not be overlooked. But against this backdrop of threat, crisis, and strategic superiority, it is striking how small an active role nuclear weapons played in Kennedy's foreign policy. The temptation to rely more heavily on US nuclear superiority to confront the threat amidst the crises must have been formidable. Another leader might have succumbed to temptation.

7

The Nuclear Education of
Nikita Khrushchev

VLADISLAV M. ZUBOK AND HOPE M. HARRISON[1]

IN the mind of the Western public there is probably no figure so linked to the gruesome image of the mushroom cloud as is Nikita Khrushchev. Yet, in the gallery of Soviet politicians and statesmen from Stalin to Gorbachev, Khrushchev was the first to realize that nuclear bipolarity dictated permanent 'peaceful coexistence' between the two antagonistic social systems. Like Stalin, long before the bomb appeared, Khrushchev was no stranger to the world of terror. In the first half of his political life, young Khrushchev passed through the eye of three historical storms: the Russian Revolution (and the Civil War it unleashed); Stalin's forced 'revolution from above' with the shattering purges; and the Great Patriotic War against the Nazi invaders. For a man who had experienced virtually limitless death and destruction, could the bomb be so radically different?

There are other questions that are of interest: How were Khrushchev's beliefs and policies affected by US nuclear superiority? How did these evolve as Soviet atomic, thermonuclear, and missile capabilities improved? Did Khrushchev's understanding of war, peace, and security change as nuclear technology and his knowledge of it advanced? In studying these questions, we will be carrying out what John Lewis Gaddis calls 'the psychological test' of the influence of nuclear weapons on the long peace: 'if we can show that one or more major leaders . . . changed their views about the utility of force as a result of the development of nuclear weapons, then the [John] Mueller argument [about the 'essential irrelevance' of nuclear weapons to the long peace] would be falsified and a strong presumption about the stabilizing effect of nuclear weapons could then be constructed.'[2] For Khrushchev this 'psychological test' started only after Stalin's death in March 1953.

The Bomb and the Dogma

When Khrushchev began his ascendancy to the heights of the Kremlin after Stalin's death in 1953, one of the first points on the agenda of the 'collective leadership' was to secure the defence of the Soviet Union against the mounting threat of a US strategic atomic strike. In the journal *Military Thought* in the fall of 1953, Colonel Nikolai Talensky pointed out, for the first time in Soviet print, that in the nuclear age a *blitzkrieg* could succeed, unlike in 1941–2, when Hitler had attacked the Soviet Union and pushed the Soviet army back to the banks of Volga.[3]

The experience of that war was very much a part of the background against which Khrushchev began to look at the issues of security and defence after the death of Stalin. Unlike all other members of the Soviet leadership, Khrushchev was deeply affected by the war. He was a witness to the slaughter of the Soviet armies and the occupation of enormous territories by the Nazis. The lack of preparedness of the Stalinist state for the war flabbergasted him. He felt that Stalin had been responsible for the disastrous outbreak of the war: Stalin let himself be 'mesmerized' by Hitler and the Nazi–Soviet pact; he refused to listen to sober advice during the first year of the war, thereby leaving millions of Soviet troops at the mercy of German *Panzers*.

The war years had left Khrushchev determined not to let anything similar happen to the Soviet Union again. Later this feeling prodded him to reject Stalin's postulate about the inevitability of war. Yet it would be wrong to conclude that in Khrushchev's mind the vision of a big war became 'obsolete' as a result of that experience. First, he was part of the generation of Soviet élites that explained the world by referring to Leninist–Stalinist 'theory,' according to which 'imperialist wars' were generated by the dominating groups and classes of capitalist societies in pursuit of material gain and redivision of markets and resources.

Second, Khrushchev also shared a common conviction of the officials of his generation, that these 'imperialist' circles unleashed the Cold War when they found out that one country after another was leaving the capitalist camp. In 1955, Minister of Defence Marshal Georgi Zhukov told President Eisenhower, that the Cold War was a result of the 'machinations of the dark forces'.[4]

This common outlook made the whole Soviet leadership, and Khrushchev in particular, believe that strength, crude and conspicuous, was the only way to deal with the United States and other capitalist countries. And it was during the decade of Khrushchev's leadership that the Soviet Union was rapidly solidifying its status as a superpower. 'The years of 1953–1962 were the most productive in the development of thermonuclear weapons' in the Soviet Union, according to a veteran of the Soviet nuclear design laboratory. Soviet developments in missile and nuclear submarine technology were impressive, and at times it was unclear which of the two main competitors would reach the next corner first.[5] The overall strategic-nuclear balance, however, was still unfavourable to the Soviet Union. This was made worse with Eisenhower's New Look policy in 1953, NATO's MC-48 in 1954, the London and Paris treaties and the integration of West Germany into NATO in 1955, and the 1957 US decision to deploy IRBMs in Europe.[6]

Khrushchev's first brush with thermonuclear power occurred several months after Stalin's death, with the test of the first Soviet hydrogen bomb on 12 August 1953. In his memoirs, Khrushchev recalls 'Sakharov's hydrogen bomb.' 'No one else, neither the Americans nor the British, had such a bomb. I was overwhelmed by the idea. We did everything in our power to assure the rapid realization of Sakharov's plans.'[7]

After the arrest in late June 1953 of Lavrenty Beria, who had been the unchallenged 'atomic czar' in the Soviet leadership under Stalin for eight years, Malenkov, Khrushchev, and Molotov claimed that Beria had concealed from them plans for a hydrogen test. However exaggerated the claim was, it is plausible that Khrushchev, still a secretary of the Central Committee (CC) of the Communist Party of the Soviet Union (CPSU) without a government position, had indeed been out of the loop. He must have been impressed when he learned about the hydrogen bomb. By that time the PGU and various components of the Second and Third Chief Directorates became merged into the Ministry of Medium Machine-Building Industry (MMB).[8] After Beria's arrest Viacheslav Malyshev, minister of the tank industry, was appointed as head. At the July Plenum, which was dedicated to Beria's 'unmasking', Malyshev's deputy, General Avraami Zavenyagin, proudly declared to the party and state élites the significance of the upcoming test: 'The Americans [after the first Soviet atomic test in August 1949] saw that their advantages had disappeared, and at Truman's order began work on the hydrogen bomb. Our people and our country are no slouches. We took it up as well and, as far as we can judge, we believe we do not lag behind the Americans. The hydrogen bomb is tens of times more powerful than a plain atomic bomb and its explosion will mean the liquidation of the second monopoly of the Americans, now under preparation, which will be an event of paramount importance in world politics.'[9]

Sergei Khrushchev recalls how happy his father was when the test succeeded: at last the Soviets managed to surpass the United States. Andrei Sakharov, a young physicist whose idea of the 'Layer Cake' (along with the proposal of another scientist, Vitalii Ginzburg) had materialized in the first hydrogen bomb, immediately became a darling of the leadership, including Khrushchev.[10]

After the test, on 26 November 1953, the Presidium of CPSU CC and the Council of Ministers approved a far-reaching plan for increasing Soviet strategic power: Sakharov's thermonuclear charge, upgraded to a one or two megaton yield, would become a staple of the arsenal, and the firm of Sergei Korolyov would build an intercontinental carrier capable of reaching the mainland United States. The tests of 'Sakharov's device' were scheduled for two years later; the test of the intercontinental missile ('semyorka' or R-7) would take place in four years. According to Sakharov, who attended the meeting and reported on his device, Malyshev, feisty and upbeat after the successful test, dominated the discussion. Molotov asked some questions, while Malenkov sat in silence. Sakharov recalled nothing about what Khrushchev said or did.[11]

There are no documentary traces of his thinking at that moment. His son Sergei, however, writes, that at some point 'perhaps already after Stalin's death', Khrushchev 'watched a film of the explosion of the atomic bomb, and came home depressed; for a long time [he] remained agitated [*ne nakhodil sebe mesta*]'.[12] We know that after August 1953 a special documentary was made for the top leadership, showing in graphic detail the destructive power of the new weapon and showing how people were knocked off their feet by the shock wave tens of miles from ground zero.[13] A witness to the first hydrogen test noticed that this time, unlike during the atomic tests of 1949 and 1951, 'the impact [of the explosion] apparently transcended some kind of psychological barrier. The effect of the first atomic bomb explosion had not inspired such flesh-creeping terror, *although it had been incomparably more terrible than any-thing seen in the still recent war*' (emphasis added).[14] No doubt, the last war also served as a base of comparison for Khrushchev.

The larger question about the significance of the new weapon for war and peace was not discussed in the Kremlin. A radical change in the security doctrine, both in its political and military dimensions, required political will and boldness—and for some time nobody in the 'collective leadership' dared to go out on a limb on this issue. Only the mounting pressures of the nuclear age made the 'collective leadership' speak up. On 8 December 1953, President Eisenhower made a proposal to the United Nations designed to dispel the image of the United States as a state preparing for thermonuclear war. Shortly afterwards, in January and February 1954, Soviet attempts to revive the negotiations with Western powers were rejected, and US Secretary of State John Foster Dulles increased the volume of his rhetoric of 'massive retaliation'. On 1 March, the United States started a new series of nuclear tests with the explosion of a 15 megaton hydrogen bomb, three times more powerful than scientists had predicted. After the huge fallout, covering 7,000 square miles over the Pacific and irradiating a Japanese fishing trawler, an international outcry arose to ban further testing of this kind. At a press conference on 10 March, Eisenhower and Lewis Strauss, head of the Atomic Energy Commission, admitted that a superbomb could destroy a whole metropolitan area, and a thermonuclear war could endanger civilization.[15]

The debate inside the Soviet leadership that reflected these developments came to be known as 'the Malenkov episode': on 12 March, Malenkov, still head of state and curator of the atomic project, said that the continuation of the arms race between the USSR and the United States would lead to war, and that this war, 'considering the modern means of warfare, would mean the end of world civilization'.[16] This was a startling departure from the accepted rhetoric. For instance, Mikoyan, on the same day, said that 'hydrogen weapons in the hands of the Soviet Union are a means for deterring aggressors and for waging peace'.[17]

On 1 April 1954, Khrushchev received a draft of an article entitled 'The Dangers of Atomic War and President Eisenhower's Proposal', written by the Minister of Medium Machine-Building, Malyshev, scientific head of the atomic project, Igor Kurchatov, and three other atomic physicists.[18] This was, perhaps, the first report from the leadership of the project to the political leaders (Malenkov and Molotov also received a copy) describing in stark terms the suicidal nature of nuclear war.

The authors of the article already knew something that Khrushchev did not: in March–April 1954, the nuclear scientists discovered a sensational new principle of radioactive implosion that made 'Sakharov's bomb' obsolete, and opened the way to making a superbomb of unlimited yield (Edward Teller and Stanislaus Ulam had discovered this principle in early 1951).[19] 'The modern atomic practice, based on the utilization of thermonuclear reaction,' they wrote, 'allows to increase, practically to an unlimited extent, the explosive energy contained in a bomb. Defence against such a weapon is practically impossible [so] it is clear that the use of atomic weapons on a mass scale will lead to the devastation of the warring countries . . . Accordingly, one cannot help admitting, that a huge threat which could obliterate all life on Earth hangs over mankind.'[20]

Still not ready to admit this, in early April, at the Plenary Meeting of the CPSU CC, Khrushchev and Molotov led an attack against Malenkov describing as defeatist and demoralizing his thesis that a nuclear war would destroy civilization. Malenkov reversed his position in April, admitting that actually a nuclear war would lead only to the 'collapse of the whole capitalist system'.[21] The aforementioned article by the physicists was never published.

The conclusions reached by Malenkov and the élite of the atomic project were revolutionary and most others were not ready to accept them, especially since they were enunciated just a year after Stalin's death. At that time Khrushchev and most of the leadership and party–state élites still remained under the spell of the dictator's dogma. The logic of the power struggle also made Khrushchev critical of the new concept, since Malenkov had become its 'father'. By that time Khrushchev had become the first secretary of the CC and was openly seeking primacy over Malenkov and the others in the 'collective leadership'.

For another year Khrushchev continued to argue publicly (and perhaps in internal discussions) that in a nuclear war between the socialist and capitalist systems, the capitalist system would be destroyed and socialism would triumph. Khrushchev was too concerned with his image as a leader for the Soviet élites, including the directors of the military-industrial complex, to give any impression of vacillation on such an important issue as the security of the Soviet state and the historical optimism of the Soviet security doctrine inherited from Stalin. He also criticized Malenkov's emphasis on the consumer sectors of the economy as erroneous and as a 'deviation' from Stalin's economic prescriptions, which focused on heavy industry and the military.

The politics of the power struggle notwithstanding, Khrushchev did not lag far behind Malenkov in understanding the message of the hydrogen bomb. Later he reconstructed his feelings to Egyptian journalist Mohammed Heikal: 'When I was appointed First Secretary of the Central Committee [in September

1953] and learned all the facts about nuclear power I couldn't sleep for several days. Then I became convinced that we could never possibly use these weapons, and when I realized that I was able to sleep again. But all the same we must be prepared. Our understanding is not sufficient answer to the arrogance of the imperialists.'[22]

Molotov, a holdover from Stalin's leadership, continued to believe, against all evidence, that nuclear weapons were just a means of deterrence, facilitating the *postponement* of a future war, not its prevention.[23] For Molotov, the world collision was just a question of the time and moment for the 'final victory' over 'the aggressive forces of imperialism'.[24]

Once Khrushchev consolidated his hold on power, he proved to be flexible and bold. He realized that the nuclear stand-off made Stalinist-Leninist dogmas about the inevitability of another global war obsolete. The thermonuclear revolution started to shape the First Secretary's thinking on a whole range of practical aspects of defence, military preparedness and planning. By early 1955 he froze Stalin's programme of construction of a 'blue-water' fleet, arguing that it could not withstand a strike by the new weaponry, conventional or atomic.[25]

Still, Khrushchev was not in a hurry to challenge Stalin's doctrine. His political platform had twin objectives as far as security and foreign policy were concerned: to consolidate the socialist camp and to promote the cause of world communism beyond the socialist camp. This dualism of communist-imperial commitments was a hallmark of Khrushchev's rule in general. He always cared a great deal about Soviet hegemony over the 'progressive forces' in the world (such as national-liberation movements in Asia and Africa) and about the Soviet 'internationalist duty' towards them.[26] Like Molotov, he feared the acknowledgement of new priorities stemming from thermonuclear danger would interfere with the theory of class struggle and 'socialist revolutions' around the world, a source of Soviet domestic and international legitimacy. The spectre of nuclear Armageddon blurred the distinction between classes and put forward the interests of all mankind. The new line smacked too much of bourgeois pacifism.

On 19 June 1954, Secretary of the CPSU CC, Pavel Pospelov, reported to Khrushchev about the 'mistakes' of chess grandmaster (and world chess champion) Mikhail Botvinnik. A man of clear logic, Botvinnik asked confounding questions in his May letter to the Party Central Committee: how to match the prospect of nuclear annihilation with an official postulate about imperialist 'war-mongers' who unleash a war in search of profits? And how to reach accommodation with those imperialist forces, while remaining faithful to the vision of 'socialist revolutions' in the West? The questions were aimed right at the heart of the ideological dogma that the next world war would lead to a series of revolutionary triumphs.[27]

At the CPSU CC Plenary Meeting on 31 January 1955 Khrushchev returned to the 'Malenkov episode' to justify the removal of his rival from the post of head of state. He called Malenkov's thesis 'theoretically incorrect and politically harmful', a statement 'capable of creating a mood of hopelessness'. He, and particularly Molotov, made it clear that Malenkov's line made it more difficult 'to prepare and mobilize all forces for the destruction of the bourgeoisie'.[28] Even if Khrushchev had grasped the frightening realities of nuclear revolution, he did not reveal it at the time. He feared he could not discard Stalin's dogmas until another 'theory' could be constructed that would satisfy both sides of the Soviet *Weltanschauung*: a search for the security of the Soviet state, and the preservation of a revolutionary perspective in the new era. Also this new theory had to be 'sold' to friends and allies around the world—no mean task given the vacuum of legitimacy and leadership in the communist camp after Stalin's death.

The New Vision and the Problems of Implementation

Only in early 1956 was Khrushchev ready to formulate the answers to Botvinnik's questions: at the Twentieth Party Congress he proclaimed a doctrine that adjusted the ideology of class struggle and 'socialist revolutions' to the priorities of the nuclear age, the doctrine of peaceful coexistence and the non-inevitability of war. Several events and developments during 1955 enabled Khrushchev to take this crucial step forward, without which his 'nuclear education' would have remained frozen in its first stage. Malenkov lost his post as head of state in February 1955, which then allowed Khrushchev to take over some of his 'heresies' in his unfolding struggle against the dogmatic Molotov. By the end of 1955, Khrushchev emerged victorious from this struggle and confirmed his reputation as a statesman: his record of successes included the Austrian State Treaty in May and the establishment of diplomatic relations with the Federal Republic of Germany in September.

Another international event helped advance Khrushchev's 'nuclear learning'—the Geneva summit in July 1955, the first such event since the Potsdam conference. Khrushchev arrived there with trepidation, expecting that Western leaders would test him and extort concessions. Instead, a reassuring exchange took place between Eisenhower and Marshal Zhukov (who, at Khrushchev's insistence, chatted with the US President as 'a soldier to a soldier'). Eisenhower stressed that 'now, with the appearance of atomic and hydrogen weapons, many notions that were correct in the past have changed. War in modern conditions with the use of atomic and hydrogen weapons became *even more senseless, than ever before*' (emphasis added). Zhukov agreed and noted that 'he personally saw how lethal this weapon is'. The President and the Marshal agreed that in case of all-out nuclear war 'nobody knows what would happen to the atmosphere'.[29] Khrushchev recalled many years later that the four-power summit in Geneva in July 1955 'convinced us once again, that there was not any sort of pre-war situation in existence at that time, and our enemies were afraid of us in the same way as we were of them'.[30]

It took more than the summit to allay Khrushchev's fears. On 22 November 1955, Soviet scientists tested their first superbomb and solved in principle the task of the unlimited increase of the nuclear arsenal. During the Twentieth Party Congress, on 20 February 1956, the successful launch of the first medium-range ballistic missile with a nuclear warhead occurred. On 27 February, Khrushchev and senior Politburo members visited Korolyov's missile firm in Podlipki for the first time and looked around in astonishment. [31]

About the same time Khrushchev 'discovered' a new frontier for the promotion of a 'socialist way of development' in the countries of Asia and the Arab Middle East. On 26 November, commenting on the Soviet hydrogen test during his state visit to India, Khrushchev said that he hoped these bombs would never be used in war. 'Let these bombs lie, let them get on the nerves of those who would like to unleash war.'[32] This formula became an official Soviet response to pacifist scientists and intellectuals: in Khrushchev's rhetoric, the nuclear age, instead of blocking revolutionary social-economic change, allowed the USSR to provide a security umbrella to developing countries who wished to move away from capitalism.

Khrushchev did not reject old dogmas outright; rather, he said that they were overshadowed by a new empirical reality—the possibility of thermonuclear war. Imperialism, according to a Marxist-Leninist precept, does breed wars, but 'the situation has changed radically, [as] today there are mighty social and political forces possessing formidable means of preventing the imperialists from unleashing war.' Khrushchev pointed out that 'signs of a certain sobering up are appearing among influential Western circles. More and more people among these circles are realizing . . . that "there can be no victor in an atomic war." [But,] these public figures do not venture to state that capitalism will find its grave in another world war, should it unleash one.'[33]

Neither did Khrushchev. In his new vision of war and peace, the Soviet leader was careful to leave room for two admissions: thermonuclear war is disastrous, but possible; capitalism would perish, but civilization would not. The causes of this half-way rethinking lay not in Khrushchev's dogmatism or lack of boldness (at the same Congress Khrushchev denounced Stalin). His dilemma was not too different from that of Eisenhower and leaders of the Western democracies: they also were not prepared to say 'better red, than dead' and to accept the legitimacy of the communist camp; instead, they continued to look for political and psychological means to undermine the Soviet Union and its satellites.

Since 1956, Khrushchev's strategic goal was to use the nuclear stalemate to undermine NATO, make the United States acknowledge the USSR as an equal power, and facilitate the dismantling of 'imperialism' in the Third World. In his opinion, all of these goals could be achieved if the United States accepted 'peaceful coexistence' on Soviet terms. 'There are only two ways,' he said at the Twentieth Congress, 'either peaceful coexistence or the most destructive war in history. There is no third way.'[34] To drive this point home, Khrushchev needed to create an impression that he was ready to use the new terrible weapons. Thus, his new vision led logically to nuclear brinkmanship and bluff.

At this stage, Khrushchev's model for emulation was the United States with its doctrine of 'massive retaliation'. Observing the US leadership, particularly after the Geneva summit of 1955, Khrushchev became convinced that his main opponent, US Secretary of State John Foster Dulles (whom he considered to be the real architect of US foreign policy), shared an understanding of the rules of brinkmanship. In 1961, Khrushchev explained to his party colleagues that he had known all along that Dulles, who had proclaimed 'a massive retaliation' doctrine, was bluffing. Dulles, said Khrushchev, 'knew where the brink was that they [Americans] should not overstep, and behaved in a circumspect way, taking our resistance into account and seeing that, with sheer force and extortion they could not get what they wanted'.[35]

For a while, the Soviet Union had no means to deliver a strike against the United States, so the first target of Khrushchev's nuclear threats were West European members of NATO. His first great success was in November 1956, during the Suez Crisis of Anglo-Franco-Israeli aggression against Egypt. The Soviets then had no means to project their conventional power to the Middle East, but Khrushchev proposed to threaten aggressors with a nuclear strike, while neutralizing the American atomic 'umbrella' with an offer to the United States to send a joint 'peace-keeping' mission to the Middle East. Afterwards, in June 1957, Mikoyan spoke to the CC Plenary Meeting triumphantly, noting that 'we found resources both to keep troops in Hungary and to warn the imperialists that, if they did not stop the war in Egypt, it might come to the use of our missiles. Everybody acknowledged that with this we decided the fate of Egypt.'[36]

The outcome of the Egyptian affair allowed Khrushchev to take another step in 'nuclear learning': he came to believe that nuclear bipolarity was a new and essential characteristic of the Cold War. Therefore, the nuclear arms race could be regarded not simply as a preparation for war or for the deterrence of an aggressor, but as a continuation of politics by other means. When the West acknowledged the meaninglessness of this race, an agreement would become possible and the Cold War would end. In May 1957, Khrushchev said in an interview that 'international tension [i.e. the Cold War] apparently boils down in the final analysis to relations between the two countries—the Soviet Union and the United States of America'.[37] This was yet another step away from ideological dogma, underlining the US–Soviet conflict, to the acknowledgement that a certain understanding between the superpowers was required in the nuclear age. This time Khrushchev himself became the target of an orthodox attack. Molotov lashed out at the idea that, because of nuclear stalemate, 'allegedly an agreement might be reached between the Soviet Union and the United States of America'.[38]

Khrushchev put an end to pre-war psychosis, that justification for Stalinist terror—a course that won support among Soviet élites.[39] At the same time, the promise of a nuclear-missile shield made Khrushchev dependent on the progress of military technology (the combination of thermonuclear power and missile technology) and on the ability of his 'atomic diplomacy' to compel, not only deter, his adversaries. In August 1957, the long-awaited technological breakthrough in missile technology occurred. The Soviet aerospace firm headed by Sergei Korolyov successfully tested 'semyorka', the world's first intercontinental ballistic missile. On 7 September, Khrushchev attended the test of 'semyorka'. He allowed Korolyov, over objections from the military, to proceed with his pioneering plans of space exploration and on 4 October, Sputnik stunned the West. Unexpectedly, it achieved something that quiet tests of Soviet ICBMs probably would never have done: it showed *all* Americans that from now on they were vulnerable to nuclear attack (if a nuclear warhead would replace the Sputnik as the rocket's payload), and it demonstrated to the whole world and American allies that the USSR was leading the technological-military race for the first time.

From that moment, Steven Zaloga writes, Khrushchev became 'obsessed with the potential of missile technology'.[40] In the following months and years he went to great lengths to convince the world of Soviet superiority in this field, and he increased the volume of his nuclear threats in his pronouncements and talks with foreign visitors. Typical of this was Khrushchev's threat in July 1961 to the British Ambassador in Moscow, Sir Frank Roberts, that 'only six of his H-bombs would be quite enough to annihilate the British isles, and nine would take care of France'.[41]

Khrushchev's possession of atomic and hydrogen weapons and missiles emboldened him to adopt risky tactics that Thomas Schelling has written about, such as the 'manipulation of shared risk' and 'competition in risk-taking'.[42] An optimistic and restless politician, he decided to achieve results even before Soviet technological achievements started to bear fruit.[43]

Existential Bluff

In Western Europe, US allies, particularly France and West Germany, reacted to Khrushchev's threats (and to the apparent unreliability of the US nuclear umbrella) with determined efforts to gain access to atomic arms. In the period leading up to the May 1955 West German rearmament and integration into NATO, the Soviets tried many tactics to stop these events. Khrushchev, in particular, abhorred the prospect of West Germany gaining access to nuclear weapons, particularly after NATO decided in December 1957 to deploy IRBMs in Europe. Andrei Smirnov, Soviet ambassador in Bonn, warned Khrushchev and the Foreign Ministry repeatedly that Konrad Adenauer and his foreign minister Heinrich von Brentano were thinking about nuclearization. On 13 May 1958, in a 'political letter', Smirnov wrote that the government of the FRG 'took the open course towards the armament of the Bundeswehr with atomic weapons'.[44]

At the same time the absence of a peace treaty with Germany became a sore in Khrushchev's eye. His leadership was suddenly at stake, both in Europe and in the Far East (with the first open signs of Mao's displeasure with the Soviet leader). Therefore, during the summer of 1958 the Soviet leader began to look

for ways to put West Germany into place and to force the three Western powers to negotiate a German peace settlement. On 11 November, the US ambassador in Moscow, Llewellyn E. Thompson, reported that Khrushchev must
have seen 'that with the completion of the next few years of West German
rearmament, including the stationing of atomic weapons there, the position
of the East German regime will become even more precarious' and 'an East
German revolt under such circumstances might confront the Soviet Union
with the choice of almost certain world war or the loss of East Germany and
subsequently of most or all of his satellite empire.' Oleg Troyanovsky, who
became Khrushchev's foreign policy assistant at that time, confirmed later
that Thompson 'hit the nail on the head'.[45]

Khrushchev's ultimatum on West Berlin triggered the international crisis
that lasted, intermittently, for about four years.[46] Both authors have written
elsewhere, on the basis of recent archival evidence, on the causes, dynamics
and outcome of this crisis.[47] It is enough to say that initially Khrushchev's
approach seemed to bring about the expected results. NATO became visibly
fractured under Soviet pressure: British Prime Minister Harold Macmillan visited Khrushchev in February 1959 in an attempt to mediate between the Soviet
leader and Eisenhower. A long-delayed conference of foreign ministers on the
'German question' took place in Geneva. Finally, in July, Eisenhower
extended an invitation to the Soviet leader to visit the United States. At the
United Nations in New York, Khrushchev announced with pomp a plan of
general and complete disarmament. The results of the Khrushchev–
Eisenhower talks at Camp David, from Khrushchev's viewpoint, were promising: Eisenhower acknowledged that the situation in Berlin (the city was
divided and located in the middle of East Germany) was 'abnormal'. He
seemed to have agreed to resume the search for a diplomatic resolution of the
German question within the framework of a four-power summit, scheduled
for the spring of 1960.[48]

All this time, unknown to most in the West, Khrushchev acted from a
position of inferiority and serious economic and technological problems.
American superiority in strategic aviation and the geographical proximity of
US airbases was a jarring reality: during the second half of the 1950s,
Americans violated Soviet airspace repeatedly, and since 1956, U-2 reconnaissance planes had flown over Soviet military installations with impunity. In
fury, Khrushchev ordered that violators be shot down (at the cost of 130
American lives), but due to a tacit agreement on both sides it remained a silent
war.[49] Another problem for Khrushchev concerned the production and
deployment of combat-ready ICBMs, which lagged behind the successes of the
nuclear project and did not provide him, between 1956 and 1960, with real
retaliatory capability against the United States. The construction of hardened
ICBM silos that could survive a US aerial attack required several years and huge
expenditures. Meanwhile, the 300–ton, liquid-fuelled R-7 had to be transported by railroad to a launching pad at Plesetsk: four of them became operational on 15 December 1959. Hastily, Khrushchev announced the creation of

the Strategic Rocket Forces (RVSN) as a new branch of the Soviet armed forces. A second missile complex became operational only in 1961 at Tyura-Tam. In case of a US first strike, the Soviets had time for one launch only, and, according to Sergei Khrushchev, they targeted four US 'hostage cities' for retaliation: New York, Washington, Chicago, and Los Angeles.[50]

The west also did not know that, at the time Sputnik was launched, the Soviet 'planned' economy was in the state of disarray: the requirements of new armament and R&D programmes far surpassed allocated resources. In 1958–61, military production in the USSR more than doubled, increasing from 2.9 to 5.6 per cent of the Soviet national income. Procurement costs for strategic missiles were about 1.4 million roubles apiece in 1962 prices; because of the construction of facilities for the mass production of strategic arms, capital investments into armament programmes sky-rocketed. To 'correct deep disproportions in the people's economy', the Soviet government had to scrap the last three years of the five-year plan.[51]

Khrushchev was unfazed by these difficulties. He plunged head over heels into nuclear romanticism which, in his opinion, was already bearing fruit. Economic pressures worked on him in the same way they had on Eisenhower in 1953: he developed his own 'New Look' approach, expecting to turn the nuclear-missile shield into a 'great economizer' in defence spending. After the Camp David summit, in the expectation of another summit in Paris, Khrushhev wrote a note to the Politburo with a proposal to scrap a huge land army, which had been crucial to the Soviet military buildup since the early Cold War, with a technological force to ensure means of 'retaliation'. The note, quickly approved by the special military conference and rubber-stamped by the CC Plenum, reveals that Khrushchev was convinced that no power could threaten a Soviet Union armed with nuclear missiles. He declared that 'we are in an excellent position with [regard to] missile-building,' and that the Soviet army could be cut by 'perhaps a million or a million and a half' people in 'no more than two years'.

Khrushchev stripped the logic of his 'New Look' to the bone: we don't need an army because we do not intend to attack anybody, and our nuclear-missile forces would provide a sufficient defence by discouraging potential aggressors with a threat of retaliation. The reform would be 'a fantastic step' that would give the USSR 'major political, moral, and economic advantages'. At the end of 1959, in anticipation of the cuts, Khrushchev's obedient Defence Minister Rodion Malinovsky, initiated a 'theoretical discussion' in the high military command, arguing that the outcome of a future war would be decided by the first exchange of nuclear strikes, whereas conventional armies and the navy would have no role at all to play. On 12 January 1960, in his speech to the Supreme Soviet, Khrushchev announced the reduction of armed forces by 1.2 million men in three years. One-quarter million officers were thrown out unceremoniously, many without adequate material compensation, retraining, or housing.[52]

The military brass could not publicly oppose Khrushchev, but the most intelligent of them took advantage of the 'theoretical discussion' on the reform in the classified journal *Military Thought* to question the Soviet version of the 'massive retaliation' doctrine, which had been imposed from the very top. In 1960–2, General P. Kurochkin, Colonel-General A. Babadzhanyan, Major-General M. Goryainov and other authors came to the same conclusions that had been formulated at about the same time by their American counterparts. (*The Uncertain Trumpet* by Maxwell Taylor, and *Nuclear Weapons and Foreign Policy* by Henry Kissinger were translated and often used in Soviet polemics.) They pointed out that the Khrushchev-Malinovsky military doctrine left no choice between surrender and nuclear suicide.[53]

Khrushchev could not ignore the barbs of the military élite. Malinovsky created a task force at the Academy of the General Staff to prepare a classified book on 'military strategy' in the nuclear age, and ordered a reluctant Vassily Sokolovsky, who had just resigned from the General Staff in protest against Khrushchev's cuts, to bring the project to fruition. Khrushchev liked the final product and approved its unclassified publication in 1962. *Military Strategy* became a classic application of Khrushchev's new vision to military thinking, and, in the opinion of the Soviet leader, was another 'sobering' reminder to American 'hotheads'.[54] The book elaborated on the thesis that the next war would be a nuclear war and described the immense importance of the opening phase of the war (the first strike), while it also established that the main point of Soviet possession of nuclear weapons was to deter an American strike, not to wage a nuclear war. Nuclear war would be too devastating and thus must be avoided.[55]

Another more serious opponent of Khrushchev and his 'New Look' was Mao Zedong, leader of the People's Republic of China (PRC). Mao could never forgive Khrushchev for his 'secret speech' denouncing Stalin. As Mao's private doctor recalls, Mao regarded the denunciation of Stalin as an attack on his own revolutionary legitimacy, a reflection of Khrushchev's 'personal character'.[56] In addition, Khrushchev's vision of nuclear bipolarity was anathema for Mao, and he began to act. In November 1957, at the world conference of communist parties, Mao hailed the new nuclear-missile might of the Soviet Union as a reason for the communist forces to be more aggressive against 'imperialism'. At the same time he asked Khrushchev to share nuclear and missile technology with the PRC. In 1957–9 the Chinese received the technology for the IRBM R-12 cruise missiles and 'some useful data' on the construction of atomic weapons.[57]

On 31 July–1 August 1958, Khrushchev, then on a secret visit in Beijing, was shocked to discover a chasm opening between his vision of the nuclear age and Mao's ambitions. He proposed to Mao the creation of a joint military fleet, but the Chinese leader rejected it as an attempt of the Soviet nuclear superpower to treat China as a location for military bases. Mao did to Khrushchev what Stalin had done to the Americans after Hiroshima: he discounted the nuclear weapons as 'a paper tiger'. 'I tried to explain to him,' recalled Khrushchev, 'that one or two missiles could turn all the divisions in China to dust. But he wouldn't even listen to my arguments and obviously regarded me as a coward.'[58] In fact, according to Li Zhisui, 'it was Mao's challenge to Khrushchev's bid to reduce tensions between the Soviet Union and the United States . . .' On 23 August, the People's Liberation Army of the PRC, without warning either Moscow or Washington, started shelling Quemoy, one of the offshore islands, still held by the Guomindang (Taiwan). Mao commented in his private circle that 'the islands are two batons that keep Khrushchev and Eisenhower dancing.'[59] By staging this provocation, the Chinese leader drew both the US and Soviet leadership into a game of nuclear brinkmanship—but according to his own scenario and for his purposes.

At a certain point, Khrushchev's patience with Mao snapped, and on 20 June 1959, the Party Presidium cancelled Sino-Soviet atomic co-operation.[60] Yet, as in Molotov's case, Mao's challenge profoundly troubled Khrushchev in his search for leadership. According to the terms of the Sino-Soviet treaty of 1950, the USSR was supposed to extend a nuclear umbrella to the PRC. From 1958 to 1962, according to Troyanovsky, China was 'always' on Khrushchev's mind.[61]

The crisis in the Far East provided Khrushchev with another lesson that the United States had learned well with NATO: whatever you think of nuclear war, there should be no 'decoupling' between your security and your ally's security. The Chinese leaders suggested that should the USA use tactical nuclear weapons against the PRC, then the Soviet Union should stay away. 'Only in the event that the United States uses large-yield nuclear weapons . . . will the Soviet Union make a retaliatory strike with nuclear weapons.' Khrushchev and the rest of the Politburo wrote to Beijing that they 'carefully considered this issue' and concluded such a scenario would be 'a crime before the world working class', and would give the enemy 'hopes that they will be able to separate us'. Undoubtedly, Khrushchev was in favour of nuclear brinkmanship, to help reunify China—only if this could be fully co-ordinated with him, and if Mao would agree with the common rules of the game.[62]

When in 1961 Khrushchev decided to resume the game of nuclear brinkmanship with a youthful John F. Kennedy, even those few military officials who had been enthusiasts for the drastic changes became uneasy. According to reports made to the CIA by Oleg Penkovsky, a high-ranking Soviet military intelligence (GRU) official who began to spy for British and American intelligence in late 1960, they grumbled: 'If Stalin were alive, he would have done everything quietly, but this fool is blurting out his threats and intentions and is forcing our possible enemies to increase their military strength.'[63] A few Soviet launching pads were highly vulnerable to SAC attack. On 28 July 1961, Khrushchev ordered the acceleration of the construction of hardened silos for missiles, and to achieve this, the Ministry of Defence sent special emissaries to the construction sites.[64] Despite working around the clock, the work was not completed until 1963. The Soviet leader took his problems—with the Chinese and his own military—as temporary difficulties. His romance with nuclear missiles continued.

Brinkmanship Falters

It is a common belief among Cold War historians that two actions of the Kennedy Administration helped to deter Khrushchev from more aggressive action during the Berlin crisis of 1961. One was Kennedy's speech on 25 July 1961, in which the US president took steps to mobilize armed forces and announced that Western allies would use all available means to defend their rights in West Berlin. The second was the speech in October 1961 by Deputy Secretary of Defense Roswell Gilpatric, sanctioned by the Kennedy administration, in which he disclosed that the United States had a large numerical superiority in nuclear missiles over the Soviet Union. 'We have a second-strike capability,' said Gilpatric, 'which is at least as extensive as what the Soviets can deliver by striking first. Therefore, we are confident that the Soviets will not provoke a major nuclear conflict.'[65]

Yet the evidence is at least equally strong that both steps may have had only a marginal impact on Khrushchev's behaviour, particularly with regard to the issue of signing a separate peace treaty with East Germany. According to Sergei Khrushchev, 'the salvo [i.e. Kennedy's speech] was fired in vain', since his father did not intend to sign a separate peace treaty with the GDR.[66] What really determined Khrushchev's policy in the Berlin crisis in the summer of 1961 and led to the construction of the Berlin Wall was the rapid deterioration of the situation in the GDR, especially as manifested in the swelling numbers of refugees fleeing East Berlin and East Germany for West Berlin and West Germany.[67]

At that time, Khrushchev believed that existential deterrence (fear of nuclear war) would help him to achieve his goals in Germany.[68] At the same time, however, he was never prepared to force a change in the status quo anywhere along the major fault lines of the Cold War. He would have been delighted, of course, if NATO had split on the proposal of the 'free city' of Berlin, and negotiations had started on a German settlement and, perhaps, even on a general superpower settlement. But his primary and *immediate* goal was to shore up the GDR. His *strategic* objective was to prove that his new vision of 'peaceful coexistence' was correct and that the Soviet nuclear shield did work as a means of deterring and 'sobering up' the West.

American experts informed Kennedy on the eve of the June 1961 Vienna summit that Khrushchev saw in the missiles the key to all doors: the forcing of the West to treat the USSR with respect, the promotion of Soviet national security and of world revolution, 'and even perhaps in the end the assurance of universal peace (Soviet style) through disarmament.'[69] They exaggerated about 'the world revolution', but the missiles in Cuba later proved they were not entirely wrong.

In the 'game of chicken' that Khrushchev played with the US leadership, he kept sizing up his opponent in the White House and his ability to hold the reins tight on 'some hotheads' in the Pentagon. During a meeting with Ulbricht in November 1960, he observed: 'luckily, our adversaries still haven't gone crazy. They still think and their nerves still aren't bad.'[70]

In Vienna, on 3–4 June 1961, he played the same game of threats with the young President that he had been playing with Western leaders since 1958. This time, however, he overreached himself. According to Soviet diplomat Georgi Kornienko, who read the original record of the meeting, Khrushchev even added: 'let the war be better now, before the emergence of new, even more terrible means of warfare.' The remark later disappeared from both US and Russian official transcripts.[71]

The Soviet leader felt that only a firm and strong leader could play the game of brinkmanship. In his eyes, Kennedy was 'too much of a light-weight'. In August 1961 he told the leaders of the Warsaw Pact, who were in Moscow for a secret meeting, that the days of Eisenhower and Dulles had been more predictable. 'If Kennedy pulls back [from the brink, like Dulles had done many times], he will be called a coward'.[72] Khrushchev was worried that Kennedy was more likely to be pushed by his advisers and others into aggressive action than Eisenhower and Dulles had been.

None the less, Khrushchev refused to take the danger of nuclear war over Berlin seriously. Just in case, the Soviet General Staff and the KGB worked out a joint plan for extensive measures of strategic deception, to discourage the United States from the use of force, if the Soviet Union signed a separate peace treaty with the GDR. Alexander Shelepin, head of the KGB, proposed to Khrushchev 'to assign the General Staff with a task to work out and to implement through KGB channels a set of measures, aimed at forming a deep conviction with the adversary' regarding the high combat readiness of the Soviet army forces 'due to their modernization by the new types of tanks equipped with tactical nuclear weapons, . . . a considerable increase of readiness of rocket forces and of the increased number of launching pads—produced by a supply of hard-liquid ballistic projectiles of medium range and by the transfer from stationary positions to mobile launching positions on highways and railroads which secure high manœuvrability and survivability'. These and other measures of strategic deception were approved on 1 August by the Secretariat of the CC CPSU. Naturally, at that moment Khrushchev was not aware of the treason of Oleg Penkovsky, who, precisely at that time, was supplying the West with detailed information about Soviet rocket forces and other branches of the Soviet army.[73]

The balance of fear had to be maintained by demonstrating the horrible potential of ever more powerful nuclear weapons. On 10 July, the Soviet leader informed the élite of the atomic complex about his decision to renounce unilaterally the moratorium on nuclear tests. He enthusiastically supported the idea of the nuclear designers to test a new 100-megaton device, albeit at half strength. When Sakharov sent him a note, arguing that the resumption of the tests at that time would favour the United States, Khrushchev gave a frank off-the-cuff rebuff to the scientists. He said, as Sakharov recalled, more or less the following: 'Only force—only the disorientation of the enemy. We can't say aloud that we are carrying out our policy from a position of strength, but that's the way it must be. I would be a slob, and not chairman of the Council of

Ministers, if I listened to the likes of Sakharov. In 1960 we helped to elect Kennedy with our policy. But we don't give a damn about Kennedy if he is tied hand and foot—if he can be overthrown at any moment.'[74]

Sakharov's collaborators in the design laboratory recall another detail of that meeting. When Sakharov and Yakov Zeldovich proposed testing a new 100-megaton device, Khrushchev said, according to Sakharov: 'Let this device hang over the capitalists like the sword of Damocles.' Later Khrushchev took the unprecedented step of announcing in public, well before the test, the potential power and actual yield of the device.[75] The explosion of the device (reduced to 50 megatons) on 30 October above Novaya Zemlya, a Russian island above the Arctic circle, was a purely 'political test', with no military or scientific consequences for the Soviet nuclear programme. The explosion 'deflected' the psychological effect of Gilpatric's speech and allowed Khrushchev to tell the Party Congress: 'When the enemies of peace threaten us with force, they must be and will be countered with force, and the more impressive force, too.'[76] At that time, a tank confrontation between the USA and the Soviet Union took place at Checkpoint Charlie in Berlin, but, according to witnesses, the Soviet leader remained 'perfectly calm.' His belief in nuclear deterrence at that time was unshakeable, and, even more importantly, at that time, a 'backchannel' between Khrushchev and President Kennedy had created an atmosphere of mutual personal predictability.[77]

The Cuban missile crisis in October–November 1962 figures prominently in the historical literature as the ultimate exercise of nuclear brinkmanship that might well have led to world war.[78] There has also been an ongoing discussion about the priorities and motivations that pushed Khrushchev to install Soviet missiles thousands of miles from the Soviet Union. Initially, American analysts saw the whole operation (its Soviet code-name was 'Anadyr') as a gamble designed to correct at a stroke the strategic disparity between the Soviet Union and the United States, and perhaps even to use Cuba as a bargaining chip to achieve American concessions in West Berlin. Kennedy also seemed to think that Berlin was the key.[79] Others believe that Gilpatric's speech triggered the missile deployment in Cuba.[80] Finally, some believe the budgetary crunch explains why Khrushchev decided to correct the nuclear balance on the cheap, by putting missiles in Cuba.[81]

On the Soviet and Cuban sides, many believed that the restoration of the strategic balance, improving the positions of the communist camp with regard to the Americans, and a deliberate affront to 'arrogant American imperialism', were Khrushchev's primary motives. Oleg Troyanovsky, who remained Khrushchev's foreign policy assistant in 1962, believes that his boss wanted to redress 'at least partially' the nuclear balance.[82]

Khrushchev did not mind redressing the disparity in existential deterrence and targeting most of the United States, rather than just a few 'hostage cities'. There is no evidence, however, that this *motive* was a main *cause* that set the high-risk operation 'Anadyr' in motion. Recently, a number of scholars have come to recognize that the defence of Cuba against possible (and credible)

American aggression had an enormous value of its own in the eyes of Khrushchev.[83] The loss of Cuba, the first communist regime in the Western hemisphere, would have laid bare the strategic inferiority of the Soviet Union and punctured Khrushchev's historic optimism and his new vision of 'peaceful coexistence' in the nuclear age as favouring the forces of communism. Troyanovsky himself acknowledges that the problem of political legitimacy was no less important for Khrushchev than the problem of disparity in existential deterrence. 'I had the impression,' Troyanovsky recalled in 1994, 'that Khrushchev constantly feared that the United States would compel the Soviet Union and its allies to retreat in some region of the world. Not without reason he believed that he would be held responsible for that.' This feeling 'had grown under the impact of the unremitting sallies coming from Beijing with accusations that the Soviet leader was appeasing the imperialists'.[84]

In the newest book on the Cuban missile crisis to make use of Soviet archival sources, Aleksandr Fursenko and Timothy Naftali maintain that the timing of Khrushchev's decision to deploy the missiles in Cuba was connected to increasing evidence at the time (spring 1962) that Chinese influence within the Cuban leadership was growing at the expense of Soviet influence.[85] Khrushchev did not want to lose his latest and most unique ally to his rival in the socialist camp. Since 'both the Soviets and Castro interpreted military supplies as a gauge of the health of their relationship',[86] on 21 May, at Khrushchev's initiative, the Soviet leadership decided to send missiles to Cuba.[87]

An additional purpose of the secret deployment was to make Americans openly accept what the Kremlin had long endured—the existence of intermediate-range nuclear missiles on their borders. (The USSR was surrounded by American 'forward-based means': SAC bases and, since 1959, IRBMs, in Turkey, Italy, and Great Britain.) Khrushchev evidently expected American pre-emptive counter-measures (otherwise, why a secret operation?), but, in a huge psychological and political miscalculation, he believed the Americans would 'swallow' the deployment.[88] Also, reversing the American practice, he thought he would first secretly deploy missiles and then publicly announce it.

Khrushchev had no fall-back position in the event that the Americans would not 'swallow' the missiles. He did not think that Kennedy would risk a war, because he strongly believed that any war between the USA and the Soviet Union would be an all-out nuclear war. But he did not quite know what would happen, and uncertainty made him nervous. His uncertainty made him take a step that significantly raised the level of risk: on 7 September, vacationing in Pitsunda, he ordered Malinovsky to ship to Cuba 'Luna' tactical missiles and warheads. Those weapons could be used by the commander of the Soviet troops in Cuba, General Issa Pliyev, to destroy the US seaborne forces in case they attacked Cuba. According to Fursenko and Naftali, Khrushchev believed 'in the value of battlefield nuclear weapons', but at the same time 'did not want to lose the control over the decision to use' them. The 'Pitsunda decision' betrayed confusion in Khrushchev's mind: His 'New Look', like Eisenhower's in 1953, sanctioned the use of nuclear weapons on the battlefield; but, in effect, the secrecy of this deployment contradicted the logic of existential deterrence. Americans, who knew nothing of the 'Lunas' during the whole crisis, could not be deterred by them and, in the event of an invasion, would have triggered escalation of nuclear war.[89]

The sudden emergence of the crisis and the subsequent wave of hysteria in the United States, along with Kennedy's proclamation of the 'quarantine', put Khrushchev's belief in nuclear deterrence to the test. For the first time, he seemed to realize that a nuclear war might result from an escalation of tensions and a series of mutual miscalculations. Contradictory signals from Soviet intelligence and the embassy in the United States, and from Cubans and Soviets in Cuba, added a great deal to the perception that the situation was rapidly spinning out of control. Under the extreme tension of the crisis, Khrushchev quickly engaged in tough bargaining with Kennedy over the heads of the Chinese and Cuban leaders, and when Kennedy proved to be tougher, he gave up. Real panic swept through the Kremlin on Sunday, 28 October, when the Main Intelligence Directorate of the General Staff (GRU) informed Khrushchev that Kennedy was about to give another televised address (it turned out to be a repetition of the 'quarantine speech'). Khrushchev stopped bargaining and accepted a compromise in a form the American leadership wanted.[90] In a meeting between Robert Kennedy and Anatoly Dobrynin at the height of the crisis on the evening of 27 October, they agreed that the Soviets would withdraw the missiles from Cuba in return for a public US pledge not to invade Cuba and a secret US pledge to take the missiles out of Turkey.[91]

The Khrushchev–Castro interaction and correspondence during and after the crisis provide revealing evidence regarding Khrushchev's thinking at the time. The Soviet leader was under the impression that Castro had ordered a shootdown of a US U-2 and, in Castro's 25 October cable, advised Khrushchev to launch (what Khrushchev believed was) a pre-emptive nuclear attack in case an American invasion or strike on Soviet missiles was imminent. In 1992, at a conference in Havana, Castro explained his cable as an attempt to prevent 'a repetition of the events of the Second World War', when the Nazis had caught the Soviets by surprise.[92]

Castro took the logic of 'massive retaliation' literally. 'We started from the assumption that if there was an invasion of Cuba, nuclear war would erupt . . . Everybody [in Cuba] was simply resigned to the fate that we would be forced to pay the price, that we would disappear. If we are going to rely on fear, we would never be able to prevent a nuclear war. The danger of nuclear war . . . cannot be prevented on the basis of fear of nuclear weapons, or by the belief that human beings are going to be deterred by the fear of nuclear weapons.'[93]

In fact, Khrushchev frequently said so himself, and had criticized Malenkov in 1954 somewhat along those lines. But now he realized that 'Fidel totally failed to understand our purpose . . . We had installed the missiles not for the purpose of attacking the United States, but to keep the United States from attacking Cuba.'[94] From Khrushchev's viewpoint, his retreat and the outcome of the Cuban missile crisis was not the defeat Castro and the Chinese perceived them to be, and not only because he knew he had gotten Kennedy to agree to take the missiles out of Turkey. Troyanovsky, who observed Khrushchev throughout the whole crisis, remarked that the events of October 'had a tremendous educational value for both sides and both leaders'. They 'made them realize, not in theory, but in practical terms, that nuclear annihilation was a real possibility and, consequently, that brinkmanship had to be ruled out and a safer and more constructive relationship between the two superpowers had to be designed and pursued'.[95]

Khrushchev had overplayed his hand, triggering a showdown under conditions that were infinitely more favourable to the United States. On the positive side, the shock of the crisis created an expectation of a 'permanent truce' between the superpowers. In other words, Khrushchev's nuclear brinkmanship achieved its goal not only in the sense of deterring aggression against Cuba, but in a larger, strategic sense—in clarifying what Khrushchev had been insisting on since 1957: that the issue of war and peace would depend on a *modus vivendi* between Washington and Moscow.[96]

A hasty deal to remove Soviet 'offensive weapons' from Cuba— in exchange for the 'gentleman's word' of the US leadership not to invade the island and the secret promise to dismantle US missiles in Turkey—looked to Beijing and hardliners in Moscow (who did not know about the secret deal regarding the missiles in Turkey) like a capitulation. Castro felt personally betrayed and believed that the communist 'cause' had been betrayed by Khrushchev, as well. Also, the deal left a bad taste for many among the Soviet élite, particularly in the military high command. Many there believed that Khrushchev should not have deployed missiles in Cuba in the first place, and, having done so, he should not have pulled them out. The combination of the high risk of the adventure and the humiliation of the withdrawal (particularly for the military) created a bitter aftertaste that overwhelmed the universal relief and appreciation of Khrushchev's realism in bringing the crisis to a peaceful conclusion.[97]

McGeorge Bundy concluded that

no one has made a larger contribution than Khrushchev to our understanding of what can and cannot be done with nuclear weapons. His four-year effort [in Berlin] constitutes the most powerful demonstration yet recorded of the limited value of attempts at nuclear blackmail undertaken in the face of opponents with weapons, commitments, and a will of their own. But the greatest teacher—and fortunately also one of the best learners—in the crisis he began and ended was Khrushchev himself.[98]

But what exactly did Khrushchev himself learn? Long before the Cuban missile crisis, he had chosen prevention of war as an overriding principle in his foreign and military policy. What had really changed was Khrushchev's perception of risk-taking. Until the missile crisis the Soviet leader was prepared to take enormous risks in response to America's 'massive retaliation' doctrine and the US buildup. He believed it was the best way to prevent war without losing Stalin's empire and authority in the communist camp. But at the same time, he had sought 'peaceful coexistence' beyond brinkmanship—what could be called 'phase two' of his vision. He tried to get Mao Zedong (unsuccessfully) and Fidel Castro (more successfully) to share this faith. He even attempted to break the back of Soviet militarism, although with the wrong means and poor results.

The fact that the US leadership long denied Khrushchev a chance to move to 'phase two' made him repeatedly play the game of brinkmanship. As a result of the Cuban Missile Crisis, Khrushchev developed special relations with Kennedy, and hoped that at last a transition to 'phase two' had become possible. After the crisis, Khrushchev's policies with regard to nuclear weapons became two-pronged: he did everything possible to accelerate the Soviet nuclear buildup, regarding it as the ultimate foundation for lasting 'peaceful coexistence'; at the same time, he supported agreements on nuclear arms control as an expression of a new bipolar world order, which, he believed, would eventually replace the Cold War.

Backing Away from the Brink

Initially, Khrushchev did not think much of the idea of slowing the nuclear arms race. In his mind, the United States was merely angling for legal opportunities to spy on the Soviet nuclear and missile arsenal. His impression of the American position on arms control was shaped by Eisenhower's 'Open Skies' proposal, which would have given America a huge advantage over the Soviets in enjoying the benefits of aerial reconnaissance. The logic was, that if Americans had learned that Khrushchev's claims of strategic parity were a bluff, they would have not been interested in talking, and would have perhaps been encouraged to get rid of the USSR. So from this perspective, arms control made the war danger greater not smaller for the Soviets. 'In the opinion of father,' writes Sergei Khrushchev, 'arms control will become effective only under conditions of disarmament, when the capabilities of both sides level off.'[99]

Meanwhile, Khrushchev viewed the proposals of both sides on nuclear arms control and disarmament as part of an important propaganda game. Mikoyan described this approach at the June 1957 Plenum: 'When [Harold] Stassen proposed to [Valerian] Zorin [in May 1957 at the UN Disarmament Commission] to conduct confidential negotiations on the issue of disarmament, we wholeheartedly supported this tactic that split the Westerners [i.e. the Western powers], and it resulted in confusion in the NATO camp. This is a result of our flexible diplomacy, and they [in the West] do not know where to run away from it.'[100]

This reaction to the Stassen–Zorin talks typified Soviet diplomacy on atomic issues in 1953–7. Later, however, Khrushchev began to view this approach as too passive and reactive. In 1959 he launched a major propaganda offensive under the slogan of 'general and complete disarmament'. He regarded it as a useful propaganda tool to gain the sympathies of 'petty bourgeois' public opinion in the West, as well as the sympathies of the non-aligned countries like India. During 1961, in the midst of tensions about Berlin, the talks on the principles of disarmament negotiations, conducted by Zorin with John J. McCloy, Kennedy's special assistant for disarmament, remained a rhetorical contest, and Khrushchev was indifferent to their substance.[101]

Yet, this does not mean that through all those years Khrushchev neglected the danger of the unregulated nuclear arms race and the need to put a check on it. The major role in the education of the leader was played by scientists, the luminaries of the Soviet atomic establishment. After Beria's arrest and the August 1953 test, the project's scientific élite gained unique access to the supreme Soviet leadership: they could immediately communicate with the leaders on the protected government line and interact with them in an informal and congenial setting.[102] As we have shown earlier, since March 1954 the scientists had informed Khrushchev and his colleagues about the dangers of nuclear contamination. One cannot over-emphasize the 'enlightening' impact that Kurchatov, the founding father of the Soviet atomic programme, had on Khrushchev. Khrushchev included Kurchatov, whose role and even whose name heretofore had been a state secret, in an official state delegation that visited Britain in April 1956. He introduced him to Churchill as 'Academician Kurchatov, who makes our hydrogen bomb'—to be sure, a subtle form of atomic diplomacy, as David Holloway writes, but also as an expression of the admiration and pride that Khrushchev at that time felt for the man. Kurchatov wisely used his position to convince Khrushchev to become interested in the 'peaceful atom' and, as a result, managed to declassify important areas of Soviet thermonuclear research. In effect, Khrushchev supported the idea of international collaboration in controlled fusion.[103] It was a remarkable step, whether it was induced by an evolution of Khrushchev's mentality or encouraged by his most respected scientist.

In the following years, Kurchatov, profoundly concerned about the threat of thermonuclear war, did not cease in his efforts to enlighten the Soviet leader. On 31 March 1958, Khrushchev announced a unilateral moratorium on nuclear testing. Of course, the Soviet leader had been driven primarily by immediate diplomatic considerations, among them the divisive tactics directed at NATO and against the nuclearization of West Germany. Yet, the considerations of Soviet atomic physicists did not escape his attention. In 1957, Andrei Sakharov, prodded by Kurchatov, wrote an article against an American project, the so-called 'clean bomb', emphasizing the dangers of low-level radiation for humankind. Before the publication of this article in a scientific journal in July 1958, Sakharov, again at the suggestion of Kurchatov, wrote another article for a wider audience on the dangers of atmospheric testing. Published in several languages by many Soviet journals that were distributed abroad, it was aimed at foreign readership. 'Khrushchev himself authorized the publication of my articles,' recalls Sakharov. 'Kurchatov discussed the matter twice with him and then referred some minor suggested editorial changes to me . . . Khrushchev approved the revised versions at the end of June and they were sent off immediately to the editors.'[104]

When Eisenhower proposed setting up an international panel of experts in Geneva to explore the problems of verification and monitoring of a nuclear test ban, Khrushchev authorized the participation of a large group of Soviet scientists in the talks during the summer of 1958. Later, however, it became clear that neither side was ready for a comprehensive ban.

When Khrushchev decided to resume testing, Kurchatov rushed to Khrushchev's dacha on the Black Sea in September 1958, trying to make him reconsider. Khrushchev, who was about to launch his campaign of pressure on the Western powers in Berlin, was so angry at the physicist that he stopped receiving him for a while. But later, relations warmed again, and Kurchatov continued nudging Khrushchev patiently towards a more responsible attitude concerning nuclear weapons.

The sudden death of Kurchatov in February 1960 certainly impeded the process of Khrushchev's 'nuclear education' from inside the Soviet atomic complex: nobody enjoyed the same authority to argue with the Soviet leader.[105] When Sakharov attempted twice (in July 1961 and in September 1962) to oppose the nuclear tests, Khrushchev unceremoniously dismissed him. He looked at Sakharov as an impractical pure scientist with odd ideas, who, unlike Kurchatov, had no appreciation of and experience in state affairs.[106]

In 1958–62, Khrushchev had many reasons to oppose a comprehensive nuclear test ban.[107] The most important, of course, was the necessity of validating existential deterrence—in the absence of a numerical parity of strategic arsenals with the United States. Fixated on this, Khrushchev was completely myopic to the fact that his brinkmanship was one of the driving forces behind the nuclear arms race. (In fact, he stuck to a crude Leninist explanation of this race, claiming it was driven by the search for capitalist profits.) He did not understand Sakharov's note of July 1961 in which the physicist argued that 'a resumption of testing at this time would only favour the USA'. 'Prompted by the success of our Sputnik,' explained Sakharov, 'they could use tests to improve their devices. They have underestimated us in the past.'[108] In fact, Khrushchev never recognized that his missile bluff and the brinkmanship around West Berlin had greatly contributed to the decision in Washington to deploy a thousand 'Minutemen' ICBMs and hundreds of missiles on nuclear submarines (SLBMs), a deterrent force that was vastly oversized by any standard.

Another important motive of Khrushchev at the time was, ironically, his growing infatuation with the 'peaceful atom', a by-product of Kurchatov's 'enlightenment'. The Soviet leader saw nuclear explosions as a powerful tool of construction in the future communist paradise, and there were many who catered to this dream by proposing grandiose schemes of canal-digging and the diversion of great Siberian rivers, etc.[109]

These illusions were only part of the general institutional inertia of the huge military-industrial complex, of which the atomic programme was the most important part. 'Beginning in the late fifties,' recalled Sakharov, 'one got an increasingly clearer picture of the collective might of the military industrial complex and of its vigorous, unprincipled leaders, blind to everything except their "job".'[110] The nuclear programmes remained the darling of the government: in addition to Avraami Zavenyagin and then Efim Slavsky at the helm of the Medium Machine-Building Ministry (the 'nuclear lobby'), they included the chairman of the military-industrial commission of the Council of Ministers (Dmitry Ustinov until 1963 and afterwards Leonid Smirnov) and the CPSU CC Department of Defence Industries (Ivan Serbin). Khrushchev's penchant for effective demonstrations of nuclear power found institutional support and encouragement among these people.

Only after the Cuban missile crisis did Khrushchev for the first time begin to view the dangers of an unregulated nuclear arms race in a more sober light. Gradually, both the Soviet leader and the Kennedy Administration began to move towards an agreement on a partial test ban.[111] It has been known that one of the major impulses for that came from inside the atomic establishment. Viktor Adamsky, a member of Sakharov's theoretical group in the nuclear design bureau Arzamas-16, wrote a proposal to Khrushchev lobbying for acceptance of a partial test ban that had been offered by the Americans earlier but rejected by the Soviet side. Sakharov approved the letter and on the next day flew to Moscow to show it to the head of the atomic ministry, Slavsky, who, in turn, transmitted it to Khrushchev. A few days later Slavsky informed Sakharov that Khrushchev had accepted the proposal.[112] The declassified document sheds light on the problems that probably were on Khrushchev's mind at the time. The letter said that

reaching an agreement banning testing in the atmosphere and in space and limiting underground testing to low-yield devices would put an end to radioactive contamination of the atmosphere, slow down the arms race, and, most likely, halt the further spread of atomic weapons to countries which do not already possess them . . . We feel that, without the ability to conduct atmospheric tests, a country which does not already have nuclear weapons will not be able to develop a sophisticated nuclear weapons system.[113]

The letter also argued that

the possibilities for the peaceful application of nuclear explosions are directly linked to underground explosions, and do not require atmospheric testing . . . We feel that there is a wide range of potential peaceful applications for nuclear explosions in many areas, including, for example, power generation, introducing thorium ores into industrial production for processing into fissionable materials, obtaining transuranic elements, oilfield regeneration, moving large masses of rock during the construction of canals and similar projects, and opening up ore and coal deposits.

It is not difficult to see why Khrushchev, who had rejected Sakharov's note in July 1961, liked this document. The Cuban missile crisis had shifted his priorities from existential deterrence through bluff and brinkmanship towards regulation of the nuclear arms race. He aimed at a world order which would be based on nuclear bipolarity, in which the Soviet Union could enjoy equal status with the United States. By 1963, it was clear that the Soviet atomic programme no longer needed large-scale tests to achieve strategic parity with the Americans.

At the same time, Khrushchev's obsession with the Chinese, and his sensitivity to their criticism after the Cuban missile crisis gave way to concern about their geopolitical adventurism and nuclear plans. After the missile crisis, the open debate with the Chinese leadership also encouraged the Soviet leader to take a much more sober, 'enlightened' line with regard to nuclear weapons than he had ever done before, publicly or privately. It also pushed Khrushchev further away from ideological dogmas on war and peace, and other doctrinal issues.[114]

In his speech to the Supreme Soviet in December 1962, Khrushchev answered the Chinese: 'If [imperialism] is a "paper tiger" now, those who say this know that this "paper tiger" has atomic teeth. It can put them to work; and it cannot be regarded frivolously.'[115] As the US embassy correctly concluded later in 1963, the 'outbreak of virtually undeclared war between Moscow and Peiping [in the] spring [of 1963] . . . explained Soviet acceptance of a partial test-ban agreement which it could have had at any time during the past year.'[116] The conclusion of the partial Test-Ban Treaty in Moscow on 4 August 1963 may be considered the final piece of the nuclear education of Khrushchev, who, according to his son, was 'extraordinarily glad, even happy' with this achievement.[117]

This evolution from brinkmanship to deterrence and regulation of the arms race does not mean that Khrushchev had reformulated his cardinal belief in the usability of nuclear weapons as an instrument of political power. In his opinion, no future war could be waged without nuclear charges—as a weapon of last resort and retaliation. For him, the fact that nuclear war would be the end of civilization did not mean that such a war should become *unthinkable* or should be excluded from political and military doctrine. At the same time, he never abandoned the concept of military 'victory' in a future war—something that only Mikhail Gorbachev did in the late 1980s. And he continued to press the military for cuts in conventional forces and armaments, while accelerating the costly buildup of strategic nuclear forces.[118]

In his last months in power, Khrushchev was moving toward something resembling the American concept of 'flexible deterrence'. But here, as with many other affairs on his political agenda, he was never able to come to anything systematic or final. There remained a huge gap in Soviet political and military thinking between the emphasis on nuclear weapons as a means of preventing war and the chief deterrent, and a pursuit of 'victory' in a future war. According to Raymond Garthoff, 'deterrence . . . was not described as a constituent element of military doctrine, even at the political level of doctrine.'[119]

Khrushchev's 'nuclear learning' was accelerated by his desire to reduce the enormous costs of the arms race: he regarded nuclear-tipped missiles as a substitute for the huge land army that kept millions of young men out of the productive economy. Of course, the costs of nuclear and missile R&D, as well as of new weapons, were enormous as well. But after the downfall of Khrushchev in October 1964 his successors sought to reach strategic parity with the United States, without reducing the Soviet army—the choice that, eventually, helped bring the Soviet economy to over-extension.[120]

Khrushchev proved to be a quick study in perceiving that the bomb made the extremes of past wars pale by comparison. He understood that the bomb could never be used in a great power confrontation, grasped that this understanding was shared by his Cold War enemies, and attempted to put this knowledge to 'rational use' by exercising the policies of bluff and brinkmanship. He had, however, enough common sense and flexibility not to test this 'rationality' to the bitter end in the Cuban missile crisis. The hallmark of his 'nuclear education' was the realization that nuclear weapons became not only the chief deterrent in a global war, but that they also introduced a new world order—that of nuclear bipolarity. Khrushchev's experience in World War II made him more willing to dismantle his ideological dogmas on war and peace, but this factor by itself had never been a crucial one. Also, contrary to the predominant view, US nuclear superiority and Soviet strategic inferiority seemed not to play a decisive role in shaping Khrushchev's approach to nuclear armament and diplomacy. From the time of the first hydrogen tests in 1953–5, until the end of his career, Khrushchev believed that the balance of mutual fear was achieved, whatever the disparity in numbers. A confrontation between two nuclear giants, he believed, did not make sense in the thermonuclear age, and therefore, an era of negotiation should replace an era of confrontation.

It was a major task of his diplomacy to ensure that the US feared war as much as the USSR did. Beginning in the fall of 1957, Khrushchev sought to force the US leadership to take the next logical step, and recognize that negotiations with the Soviet Union were the only way of settling the disputed issues and stabilizing global affairs. In this sense, his nuclear diplomacy was not only one of deterrence, but one of coercion.

No doubt, the strongest factor that influenced Khrushchev's tactics was the rapid progress in the nuclear field and in missile technology. Even though the Soviet Union had been outraced by the United States in the early 1960s, Soviet achievements were very impressive, and parity, i.e. a strategic deadlock, was already within sight. The development of missiles and nuclear weapons contributed to Khrushchev's conviction that traditional Stalinist dogmas on war and peace were no longer applicable. That led him in late 1959 to take a radical step towards a thorough reform of military doctrine and the structure of the armed forces. Khrushchev evidently came to believe that nuclear power, the most important scientific discovery of the age, could work miracles in security and economics.

Economic and budgetary problems played a major role in stimulating Khrushchev's reliance on the nuclear-missile 'shield', while he cut drastically conventional forces. His thinking is remarkably reminiscent of Eisenhower's 'New Look' of 1953; and some of the developments of Soviet political-military doctrine in the early 1960s certainly prove that 'massive deterrence' imposed a logic of its own (e.g. reliance on tactical nuclear weapons in the battlefield) on statesmen, no matter in which political regime they operated.

The growth of Soviet capabilities emboldened Khrushchev to unleash the Berlin crisis in 1958 and to send missiles to Cuba in 1962. Yet it would be wrong to overlook other important factors that contributed to these decisions. The record indicates that Khrushchev's goals in both the Berlin and Cuban missile crises were predominantly defensive, not expansionist or aggressive. In Berlin, his primary goal was to shore up East Germany and use the weakest spot of the United States' alliance system to force it to begin to negotiate a general settlement in Germany, and, *ipso facto* of the Cold War in Europe. In Cuba, Khrushchev primarily sought to protect the Cuban revolutionary regime and improve the strategic balance of power. After the missile crisis, Khrushchev's nuclear priorities shifted from brinkmanship towards joint efforts with the United States to prevent war and co-ordinate the arms race.

Again, it would be an oversimplification to see this shift as a mere result of Khrushchev's submission to superior US force. The Soviet leader's orientation toward a settlement with the United States had started long before the missile crisis, but the rejection of such a settlement by the US leadership—as well as a continuing commitment by the Soviet leader to revolutionary movements and 'wars of independence' around the world—made this goal unfeasible. The crisis in Cuba painfully reminded Khrushchev that the security of the USSR should be put above the support of revolutionary movements. And the split with the People's Republic of China freed his hands for the conclusion of the first significant treaty regulating the arms race.

Aside from technological progress and interaction with international actors, various domestic groups influenced Khrushchev's nuclear evolution. One should particularly mention the attempts of some nuclear scientists to bring to the leader's attention the dimensions of nuclear danger and the hazards of the nuclear arms race. The military, by contrast, had little impact on Khrushchev; he pulled them, kicking and screaming, into the new age. The group that eventually had the largest leverage on Khrushchev, were the most advanced (nuclear and missile) parts of the military-industrial complex.

Khrushchev's political biography is a remarkable testimony to the significance of nuclear weapons in contemporary history. With regard to Gaddis' 'test', Khrushchev's views on the utility of force changed greatly due to the development of nuclear weapons. Without the development of thermonuclear weapons, it is hard to see how any Soviet leader, including Khrushchev, could have managed to reject so quickly the ideological dogmas about war and peace that had been the basis of Stalin's rule.

From the present vantage point, Khrushchev stands out as a rare case of a nuclear optimist. Although he never quite abandoned the idea of the usability of nuclear weapons, he regarded them primarily as a positive force and was eager to use them in his gamble for peace—an attempt to negotiate a permanent 'truce' with the United States and the other great capitalist powers, which would have liberated Soviet resources for the 'construction of communism' and the assistance of 'progressive' movements and regimes around the world. Khrushchev had little doubt that behind the nuclear shield, the Soviet Union would win a peaceful economic competition with the capitalist camp.

PART II

Allies

8

Before the Bomb and After: Winston Churchill and the Use of Force

JONATHAN ROSENBERG

SEATED at his dining-room table one evening in 1928, Chancellor of the Exchequer Winston Churchill refought the Battle of Jutland. The Chancellor's barking provided the roar of the great guns, while decanters and wineglasses, the ships of the opposing fleets, manœuvred to and fro. Churchill's cigar supplied a haze of gun smoke, which floated over the battle scene, as the former First Lord of the Admiralty, excited as a schoolboy, spent two hours recreating the historic engagement of the First World War.[1] Winston Churchill was not averse to revelling in the glory of past martial encounters; the use of force caused him little discomfort. As an observer wrote in 1913, Churchill was always playing 'an heroic part. . . . Moving through the smoke of battle . . . his brow clothed with thunder . . . He thinks of Napoleon . . . of [Marlborough]. . . . There are always great deeds afoot with himself cast by destiny in the Agamemnon role.'[2]

On the battlefield and in politics, Winston Churchill's active life spanned nearly six decades. These were years of enormous change: Britain's power and influence depreciated sharply; a bipolar system emerged from the multipolarity of the pre-World War II years; and most significantly for this essay, the development of the atomic and hydrogen bombs profoundly transformed the technology of war. The young soldier who had fought on the bloody fringe of empire in the 1890s, and would someday lead his country to victory over Nazi Germany, would, in the years after 1945, confront one of the great diplomatic challenges of the age: the development and deployment of nuclear weapons. For the man who had enthusiastically confronted the Dervishes at Khartoum, and had experienced feelings of happiness on the eve of World War I, the emergence of the bomb would transform his attitude toward the use of force. But this was no sudden transformation, for the first light of the atomic age did not cause the great war leader immediately to abjure force as an instrument of state action. Instead, between 1945 and 1955, Churchill's thinking evolved, his attitude toward the use of force becoming more and more circumspect. During these ten years, Churchill became increasingly convinced that the bomb imposed novel constraints upon the world's leaders—constraints unlike any statesmen had known before. By 1955, Churchill had come to believe that the cost of war—in a world in which both sides possessed the bomb—had grown intolerably high.

'A Warrior at Heart'

War was never far from the centre of Winston Churchill's life. Fascinating him more perhaps than any other human activity, the drama of the battlefield occupied his physical and intellectual energies for more than six decades. A graduate of Sandhurst, Churchill first heard shots fired in anger in 1895 in Cuba, where he was working as a war correspondent for a London periodical. Over the next sixty years, as a soldier, politician, and writer, Churchill devoted a vast quantity of time to fighting, planning, directing, and chronicling war. Even as a boy, young Winston was drawn to martial affairs. In *My Early Life*, he described his collection of nearly 1,500 toy soldiers, which he organized as an infantry division with a cavalry brigade. His younger brother Jack commanded the opposing force, which, due to an inequitable arms-limitation treaty, was denied artillery.[3] Not content to command toy soldiers, Winston also drilled more life-size companions, including his brother and cousins, whom he marched about the family's summer residence.[4]

But Churchill was no mere backyard soldier, for in a life often punctuated by the sound of battle, he regularly manifested great personal courage. As a soldier confronting the prospect of dying in the field or as a member of the government on official business in the battle zone, Churchill went forth fearlessly. Writing to his mother from the Sudan in 1898, Churchill warned that he might be killed in action. She would have to avail herself of 'the consolations of philosophy and reflect on the utter insignificance of all human beings', he wrote, noting that while he hoped to escape with his life, he would not flinch. 'Nothing—not even the certain knowledge of approaching destruction would make me turn back now—even if I could with honour.'[5] Such fearlessness was clear a generation later, when, as First Lord of the Admiralty, Churchill was in Antwerp on naval business during a heavy German bombardment. Having decided to remain in the city to direct its defence, Churchill ventured to the battle line near Lierre, where an Italian war correspondent witnessed the following scene:

. . . in the midst of a group of officers stood a man. He was still young, and was enveloped in a cloak, and on his head wore a yachtsman's cap. He was tranquilly smoking a large cigar and looking at the progress of the battle under a [fearful] rain of shrapnel... It was Mr Churchill, who had come to view the situation himself . . . It is not easy to find in the whole of Europe a Minister who would be capable of smoking peacefully under that shellfire. He smiled and looked quite satisfied.[6]

Even as prime minister, Churchill's disregard for his own safety remained striking. On several occasions, he was drawn to the battle zone, and it is clear that, beyond possessing great courage, Churchill found the fury and romance of the battlefield deeply alluring. In his memoirs, Churchill recalled enthusiastically a visit to the Italian front with Field Marshal Alexander in 1944. As Alexander later recalled: 'I took him right up to the front line. You could see the tanks moving up and firing and the machine-guns in action a few hundred yards ahead of us. There were . . . shells flying about and land-mines were all over the place. He absolutely loved it. It fascinated him—the real warrior at heart.'[7]

On a 1945 trip to the front with General Montgomery, Churchill witnessed an engagement with the Germans along the Rhine. With shells landing closer and closer to the prime minister's party, the American General Simpson decided he had seen enough. It was time to depart. Simpson told Churchill:

There are snipers in front of you; they are shelling both sides of the bridge and now they have started shelling the road behind you. I . . . must ask you to come away. The look on Winston's face was just like that of a small boy being called away from his sandcastles on the beach by his nurse! He put both his arms around one of the twisted girders of the bridge and looked over his shoulder at Simpson with pouting mouth and angry eyes. . . . He came away quietly. It was a sad wrench for him; he was enjoying himself immensely.[8]

And back in the capital, Churchill longed to taste the action. Upon hearing that a German raid was imminent, he would climb to the roof and step out to view the spectacle. He was often heard to say: 'Let 'em come. We can deal with 'em.' According to an aide, 'the question of taking shelter never seemed to enter his head and it was only . . . [the] pressure of his personal staff' that made him realize that he might be in danger.[9]

Churchill not only loved the smell of battle, but he also relished the opportunity to devise tactics and plan strategy. Indeed, few modern statesmen were as conversant in the language of military planning as was the British leader. He revelled in seizing the initiative in battle and was highly innovative in the pursuit of military objectives. If his plans were at times unfeasible or went awry, there was an undeniable energy in his approach to warfighting. Churchill's willingness to take risks and to employ force vigorously were legendary among his government colleagues, and his dynamism made life difficult for many an officer, whom the prime minister encouraged, prodded, and occasionally browbeat into action. The battlefield was no place for the reticent.[10]

It was not unknown that war exerted a powerful hold on Churchill. As Prime Minister Herbert Asquith observed in 1914: I am inclined 'to shiver when I hear Winston say that the last thing he would pray for is peace'. During World War I, people came to see Churchill as 'a man of blood', a politician who seemed, in Martin Gilbert's words, 'to have a lust for battle'.[11] Indeed, on the eve of the Great War, Churchill wrote to his wife: 'Everything tends towards catastrophe and collapse. I am interested, geared up, and happy. Is it not horrible to be built like that? The preparations have a hideous fascination for me.

I pray to God to forgive me for such fearful moods of levity.' And a few months later, Churchill told Henry Asquith's daughter, Violet: 'I think a curse should rest on me because I am so happy.' With the battle raging in Europe, he remarked, 'I know this war is smashing and shattering the lives of thousands every moment—and yet—I cannot help it—I love every second I live.'[12]

But it must be said that Churchill was not oblivious to the horrors of war. In 1915, he condemned unambiguously the bloodshed and destructiveness of the world conflict: the 'war is terrible; the carnage grows apace . . . It fills my mind with melancholy thoughts. The youth of Europe—almost a whole generation—will be shorn away.'[13] Nevertheless, despite the horrors of war, Churchill could not deny that it fascinated him. In a 1909 letter to his wife, written while on a visit to observe German army manœuvres, he articulated these conflicting feelings: 'Much as war attracts me and fascinates my mind with its tremendous situations—I feel more deeply every year . . . what vile and wicked folly and barbarism it all is.'[14]

But if the British leader found war to be both attractive and repellent, it is undeniable that he believed international conflict was supremely important in the movement of history. In 1940, he declared that it was nonsense to say that 'nothing was ever settled by war', claiming that 'nothing in history was ever settled *except* by wars.'[15] But when was it legitimate to use force, and could Britain preserve her vital interests without resort to the sword?

Fighting and Deterring War before the Bomb

Before the turn of the century, Churchill had reflected on Britain's use of force in the Boer War, expressing ideas that were consistent with his later views on the challenges that would befall Europe. Against the Boers, there 'must be no half measures', he said. We must fight them for 'the sake of our Empire, for the sake of our honour, for the sake of our race . . .'[16] During the next two generations, he would frequently argue that force might honourably be employed against any foe that threatened these vital interests. Speaking in London in September 1914 about the conflict that had just erupted in Europe, Churchill observed:

However the war began, now that it is started it is a war of self-preservation for us. Our civilization, our way of doing things, our political and Parliamentary life, with its voting and its thinking, our party system, our party warfare, the free and easy tolerance of British life, our method of doing things and of keeping ourselves alive and self-respected in the world—all these are brought into contrast, into collision with the organized force of bureaucratic Prussian militarism.

The struggle 'must go forward without pause or abatement until it is settled decisively', he declared. 'On that there can be no compromise or truce. It is our life or it is theirs.'[17]

During the 1930s, in response to the darkening skies in Europe, Churchill was notably forceful in warning his countrymen of the dangers that lay before them. In 1932, responding to Germany's plea that she sought nothing but equality of arms with France, Churchill stated:

Do not delude yourselves . . . that all that Germany is asking for is equal status . . . That is not what Germany is seeking. All these bands of sturdy Teutonic youths, marching with the light of desire in their eyes to suffer for their Fatherland . . . are looking for weapons and, when they have [them] . . . they will then ask for the return of lost territories and lost colonies [which will] shake and possibly shatter [the] foundations [of many countries throughout Europe].[18]

Recognizing the severity of the German threat, Churchill repeatedly inveighed against Britain's policy of appeasement. He argued against British disarmament, claiming that the best way to preserve peace was by maintaining a potent military force. Disarmament, he declared in 1933, would no more lead to peace 'than an umbrella would prevent rain'.[19] The following year, Churchill called for a large and rapid increase in air-force expenditures, observing that allowing Germany to build an air force larger than that of Britain should be considered 'a high crime against the state'. Employing reasoning not unlike that used by the nuclear strategist of a later time, Churchill claimed that one must 'possess the power to inflict simultaneously upon the enemy as much damage as he himself could inflict'. It was vital, he declared, to increase air-force spending.[20]

In addition to calling for rearmament in the 1930s, Churchill also advocated the establishment of security arrangements with France (and other countries) in order to deter potential German aggression. Arguing in 1934 that peace could be achieved through strength, Churchill stated:

There is safety in numbers. If there were five or six on each side, there might well be a frightful trial of strength. But . . . [with] eight or ten on one side, and only one or two upon the other, and if the collective armed forces of one side were three or four times as large as those of the other, then there will be no war. . . .[21]

Supporting an Anglo-French agreement, Churchill observed in 1938 that 'great security' would be gained on both sides. 'Treat the defensive problems of the two countries as if they were one. Then you will have a real deterrent. . .' Should an attack occur 'you will have a highly organized method of coping with the aggressor'.[22] Throughout the 1930s, Churchill argued vigorously that the best way to preserve peace in Europe was by maintaining powerful forces that could deter German aggression. Recognizing that Germany threatened the continent's security, Churchill rejected disarmament in favour of a policy that would counter German aspirations by arraying powerfully armed forces on her borders. The British leader's advice went unheeded, and in September 1939, Europe was again at war.

Throughout the war, Churchill spoke repeatedly about Britain's reasons for fighting. In his public remarks, one sees the clearest exposition of Britain's reasons for waging war. Beyond recognizing the undeniable power of Churchill's wartime rhetoric—rhetoric that sought to embolden the British people as they confronted a threat unlike any they had ever known—one notices how consistent Churchill's wartime language is with views he had articulated in the past. In a much-quoted June 1940 speech, Churchill told his countrymen that the Battle of Britain was about to begin:

Upon this battle depends the survival of Christian civilization. Upon it depends our own British life, and the long continuity of our institutions and Empire. . . . If we can stand up to [Hitler], all Europe may be free and the life of the world may move forward into broad sunlit uplands. But if we fail, then the whole world . . . will sink into the abyss of a new dark age . . .[23]

Britain was fighting not only to defend her national integrity and imperial position, but also to permit the continued advance of human progress. Consistent with the views he had expressed for decades, Churchill advocated the use of force for two reasons: to preserve Britain's national interest—which for the wartime leader meant the continued security of the British Isles and the maintenance of the Empire—and because it would benefit mankind. By waging war, Britain would defend herself and serve humanity.

Force without Reluctance 1940–1945

Churchill's leadership of the British people, who held the line until America entered the fray, remains one of the century's more inspiring tales. Of significance here is the ardour with which Churchill prosecuted the war against Germany. The British leader displayed little reluctance to strike at the enemy with complete abandon.[24] Evincing little aversion to bloodshed, Churchill spoke in 1940 about a proposed inland raid, which he hoped would leave 'a trail of German corpses behind . . .'. Faintheartedness in war was no virtue; the commitment to destroy the enemy would be total. Meeting with Stalin in 1942, Churchill spoke of bombing Germany, and discussed specifically the idea of striking the German civil population: 'We looked upon its morale as a military target. We sought no mercy and we would show no mercy.' Churchill hoped his air force would 'shatter twenty German cities', as several had already been shattered, and, should it be necessary, 'as the war went on, we hoped to shatter almost every dwelling in almost every German city'.[25] Later that year, the British leader savoured the defeat of Rommel at El Alamein: The 'enemy were stuck to the . . . position like limpets to a rock. We cut them out,' he said, and 'we detached them utterly. . . . [When] a limpet loses its rock, it dies a miserable death.'[26]

Even poison gas was not beyond the pale. Upon learning in 1943 that the Germans were considering using gas against Russian forces, Churchill minuted the following to his chiefs of staff: should gas be used, 'We shall retaliate by drenching the German cities with gas on the largest possible scale.' Although he hoped Britain's threat to retaliate with gas would deter Germany from moving first, he declared, 'we must be ready to strike and make good any threat we utter with . . . promptitude and severity.'[27] The following year, the question of using gas came up again, and Churchill decided that if the Nazis used gas against the D-Day invasion forces, Britain would respond in kind, drenching 'the German cities and towns where any war industry exists'.[28]

Considering retaliation against German flying-bomb attacks, Churchill minuted the Chiefs of Staff Committee in July 1944, noting that he wanted very serious thought to be given to 'this question of poison gas'. Describing the limits he considered on the use of gas, Churchill wrote:

I would not use it unless it could be shown either that (a) it was life or death for us, or (b) that it would shorten the war by a year. It is absurd to consider morality on this topic when everybody used it in the last war without a word of complaint from the moralists . . . [But] in the last war the bombing of open cities was regarded as forbidden. Now . . . it [is] a matter of course. It is simply a question of fashion changing as she does between long and short skirts . . .

Churchill wanted his commanders to make a 'cold-blooded calculation' in assessing whether it would pay for Britain to use the deadly substance, and declared it was not because of 'moral scruples or affection for us' that Germany had not used it. They have not used gas, he argued, because 'it does not pay' and because they 'fear retaliation. What is to their detriment is to our advantage.'

Churchill went on to suggest a potential response if the German rocket danger worsened and London was severely hit. He would use poison gas, and was prepared to

drench the cities of the Ruhr and many other [German] cities [so that] most of the population would be requiring constant medical attention. . . . I do not see why we should always have all the disadvantages of being the gentlemen while they have all the advantages of being the cad. . . . I want the matter studied in cold blood by sensible people and not by . . . psalm-singing uniformed defeatists . . . Just try to find out what it is like on its merits.[29]

Clearly, Churchill was determined to win the war at any cost. To do so, he advocated vigorous—indeed merciless—action, and would stop at nothing in employing force against the enemy. The war against Hitler's Germany represented a struggle for national survival, and the Prime Minister believed he could afford nothing but total victory. And the quest for total victory, he was convinced, legitimized even the use of gas against the civilian population of Germany. Churchill was fully prepared to subordinate moral concerns to the demands of reason of state.

Developing the Bomb 1939–1945

Beneath the drama of the world war, a critical sub-plot would unfold, the climax of which would bring the struggle to a shattering and unprecedented conclusion. Throughout the war, in Britain and America, a group of scientists toiled in secret to unlock the mysteries of the atom. Not only would their successful effort end the war, but it would also transform international politics in the post-war era. The story of this great scientific enterprise, which has been told elsewhere, does not merit comprehensive discussion here.[30] The focus, instead, is on Britain's contribution to the effort and on Anglo-American relations during the period. While Churchill did not play a critical role in the overall project, this chapter of the story is an intrinsic part of the larger tale of his evolving attitude toward the use of force in the atomic age.

The year 1939 looms large in twentieth-century history not only because a European war broke out for the second time in a generation, but also because critical developments in physics would have a significant impact on the quest to build the atomic bomb. While important research had been conducted since the end of the nineteenth century, 1939 was, in Margaret Gowing's words, 'a year of dramatic advance in nuclear physics'.[31] That spring, scientists recognized that the nucleus of the uranium atom could be split, releasing great amounts of energy. Just two days before the war began, the eminent physicist Niels Bohr and an American colleague published a paper that shed light on the process of uranium fission.[32] Scientists speculated on the question, with some wondering if this energy could be used to construct a devastating weapon. At first, the scientific community's response was sceptical, with most researchers believing that practical application of a fission bomb was years away. Churchill himself expressed this view in a minute to the Secretary of State for Air on 5 August 1939: 'There is no danger that this discovery, however great its scientific interest, and perhaps ultimately its practical importance, will lead to results capable of being put into operation on a large scale for several years.'[33]

But scepticism gave way to optimism in 1940 as two physicists in Birmingham, England reached a startling conclusion. Otto Frisch and Rudolf Peierls, refugees of Nazism, prepared a seminal paper that spring, which Gowing calls 'the first memorandum in any country which foretold with scientific conviction the practical possibility of making a bomb and the horrors it would bring'. Having returned to Bohr's pre-war paper, Peierls and Frisch theorized (they conducted no experiments) that an atomic bomb was possible. In Gowing's words, they had 'asked the right questions' and had 'answered them correctly'.[34] While the two men could not estimate with certainty the effects of the bomb's radiation, they argued in 1940 that 'the cloud of radioactive material [would] kill everybody within a strip estimated to be several miles long', adding, 'effective protection is hardly possible. Houses would offer protection only at the margin of the danger zone.'[35] Thus had science confronted the potentially awesome consequences of war in the atomic age.

The Peierls–Frisch Memorandum led to the formation in Britain of the Maud Committee, which would guide the next phase of atomic research. Under the direction of Sir George Thomson, the Maud Committee held its first meetings in April 1940. Working at breakneck speed (to stay ahead of the Germans) the team of scientists studied the problem of the bomb's feasibility and explored 'whether the possibilities of producing atomic bombs during the war . . . were sufficient to justify the necessary diversion of effort for this purpose . . .'[36] Issuing reports in the summer of 1941, the Committee described its initial scepticism at the practicability of such a project, but went on to state that further investigation led them to conclude that the

release of atomic energy on a large scale [was] possible and that conditions can be chosen which would make it a very powerful weapon of war. We have now reached the conclusion that it would be possible to make an effective uranium bomb . . . the destructive effect [of which], both material and moral, is so great that every effort should be made to produce [it]. . . . The committee considers that the scheme for a uranium bomb is practicable and likely to lead to decisive results in the war.[37]

The impact of the Committee's conclusions was significant for at least two reasons: It marked the origin of Britain's conception of itself as an atomic power, and it 'galvanized' the United States to act.[38]

Anglo-American co-operation on developing the bomb flowed from the Maud Reports, and due to America's strong commitment to develop the weapon, Britain's early lead in atomic research soon disappeared. But despite the American effort, Britain was determined to take an active part in atomic research and development. While it was clear by 1942 that the United States would become pre-eminent in the atomic project, the British were unwilling to sacrifice their position altogether. As Churchill observed to his science adviser, Professor Lindemann, 'However much I may trust my neighbour, and depend on him, I am very much averse to putting myself completely at his mercy.'[39]

As early as 1942, the British had become aware of the bomb's potential and recognized they could not enter the post-war world without it. Sir John Anderson, Lord President of the Council, who came to exercise great responsibility in Britain's effort to develop the bomb, believed that after the war his country could not afford to be without the weapon, and 'rely entirely on America should Russia or some other power develop it'.[40] Among the small group that knew of developments in the atomic sphere, there was agreement that Britain had to remain in the game.[41] While Britain would occupy a subordinate position in the atomic project, decisions made at this time reflected the British belief in the importance of developing what would later be called the 'independent deterrent'.

The co-operative venture began to take shape at a June 1942 meeting between Churchill and Roosevelt, where it was decided that the United States would be the site of the project. While rapid scientific progress was achieved, the collaborative spirit dissipated quickly as relations between Washington and London grew strained due to America's growing unwillingness to share fully its findings with the British.[42] Nevertheless, meetings in August 1943 between Churchill and Roosevelt produced the Quebec Agreement, which helped ameliorate the differences between the two countries and provide a secure foundation for co-operation during the rest of the war. According to the terms of the document, the two nations agreed on the following: not to use the bomb against each other; not to use it against third parties without the other's consent; to restrict dissemination of research information; and finally,

Britain granted to the United States any post-war industrial or commercial advantages that atomic research might provide. Although Britain had become a 'junior partner' in the project, Margaret Gowing writes that the 1943 Quebec Agreement allowed Anglo-American relations to be 'pretty smooth and friendly' for the rest of the war.[43] In September 1944, Churchill and Roosevelt met again (at Hyde Park) and amended the Quebec Agreement somewhat by signing a brief agreement that provided for 'full collaboration between [the two governments] in developing tube alloys for military and commercial purposes' after the defeat of Japan.[44] ('Tube alloys' was the code-name for the wartime effort to develop the bomb.) The Hyde Park Agreement was something of a victory for Britain, for this 1944 *aide-mémoire* cancelled the concessions that had been granted previously by the Quebec Agreement.[45]

It is worth remembering that during this period the bomb's potential impact on the post-war world was not unknown. Meeting with the president in July 1943 at the White House, Churchill explained that Britain wanted a total interchange of information between the two countries because he was 'vitally concerned with being able to maintain her future independence in the face of the international blackmail that the Russians might eventually be able to employ'.[46] That same year, John Anderson told Canadian Prime Minister Mackenzie King that atomic weapons would 'give control of the world to whatever country obtains them first . . . [the bomb] would be a terrific factor in the post-war world as giving absolute control to whatever country possessed the secret.'[47]

Into the Atomic Age

Although Britain and the Allies would win the war, Churchill faced the post-war period with a sense of gloom. While he hoped for co-operation between East and West, he feared a rift was unavoidable. Even before the war in Europe had ended, Churchill wrote to Anthony Eden: 'I fear that very great evil may come upon the world. . . . The Russians are drunk with victory and there is no length they may not go.'[48] Standing on the threshold of victory, Churchill described his feelings: the 'climax of apparently measureless success was to me a most unhappy time. I moved amid cheering crowds . . . with an aching heart and a mind oppressed by forebodings.'[49] Moreover, Churchill's fear of Russia's strength was exacerbated by his recognition of Britain's weakness. Speaking about the Polish question, which was one of the key points of East–West contention in this period, Churchill said: 'Great Britain and the British Commonwealth are very much weaker militarily than Soviet Russia, and have no means, short of another general war, of enforcing their point of view.'

In the final year of the war, Churchill wondered what lay between 'the white snows of Russia and the white cliffs of Dover', and was unsure if the Russians might not sweep across Europe. There was, he noted, 'an unspoken fear in many people's hearts'.[50] After the war, Britain would be weak and without money, and would 'lie between two great powers . . .' His description of post-war Britain was memorable: 'a small lion . . . walking between a huge Russian bear and a great American elephant . . .' But perhaps, he noted, 'it would prove to be the lion who knew the way'.[51] And over the 'poisonous politics and deadly international rivalries'[52] of the post-war period hung the atomic bomb. The impact the weapon would come to have on Churchill's post-war attitude toward the use of force would be undeniable.

At the Potsdam meeting on 17 July 1945, Churchill learned that the Americans had successfully tested the atomic bomb in the sands of New Mexico. According to his physician, Lord Moran, Churchill observed: 'Fire was the first discovery. This is the second.' Had the Russians got it, 'it would have been the end of civilization'. But now, he asserted, the Americans had 'the power to mould the world'.[53]

While not inattentive to the effect the bomb would have on ending the war, Churchill was especially concerned about the weapon's potential impact on the Soviet Union. Certainly, 'the nightmare picture of enormous Allied casualties had disappeared—to be replaced by "the vision—fair and bright indeed" of the end of the war in "one or two violent shocks".'[54] But the British leader was also moved by thoughts of the future. Britain's Admiral Cunningham described the Prime Minister as 'most optimistic'; he placed 'great faith in the new bomb . . . [and] thinks it a good thing that the Russians should know about it' because 'it may make them a little more humble'.[55]

If the decision to drop the atomic bomb on Japan would generate controversy in the decades after the war, in the summer of 1945 policy-makers overwhelmingly supported the action.[56] As Churchill wrote in his memoirs:

There was never a moment's discussion as to whether the atomic bomb should be used or not. To avert a vast, indefinite butchery, to bring the war to an end, to give peace to the world . . . at the cost of a few explosives, seemed . . . a miracle of deliverance.[57]

Indeed, according to Margaret Gowing, who has examined closely the British sources, among those connected with the atomic project, there was virtually no reluctance to drop the bomb on Japan. This was not the case in the United States, however, where some—particularly among the scientists—harboured reservations about using the weapon. Nevertheless, after the Alamogordo test, there was no further reconsideration of the decision to bomb Japan.[58] While the decision about whether and where to use the bomb was essentially an American one (see n. 58), the British fully supported the American action.

On 6 August 1945, America dropped the atomic bomb on Hiroshima. Three days later, America dropped a second bomb on Nagasaki. The first bomb killed 64,000 people within four months. The second killed 39,000 people. In Hiroshima, 72,000 people were injured. In Nagasaki, 25,000 people were hurt. The American government asserted the decision to drop the bomb was based on strategic considerations, and declared later that it had done so in order to avoid conducting a land invasion of Japan. In order to end the Pacific war quickly, the American government argued, it had decided to use the atomic bomb against Japan. On 14 August 1945, Japan surrendered, and the greatest war humanity had ever known was over. Thus, less than six years after the preparation of the Frisch–Peierls Memorandum, the atomic bomb had been used to end the war. After the weapon was dropped on Hiroshima, the Attlee Government issued the following statement:

This revelation of the secrets of nature, long mercifully withheld from man, should arouse the most solemn reflections in the mind and conscience of every human being . . . We must indeed pray that these awful agencies will be made to conduce to peace among the nations, and that instead of wreaking measureless havoc upon the entire globe they may become a perennial fountain of world prosperity.[59]

The words were those of Winston Churchill; he had penned them before Clement Attlee succeeded him as Prime Minister in July 1945.

In Opposition, 1945–1951

In one of history's less charitable acts, the British electorate voted Churchill out of office in July 1945. For the next six years he would lead the opposition to the Attlee government, until returning to the premiership in 1951. During Labour's years in power, the British atomic energy programme received significant funding and support, so that by October 1952, with Churchill again at the helm, it was possible for Britain to conduct its first atomic test. Why Britain decided to build its own bomb is worth a brief detour, as are the views of key Labour leaders who strongly advocated the development of Britain's independent deterrent.[60]

After the war, the Attlee government confronted the sobering reality of Britain's diminished power and influence in the international arena. In the political, military, and economic spheres, Britain faced the post-war world as, at best, a middle-level power. The country's economic weakness, especially, left the government to ponder how it might maintain Britain's military establishment and thus its global influence.[61] In order to resist what many believed were Moscow's expansionist aspirations, it seemed necessary to develop the atomic bomb. Moreover, British officials, having recognized that the United States would become the leader of the western alliance, believed it was necessary to possess the bomb to 'exert influence over the United States'.[62] Indeed, Anglo-American relations, which continued to falter on the shoals of America's unwillingness to exchange information freely with Britain, led rather directly to Britain's decision to pursue the independent deterrent. With congressional passage of the McMahon Act in 1946, which ended hopes for Anglo-American partnership in the atomic field, the British decided to move ahead on their own without delay. As Attlee recalled:

Once Congress proceeded to pass the McMahon Bill, we had to go ahead on our own. . . . [The bomb] had become essential. We had to hold up our position *vis-à-vis* the Americans. We couldn't allow ourselves to be wholly in their hands . . . [Building] a British atom bomb was therefore at that stage essential to our defence.[63]

A notable aspect of the Attlee Government's atomic policy was the absence of full cabinet participation in the atomic decision-making process. The infrequency with which the full cabinet discussed atomic matters is striking, and it was, according to Margaret Gowing, 'completely excluded' from decisions concerning atomic policy during Attlee's premiership. Instead, small groups and committees were charged with formulating atomic policy as the Prime Minister relied on an 'inner circle' for advice on atomic matters. Consequently, parliament and the press had little opportunity to examine questions pertaining to atomic policy. As Gowing observes, Attlee worked in this fashion mainly due to 'awe and fear', the nature of the atomic problem being qualitatively different from any other. Another factor, albeit less important, was the divergence of views within the Labour Party, which might have made Attlee loath to include his more left-wing colleagues in the decision-making sphere. Nevertheless, during the Attlee years, Britain's atomic programme was successful, a point underscored by the atomic test conducted at Monte Bello, Australia in October 1952.[64]

Britain's first post-war Prime Minister was clearly struck by the bomb's transformative impact on international relations. Declaring as early as August 1945 that the nature of warfare had changed, Attlee claimed it was difficult for people to realize that 'the modern conception of war to which in my lifetime we have become accustomed is now completely out of date'.[65] In a letter to Harry Truman a month later, Attlee again stressed this point, writing that the 'terrible effectiveness' of the atomic bomb had made him 'increasingly aware of the fact that the world is now facing entirely new conditions. . . . The emergence of this new weapon has meant, taking account of its potentialities, not a quantitative but a qualitative change in the nature of warfare.'[66]

Given Attlee's views on the revolutionary character of the bomb, it is hardly surprising that he was determined that Britain should possess it. While just after the war, he had discussed the need for international control of the bomb and even about the need for restructuring international society,[67] as we have seen, he soon supported Britain's efforts to develop the weapon. Later, he recalled that Britain

couldn't take risks with [her] security . . . we had worked from the start for international control of the bomb. We wanted it completely under the United Nations. That was the best way. But it was obviously going to take a long time. Meanwhile we had to face the world as it was. We had to look to our defence.[68]

In weighing Britain's need to develop the bomb against the desire to achieve international control, Foreign Minister Ernest Bevin expressed similar thoughts in a high-level meeting in 1947. According to Bevin, Britain had to

press on with the study of all aspects of atomic energy. We could not afford to acquiesce in an American monopoly of this new development. Other countries might also well develop atomic weapons. Unless therefore an effective international system could be developed under which the production and use of the weapon would be prohibited, we must develop it ourselves.[69]

Indeed, Britain's determination to build the bomb was fortified by American actions in 1945 and 1946, including the sudden termination of Lend-Lease and Truman's cancellation of earlier collaborative efforts on atomic matters. Bevin's view was crucial in an important 1946 meeting, in which it was decided to build a gaseous diffusion plant, an essential component of Britain's atomic programme:

We've got to have this. . . . I don't want any other Foreign Secretary of this country to be talked at or by [an American] Secretary of State as I have just had [sic] in my discussions with Mr Byrnes. We have got to have this thing over here whatever it costs. . . . We've got to have the bloody Union Jack flying on top of it.[70]

Thus, with the strong support of Attlee and Bevin, and a capable team of scientific and military people behind it, Britain's atomic bomb programme proceeded steadily toward its goal. With the Monte Bello Test in 1952, Britain had acquired an independent deterrent.

As opposition leader during the Attlee years, Churchill frequently expressed his views on the way in which the bomb might serve the West's advantage. During the years of the American atomic monopoly, Churchill continued to talk in the forceful manner that had long characterized his outlook on and approach to international politics. In Churchill's estimation, the West—in sole possession of the bomb—could check Russian expansionism; the bomb, he believed, helped keep the peace. At the same time, Churchill spoke occasionally about actually using the weapon against Russia if she failed to cooperate with the west. And significantly, in these years, the opposition leader began to speculate on how Russia's acquisition of the bomb would change the strategic equation.

Believing the West derived great strategic advantages from the bomb and also that the atomic monopoly helped restrain Soviet ambitions, Churchill thought the West should press Moscow in order to extract maximum political benefits from its dominant position. Writing to Attlee in 1946, Churchill expressed wryly his thoughts on the bomb's significance in Europe: 'only two reasons prevent the westward movement of the Russian armies to the North Sea and the Atlantic. The first is their virtue and self-restraint. The second, the possession by the United States of the Atomic Bomb.'[71] While he continued to speak out on atomic matters, Churchill regretted that, out of office, his influence on events had diminished. Nevertheless, he supported a vigorous policy of reining in the Russians, and believed the bomb enabled the United States to proceed confidently. As Churchill told Lord Camrose of the *Daily Telegraph*:

With the manufacture of this bomb in their hands, America can dominate the world for the next five years. If [I] had continued in office [I am] of the opinion that [I] could have persuaded the American Government to use this power to restrain the Russians. [I] would have had a show-down with Stalin and told him he had got to behave reasonably and decently in Europe.[72]

While Churchill was not entirely clear what he meant by such a 'show-down', it is apparent that he believed the bomb conferred upon the United

States the pre-eminent position in world politics. Moreover, American primacy led him to hope that a settlement of international differences could be reached, which would force the Soviets 'to retire to their own country and dwell there . . .' And it was critical to move quickly to achieve this settlement because the atomic monopoly would not last forever. As Churchill wrote to Eisenhower in 1948, 'the moment for this settlement should be chosen when [the Soviets] will realise that the United States and its allies possess overwhelming force.'[73]

As long as the West's atomic monopoly lasted, Churchill favoured a forceful orientation toward Moscow. He told a New York audience in 1949 that it was essential to maintain the great power that the bomb afforded the United States because one could deal with the communists only if one possessed superior force. Furthermore, it was critical for the communists to believe that the West would use this great power without hesitation and ruthlessly, if necessary; moral considerations had to be cast aside. He was 'certain that Europe would have been Communized and London would have been under bombardment some time ago, but for the deterrent of the atomic bomb in the hands of the United States. That is my firm belief.'[74]

During most of his tenure as opposition leader, Churchill advocated the view that peace could best be maintained through strength, believing this to be the best way to restrain the Soviet Union. By relying on atomic superiority—which was, in fact, a monopoly—Churchill believed the West could prevent the absorption of Europe into the Soviet sphere. This posture—the maintenance of peace through strength—was not unlike Churchill's response to the international security challenges of the 1930s. During those years, he had believed it would be possible to deter Nazi aggression by arraying powerful forces against Germany. In this sense, Churchill's response to the Soviet problem after 1945 resembled his approach to the threats Western Europe had confronted a decade before. In another sense, too, Churchill approached the security problems of the two periods similarly.

Just as he had before World War II, after 1945, Churchill advocated a collective response to the problem of European security. In a landmark speech given in Zürich in 1946, he spoke of a United States of Europe, noting that while the 'fighting has stopped . . . the dangers have not . . .' At the centre of Churchill's vision was 'a partnership between France and Germany', without which, he said, there could be 'no revival of Europe'.[75] Churchill's support for European unity flowed from his realization that British power had declined; the consequences of this decline, he believed, might be ameliorated by participation in a collective security arrangement. Commenting on European unity in 1950, Churchill noted that there would be 'no revival of Europe, no safety or freedom for any of us, except in standing together united and unflinching.'[76]

That same year, Churchill lamented Britain's dependence 'upon the United States both for the supply of the bomb and largely for the means of using it. Without it, we are more defenceless than we have ever been. I find this a terrible thought.'[77] The notion that Britain had no bomb in a world where the bomb reigned supreme intensified Churchill's concern about Britain's increased vulnerability and decreased power. He spoke of this reality in 1951, discussing an atomic war in which the 'decision and timing of the terrible event would not rest with us'. Regrettably, Britain's 'influence in the world is not what it was in bygone days . . .'[78]

In the first few years after the war—and prior to the Soviet atomic test in 1949—Churchill spoke occasionally in favour of an atomic strike against the Soviet Union. While he always made these remarks privately, they were consistent with his then-current belief in a vigorous approach to the conduct of East–West diplomacy. Several statements suggest Churchill's willingness to strike the Soviets before they acquired the bomb. Discussing the prospects for another war in a 1946 conversation with Lord Moran, Churchill advocated an attack before Russia had the bomb:

We ought not to wait until Russia is ready. I believe it will be eight years before she has these bombs. America knows that 52 per cent of Russia's motor industry is in Moscow and could be wiped out by a single bomb. It might mean wiping out three million people, but they would think nothing of that. [He smiled.] They would think more of erasing an historical building like the Kremlin.[79]

The following year, in a conversation with Canadian Prime Minister Mackenzie King, Churchill discussed an American attack on the Soviet Union, claiming that the Americans had plans 'all laid for this, for over a year'. We should tell the Russians that

if they are unwilling to co-operate . . . that the nations that have fought the last war for freedom have had enough of this war of nerves and intimidation. . . . We fought for liberty and are determined to maintain it. . . . We will not allow you to destroy Western Europe; to extend your regime further there. If you do not agree to that here and now, within so many days, we will attack Moscow and your other cities and destroy them with atomic bombs from the air. . . . If that stand is not taken within the next few weeks, within five years [or less] . . . there would be another world war in which we shall all be finished.[80]

And again, in 1948, Churchill expressed similar thoughts in conversations with the American Ambassador to Great Britain, Lewis Douglas. According to Douglas, Churchill

believes that now is the time . . . to tell the Soviet that if they do not retire from Berlin and abandon Eastern Germany . . . we will raze their cities. [He believes] we cannot appease, conciliate, or provoke the Soviet; and the only vocabulary they understand is the vocabulary of force.[81]

According to Martin Gilbert, in private conversations with President Truman in 1949, Churchill 'urged the President to make plain, and to make public, that the United States would indeed be prepared to use the atomic bomb in order to defend democracy'.[82] As Churchill wistfully told Lord Moran in 1954: 'I wanted America to have a show-down with the Soviet Republic before the Russians had the bomb.'[83]

Toward the end of Churchill's tenure as opposition leader, the Soviets successfully tested the bomb, a development that led Churchill to speculate on how the end of the Western atomic monopoly would transform the nature of international relations. In these remarks, one sees that a new circumspection had begun to influence Churchill's outlook on world politics. Evincing this evolving view, he told the House in 1950:

Our whole position in this atomic sphere has been worsened since the war by the fact that the Russians . . . have acquired the secrets of the atomic bomb, and are said to have begun its manufacture. Let us therefore labour for peace, not only by gathering our defensive strength, but also by making sure that no door is closed upon any hope of reaching a settlement which will end this tragic period.[84]

In the electoral campaign of 1951, Churchill again talked of peace, saying he was determined to disprove the 'false and ungrateful charge' that the election of a Conservative Government would increase the chance of war. By remaining in public life, he asserted, he sought to help prevent another war, and to achieve the peace all peoples desired. 'I pray indeed that I may have this opportunity. It is the last prize I seek to win.'[85] On the eve of his re-election, a new impulse had begun to move the ageing leader.

Return to Downing Street, 1951–1955

During his second premiership, Churchill would come to embrace the idea that the maintenance of peace depended upon the bomb, and throughout these years, he expressed a cautious optimism that nuclear weapons served to deter war. Before the American Congress in 1952, the Prime Minister said the atomic bomb was not only 'the supreme deterrent' against a third world war, but was also the 'most effective guarantee' of victory in the event of war. He urged America's lawmakers 'not to let go of the atomic weapon until you are sure . . . that other means of preserving peace are in your hands'.[86] At a dinner honouring General Matthew Ridgway that same year, Churchill explained why a third world war was unlikely:

It would be entirely different in certain vital aspects from any other war that has ever taken place. Both sides know that it would begin with horrors of a kind and on a scale never dreamed of before . . . The torments would fall . . . upon the whole civilian population of the globe.[87]

Clearly, Churchill was referring here to atomic weapons, which, he believed, would make any future world war 'entirely different'. In a 1952 speech to the Commonwealth prime ministers, Churchill again discussed the notion that atomic weapons had reduced the possibility of war: 'The development of atomic warfare would deter the [Soviet] regime, since it would face them with the certain loss of power to wage modern war.' War was unlikely because the Kremlin feared the 'results of the use . . . of the overwhelming atomic power . . . [by] the United States'.[88]

With their return to power in 1951, the Conservatives' atomic problems combined 'tidying-up' the Labour inheritance and deciding upon the course of future atomic development. Impressed by Labour's effort in the atomic sphere, Churchill was surprised that the party had, without parliament's knowledge, spent almost £100 million on the project.[89] In February 1952, he told the House that he was unaware until taking office

that not only had the Socialist Government made the atomic bomb as a matter of research, but that they had created at the expense of many scores of millions of pounds the important plant necessary for its regular production. This weapon will be tested in the course of the present year by agreement with the Australian Government [in Australia].[90]

And on 3 October 1952, in an event which, according to one scholar, attracted 'remarkably little public interest', Britain conducted its first atomic test off the Australian coast.[91]

Much can be learned about Britain's atomic policy during Churchill's second premiership by considering the annual Defence Reviews. Particularly significant are the 1954 and 1955 reviews, the former serving as something of a watershed, especially in its emphasis on the importance of nuclear weapons. In the words of the document: 'The primary deterrent . . . remains the atomic bomb and the ability of the highly organized and trained United States strategic air power to use it.'[92] Still more important was the 1955 White Paper, which greatly influenced post-war British defence policy, particularly in its emphasis on the hydrogen bomb: 'Overshadowing all else in the year 1954 has been the emergence of the thermonuclear bomb. This has had, and will continue to have, far-reaching effects on the defence policy of the United Kingdom. . . . [Facing a dual problem,] we have to prepare against the risk of a world war and so prevent it.' The 1955 document asserted that the development of thermonuclear weapons was a key to Britain's maintaining an important role on the world stage, an assumption that led the government, after careful consideration, to develop the hydrogen bomb.[93] As we shall see, in March 1955, in one of Churchill's last appearances before the House, he articulated publicly the thinking embedded in the 1955 White Paper—which was a crucial guide to Britain's post-war defence strategy.

In what was perhaps the most striking goal of his second premiership, Churchill longed for a summit meeting with the United States and the Soviet Union. Indeed, as early as February 1950, while still in opposition, Churchill discussed a possible meeting with Soviet leaders:

The idea appeals to me of a supreme effort to bridge the gulf between the two worlds, so that each can live their life, if not in friendship at least without the hatreds of the cold war. . . . It is not easy to see how things could be worsened by a parley at the summit, if such a thing were possible.[94]

As Prime Minister, Churchill repeatedly asserted that a summit meeting could mitigate East–West tensions. While he recognized that the conflict was not susceptible to easy answers and appeared 'intractable' at times, Churchill

stated in November 1951 that a high-level meeting might create 'a new atmosphere and climate of thought and [lead to] a revived relationship and sense of
human comradeship . . .'[95]

Churchill's desire for a summit reflected a novel impulse in a changed world.
With the passing of the West's atomic monopoly and his growing recognition
that war between the superpowers would cause unimaginable devastation,
Churchill's long-held belief that war was the critical agent of change in history
began to dissolve. In 1954, Lord Moran wrote that the idea of a meeting with
the Soviet leadership had 'completely taken possession of him. It has indeed
become an article of faith . . . To hold off the threat of war until it is no longer
worthwhile for anyone to break the peace—that is . . . his one consuming purpose.' According to Moran, Churchill dreaded another war because he did 'not
believe England could survive'. And significantly, the British leader had come
to believe with 'almost religious intensity—that he, and he alone, [could] save
the world from a frightful war which will be the end of everything in the
civilized globe . . .'[96]

While Churchill's hope for a meeting with Soviet and American leaders
would go unrealized, it did cause significant tensions in the Anglo-American
relationship (and even sometimes within the British cabinet) during the
Eisenhower years.[97] What is critical here, though, is the fact that the Prime
Minister's longing for a great power meeting indicates his evolving orientation
toward the conduct of international politics. Summitry might serve to lessen
East–West tensions, and Churchill's desire for a summit flowed from his conviction that great power rivalry—in a world in which both sides possessed the
bomb—could not be allowed to result in war. Churchill had come to believe
that it was essential to replace conflict with negotiation in world politics, and
this, it is clear, marked a dramatic shift in his approach to interstate relations.
As he told parliament in May 1953, a conference might achieve 'no hard-faced
agreements . . . but there might be a general feeling among those gathered
together that they might do something better than tear the human race,
including themselves, into bits'.[98]

In addition to his new-found passion for summitry, in working to keep the
peace during his second premiership, Churchill simultaneously employed an
older approach to world politics. As he had long held, the Prime Minister continued to believe that the maintenance of one's military strength could help
to preserve peace. Thus, Churchill melded the novel idea of peaceful coexistence—which, in the nuclear age meant there was no rational alternative to
peaceful relations between the great powers—to a more traditional view of
international politics. Consequently, to maintain British strength—which
would enhance the prospects for peace—Churchill supported Britain's development of the hydrogen bomb. Churchill thus not only worked for a great-
power summit, but he also sought formal cabinet approval for development of
the new weapon, telling the cabinet in July 1954:

We could not expect to maintain our influence as a world power unless we possessed the
most up-to-date nuclear weapons. The primary aim of our policy was to prevent major

war; and the possession of these weapons was now the main deterrent to a potential aggressor. . . . The best hope of preserving world peace was to make it clear that they had no hope of shielding themselves from a crushing retaliatory use of atomic power. . . . The Western Powers . . . must put themselves in a position to ensure that no surprise attack . . . could wholly destroy their power of effective retaliation.[99]

Two weeks later the cabinet decided to approve 'in principle' the proposal to produce the hydrogen bomb.[100]

In Churchill's world-view in these years, one sees the emergence of a novel formulation: he believed it remained essential to maintain one's military might, while he also thought it was vital to co-operate with one's adversaries. In the nuclear age, the leader who had harboured a deep and longstanding antipathy for communism had come to speak about living with the Soviet state. He discussed the idea of 'peaceful coexistence'—Anthony Eden had coined the phrase in 1954—in a House speech in July of that year. After praising Eden for his 'remarkable phrase' and describing it as a 'fundamental and far-reaching conception', Churchill told the House:

What a vast ideological gulf [there is] between the idea of peaceful coexistence vigilantly safeguarded, and the mood of forcibly extirpating the Communist fallacy and heresy. It is, indeed, a gulf. This statement is a recognition of the appalling character which war has now assumed and that its fearful consequences go even beyond the difficulties and dangers of dwelling side by side with Communist states.[101]

At times, Churchill wove the two ideas together, claiming there was no inconsistency in maintaining a strong defensive posture against the Soviets, while seeking to live in peace with the enemy. Early in 1954 he told the House:

there is no contradiction between our policy of building up the defensive strength of the free world against Communist pressure and . . . potential armed Soviet aggression and trying, at the same time, to create conditions under which Russia may dwell easily and peacefully side by side with us all.

While many would say they were 'trying to have it both ways at once', Churchill declared 'it is only by having it both ways at once that we shall get a chance of getting anything of it at all.'[102]

It seems clear that Churchill believed nuclear weapons might usher in an era of concord between the great powers, and during his second premiership he frequently explored the idea of nuclear peace. In November 1953, he spoke to the House on a range of subjects, including the Korean War and the death of Stalin.[103] But one event, he said, overshadowed the other two: 'the rapid and ceaseless developments of atomic warfare and the hydrogen bomb'. He believed 'the probabilities of another world war have diminished', despite 'the continual growth of weapons of destruction such as have never fallen before into the hands of human beings'. Wondering whether the 'annihilating character of these agencies [might] bring an utterly unforeseeable security to mankind', Churchill concluded with a compelling metaphor:

When I was a schoolboy I was not good at arithmetic, but I have since heard it said that certain mathematical quantities when they pass through infinity change their signs from plus to minus. . . . It may be that this rule may have a novel application and that when the advance of destructive weapons enables everyone to kill everybody else nobody will want to kill anyone at all . . . a war which begins by both sides suffering what they dread most—and that is undoubtedly the case at present—is less likely to occur than one which dangles the lurid prizes of former ages before ambitious eyes.[104]

Returning to the theme of nuclear peace the following April, he told the House that 'the new terror brings a certain element of equality in annihilation. Strange as it may seem, it is to the universality of potential destruction that I feel we may look with hope and even confidence.'[105]

Throughout these years, one sees Churchill engaged in the process of what can be described as 'nuclear learning'. As he became increasingly knowledgeable about the bomb and its destructive potential, the Prime Minister began to confront its strategic implications. He came to believe that a more peaceful world was the likely product of nuclear weapons, and he began to question the validity of traditional strategic assumptions. Writing to President Eisenhower in March 1954, Churchill discussed the hydrogen bomb and reacted to a February speech on the subject made by Sterling Cole, Chairman of the Joint Committee on Atomic Energy. Churchill questioned whether the concept of superiority had become outmoded, noting that 'after a certain quantity had been produced on either side the factor of "over-taking", "superiority", etc. loses much of its meaning. If one side has five hundred and the other two hundred both might be destroyed.' In this observation, one sees the ageing Prime Minister beginning to consider the arcana of nuclear strategy. As he told the President, those in power had 'to drive their minds forward into these hideous and deadly spheres of thought'.[106]

The product of Churchill's nuclear learning was clear on 1 March 1955, when the eighty-year-old leader made his final important speech before the House. He told his physician Lord Moran that he had 'taken a hell of a lot of trouble' over the speech, noting that he had devoted twenty hours to its preparation and eight to checking the facts.[107] A fascinating document, it reveals Churchill's keen understanding of the nuclear dilemma. After describing the great rift that divided the communist from the free world—and how it was accompanied by the 'obliterating weapons of the nuclear age'—the Prime Minister considered several aspects of the nuclear problem. While his language was not strictly that of the strategist, the concepts embedded in the speech would become central to the emerging field of nuclear strategy. The speech was centred on 'deterrents' [sic], and how the possession of nuclear weapons allowed one to enhance stability, thereby strengthening one's defensive position. In fact, Churchill argued, such 'deterrents' might one day become the 'parents of disarmament'.

The March 1955 address is striking for the manner in which Churchill blended strategic sophistication with prescient analysis. Although he employed no contemporary strategic jargon, Churchill discussed the importance of a second-strike capability (and the necessity for having varied delivery systems to ensure survivability), and explored the reasoning behind what would later become known as mutual assured destruction, arguing that it decreased the likelihood of war. Moreover, he foresaw the phenomenon of 'limited war', suggesting that in the nuclear age, Korea might be a model for future communist incursions. He outlined, too, the importance of maintaining strong conventional forces, believing that the West could not rely solely on a full-scale nuclear response to a minor incident. (This, of course, would become one of the important strategic issues in later years.) Given Soviet nuclear inferiority, Churchill claimed that war was unlikely in the current period, and he closed on an optimistic note, declaring that deterrents would 'improve and gain authority' during the next decade. A remarkable performance by the eighty-year-old leader, the speech revealed a wisdom and mental acuity rare among statesmen of any age. And more than that, it reflected how much Churchill had learned in the preceding ten years.[108]

Between 1945 and 1955, Winston Churchill's attitude toward the use of force had undergone a dramatic transformation. In the period of the American atomic monopoly, Churchill's views were largely consistent with those he had held for many years: It was possible to maintain peace through strength, and, more specifically, the bomb could preserve European democracy against the threat of Soviet expansionism. Moreover, in keeping with his lifelong vigour as a soldier and statesman, Churchill spoke privately about attacking the Soviet Union and forcing a show-down—before the Soviets acquired the bomb. One could employ force to achieve a diplomatic objective: reining in Soviet Russia. Without question, it was essential to take this extraordinary step—to raze Moscow and other Soviet cities—during the period of America's atomic monopoly. With the disappearance of that monopoly, Churchill would come to articulate a markedly different view.

With the West's atomic monopoly gone, Churchill came to realize that the bomb could do far more than preserve democracy in Western Europe. Over time, it could decrease the likelihood of war and perhaps someday eliminate great-power conflict altogether. Accordingly, the idea of 'peaceful coexistence' became an integral part of Churchill's approach to international politics. If it is true that the transformation flowed from the realization that Soviet acquisition of the bomb left no other option, this did represent a new and powerful impulse for the British statesman. In a world in which both sides possessed the bomb, the pre-eminent objective of statesmen, Churchill now believed, was to avoid war rather than to extirpate communism. This implied that a more peaceful and increasingly stable international order was possible.

When compared with Churchill's lifelong attitudes toward force and conflict, these newly developed views are striking. Gone was the belief that the decision to use force imposed few, if any, moral constraints on statesmen. Gone, too, after 1949, was the belief that Soviet Russia could be threatened—and attacked, if necessary—to curb her hegemonic impulses. And Churchill's strongly held view that Soviet communism was a cancer, which one had to remove before it overwhelmed the international system, disappeared, as well. In its place stood a novel approach to Moscow: peaceful coexistence. The bomb had tempered Winston Churchill: the martial vigour of the past had been supplanted by a passion for peace.

Having spent a lifetime preoccupied with fighting, directing, and writing about war, Churchill was uniquely situated to perceive the meaning of great-power conflict in the nuclear age. His belief that nuclear war—by causing unparalleled destruction—would be 'entirely different' from past conflicts, led Churchill to devote his final years in office to seeking a rapprochement with the Soviet Union. His lifelong advocacy of a vigorous and forceful statecraft, along with his deeply held view that 'nothing in history was ever settled except by war' gave way to the idea that the use of force in the nuclear age would be an act of supreme folly. If, as Churchill had argued in earlier days, nations might legitimately fight great wars to sweep obstacles from the path of human progress, by 1955, he had come to believe that such wars themselves would impede the advance of nations.

9

Between 'Paper' and 'Real Tigers':
Mao's View of Nuclear Weapons

SHU GUANG ZHANG

NUCLEAR weapons have shaped China's military and foreign policy
over the last four decades. When the Chinese Communists took
power in 1949, their armed forces—the People's Liberation Army—
consisted of a large number of light infantry troops. But by 1955, Beijing was
developing its own nuclear arsenal, and the People's Republic has since
become a major nuclear power.

A recent study by John Lewis and Xue Litai documents how Beijing went
about building the bomb.[1] This essay focuses on two more specific issues: how
Mao Zedong, the Chinese Communist Party's (hereafter, CCP) Chairman, perceived the military and strategic value of nuclear weapons; and how that perception changed China's national defence policy. It will also consider lessons
China's 'nuclear revolution' reveals.

'The Nuclear Bomb Is a Paper Tiger'

Mao at first did not seem to believe that nuclear weapons had changed basic
military and political realities. Reflecting Chinese traditional thinking, he
insisted that technology was not a decisive factor in warfare.

In his *Art of War*, the ancient Chinese strategist Sun Tzu wrote of five strategic assets crucial to victory or defeat, including: '(1) The Moral Law; (2)
Heaven; (3) Earth; (4) The Commander, and (5) Method and discipline'. To
him, proper morale, the best timing, the most favourable positioning, domestic harmony, and the fighters' virtues of wisdom, sincerity, benevolence,
courage, and strictness were the main components of military thinking. Sun
Tzu further wrote that 'the elements of the art of war are first, the measure-
ment of space; second, the estimation of quantities; third, strategic calculation; fourth, strength comparison; and fifth, chances of victory'. This
traditional strategic thought taught, in short, that one should not overesti-
mate the power of weaponry.[2] As a firm believer in Sun Tzu, Mao had long
asserted that victory or defeat in war was not determined by military weapons

but by the masses who operated them. He had consistently objected to the notion that 'weapons decide everything'. In his famous essay 'On Protracted War', written in May 1938, the CCP Chairman condemned this thesis as 'a mechanical approach to the question of war and a subjective and one-sided view'. He argued:

Our view is opposed to this; we see not only weapons but also people. Weapons are an important factor in war, but not the decisive factor; it is the people, not things, that are decisive. The contest of strength is not only a contest of military and economic power, but also a contest of human power and morale. Military and economic power is necessarily wielded by people.[3]

In his view, 'whatever is done has to be done by human beings'. Mao thus maintained that the outcome of a war was decided by such factors as (a) 'the military, political, economic and geographical conditions on both sides'; (b) 'the nature of the war each side is waging', (c) 'the international support each enjoys', and (d) 'the directing and waging of war, man's conscious activity in war'.[4] Mao's thesis that new types of weapons could not determine the outcome of wars persisted in his writings on military affairs. Viewing 'war as "man's politics with bloodshed", [and] as mutual slaughter by opposing armies', he believed that 'the object of war is specifically "to preserve oneself and to destroy the enemy". To destroy the enemy is to disarm him or "deprive him of the power to resist", and not to destroy every member of his forces physically'. Weapons were to serve this object of war and nothing else. He explained in 1938:

In ancient warfare, the spear and the shield were used, the spear to attack and destroy the enemy, and the shield to defend and preserve oneself. To the present day, all weapons are still an extension of the spear and the shield. The bomber, the machine-gun, the long-range gun and poison gas are developments of the spear, while the air-raid shelter, the steel helmet, the concrete fortification and the gas mask are developments of the shield. The tank is a new weapon combining the functions of both spear and shield.[5]

Any new inventions of weaponry, in Mao's judgement, had to comply with the principle of preserving oneself and destroying the enemy; otherwise, they would ultimately lose their military value. Mao indeed saw no difference between the atomic bomb and conventional weapons in the immediate post-World War II years. The first time Mao publicly commented on atomic weapons was in August 1946, when he spoke with an American correspondent Anna Louise Strong in Yanan, Shaanxi province, then the CCP headquarters. In his conversation, Mao put forward his famous slogan, 'All reactionaries are paper tigers'. Just as Lenin considered imperialism as a 'colossus with feet of clay', so Mao regarded American power as illusory: 'In appearance, the [U.S.] reactionaries are terrifying, but in reality they are not so powerful. From a long-term point of view, it is not the reactionaries but the people who are really powerful.'

When Strong asked: 'But suppose the United States uses the atomic bomb? Suppose the United States bombs the Soviet Union from its bases in Iceland, Okinawa and China,' Mao responded:

The atomic bomb is a paper tiger which the US reactionaries use to scare people. It looks terrible, but in fact it isn't. Of course, the atomic bomb is a weapon of mass slaughter, but the outcome of a war is decided by people, not by one or two new types of weapon.

To Mao, the atomic bomb was nothing but a new conventional weapon just like tanks and aeroplanes. In the same interview, the CCP Chairman was confident that 'we have only millet plus rifles to rely on, but history will finally prove that our millet plus rifles is more powerful than [the enemy's] aeroplanes plus tanks'.[6]

Mao's contempt for the atomic bomb played an important role in Beijing's decision for military involvement in the Korean War. Shortly after the outbreak of the conflict in June 1950, the Chinese government began military preparations to intervene on North Korea's behalf. When the deployment of a large number of PLA troops along the Sino-Korean border failed to dissuade the US/UN forces from crossing the 38th parallel, the CCP central leadership seriously considered the immediate dispatch of the troops across the Yalu River. Mao vigorously advocated engaging American forces in Korea. However, others who opposed China's intervention worried that Chinese military action might provoke the US into large-scale retaliation, including the use of the atomic bomb. Mao was not frightened by such a prospect. Speaking at the ninth meeting of the Central People's Government Council on 5 September 1950, the CCP Chairman asserted:

We will not allow you [the Americans] to use the atomic bomb [against us]. But if you won't give it up, you may just use it. You can follow the way you choose to go, and we will do whatever is to our [best] advantages [in encountering you]. You may bomb [us] with the atomic bomb, but we will respond with our hand-grenades. We then will catch your weakness to tie you up and finally defeat you.

Mao clearly regarded the atomic bomb as nothing more than a conventional weapon of high explosiveness. He believed that the atomic bomb would not guarantee a US victory in a war against China, and that the Chinese people should not be scared of it.[7] The CCP's propaganda machine then launched a campaign to urge the CCP cadres and masses not to fear US nuclear weapons. A CCP political study document, 'The Bankruptcy of US Imperialist Nuclear Diplomacy', issued by the Ministry of Foreign Affairs in December 1950, pointed out that 'we should smash the myth of the atomic bomb' with scientific evidence. 'One atomic bomb,' this book calculated, 'is merely as powerful as the yield of 3,000 tons of conventional bombs.' It then referred to the fact that 'within one month, Nazi Germany had dropped hundreds of thousands of tons of bombs on the Soviet Union in 1941, of which the explosive force was equal to that of several hundred atomic bombs. But the Soviet Union won the final victory.' With regard to the Korean battlefield, this study pointed out that 'the United States has so far bombed [North] Korea with conventional bombs equal to more than 20 atomic bombs. However, the glorious Korean people are still fighting vigorously in the war of resisting US aggression.' The study concluded: 'In short, the atomic bomb cannot play a decisive role in modern warfare or determine success or defeat in war.'[8] CCP propaganda also argued that the US government would have to think twice before deciding to use the atomic bomb again. Since the United States had dropped two bombs on Japan at the end of World War II and killed thousands of 'innocent people', another analysis of current affairs asserted on 25 December 1950, it would offend the 'dao', or morality, should it use the bomb again in Asia. 'If the U.S. imperialists venture to do so,' this study maintained, 'the peoples of Asia and around the world will rise against [the US].' It further pointed out that 'the prospect of losing moral grounds and consequently political support' would inhibit Washington from attacking Korea or China with atomic bombs.[9] The Chinese Communists also believed that the possibility of Soviet nuclear retaliation would deter the American use of atomic bombs. On 7 October 1951, an editorial in *Renmin Ribao* (People's Daily) commented on a public statement on the US nuclear threat made by Stalin on 6 October. 'Comrade Stalin's statement on atomic weapons,' the editorial proclaimed, 'is the greatest gospel [*fuyin* in Chinese] for the world peace and security, [because] it has once again seriously smashed the US imperialist aspiration for nuclear aggression and greatly enhanced our confidence in defending the course of world peace.' The Soviet acquisition of atomic weapons would 'force our common enemy to lay down its own bomb . . . [since] Soviet production of atomic weapons and our military intervention to resist America and aid Korea are serving the same purpose'.[10] Even if the US were to launch a nuclear attack against China, the Chinese Communists held, it would not guarantee the enemy final victory. The CCP study document of 25 December 1950 conceded that atomic bombs would 'inflict massive destruction and cause tremendous psychological fear'. However, it asserted, the bomb had 'little military value regarding battlefield and combat operations'. It explained:

The atomic bomb can only be used against big objects or targets such as big cities, industrial complexes, and naval vessels concentrated in large numbers. The bomb will definitely inflict heavy damage on these targets; it is, however, of no use in ground war no matter how concentrated men forces or military materials are. This is because, although the use of the atomic bomb at the front may kill combat personnel in the open field, the forces underground and in the rear will survive the attack and continue to operate. It will cost a great deal of money to launch numerous and massive nuclear assaults on either the front or small cities, railway stations and other targets.

The CCP study concluded that 'since China and its ally, the Soviet Union, are countries of such a vast land that we can easily disperse our people, industries, and military materials, the atomic bomb has no use in a war against our countries.' Moreover, this study pointed out that 'we can protect ourselves from atomic attack by conventional methods', including: '(a) construction of strong and solid defence works such as tunnels and bunkers; (b) hiding our people and materials in big mountains; (c) bombing the enemy airfields [in South Korea or Japan] so as to destroy its bombers of nuclear components; and (d) building a close-knit network of air defence with attackers and anti-aircraft guns'.[11]

There can be little doubt that Mao endorsed these CCP study materials and that he saw the atomic bomb as having little military value. The CCP Chairman later told a group of local party officials that it was better not to be afraid of nuclear weapons. The purpose of imperialist policy was exploitation, he insisted, and 'the object of exploitation is man. . . . If man is killed, what's the use of occupying soil? I don't see the reason for the atomic bomb. Conventional weapons are still the thing.'[12]

For the moment, though, conventional weapons were all Mao had, and he was determined to make the most of them. Beijing authorities thus concentrated on building modern air and naval forces and developing heavy artillery, tanks, and machine-guns during the early 1950s.

'The US Nuclear Threats Are Becoming Real'

The Korean experience, however, brought about some changes in Beijing's strategic thinking. Although the Chinese leaders believed that China's 'success' in Korea had shattered the myth of US invincibility, they conceded that advanced technology was playing an increasingly important role in modern warfare. Mao explained in September 1953 that China's 'glorious people's war' had smashed the doubts as to '(a) whether we are capable of fighting; (b) whether we are able to defend [our positions]; (c) whether we can assure logistic supplies; and (d) whether we can beat the enemy's bacteriological warfare'. He admitted, however, that the Chinese People's Volunteers had paid a huge price for their simple and crude equipment and inferior firepower.[13] China's commander-in-general in Korea, Peng Dehuai, was even more cautious. Reporting to the Central People's Government Council on 12 September he asserted: '[although] the Chinese-[North] Korean people's armies of inferior equipment have achieved a brilliant victory in fighting the invading forces of superior equipment, [we must pay closer attention to the] new weapon's "omnipotence" which US imperialists have applied in bluffing, threatening, and scaring people.'[14]

The Chinese military commanders believed that the Korean War offered important lessons and insights. During a meeting of high-ranking commanders on 7 December 1953–26 January 1954, Peng pointed out that 'the war to resist US aggression and aid Korea was an important challenge to our army . . . its importance lies in the fact that we must raise the military art of our armed forces to a new level'.[15] At the same meeting, deputy CPV Commander Deng Hua also asserted that 'since we beat the highly modernized invading forces led by US imperialists with [our] inferior equipment, [our] experience in the Korean War is evidently valuable and realistic.' To him, it was urgent and imperative that the Chinese forces should enhance the People's Liberation

Army's capacity to fight anti-amphibious, anti-airborne, and anti-nuclear war-fare. Deng explained: 'We must study hard to catch up and master modern military technology so that [we] will be able to reduce the advantages of enemy's technology and equipment.'[16] In examining the Korean lessons, the Chinese military commanders seemed to have firmly believed that advanced technology was as important as manpower in modern wars. In early 1954, Deng Hua wrote a lengthy report on 'principles and guidelines of combat oper-ations' in Korea. 'My general observation . . . is,' he maintained, 'that although nature of war and the army's political quality will still play a decisive role in modern warfare, [our army's] sources of military materiel and technological conditions will be indispensable factors.'[17] Interestingly, there is no evidence that Mao was aware of the possibility that the US might use tactical nuclear weapons to end the Korean War in the spring of 1953; or that he took seriously the Eisenhower Administration's warning that it would launch a nuclear assault against China if Beijing sent armed forces into Indo-China to support the Viet Minh in 1954.[18] Since the mid-1950s, however, China's national security policy had been shaped by the consensus, which emerged among the Chinese high-ranking commanders, that China had to prepare to 'fight a gen-eral war on the assumption that it will break out any time soon and it will be on a grand scale and nuclear [zaoda dada dahezhanzheng in Chinese]'.[19]

To prepare for a general nuclear attack, Beijing stressed the importance of a national defence system. The Central Military Commission had already decided on the construction of national defence works in August 1952. Mao Zedong ordered in October that '[we] must plan to build permanent defence works step by step in strategic key points and important directions of military operations.' Accordingly, Deputy Chief of Staff Su Yu designed detailed oper-ational plans.

During 1954 and 1955, Peng Dehuai twice called high-ranking commanders to discuss this matter and personally inspected the East China Coast to com-plete defence projects. As the defence works were under construction, Su Yu pointed out at the fifth meeting on the national defence system in February 1955 that '[we] should adjust and improve designs so as to be anti-nuclear'. Accepting Su's suggestion, the Ministry of National Defence ordered changes in the projects to add anti-nuclear, anti-chemical, and anti-bacteriological installations.[20] During this period, the Soviet Union assisted China in con-structing 150 defence industry projects. When the CCP leaders considered where to build them, they were largely concerned about how to escape American air or nuclear assaults. For every factory, Zhou Enlai would ask his aides to mark out on a map the distance between perspective sites and the US military bases in South Korea, Taiwan, or Japan. Zhou often questioned what type of US bombers would be capable of attacking these factories and how much damage they would cause.[21]

Washington's response to China's bombardment of Jinmen (Quemoy) and Mazu (Matsu) offshore islands in late 1954 made the CCP leadership worry seriously about the US nuclear threat. Zhou Enlai claimed in late January 1955 that the US was 'brandishing atomic weapons' in an attempt to maintain its position on Taiwan. He also accused the Eisenhower administration of 'openly boasting of nuclear missiles as conventional weapons and preparing for nuclear war'. The Chinese press clearly noted a *Washington Star* report on 22 January that 'the 7th Fleet was equipped with tactical nuclear-bombs and any action to attack Taiwan would have to go through atomic bombs first'. A *Shijie Zhishi* (World Knowledge) analysis also indicated that it was 'not an accident' for Secretary of State Dulles on 15 March, President Eisenhower on 16 March, and Vice-President Nixon on 17 March, all to have mentioned publicly the possibility of using nuclear weapons either to 'stop the PLA's action aimed at liberating Taiwan' or 'to fight a war against China in the Far East'.[22]

This was the first time the PRC leadership had taken the US nuclear threats seriously; the explicit warnings coming directly from the US top leaders impressed the Chinese leaders more this time than before. Throughout the spring of 1955, the Chinese press had repeatedly stressed that 'we are not afraid of atomic bombs but we don't want a nuclear war'. In his 28 January talk with Carljohan Sundstrom, Finland's first ambassador to China, Mao specially commented on the possibility of the US 'wanting to launch an atomic war' in the Taiwan Strait. He asserted that 'we do not want [such a] war', but 'if anybody commits aggression against us, we'll resolutely strike back'. Mao claimed that 'because we have a population of 600 million, and a territory of 9.6 million square kilometers, . . . the US cannot annihilate the Chinese nation with its small stack of atom bombs'. But he explicitly admitted: 'Even if the US atom bombs were so powerful that, when dropped on China, they would make a hole right through the earth, or even blow it up, that would hardly mean anything to the universe as a whole, though it might be a major event for the solar system.'[23] Although Mao still insisted on his thesis that nuclear weapons were 'paper tigers', his statement was, as a China specialist put it, 'a somewhat atypical excursion into hyperbole about nuclear weapons'.[24]

Fearing the danger of nuclear war, the CCP leaders began preparations for possible US nuclear strikes. On 12 February 1955, Guo Moruo, the Chairman of the Sino-Soviet Friendship Organization, spoke to the Chinese public on the issue of nuclear war. Guo went to considerable length to tell the nation that US nuclear weapons should not be feared because (a) 'our land is so vast and our industry is in such an initial stage that nuclear weapons would not hurt us'; and (b) 'our ally, the Soviet Union, already has both atomic and hydrogen bombs, as well as long-range strategic bombers, which can be used to retaliate against US use [of nuclear weapons] against China'. But at the same time, Guo warned that 'we must not be over-optimistic and we must prepare for any such contingency, . . . [because] the US imperialists cannot be accounted for on the basis of a general logic and "a mad dog" may jump over the wall.'[25] On 31 March although asserting that 'there is no "magic weapon" that cannot be defeated', Mao warned other Party leaders that 'no matter what kind of work we do, we should think in terms of and prepare for the worst possibilities'. Based on this consideration, he argued that 'if we are prepared beforehand, . . .

the atomic and hydrogen bombs which the imperialists use to scare us are not that terrifying.'[26]

After the first Taiwan Strait crisis, the Chinese leadership's perception of an increased danger of nuclear war greatly intensified. By early 1958, Beijing authorities had detected a significant change in the Eisenhower administration's strategic thinking from an emphasis on massive nuclear retaliation to the possibility of limited or local nuclear attack. With such a change, the leaders feared, the United States might be less restricted in using tactical nuclear weapons to protect its interests in a local crisis, and the likelihood of 'bold' American action in East Asia would thus greatly increase.

A Ministry of Foreign Affairs expert on US strategy pointed out at the end of 1957 that Washington had started to prepare for such a change as early as the previous spring, when Secretary of Defense Charles Wilson told Congress that the administration undertook to 'distinguish between all-out nuclear weapons and nuclear weapons with military feasibility for local or limited war'. Henry Kissinger's new book, *Nuclear Weapons and Foreign Policy* (Kissinger was described as a special counsel to the Joint Chiefs of Staff), the analyst believed, laid down 'a theoretic basis for developing limited nuclear war strategy for local conflicts'. This US policy specialist also found that Dulles had endorsed such a strategy in his article in the October 1957 issue of *Foreign Affairs*, stressing 'the possibility of less and less relying on the deterrence of massive retaliation'.[27] The same specialist explicitly warned in early 1958 that the United States, realizing the difficulty involved with the massive retaliation strategy, had begun to shift to a strategy of 'a limited but actual use of nuclear weapons'.[28] The 19 January editorial in *Renmin Ribao* noted that in his budget request to Congress, Eisenhower asked for 'an increase of $1.3 billion for military expenditures, . . . [of which] the primary proportion will be spent on building missiles and tactical nuclear weapons'.[29]

The US decision, early in 1957, to deploy tactical nuclear weapons in Taiwan seemed to have confirmed this perceived change in American strategic thinking. Intelligence regarding this reached Beijing two months before the State Department announced, on 7 May, the planned deployment of Matador surface-to-surface tactical nuclear missiles. In a 5 March report on his trip to several Asian and European countries, Zhou Enlai mentioned that Washington was planning to spend $25 million to build more air-force bases in Taizhong (Central Taiwan), and to deploy nuclear missiles there as well. Zhou believed that the US 'aimed to increase the tension in the Taiwan area'.[30]

A spokesman of the Ministry of Foreign Affairs pointed out on 11 May that Washington's decision to deploy nuclear weapons on Taiwan 'not only reveals the warlike nature of America's policy to deploy nuclear weapons everywhere around the world, but indicates a US conspiracy to turn Taiwan into a nuclear base against China'.[31]

China's concern about US nuclear missiles grew during the spring of 1958. An analysis of US China policy, appearing in the 15 July *Renmin Ribao*, pointed out that 'the US Defense Department announced in April that a study is being undertaken on setting up intermediate ballistic missiles in the Far East, with Taiwan and South Korea the first priority. The first test-firing of such missiles took place in May'. This analysis then asserted that the USA was no longer 'bluffing the Chinese people' but was actually 'speeding-up its preparations for a nuclear war against China'.[32] Moreover, the CCP's press network clearly regarded American military activities in South Korea as part of America's scheme. As a *Renmin Ribao* commentary had pointed out in January, the United States had transformed two of its regular divisions into five units of a special force so as to be equipped with nuclear missiles. American forces, it noted, had conducted a joint manœuvre with South Korean forces simulating a nuclear offensive near the 38th Parallel, which, the analysis found, was the largest military activity since the truce of 1953. The study cited Syngman Rhee's recent announcements on several occasions that 'the matter is not whether South Korea would accept US nuclear weapons but how soon these weapons can be deployed'.[33]

Given these indications of a US nuclear threat, Mao felt that nuclear weapons were becoming 'real tigers'. He called upon the whole nation to prepare for the worst outcome of a nuclear attack. In the spring of 1958, at the landmark Second Session of the Eighth Party Congress that sparked the Great Leap Forward, Mao pointed out that preparations were needed because 'the maniacs' might launch a war. If the atomic bomb was resorted to, he asserted, the duration of atomic war would be short, 'three instead of four years'. Mao stressed: 'We have no experience in atomic war. So, how many [people] will be killed cannot be known. The best outcome may be that only half of the population is left, and the second best may be only one-third.' He thus made it clear that the communes would be 'organized along military lines' so that 'the whole population would be citizen soldiers ready to cope with the imperialist aggressors'. The CCP Chairman maintained that the party should adopt an appropriate attitude toward nuclear threat:

We are afraid of atomic weapons and at the same time we are not afraid of them. . . . We do not fear them because they cannot fundamentally decide the outcome of a war; we fear them because they really are mass-destruction weapons. Therefore, we have to deal with [the atomic bomb] with a scientific attitude.[34]

To the Chinese leader, the possible American use of nuclear weapons may not have been 'an empty threat'. Tigers were capable of eating people. However, Mao was not sure of the extent to which Moscow would be willing to retaliate for a US nuclear strike against China, nor was he certain whether the Chinese people would be willing to sacrifice in face of the risk of massive destruction. He needed to reconsider how China could deal with the perceived US nuclear threat.

'We Must Build Our Own Bomb'

As a direct consequence of his concern about the US nuclear threat, Mao and other Chinese leaders decided to build China's own nuclear weapons early in

1955. There had been a concern that nuclear technology would be too complicated for the Chinese scientists to master and that building bombs was too expensive. It is interesting to note that some Western ban-the-bomb advocates had dismissed these concerns, urging the Chinese leaders not to be intimidated by the prospect of building atomic weapons. In October 1951, Nobel prize winner Frederic Joliot-Curie urged the Chinese radiochemist Yang Chengzhong, then in Paris, to see Mao upon his return to China. 'Please tell Chairman Mao Zedong,' he asked Yang, 'that he should oppose the atomic bomb, and he should own the atomic bomb. The atomic bomb is not so terrifying.' Joliot-Curie also stressed that the 'fundamental principles of the bomb had not been discovered by the Americans', and the Chinese could easily master the nuclear secret. Irene Joliot-Curie then gave Yang ten grams of radium salt standardized for radioactive emissions, because she wanted 'to support the Chinese people in their nuclear research'.[35]

Indeed, a number of Western-educated Chinese scientists returned during the early 1950s. Many of them had studied nuclear, high-energy, and experimental physics, and some were specialists in accelerator, computer, and vacuum technology, as well as radioactivity and geology. From America, England, and France, they brought back nuclear science literature and equipment for nuclear research of which most were on the US list of items embargoed against shipment to the PRC. More important, many of these scientists were inspired by the nationalist sentiment that China must develop its own nuclear weapons so that it would no longer be humiliated by others. Late in 1952, to lay the groundwork for nuclear research, these scientists drafted a first five-year plan, which called for construction of a nuclear laboratory and a reactor by 1957.[36]

Discoveries of uranium mineral in Guangxi province in 1954 were immediately brought to Mao's attention. He was very excited when Deputy Geology Minister Liu Jie explained to him and Zhou Enlai that uranium was the key material in nuclear fission and that with it, China could overcome a major obstacle in building its own atomic bomb. Mao asked to see a sample of uranium right away. While inspecting it with a detector, he commented: 'There are a lot of minerals [in China] which have yet to be found. We are very hopeful. [We must] look for them and we will find lots of uranium mines.' With rich mineral resources, he believed that 'our country is capable of building nuclear [weapons]'.[37]

Mao wanted to know more about nuclear bombs. Under his instruction, Zhou Enlai invited China's leading nuclear scientist Qian Sanqiang and geologist Li Siguang to a meeting in his office on 14 January 1955. Qian briefed Zhou on the technology of atomic bomb and China's nuclear research facilities. The two scientists also helped Zhou review the fundamentals of atomic reactors and nuclear weapons. At the end of this meeting, Zhou asked Qian and Li to prepare for a full-dress meeting with Chairman Mao and other CCP Politburo members. He also wanted them to bring a sample of uranium and prepare for a demonstration of nuclear fission. Zhou made it clear that Mao and other leaders were anxious to acquire some knowledge about atomic bombs.[38] The CCP Secretariat called an enlarged meeting to discuss the possibility of starting a nuclear-weapon programme on 15 January 1955. Mao presided over it and 'attentively listened to' Qian Sanqiang and Li Siguang's lectures. The conference room in Zhongnanhai became a classroom for introductory nuclear physics and uranium geology. With a sample of uranium on a table, Mao and other CCP leaders 'took turns playing with a Geiger counter to hear it click'. The CCP Chairman frequently asked questions and Zhou kept 'reminding the scientists to report in more detail'.[39]

After the scientists finished the lectures, Mao made an important comment:

during the past years we have been busy doing other things and there has not been enough time for us to pay attention to this matter [of nuclear weapons]. [We knew that] sooner or later, we would have had to pay attention to it. Now, it is time for us to pay attention to it. We can achieve success provided we put it on the order of the day.[40]

It was possible, he thought, for China to build its own bomb. 'Now we know,' he explained, 'that our country has uranium mineral and [we'll] find more mines in [our] further prospecting.' Moreover, he pointed out that 'we have trained a group of [nuclear] experts since the liberation and created necessary conditions for [nuclear] research.' Mao was confident that '[w]e possess the human and natural resources, and therefore every kind of miracle can be performed.' Then he invited all the attendees to dinner, where he toasted: 'Let's drink a toast to the development of our country's atomic energy cause!'[41]

Mao had considerable confidence in China's nuclear programme. In his view, the physics of the atomic nucleus, which was as simple as 'positive and negative electricity', merely proved the validity of the basic law of materialist dialectics (the division of a unity into mutually exclusive opposites). He praised a Japanese particle physicist, Sakata Shiyouchi, for applying the principle of dialectics to nuclear physics, and had *Hongqi*, CCP's official journal of communist theories, publish one of Sakata's articles. 'When one lectures on nuclear physics,' the CCP Chairman later pointed out, 'it will suffice to talk about the Sakata model: one needn't start from the theories of Bohr of the Danish school; otherwise you won't graduate even after ten years of study. Even Sakata uses dialectics—why don't you use it?' Mao, who finally met the Japanese physicist in 1956, claimed that he had never been intimidated by nuclear physics.[42]

While preparing for building the atomic bomb, the CCP leaders also began to pay attention to missile programmes. Through the Sino-American ambassadorial talks at Warsaw in 1955, Beijing had persuaded the Eisenhower administration to allow a group of Chinese scientists to return to China. Among them was Qian Xuesen, a Ph. D. from the California Institute of Technology, who had worked in the Jet Propulsion Laboratory. Shortly after his return in early 1956, Qian submitted to Zhou a written report, 'My Suggestions on Constructing National Defence'. He pointed out that 'developing missiles and developing atomic energy should be the two key projects in China's defence modernization'. He urged the CCP leadership to give priority to strategic missiles, the construction of nuclear fuel production plants, and the development of atomic bombs. These recommendations having been approved by Mao, Zhou presided over a Central Military Commission meeting in February at which Qian briefed the military leaders on why China should develop a strategic missile programme and how. Two months later, Mao and Zhou had the CCP Central Committee pass a resolution on developing and manufacturing strategic missiles. The Fifth Academy under the Ministry of National Defence, China's first missile research agency, was formed in October, with Qian being appointed as its director.[43]

Clearly, Mao had taken a new look at the role of nuclear weapons in international security and warfare. He appeared to have understood that the bomb was more important than conventional weapons in assuring China's security interests. Proclaiming to the enlarged Politburo meeting in April 1956 that China would build the atomic bomb and develop strategic missiles, Mao explicitly stressed that 'in today's world, if we don't want to be bullied by others, we should have atomic weapons by all means'. He insisted that China would give first priority to atomic bombs, missiles, long-range delivery systems and strategic bombers, and that 'this is an issue of strategic policy'.[44] Beijing's new emphasis on nuclear-energy research was immediately reflected in the state budget. Funds for science and technology rose from about $15 million in 1955 to about $100 million in 1956; the Chinese Academy of Sciences received three times as much money in 1957 as it had received in 1953, with a large portion going to purchase scientific literature from the West.[45]

Mao evidently showed considerable respect for the power of the atomic bomb he had already decided to acquire. He said in 1955 that the atomic bomb was not 'an invincible "magic weapon"'. However, the CCP leader recognized that militarily the United States had 'claws and fangs' that would definitely hurt the Chinese people. The task of the socialist states, in his view, was to remove the 'paper tiger's' claws 'step by step'.[46] China could have relied on Soviet nuclear protection. Khrushchev had invited the Chinese to attend the Warsaw Pact conference in 1955, and Mao had sent Peng Dehuai, then Minister of National Defence. Peng talked with Khrushchev twice in Moscow about co-ordinating military action between the two countries. At one meeting, Khrushchev lectured Peng on the strength of Soviet advanced weaponry, especially long-range strategic bombers and guided nuclear missiles, which, he stressed, could help the Chinese in defending China's coast if necessary. He also assured Peng that 'Russia's powerful Navy and Air Force in the Far East can be at Chinese disposal at any time'. The Soviet leader further claimed that the Warsaw Pact was not only for the defence of Europe but for East Asia as well, and that measures had to be taken to incorporate China into this defence system. With strong Sino-Soviet military co-operation in defending East Asia, Khrushchev believed, the United States would have to 'consider it twice' before attempting to risk a war against either China or the Soviet Union. Peng was very pleased with the offer, and presented a copy of 'China's Strategic and Military Planning in the Far East' to the Kremlin leader for Soviet consultation.[47]

Mao was also pleased with Khrushchev's offer. In November 1957, he asked Peng to lead another military mission to Moscow including almost all the top commanders of the Chinese Army, Navy, Air Force, Artillery Force, and Logistic Services. When Khrushchev met the Chinese generals, he reconfirmed his offer, and directed Marshall Georgii K. Zhukhov to discuss details of Sino-Soviet military co-operation.[48] Mao believed in 1957 that the military achievements of the Soviet Union had drastically lessened the threat of overt American aggression and the use of nuclear blackmail. His great enthusiasm stemmed from the key event of that year, the launching of the Soviet satellite, Sputnik I, in October. As he saw it, this event heralded a shift in the 'correlation of forces' and placed the United States in a paralysed position of strategic inferiority. In November, when he visited Moscow to celebrate the fortieth anniversary of communist victory in Russia, Mao addressed an audience of Chinese students at Moscow State University: 'The direction of the wind in the world has changed. . . . At present, it is not the West wind that prevails over the East wind but the East wind that prevails over the West wind.' On another occasion during his visit, Mao further pointed out that the year of 1957 constituted a 'new turning point', by which he meant that the 'socialist forces are overwhelmingly superior to the imperialist forces'.[49]

However, Mao soon found out that the Soviets were willing to extend a nuclear umbrella over China, but not to help the Chinese build an atomic bomb. Moscow had sent a group of geologists to China to prospect for uranium early in 1950 and on 20 January 1955, signed an agreement for a Sino-Soviet joint venture to mine uranium. In response to China's request, the Soviet leaders, late in April 1955, agreed to provide the Chinese technology and equipment to construct a high-water-moderated reactor and a cyclotron accelerator. They also promised to help the Chinese build a laboratory for nuclear research in August 1958. All these agreements, however, provided that Soviet nuclear technology would be 'for peaceful use' only.[50]

Nevertheless, the Chinese leaders wanted to acquire Soviet nuclear technology for military purposes. In September 1957, Marshall Nie Rongzhen, the Vice-Premier in charge of military and nuclear industries, led a mission to Moscow to procure Soviet assistance for building a Chinese bomb. Nie's trip brought about the signing of another Sino-Soviet protocol in October, in which the Soviets agreed to provide a training model of an atomic bomb and related equipment. But the Soviets deliberately left it open as to exactly what equipment would be delivered and when and how. When Nie pressed for a succinct answer, the Soviet leaders replied that 'we are not ready to discuss these issues and we won't be ready in the near future'.[51] In August 1958, Moscow did send a delegation to Beijing to make specific arrangements concerning the transformation of Soviet atomic technology. The Chinese leaders, however, found that 'the Soviets tried to find all possible excuses not to help us'. Although Moscow had dispatched, late in 1957, 102 Soviet missile specialists and two Soviet P-2 short-ranged ground-to-ground missiles, it never fulfilled its promise regarding atomic bomb technology and equipment.[52]

Rather than helping the Chinese build an atomic bomb, Moscow wanted to incorporate China's coastal defence into its East Asian defence system. On 18 April 1958, in a letter to Peng Dehuai, Marshal Radion I. Malinovskii, Soviet Minister of Defence, suggested 'jointly' building a powerful long-wave radio station linking the Chinese Navy with the Soviet Navy in East Asia. Malinovskii made it clear that the Soviet Union would provide the technology and most of the money needed.[53] Shortly after, Soviet Ambassador to Beijing Pavel F. Iudin also proposed on behalf of Khrushchev that the USSR would like to establish a joint fleet of nuclear-powered submarines with China 'for a common defence in the Far East'. Iudin explained that Russia's coastal conditions were not appropriate for the Soviet Navy's newly developed submarines, and that China had a long coast and better 'harbour conditions for our advanced [nuclear] submarines to demonstrate their strength'.[54] Moscow's suggestion made the Chinese leaders suspect that Russia might be seeking to control China militarily in the long run. Mao in particular wanted to make sure that China would have complete authority over both the radio station and the joint submarine fleet.

On 12 June, he directed Peng to cable Malinovskii stressing that China welcomed the Soviet offers but insisting that China would only accept Russia's technological assistance.[55] At a 22 July meeting with Iudin, Mao explicitly stated that 'the Soviet Union's request for building a joint [nuclear] submarine fleet is a political issue involving China's autonomy.' He lectured the Soviet ambassador: 'If you want to talk about political conditions [for assisting us in building the fleet], we will never accept [your offer]. . . . You may accuse me of being nationalist, but I then can accuse you of bringing Russia's nationalism over to China's coast.'[56]

This dispute was not settled until Khrushchev's visit to Beijing on 31 July. The Soviet leader accommodated the CCP's concerns by confirming that the Soviet Union would only provide loans and technology for building the radio station, which China would completely own. Khrushchev also explained to Mao that Moscow never had the intention of establishing a joint nuclear submarine fleet in China, and that Iudin had passed the wrong message thus resulting in the 'misunderstandings'.[57]

Mutual suspicion in the Sino-Soviet relationship nevertheless continued. When Beijing began another massive bombardment on Jinmen and Mazu offshore islands on 23 August 1958, the Kremlin was shocked at the CCP's bold action. Khrushchev immediately sent Andrei A. Gromyko to Beijing. Arriving on 6 September, the Soviet Minister of Foreign Affairs explicitly expressed Moscow's concern that China's military action might trigger off a general conflict between Russia and America in East Asia. Gromyko later recalled that while discussing a possible US attack on China as a result of mounting tensions in the Taiwan Strait, Mao had told him that the Chinese would react according to the principle of 'blade against blade', Chinese forces would evacuate the coastline and let American forces enter China's heartland; once American forces were deep within Chinese territory, the Soviet Union should then help the Chinese retaliate 'with all the possible means'. Gromyko told Mao that 'the scenario of war described by you cannot meet a positive response by us'. But according to recently available Chinese sources, Mao and Zhou made it clear to Gromyko: (a) that China's bombardment of Jinmen and Mazu was intended mainly to 'punish the KMT' and 'pressure the US not to pursue a "two-Chinas" policy'; (b) that China had no intention of attacking Taiwan; and (c) that China would be fully responsible for the Taiwan problem, and if it 'came out disastrously', China would bear it alone and would not 'pull the Soviet Union into the water'.[58]

Rather unexpectedly to the Chinese leaders, Khrushchev then acted on his own initiative. On 7 September, he addressed a letter to Eisenhower, directly warning that an attack on China would mean an attack on the Soviet Union, and clearly stating that any US nuclear strike on China's mainland would result in Soviet nuclear retaliation on the 'once formidable surface warships of the US Navy with right types of rockets'. The Soviet leader also urged Washington to go back to the negotiating table.[59] This stated Soviet policy differed significantly from Moscow's stand prior to the crisis. There is as yet no evidence from the Chinese as to why the Kremlin did this. A few days later, Khrushchev called in Chinese Ambassador Liu Xiao to talk about 'how the Soviet Union can further help China'. Once again, the Soviet leader showed his concern that the US brinkmanship policy in the Taiwan Strait might lead to a larger—probably nuclear—conflict in East Asia. He repeatedly urged Liu to report back to Beijing that 'the Soviet Politburo has already decided to strengthen the Soviet Air Force in the Far East for the purpose of effectively deterring the US-KMT naval forces from attacking China'.[60]

Moscow explicitly expressed its intention to extend Soviet nuclear deterrence over the Taiwan Strait. But in a personal letter to Khrushchev two weeks later, Mao firmly rejected Khrushchev's offer. He told the Soviet leader that the Taiwan Strait situation was well under control. He also claimed that the USA was not ready to attack China with nuclear weapons, and that even if it was, China had already fully prepared and would not appeal for any Soviet assistance. When Ambassador Liu presented Mao's letter to Khrushchev, the Soviet leader responded that 'the Chinese comrades may know better than we do on the Taiwan Strait situation'.[61]

Nevertheless, the Mao–Khrushchev dispute over the Taiwan Strait crisis paved the way for an open Sino-Soviet split. What particularly bothered Khrushchev, he wrote in his memoirs, were Mao's views on nuclear weapons. The Soviet leader found 'incredible' the CCP Chairman's slogan that 'the atomic bomb itself was a paper tiger'.[62] In his letter to Mao on 20 June 1959, Khrushchev informed the Chinese leader that the Soviet government had decided to postpone the delivery of a training model of an atomic bomb and atomic technology to China. Meanwhile, many Soviet nuclear scientists left China 'for vacation'.[63]

Khrushchev stopped in Beijing on his way back from his visit of the United States in September 1959; and on 2 October, Mao had a more than seven-hour talk with the Soviet leader. They fiercely attacked each other's policies regarding nuclear weapons and the American threat. Khrushchev made it clear that if China insisted on its 'bold and risky' course, the Soviet Union would offer no protection or assistance. Mao firmly rejected the Soviet leader's position on the grounds that China would never tolerate Moscow's 'imperious and despotic attitude'. As a result, the Soviet Union tore up the agreement of October 1957 to assist the Chinese in developing the atomic bomb, and withdrew all the Soviet military and technological advisers from China in July and August of 1960.[64] Soviet unwillingness to help the Chinese build an atomic bomb had a chilly effect on Mao. He had greater reason to suspect Soviet willingness to extend a nuclear protection over China. More importantly, he was worried that China's reliance on a Soviet nuclear 'umbrella' would lead to a Soviet military control of China in the future. Lacking confidence in Soviet extended deterrence, he was more anxious late in the 1950s than before to acquire a Chinese bomb.

'We Must Break the Nuclear Monopoly of the Superpowers'

In retrospect, Khrushchev overreacted to Mao's views on the atomic bomb and American power. The CCP Chairman did not deny that the 'unprecedented concentration of [US] nuclear weapons' in the Taiwan Strait had restricted China's freedom of action. He later explained his caution in dealing with the second Strait crisis by saying that those critics who wondered why China did not attack Taiwan did not 'understand the paper tiger [the atomic bomb] problem'.[65] On 1 December 1958, at a meeting of the Politburo of the CCP Central Committee held in Wuchang, Mao argued that just as there was not a single thing in the world without a dual nature (this was the law of unity of opposites), so imperialism and all reactionaries had a dual nature—they

were real tigers and paper tigers at the same time. . . . The reactionary, backward, decaying classes retained this dual nature even in their last life-and-death struggles against the people. On the one hand, they were real tigers; they ate people, ate people by the millions and tens of millions. . . . But in the end they changed into paper tigers, dead tigers, bean-curd tigers. These are historical facts.

Nuclear weapons, to Mao, were no exception. 'In essence, from a long-term point of view, from a strategic point of view,' he argued, '[they] must be seen for what they are—paper tigers. On this we should build our strategic thinking. On the other hand, they are also living tigers, iron tigers, real tigers which can eat people. On this we should build our tactical thinking.'[66]

Recognizing the atomic bomb's threat to China, Mao had set the nation on a firm course to acquire nuclear weapons: 'If we are not to be bullied in the present-day world, we cannot do without the bomb. Then what is to be done? One reliable way is to cut military and administrative expenditures down to appropriate proportions [in order to build nuclear weapons].'[67] In June 1958, he set ten years as a deadline. 'Let us work on atomic bombs and nuclear bombs,' he urged other CCP leaders, 'Ten years, I think, should be quite enough.'[68]

At a conference of the Central Military Commission held from 27 May to 22 July 1958, Mao supervised the production of 'The Guidelines for Developing Nuclear Weapons', which further established the main objectives of acquiring the atomic bomb as follows:

1. Our country is developing nuclear weapons in order to warn our enemies against making war on us, not in order to use nuclear weapons to attack them.

2. The main reason for us to develop nuclear weapons is to defend peace, save mankind from a nuclear holocaust, and reach an agreement on nuclear disarmament and the complete abolition of nuclear weapons.

3. To this end, we have to concentrate our energies on developing nuclear and thermonuclear warheads with high yields and long-range delivery vehicles. For the time being we have no intention of developing tactical nuclear weapons.

4. In the process of developing nuclear weapons, we should not imitate other countries. Instead, our objective should be to take steps to 'catch up with and keep pace with the advanced world' and to 'proceed on all phases [of the nuclear programme] simultaneously'.

5. In order to achieve success rapidly in developing nuclear weapons, we must concentrate human, material, and financial resources. . . . Any other projects for our country's reconstruction will have to take second place to the development of nuclear weapons.[69]

The break with the Soviets and consequently the withdrawal of all the Soviet advisers made Mao assign even higher priority to building nuclear weapons. Late in 1959, the CCP Chairman urged other Chinese leaders to 'ignore Khrushchev's suggestion that China need not build its own nuclear bomb'.[70] At the enlarged meeting of the Politburo in January 1960, he directed the approval of an emergency decision on developing the atomic bomb without Soviet aid. He called for solving the key technical problems in three years, building the bomb in five years, and attaining 'appropriate [nuclear weapons] reserves' in eight years.[71] Meeting with Vice-Premier Li Fuchun on 18 July, Mao instructed that 'we must make up our minds to develop sophisticated [nuclear] technology'. He pointed out that 'it is perfectly all right that Khrushchev won't offer us help; otherwise, it would be too costly to pay his debt.' He was determined that 'we must not relax our efforts or discontinue [the sophisticated defence projects].'[72] Among these projects was the construction of nuclear submarines and guided missiles. The CCP Chairman proclaimed at one point that 'China is determined to develop nuclear weapons even if it would take us ten thousand years.'[73]

Indeed, the CCP leadership came to believe that the future of the nuclear programme would determine the destiny of the state. At a special Politburo meeting in the summer of 1961, Chen Yi, then Vice-Premier and the Minister of Foreign Affairs, asserted that China should continue the development of nuclear weapons at any cost, 'even if the Chinese people have to pawn their trousers for this purpose'. He stressed that 'as China's minister of foreign affairs, at present I still do not have an adequate back-up. If we succeed in producing the atomic bomb and guided missiles, then I can straighten my back.' Mao concurred in Chen's argument.[74] Urging the scientists to speed up the nuclear research, Mao instructed:

We are stronger than before and will be stronger in the future. We will have not only more planes and artillery but atomic bombs as well. If we are not to be bullied in this present-day world, we cannot do without the bomb. It is really time for China to develop an atomic energy programme. We possess the [necessary] natural and human resources. We also have laid a certain foundation of scientific research. We will undoubtedly achieve success in speeding the atomic energy programme if we pay close attention to it.[75]

Clearly, Mao had adopted the belief, as a China specialist put it, that 'China could not do without the bomb'.[76]

Mao came to realize that nuclear weapons placed the USA and the USSR in a privileged position in international affairs. In a letter to Khrushchev on 6 June 1963, the CCP Chairman argued that the Soviet Union aimed at 'maintaining dominance over other socialist states' by providing them nuclear protection but not nuclear technology. 'That is why you want to develop [nuclear weapons] alone and prohibit other brother states from building [the bomb], . . . so that all the [socialist states] would obey you and you control [us] all.' He declared: 'The Chinese people will never accept the privileged position of one or two superpowers because of their monopoly of the nuclear weapons in today's world.'[77]

When the CCP Chairman was informed by Zhou Enlai on the night of 16 October 1964 of China's first successful test of an atomic bomb, he directed Zhou to 'verify once again whether it really was a nuclear explosion so as to convince the foreigners!' The scientists on the research site immediately confirmed that there had indeed been a nuclear detonation. Mao then asked Zhou to release the 'good news' to the world right away. So the whole world heard from *Radio Beijing* that 'China exploded an atomic bomb at 15.00 hours on 16 October 1964, thereby successfully carrying out its first nuclear test.' A message of congratulation from the CCP central leadership—approved by Mao— was also broadcast in Beijing, proclaiming:

This is a major achievement of the Chinese people in their struggle to strengthen their national defence and oppose the US imperialist policy of nuclear blackmail and nuclear threat. To defend oneself is the inalienable right of every sovereign state. To safeguard world peace is the common task of all peace-loving countries. China cannot remain idle in the face of the ever-increasing nuclear threats from the United States. China is conducting nuclear tests and developing nuclear weapons under compulsion.

Although the message of congratulation repeated Mao's famous statement that 'the atomic bomb is a paper tiger', it stressed that 'China's aim is to break the nuclear monopoly of the nuclear powers, . . . China's success in making nuclear weapons is a great encouragement to the revolutionary people of the world in their struggles and a great contribution to the cause of defending world peace.'[78]

Rather than acquiring just a nuclear 'have' status, Beijing wanted to become a major nuclear power. Meeting with the State Planning Commission in January 1965, Mao pointed out that 'we must have both atomic and hydrogen bombs'. In particular, he ordered a rapid progress in 'breaking through the technology of the hydrogen bomb'.[79] The CCP Chairman was satisfied when he heard from Zhou Enlai in February that China's nuclear tests during 1965–7 would focus on developing a delivery system for the atomic bomb, nuclear power plants for submarines, and a hydrogen bomb. He approved a suggestion of the nuclear scientists that China explode its first hydrogen bomb in 1968.[80] When China succeeded in its first nuclear missile test on 27 October 1966, Mao proudly proclaimed: 'Who says we Chinese can't develop nuclear missiles? Now we have done it, haven't we?'[81] China's first successful explosion of a hydrogen bomb on 17 June 1967, made Mao even more proud, because 'China's nuclear success has evoked worldwide repercussions and our country is recognized as an advanced nuclear power in the world.'[82]

China also wanted to encourage other countries to build atomic weapons. When asked at a press conference on 29 September 1965, whether China would share nuclear technology with other developing countries, Minister of Foreign Affairs Chen Yi referred to Mao's statement that 'China sincerely wishes that the Asian and African countries would be capable of developing their own atomic bomb, [because] the more countries can build the bomb the better.' What Chairman Mao meant, Chen explained, was that 'as soon as the small and weak nations acquire their own atomic weapons, the nuclear monopoly would be broken, the one or two superpowers could no longer wave nuclear weapons to blackmail [us], and the nuclear overlords could not but sob out their grievances in the corner [of the world].'[83]

Mao understood that China's acquisition of nuclear weapons was aimed primarily at enhancing national security through deterrence. Deterrence strategy was not alien to him. The ancient Chinese strategist Sun Tzu had pointed out that 'attacking the mind is superior to engaging in diplomatic negotiations; engaging in diplomatic negotiations is superior to fighting field operations; and fighting field operations is superior to attacking fortifications'.[84] Mao seemed to have adopted the notion that nuclear weapons, with their tremendous psychological impact, were indispensable for strategic deterrence, that is, to deter the enemies from using the nuclear bomb. He had long held that a balance must exist between maintaining sizeable regular forces to deter or repel conventional attack and building a small nuclear capability to deter nuclear attack.[85] This became a major theme that Mao stressed over and again through the 1960s. At different points, he stated that China's nuclear weapons 'will not be numerous even if we succeed [in the strategic weapons programme]', that 'the success [of our strategic weapons programme] will boost our courage and scare others', and that 'in any case, we won't build more atomic bombs and missiles than others'. More important was his statement in the mid-1960s that China would adhere to the principle of 'building a few [nuclear weapons] with small quantity but high quality [*you yidian, shao yidian, hao yidian* in Chinese]'.[86] Mao's instructions became Beijing's official policies toward nuclear weapons in the 1960s and 1970s, and most of them remain in effect to this day.

Mao's perception of the atomic bomb was an interesting case of how Western military technology challenged Chinese strategic thinking. The CCP Chairman originally saw a new China's struggle for security in terms of conventional warfare and in 1946 satirized the atomic bomb as a 'paper tiger'. His initial reaction to the bomb was consistent with his belief that 'political power grows out of the barrel of a gun'. Mao had found it difficult to understand why the imperialists would venture to use nuclear weapons in a war if they wanted to dominate other nations, because a massively destructive weapon such as the bomb would not serve the purpose of acquiring political control, but would instead destroy that which was to be controlled. As someone well versed in oriental strategic culture, Mao originally found it hard to understand the bomb's value. The use of nuclear weapons in modern warfare, he had thought, would be amoral, or in Chinese terms, offensive to *dao* or morality; anyone who offended *dao* would lose popular support and inevitably lose political control. He thus maintained that the bomb had no political utility. Moreover, Mao had difficulty accepting that advanced military technology would prevail over the human factors in determining victory or defeat. No matter how advanced they would be, he insisted, weapons had to be operated by men; the development of nuclear weapons did not invalidate this logic.

Nevertheless, Mao gradually changed his position regarding the atomic bomb. Stressing the bomb's deterrent value, he conceded that 'China cannot do without it' in international relations. Several factors contributed to Mao's 'nuclear revolution'. There can be little doubt that frequent US nuclear threats against China forced Mao to reconsider how atomic weapons had transformed modern warfare and international relations. Soviet pressures, especially from Khrushchev, who seemed to have acquired a more solid understanding of the bomb than Mao, caused the CCP Chairman to take the nuclear threat more seriously. More important than this, though, was pressure from other Chinese leaders such as Zhou Enlai, Chen Yi, and Nie Rongzhen, who kept pushing Mao to pay more attention to nuclear-weapon programmes. Western and Russian educated scientists such as Qian Sanqiang and Qian Xuesen broadened Mao's knowledge and led the CCP Chairman to a more 'scientific' understanding of nuclear weapons. With China's development of modern nuclear bombs and missiles, Mao seemed to have recast the struggle for security into one with a military-technical emphasis on assured nuclear destruction to ensure deterrence. He constantly cautioned against the danger of 'real tigers' throughout the Cold War years, and the Chinese government became more and more cautious in its attempts to resolve conflicts by military means. Also, realizing that nuclear weapons would grant his regime political prestige, both at home and outside, Mao was even more determined to speed up China's nuclear weapons programmes. Consequently, the CCP Chairman's thinking on the atomic bomb came to dominate China's defence policy and the changes in Mao's views brought about the policy changes which turned China into a major nuclear power.

Mao's 'nuclear revolution' was indeed of significance in connection with the question of how the development of nuclear weapons has shaped post-World War II international relations. Nuclear weapons caused him to change his strategic thinking in several aspects. First, regarding power, Mao seemed to have abandoned the Chinese calculus of strength. Traditional Chinese strategists thought that a strong nation must have a vast land, huge population, abundant resources, and troops of high morale. Only such a nation could afford to fight a protracted war or a war of attrition for ultimate victory. The massive destructiveness of the atomic bomb, however, made these strategic assets irrelevant. Nuclear weapons and advanced technology became the most important indicator of one's war-fighting capability. Deviating from his 'people's war' strategy, Mao came to believe by the mid-1950s that China would not be respected as a major power without the nuclear bomb.

Second, nuclear weapons made the Chinese leaders redefine China's security interests. Chinese northern and western land borders, given the mountainous terrain, uninhabited desert, and the oldest defence system, the Great Wall, were historically safer than the southern and eastern coastline. Mao inherited this tradition and, indeed, placed a great emphasis on coastal defence through the 1950s. Nuclear weapons, especially with sophisticated delivery systems, challenged this Chinese tradition. Suddenly, land borders, heartland, and coast all became vulnerable. Mao had to worry at least as much about the Soviet threat from the north as the American threat from the east and south-east throughout the 1960s and 1970s.

Third, Mao tended to manage crises differently because of the advent of nuclear weapons. The Chinese understanding of crisis as both danger and opportunity taught that short-term belligerency or initiating an offensive action were the best ways to prevent potential danger. By doing this, one could demonstrate one's strength and resolve before one was invaded. Mao applied this principle in Korea, Indo-China, and the first Taiwan Strait crisis. He soon realized, however, that to initiate a crisis against a nuclear power would entail incalculable and uncontrollable risks. He exercised a great deal of caution when China was faced with the American challenge in Vietnam and the Soviet threat from the northern border during the late 1960s. The fear of nuclear retaliation against China haunted Mao and the Chinese people during the late 1960s and early 1970s, when the CCP Chairman mobilized the entire nation 'to dig tunnels deep, store grains everywhere, and never seek hegemony [*shen wa dong guang ji liang bu cheng ba* in Chinese]'.[87]

Finally, nuclear weapons made Mao reappraise the traditional value of military alliances. What made an ally trustworthy, he thought, were common interests in national security. This was why he vigorously sought a military alliance treaty with the Soviet Union right after the People's Republic was founded in October 1949. He believed, in particular, that China needed Soviet nuclear protection. However, it did not take him too long to find out that Soviet extended deterrence was not credible and thus, the Sino-Soviet alliance was not reliable. Having been bothered by Stalin's caution during the Korean War and Khrushchev's fear of nuclear war with the USA, he came to believe that no Soviet leader would be willing to risk nuclear retaliation against the Soviet Union in order to protect China. Rather than relying on an untrustworthy ally, Mao—like Charles de Gaulle in France—was determined to build his own bomb. Cultural differences may have caused misunderstanding, miscalculation, and consequently conflict, but the bomb seems to have bridged the gulf between the nuclear powers and the nuclear have-nots, or at least provided an incentive for policy-makers to seek solutions to these differences. Nuclear threats—for both deterrence and compellance—became a universal language in Cold War international relations.

10

Charles de Gaulle and the Nuclear Revolution

PHILIP H. GORDON

C HARLES de GAULLE was among those post-war leaders whose views about the utility of military force changed with the advent of atomic weapons. De Gaulle concluded that nuclear weapons would tend to produce caution—as well as collusion—among nervous nuclear powers; that the bomb would dissuade an aggressive state from threatening a nuclear-capable state; that the existence of two nuclear superpowers exacerbated the fissiparous tendencies of a bipolar world; and, not least important, that France itself could derive manifold benefits from possessing the bomb. A case-study of de Gaulle's thinking about nuclear weapons, then, helps support the hypothesis that nuclear weapons have indeed changed the character of international relations, and that they have thereby had great significance in the post-war world.

I. The Impact of the Bomb on International Relations

Gaullist Thinking and the Nuclear World

In order to understand how nuclear weapons may have changed de Gaulle's thinking about the uses of military force, we must first briefly recall what his thinking was. And it should be made clear from the start that Charles de Gaulle—much more than the average middle-ranking French officer of the interwar period—already had well-developed conceptions of history, diplomacy, and statecraft by the time he was confronted with the nuclear age. The son of a history teacher, de Gaulle read voraciously as a boy and young man—Jacques Bainville, Henri Bergson, Friederich Nietzsche, Maurice Barrès—and was steeped in conservative French historical and philosophical traditions. He was chosen for his sense of history and leadership to lecture at the Ecole de Guerre in the 1920s, and in the following decade wrote several books on war, politics, and international relations. De Gaulle was far from a narrow-minded soldier trained to execute but not reflect.

De Gaulle's early world-view was one later scholars would have described as a brand of 'realism': nation-states were the pillars on which the international system was built; those nation-states could form temporary alliances but ultimately could not trust one another; power was the basis of international politics; states were ambitious but often cloaked their ambitions in ideology; morals had little place in international affairs; the world was inevitably hostile and involved human and national competition. It goes without saying that for de Gaulle—a soldier since his teens, a tank commander, and an army general—military force was a viable tool of statecraft. Countries had vital national interests to protect in a dangerous and anarchic international system, and it was often necessary—and sometimes even noble—to bear arms to protect them. Indeed, for de Gaulle, military genius and national achievement went together: 'no statesman had ever attained glory without having been gilded with the lustre of national defence.'[1]

It is important to note that de Gaulle's vision of nations, competition, and armed struggle came not merely from reading Machiavelli or Hobbes, but rather from his own personal experience. By the time he was 24, in 1914, de Gaulle had watched the blatant competition of European states for power, the emergence of two rigid alliance systems, and the outbreak of World War I. During the interwar period, he saw how Anglo-Saxon 'guarantees' had been worthless—not only to France in the 1936 Rhineland affair but later to Czechoslovakia at Munich—and he watched the Germans build the power that would eventually crush the isolated France. When war did come in 1939, de Gaulle was not surprised to see that the Americans would wait two years before joining the fight for democracy in Europe—and this only after the United States itself was attacked by Japan. France would have to stand up for itself in war and in peace, and it could count on no one but itself for survival. De Gaulle's own early experiences simply confirmed what his intellectual bias had already led him to believe: that nations act according to their interests, and that this was never more true than during time of war.

By the time the nuclear age dawned in 1945, then, Charles de Gaulle already had a very particular set of beliefs about nation-states, military force, and international relations. How did the invention and deployment of nuclear weapons alter this set of beliefs? Did the existence of the bomb influence de Gaulle's foreign policy? Was France ever deterred by another country's nuclear weapons, and did France ever deter anyone else? Such questions are difficult to 'test', for two reasons. First, the France of the Gaullist years had no overriding claims that might have brought it into military conflict with one of the nuclear powers. To be sure, France took exception to Soviet behaviour in Eastern Europe and the Third World, vociferously opposed the exercise of American 'hegemony', and clashed with the United Kingdom over the Common Market. But none of these issues was ever great enough to lead to potential military actions by France. Second, de Gaulle was never in a position to use, or to threaten to use, nuclear weapons. During the years of colonial conflicts in Indo-China, Algeria, and Suez (when French nuclear threats might have been conceivable), France had no deliverable atomic bombs, and by the time it became an operational nuclear power—in 1964 with the delivery of the first Mirage IV bombers—all those conflicts were over. France's nuclear deterrent throughout the 1960s was an 'existential' one, and France's existence, happily, was never in question. Thus, unlike in the cases of Truman, Eisenhower, Stalin, or Khrushchev, we have no direct evidence that might help us determine how de Gaulle would (or would not) have used nuclear arms or threats, or how his own actions might have been deterred by the nuclear threats of others.

This does not mean, however, that we have no way of assessing the atomic bomb's impact on de Gaulle. Instead, it means that in order to understand this impact we must look not only at the particular French experience with nuclear weapons (explored in part 2 of this essay) but also at how de Gaulle expected other nuclear powers—the United States and the Soviet Union—to behave. And here we have a wealth of rhetoric, action, policy, and analysis that dates back to the very beginning of the nuclear age.

The 'Immense Consequences' of Hiroshima

Charles de Gaulle first learned of the existence of the 'apocalyptic work' that would produce nuclear weapons during a visit to Ottawa, Canada on 11 July 1944. Excluded by the 'Anglo-Saxons' from any information regarding the top secret Manhattan Project, the French leader only became aware of that effort when three French scientists—Pierre Auger, Bertrand Goldschmidt, and Jules Guéron (who were working on plutonium with the Canadians at the time)— took it upon themselves to 'inform the General of the importance of the project'. The Frenchmen wanted de Gaulle to be aware of 'the considerable advantage that possession of the new weapon would represent for the United States'.[2] The General 'understood very well' what his compatriots were suggesting and, following their advice, got in touch with France's leading physicist, Frédéric Joliot-Curie, after returning to Paris.[3] Obviously, however, occupied France was in no position to do much of anything in this great matter, and with the liberation of Paris set to take place within a month it is safe to presume that the leader of the Free French had other things on his mind.

The real message that got through to de Gaulle about nuclear arms, of course, took place not in Canada in 1944 but in Japan in 1945, and his first public comment about the nuclear era came on 11 August, two days after the Nagasaki bomb.[4] In a speech primarily focused on France's own efforts of national renewal, de Gaulle noted that 'the frightful explosion of atomic bombs suddenly demonstrates the immense forces that can be unleashed onto the world, either for destruction, or for the good of humanity . . .'[5] The observation, if perfectly accurate, is relatively unoriginal and very much like other comments of the time, except perhaps in one respect: already, de Gaulle was suggesting that the forces released by these weapons might not only be used for 'destruction', but also for 'good'. It would be interesting to know whether by this de Gaulle was referring to their capacity to end a tragic war sooner—as they had just done—or to the prospect that the bomb might be so destructive, so 'frightful', that it would deter aggression in the first place. Because de Gaulle makes a clear distinction between using the bomb for 'destruction' and using it 'for the good of humanity', the hypothesis that de Gaulle was an early believer in nuclear deterrence cannot be excluded. There is, however, little other evidence to support this view.

Several months after Hiroshima and Nagasaki, de Gaulle had more to say about the 'immense consequences' of the atomic bomb. In a press conference on 12 October 1945 he commented:

In the end this bomb was built by our allies, and it is true that as a government, as France, we had nothing to do with it. What can I say, a number of things have been handled without our being present. These were not always the best handled of things. As for the atomic bomb, we have time. I am not convinced that atomic bombs will have to be used in this world in the near future. In any event, the French government is fully aware of this question which is very grave for the entire world and whose consequences are obviously immense. This bomb shortened the war. For the time being we must recognize this merit. We must now see to it that it does not become a global cataclysm.[6]

Several observations emerge from a close reading of this short text. First, it should not be surprising that Charles de Gaulle, a patriot who had spent the past five years battling both enemies and allies on a single-minded mission to prevent the disappearance of his country, should discuss the atomic bomb first in terms of France's own role. That the Anglo-Saxons pursued this grand enterprise without France (though not without the help of French scientists!), and that they would continue to refuse to share their knowledge and responsibility with de Gaulle, was perfectly consistent with the General's wartime (and pre-war) experience. The leader of the Provisional French Government had been frozen out of Yalta and Potsdam, and he was not surprised to be likewise excluded from this latest great event.[7]

Second, de Gaulle seems to have recognized not only the immense but also the paradoxical consequences of the new weapon. The nuclear question was both 'very grave' and at the same time the bomb was worthy of 'merit'. Nuclear weapons were capable of shortening—and perhaps deterring—a long, bloody war, but at the same time they could cause unprecedented destruction. It was the same point de Gaulle had referred to in his remarks about 'the good of humanity' on 11 August.

Finally, and more important where we are concerned, is de Gaulle's comment, 'As for the bomb, we have time.' While far from an outright assertion that France, too, would be heading down the path to atomic power—an absurd suggestion given the circumstances of late 1945—this was an obvious reflection for Charles de Gaulle to make; the man who had written about the French army in terms of cycles going back to the Merovingians was in no hurry, but he was already thinking of France's own place along this new frontier of military affairs. For the memorialist who would also later write that 'France is not really herself unless she is in the front rank', it went without saying that if other countries would have these extraordinary weapons, so, eventually, would France.[8]

Indeed, just a few days after this press conference, de Gaulle made a decision that would later prove to have been a key step in the creation of France's own *force de frappe*: on 18 October 1945 he founded the Commissariat à l'Energie Atomique (CEA). This new body, to be sure, was designed to study atomic energy for civilian use, and no specific plans whatever were made to work on a bomb: it would be wrong to call the founding of the CEA an unambiguous decision to produce atomic weapons.[9] Still, given de Gaulle's preoccupation with 'rank', his initial conclusions about the bomb's importance and his tendency to think about the long-term ('as for the bomb, we have time'), it seems certain that the door to nuclear weapons was meant to be left open. Indeed, the CEA's unique statute not only specifically mentioned 'national defence' as one of its areas of competence, but also gave it complete administrative and financial autonomy to free it from bureaucratic interference.[10] In addition, archives reveal that a 27 October letter written by Raoul Dautry, the CEA's main administrator, refers to 'the atomic bomb', but that 'bomb' is scratched out and replaced by 'energy'.[11] It is likely that already when he founded the CEA in 1945, an eventual military role for French nuclear energy was not far from de Gaulle's mind.[12]

What can we conclude about de Gaulle and the bomb from this early evidence? Did the General believe from the very beginning that military force would lose some of its former utility, and that international relations would forever be changed? It would not be surprising, of course, if de Gaulle—the strategist who had made his name in the first place by presciently analysing the impact of new weapons—did indeed understand a great deal about the nuclear revolution from the start. The General was certainly enough of an intellectual to comprehend the dialectic of fear that would come to replace the dialectic of force, and he was certainly flexible and pragmatic enough to accept that the old ways of warfare he had learned might irrevocably be changed. As a national leader—and as a Catholic—he was also certainly sensitive to the power that moral force and public opinion could have on a leader's willingness to wreak such biblical destruction. In short, de Gaulle had all of the personal characteristics—foresight, flexibility, intellect, and sensitivity—to be capable of understanding the potential impact of the nuclear revolution sooner and more fully than most.

But the evidence we have from 1945 is not enough to make such a case definitively. Clearly, de Gaulle recognized right away that the bomb would have 'immense consequences', and he—who had so fiercely criticized the French military's tendency to 'fight the last war'—was certainly not, this time, going to be caught doing the same thing.[13] At no time did de Gaulle—unlike a number of other military leaders of his time—think of the bomb as 'just another weapon'.[14] But as prescient and sensitive as de Gaulle was in 1945, there is no compelling evidence that he was immediately prepared to revise his views about military force and international relations. Indeed, if we follow de Gaulle's 'nuclear learning process' into the next two decades, we are able to see that he continued for a time to believe in the continuation of past patterns of great-power conflict, war, and behaviour before finally coming to the conclusion that the development of the bomb would significantly change those patterns. De Gaulle was a precocious nuclear student in 1945, but he still had more to 'learn'.[15]

Reaching Conclusions about the Bomb

If the de Gaulle of 1945 was not yet convinced that nuclear weapons had changed the world, when does he come to such a conclusion? When and why does he fully come to believe—as he asserted in 1964—that the bomb 'has opened a completely new phase in the history of our universe'?[16] A look at Gaullist thinking from the 1940s into the 1950s and 1960s shows how de Gaulle's views of the nuclear revolution developed with time, technology, and nuclear proliferation to the point where he had become one of the world's most convinced believers in the power of the atomic bomb.

From 1945 to 1949, of course, the United States had a nuclear monopoly, and could threaten to use nuclear weapons without having to worry about a nuclear response. Logic would suggest that, under these circumstances, the United States was in a position to deter whatever it wished. If, for example, the Soviet Union were to threaten to invade Western Europe as Germany had several years before, the United States would be in a position to stop this invasion with much greater ease than the last time: the spectre of Hiroshima was still strong, and it should have been enough to keep the Red Army in place.

Yet de Gaulle, during these years, was consistently pessimistic about war in Europe. As the leader of the anti-communist Rassemblement pour la France (RPF) that he founded in 1947, the General regularly warned against the possibility—one might even say the *likelihood*—of a coming war.[17] The menacing Soviet bloc of 'almost 400 million men' had already imposed its 'totalitarian dictatorship' on two-thirds of Europe, and now stood poised only 'two stages of the Tour de France' away from France.[18] 'Of course,' he told Claude Mauriac later that year, 'we will be going to war'.[19] By the time of the Soviet coup in Czechoslovakia and blockade of Berlin in 1948, and particularly after the June 1950 launching of war in Korea—which de Gaulle saw as a mere prelude of what was to come in Europe—the General's pessimism had become acute: 'The tempest is approaching . . .' he warned in August 1950. 'The Korean war is the preliminary sign. The whole world knows that one day or another the aggression could be unfurled on Europe and on France.'[20] Three months later, de Gaulle told Georges Pompidou that 'war is encroaching and will not stop . . . France will not recover in time [and] will be invaded, bombarded. [Her leaders will be] hung, because the communists are tough, and the people will have suffered.'[21] Thus, de Gaulle's statements of these years—both public and private—hardly suggest the reassurance of someone convinced that nuclear weapons were 'frightful' enough to deter the use of military force.[22]

Why, though, did the man who later argued that his own country could deter the Soviets with a small nuclear force expect war when in this case the Americans still had a monopoly on the bomb? Why did France have to 'renovate its forces' and 'prepare to act as an Atlantic bridgehead'?[23] How could deterrence possibly fail under these circumstances? Does this not suggest that de Gaulle—at least during the late 1940s—believed nuclear weapons to be something close to 'irrelevant'? The first possible response, of course, is that de Gaulle did believe in nuclear deterrence, but that he was never convinced that the Americans—even with their nuclear monopoly—could be trusted to come to Europe's defence. No one could be certain that the very limited number of fission bombs held by the United States would be enough to ensure military victory in Europe over the huge Red Army, and no one could be sure that the United States would be prepared to find out. Having only recently demobilized under popular demand, it was not clear that the Americans would come back to Europe even with their atomic bombs, nor was it evident that they would be willing to use them if they did come back. In this view, de Gaulle might have already believed that atomic weapons could deter, but not if deterrence depended on one country using them in the defence of another.

Such a hypothesis can surely not be excluded, and indeed it fits well with later Gaullist perspectives on international relations in the nuclear world. But another—and more persuasive—hypothesis suggests that de Gaulle was in fact not yet a firm believer in nuclear deterrence of any kind, and that he was not yet convinced that the bomb was 'unusable'. While he knew that nuclear devastation would be horrible and potentially 'cataclysmic', de Gaulle also knew that atomic bombs had in fact been used only several years before, and that nothing could with certainty prevent them from being used again. The Soviet Union, after all, was many times larger than Japan, and its leaders might not be so fearful of the new (and few) American weapons. Practically *all* of Japan had been within easy striking range of US atomic-capable bombers; Moscow, on the other hand, was hundreds of well-protected kilometres away from American bases. With the Americans controlling only a small fraction of the destructive power they would later possess, and with uncertain means of accurate delivery, de Gaulle still believed that nuclear weapons might easily fail to deter war, and that if deterrence did fail, atomic weapons would be used. At the start of the Korean war de Gaulle told Georges Pompidou that 'there will be atomic bombings, the Americans too are brutes . . .'[24]

In any event—whether he failed to believe only in *extended* nuclear deterrence or in any nuclear deterrence at all—what does seem clear is that the de Gaulle of 1945–54 was not yet persuaded that the simple *existence* of nuclear weapons would be enough to deter war and aggression. This was a far cry from the de Gaulle of the 1960s, the apostle of 'existential deterrence' who was confident that the nuclear superpowers would go to great lengths to avoid war with each other. Whether because the early atomic bombs were not yet destructive enough to scare national leaders, because the limited means of delivery then available might convince the Russians they were not really vulnerable, or because US invulnerability to a Soviet nuclear response might encourage the Americans to use atomic bombs to defend Europe, de Gaulle was still in the early 1950s not yet a believer in 'deterrence by nuclear danger'.[25] He feared both a conventional war in which nuclear weapons would have failed to deter and a nuclear war in which they would actually be used.

This view was not to last. It is difficult to say precisely when de Gaulle came to the opinion that the potential for nuclear war would itself be enough to deter aggression against a nuclear power, but sometime during the mid-1950s seems to be a reasonable guess. After 1954, de Gaulle's repeated public warnings about war in Europe cease; by 1956 his confidence even in the concept of a 'minimal' French deterrent becomes clear; after 1957 his arguments that the United States would not risk nuclear war for Europe intensify; and by 1959 de Gaulle appears fully confident that the Soviets do not want war in Europe. There are obviously factors other than the nuclear one that explain some of these changes, but de Gaulle's own comments and policies, as well as the timing of the changes, seem to suggest that nuclear weapons also played a major role. By the time de Gaulle came back to power in 1958 he was convinced that the very existence of nuclear weapons in the hands of one country would be enough to make others think twice before confronting it.

That the mid- to late 1950s should be the period in which de Gaulle decisively reaches this conclusion corresponds well with developments taking place at that time. From the beginning to the end of the 1950s the destructiveness and deliverability of nuclear weapons increased manifold: Thermonuclear fusion bombs (hundreds of times more powerful than the Hiroshima device) were invented and were now held by the Soviets as well as the United States; long-range bombers had multiplied and improved; and by the end of the 1950s ballistic missiles suddenly made possible the destruction of every country in the world. Moreover, the American experience of nuclear 'non-use' in Berlin, Korea, Indo-China and the Taiwan Strait had demonstrated that US policy-makers were well aware of the nature of the new weapons and were consequently awed by the idea of their use. If leaders were so afraid of the result of nuclear use even when they would be the 'users', it could reasonably be concluded that they would be even more intimidated by bombs that might be used against them. For de Gaulle, all of this seems to have led to the belief that the old ways of armed confrontation among the great powers had passed.[26]

For evidence of this belief, we can look in a number of different places. First, for example, is the startling contrast between de Gaulle's great concern about war in Europe during the late 1940s, and his apparent confidence that there would *not* be war a decade later, despite crises as serious as those in Berlin in 1958–61 or Cuba in 1962. As is often pointed out, the otherwise rebellious de Gaulle was always one of the staunchest defenders of Western positions when crises broke out between East and West. In the second Berlin crisis, for example, de Gaulle consistently warned Konrad Adenauer about an Anglo-Saxon 'sellout', and despite the local Soviet preponderance of force, refused to concede anything to Moscow.[27] One reason for de Gaulle's self-assurance, a March 1959 letter written to Eisenhower reveals, was that de Gaulle had 'the impression that the Soviets don't want to turn this into war'.[28] For de Gaulle, it would not only have been 'odious' but 'absurd' for the Soviets to try to intimidate the West, given 'the risks run by our species . . . [with] everything arranged so that means of destruction capable of annihilating continents could be unleashed in the space of a few seconds'.[29] Similarly, during the Cuban missile crisis, de Gaulle was solidly behind the firm American response to the Soviet deployment of IRBMs in Cuba, despite the potential retaliation US action might provoke and the fact that the Cuban missiles posed no threat whatever to France. As de Gaulle told President Kennedy's special emissary to Paris, Dean Acheson, 'If there is a war, I will be with you. But there will be no war.'[30]

As the 1960s proceeded, de Gaulle's confidence that the superpowers would earnestly seek to avoid conflict increased, and by the middle of the decade he was travelling to Moscow and arguing that the conditions for détente had emerged. That de Gaulle in 1966 was thumbing his nose at NATO—which he had strongly supported in 1949—and courting the Soviet Union is a powerful suggestion that he was no longer concerned about war in Europe; it is hardly reminiscent of his warnings of a Third World War in 1948. By the mid-1960s, de Gaulle was clearly convinced that the Russians '[would] not dare'.[31]

As already noted, there are plenty of reasons for this change in attitude that had nothing to do with nuclear weapons. By the end of the 1950s, Stalin was dead, NATO was in place, the Western European democracies were no longer so susceptible to communism, and China was in the process of leaving the Socialist bloc: the balance of power in Europe seemed to be shifting away from the Russians. But it is also clear that a major factor—perhaps the decisive factor—in de Gaulle's new faith in peace came from the realization that the superpowers would not risk confrontation in a world of mutual assured destruction. 'More than anything,' de Gaulle later wrote, 'the general situation has changed' because 'it would be folly for Moscow—as for anyone else—to set off a global conflict that could end up, after the dropping of bombs, in general destruction. And, if one does not make war, one must sooner or later make peace.'[32] This analysis (written in 1969) was not, moreover, a mere retrospective judgement, but one that de Gaulle asserted clearly as the situation developed in 1959: 'A few signs of détente are starting to become clear,' de Gaulle said, because 'Russia . . . accepts that a conflict, no matter which side started it, would lead to general annihilation.'[33] The Soviet Union was still a 'totalitarian Empire that muzzled fourteen nations and openly envisaged doing the same to all the others', but none the less, there would be no war in Europe.[34]

A second persuasive piece of evidence that de Gaulle believed by the late 1950s, that nuclear weapons could have a great effect on the way statesmen would act, has to do with his views about the not yet existent French nuclear force. Throughout his years in 'exile', of course, de Gaulle formally had nothing to do with the Fourth Republic's nuclear programme, which only directly began to undertake military research in 1952. De Gaulle, however, was surely interested in the nuclear question and was eminently well connected at the CEA, many of whose top administrators and scientists were Gaullists.[35] It was during these years that de Gaulle apparently came to the conclusion that even a 'minimal' deterrent force could have very powerful effects.

In an April 1956 meeting with a French general (Pierre Gallois) sent by NATO to inform de Gaulle about nuclear strategy, de Gaulle showed he was already rather well informed, and first used a formula that revealed his confidence in the concept of proportional nuclear deterrence. 'Yes,' de Gaulle said in plain language after Gallois' long personal seminar on the emerging theories and jargon of deterrence, 'all France has to be capable of is tearing off the arm of an aggressor . . .'[36] De Gaulle, it seems, already by this time had great faith in the process of nuclear deterrence, at least for the country that possessed the deterrent.

It is important to understand why in de Gaulle's mind the bomb would have such an effect because this explains why he believed the superpowers would shy away from conflict. Nuclear weapons would induce caution and restraint in national foreign policies simply because no country could risk the immense destruction they would wreak. There were only two prerequisites for deterrence—means and will—and de Gaulle believed both were available in sufficient quantities, even for a country the size of France. As he put it in 1964:

We are in a position to think that six years from now our deterrent means will reach a total instantaneous power of 2,000 Hiroshima bombs . . . The field of deterrence is thus henceforth open to us. For to attack France would be equivalent, for whomever it might be, to undergoing frightful destruction itself. Doubtless the megatons that we could launch would not equal in number those that Americans and Russians are able to unleash. But, once reaching a certain nuclear capability, and with regard to one's own direct defence, the proportion of respective means has no absolute value. Indeed, since a man and a people can die only once, the deterrent exists provided that one has the means to wound the possible aggressor mortally, that one is very determined to do it and that the aggressor is convinced of it.[37]

In other words, de Gaulle believed that world leaders would indeed be influenced in the way they used military force. Even a small atomic force would 'have the sombre and terrible capability of destroying in a few seconds millions and millions of men. This fact cannot fail to have at least some bearing on the intents of any possible aggressor.'[38] It is difficult to make the point any more clearly than that.

Finally, de Gaulle's conviction that nuclear weapons had changed the nature of international relations is strongly suggested by the fact that he was willing to devote as much as 50 per cent of France's military-equipment budget on nuclear forces while French conventional forces were starved of modern weapons.[39] He was convinced that a credible strategic nuclear deterrent would keep the Soviets from threatening the West, and that such a deterrent would only be credible if the Europeans themselves had some say over it. Nuclear weapons were the modern equivalents of the tanks and aeroplanes that revolutionized warfare after World War I, and it was necessary to recognize and adapt to this fact. The bomb, de Gaulle argued to France's top military officers in early 1968, was a 'fundamentally new weapon [that] required a reorganization of military thought and a redefinition of power . . . without comparison to what we have known before.'[40]

By the end of the 1960s, then, de Gaulle was clearly convinced that the bomb would have profound effects on how statesmen would use military force. He was uninterested in the elaborate and arcane theories of the so-called 'wizards of Armageddon', and simply considered that rational states—the entities that made up his world—would not initiate conflict if by doing so they put their very survival at stake. For him, nuclear weapons 'held the destiny of every people and every individual in suspense'.[41] Any war with such weapons would be 'a disaster for everyone, because . . . after the conflict, there might be neither powers, nor laws, nor cities, nor cultures, nor cradles, nor tombs'.[42] The spectre of such an outcome was enough to change the way leaders would use or threaten to use military force.

The Effect of the Bomb on International Relations

We have concentrated so far on the point that the nuclear revolution changed the way de Gaulle thought about the utility of military force, but the bomb had an effect on other aspects of Gaullist thinking. This is most notably the case in terms of Gaullist perspectives on international structures and relations between states. While it can probably not be said that the bomb actually *changed* Gaullist conceptions of the international system, it is clear that it significantly reinforced those conceptions. The point is important because it suggests another way in which nuclear weapons may have been 'relevant' in the postwar world and it confirms that de Gaulle thought they would be seen as such.

The 'nuclear reinforcement' of the Gaullist world-view took place in two main ways. First, the existence of nuclear weapons bolstered de Gaulle's view that the nation-state was the only legitimate international actor and the only conceivable foundation for national defence. Because states in the nuclear era had the capacity to annihilate one another, no state would be willing to take a nuclear risk for another one, since its very survival would be at stake.

States, de Gaulle had always believed, could never fully trust one another, and now, in a nuclear world, the idea that they could do so was patently absurd. It was one thing, perhaps, to risk an expeditionary professional army, as countries had done in the past. The Americans, for example—if late and grudgingly—had intervened in World Wars I and II on behalf of Britain and France when US interests seemed at stake. But could they have done so had Germany in either period been able to threaten the United States' very existence? The answer seemed to de Gaulle self-evidently negative. As he put it in 1963:

Above and beyond everything, the deterrent is now a fact for the Russians as for the Americans, which means that in the case of a general atomic war, there would inevitably be frightful and perhaps fatal destruction on both sides. In these conditions, no one in the world—particularly no one in America—can say if, where, how, and to what extent the American nuclear weapons would be employed to defend Europe.[43]

Consequently, the nation-state was more fundamental than ever because it was the only actor that could ever be counted on to take responsibility for matters as important as nuclear war. Just as France and Europe could not count on the United States to risk annihilation for it, no European state could count on another. The European Community, then, was ultimately not viable as a supranational federation that would deal with defence. In such a federation, who could possibly be responsible for a decision as momentous as that of pushing—or even threatening to push—the nuclear button? Such an act, de Gaulle believed, could never come from anything but the nation-state.

The second major 'reinforcing' effect of nuclear weapons on de Gaulle's view of international relations was that they tended to divide an emerging bipolar world even more sharply between the two hostile blocs. The post-war world, de Gaulle doubtless acknowledged, would have been split between East and West whether fission had been discovered or not; the ideological competition (or at least the struggle for power) between the United States and the Soviet Union was not the result of the bomb. But the bomb did reinforce this bipolar structure by forcing almost every state in the world to align with one of the nuclear powers for its ultimate protection. Nuclear weapons also strengthened the alliance leader's insistence that decision-making be centralized and at the same time made that leader suspicious of smaller allies who might drag it into a nuclear war. The whole situation, de Gaulle believed, only reinforced the subordination of non-nuclear countries to one or the other major nuclear countries:

those non-nuclear countries that are threatened by one of the two giants are led to accept a strategic *and thereby political* dependence *vis-à-vis* the other giant, because this is the only way they believe they have any hope for security.[44]

This mechanism might best be illustrated with an analogy to civil society, the sort of which John Foster Dulles was fond. The nuclear world might be compared in de Gaulle's mind to a dangerous city, divided between numerous rival gangs.[45] For years, all the gangs have approximately similar kinds of weapons: handguns, slingshots, and the like. Suddenly, the two largest gangs come to possess new, much more powerful weapons—say, hand grenades— while the others do not. What does this new development do to the relations between all the rest of the gangs?

Clearly (in de Gaulle's mind), it forces them to ally, or rather, to subordinate themselves, to one of the gangs with the new capability to destroy all of the others. In the old situation, varying combinations of smaller gangs could offset the strength of the larger, and even single groups with enough intelligence and pluck could stand up for themselves. Now, with ultimate security only available from one of the two gangs with the new weapons, polarization is inevitable, much to the detriment of all but the two largest gangs.

Without getting into the implications for 'gang policy' (come up with your own grenades), the point of the story is simple: for de Gaulle, the division of the world between those that could destroy and those that could not was a pernicious one. It would lead either to a polarization in which all non-nuclear countries had to align with one or the other of the nuclear countries, or, under different circumstances, to collusion between the nuclear countries, in which case the non-nuclear ones would be subordinates all the same. In de Gaulle's own words:

The world situation in which two super-states would alone have the weapons capable of annihilating every other country . . . over the long run could only paralyse and sterilize the rest of the world by placing it either under the blow of crushing competition, or under the yoke of a double hegemony that would be agreed upon between the two rivals. . . . Under these conditions, how could Europe unite, Latin American emerge, Africa follow its own path, China find its place, and the United Nations become an effective reality?[46]

Nuclear bipolarity was thus even more divisive than the previous version; it forced all non-nuclear states to line up in their respective blocs, and prevented the legitimate emergence of other independent actors.

It seems, then, that in the mind of Charles de Gaulle nuclear weapons strengthened the most basic features of the international system.[47] They reinforced the fundamental role of the nation-state and froze the world into a bipolar order. In and of itself, of course, the fact that de Gaulle came to such conclusions does not tell us that he was right; indeed, other thinkers thought the post-war world was leading to the *end* of the nation-state (because defence was only possible via alliances), and most believed the world would have been a bipolar one anyway. What this conclusion does tell us, however, is that de Gaulle, at least, believed nuclear weapons and nuclear threats would indeed have an impact on the way states and statesmen would act. If nuclear weapons were 'irrelevant' in practice—and would be seen as such by national leaders— there would be no reason to conclude that they would have such an impact. For all the reasons we have seen, atomic bombs could not, and would not, be ignored.

II. France's Own Bomb

Whenever de Gaulle may have concluded that nuclear weapons would 'revolutionize' international relations, it is clear that he never wavered in his view that France should have its own bomb. Indeed, the determination with which the French nuclear programme was pursued under de Gaulle is itself testimony to the fact that the General, at least, did not believe nuclear weapons to be 'irrelevant'. Why, though, was French possession of nuclear weapons so important to de Gaulle? What did he believe he could do with them? In practice, has the French bomb played a role in the post-war world? While a long discussion of the French nuclear force is obviously beyond the scope of this essay, there is no better testing ground for the conclusions reached above than de Gaulle's own actions as president of France. And a look at those actions reveals that de Gaulle's decisions as a nuclear leader were highly consistent with those conclusions: France had to have the bomb, because for a number of different reasons, the bomb 'mattered'.

The Logic of the French Nuclear Force

At least six different justifications of the French bomb can be identified: status; influence; independence; national security; technological gains; and strong domestic leadership.[48] While all were used at different times and to varying degrees, the first four are those that have most to do with the international system and thus concern us here.[49] It should be kept in mind, of course, that all these justifications were often used—and even exaggerated—in order to rally public or international support. But it should also be clear that they cannot *all* be dismissed as self-serving: The existence of the *force de frappe* itself is proof enough that for *some* reason, the French believed it was worth it.

Many knowledgeable observers would argue that the primary justification of the French bomb was not national security but national status. De Gaulle could not accept that France—which 'could not be France without grandeur'—would be excluded from a private club of two or three. Nuclear weapons were symbols of technological achievement and military prowess in the modern world, and it was inconceivable for France not to possess them. Minutes after the first French atomic test in 1960—before French leaders could ever imagine defending or deterring, France was already, in de Gaulle's mind, 'stronger and prouder'.[50] The next day, de Gaulle proudly claimed in a letter to his son Philippe that 'Our bomb is going to change the ideas of a lot of people. It is a success, especially as proof of our capacity to assimilate the most arduous and most complicated techniques.'[51] What was most important was that France could count itself among *les Grands*.

Geoffrey de Courcel, de Gaulle's former secretary-general, has stated that 'for [de Gaulle] what mattered was to be able to say that France was politically a nuclear power, and to talk as equal to equal with the Anglo-Saxon powers.'[52] General Albert Buchalet, former director of military applications at the CEA, has agreed:

From my meetings with General de Gaulle on this subject, I was left with the impression that he considered, during this period, the success of the nuclear explosion more than anything to be a political means permitting him to sit at the *table des Grands*. Naturally, as a military leader, he measured fully the revolution that atomic weapons brought to the military domain.[53]

In a world of nuclear 'haves' and 'have-nots', it was critical for France—if it was to 'remain France' in de Gaulle's words—to be in the former category and to get out of the latter.[54]

A by-product of nuclear status, in the Gaullist view, was influence through-out the world. This was the case not only in terms of encouraging superpower disarmament, one of the early justifications of the *force de frappe*, but also in terms of political influence. 'When we become an atomic power,' de Gaulle said in November 1961, 'we will have all the more means to make our actions be heard in the domains which are dear and useful to all men: those of world security and disarmament.'[55] After the Reggane test de Gaulle issued a communiqué stating that 'the French Republic is better able to make its action felt for the conclusion of agreements between atomic powers with a view toward realizing nuclear disarmament.'[56]

Indeed, the bomb would help endow France with the world-wide political responsibilities de Gaulle sought:

our country, becoming for its part and by its own means a nuclear power, is led to assume for itself the very extensive political and strategic responsibilities that this capability brings with it, responsibilities whose nature and dimensions evidently make them inalienable.[57]

By earning France the respect of its allies, and by giving Paris a say in when to start or how to fight a nuclear war, the *force de frappe* would allow France to play the sort of leading role in the Atlantic Alliance that it felt it deserved. As de Gaulle wrote to his top advisers in a private 1961 note: 'the American attitude will change only once we have acquired atomic bombs.'[58]

An autonomous French nuclear force was also the key to the political independence so critical to de Gaulle. As seen earlier, the General believed that in a world with just two nuclear powers, all other states would be obliged to accept the leadership, and ultimately the hegemony, of one of the two. It was only by breaking this bipolar nuclear monopoly that a state could break the political monopoly as well. 'National independence', de Gaulle was convinced, was 'unimaginable for a country [that] does not dispose of nuclear arms'.[59]

As he writes in his memoirs, de Gaulle explained this conviction to John Foster Dulles in their first meeting, in July 1958. 'There is no France worth its mettle,' de Gaulle said, 'especially in the eyes of the French, without world responsibilities.'

That is why she does not approve of NATO, which does not give her proper due in its decisions and which is limited to Europe alone. That is also why she is going to acquire atomic weapons. In that way, our defence and our policies can be independent, which is what we find important above all else.[60]

When the first French nuclear test at Reggane was successful two years later, France had 'taken her independence back in hand'.[61]

In making the link between the bomb and political independence, de Gaulle's deputies were sometimes even more zealous than the General himself. Michel Debré, for example, argued in the National Assembly as early as

1956 that 'nations without bombs are satellites', and Alexandre Sanguinetti (even more colourfully) asserted that 'countries without their finger on the [nuclear] trigger will be auxiliaries, playing the role of Moroccan soldiers in the French army of the last war'.[62]Somewhat more restrained, but equally illustrative, was Couve de Murville in 1958:

As the nuclear bomb . . . remains the essential element of a modern army, all those . . . countries [which remain non-nuclear] would be renouncing the possession of the elements of a true defence, and consequently would be placing the responsibility for their defence completely in the hands of the nuclear powers. It is easy to see what the consequences of this would be in five, ten or twenty years. A country like France can envisage no such thing.[63]

In short, for de Gaulle and for those around him, nuclear weapons were the key to national independence.[64]For France to depend on its allies for nuclear protection would be to subordinate itself both militarily and politically to them.[65] 'A great state which does not possess [nuclear weapons]', de Gaulle believed, 'does not command its own destiny.'[66] And commanding its own destiny was essential for France.

We have already seen why de Gaulle believed an independent nuclear force was essential to French security and the point need not be laboured here. When the Americans had a nuclear monopoly, France, perhaps, was protected. But now that the Russians also had the capability of destroying the other superpower's homeland, 'extended deterrence' could not be guaranteed. Neither superpower would be willing to run the risk of total destruction that global nuclear war would bring and as a result would seek to limit any war to Europe itself. The only way to prevent this, de Gaulle believed, was for the Europeans themselves (and this meant France) to possess atomic capabilities. For if France could guarantee an aggressor that it could 'tear off' that aggressor's 'arm', there would be no attack. By endowing itself with nuclear weapons, France was making sure that deterrence would work.

For all these reasons, Charles de Gaulle and those around him believed that the possession of nuclear weapons was a path toward bigger and better things in the world. Even at the cost of billions and billions of francs, and in the face of domestic and international opposition, de Gaulle and his governments went ahead with the construction of the *force de frappe*. Nuclear weapons would not only help to ensure French national security but would provide great-power status, respect, national independence, political influence, technological benefits, and a strong executive state. French leaders of the 1960s were convinced—and their successors appear to have been convinced as well—that joining the nuclear club was worth the price.

The 'Relevance' of the *force de frappe*

The final question that remains to be addressed here, then, is whether de Gaulle and these other Frenchmen were right. To assess the impact of French nuclear weapons on world stability and international relations, it is not enough to show that Charles de Gaulle and his supporters believed that they would have such an impact. It is instead necessary—though immeasurably more difficult—to ask whether the French bomb actually did matter, and if so, how.

A number of observers who have studied the question have concluded that the French *force de frappe* has had little effect on international relations. Not surprisingly, opponents of the cost and morality of nuclear weapons in France, and also those who have seen all nuclear weapons as 'essentially irrelevant', have argued that de Gaulle was wrong to count on the increased status or security the bomb was supposed to bring.[67] What is more interesting, though, is that even many of those who believe that nuclear weapons have generally played a stabilizing role in international politics have seen the *French* deterrent as inconsequential. For example, Raymond Aron—France's top strategic thinker and a firm believer in nuclear deterrence—argued in 1976 that:

as long as the present conjuncture lasts, as long as American troops are stationed in Western Europe, no one can imagine a scenario in which the French nuclear force would deter the Soviets from an aggression that would not have been deterred by the American force.[68]

Going even further, McGeorge Bundy—a believer like de Gaulle in the concept of 'nuclear danger'—has asserted that:

It is not easy to find evidence of the exercise or even the existence of . . . [the] responsibilities [de Gaulle believed nuclear status would confer on France.] Where has the international role of France been larger because of the French bomb? Has that bomb had a role in Africa or in the Middle East? Have the non-nuclear neighbors of France been willing to accept French leadership because France has bombs and they do not? Has French influence been visibly greater in Moscow or London or Washington? Surely if the possession of the bomb had the political meaning that de Gaulle so confidently asserted, one would expect to find traces of that meaning in the historical record of the decades since he spoke. Ardent defenders of the Gaullist view often assert that the French bomb has reinforced French diplomacy, but I am aware of no concrete demonstration of these assertions.[69]

Both Aron and Bundy have a point. Looking back over the more than three decades of French nuclear history, it is difficult to find a single specific, concrete case where it can be demonstrated that the French bomb has played a deterrent role, or even contributed greatly to general 'nuclear danger'. Still, the fact that the archives—even if they were open—would not reveal any 'smoking guns' does not mean that the French nuclear adventure has been a waste of time. A careful reflection on the French experience reveals that even if few explicit 'traces of the meaning of nuclear weapons' can be found, the 'irrelevance' of the French nuclear force cannot be taken for granted. De Gaulle and the Gaullists often exaggerated the potential impact of the French atomic bomb, but their logic was not unfounded, and it has not lost its power over the years.[70]

First, it is important to acknowledge the importance of the psychological benefits that de Gaulle believed would result from the bomb. After ignominious defeat in World War II, followed by not much better results in Indo-China and Algeria, the French in the late 1950s—and in particular the French military—needed something to stand for. They had known war (and frustration) for nearly two decades, and it had left a sour taste in their mouths. By endowing the country with nuclear weapons—rightly or wrongly the modern sign of great power status—de Gaulle was showing his countrymen that they could indeed accomplish great things. To the extent that de Gaulle's grand design was to restore French self-confidence, the bomb can be seen as a key step toward that goal. More than anything, de Gaulle was a national psychologist, and for him nuclear status was a therapy that could not be forgone.[71]

Closely related to these psychological factors, it may well be that the French bomb also contributed to the feeling—and in part even the reality—of the national independence with which it was so often rhetorically linked. To be sure, it is difficult to imagine how France's possession of even the most powerful tactical or strategic nuclear weapons would have altered the course of events of some of the crises of the Cold War. For example, in the classic test-case of the 1956 Suez crisis—after which the French government of Guy Mollet reversed its opposition to French nuclear weapons—how would a *force de frappe* have played a role? Would the Russians have been less ready to brandish their nuclear 'threat' had France possessed nuclear missiles of its own? The fact that the British, a nuclear power fighting alongside the French, were subject to a similar threat (along with the fact that this Russian posturing in fact played little or no role in the denouement of the crisis anyway) suggests not. Would the Americans, whose financial manœuvres *did* have an effect on the British and French, have decided not to pressure the colonial powers? Because a French nuclear attack on Washington in response to such pressure is hardly credible, it is difficult to imagine why this might have been the case. Finally, would a French bomb have changed the course of events on the battlefield itself? That the French-British-Israeli armies were easily winning the military battle anyway suggests that there was no need for the bomb here even if one could come up with a practical way to use it. Suez (or indeed any other factual or counterfactual case-study of the French bomb), would seem to contradict Gaullist logic.

Yet Suez does suggest, at least, how the possession of atomic weapons might contribute to political and military independence under these or other circumstances. The mechanism that would come into play would be the complex and difficult-to-measure one of confidence. If a nuclear France were sufficiently self-assured in its possession of a nuclear force that it knew it would not have to depend on the United States for its security, it just might be willing to stand up more forcefully to the United States. And the United States, knowing this, would be somewhat less willing to exert pressure that might not work. If the issue at stake in Suez had been something greater than a colonial dispute—and instead something in which the French had an overriding vital interest like Berlin, Germany, or even France itself—it is easy to see how the French possession of a deterrent force would allow France to act independently of its Atlantic ally. If the Americans had been willing to make concessions over Berlin or Cuba, for example—something that de Gaulle feared and certainly could not exclude—would the ultimate security afforded by a proportional deterrent not give de Gaulle the confidence to make his own voice heard? The French argument was not so much that the bomb would permit them to *resolve* crises like Suez with the atomic bomb, but rather that by believing themselves more secure because of the bomb, they could take risks that a non-nuclear power would not dare take.

Did it ever work out this way in practice? Was de Gaulle better able to pursue his revisionist diplomacy because of the existence of a French bomb? One is easily tempted to doubt it. Though many Gaullists assert a link between the deployment of the *force de frappe* and the beginning of France's global diplomacy in the mid-1960s,[72] the timing of this concurrence is probably due to other factors, such as the end of the Algerian War, de Gaulle's re-election by universal suffrage in 1965, and the fact that the 75-year-old de Gaulle knew he had little time left to implement the rest of his grand design. It is surely a great exaggeration to suggest that the possession of nuclear weapons somehow permitted de Gaulle to criticize the Bretton Woods monetary system, recognize China, withdraw from NATO commands, castigate American policy in Vietnam, pursue détente with the Soviet Union, and call for a free Quebec. Finally, it should not be forgotten that de Gaulle was hardly one to bow to 'realities' because of an absence of means. He was, after all, the man who stood up to the Germans, British, and Americans in World War II as the leader of a country that had hardly any means at all; the General did not necessarily need powerful weapons to speak his mind.[73]

Instead, a much more viable thesis is that de Gaulle was preparing his country for the future. So long as he was running the show himself, French interests as he saw them would surely be asserted, even in the absence of a truly 'independent' defence. But would the same be true in the years to come? Would French leaders not revert back to what de Gaulle saw as the subordination of the Fourth Republic, when French foreign policy was constrained because of a dependence on the United States for defence? De Gaulle did not want to take the chance. He would endow France with a powerful and invulnerable nuclear force that would make it possible for his successors—if warranted by events—not to follow quietly the policies of their protector, the United States. If another Suez ever took place, the French would not be obliged to give in over Strasbourg (as in late 1944) as they had done.[74]

Finally, and most important, the French have developed over the years the capability to remove instantaneously whole civilizations from the face of the earth, the same capability that has supposedly contributed to international stability in the case of the superpowers. To be sure, few would argue that the French force of 62 Mirage bombers in the 1960s ever deterred the Soviets, who probably appreciated it as a divisive factor within the Atlantic Alliance more

than they feared it as a deterrent. Even de Gaulle himself may have believed—
though he could never admit it—that the French of the mid-1960s could not
really 'tear off' enough of the Russian Bear's arm to scare it, and anyway, that
the American threat to tear off its head was enough.[75] But once again, de
Gaulle's nuclear force was primarily a project for the long term. As de Gaulle
explained as late as 1968,

Yes, we are building a nuclear armament. . . . It is a long-term project. . . . We are not
making it for tomorrow, but for generations, in a completely new system of defence and
deterrence. And in this long space of time, who can say what the evolution of the world
will be?[76]

De Gaulle was working at that time to build a force of nuclear submarines and
ballistic missiles—deployed only after his departure—that was meant to be a
significant threat in later decades, after the American guarantee had continued
to erode. Today, with the modernization of the French strategic nuclear force
(ironically under François Mitterrand, de Gaulle's historic adversary and the
greatest opponent of the original *force de frappe*) enabling France to deploy
hundreds of relatively invulnerable warheads, who can say that the French
bomb is not capable of playing a deterrent role? If one accepts the mechanism
by which any deterrent works, surely France's capacity to set off that mechanism must be taken into account.

In conclusion, the significance of the *force de frappe* should not be sought in
the same way that we have tried to understand the role of the American or
Soviet nuclear forces. As Bundy and Aron argue, if we look for concrete documentation affirming the success of French deterrence, we will not find it.
Instead, the 'relevance' of the French nuclear force should be assessed in terms
of the context in which it was built: it was designed as a source of pride and
unity—the sort of *vaste entreprise* to which de Gaulle's memoirs allude—in a
country that badly needed both; it has given French leaders added fuel in their
claims to world-power status and in their ambitions to play an active role in
the world; it has been an ultimate shield in an uncertain world; and finally—
as France's Atlantic allies recognized formally in 1974—it has contributed, as
one more element of uncertainty, to deterrence based on nuclear danger.[77]
These are perhaps modest conclusions for a project with sometimes immodest
aims; but where nuclear weapons are concerned, a little bit can go a long way.

11

Konrad Adenauer: Defence Diplomat on the Backstage

ANNETTE MESSEMER

The Heritage of the Holocaust

At the dawn of the nuclear age, Konrad Adenauer was not yet involved in international politics. Unlike Churchill, Eisenhower, de Gaulle, and Stalin, he did not have any major experience in military strategy, warfare or international politics before or during World War II, and until the beginning of 1945 he did not know that the future still held a second political career for him. Adenauer was reinstated by the Allies as mayor of the Rhineland city of Cologne in May 1945, a post he had been forced to leave at the age of 57 in 1933 in order to escape persecution from the National Socialists. He spent twelve years as a pensioner in the politically less dangerous environment of Rhöndorf, a sleepy village on the banks of the Rhine, 15 miles south of Cologne. Back in office, he once again had to reconstruct the city as he had done after World War I, and even more important to his future career, he had to gain confidence from the Western powers.

Worse than in 1918–19, two-thirds of Cologne lay in ruins. In a letter to a friend Adenauer wrote: 'The major parts of Cologne are devastated. Although the city again numbers approximately 500,000 inhabitants, one-third are living in cellars or partially destroyed homes. I visited several German cities over the last weeks, but I have not seen any city that is as destroyed as Cologne. The cathedral is still there, but most of the roof is shattered. . . There is barely anything left of the city hall.'[1] The political legacy of the National Socialists further complicated the reconstruction of post-war German political life. The Allied Powers took necessary precautions to ensure that once and for all a totalitarian system had no chance of regaining power on German soil. It was not until 6 August 1945, the day of the atomic bombing of Hiroshima, that British military authorities reduced restrictions on the organization of political parties, unions, and newspapers in their zone. It was during these following months that Adenauer seized the opportunity to create a new Christian Democratic Party—Adenauer was once a member of the Catholic *Zentrumspartei*—and to push for the unification of the Western zones.

Adenauer first had to make his way to the top of the Christian Democratic Party, as well as the first German post-war government, before he could consider issues of international politics other than those which had an immediate impact on the domestic development of West Germany. Even after he became the first Chancellor of the Federal Republic in September 1949, it took several years before he needed to make decisions about nuclear issues in the context of the revision of the Occupation Statute. At that time Adenauer already showed a very pragmatic and rational attitude towards nuclear issues. His policy for the re-establishment of German atomic energy research designated for *civilian* purposes further reveals the secondary importance of the nuclear issue in Adenauer's overall political goal of making West Germany a sovereign and integrated part of the Western community.

It was only at the instigation of one of Germany's leading physicists, Werner Heisenberg, who emphasized the necessity of civilian atomic energy research to keep up with international standards, that Adenauer tried to reduce Allied restrictions on German atomic energy research. Although the High Commission had allowed theoretical research in 1950, German scientists were hampered in their efforts due to the limited amount of uranium at their disposal. Adenauer was ultimately able to reduce restrictions on civilian research, but kept a low profile on the other aspects of atomic energy. He considered it unwise for the Federal Government to create the impression that West Germany was violating Allied restrictions or was even aiming for nuclear weapons.[2] That Adenauer had no other alternative than a very cautious policy can be illustrated by various Allied sensibilities toward the potential emergence of West Germany as a nuclear player; in the negotiations between the German government and the Allies, the High Commissioner of Great Britain, Sir Ivone Kirkpatrick, particularly opposed further concessions to German civilian nuclear research. He argued that news of any kind of German nuclear research had to be considered in the context of nuclear weapons and would consequently be taken as evidence that Germany was trying to become a nuclear player—an unthinkable scenario for the population of Great Britain just seven years after the end of the war.[3]

Allied sensibilities were further illustrated by their handling of the military aspect of German nuclear energy research. During the last period of negotiations over the European Defence Community (EDC) in the fall of 1951, the Allies did not even consider placing the issue on the agenda. They had agreed beforehand that West Germany had to sign an agreement restricting any kind of activity in the field. The legislation was laid down in Article 107 of the EDC Treaty as well as in three accompanying letters which Adenauer signed.[4] The Chancellor emphasized that it was not worth it 'to shed tears' over the Allied prohibition to build nuclear weapons: 'We would have to invest so much capital and scientific effort to manufacture the weapons—they would attract our potential enemies like honey bees. We could not even build them if we had the money because our scientific efforts came to a standstill in 1945.'[5]

The exclusion of nuclear weapons from Adenauer's policy reflected most importantly Allied resistance against a German nuclear role. It also demonstrated the evolution of nuclear strategy, and the very limited sharing of strategic information between the United States and its Allies, in general, at the time.[6] The German internal deliberations, which took place among the small circle of Adenauer's military advisers, illustrated this situation. As a follow-up to the New York conference in September 1950, at which Germany's rearmament was finally agreed upon, Adenauer asked his advisers to draft a plan for a German military contribution to Western defence efforts. For reasons of secrecy, they gathered at the Himmerod monastery near Bonn during the first weekend of October. It was at the opening session on 3 October that the issue of nuclear weapons was brought up for the first time. The point at issue was whether the existence of the weapons was of any importance for German strategic planning; the answer was 'no'. It was common sense that the United States and the Soviet Union—in so far as the latter already had the opportunity—would only direct atomic strikes at their respective territories. As a consequence, Adenauer's defence experts decided to give priority to conventional planning: 'We argued that they could destroy a lot in their respective countries. However, the destruction was to happen on their territory. It would take four to six weeks, perhaps even eight weeks, until nuclear strikes would have any consequences for the front in Germany.'[7] The *Himmeroder-Memoire* did not include a single line on nuclear weapons, and it seems as if nuclear weapons were also of peripheral importance for decision-making in the following years.[8]

The planning of his advisers reflected Adenauer's overall thinking about the challenges for post-war German national security policy, namely Europe's decline and the emergence of superpower rivalry. He argued that Germany's geopolitical situation did not only make it an object of this rivalry, but that it also created a new kind of vulnerability. Adenauer was convinced that Stalin's intention was to bring the economic and military potential of West Germany under his control, as he had done with East Germany and the central European countries. However, Adenauer did not believe that Stalin would make use of nuclear weapons for two reasons: first, he thought that Stalin wanted Germany (as well as France and Italy) delivered into his hands undestroyed because he needed Germany's economic potential to win the upper hand in his rivalry with the United States. Second, Adenauer was convinced that the Soviet Union would be deterred from any sort of attack as long as the United States maintained a nuclear monopoly. Although Adenauer expected the Soviet Union to restrain its aspiration for communist world rule until it had built up its own nuclear arsenal, he did not expect a nuclear war in this case either. Instead, Adenauer pictured a nuclear stalemate, which, he argued, would probably not be very different from the experience of the last war when both parties had poison gas at their disposal without making any use of it. If the superpowers achieved a nuclear equilibrium, they would have no choice but to return to the fighting power of land forces and airpower.[9]

Adenauer's approach to post-war international politics was therefore of a realistic nature: he was a strong believer in power as the basis of international politics. Morals had little place. Past patterns of great-power conflict and warfare would continue. During all of his seventeen years as Chancellor he would consider military power and economic strength as the determining factors in resisting the expansionist efforts of a totalitarian state like the Soviet Union. Adenauer's thinking on nuclear weapons, therefore, has to be seen in the overall context of German defence, self-defence being an integral part of the natural rights of a nation. Rearmament, then, could only be considered to be a moral problem if Germany was planning a provoked attack.[10] Marc Cioc describes Adenauer's attitude correctly: 'Nuclear weapons are not immoral. A gun in the hand of a murderer is immoral. Effective defence weapons are not immoral. A totalitarian state that considers the use of force a permissible principle when its goal can be achieved with little risk is immoral.'[11]

Adenauer's former aides agree that if there was any deep anxiety about the development of international politics in post-war Europe, it was more the fear of Russian expansionism than the impact of nuclear weapons on the international system. Adenauer's conviction that the free part of Germany would come under the control of communist Russia, if it was not integrated into the Western community, was also shared by the majority of Germans for whom the flight of millions of their fellow citizens from communist rule in Poland and Russia, and the communist repression in Eastern Germany, was a troublesome experience in daily life. Adenauer's son, Paul, remembers a delirium of his father's shortly before he died, in which he mumbled something about the Russians pushing forward to the Rhine and pictured a scenario of the destruction of all European culture.[12]

The fact that Adenauer was much more worried about the way communism threatened the survival of Europe than about the way the bomb threatened the survival of humanity resulted from this very German notion of vulnerability. However, the political impact of German vulnerability towards the Soviet Union might not be seen the same way in the United States, which was, for the first time since its founding, exposed to direct enemy attack. The impact of nuclear weapons on the international system consequently had, from the very beginning of the nuclear age, a different magnitude of importance for American statesmen and military officials than for their German counterparts.

In the first years after World War II Adenauer did not consider nuclear weapons to be a crucial security guarantee for West Germany. He perceived them simply as another new, purely military instrument and had not yet discovered them as a political instrument. There is no early evidence of any consideration of the revolutionary scale of death and destruction that nuclear weapons could bring. Adenauer's biographer, Hans-Peter Schwarz, stresses that the Chancellor was dependent on 'old thinking' and that as always during revolutions, old thinking hesitates. In the eyes of Schwarz, Adenauer displayed the attitude of a political leader who was unwilling and unable to place himself at the head of a technological revolution.[13]

The reason for this lies in the 'World War II factor', but not as interpreted by John Mueller, who argues that the 'memory' of new developments in warfare, which had made war 'spectacularly costly and destructive, killing 50 million world-wide', prevented its repetition.[14] Although the Federal Republic of Germany, as the country responsible for this most catastrophic battle of mankind, was haunted by this heritage, its political and military leadership saw the possibility of another major military confrontation in Europe, possibly even another world war, as a consequence of communist expansionism. The horrible memory of World War II was therefore no reason for Adenauer to believe that the enormous suffering of nations would save them from a similar experience in the future. On the other hand, the memory of World War II became an important factor in the resistance of German public opinion against any kind of German rearmament. Such resistance would peak during strong anti-nuclear movements in various parts of post-war German society: in the scientific community, church synods, trade union congresses, the political parties, and on the streets. Strong as nuclear pacifism might have been in the second part of the 1950s, there were no anti-nuclear movements during Adenauer's first term as Chancellor: Germany was still a 'quasi-protectorate', its population challenged by the gigantic task of reconstruction.

'Old Thinking' in a Nuclear World

During Adenauer's first term in office, the West Germans were kept completely in the dark about American technological development, strategic evolution, or military programmes: 'We did not have a grasp of anything. We were lucky if an American military official, with whom one or another of us had good relations, showed us a document providing us some insight. These documents always bore the stamp 'for American eyes only'.[15] Of course, such words cannot be taken at face value because it was considered a gesture of 'courtesy' by the Americans to have German officials view privileged documents. This also points out the beginning of a working relationship between the German leadership and the American military authorities. But there was still a long way to go before institutionalized consultation on nuclear issues became common; information was like breadcrumbs falling off the American table. This became particularly obvious in 1953 when the first American nuclear weapons were deployed on German soil. Germany was still under occupation law, and the Allies were not obliged to provide the German government with any detailed information. The Chancellor was lucky enough that the deployment was postponed until after federal elections, which were scheduled for 6 September 1953.[16] The German military hardly knew of the existence of tactical nuclear forces. They were only concerned about strategic weapons and all German planning focused on them. German Air Force general Steinhoff agrees with Kielmansegg's perspective: 'When the ambitious American nuclear programme took off [Steinhoff refers primarily to NSC-68], we were stumbling into the equipment with nuclear weapons', and he added, 'people always ask me why Lägeler [a general in the German Air Force] was not concerned with the moral aspect of the weapons and so on. In fact, we were . . . damned ignorant'.[17]

The perspectives of the German military officials are of great importance because they reflect Adenauer's views. Unlike de Gaulle or Eisenhower, for whom military strategy was a lifetime interest, Adenauer had never been, nor would he ever become, a sophisticated strategist. He relied on his advisers for strategic information and analysis. His own 'old thinking' was therefore reinforced by their ideas on warfare, which had been determined by World War II, or even, as in the case of General Heusinger, by World War I.[18] The strategic thinking of Adenauer's advisers was 'limited and unsophisticated',[19] and it seems as if the World War I and World War II generation of the German military played their part in the Chancellor's misconceptions about nuclear issues. There is an amazing similarity between Adenauer's analysis and those of his advisers, and it is difficult to say who was more influenced by the other.[20]

Germany's understanding of nuclear issues was still all the more delayed because of the personalities of the German political and military leadership. Adenauer considered himself a statesman who did not base his policy on purely military considerations, but rather, he thought in the context of his overall goal of making West Germany an equal partner within the Western community. He made it clear to his military that he did not want the 'primacy of politics' to be questioned. In this respect, Adenauer's self-perception as a defence diplomat was his major political strength. While some scholars go so far as to conclude that 'Adenauer had little instinct for military affairs',[21] they must also concede that he had a strong idea of the implications of nuclear weapons on the *political status* of West Germany. It was thanks to this political instinct that Adenauer brought his country back to near equal status among the Western powers.[22] The Chancellor used the future German army as leverage to regain German sovereignty as he would later use nuclear weapons. Particularly in the second part of the 1950s, Adenauer's nuclear policy involved broader considerations than those of direct national possession or strategic military preferences. It was during these years that nuclear weapons became a major factor in his political thinking, as well as in his overall foreign policy.

Adenauer's Perception of the Nuclear Revolution

There is no consensus as to when Adenauer finally sensed the awesome destructive power of nuclear weapons or their importance as a policy instrument. It seems that the second half of the 1950s must be considered decisive, although there are also earlier statements by Adenauer, which show that the Chancellor gradually realized the genuine destructive power of the weapons as well as their particular impact for the security of his country.[23]

What is probably Adenauer's earliest statement on this issue dates back to 11 December 1953. At a speech before the 'Association de la Presse

Diplomatique Française', he joined the chorus of those asserting that nuclear weapons would make war impossible:

Once the development of nuclear weapons is advanced enough that countries having enough of them in stock might destroy life in any other country, then war destroys itself . . . Nations and their leaders will see that war is no longer a means to settle disputes. Nations will be forced to use peaceful means to settle their disputes. Ultimately, the development of the bomb will destroy war itself.[24]

This change of mind can easily be attributed to two decisive events at the beginning of the 1950s: the first successful explosion of a Soviet hydrogen bomb and the reassessment of American nuclear policy. As a result of the American 'New Look', the first battalions of the US Army in Germany were equipped with 280mm cannons at the end of 1953. The United States now established information channels with their German ally that were supposed to provide the German military with more insight about American progress in the technical development of its nuclear arsenal as well as in strategic planning. However, it was soon obvious that not only West Germany but all of the other 'nuclear have-nots' were not given access to certain information, particularly that pertaining to operational planning. Although there clearly had been some progress in the information process since General Speidel in 1954 represented the German interests at NATO headquarters in Paris, there were still no formal consultations with German authorities until 1962 when the NATO allies adopted the Athens guidelines. The Supreme Allied Commander in Europe, General Lauris Norstad, informed the Chancellor only verbally about the nuclear weapons deployed on German territory, and it took until the early 1960s before German military officials could be trained in the United States to understand the psychological, technical, and strategic aspects of the weapons.

The Allied simulation of a nuclear war in Europe in 1955, the so-called *Carte blanche* manœuvre, played a crucial role in Adenauer's nuclear education: he now realized that his country could become a major battlefield in a nuclear confrontation. Another more general consequence of the manœuvre was that public resentment grew and nuclear protest movements like Campaign Against Nuclear Death (*Kampf dem Atomtod*) mushroomed. Whereas the events of the early 1950s played a part in his learning, it took the public controversy over *Carte blanche* for Adenauer to realize the potential destruction of his country through nuclear weapons. His speeches during the latter half of the 1950s were full of apocalyptic scenarios which presented nuclear confrontation as the ruin of mankind. He also demonstrated his awareness of the consequence of nuclear strikes against German cities: 'If a bomb the size of the one dropped over Hiroshima exploded over one of our cities, we would, at one stroke, easily count 300,000 casualties; I doubt that one can still differentiate between tactical and strategic warfare in such a case. This is a whole new ball game.'[25] The fear of escalation therefore became another reason why he could not imagine a nuclear war. In his eyes, any responsible statesman had to make all possible efforts to save his country from the inevitable self-destruction of a nuclear war.

This strong feeling of responsibility, together with his religious beliefs as a Catholic, were the main reasons for Adenauer's belief that a nuclear war was impossible. On the other hand his experience in two world wars, the instability of the interwar period, and the rise of the communist threat in post-war Europe, deepened his pessimism about a peaceful development of international politics and prevented him from excluding the possibility of war at all. Although he concluded that nuclear weapons might deter war at a nuclear level, and even play some role in deterring conflict at a conventional level, he was convinced that they could not credibly serve as a deterrent at all levels of possible aggression. In the same meeting of the Council of the Christian Democratic Party (*Parteivorstand*) in which he argued in favour of 'pax atomica', Adenauer presented a conventional confrontation as the most likely military conflict in the future:

If the possibility of nuclear warfare is excluded, the Soviets will fight conventional wars comparable with Korea, Indo-China, Egypt, Israel or now Suez in order not to provoke nuclear retaliation of their enemy. This is why a certain level of conventional weapons . . . has to be maintained. However, I caution against the assumption that a major war even on a conventional or tactical nuclear level is still possible.[26]

Adenauer did not go so far as to state that because of a potential escalation, the chief purpose of a political leader had now changed from that of winning wars to averting them. Adenauer instead concluded, as had many scholars of post-war international politics, that 'nuclear war is possible, but it is also improbable.'[27]

In Adenauer's case it is of particular interest that his perception of the nuclear age stood side by side with a very traditional attitude towards warfare, which resulted in the use of simplistic, naïve, or even ignorant language when he talked about the evolution of warfare. He knew the qualitative difference between nuclear and conventional warfare, but he showed the same attitude towards the moral challenge of nuclear weapons with respect to the lethal technology that was used in World War I and World War II; to the extent that the destructive consequences of poison gas forbade its use in the first half of the century, one would logically think it irresponsible for a statesman to use nuclear weapons in the second half of the century. This paradoxical assessment of modern warfare sometimes brought him controversy and created an image of a Chancellor who could not adapt to the nuclear age. The records of the Council of the Christian Democratic Party offer many examples of Adenauer's simplistic categorization of nuclear weapons in the overall evolution of warfare. In a speech before the Council on 11 May 1957 he gave a revealing statement of his simplistic perception of the evolution of modern warfare:

There are big and there are small bombs. The big weapons were first called strategic weapons, and the small ones tactical weapons. Although the Hiroshima bomb now falls into the smaller category, the strategists are right in emphasizing the possibility of a strategic use for these small weapons. It would therefore be better if one no longer made a difference between strategic and tactical weapons, but between big and small weapons.

The researchers are still looking for solutions to miniaturize the bomb. Therefore, the question of whether the German army had to be equipped with the weapons cannot be answered before the tests will have shown any results.[28]

Adenauer himself considered it an open question whether one would be able to fit the bomb to the size of cannons (*Geschütze*) measuring 10–12 centimetres. To explain to the leading party officials the various steps in the evolution of nuclear weapons, he continued with the following historical overview:

Einstein was the first to point out the possibility of nuclear fission in a letter to Roosevelt [Adenauer refers to Einstein's letter of 2 August 1939]; and asked the latter to develop the bomb during the war against Germany. The Americans then began the research. The result of Einstein's letter was the Hiroshima bomb. However, and that is the reason why I mention this, Einstein had mentioned in the same letter that the bomb would be so heavy and big that it could not be transported by plane, but only by ship. It was known that when a ship transporting such a weapon would fall into the hands of the enemy the port as well as all of the anchoring ships would be destroyed.[29]

And with a reference to the development of the technology he concluded:

Today, we transport the bomb by plane, and besides the atomic bomb we also have the hydrogen bomb, which works through a completely different physical mechanism. I do not want to explain the difference of the hydrogen bomb in more detail because I do not want to deck myself out in borrowed plumes. It is enough to say that its functioning relies on a completely different mechanism. I rather want to stress that the whole field of the production of nuclear energy is still full of technical surprises so that nowadays even physicists consider the uranium atom obsolete. That's why the price of the uranium went down so abruptly. Nobody knows where the technical progress will lead. It is good that it is the way it is. If we tell the people, they would get scared even more.[30]

Adenauer's elaboration illustrates that the Chancellor's controversial statement about tactical atomic weapons was not a singular one. In a press conference on 4 April 1957 he said:

Tactical atomic weapons are basically nothing but the further development of artillery. It goes without saying that, due to this powerful development in weapons technique (which we unfortunately now have), we cannot forgo these weapons for our troops. We must follow the lead of others and have these new weapons—they are after all practically normal weapons.[31]

The remarks provoked the protest by eighteen of Germany's most distinguished physicists in addition to Albert Schweitzer. These respected personalities warned that in the nuclear age tactical weapons would have the same destructive power as the Hiroshima bomb, and they also illustrated that the explosion of a hydrogen bomb would extinguish life in Germany's most vibrant regions. Although the scientists admitted that defensive efforts by the

West were a necessary counterweight to communist expansionism and argued that the weapon would contribute to stability, they concluded that the potential risks of the weapons were too dangerous to be relied upon in the long-term.[32] For the first time German public opinion reacted against nuclear weapons; such controversy would not be seen again until the NATO 'Dual Track Decision' in 1979.

In 1957, Adenauer had to mobilize all his abilities to calm not only the physicists' worries, but also internal party criticism. The controversy was potentially quite harmful to Adenauer's chances in the federal elections scheduled for the fall of that year.[33]

The incident reveals Adenauer's self-perception as a 'statesman', a position which in Adenauer's mind implied a differentiation of the responsibilities of political actors and those of pure political observers. He argued that a statesman, unlike a scientist, must not only act to the best of his beliefs, but also must recognize that the failure to act might make him as culpable as if he had taken the wrong decision.[34] Adenauer's strong sense of responsibility was rooted in his religious beliefs. In this sense, he perceived nuclear weapons more as an ethical than a moral or even emotional challenge. As a realist he emphasized the weight of political, military, and economic factors: 'it is absurd to think that through the surrender of the German people, or of Europe for that matter, the rivalry between the United States and the Soviet Union will be solved.'[35] And in the Council meeting of the Christian Democratic Party on 11 May 1957 he concluded with respect to the atmosphere in Germany at the time: 'We are in a kind of a ray psychosis. Everybody knows that radioactive rays might be dangerous and that a physician normally avoids X-raying a pregnant woman. It is also well known that one takes precautions in an X-ray room . . . and that still there are injuries. However, this whole debate is completely exaggerated, and the population is somewhat in a panic.'[36] The statement is another example of how the Chancellor perceived his relationship with the public. He took on the role of elder statesman, whose task was to educate, inform, and calm the thinking and emotions of the masses, though he had little respect for public opinion.

As a highly talented political strategist, he had his own way of dealing with the impact of public opinion on the nuclear debate. His strategy was to be as vague as possible in the public discussion of unpleasant topics, particularly military affairs. In the case of nuclear weapons in the German army he simply pretended the whole issue was not yet on the political agenda, a tactical approach coming, as it did, shortly before federal elections in the fall of 1957.

Adenauer none the less realized that fear of the bomb would be too difficult to overcome in a society which had suffered through two world wars. In a nuclear weapons analysis he used in the campaign of 1957, he concluded: 'We will not be able to eliminate the fear of weapons in this country. This is something we have to face.'[37] The postscript shows that Adenauer himself was not immune to irrationality and emotions: 'I am afraid that the fear of the atomic bomb has a major impact on women. They are our largest voting bloc, and therefore the issue could have very serious consequences for the party.'[38]

However simplistic, naïve, or ignorant Adenauer's ideas on nuclear weapons might have been, one should not draw wrong conclusions about Adenauer's thinking regarding the political impact of these weapons; he had a very good feeling for the weapons as a policy instrument.

Adenauer's Nuclear Options: Playing the National, Transatlantic, and Western European Cards?

Adenauer's perception of the post-war international system centred around two revolutionary developments: the decline of Europe and the rise of the United States and the Soviet Union to superpower status. During his thirteen years at the top of German political life, Adenauer was deeply afraid that the two superpowers would divide the world between themselves. In a cabinet meeting on 9 November 1956, he elaborated this view: 'That's exactly what I already told the American governor of Cologne in 1945. If they [the Americans] face the possibility of war against Russia, they'll compromise on division'.[39] Nuclear weapons could have significant consequences: 'either the two powers will have to fight, which would be devastating, or they'll divide the world between themselves; thus, all the other countries won't be of any importance.'[40] With its indispensable economic productive capacity, Western Europe was in great danger of becoming the prize of this superpower rivalry.[41] The Chancellor considered it therefore an 'unbearable thought'[42] that the United States and the Soviet Union were the only nations to have a nuclear arsenal.

Adenauer argued that the United States did not wish a permanent presence in Europe. Citing the example of the Suez crisis, he predicted that this under-lying rationale was going to be strengthened by conflicts of interest between Western Europe and its transatlantic ally. America's claim of leadership on the one hand and the dependence of the European powers on the United States on the other hand would lead Western Europe into decadence in the long run. This fear was magnified by the appearance of non-white peoples on the world stage; Adenauer wondered whether Western Europe could maintain its cul-tural supremacy under this condition. This would only be the case if Europe resisted any kind of dependence in the long run. Otherwise, he concluded that Europe, like other cultures before, was doomed to disappear.[43]

The combination of power politics and belief in European cultural supremacy made nuclear weapons a crucial factor in determining the inter-national status of Western Europe as well as that of Germany. The Chancellor showed the same underlying rationale in his attitude towards nuclear weapons as did the French leadership for example. However, the heritage of the Holocaust made a difference between French and German aspirations: the French leaders of the Fourth Republic, and in particular de Gaulle at the beginning of the Fifth Republic, considered the unification of Europe as a means of rivalling the two superpowers as well as a method of gaining political dominance over continental Western Europe. Adenauer, on the other hand, could only use Western European unification as a way to make Germany an equal member of the post-war international order. Unlike de Gaulle, he could not afford to think of his country's international standing for its own sake. Status had to serve the triple goal of national equality, security, and unification.

Statements like that of former French Prime Minister Michel Debré in 1956, that 'nations without the bomb are satellites' only opened old sores and made him suspicious of French nuclear oligopolism.[44] Furthermore, the Chancellor's fears of the division of the world between the two superpowers was nourished by the variety of proposals during the 1950s to impose upon Germany a secondary status: it did not matter to the Chancellor whether those plans came from Allied desks as for example the American Radford Plan of 1956 or French plans for a Tripartite (*Dreierdirektorium*) of 1958, or from the Warsaw Pact desk, as for example the Rapacki Plan of 1956. The status question was also the driving force behind Adenauer's claims for nuclear co-operation. He welcomed the French proposal for a co-operative trilateral nuclear effort in 1957–8 and the American proposal for a multilateral nuclear force (MFN) in 1959–60.

Playing the National Card

Adenauer was by no means willing to accept the status of a 'nuclear have-not' and this became particularly obvious during his second and third terms in office. One could even argue that this was the principal difference between Adenauer's nuclear policy and that of his successors who eagerly accepted Germany's status as a non-nuclear power.

Because of Germany's recent past, Adenauer's policy was restrained. During his first term in office, there was only a nuclear policy in West Germany. The Federal Republic was not yet sovereign, and the German government had to accept unconditionally the nuclearization of the American forces on German territory. When West Germany gained more political weight after the failure of the European defence community in the French parliament in August 1954, Adenauer saw his chance and took it. The German government declared, even before the opening of the second round of negotiations on the German contribution to European defence, that any kind of military restriction would henceforth be based first on a 'voluntary letter of renunciation' and, second, would only relate to a quantitative rather than a qualitative restriction.[45] Adenauer could not achieve his maximum goal of acquisition and production of nuclear weapons in the nine-power conference in London in the fall of 1954. Adenauer's compromise renunciation of the production of those weapons was not only the breakthrough in negotiations, but it also granted the Federal Republic the nuclear option: *the compromise prohibited the production of the weapons; it implicitly allowed acquisition.*[46]

When Adenauer brought up his renunciation in a Council meeting of the

Christian Democratic party in October 1954, he did not attach much value to it. He presented his decision not to pursue the development of a West German nuclear force for the moment purely in terms of cost–benefit analysis. He still did not think that Germany had the scientific and financial capacities to develop its own nuclear arsenal and therefore accepted West Germany's dependence on Allied protection:

On what concerns nuclear weapons, the development of a new H-bomb costs around 10 million dollars today. We do not know anything about the costs in the future. It is obvious that we do not have the facilities for their production; we renounced production in the EDC-treaty. When I declared the renunciation in London, the Belgians and Dutch followed voluntarily. We do not have to worry about discrimination.[47]

However, Adenauer did not regard his declaration as Germany's last word:

When I gave the declaration, Dulles got up at the other side of the table. He walked towards me speaking with a loud voice: 'Mr Chancellor, you just declared that the Federal Republic of Germany renounced the production on nuclear weapons on its territory. Do I understand you correctly that this declaration, like all other declarations and responsibilites in international law, has to be considered *rebus sic stantibus*?' I answered him equally with a loud voice: 'You interpreted my declaration correctly!' The other participants were silent.[48]

Hans-Peter Schwarz remarks that Adenauer, who usually was not shy about making decisions on his own at international conferences, would even follow up with a kind of excuse because of the importance of the issue in the long run.[49] The Chancellor continued his account of the London conference:

It is often said about me that I am a man of solitary decisions. This is not correct. The only really lonely decision I ever took during all of my chancellorship—not to bring it up in the cabinet, the parliamentary group of the Christian Democrats, or the Council of the party—was the declaration of renunciation. Because of the course of the negotiations I had no other choice.[50]

Adenauer's military adviser and translator at the London conference, Count Kielmansegg, does not exclude that Dulles brought up the formula of the *clausula rebus sic stantibus* at another time. He remembers that the conference had been interrupted after Adenauer's renunciation on ABC-weapons. During the break, first the Dutchman Paul-Henri Spaak asked Kielmansegg to express his respect for the Chancellor's decision: 'Tell the Chancellor that he is a greater European than I am'. According to Kielmansegg's account, Adenauer did not bat an eye nor did he say anything. Then Dulles had walked towards the Chancellor saying: 'Mr Chancellor, I would like to thank you. I know very well what the renunciation means to you. I understand that you are worried about the future implications of this'. Adenauer had responded: 'Well, Mr Dulles, let us first have the twelve divisions. Then we will talk about this issue'. Dulles had smiled and left the room.[51] Kielmansegg emphasizes that Dulles did not use the term *clausula rebus sic stantibus*.

Whichever of the two accounts is correct makes no difference; both show that Adenauer did not think of his renunciation as permanent. In the fall of 1954 nothing was yet decided. Each time the Allies made attempts to impose a secondary status on Germany, Adenauer would come back to his version of the London conference. This, for example, was the case during the negotiations about EURATOM in 1956, which coincided with the first major post-war American-German crisis over the Radford Plan to reduce American conventional forces in Germany. Adenauer not only pushed hard for European unification, but also emphasized a national nuclear option.

The French side had never left any doubt about treaty exceptions for the production of French nuclear weapons. However, it was not willing to grant such a provision for Germany. In the cabinet meeting on 5 October 1956, the Minister of Nuclear Energy Strauss and the Minister of Economics, Erhard, were at the forefront of the criticism of France's one-sided position: 'The EURATOM-treaty is more a sacrifice than an advantage for us. It controls German nuclear research rather than helps it.'[52] Because of his scepticism about NATO at the time, Adenauer brushed the critique aside. Two weeks before Strauss he had stated his position on the issue: 'Germany can no longer remain a nuclear protectorate.'[53] He presented the EURATOM treaty as a detour in Germany's long-run goal to become a nuclear power. Notes by Minister von Merkatz express Adenauer's position more explicitly: 'The establishment of EURATOM will give us the possibility to legitimately acquire nuclear weapons in the long run. For the moment, others, including France, are ahead of us.'[54]

Another example of Germany's claim for a nuclear option, this time in transatlantic politics, was Adenauer's visit to Washington in the fall of 1961, during which President Kennedy raised the possibility of German nuclear weapons. Again, Adenauer gave his version of the London conference. Kennedy made it clear that the United States still thought of German renunciation as most desirable. The President argued that a German nuclear arsenal would only increase the potential for war without strengthening security. Adenauer had no other choice than to accomodate US policy, taking into account that the meeting took place during the second Berlin crisis (1958–63).[55] Hans-Peter Schwarz concludes that both statesmen were well advised to ask their translators at the end of their talk to destroy their notes.[56]

However, Adenauer never really revolted against Germany's political constraints, which were forced on the country because of the Holocaust and the Cold War. The Chancellor knew only too well that West Germany could not take the path France had chosen and aim for its own nuclear arsenal. That would have been too great a challenge to the three Allied nations, on whom West Germany, and particularly West Berlin, would be depending in a crisis: the United States, France, and Great Britain. His statements about the national option were of a rhetorical nature. This became particularly clear in Adenauer's last fight, the opposition to the non-proliferation treaty, just a few months before his death in April 1967. He thought that a renunciation according to the wishes of the Soviet Union would be the end for any German hopes for nuclear equality, and argued polemically against the treaty as a 'Morgenthau Plan in quadrate'. This last desperate rebellion shows that Adenuaer actually experienced the failure of his nuclear policy.

Playing the Transatlantic Card

The constraints put on post-war German defence policy made Adenauer into a highly flexible statesman with respect to his conduct of alliance politics: he was bouncing back and forth between close co-operation with the United States and close co-operation with the European powers, particularly France. Until 1962–3 Adenauer's alliance politics were of an accommodating nature; he tried to suit the security interests of all of Germany's Western Allies. This meant that Adenauer was not only trying for a settlement that took into account the security interests of the United States, France, and Great Britain. He was also sensitive to the smaller powers like Italy and the Benelux countries.

During the 1950s and the early 1960s, the Chancellor still paid tribute to Germany's overall dependence on American protection, and became eager to express his transatlantic credo: 'The idea of European unification will either lead to a federalist structure and will therefore survive, or Europe will disappear in its hitherto existing form and culture. A militarily neutral Germany or a German refusal to join the Western countries means the failure for European unification'. And he continued, that 'Europe would fail without the support of the United States'. Only a strong and unified West would be able to survive.[57]

First doubts about American security guarantees arose during the 'Radford crisis' of the summer of 1956. Adenauer realized that a significant reduction of American conventional forces would imply stronger emphasis on nuclear weapons. He was very critical of the strategic reorientation of the Anglo-Saxon powers, for which he found not only evidence of the recent American plans, but also of the British decision to go ahead with the development of a hydrogen bomb. From Adenauer's perception, this worsened Germany's 'nuclear dilemma'.[58] This means that he was aware of nuclear deterrence as a guarantee against any major war on the one hand, and the fear that any nuclear war would be particularly difficult for West Germany, whose territory would be the potential nuclear battlefield, on the other. Adenauer argued that the possibility of nuclear war would be increased if conventional forces were reduced because nuclear weapons would be the only recourse in the event of a military confrontation and the two superpowers would be under less pressure to make progress with a disarmament agreement, which Adenauer considered as the only effective way to ban nuclear war.[59]

Adenauer's reaction in the summer of 1956 offers evidence for McGeorge Bundy's conclusion that it was not American doctrine, and not American nuclear warheads in particular locations, but the American military presence in Europe and the American political commitment which it represented and reinforced, that established nuclear danger. Kennedy's former aide quotes Michael Howard, who argued that American military presence was needed in the first place 'not just in the negative role of a *deterrent* to Soviet aggression, but in the positive role of a *reassurance* to the West Europeans'.[60]

Adenauer's thinking was contradictory: he stressed both the necessity of a linkage between nuclear and conventional weapons to avoid war and the need for world-wide nuclear disarmament. This becomes obvious in the three different tracks of German nuclear policy which developed in the aftermath of the Radford crisis.

The crisis resulted primarily in a strong reorientation towards NATO, particularly with Germany's backing of equipment from its army with American controlled tactical nuclear weapons in the aftermath of the annual NATO-review conference of 30 October 1956. It was at this time that Adenauer finally appointed Franz-Josef Strauss as Secretary of Defence.[61] In particular, the German ambassador to NATO, Herbert Blankenhorn, pushed hard for a change at the top of the Defence Department: 'What counts now is to make our new course on the issue of rearmament credible with a new person . . . It will be much easier for the new secretary to convince the Council of our efforts than for a Defence Secretary, who was for years the symbol for German delay in rearmament.'[62] It was in his talk with Adenauer on 10 October 1956 about the appointment, that Strauss was given a free hand in the nuclearization of the German Army.

At the conference of the NATO Council in December 1956, Strauß requested the equipment of Germany's army with tactical nuclear weapons on the divisional level. Unlike the Chancellor, Strauss had a grasp of the complex issues of nuclear deterrence from the very beginning. Adenauer had a defence secretary who was eager to integrate nuclear weapons into defence planning, whether it was on the national level as for example in the EURATOM negotiations or on the transatlantic level as during the equipment of the German army with tactical nuclear weapons in 1956–7.[63] In general, Strauss became the driving force behind the integration of nuclear weapons into German defence planning. Strauss often chose his own way in negotiations with the Americans or the British and did not always report his activities to the Chancellor.

The second aspect of Adenauer's nuclear policy following the Radford crisis relates to initiatives for nuclear disarmament. From his perspective, the Radford Plan had discredited the concept of world-wide disarmament. With reference to Germany's particular nuclear dilemma, Adenauer argued that Germany depended on disarmament agreements between East and West more than any other European nation: 'It is very likely that something as frightening as a nuclear war might really induce the Russians to negotiate with the Americans. If we should achieve an agreement on nuclear weapons between the two powers, our fear of Russian expansionism would be much less. At that moment the bells of liberty would also ring for Eastern Germany.'[64] Adenauer's rhetoric for general controlled disarmament was first of all founded upon West Germany's geopolitical situation, but was further strengthened by Adenauer's aversion to having technological developments dictate politics. The Chancellor argued that in contrast to earlier periods in history, when politics took advantage of technological developments, politics were now driven by technology. That is why he could think of nuclear weapons as a stabilizing force in the international system and also repudiate them as an unbearable burden for modern statesmanship. Adenauer pictured a political process which would start with a conference on the German question and a European security system, and then lead to an overall disarmament conference aiming for a peace mechanism, namely nuclear and conventional disarmament.[65]

This thread of Adenauer's policy can be illustrated with internal German plans linking disarmament and unification. Parallel to Germany's reorientation towards NATO, Adenauer's aides, Blankenhorn, von Eckart, and Heusinger, worked on a complex plan in case the Eisenhower Administration should undertake 'a profound reexamination' of its foreign policy after the presidential elections: 'There is no doubt that the American troops will leave Germany, and perhaps even from all of Europe, in no later than four years.'[66] The advisers thought that the United States might begin to put more emphasis on the United Nations than it had before, at the expense of NATO. They also stressed possibilities for a peaceful arrangement with the Soviet Union.

The latter consideration has to be seen in the overall context of Adenauer's policy towards the Soviet Union as it had emerged by 1952. By that time Adenauer had given up his fears of an Eastern German or Soviet invasion in Germany, which had guided his thinking in 1950 and 1951. Adenauer now believed in the possibility of a peaceful settlement of the differences between the Soviet Union and West Germany, believing that because of its own national interest the Soviet Union would contribute to a peaceful settlement of European problems.[67]

With the first draft of his disarmament plan in 1956, von Eckart followed up on Adenauer's new perception of the Soviet threat. He concluded that Germany's foreign policy had to take advantage of this new situation for German reunification. According to the handwritten draft, von Eckart, as a first step, proposed a parallel retreat of Soviet forces from the Eastern European countries, including the German Democratic Republic, and of the American forces from Germany, both to be started in 1957 and 1959. In a second step, both sides should remove their air forces from German territory. And finally in a third step, both countries should meet at an all-round disarmament conference in 1959 in order 'to achieve a general disarmament agreement that would eliminate *all* foreign troops on *European* territory'.[68]

However, Adenauer's advisers did not believe that the Soviet Union, with respect to its interests in its Eastern European sphere of influence, would accept free elections in Germany at the beginning of this process. Von Eckart therefore planned an alternate way to achieve that goal, and linked the disarmament plan with two plans aimed respectively at German reunification and an all-European unification. Here, too, he imagined a three-step procedure: first a German plebiscite, then the establishment of a 'National Council' responsible for the operational details of German reunification, and finally, free elections. The plan for German reunification would be complemented by another plan, which aimed for the establishment of an all-European organization.

Although Adenauer first backed the work of his advisers, he became sceptical of such a new course at the beginning of 1957. His reservations were based on an increased feeling of insecurity in German public opinion following the Soviet invasion in Hungary. Adenauer continued to focus on the re-establishment of NATO unity.[69]

From the perspective of the events of 1957, it is all the more surprising that Adenauer considered such proposals even if it was only for a brief moment at the turn of the year. Had the American side known about the internal German plans, it would have been even more suspicious in its reaction towards the third thread of German policy in the aftermath of the Radford crisis: the secret project of French-Italian-German nuclear co-operation.

Playing the European Card: French–German–Italian Nuclear Co-operation

The French administration of Felix Gaillard launched the project for trilateral nuclear co-operation in the fall of 1957. Earlier contacts about a possible continental European nuclear co-operation existed but had not led anywhere. Since 1955 the French approached the German government, for example, during the negotiations of the accord of Colomb-Béchar in January 1957, to build a particle accelerator.[70] However, it took the critical mass of events in international politics of 1956–7 for the French government to put a precise project together. Those events included the NATO crisis following the Radford Plan in the fall of 1956; the perception of a more imminent threat by the Soviet Union after the successful launching of the first intercontinental missile on 26 August 1957 and the satellite 'Sputnik' on 4 October and 3 November 1957; the failure of the British-French military intervention in the Suez crisis in November 1956; the American-British agreement during the Bermuda Summit in March 1957; and the British decision to develop its own hydrogen bomb.[71]

With regard to the US nuclear guarantee, the French concluded that Europe would have to prepare for the retreat of the American forces, and the eventual weakening of American nuclear protection. Although the French did not think that the United States would remove its forces soon, they thought such a move likely as soon as the United States had developed intercontinental nuclear weapons.[72]

The French made the principal decisions for co-operation with Germany and Italy in November and December 1956. Three factors finally convinced the French government and its military officials that they could only undertake the development of the 'bomb' with foreign support: the political instability of the Fourth Republic; the need for scientific and technical support; and the financial constraints imposed on French defence planning by the Algerian war. Paris, of course, also had in mind Germany's renunciation of the production of nuclear weapons, including intermediate-range missiles of 1954. Research and development therefore had to be done on French or Italian territory. And the French did not specify to whom the weapons, which would be developed on French territory, would belong. France also did not intend to give up its leading role in the WEU.

In a first phase running from September 1956 through October 1957, the French side prepared the ground, but did not present an invitation to the German government before November 1957. In a second phase, then, it started bilateral and finally trilateral negotiations.[73] Assistant Secretary of State Maurice Faure, and the French Ambassador in Germany, Maurice Couve de Murville, presented their strategic analysis in a secret meeting to the German Chancellor at Adenauer's home in Rhöndorf on 16 November 1957. The French did not present the project as a strictly European undertaking, but as one that could very well be integrated into NATO. The delegation told the Chancellor that Minister President Gaillard wanted to inform the Allies as early as the NATO conference the following December in Paris.

From the very beginning it was obvious for the German interlocutors that this approach concealed the French aim for a national option that was transformed into a European one only because of political and financial constraints. However, Adenauer was interested in the establishment of a European nuclear consortium that would produce nuclear warheads and delivery systems. In his response, Adenauer presented his usual doubts about the American security guarantee and approved the underlying rationale of the proposal to readjust NATO symmetry as well as to increase the Western defence with regard to the Soviet Union. To this extent, German and French interests were the same.

They parted where France's political concern came into play. As before, during the EURATOM negotiations, the Chancellor regarded the project as just another milestone on the way to German equality, but not as a goal in itself. Adenauer also opposed France's general antagonism towards the Atlantic powers, the United States and Great Britain. He made it clear that the German government did not want to get into another crisis with the Americans; one must keep in mind that the Chancellor's nuclear policy at the time was under heavy fire because of the public arousal provoked by his 'Artillery statement', and the equipment of the *Bundeswehr* with tactical nuclear weapons.

The Chancellor also did not want to exclude Great Britain and the United States to the extent the French did. The French plan precluded any kind of co-operation with Great Britain for the above described reasons. Adenauer, on the other hand, did not discount the chance that Great Britain would change its course once the United States and/or continental Europe went their own ways. And indeed, until the very end of the project, Adenauer made every effort to keep the project open for British co-operation.[74]

Adenauer was willing to pursue the French proposal and both sides agreed to have their defence secretaries negotiate details. Jacques Chaban-Delmas and Franz-Josef Strauss, were asked to talk about operational issues concerning the production of tactical and strategic weapons as well as about general scientific co-operation between the two countries. With his usual distrust for defence officials, Adenauer emphasized that he did not want the defence secretaries to discuss overall political implications. Beginning with a meeting of the two ministers four days later in Paris, a whole series of bilateral and/or trilateral talks started, which took place by turns in Paris, Bonn, and Rome. Until May 1958, the three countries negotiated an ambitious nuclear programme that included the building of a common particle accelerator in Pierrelatte (France) as well as common research, development, and production of nuclear warheads for tactical and strategic weapons, delivery systems, and intermediate-range missiles.[75]

The French were determined to go ahead with the project even if the United States should refuse co-operation. That at least Chaban-Delmas and Strauss did not want the United States or Great Britain to co-operate with the continental powers was illustrated by their decision to keep the talks secret. Strauss also knew that it was politically smart to keep the project secret because of Germany's foreign policy constraints. A change of the pertinent clauses of the Paris treaties could have only been undertaken by the German parliament. In that case, the government would have had to inform the public. Such a decision, German officials argued, might not only endanger the project because of German pacifism, but, because of Germany's division, might also lead to ultimatums by the Soviet Union to stop the project. They agreed that the German government would hide the project from the Treasury and the parliament behind a German contribution for a 'European Research Institute for Aeronautics'.[76]

The Chancellor took account of Germany's foreign policy constraints in still another fashion. He informed Dulles before the NATO conference about the trilateral talks. He said that he had charged Strauss with negotiations but emphasized that the cabinet had not yet sanctioned them. The project therefore was not a secret to the Allies. The Americans knew as early as the spring of 1957 of the French-German undertaking, and from November 1957 on were informed by the Chancellor personally.[77]

The Eisenhower administration worried most about the project's implications for nuclear proliferation, and from the beginning was critical of the European initiative. However, the Eisenhower administration was not as dogmatic on non-nuclear proliferation as the Kennedy administration would be during the 1960s. And it seems that the Americans approved the trilateral co-operation shortly before and during the NATO conference in Paris. However, soon after, Dulles countered the trilateral co-operation with the proposal of a five-nation nuclear agency in which France, Germany, and Italy would have the same rights as the United States and Great Britain.[78]

Meanwhile, the trilateral negotiations went ahead and the three defence secretaries signed a 'Memorandum of Understanding' on Easter Sunday 1958 in Rome. However, it was immediately cast into doubt by the fall of the Fourth Republic in France. Nevertheless, during a meeting with French defence officials on 17 June 1958, General de Gaulle decided to go ahead with a national nuclear programme: *'La capacité atomique . . . ne se partage pas'.*[79]

The trilateral project shows that Adenauer again and again tested Germany's political constraints. The trilateral experiment is also revealing with respect to three other features of Adenauer's nuclear policy. First, it illustrates once again the Chancellor's willingness in principle not only to aim for acquisition of nuclear weapons, but also for production. Second, the project throws some light on Adenauer's rhetoric on the disarmament issue, showing that one could not take these proposals seriously. And third, the German decision to play the European card did not illustrate a turning away from close co-operation with the United States to closer co-operation with other European powers. Instead, it does clarify Germany's foreign policy constraints during the Cold War, which made German policy bounce back and forth between transatlantic and European co-operation.

Nuclear Weapons and the Second Berlin Crisis

De Gaulle's national nuclear course, together with his ideas concerning a Tripartite Agreement, made Adenauer move back toward NATO at the end of the 1950s. Adenauer's course was strengthened by proposals for nuclear sharing in the late Eisenhower period.[80] NATO Supreme Commander in Europe, General Lauris Norstad, for example in 1958, made arrangements with German military authorities to train a German fighter-bomber unit with some nuclear capability. Norstad's plan also included the construction of a nearby storage container area. This project, known as 'Wagon Train', was successfully completed in late 1958. Norstad followed up in 1959–60 with a proposal to make NATO the fourth atomic power to accommodate European claims for more nuclear rights. This plan, which Norstad presented to Adenauer at a meeting in the summer of 1960, aimed at a reform of Allied rights concerning the storage and use of nuclear weapons stationed on Allied territory, including Germany. Norstad proposed that the United States should share those rights with Great Britain, France, Italy, and Germany in an emergency.[81] Thus, about the same time as the Soviets provoked the Berlin crisis, the German nuclear issue was coming to a head.

Khrushchev's ultimatum of 26 November 1956, in which the Soviets claimed to transform Berlin into a 'free city' and asked for the removal of the

Western powers, had been taken back by the Soviets during the summit at Camp David a year later. However, contingency planning about when and how the Western powers would go to war over Berlin were henceforth a permanent topic on the Allied agenda between 1959 and 1963.[82]

It was during the five years of the second Berlin crisis that Adenauer was directly confronted with Germany's nuclear dilemma: was Germany willing to integrate the eventual *use* of nuclear weapons into Allied contingency planning? Although German representatives were only integrated in July 1961 into the actual planning for 'Live Oak', the cover name for Allied contingency planning in a war over Berlin, Adenauer from the beginning had to take a stand in his meetings with United States officials.[83]

The records of Adenauer's talks with his advisers and with American officials show that the Chancellor did not have any desire to push the confrontation to its bitter end and turn his country into a nuclear battlefield. This became clear after the Soviets stopped a US military convoy in November 1958 as well as during the deliberation on the West's response to the Soviet 'agent theory' and when East Germany started to seal itself off with the construction of the Wall in August 1961.

In an internal meeting with his advisers before Dulles' visit to Bonn in February 1959, Adenauer formulated three principles which should guide Allied action. The Chancellor brought them up during his meeting on 7 February 1959 with the Secretary of State. First, he told Dulles that the Allies had to avoid any situation which would bring their differences over the German question into the public eye. Second, the United States, Great Britain, and France had to keep various options open in order not to get into a defensive position. Third, nuclear weapons should not be used by any means. The three principles were vague, but considering internal German planning at the time one could interpret them as follows: Great Britain as the least aggressive Western power should determine the speed and intensity of military action. The Chancellor wanted to exclude any attack because of Soviet conventional superiority. The Chancellor saw the danger of Western humiliation in the event that the Allies were not united behind a course of defence. In this case, the Allies would have no choice other than to use nuclear weapons—the worst-case scenario that the Chancellor wanted to avoid by all means.

Dulles, who was not willing to exclude the use of nuclear weapons, did not agree with the Chancellor. If the Soviets should block access to Berlin, he argued, the Allies would have to use force. The use of force, he added, meant ultimately the use of nuclear weapons. The Secretary of State could not imagine anything more dangerous to Allied planning than the exclusion of the use of nuclear weapons because of the Soviet superiority in the conventional sphere in Europe. Adenauer, facing Dulles' staunch will ultimately to use nuclear weapons gave up his resistance. Dulles then explained to the Chancellor the contingency planning the Allies had agreed on at the end of January in Washington in more detail. At the end of the talk, Dulles made it clear that there were not only three Western powers, but four; Germany had to take its share of responsibility. After all it was Germany that was concerned first of all. Dulles simply expected Bonn to agree fully with Allied planning.[84]

There were only a few months during Adenauer's Chancellorship in which his attitude toward the actual use of nuclear weapons was tested to the extent it was at the end of the Eisenhower administration. When the topic was brought up once again at the end of 1961, Adenauer was in favour of using nuclear weapons, although he knew that Kennedy was much more reluctant than was his predecessor in the Oval Office to risk a nuclear war over Berlin.[85] After East Germany's efforts to seal itself off in August of that year, Adenauer was also in a more defensive position than two years previously.[86] This scheme of Allied thinking with regard to the use of nuclear weapons would continue until the spring of 1963.

Although the possibility of the actual use of nuclear force was the major challenge for German policy between 1958 and 1963, Adenauer also stood up against Allied attempts to impose a secondary status on Germany in those years. It was General Norstad, who, parallel to his plans for nuclear sharing, came up with a plan for a security zone in Europe in the spring of 1960. The NATO official presented a plan, in which both Germanys, the Benelux countries, Denmark, and Norway—as well as Poland and Czechoslovakia—would be controlled by three thousand international observers to prevent any surprise attack.

Adenauer at no time believed in security zones. He had taken a negative stance towards such proposals since the interwar period. The existence of nuclear weapons only strengthened his resistance. Particularly in the context of the Rapacki Plan in the fall of 1956, Adenauer argued that such agreements had been disregarded in periods of crisis, and stressed that nuclear-free zones would probably not save countries like West Germany, Poland, Czechoslovakia, or East Germany from strategic or tactical nuclear strikes.[87]

In general, Adenauer's thinking on the impact of nuclear weapons on the post-war system was limited to the European and transatlantic sphere. It was not until the experience of the Cuban missile crisis that he considered the impact of nuclear weapons in a global context. In the last volume of his memoirs, which he never completed because of his death in April 1967, he concluded:

Nuclear technology overcomes long distances, and therefore brings dangers in distant areas of the world as for example the Far East, very close to us. Thinking of the extent to which the influence of modern weapons is felt . . . I am convinced that the distance between East Asia, where the Chinese prepare a nuclear war, and European cities no longer presents a security guarantee for us.[88]

From Adenauer's perspective, the challenges for German nuclear policy did not change during the 1950s and early 1960s. The theme of Germany's status and Europe's decline were as prominent at the end of his thirteen years in office as they were when he first came to power. The Chancellor was still preoccupied with the fear that Germany would be the first country to be turned into a nuclear battlefield in a military conflict between the United States and the Soviet Union. The difficult choices that Adenauer confronted were different from those faced by any other statesman during the Cold War.

12

Conclusion

JOHN LEWIS GADDIS

W HAT, then, was the effect of nuclear weapons on Cold War state-craft? Will the Cold War be remembered as the point at which the prospect of war among great powers shifted from the realm of rationality to that of absurdity? If such a shift occurred, did the nuclear revolution bring it about, or would it have happened in any event? What do the answers to these questions suggest about the role of nuclear weapons specifically—as well as the use of force generally—in the post-Cold War world?

One of these questions is easy to answer: it is clear enough now that during the Cold War the likelihood of a hot war involving the world's most powerful states did diminish to the point of being ludicrous. So when John Mueller published *Retreat from Doomsday: The Obsolescence of Major War* in 1989, the thesis suggested in his subtitle was relatively uncontroversial. The end of the Cold War and the subsequent collapse of the Soviet Union have, if anything, reinforced it.[1]

Mueller's explanation of how war became obsolete, however, was and remains controversial. Few other historians or theorists of international relations have accepted his argument that nuclear weapons had little or nothing to do with this outcome—that the global aversion to great-power war would have evolved even if such devices had never been invented.

As Ernest May points out in his introduction, there is no way to prove or disprove Mueller's 'irrelevancy' thesis. We cannot rerun the experiment, assuming away nuclear weapons to see what happens. History is not like chemistry. But we can try to specify more clearly the effects this breakthrough in the technology of destruction had upon the human propensity, when angered, to destroy.

That there was such an effect is undeniable. For after having been demonstrated against human targets at Hiroshima and Nagasaki in August 1945, tens of thousands of nuclear weapons were produced and deployed provocatively around the world—yet, not one of them was ever again used. Even if someone should someday violate that taboo, it would be hard to find a comparable example of so great a gap between the expected and actual utility of weaponry. Mueller's thesis challenges us to specify, more clearly than scholars of this subject have done in the past, just what brought it about.

I

Without exception, each of the ten statesmen discussed in this volume, as late as the summer of 1945, would have regarded war among great powers to be entirely within the realm of rational behaviour. It could hardly have been otherwise, given the extent to which their countries—and they themselves—had fought in World War II. There were no pacifists among them; indeed because of the clarity of the moral issues involved, there were fewer pacifists anywhere during that conflict than in any other major modern war. These men looked to the future with the *hope* that there would be no new conflagration—but with no great confidence.

Hiroshima and Nagasaki came as a shock to all of them, even to Truman, who decided to use the bomb, and to Churchill, who knew what the president's decision would be. The revelation that so many people and so much of a city could disappear in a single flash unsettled everyone. There was little rejoicing over what had happened: only a grim relief that the war would now end, together with a vague sense that the world—and warfare—would never be the same.

What surprised us though, as we reviewed the evidence, is how quickly that shock effect wore off. As post-war leaders tried to figure out what one actually *did* with atomic bombs, old ways of thinking reasserted themselves. They came to be seen, neither as so effective a weapon that they would guarantee victory to anyone who possessed and used them, nor as so terrible a weapon that they would render war itself impossible. There was, in between, a powerful psychological tug toward normality: toward trying to fit this new weapon within familiar categories of thought and practice.

One can see this most clearly with Winston Churchill. At the time of Hiroshima, he had known about the possibility of atomic bombs longer than any statesman then living. He found their physical effects awesome, but he had no doubt about the wisdom of using them against the Japanese—or about threatening to do the same in the contest with the Soviet Union that he saw as sure to come. The bomb, Churchill believed, might be the *only* means by which the Western democracies could stop the Soviet Union from taking over Europe.

The former prime minister argued vigorously, therefore, for a strategy that would confront the Russians with the prospect of atomic attack if they did not withdraw from their advanced positions in Europe. There is no hint that he regarded this as a hollow threat, nor does he appear to have worried about its moral implications. As long as the Russians could not retaliate, Churchill favoured using nuclear weapons in any way that would serve Anglo-American interests. They made appeasement obsolete, therefore, but by no means war itself.[2]

Churchill's hopes corresponded precisely with Stalin's fears. The possibility of atomic weapons was hardly new to him either, thanks to Soviet wartime espionage. But Hiroshima came as a double shock, in that it showed the

Americans to be capable both of building the bomb and of using it. Stalin had not pushed bomb development hard prior to Hiroshima, but—surprised and impressed by the Americans' success—he did so afterwards with remarkable purposefulness and without regard to costs.

Publicly Stalin feigned lack of concern about the bomb, but it is clear now this was a tactical ploy intended to deny the Americans leverage should they seek to extract political or psychological benefits from their new military capability. He understood that atomic weapons might not be decisive in war; but he was also certain that without them his country would be defenceless— hence his obvious relief when the Soviet Union at last perfected its own bomb. The advent of such weapons did not in any way alter Stalin's ideologically based view of the international system, however, or of the inevitability of conflict within it, or of the rationality, when necessary, of using force to ensure that one prevailed.[3]

Dwight D. Eisenhower also incorporated atomic weapons within an existing strategic framework. Horrified—initially—by the damage at Hiroshima and Nagasaki, he none the less adjusted quickly. As Army Chief of Staff and later as SACEUR, Eisenhower presided over the formulation of war plans that would have involved the use of many atomic bombs, but only in combination with World War II weaponry. It was not at all clear to him that these new devices alone would defeat the Soviet Union, even if only the United States possessed them. Eisenhower continued to place his primary faith in what Mueller has called the 'Detroit Deterrent': the capacity of the American economy to turn out so wide a *spectrum* of armaments that no other country could match it. War, for him, was by no means obsolete.[4]

John Foster Dulles paralleled Eisenhower's thinking. From having publicly condemned the bomb's use as immoral in 1945, he moved toward the view that if the Russians could get such a weapon, the Americans would have to retain it: the prospect of *their* possession expanded *our* moral latitude. By the time of the 1952 presidential campaign, Dulles had come around to condemning as *immoral* the Truman administration's strategy of containment, precisely because it had failed to threaten the use of nuclear weapons in resisting the expansion of international communism.[5]

For those leaders who had no atomic bomb and no immediate prospect of getting one, the tendency to incorporate the new weapon within old habits of thinking was even more pronounced. Mao Zedong dismissed the atomic bomb, famously, as a 'paper tiger'.[6] Charles de Gaulle thought it important as a symbol of national authority, but not as something that would change past patterns of great power conflict.[7] Konrad Adenauer, denied even the most basic information about atomic bombs, also fell back on familiar assumptions about war and world politics: the new weapons, he believed along with Mao and de Gaulle, would not greatly change things.[8]

The Cold War statesman who came closest to regarding atomic bombs as revolutionary was the only one to have authorized their use—Harry S. Truman. More than any of his contemporaries the president resisted the urge to 'normalize' atomic weapons. He alone seems to have retained the view that these devices were so exceptional that they might not be usable as other weapons of war had always been. He appears to have had the sense, from the start, that atomic bombs might render warfare itself obsolete. Truman at no point relinquished his conviction that nuclear weapons were somehow differ- ent: hence his determination not to delegate responsibility for their use; hence his reluctance to brandish them in his public statements.

Beyond this, though, Truman was unwilling to act on his intuition that the nature of warfare had changed. He allowed war planning to proceed as if such weapons would be used, albeit only with his permission. He authorized the expanded production of atomic weapons and initiated the world's *second* pro- gramme to develop a thermonuclear bomb—Soviet scientists, we now know, were already working on such devices.[9] He made a sincere effort, through the Baruch Plan, to achieve the international control of atomic weapons; but it was nevertheless a *narrow* effort, presented on a 'take it or leave it' basis that required the Soviet Union simply to trust—not to negotiate with—the United States. The president himself would never have accepted it, had the circum- stances been reversed.

Truman did, in one way, translate his instinct that nuclear weapons were revolutionary into practical policy: he established, in the Korean War, the important precedent that they would not be used each time a great power got into conflict, even if the other side lacked the full means of retaliation. But it is too much to conclude from this that Truman regarded the use of force by great powers against other great powers as henceforth impossible. What deterred him as much as anything else was the prospect of a hostile public response, both at home and abroad, if the United States should again be the first to use nuclear weapons. Truman's sense that the world had changed, one has to conclude, grew to a considerable extent out of tightly held feelings of guilt over the fact that he himself had changed it.[10]

The 'atomic revolution', therefore, was not particularly revolutionary. Once they got over the initial shock that such a thing was possible, early Cold War statesmen found ways to incorporate atomic bombs within existing frame- works of thought. With the possible exception of Truman, they did not sig- nificantly alter their conviction that war among great powers could still be a rational act. They may well have regarded a new world war as a remote prospect; certainly all of them saw it as an undesirable one. But they still thought it possible to fight and win such a conflict.

We can never know for certain what kept them from trying to do so. But as Mueller has suggested, the deterrent during the first half-decade of the Cold War could as plausibly have been the fear of *non-nuclear* as of nuclear war. Removing atomic weapons from the history of that era would not fundamen- tally have changed it. There was as yet no consensus that a new world war would be much worse than the two earlier ones. And they had been bad enough.

II

That consensus would soon emerge, though, and the reason was the 'thermonuclear revolution' of the mid-1950s—an event that now looks to have been at least as important as the 'atomic revolution' of 1945. We tend today to lump together fission and fusion weapons, regarding both as equally horrible. That was not the view at the time, though. For just as most people had begun to assure themselves that atomic weapons had not indeed turned their world upside down, there came a weapon at least *a thousand times more powerful*—together with intermediate and intercontinental ballistic missiles, the means of delivering it on targets thousands of miles away in thirty minutes or less. In the wake of this development, none of the leaders we have studied (with the exception, of course, of Stalin, who died in 1953) found it possible to believe, any longer, that the world had not changed.

The effect, again, was most dramatic with Churchill. None of the leaders we studied had so obviously *enjoyed* war: one gets the impression at times, even in World War II, that he saw military conflict as some gigantic sporting event. His recklessness in exposing himself to battle, his petulance when not allowed to do so, suggests an almost boyish glorification of combat that would be chilling were it not for the fact that the wars he relished seem, on the whole, justifiable. No other post-war leader spoke so bluntly of actually *using*, not just threatening the use, of atomic weapons. Even after the Soviet Union had successfully tested its atomic bomb, Churchill could still insist, in 1952, on the probability of prevailing if war should come.[11]

And yet—by 1954 the prospect of war had become utterly repugnant to him. Great Britain, he thought, might not survive; the world itself could be at risk. What made the difference here, by Churchill's own testimony, was the hydrogen bomb, especially the unexpectedly powerful test of an American weapon, on 1 March, that spread radioactive fallout throughout the northern hemisphere. 'After a certain quantity had been produced on either side the factor of "over-taking", "superiority", etc. loses much of its meaning,' Churchill wrote Eisenhower later that month. 'If one side has five hundred and the other two hundred, both might be destroyed'.[12]

The great Englishman did not, to be sure, abandon hope. The capacity for mutual destruction might in time, he thought, lead the United States and the Soviet Union to settle their differences, if only for reasons of self-preservation. The new weapons were so horrendous that they could make geopolitical and ideological disputes seem insignificant. They could *force* the great powers to learn to live together. What that would mean, though, was nothing less than that they would have to give up war as a rational act of policy.

There was here, then, a remarkably abrupt shift in the views of a major Cold War leader—all the more surprising, as Jonathan Rosenberg points out, for the fact that Churchill was approaching his ninth decade when he made it. Old men do not normally repudiate the views of a lifetime. The fact that Churchill did so provides the most compelling evidence we have seen for the 'relevance' of nuclear weapons to the obsolescence of major war, precisely because he had gloried in war for so long, and now so decisively rejected it.

Somewhat surprisingly in the light of his reputation for favouring 'massive retaliation', Dulles went through a similar if less public shift in thinking. He had taken office as Secretary of State in 1953 determined to blur the distinction between nuclear and conventional weapons. But the first hydrogen bomb tests made it clear to him that their physical effects were so disproportionate to any conceivable reason for using such weapons that to do so would be disastrous. Even threatening their use might not be believable. Hence Dulles quietly began challenging the Eisenhower administration's reliance on nuclear deterrence, advocating what would later become known as a strategy of flexible response.[13]

As Neal Rosendorf has pointed out, the evolution of Dulles' thinking was indeed 'tortured', partly because he oscillated between highly principled and coldly realistic approaches to world politics, partly because his public rhetoric was often at odds with the positions he took behind the scenes. But the overall trend in Dulles' thinking after 1954 is clear: atomic weapons might fit within the Clausewitzian concept that war could be an extension of policy by other means. Thermonuclear weapons could never do so.

There is little reliable information regarding Nikita Khrushchev's views on the feasibility of using atomic weapons; but the first hydrogen bomb tests impressed him—and his colleagues in the post-Stalin leadership—very powerfully. Khrushchev's rival, Georgii Malenkov, may well have been the first leader anywhere to raise the possibility in public that a war fought with thermonuclear weapons might end world civilization. Because Khrushchev was challenging Malenkov at the time, he continued to argue Stalin's old position that socialism would triumph in any new world war, even if fought with atomic weapons. He did not really believe this, though, and after succeeding to the leadership in 1955, he set about revising some of the most basic assumptions of Marxist-Leninist ideology to reflect this new reality.

The old view had been that wars among capitalists, perhaps involving the Soviet Union, were inevitable: only through the destruction of warfare could the socialist revolution advance and eventually triumph. But at the Twentieth Party Congress early in 1956, Khrushchev acknowledged that a thermonuclear war would be so devastating that no one would survive it, whether capitalist or communist. It was necessary, then, to shift the class struggle from the anticipation of conflict to the necessity of 'peaceful coexistence'. The competition would continue, but within certain 'rules of the game', born of the need to avoid mutual destruction.[14]

Mao Zedong and Charles de Gaulle, too, found it difficult, in light of the thermonuclear revolution, to retain their views that nuclear weapons had not changed much: indeed there is a remarkable parallelism in their thinking, all the more striking for the cultural and ideological differences that separated them. Both had seen no immediate need to develop nuclear weapons because their countries could look to a superpower ally for its protection: France to the United States, by virtue of the North Atlantic Treaty of 1949, Mao to the Soviet Union through the Sino-Soviet Treaty of 1950. Such reassurance, however, required the superpowers to be willing to defend their smaller clients; and as the potential devastation of such a war took a quantum leap during the early 1950s, the credibility of such guarantees diminished.

Throughout his costly involvement in the Korean War, Mao had shown no interest in developing his own nuclear capability. The Soviet deterrent, he appears to have believed, would be enough; American threats to use nuclear weapons in Korea did not impress him. Then came the first big hydrogen bomb tests, followed by the Quemoy-Matsu crisis of 1954–5, in which the communists began shelling Nationalist-held islands off the China coast. The Americans threatened the use of nuclear weapons once again, and this time Mao took them seriously: to the point, in January 1955, of authorizing his own programme to build an atomic bomb. Implied in this decision was another consideration that became explicit later on: the credibility of Soviet commitments to defend China were much less in a thermonuclear age than they had been when it was only a matter of fighting wars with atomic bombs.[15]

De Gaulle went through a similar evolution in his thinking. From having held the view, during the late 1940s, that atomic bombs had not significantly revolutionized modern warfare, he had shifted by the mid-1950s to wondering what if anything would cause the Americans ever to use their nuclear weapons, given the levels of destruction that might then ensue. It followed from this that NATO's guarantee of French security could not be taken seriously. De Gaulle therefore came around to the view that the French—like the Chinese, would have to have their own bomb. The thermonuclear revolution, in both cases, had rendered superpower defence commitments problematic: the smaller powers would have to take matters into their own hands.[16]

Konrad Adenauer, too, found the thermonuclear revolution impressive. As early as December 1953, he had suggested that nuclear weapons might end civilization, but also that the prospect of such a thing might end war. He understood clearly that whatever happened to civilization, not much would be left of Germany if such a conflict should take place on its soil. Left to make his own choices, Adenauer would probably have followed the examples of Mao and de Gaulle, and developed an independent German nuclear capability. But since the legacy of World War II denied him that option, he fell back on making the American nuclear deterrent as credible as possible. The Americans reciprocated by treating West Germany as a virtual, if not an actual, nuclear ally. Despite this ambiguous outcome, Adenauer would in no way have thought nuclear weapons as irrelevant to German interests at the end of the 1950s as he had at the beginning.[17]

And what about Eisenhower, who commanded far more nuclear weapons than anyone else? Unconvinced, prior to becoming president, that atomic weapons had significantly changed the nature of warfare, he did not immediately change his thinking upon entering office. He was certainly aware of the conclusions that friends like Churchill and Dulles were coming around to as a result of the first hydrogen bomb tests. But he resisted the alternative courses of action they proposed: negotiations with the Russians, Churchill's preference, and the development of a flexible response strategy that would place less weight on nuclear deterrence, which Dulles favoured. Andrew Erdmann has argued that Eisenhower retained the view that it would be possible to fight and win a nuclear war at least through the end of 1955.

When shown the first assessments of the damage a Soviet nuclear attack would inflict upon the United States, though, Eisenhower shifted his position radically. 'We are rapidly getting to the point that no war can be *won*,' he wrote privately in April 1956. 'War implies a contest', but the point was approaching at which war would mean no contest at all but rather 'destruction of the enemy and suicide for ourselves'. The thermonuclear revolution had changed the nature of warfare so drastically that 'today we are further separated from the end of World War II than the beginning of the twentieth century was from the beginning of the sixteenth century.' By 1959, he was acknowledging publicly what he had already repeatedly said privately: that an all-out war fought with thermonuclear weapons might make the northern hemisphere, perhaps even the world, uninhabitable.[18]

John F. Kennedy needed no convincing of that, because unlike the other leaders we have considered, he had found the thermonuclear revolution an accomplished fact by the time he emerged as an influential actor on the American political scene. Quick to sense the illogic of trying to make incredible weapons a credible deterrent, he had called publicly during the late 1950s for what Dulles had been seeking behind the scenes: a flexible response strategy that would lessen—Kennedy never thought it could eliminate—reliance on thermonuclear weapons. There was no learning in Kennedy's case: as Philip Nash has shown, his views were remarkably consistent from the beginning. 'The prospect of a nuclear exchange is so terrible,' the new President wrote shortly after taking office, that 'it would be preferable to be among the dead than among the quick.'[19]

It fell to Kennedy to confront the meaning of those words at the most dangerous moment of the Cold War. What is striking about the Cuban missile crisis is how the nuclear danger hovered *around* it, but how little the nuclear balance meant *during* it. Kennedy's Secretary of Defense, Robert McNamara, estimated that the United States possessed a 17–1 advantage over the Soviet Union in strategic weapons during that crisis.[20] Yet the Americans compromised in resolving it: they promised to refrain from invading Cuba, to remove American missiles from Turkey—and the evidence now suggests that Kennedy would have compromised even more, if necessary, to avoid an invasion of the island that might trigger an all-out war.

One can read that evidence, as Mueller does, to suggest that nuclear weapons were irrelevant to the outcome of the crisis. An alternative reading, though, is that they were supremely relevant: that they had so changed the nature of warfare that even a 17–1 advantage in military capability could not ensure victory; that balances of military forces themselves had become irrelevant; that when the capacity existed to get *only a few nuclear weapons through*, deterrence would have been achieved. Mao and de Gaulle appear to have understood this instinctively: it was enough to have just a few. What Kennedy discovered—and this may well have been the most significant implication of the thermonuclear revolution—was how little good it did to have many.[21]

The evidence is compelling, then, that the thermonuclear revolution really did make a difference. If one could have assembled our group of Cold War leaders in 1950 and asked them whether the atomic bomb had changed the nature of warfare, the answer from all of them—except perhaps for Truman—would have been: 'not really'. Future wars would occur, they would probably have argued, and they would probably be fought much as past wars had been. The bombs would be bigger, but the logic of great-power war would be close to what it had always been.

The same group assembled in 1960 (minus Stalin), would have had a radically different view. Every one of them would have come around to the position that only Truman had been approaching a decade earlier: the new weapons really were unusable. They had not only changed the nature of warfare, they had changed the meaning of self-reliance and the commitments of allies, the distinction between civilian and military casualties, indeed the very framework of time and space upon which traditional military strategies had been based. They had raised the possibility, a decade before the war in Vietnam originated the terminology, of destroying not villages but entire countries, perhaps even the world itself—in order to save them.

III

In his introduction to this volume, Ernest May suggested asking three questions of the evidence presented in it:

1. Where would one locate each of our Cold War statesmen on a graph that would plot the usability versus non-usability of nuclear weapons against the effectiveness versus ineffectiveness of deterrence?

2. To what extent did learning take place? Did our statesmen incorporate nuclear weapons within an existing frame of reference that predated their development? Or did Cold War leaders revise their frame of reference in the light of their experiences in dealing with nuclear weapons?

3. Did it make all that much difference what individual leaders thought or did in the first place? Or were the circumstances such that any group of leaders would have moved more or less in the direction that these leaders did?

Definitive judgements in history—conclusions one is *so* certain of that one would *never* expect to see them revised—are very rare. Historians are always reconsidering the past, even the very distant past, whether in the light of new sources or as a result of their own shifting perspectives. Since we are dealing with the very recent past, our conclusions must necessarily be highly tentative. This is how things look to us *now*—but the story will by no means end with our particular telling of it.

With that important qualification in mind, let us address the first of May's three questions. The only statesman we dealt with who seems consistently to have regarded nuclear weapons as unusable was—whether ironically or logically—the only statesman who ever ordered their use. Truman's experience with nuclear weapons was unique, and so too was his thinking about them. It was as if the act of using such weapons in itself created a strong psychological resistance against ever doing so again.

We can never know what Truman would have done if the nation's survival had really been at risk. We do know that United States forces suffered their most humiliating military defeat since the Civil War under his command, and that he chose *not* to use such weapons. And that—to anticipate May's third question—may have been the most important point at which the action of an individual changed the course of nuclear history. Refraining from using one's most powerful weapon at a time when one's forces were in abject retreat and yet there was no immediate possibility of enemy retaliation is not what past military practice might have suggested. Truman's decision to keep the Korean War non-nuclear created a new kind of practice—that of 'limited' war—and that in itself is an argument in favour of the 'relevance' of nuclear weapons to the 'long peace' that eventually emerged.

Each of the other statesmen in our group fudged the issue of usability; and perhaps because they could be vague about that, they were able to move toward a greater reliance on deterrence than Truman was ever able to manage. Different leaders did this in different ways, but it seems accurate enough to conclude that all of them, by the 1960s, had converged near the top of May's semi-circle: around the view that nuclear weapons could indeed deter war— *but only if one refused to resolve the issue of whether or not they were usable in war.*

Ambiguity, therefore, became the path to stability. It is remarkable how widely this view came to be shared, despite the enormous differences in personality, history, culture, and ideology, among those who shared it. We need to be clear, though, on what this required. It was nothing less than a repudiation of rational choice as traditionally understood: the rationality that asked why one would build and deploy weapons if one were not prepared to use them. Instead a new kind of rationality emerged: it was based on making the incredible credible—what might seem at first a wholly improbable task—and in retrospect it is surprising that it worked as well as it did.

Mueller might well deny the centrality of nuclear weapons in this process, arguing that the experiences of the two world wars were in themselves enough to deter a new one. Our evidence suggests the need, though, to distinguish between the prospect and the rationality of war. Prior to the development of thermonuclear weapons, it seems fair to say that war was indeed regarded as a remote prospect because the costs of the recent war were still so evident. But war was not at that time seen as an *irrational* act, in which there could be no correspondence between expected costs and intended benefits. That view did not survive the thermonuclear bomb tests of the mid-1950s, and that seems to us the most convincing confirmation of a determining role for nuclear weapons in the obsolescence of great-power war.

It is not that Mueller's argument about the legacies of the two world wars is wrong—it is just remote, overshadowed by the immediacy of having to grapple with *two* revolutions in weaponry in a single decade. The first of these could be rationalized as an abnormality, from which a reversion to the normal was still possible. The second could never be. In this sense, we think, it was circumstances and not individuals that determined the outcome: *anyone* would have been impressed.

IV

If thermonuclear weapons did indeed make war among the great powers obsolete, does it follow that we should welcome the proliferation of these weapons to middle and smaller states, perhaps even factions within states, in the belief that it would thereby eliminate the possibility of war at any level?[22]

We think not. For even if one buys the evidence for nuclear weapons as an instrument of cross-cultural education—and we do think they worked that way during the Cold War—the question arises as to how far down the spectrum of violence we can expect that effect to persist. Would one want to place such devices in the hands of the warring factions in the Balkans, for example, or of the paramilitary groups in Northern Ireland, or of the Khmer Rouge in Cambodia? What about the Aum Shinrikyu cult, or the Montana militia?

There is clearly a point of diminishing rationality, even when it comes to the unconventional logic of nuclear deterrence: we would be most unwise to assume that because that logic crossed the cultural barriers that separated the Americans, the Russians, the Europeans, and the Chinese during the Cold War, it can cross all such barriers.

But there is another consideration as well, the significance of which we are only now beginning to appreciate. It is that the world was extraordinarily lucky during the Cold War. There were no accidental detonations of nuclear weapons, but what we have learned of the limitations of command and control systems—especially of what happens when such systems operate in periods of crisis—suggest that there could easily have been.[23] Whether such an event would have triggered a full nuclear exchange we can never know; but we do know that the superpowers operated for decades with tens of thousands of nuclear weapons poised for use on a hair-trigger basis. One needn't be a rocket scientist, or a pastry chef for that matter, to figure out how fortunate we were. And it is surely an element of wisdom to know when not to push one's luck too far.

We conclude, then, that nuclear weapons did play the determining role in making great-power war obsolete, at least during the Cold War. And it seems reasonable to assume that as long as the great powers continue to possess nuclear weapons—even if in far smaller numbers than in the past—that deterrent effect will continue. That it will do so for all times and in all places, though, seems a very shaky proposition. What we have here, then, is the presumption of a confirmed *contingent* generalization. That is about as far as we would want to go.

EPILOGUE

Duelling Counterfactuals

JOHN MUELLER

MOST of the essays in this volume defend, or seem to want to defend, a widely accepted proposition that can be called the 'Churchill counterfactual'. As reproduced in Ernest May's introduction, this proposition stresses the emergence after World War II of a 'curious paradox' and a 'sublime irony' in which, Churchill suggests, nuclear weapons vastly expanded 'the area of mortal danger' with the potential result that 'safety will become the sturdy child of terror, and survival the twin brother of annihilation'. Elsewhere, and more specifically, Churchill advanced the 'melancholy thought' that 'nothing preserves Europe from an overwhelming military attack except the devastating resources of the United States in this awful weapon'.[1]

Rendered in more pointed, if less eloquent, phraseology, the Churchill counterfactual holds that if, counter to fact, nuclear weapons had not been invented, disaster was pretty much inevitable. That is, the people running world affairs after 1945 were at base so risk-acceptant, so incautious, so casual about the loss of human life, so conflagration-prone, so masochistic, so doom-eager, so incompetent, and/or simply so stupid that in all probability they could not have helped plunging or being swept into a major war if the worst they could have anticipated from the exercise was merely the kind of catastrophic destruction they had so recently experienced in World War II.

As John Gaddis puts the Churchill counterfactual (but with my emphasis), at least during the Cold War nuclear weapons played '*the determining role* in making great power war obsolete'. In other words, without the vivid images of mushroom clouds, statesmen like those discussed in this book would likely have tumbled into another massively self-destructive war.[2] Accordingly, those of us who abhor catastrophe presumably should take the advice of Kenneth Waltz and 'thank our nuclear blessings' or, as Elspeth Rostow proposes, bestow upon it the Nobel Peace Prize.[3]

To me, the opposite counterfactual seems more plausible. It suggests that if, counter to fact, nuclear weapons had not been invented, the history of world affairs would have turned out much the same as it did. Specifically, it seems to me that nuclear weapons and the horrifying image of warfare they so vividly inspire were not necessary to induce the people who have been running world affairs since World War II—in particular the Cold War figures so ably discussed in this book—to be extremely wary of repeating the World War II (or for that matter, the World War I) experience.

After all, most of these figures are either the same people (Stalin, Churchill, Dulles) or the direct intellectual heirs (Truman, de Gaulle, Khrushchev, Eisenhower, Kennedy) of the people who tried desperately, frantically, pathetically, and ultimately unsuccessfully to prevent World War II. They did so in part because they feared—correctly, it gave them no comfort to discover—that another major war would be even worse than World War I. I find it difficult to understand how people with those sorts of perceptions and with that vivid and horrifying experience behind them would eventually become at best incautious about, or at worst eager for, a repeat performance. But that, essentially, is what the Churchill counterfactual asks us to believe.

War Aversion among the Cold War Statesmen

Taken either as a whole or individually, the essays in this volume certainly do not seem to suggest that the figures examined were either eager for, or complacent about, major war. On the contrary, they depict a group of leaders who were substantially war averse—sometimes to their very bones. As David Broscious notes, it was in 1938 that Harry Truman declared 'I am for peace now and forevermore.' Eisenhower, observes Andrew Erdmann, 'viscerally abhorred war, condemning it into his old age as the height of human folly' and 'consistently stressed that another world war would bring unspeakable horrors, perhaps worse than those of the Second World War'. In 1939 John Foster Dulles had published a book devoted to exploring mechanisms by means of which it might be possible to 'eradicate' war, an institution that the 'peoples of the world', Dulles approvingly noted, had come to consider 'no longer tolerable'.[4] This was the focus, too, of John Kennedy's 1940 book, *Why England Slept*, and Kennedy's cautious wariness about war—even in crisis situations when he knew the US enjoyed a 'towering' advantage militarily—is made abundantly clear in Philip Nash's discussion.

As Annette Messemer observes, Konrad Adenauer was deeply fearful of communist expansionism and was particularly concerned that the Soviet Union might try to take over Germany, probably without direct warfare. But given Germany's dismemberingly devastating experience—the 'horrible memory'—of the recently concluded 'most catastrophic battle of mankind', and given the deep antipathy toward war within the German public, Adenauer was hardly likely to advocate anything that could resemble a repetition, even though he sometimes anticipated that a major war might possibly be carried out under a stalemate in which nuclear weapons, like gas in World War II, would not actually be used.

As for the communist side, Vladislav Zubok points out that Stalin did anticipate that a war between East and West might eventually break out although 'he did not expect a war at any time soon'. Nevertheless, he and other Soviet leaders were hardly enthusiastic about repeating the 'terrible experience' they had just been through.[5] And Zubok and Hope Harrison stress that Nikita Khrushchev 'was deeply affected' by World War II and that the war had left him 'determined not to let anything similar happen to the Soviet Union'.

At a conference of the Nuclear History Program in Washington, in September 1990, Georgy Kornienko, a member of the Soviet foreign ministry since 1947, said he was 'absolutely sure' the Soviets would never have initiated a major war even in a non-nuclear world. The weapons, he thought, were an 'additional factor' or 'supplementary', and 'not a major reason'. In his memoirs, Nikita Khrushchev is quite straightforward about the issue: 'We've always considered war to be against our own interests'; he says he 'never once heard Stalin say anything about preparing to commit aggression against another [presumably major] country'; and 'we Communists must hasten' the 'struggle' against capitalism 'by any means at our disposal, excluding war'.[6] The Soviets had always been concerned about wars launched against them by a decaying capitalist world, but at least since 1935 they had held such wars to be potentially avoidable because of Soviet military strength and of international working-class solidarity.[7]

The one leader from those examined in this book who seems still to have relished war—or, at any rate, considered it inevitable, potentially productive, and perhaps desirable—was Mao Zedong. But even Mao, like the Soviet Communists, stressed advancing the class struggle through revolution, revolutionary war, and various kinds of class warfare, not through direct major war.

Then there is the man of the hour, Winston Churchill. As Jonathan Rosenberg stresses, Churchill was something of a 'warrior at heart', and during World War I he seemed to display 'a lust for battle'. He found something fascinating and exciting about war: 'nothing in life is so exhilarating as to be shot at without result', he observed in his first book.[8]

But because something is held to be fascinating, doesn't mean people will still want to do it. Formal duelling retains its fascination, but it has still become obsolete. Chainsaw massacres apparently continue to intrigue, but that does not mean people will necessarily rush out to engage in the practice. The people writing this book find something fascinating about atomic bombs, but that, I strongly suspect, doesn't mean they would want to drop one on somebody.[9] Moreover, as Rosenberg notes, Churchill was fully aware of the 'horrors of war', and, even before World War I he reflected that 'much as war attracts me and fascinates my mind with its tremendous situations', he could still see what a 'vile and wicked folly and barbarism it all is'.

In addition, and more to the point for the purposes of this book, Churchill's experience with World War I convinced him that 'War, which was cruel and magnificent, has become cruel and squalid.' In fact, Churchill continued, 'it has become completely spoilt', the fault, he concluded, of 'Democracy and Science. From the moment either of these meddlers and muddlers was allowed to take part in actual fighting, the doom of War was sealed.'

No longer, he bemoaned, could the Dragoon, the Lancer, and the Hussar claim their 'time-honoured place upon the battlefield' where one could find 'wheeling or moving in échelon a front' and 'that greatest of all cavalry events—the Charge'. He pronounced it 'a shame that War should have flung all this aside in its greedy, base, opportunist march, and should turn instead to chemists in spectacles, and chauffeurs pulling the levers of aeroplanes or machine-guns'. Thus, 'instead of a small number of well-trained professionals championing their country's cause with ancient weapons and a beautiful intricacy of archaic manœuvre sustained at every moment by the applause of their nation, we now have entire populations, including even women and children, pitted against one another in brutish mutual extermination, and only a set of blear-eyed clerks left to add up the butcher's bill'.[10]

In a more sombre essay, entitled 'Shall We All Commit Suicide?' written in 1925, and reprinted in a collection in 1932, Churchill expounded further on this profound, and perhaps regrettable, change. 'In barbarous times,' Churchill noted approvingly, 'superior martial virtues—physical strength, courage, skill, discipline—were required' to win wars, and 'in the hard evolution of mankind the best and fittest stocks came to the fore'. But he argued that war had now lost 'the crude but healthy limits of the barbarous ages'. And, expressing a view that was common at the time, he concluded that war had now become 'the potential destroyer of the human race. . . . Mankind has never been in this position before. Without having improved appreciably in virtue or enjoying wiser guidance, it has got into its hands for the first time the tools by which it can unfailingly accomplish its own extermination.'[11]

Accordingly, however fascinating and exhilarating war might be—or might once have been—Churchill considered the avoidance of another major war to be 'the first aim of all who wish to spare their children the torments and disasters compared to which those we have suffered will be but a pale preliminary'.[12] In that state of mind, Churchill in the 1920s and 1930s, as William Manchester observes, 'though a born warlord', was 'prepared to sacrifice all save honor and the safety of England to keep the peace'.[13] Or as Churchill put it, 'War ceased to be a gentleman's game. To Hell with it! Hence the League of Nations.'[14] And, on the eve of the war he had been unable to prevent, Churchill predicted, gloomily if accurately, that it would be characterized by 'indescribable horrors'.[15]

It seems hugely unlikely to me that it was only the arrival on the scene of the atomic bomb that kept leaders with such views from altering their deep aversion to major war, especially after the confirming cataclysm of World War II.[16]

The Bomb and Diplomatic Thinking

Many of the chapters in this book propose to undermine my counterfactual by applying a test which I consider invalid. They seek to demonstrate that nuclear weapons had a conspicuous impact on diplomatic thinking. In their chapter on Khrushchev, for example, Vladislav Zubok and Hope Harrison cite a test once proposed by John Gaddis: 'if we can show that one or more major leaders . . . changed their views about the utility of force as a result of the development of nuclear weapons, then the Mueller argument would be falsified and a strong presumption about the stabilizing effect of nuclear weapons would then be constructed'.

But I readily acknowledge that nuclear weapons helped leaders change their views about the utility of force at least as it pertained to major war and therefore, to that degree, I agree that nuclear weapons had a stabilizing effect. I maintain, however, that, while this change may have been *notable*, it was not *consequential*: the Cold War figures examined in this book would deem a World War III prosecuted *without* nuclear weapons to be an excruciatingly bad idea, while they would deem a World War III carried out *with* them to be an unbelievably excruciatingly bad idea. Erdmann's discussion of the evolution of Eisenhower's thought processes nicely catches the point: in Eisenhower's mind major war went from being (merely) unspeakably horrible to being utterly preposterous.

Similarly, I don't particularly disagree with Philip Gordon's conclusion that nuclear weapons have 'changed the character' of international relations, John Gaddis' argument that nuclear weapons 'changed the nature of warfare', or Philip Nash's observation that Kennedy had come to the view that 'atomic weapons had decisively altered the nature of war'. The world *is* different with nuclear weapons around and so, clearly, are military calculations. I question, however, whether such changes have made any truly substantial difference in the diplomatic behaviour of the war-averse statesmen who have been running world affairs since World War II.

It seems to me that international stability was vastly overdetermined in that era—nuclear weapons may have been sufficient for the stability, but they were not necessary for it. I have likened the effect to the difference between a jump from a fifth storey window and a jump from a fiftieth storey one.[17] The latter is surely much more horrifying to contemplate, but anyone who finds life even minimally satisfying is readily dissuaded from either adventure.[18]

Rationality and the Thermonuclear Revolution

In his provocative and nuanced concluding chapter John Gaddis shifts the focus somewhat. He suggests that during the first decade of the Cold War, the atomic bomb did not actually alter the military situation terribly much, and in consequence 'there was as yet no consensus that a new world war would be much worse than the one that had preceded it.'[19] He then argues that a consensus that a nuclear war would be much worse than World War II emerged only with the arrival of thermonuclear weapons in the mid-1950s.[20] Until that point, he contends, at least some of the Cold War figures held atomic war to be 'rational' in some sense. After that, major war became, to use Eisenhower's expression, preposterous.[21]

Yet, even though military realities, in his view, had not changed very much in the pre-thermonuclear era, Gaddis observes that 'certainly all' of the early Cold War statesmen still held a 'new world war' to be 'undesirable' (a bit of an understatement in my view).

Because something may be 'rational' in some sense, however, doesn't mean it will take place. In fact, rational people do not, essentially by definition, select alternatives they consider undesirable. It happens that they *also* tend to avoid ventures they consider preposterous. That is, in Gaddis' assessment, a policy that was already universally held to be undesirable became even more so with the arrival of the thermonuclear bomb. But for rational people there are no differences in the behavioural consequences of these evaluations. Gaddis may be correct when he suggests that 'nuclear weapons, from the very beginning, gave rational people pause'.[22] But in my view, they were already dead in their tracks.

If all the people who could start one hold major war to be undesirable, and if, in addition, they remain rational and in control, no major war will take place. It is this, it seems to me, that explains the long peace, not the novelty of the dramatic and impressive weaponry that accompanied it.

Indeed, it is difficult to see how a major war could have taken place among the war-averse statesmen assessed in this book. Clearly if one of them had come, like Hitler, to desire or to be willing to risk a major war or, like some leaders in 1914, at least to look upon the prospect with fondness, the others might find themselves unwillingly dragged into one. But there clearly were no Hitlers in this group. Some of the communist leaders did still hold lesser forms of conflict, like civil war and revolutionary uprising, to be natural, necessary, and desirable, and as Shu Guang Zhang notes, Mao in particular could get quite romantic about such ventures. But none held major war to be sensible or desirable, and when lesser-scale warfare did erupt, as in Korea and Vietnam, the world leaders were careful to keep them limited.

Many people have been concerned that a major war might have emerged from the various crises in the Cold War. But even here, especially in retrospect, it is clear that the people in charge—Kennedy and Khrushchev in the Cuban missile crisis, most notably—were determined from the start to keep such conflicts from escalating dangerously and to accept very substantial political embarrassment to do so.[23] It is possible, perhaps, that things could have somehow gotten out of control, but that is not the way wars tend to start—the popular notion that World War I began that way has been rather substantially debunked.[24]

Despite his belief in the deep international stability that thermonuclear weapons inspired during the Cold War, Gaddis still suggests that we have been 'extraordinarily lucky' that none of those peace-inspirers so hallowed in the Churchill counterfactual went off accidentally. Perhaps we have been, but, given how war-averse the statesmen were, it is far from clear that any sort of accident would have escalated to anything like major war: as Henry Kissinger puts it 'despite popular myths, large military units do not fight by accident.'[25]

Essential Versus Complete or Conceivable Irrelevance

While I maintain that nuclear weapons have been *essentially* irrelevant to the course of post-World War II history, I do not maintain that they have been *completely* irrelevant. The question in all this is not whether nuclear weapons have made any difference whatever, but whether they have been a crucial—determining—influence in keeping leaders cautious and the world free from major war.

As Neal Rosendorf notes, my position is that 'while nuclear weapons may have substantially influenced political rhetoric, public discourse, and defence budgets and planning, it is not at all clear that they have had a significant impact on the history of world affairs since World War II.' He then goes on to suggest, in apparent refutation, that nuclear weapons 'consumed much of the psychic energy of America's policy formulators'.

I do, of course, agree that nuclear weapons very strongly affected planning and rhetoric and budgets and psychic energies—they 'irrevocably transformed the requirements' for national security, as Erdmann suggests. But I maintain that these effects were essentially inconsequential to the broader course of world affairs.[26]

I have also acknowledged that nuclear weapons 'added a new element to international relations—new pieces for the players to move around the board, new terrors to contemplate'.[27] The players could not have spent money on nuclear weapons had they not been in existence, nor could France (and more lately India and Pakistan) have taken them on as status or virility symbols or, like China, acquired them in an effort to garner respect, nor could we have had a nuclear crisis over Cuba,[28] nor could they have rattled their rockets (Eisenhower, Dulles, Khrushchev, and Kennedy all did that from time to time), nor, for that matter could this book ever have been written. Nor do I dispute Philip Gordon's contention that France's bomb generated 'psychological benefits' and a 'feeling . . . of national independence' and that it served as 'a source of pride and unity' for at least some Frenchmen (including, of course, Charles de Gaulle). But as far as he can determine, the French bomb had little actual impact on international relations.

And, while I maintain that nuclear weapons have not been necessary to keep the war-wary and risk-averse world leaders who have actually been in place, like those chronicled in this book, from plunging or being swept into major war, I do not argue that nuclear weapons are irrelevant under all *conceivable* circumstances. There are imaginable circumstances under which the weapons might be decisive in altering the course of events.[29]

For example, if Khomeini had had nuclear weapons in 1980, Iraq might not have invaded Iran. If Grenada had had nuclear weapons in 1983 or if Noriega's Panama had had nuclear weapons in 1989, the United States might well have been able to contain its enthusiasm for attacking them. It seems possible, moreover, that nuclear weapons could have deterred Hitler in the 1930s (though determined and credible warnings from an effective, armed East-West alliance of the sort he eventually confronted in the war might have done so as well). And it is always possible that nuclear weapons could be useful in the future should such a risk-acceptant, war-eager, and highly skilled fanatic once again rise to a position of world leadership in an important country.

Proof and Disproof

It is argued in the introductory and concluding chapters of this volume that my counterfactual—and by extension the popular and attractive Churchill counterfactual implicitly and explicitly maintained in most of the book—can be neither proved nor disproved because there is no way to rerun the history of the Cold War without nuclear weapons to see if things would come out importantly different.

It is true, of course, that history is not an experimental science, but sensible analysis over the validity of a historical counterfactual can still often be accomplished. Historians are often intensely interested in cause and effect and in weighing elements that went into an important decision. With such skills and interests, it might be possible to establish that the fear of nuclear weapons was a crucial or determining reason (not simply an embellishing or reinforcing one) in causing a Cold War statesman to refrain from a military attack or adventure—or perhaps to take one.

For example, in late 1990, George Bush was clearly eager for a war against his nemesis, Saddam Hussein. If, however, Hussein had had a nuclear weapon or two to lob on attacking American troops, Bush would very probably have been able to contain his war-eagerness since the likely costs to American troops in a war with Iraq would have been prohibitive.[30] That is, in that instance, nuclear weapons would have been decisive—highly relevant indeed—and it is likely that the historical record would show that.

Similarly, Shu Guang Zhang notes that some Chinese Communist leaders apparently opposed intervention in the Korean War out of fear of the American atomic bomb. Their view, of course, didn't prevail; but had it done so, it would form a case in which it could be said that the bomb altered the course of international history significantly, though it would have to be established that the atomic argument was the decisive one.[31]

Or perhaps historical research could indicate that Truman was correct in his memoirs when he claims that it was his nuclear-backed ultimatum that forced the Soviet Union to withdraw from Iran in 1946—though it would be important in the process to be able to demonstrate in the process that any such ultimatum would not have been effective without the nuclear backing. However, as Zubok observes, the accumulating evidence does not seem to support Truman's assertion.[32] And Eisenhower and others have argued that his threat to use nuclear weapons caused the Korean War to end. This proposition can be examined, although when that has been done, the conclusion seems to be, as Erdmann notes, that any threats were 'ambiguous and equivocal' and probably of less than central import. Moreover, as Zhang puts it, 'there is no evidence that Mao was aware of the possibility that the US would use tactical nuclear weapons to end the Korean War in the spring of 1953.'[33] Nash suggests that Kennedy decided not to send troops to Laos in 1961 'probably in part because such a decision might have led to nuclear use'. If a study could show that this aspect of Kennedy's decision calculus was decisive or determining, rather than simply contributing, it would indicate that the existence of nuclear weapons was of substantial consequence in this instance.

Or support might be found for the proposition that Stalin was impelled to initiate the Korean War in a spirit of over-confident arrogance after the successful Soviet atomic test of 1949. Zubok does not completely dismiss this speculation, though it seems clear from his analysis that other factors were far more important, and probably fully sufficient, to explain the origins of the communist attack in Korea. And John Gaddis speculates that 'it is possible that without [the bomb] the Americans would never have run the risks involved in defending Berlin, encouraging the formation of an independent West German state, and creating the North Atlantic Treaty Organization.'[34]

I suspect that the best case against my counterfactual might be found in the Taiwan Strait crisis of 1954–5. As Zhang notes, there seems to have been a great deal of self-conscious bluster by the Chinese during and after the crisis boasting that 'we are not afraid of atomic bombs'. The impression arising from such protesting-too-much activity and from other evidence is that perhaps they would have been engaged in far more belligerent acts but for the US atomic threat. Historical analysis might be able to determine that.[35]

However, as it stands, none of the essays in this book seems to have been able to come up with such evidence and so, to that degree, it seems to me that the Churchill counterfactual has been disconfirmed and mine confirmed.

The Broader Issue: The Rise of War Aversion

As Ernest May's Introduction observes, my conclusions about the essential irrelevance of nuclear weapons and my efforts to refute the eternally popular Churchill counterfactual arise from the proposition that there has been, particularly over the course of the last 100 years, a broad secular trend in which people and relevant decision-makers have come to believe that major war— war among developed countries—is, to apply Gaddis' word again, 'undesirable'. It is also my contention that this change has been highly consequential and that it, not the advance of weaponry, best explains the long peace.

At one time Europeans—certainly including Winston Churchill—widely viewed warfare as something that was natural and normal: as Michael Howard has observed, 'war was almost universally considered an acceptable, perhaps an inevitable and for many people a desirable way of settling international differences.'[36] In partial consequence of this point of view, Europe was a cauldron of both international and civil conflict—the continent was, in fact, the most warlike in the world. Thomas Jefferson, with a mixture of amazement and disgust, called it an 'arena of gladiators' where 'war seems to be the natural state of man'.[37]

Attitudes toward war have changed profoundly in the twentieth century in Europe. This change is reflected in the intellectual development of Winston Churchill as discussed above, and it can be seen perhaps through a rough sort of content analysis: a hundred years ago it was very easy to find serious writers, analysts, and politicians in Europe and the United States who hailed war 'not merely as an unpleasant necessity', as Roland Stromberg has observed, 'but as spiritual salvation and hope of regeneration'.[38] By now, however, such views have become extremely rare. This suggests that the appeal of war, both as a desirable exercise in itself and as a sensible method for resolving international disagreements, has diminished markedly on that once war-racked continent. War has hardly become obsolete, but international war in the classic European sense has, I think, started to become so—it has begun to go out of style.

Much of this change took place at the time of World War I, not at Hiroshima. Attitudes toward war did not change, I think, simply because World War I had been peculiarly painful—there had been plenty of massively destructive, even annihilative, wars before. Rather, the war seems to have been quite unique in two important and somewhat related respects.

First, it was the first major war in history to have been preceded by substantial, organized anti-war agitation. Individual voices, some of them very eloquent, had been raised against war in the past, but as a significant political issue, the notion that war is a bad idea and ought to be abolished is only about a century old. Thus, in the decades before 1914 anti-war agitators were preparing international thought to be receptive to their notions, and they were assiduously developing the blueprints for institutions that might be viable substitutes for war should the desire for such plans become general.[39]

And second, the war followed a century that was most peculiar in European history, one in which the continent had managed to savour the relative blessings of substantial periods of peace. As a result, in the century before 1914 Europeans gradually became, perhaps without quite noticing it, accustomed to the benefits of peace, and they garnered an enormous and historically unprecedented improvement in material well-being and in life expectancy.[40]

Nevertheless, the traditional appeals of war persisted. For the abolition of war to become a widely accepted idea, it was probably necessary for there to be one more vivid example of how appalling the hoary, time-honoured institution really was. World War I may not have been all that much worse than some earlier wars, but it destroyed the comforting notion—so beloved by romantics like Churchill—that wars in Europe would necessarily be long on dashing derring-do and short on bloodshed, and it reminded Europeans of how horrendous wars on their continent could become. Thanks to the pre-war fulminations of the peace movement and thanks to the experience with an unprecedented century of comparative warlessness, people in the developed world were at last ready to begin to accept the message.[41]

Because of the change, it became the central policy of almost all countries in the developed world after World War I to avoid war—at least war with each other. The experience of World War II embellished this process (and it was probably crucial for the distant Japanese), but I think that war came to Europe in 1939 not because it was in the cards in any important sense, but because it was brought about by the maniacally dedicated machinations of an exceptionally lucky and skilled entrepreneur, Adolf Hitler—history's supreme atavism.[42]

To opt out of the war system there were two paths war-averse countries could take. One was the pacifist (or Chamberlain) approach: be reasonable and unprovocative, stress accommodation and appeasement, and assume the best about one's opponent. The other was the deterrence (or Churchill) approach: arm yourself and bargain with trouble-makers from a position of military strength. The chief lesson garnered by the end of the 1930s—strongly advocated by John Kennedy in his 1940 book, *Why England Slept*—was that, while the pacifist approach might work well with some countries, an approach stressing deterrence and even confrontation was the only way to deal with others. To that degree, war remained part of the political atmospherics even for the war-averse.[43] It does not follow, therefore, that because countries maintain strong militaries and the will and ability to use them, that they are necessarily in favour of war. Rather, it seems that, as Michael Howard has put, 'today everyone in developed societies belongs to the "peace movement", even those who, in the name of stability, are most zealously building up their national armaments'.[44]

After World War II, there was an important contest between East and West. It stemmed, I think, from the essential belief by many important Communists that international capitalism, or imperialism, was a profoundly evil system that must be eradicated from the face of the globe. As I have suggested above, it does not appear that the Soviets and their ideological allies ever envisaged that the initiation of major war was a sensible (or desirable) method for carrying out this scheme, though they did consider valid such tactics as violent revolution, bluster and crisis, and revolutionary wars in what came to be called the Third World.

By the time *Retreat from Doomsday* left my hands at the end of 1988, it seemed to me that communist ideology—which I take to be the central cause of the Cold War confrontation—was in the process of very substantially mellowing, and therefore that the Cold War might end, that the arms race might reverse itself, and that East and West might soon find themselves linked in previously inconceivable alliance relationships.[45] In the period since the book came out, much of that has transpired, though with a speed and thoroughness I still find breathtaking. And, while armed conflict has hardly vanished from the globe, the likelihood of a major conflagration among developed nations—the kind of war most feared during the Cold War—has further diminished.[46] We seem to have retreated even farther from doomsday.

An important consequence of the change in attitudes about the desirability of major war is that Europe (and the developed world in general) has experienced a complete absence of major international warfare for over half a century—a condition unknown in Europe, as Paul Schroeder has pointed out, since the days of the Roman Empire.[47]

Throughout all these remarkable historical changes, in my opinion, nuclear weapons, while very noticeable, have been essentially irrelevant.[48] In counter to Albert Einstein's oft-quoted remark that 'the atom has changed everything save our modes of thinking', it might be suggested that nuclear weapons have changed little *except* our modes of thinking—or, more specifically, our way of posturing and spending money.

In one of his central questions for writers and readers of this book, Ernest May asks them to consider whether the Cold War statesmen considered war—or major war—to be *obsolete* before the arrival of nuclear or thermonuclear weaponry. It is not my contention that they have ever considered major war to be obsolete (or even that anyone does now), nor do I contend that major war has become either impossible or infeasible.

In so far as military considerations have been relevant, it is the fear of escalation (whether to the nuclear or World War II level) that deterred major war, a fear that may well be something of a myth. Indeed, the lesson of the Cold War era could be taken to suggest not that escalation is dangerously easy or automatic, but that it is quite possible to keep conflict contained at a bearable level and that mutually self-interested limits of the sort imposed in the Korean War could be applied in other, broader conflicts. In fact, it is conceivable that a major war between the United States and the Soviet Union could have been fought entirely with conventional weapons (following the pattern of World War II where as an important weapon, gas, went unused), and that the economic costs and casualty levels of such a war could have been kept well below those of World Wars I and II. Thus even in the nuclear era a sufficiently discontented or quarrelsome country led by a Hitler-like figure could be tempted to try out a war to advance its interests.[49]

I think, however, that, myth or no myth, war in the developed world is highly and increasingly unlikely. It has been rejected not so much because it has become unfeasible or impossible but because people have come to consider it to be, to use Gaddis' mild word, singularly undesirable. As the experience with slavery and duelling suggests, institutions which fall into disrepute because they are increasingly held to be undesirable do go out of style, and, in due course, can become obsolete. But they become obsolete—subrationally unthinkable, in my jargon—because they are deemed undesirable, not the other way around.

NOTES

Chapter 1

1. John M. Blum (ed.), *The Price of Vision: The Diary of Henry A. Wallace, 1942–1946* (Boston: Houghton Mifflin, 1973), 474. Some of Truman's key advisers had recommended that he halt all bombing of Japan, hoping for a surrender announcement. The fact that he suspended only nuclear bombing is significant of an early drawing of a line between nuclear weapons and other weapons. For a full analysis, see Barton J. Bernstein, 'The Perils and Politics of Surrender: Ending the War with Japan and Avoiding the Third Atomic Bomb', *Pacific Historical Review*, 46/1 (Feb. 1977), 1–28, and 'Understanding the Atomic Bomb and the Japanese Surrender: Missed Opportunities, Little-Known Near Disasters, and Modern Memory', *Diplomatic History*, 19/2 (Spring 1995), 227–74.
2. *Public Papers of the Presidents: Harry S. Truman, 1945* (Washington: Government Printing Office, 1961), 362–3. (Needless to say, most quotations from and other specifics about the individual statesmen treated in this book are to be found in the appropriate chapters. Each note to this introduction has an implicit 'See below' clause.)
3. Diary of Henry L. Stimson, 22 July 1945, quoted in Herbert Feis, *The Atomic Bomb and the End of World War II* (Princeton: Princeton University Press, 1966), 87.
4. Address in the House of Commons, 1 Mar. 1955, reproduced in *Vital Speeches of the Day*, 21 (15 Mar. 1955), 1090–4.
5. *Pravda*, 25 Sept. 1946. See, in addition to the essay on Stalin below, David Holloway, *Stalin and the Bomb: The Soviet Union and Atomic Energy, 1939–1956* (Stanford: Stanford University Press, 1994).
6. Yuli Khariton and Yuri Smirnov, *Mifi i realnost sovenskogo atomnogo proekta* (The Myths and Reality of the Soviet Atomic Project) (Russian Federal Nuclear Centre: Arzamas-16, 1994), 15.
7. Hermann Hagedorn, *The Bomb That Fell on America* (Santa Barbara, Calif.: Pacific Coast Publishing Co., 1946), quoted in Paul Boyer, *By the Bomb's Early Light: American Thought and Culture at the Dawn of the Atomic Age* (New York: Pantheon books, 1985), 280.
8. Spencer Weart, *Nuclear Fear: A History of Images* (Cambridge, Mass.: Harvard University Press, 1988), 193.
9. John Mueller, *Retreat from Doomsday: The Obsolescence of Major War* (New York: Basic Books, 1989).
10. Norman Angell, *The Great Illusion: A Study of the Relation of Military Power to National Advantage* (London: Heinemann, 1914).
11. Alexander L. George, *Bridging the Gap: Theory and Practice in Foreign Policy* (Washington: United States Institute of Peace Press, 1993) is a thoughtful and penetrating essay, arguing the affirmative side of the case—that history can be used to build a body of more or less verifiable theory. Ernest R. May, 'History—Theory—Practice', *Diplomatic History*, 18/4 (Fall 1994), 589–603, partly an essay on George's book, summarizes some arguments to the contrary.

12. John Lewis Gaddis, *The Long Peace: Inquiries into the History of the Cold War* (New York: Oxford University Press, 1987).

13. Cited in Arthur M. Schlesinger, 'The Measure of Diplomacy', *Foreign Affairs*, 73/4 (July–Aug. 1994), 150.

14. The language here is influenced by Imre Lakatos, 'Falsification and the Methodology of Scientific Research Programmes', in Imre Lakatos and Alan Musgrave (eds.), *Criticism and the Growth of Knowledge* (Cambridge: Cambridge University Press, 1970), 91–196.

15. Curtis E. LeMay with MacKinlay Kantor, *Mission with LeMay: My Story* (Garden City, NY: Doubleday, 1965), 380–1.

16. Neustadt has not yet put this anecdote in print.

17. Speech delivered before the Association de la Presse Diplomatique Française and the Association de la Presse Étrangère in Paris, 11 Dec. 1953, quoted in Hans-Peter Schwarz, 'Adenauer und die Kernwaffen', *Vierteljahrshefte für Zeitgeschichte*, 37 (Oct. 1989), 586.

18. Konrad Adenauer, *Erinnerungen 1955–1959* (Stuttgart: Deutsche Verlagsanstalt, 1967), 296.

19. For details, follow index entries for Mk 7, W 7, Mk 10, W 9, Mk 12, W 12, W 19, W 23, W 25, and W 33 warheads in Chuck Hansen, *U.S. Nuclear Weapons: The Secret History* (Arlington, Tex.: Orion Books, 1988). See also Ernest R. May and Catherine McArdle Kelleher, 'History of the Development and Deployment of BNW', in Stephen D. Biddle and Peter D. Feaver (eds.), *Battlefield Nuclear Weapons: Issues and Options* (Cambridge, Mass.: Center for Science and International Affairs, Harvard University, 1989), 13–32.

20. Stephen Ambrose, *Eisenhower, the President* (New York: Simon and Schuster, 1984), 262–3; Memorandum of Discussion at the 131st Meeting of the National Security Council, 11 Feb. 1953, United States Department of State, *Foreign Relations of the United States, 1952–1954*, 15, pt. 1: *Korea* (Washington: Government Printing Office, 1984), 770; *Public Papers of the Presidents: Dwight D. Eisenhower, 1955* (Washington: Government Printing Office, 1961), 332.

21. See Catherine McArdle Kelleher, *Germany and the Politics of Nuclear Weapons* (New York: Columbia University Press, 1975), 34–44, and Mark Cioc, *Pax Atomica: The Nuclear Defense Debate in West Germany during the Adenauer Era* (New York: Columbia University Press, 1988), 29–32.

22. Anticipating twentieth-century experimental psychology, Kant used the term 'schemata' to describe the compartments developed by the mind to sort and re-sort sensory experience: Kant, *The Critique of Pure Reason*, trans. Norman Kemp Smith (New York: St. Martin's Press, 1965), orig. p. 180. For modern usage, see John H. Holland *et al.*, *Induction: Processes of Inference, Learning, and Discovery* (Cambridge, Mass.: MIT Press, 1986).

23. Leon Trotsky, *My Life* (London: Butterworth, 1930), 425, cited in E. H. Carr, *What Is History?* (New York: Alfred A. Knopf, 1962), 129.

24. Karl R. Popper, *The Open Society and Its Enemies*, rev. edn. (Princeton: Princeton University Press, 1950), 663–4.

25. See Ernest R. May, 'The Nature of Foreign Policy: The Calculated versus the Axiomatic', *Daedalus*, 7 (Fall 1962), 653–7.

Chapter 2

1. I would like to thank Dennis Bilger of the Truman Library, John Lewis Gaddis, Alonzo L. Hamby, Ernest R. May, Philip Nash, Anne Wallace, and the Nuclear History Program for their assistance.
2. Congress established the rank of five-star general in December 1944. At the time, the presidential seal displayed the traditional eagle surrounded by four stars.
3. Clark Clifford, *Counsel to the President: A Memoir* (New York, 1991), 62; Clifford memorandum, 27 Aug. 1945, and Elsey to Dubois, 28 Aug. 1945, Presidential Flag and Seal folder, Box 95, George M. Elsey Papers, Harry S. Truman Library (hereafter cited as HSTL). Clifford also reveals that during the train ride to Fulton, Missouri in March 1946, Truman showed the newly crafted presidential seal to Winston Churchill, who teasingly suggested that 'the berries on the olive branch looked . . . like atomic bombs to him' (Clifford, *Counsel to the President*, 102; and Charles G. Ross Personal Diary (typed draft), 9 Mar. 1946, Box 21, Charles G. Ross Personal Diary folder, Charles G. Ross Papers, HSTL).
4. Paul Boyer, ' "Some Sort of Peace": President Truman, the American People and the Atomic Bomb', in Michael J. Lacey (ed.), *The Truman Presidency* (Cambridge, 1989), 174.
5. See John Mueller, *Retreat from Doomsday: The Obsolescence of Major War* (New York, 1989); and John Lewis Gaddis, *The United States and the End of the Cold War: Implications, Reconsiderations, Provocations* (New York, 1992) for contrasting assessments of the essential relevance or irrelevance of nuclear weapons in explaining the long post-war peace.
6. Truman's committee was beginning an investigation of the Oak Ridge and Hanford sites when Stimson asked Truman, who readily agreed, to suspend his inquiry (Harry S. Truman, *Year of Decisions* (Garden City, NY, 1955), 10–11). Robert Ferrell contends that Roosevelt told Truman, then on the same presidential ticket, about the atomic bomb project on 18 Aug. 1944 (Robert H. Ferrell, *Harry S. Truman: A Life* (Columbia, SC, 1994), 172).
7. At the time, Byrnes was Director of War Mobilization. James F. Byrnes, *All in One Lifetime* (New York, 1958), 282; and Robert L. Messer, *The End of an Alliance: James F. Byrnes, Roosevelt, Truman and the Origins of the Cold War* (Chapel Hill, NC, 1982), 84. According to Truman, 'Byrnes had already told me (prior to 25 April) that the weapon might be so powerful to be potentially capable of wiping out entire cities and killing people on an unprecedented scale' (Truman, *Year of Decisions*, 87).
8. Ibid. 419. According to David McCullough, Groves joined Stimson and the president only after the Secretary of War had discussed his memo (David McCullough, *Truman* (New York, 1992), 377–8).
9. Henry L. Stimson and McGeorge Bundy, *On Active Service in Peace and War* (New York, 1947, 1948), 635–6. Point 2 in the text subsumes points 2 and 3 in Stimson's memo. The meeting, which was scheduled for fifteen minutes, actually lasted forty-five minutes (Henry Lewis Stimson Diaries, LI, 69 (microfilm edition, reel 9), Manuscripts and Archives, Yale University Library; and Truman's appointment schedule, 25 Apr. 1945, Memo re Appointment File Data Sheets, April folder, Box 82, Appointment File, President's Secretary's Files (hereafter cited as PSF), HSTL). Gregg Herken incorrectly suggests that this meeting lasted only the scheduled fifteen minutes, and thus erroneously concludes that the meeting was 'remarkably

brief considering the complexity and importance of the subject' (Gregg Herken, *The Winning Weapon: The Atomic Bomb in the Cold War, 1945–1950* (New York, 1980), 15–16).

10. The full depth of Truman's inexperience emerges only when one considers that as a senator (since 1935) Truman had devoted little attention to foreign affairs, and that as vice president he had been excluded from Roosevelt's inner circle of advisers. McCullough adds that despite Truman's intimation that Roosevelt would not survive a fourth term, he made no effort to prepare for the possibility of Roosevelt's death (McCullough, *Truman*, 335).

11. Transcript, J. Leonard Reinsch Oral History Interview, 13 Mar. 1967, 61, HSTL; Robert J. Donovan, *Conflict and Crisis: The Presidency of Harry S. Truman, 1945–1948* (New York, 1977), 49; and Clifford, *Counsel to the President*, 58.

12. Margaret Truman (ed.), *Where the Buck Stops: The Personal and Private Writings of Harry S. Truman* (New York, 1989), 204. An indirect illustration of the bomb's impact on Truman's thinking appears in April 1947, when the president mistakenly remembered the date of his famous 23 Apr. 1945 meeting with Soviet Foreign Minister V. M. Molotov as 25 Apr. 1945—the day he was formally briefed about the bomb (*Public Papers of the Presidents, Harry S. Truman, 1947* (Washington, 1963), 208 (hereafter cited as *PPP 1947*)). Similarly, in a personal note dated 2 Dec. 1950, Truman referred to the 1945 Potsdam Conference as 'the Atomic Bomb Conference in Berlin' (Longhand Personal Memos, 1950 folder, Box 333, 'Longhand Notes' File, PSF, HSTL).

13. McGeorge Bundy, *Danger and Survival: Choices about the Bomb in the First Fifty Years* (New York, 1988), 54. Herken contends that Truman fell 'heir to the assumption that the bomb would be used', if and when it was ready (Herken, *The Winning Weapon*, 13). In a similar vein, McCullough asserts that Truman most likely 'never seriously considered not using the bomb' (McCullough, *Truman*, 437). Also see J. Samuel Walker, 'The Decision to Use the Bomb: A Historiographical Update', *Diplomatic History*, 14 (Winter 1990): 97–114; Allan M. Winkler, *Life Under A Cloud: American Anxiety About the Atom* (New York, 1993), 21–2; and Lawrence S. Wittner, *One World Or None: A History of the World Nuclear Disarmament Movement Through 1953*, i. *The Struggle Against the Bomb* (Stanford, Calif., 1993), 26.

14. Byrnes, *All In One Lifetime*, 286; and Donovan, *Conflict and Crisis*, 67. The Interim Committee was the group of advisers established in May 1945 to provide the president with advice on atomic policy. It included Stimson, Byrnes (as Truman's special representative), George L. Harrison, Vannevar Bush, James B. Conant, Karl T. Compton, Ralph A. Bard, and William L. Clayton. The Committee gave its recommendations to the president on 1 June 1945 (See Notes of the Interim Committee Meeting, June 1, 1945, no. 671, Miscellaneous Historical Documents Collection, HSTL).

15. *PPP 1945*, 97.

16. Truman, *Year of Decisions*, 419. Also see Leslie R. Groves, *Now It Can Be Told: The Story of the Manhattan Project* (New York, 1962), 264.

17. Bundy, *Danger and Survival*, 58. Also see Thomas B. Allen and Norman Polmar, *Code-Name Downfall: The Secret Plan to Invade Japan—and Why Truman Dropped the Bomb* (New York, 1995), 291; Ferrell, *Harry S. Truman*, 210–15; Robert James Maddox, *Weapons for Victory: The Hiroshima Decision Fifty Years Later* (Columbia, 1995), 129, 154; J. Robert Moskin, *Mr. Truman's War: The Final Victories of World War II and the Birth of the Postwar World* (New York, 1996), 215, 255, 281, 323; and Robert P.

Newman, *Truman and the Hiroshima Cult* (East Lansing, Mich., 1995), 1–31. For a concise and superb examination of Truman's decision to use atomic bombs against Japan, see J. Samuel Walker, *Prompt and Utter Destruction: Truman and the Use of Atomic Bombs Against Japan* (Chapel Hill, NC, 1997).

18. John Newhouse, *War and Peace in the Nuclear Age* (New York, 1989), 42.

19. Quoted in Newhouse, *War and Peace in the Nuclear Age*, 43. For the argument that Truman's decision to drop the atomic bomb stemmed more from concerns about maximizing diplomatic leverage against the Soviet Union than from irresistible momentum, see Gar Alperovitz, *The Decision to Use the Atomic Bomb, and the Architecture of an American Myth* (New York, 1995).

20. Murray to Truman, 16 Jan. 1953, and Truman to Murray, 19 Jan. 1953, Atomic Bomb folder, Box 112, General File, PSF, HSTL. Murray's letter was elicited by the president's 15 Jan. 1953 Farewell Address, in which Truman stated that 'starting an atomic war is totally unthinkable for rational men' (*PPP 1952–3*, 1201). Truman's mistaken belief that chemical and biological weapons could not affect civilian populations 'by the wholesale' was based most likely on his World War I experience.

21. Truman's Potsdam Diary (typed copy), 16 July 1945, Atomic Bomb folder, Box 7, Ross Papers, HSTL; and Robert H. Ferrell (ed.), *Off the Record: The Private Papers of Harry S. Truman* (New York, 1980), 52–3. A little less than a year later (17 April 1947), Truman would express this sentiment publicly: 'We must catch up morally and internationally with the machine age. We must catch up with it, and we must catch up with it in such a way as to create peace in the world, or it will destroy us and everybody else. And that we don't dare to contemplate' (*PPP 1947*, 209). Also see Truman to Acheson, 17 Mar. 1954 (quoted in McCullough, *Truman*, 942).

22. *PPP 1945*, 362–3, 365. Clark Clifford suggests that Truman's speeches provide reliable evidence regarding the president's thinking. Reflecting on his days as one of Truman's speech-writers, Clifford reveals that 'all an advisor does is to *help* a President draft [a speech]. You get his ideas and then you try to formulate his ideas. You turn them over to him and he does what he wants with it. It becomes the President's statement.' Elaborating on this point, Clifford contends that as a speech-writer 'you don't write the President's speeches. You just take his ideas, you try to put them in written form, and then you resubmit them. You and he then work on the speech together. That's the way we did it' (Transcript, Clark M. Clifford Oral History Interview, 13 Apr. 1971 and 23 Mar. 1971, 49–50, 11, HSTL (emphasis in the original)).

23. Ferrell, *Off the Record*, 99. The date of the entry is 26 Sept. 1946. Lawrence Wittner makes clear that Truman was by no means exceptional in this belief. In fact, Truman's reaction to the atomic bomb was shared by legions around the world (Wittner, *One World Or None*, 167).

24. Writing to his wife Bess in September 1946, Truman invoked this phrase to describe the White House (Robert H. Ferrell (ed.), *Dear Bess: The Letters from Harry to Bess Truman, 1910–1959* (New York, 1983), 536). Also see *PPP 1946*, 142.

25. *PPP 1950*, 3. The date of the speech was 4 Jan. 1950.

26. According to Allan Winkler, 'the government's focus on military uses of atomic energy meant that it was less able to pursue peaceful applications aggressively' (Winkler, *Life Under A Cloud*, 143).

27. The president referred to the *Nautilus* keel-laying as 'a milestone . . . in the historical setup of the discovery of the breaking of the atom and using it for energy for

peaceful purposes' (Luncheon remarks of the president, 14 June 1952, Atomic Submarine Nautilus folder, Box 8, David D. Lloyd Files, Harry S. Truman Papers, HSTL).

28. *PPP 1952–3*, 425, 429. In November 1949, Truman talked with retiring Atomic Energy Commission Chairman David Lilienthal about the qualities he sought in a new chairman. According to Lilienthal, the president said, 'We don't want someone who will let that Joint [Congressional] Committee [on Atomic Energy] run things; we don't want a military-minded civilian, he must be someone who sees the necessary military setting, how it fits in, but he must be someone who doesn't regard that as our objective—and we're going to use this [i.e. atomic energy] for peace and never use it for war—I've always said this, and you'll see. It'll be like poison gas (never used again)' (David E. Lilienthal, *The Atomic Energy Years, 1945–1950*, ii. *The Journals of David E. Lilienthal* (New York, 1964), 594; also see page 475).

29. Ibid. 426.

30. Harry S. Truman, *Years of Trial and Hope* (Garden City, NY, 1956), 314–15.

31. Allan Winkler contends that this simultaneous embrace of both hope and fear was rather widespread among Americans (Winkler, *Life Under A Cloud*, 4, and 136).

32. *PPP 1952–3*, 1124, 1125. Truman continued, 'there is something I would like to say, to Stalin: You claim belief in Lenin's prophecy that one stage in the development of communist society would be war between your world and ours. But Lenin was a pre-atomic man, who viewed society and history with pre-atomic eyes. Something profound has happened since he wrote. War has changed its shape and dimension.'

33. *PPP 1945*, 381. There was no formal draft of this speech delivered in Caruthersville, Missouri, and Truman's notes indicate that he was planning to say only that 'We must used [sic] this great discovery [atomic energy] for the good of man and not for his destruction. That I am sure we will do' (7 Oct. 1945 folder, Box 46, Speech File, PSF, HSTL).

34. *PPP 1946*, 245. The occasion of the president's 11 May 1946 speech was his acceptance of an honorary doctorate.

35. Lilienthal, *The Atomic Energy Years*, 342. The Atomic Energy Commission was established under the terms of the Atomic Energy Act of 1946 and began operations on 1 Jan. 1947.

36. Ibid. 474.

37. Walter Millis (ed.), *The Forrestal Diaries* (New York, 1951), 487. The occasion of Truman's remarks was a 13 Sept. 1948 meeting, the subject of which was presidential authorization of the use of nuclear weapons in an emergency. Also attending the meeting were Secretary of the Army Kenneth C. Royall, General Omar N. Bradley (Army Chief of Staff), and General Hoyt S. Vandenberg (Air Force Chief of Staff).

38. *PPP 1952–3*, 1125.

39. *PPP 1945*, 366. For a negative assessment of Truman's sincerity on this point, see Barton J. Bernstein, 'Crossing the Rubicon: A Missed Opportunity to Stop the H-Bomb?' *International Security*, 14 (Fall 1989), 158–9.

40. Truman to Osborn, 19 Dec. 1945, 692A-Atomic Bomb folder, Box 1527, Official File, White House Central File (hereafter cited as WHCF), HSTL.

41. The tone of Truman's pleas for international control of atomic energy changed with the onset of the Cold War. As Soviet–American relations deteriorated and the prospect of an international agreement on atomic energy faded from sight, the president's references became more polemical. Virtually every call for international

control was combined with a reference to Soviet obstructionism in the matter. By 1948, Truman seems to have employed his pleas for international control mainly as propaganda. This, however, in no way indicates that Truman lost faith in international control as the primary mechanism for dealing with atomic energy, only that he did not anticipate the establishment of that mechanism in the foreseeable future. See, for example, Truman to Folger, 20 May 1948, Russia 1945–8 folder, Box 187, Subject File, PSF, HSTL; *PPP 1948*, 337; *PPP 1949*, 519; *PPP 1950*, 152; Truman to Flanders, 14 Mar. 1951, 394B-Disarmament (1945–Apr. 1951) folder, Box 1075, Official File, WHCF, HSTL; Truman to Borst, 12 Dec. 1951, Atomic Bomb folder, Box 112, General File, PSF, HSTL; and *PPP 1951*, 358.

42. Truman, *Year of Decisions*, 523.

43. Truman, *Years of Trial and Hope*, 306. Also see *PPP 1947*, 120; *PPP 1948*, 236, 414–16; *PPP 1950*, 4–5; and *PPP 1951*, 624.

44. *PPP 1945*, 212, 213.

45. Bundy contends that Truman applied four 'clear and simple standards' to nuclear issues: without international control, the United States had to retain its lead in nuclear developments; the nuclear stockpile should be under civilian control; nuclear weapons were not ordinary weapons; and, nuclear weapons were all the United States had to counterbalance the Soviet Union in Europe (Bundy, *Danger and Survival*, 199–200). Bundy's three additional standards are by no means off the mark. However, they reflect more of a tactical or second-order response to Truman's nuclear-induced hope and fear, whereas the first standard constitutes a strategic or first-order response. For a contrasting assessment of the intellectual directions in which atomic energy pushed people, see Wittner, *One World Or None*, 35–6.

46. Melvyn P. Leffler, *A Preponderance of Power: National Security, the Truman Administration, and the Cold War* (Stanford, Calif., 1992), 26. Also see Alonzo L. Hamby, *Man of the People: A Life of Harry S. Truman* (New York, 1995), 200–73.

47. Wilson D. Miscamble, 'The Evolution of an Internationalist: Harry S. Truman and American Foreign Policy', *Australian Journal of Politics and History*, 23 (Aug. 1977), 270. Also see Mark Steven Wilburn, 'Keeping the Powder Dry: Senator Harry S. Truman and Democratic Interventionism, 1935–1941', *Missouri Historical Review*, 84 (Apr. 1990).

48. Alonzo L. Hamby, 'The Mind and Character of Harry S. Truman', in Lacey (ed.), *The Truman Presidency*, 49.

49. Richard Lawrence Miller, *Truman: The Rise to Power* (New York, 1986), 364; and Wilburn, 'Keeping the Powder Dry', 328–9.

50. *Congressional Record* (31 Oct. 1939), vol. 85, app. 609.

51. Miller, *Truman*, 367–8; and Hamby, *Man of the People*, 264–5.

52. McCullough, *Truman*, 287. Robert A. Divine contends that while Senator Joseph H. Ball (rather than Truman) was the guiding spirit, the only reason Truman did not act as one of the resolution's sponsors was because 'he had his hands full' with the work of the Truman Committee (Robert A. Divine, *Second Chance: The Triumph of Internationalism in America During World War II* (New York, 1967), 92). The resolution took its name from its sponsors—Senators Harold H. Burton, Joseph H. Ball, Lister Hill, and Carl A. Hatch. Also see Hamby, *Man of the People*, 268.

53. *Congressional Record* (16 Mar. 1943), vol. 89, pt. 2, 2030.

54. Divine, *Second Chance*, 145–8.

55. *Congressional Record* (7 Mar. 1944), vol. 90, pt. 2, 2299. Also see Alfred E. Eckes, Jr., *A Search for Solvency: Bretton Woods and the International Monetary System, 1941–1971* (Austin, Tex., 1975), 108.

56. Truman to his future wife, Bess Wallace, 12 Jan. 1919 (Ferrell, *Dear Bess*, 292).

57. Miscamble, 'The Evolution of an Internationalist', 270; and Wilburn, 'Keeping the Powder Dry', 319–21.

58. 7 Mar. 1938 speech folder, Box 1, Senatorial and Vice-President Speech File, Truman Papers, HSTL. Also see *Congressional Record* (24 Nov. 1937), vol. 82, app. 185–6.

59. 16 Apr. 1938 speech folder, Box 1, Senatorial and Vice-President Speech File, Truman Papers, HSTL. Also see *Congressional Record* (1 July 1940), vol. 86, app. 4192–3.

60. John Lewis Gaddis, 'Harry S. Truman and the Origins of Containment', in Frank J. Merli and Theodore A. Wilson (eds.), *Makers of American Diplomacy: From Theodore Roosevelt to Henry Kissinger* (New York, 1974), 193–4.

61. Robert H. Ferrell (ed.), *The Autobiography of Harry S. Truman* (Boulder, Colo., 1980), 41. In a November 1939 letter to his wife, Truman referred to World War I as 'that Crusade' (Ferrell, *Dear Bess*, 428).

62. McCullough, *Truman*, 271, 735.

63. J. Phillipp Rosenberg, 'The Belief System of Harry S. Truman and Its Effect on Foreign Policy Decisionmaking During His Administration', *Presidential Studies Quarterly*, 12 (Spring 1982), 227. Also see McCullough, *Truman*, 43–4.

64. Ibid. 234.

65. Ibid. 325. Also see Margaret Truman, *Souvenir: Margaret Truman's Own Story* (New York, 1956), 174.

66. Transcript, Clark M. Clifford Oral History Interview, 10 May 1971, 170, HSTL.

67. Ferrell, *Dear Bess*, 549.

68. Asked by Arthur Krock in an 8 Apr. 1948 interview if he had noticed any change in his 'makeup' since becoming president, Truman 'could think of nothing . . . except that he felt a growing sense of being "walled-in"' (Arthur Krock, *Memoirs: Sixty Years on the Firing Line* (New York, 1968), 242).

69. Truman, *Year of Decisions*, 524. Also see Truman, *Where the Buck Stops*, 206; and *PPP 1948*, 859.

70. John Lewis Gaddis, *The Long Peace: Inquiries into the History of the Cold War* (New York, 1987), 108–9. Also see Leffler, *A Preponderance of Power*, 38–40; and Wittner, *One World Or None*, 27–8.

71. Messer, *The End of an Alliance*, 76.

72. Stimson gave Truman a memorandum to this effect on 4 July 1945 (*Foreign Relations of the United States, 1945* (Washington, 1967) 2: 13 (hereafter cited as *FRUS 1945*, 2)). Stimson modified his position on disclosure while Truman was at Potsdam. In a 19 July memo, the Secretary of War told the president that 'we must go slowly with any disclosure of atomic information', because Soviet autocracy dramatically lowered the likelihood of effective international control of atomic energy (*FRUS, The Conference in Berlin, 1945*, 2: 1155–7). On Byrnes' desire to exploit atomic weapons for diplomatic gains, see Alperovitz, *The Decision to Use the Atomic Bomb*, 195–219.

73. Messer, *The End of an Alliance*, 111.

74. Truman, *Year of Decision*, 416.

75. Martin Sherwin refers to this as 'reverse atomic diplomacy' (Martin J. Sherwin, *A World Destroyed: The Atomic Bomb and the Grand Alliance* (New York, 1975), 238). For Soviet reactions to America's new weapon, see David Holloway, *Stalin and the Bomb: The Soviet Union and Atomic Energy, 1939–1956* (New Haven, 1994), 150–71; and Vladislav Zubok and Constantine Pleshakov, *Inside the Kremlin's Cold War: From Stalin to Khrushchev* (Cambridge, Mass., 1996), 40–6.

76. Messer, *The End of an Alliance*, 132; Donovan, *Conflict and Crisis*, 97, 137; Gaddis, *The Long Peace*, 109–10; David Alan Rosenberg, 'American Atomic Strategy and the Hydrogen Bomb Decision', *Journal of American History*, 66 (June 1979), 66; and Boyer, 'Some Sort of Peace', 196, 199.

77. Quoted in Gaddis, *The Long Peace*, 106.

78. Dean Acheson, *Present at the Creation: My Years in the State Department* (New York, 1969), 36. At the time, Acheson was Assistant Secretary of State for Congressional Relations and International Conferences. He was promoted to the position of Under Secretary of State on 27 Aug. 1945. He remained in that post until he left government service on 1 July 1947—only to return as Secretary of State in January 1949.

79. Ibid. 113.

80. *FRUS 1945*, 2: 48, 49.

81. For Stimson's 11 Sept. memo, see *FRUS 1945*, 2: 40–4; and Stimson and Bundy, *On Active Service*, 642–6.

82. David S. McLellan, *Dean Acheson: The State Department Years* (New York, 1976), 397.

83. Compare, for instance, the following section of Acheson's memo with the section of the president's speech quoted earlier (see n. 22): 'This scientific knowledge does not relate merely to another and more powerful weapon. It relates to a discovery more revolutionary in human society than the invention of the wheel, the use of metals, or the steam or internal combustion engine' (*FRUS 1945*, 2: 48; and *PPP 1945*, 362).

84. *PPP 1945*, 366.

85. In fact, Stimson's 11 Sept. memo raised the point that unless the Soviets were brought in on talks about atomic energy, they would perceive the existence of an Anglo–American bloc aligned against them (Stimson and Bundy, *On Active Service*, 643).

86. See, for example, Truman's 8 Oct. 1945 news conference (*PPP 1945*, 382).

87. Ferrell, *Dear Bess*, 523. The Cabinet meeting referred to by Truman was the 21 Oct. meeting.

88. Quoted in John Lewis Gaddis, *The United States and the Origins of the Cold War, 1941–1947* (New York, 1972), 273.

89. *PPP 1945*, 474. Although Secretary of State Byrnes may have forced the decision to work through the United Nations, there can be little doubt that the decision accorded with Truman's outlook. Byrnes, apparently, returned from the London Council of Foreign Ministers meeting less than satisfied with Truman's 3 Oct. speech (Bundy, *Danger and Survival*, 156). Acheson, in turn, was 'dismayed' by the mandate contained in the 15 Nov. Joint Declaration (McLellan, *Dean Acheson*, 65; and Acheson, *Present at the Creation*, 151).

90. The irony here lies in the fact the Acheson had argued in favour of approaching the Soviets bilaterally, not through the United Nations. The other members of the Acheson committee were John J. McCloy, Vannevar Bush, James B. Conant, and Major-General Leslie R. Groves.

91. The board of consultants comprised David E. Lilienthal (chairman), Chester I. Bernard, J. Robert Oppenheimer, Charles A. Thomas, and Harry A. Winne.

92. For excerpts of the report, see *Department of State Bulletin* 14 (7 Apr. 1946), 553–60 (hereafter cited as *DSB*). The report defined 'intrinsically dangerous operations' as 'all activities relating to raw materials, the construction and operation of production plants, and the conduct of research in explosives' (*DSB* 14 (7 Apr. 1946), 558).

93. McLellan, *Dean Acheson*, 82; transcript, R. Gordon Arneson Oral History Interview, 21 June 1989, 53, HSTL.
94. *DSB* 14 (5 May 1946), 776.
95. Lilienthal, *The Atomic Energy Years*, 27.
96. This was a direction which the Acheson committee had considered and rejected as too likely to perpetuate mutual distrust (Acheson, *Present at the Creation*, 155).
97. See 'Statement of United States Policy', 7 June 1946, Box 4, Confidential File, WHCF, HSTL.
98. Bundy, *Danger and Survival*, 164; Bernard M. Baruch, *The Public Years* (New York, 1960), 368.
99. See n. 88. Also see Truman to Mitchell, 7 Nov. 1950, 394B-Disarmament (1945–Apr. 1951) folder, Box 1075, Official File, WHCF, HSTL.
100. The Acheson–Lilienthal report called for the construction of nuclear facilities within the borders of any number of nations. Conceivably, a nation hosting an ADA facility and seeking to subvert the international control regime would find it relatively easy to seize the facility and convert it to bomb production. Although the Acheson–Lilienthal report recognized the possibility of this scenario, it concluded that no plant conversion could take place before the rest of the world knew of the violation and had a chance to respond (*DSB* 14 (7 Apr. 1946), 557). The UN would possess three possible responses: a diplomatic solution, a military solution (i.e. armed intervention against the violating nation), and a reciprocal conversion of ADA plants to weapons production. Of these options, the last would have been undoubtedly the easiest to pursue, but in all probability this course would produce an arms race. Since Truman and Baruch seemed to envisage intrusive measures to guarantee swift and sure punishment of any violations, the likelihood of an arms race emerging from an international control regime would be minimized from the outset.
101. Truman, *Years of Trial and Hope*, 11; and Truman to Baruch, 10 July 1946, Bernard M. Baruch folder, Box 113, General File, PSF, HSTL.
102. Gaddis, *The United States and the Origins of the Cold War*, 282–315. Also see Hamby, *Man of the People*, 351–2.
103. For a transcript of the speech, see *DSB* 14 (23 June 1946), 1057–62.
104. Bundy, *Danger and Survival*, 166.
105. *FRUS 1947*, 1: 822.
106. *PPP 1948*, 790. Truman spoke these words on the presidential campaign trail in October 1948.
107. Millis, *The Forrestal Diaries*, 458.
108. Truman, *Years of Trial and Hope*, 3; Truman to McMahon, 1 Feb. 1946, 692 (1945–7) folder, Box 1523, Official File, WHCF, HSTL. For a recapitulation of the basic points contained in the 30 Nov. memo, see Truman memorandum to the Secretaries of War and Navy, 23 Jan. 1946, Atomic Bomb-Cabinet folder, Box 199, NSC-Atomic File, PSF, HSTL. For what is either a misdated copy (assuming that 30 Nov. is the correct date) or draft of the 30 Nov. memo, see Truman memo to the Secretaries of Navy and War, 28 Nov. 1945, National Defense-Atomic Energy, 1945–6 folder, Box 88, Elsey Papers, HSTL.
109. *PPP 1945*, 403.
110. Steven L. Rearden, *The Formative Years, 1947–1950*, i. *History of the Office of the Secretary of Defense* (Washington, 1984), 426–7.
111. See Forrestal to Truman, 21 July 1948, and Lilienthal to Truman, 21 July 1948, Atomic Weapons-Stockpile folder, Box 202, NSC-Atomic File, PSF, HSTL.

112. Millis, *The Forrestal Diaries*, 460–1.
113. Lilienthal, *The Atomic Energy Years*, 391.
114. Ferrell, *Dear Bess*, 555.
115. Doris M. Condit, *The Test of War, 1950–1953*, ii. *History of the Office of the Secretary of Defense* (Washington, 1988), 467.
116. *FRUS, 1952–1954*, 2: 1010–13.
117. David Alan Rosenberg, 'The Origins of Overkill: Nuclear Weapons and American Strategy, 1945–1960', *International Security*, 7 (Spring 1983), 11.
118. Robert J. Donovan, *Tumultuous Years: The Presidency of Harry S. Truman, 1949–1953* (New York, 1982), 100.
119. An edited version of HALFMOON, dated 21 July 1948, appears in Thomas H. Etzold and John Lewis Gaddis (eds.), *Containment: Documents on American Policy and Strategy, 1945–1950* (New York, 1978), 315–23.
120. Rearden, *The Formative Years*, 434.
121. *FRUS 1948*, 1: 572.
122. Ibid. 628.
123. For affirmations that NSC 30 remained US policy, see *FRUS 1951*, 1: 872; and *FRUS 1952–1954*, 2: 864, 974. Rosenberg contends that NSC 30 continued as official policy through at least 1959 (Rosenberg, 'The Origins of Overkill', 13).
124. Truman, *Years of Trial and Hope*, 382.
125. *PPP 1949*, 200.
126. In a 1972 interview, Frank Pace, Jr. (Assistant Director, Bureau of the Budget, 1948–9; Director, Bureau of the Budget, 1949–50; and Secretary of the Army, 1950–3) indicated that he never heard Truman spell out the conditions that he thought would justify the use of nuclear weapons (Transcript, Frank Pace, Jr. Oral History Interview, 26 June 1972, 138, HSTL). Also see Hickerson memo, 14 Sept. 1948 in *FRUS 1948*, 1: 629.
127. Irving L. Janis and Leon Mann, *Decision-Making: A Psychological Analysis of Conflict, Choice, and Commitment* (New York, 1977), 6, 87. Other forms of defensive avoidance include shifting responsibility and bolstering.
128. Returning to the question of why Truman allowed the military to increase its custodial responsibilities regarding nuclear weapons in the summer of 1950, he did so for several reasons: NSC 30 mandated that the military establishment plan to fight a nuclear war; Truman's pre-1950 military budget ceilings turned military planners away from a conventional, toward a nuclear-oriented defence posture; there was within the administration an increasing perception of an unstable and threatening international context, peaking with the outbreak of the Korean conflict; and the Korean war itself increased the leverage of the military establishment (see Rosenberg, 'American Atomic Strategy', 71; and Condit, *The Test of War*, 455). Over time, the first two conditions worked to make the United States increasingly dependent on nuclear weapons in order to deter Soviet aggression and prevail in the event of general war (see *FRUS 1952–1954*, 2: 202–5). Consequently, according to Doris Condit, when Truman confronted an increased likelihood of war in the summer of 1951, he found it necessary to accede to the military's request for greater custodial responsibility. By that point, preparing for war entailed being prepared to use nuclear weapons. This, in turn, was facilitated by giving the military authority to pre-position nuclear weapon components in forward-base areas (Condit, *The Test of War*, 456).
    Truman's dispatch of B-29s to Germany and England in June–July 1948, his

authorization of the transfer of the non-nuclear components of nuclear weapons to England in mid-July 1950 and to Guam at the end of July, and his approval of the transfer of both non-nuclear components and complete nuclear weapons to the Pacific at the beginning of April 1951 should be interpreted in the same fashion—i. e. contingency preparations for war. See Richard K. Betts, *Nuclear Blackmail and Nuclear Balance* (Washington, 1987), 72; Roger Dingman, 'Atomic Diplomacy During the Korean War', *International Security*, 13 (Winter 1988/9), 59, 69, 72, 78; Condit, *The Test of War*, 464; Gaddis, *The Long Peace*, 110; Herken, *The Winning Weapon*, 257–62; Richard G. Hewlett and Francis Duncan, *Atomic Shield, 1947–1952*, ii. *A History of the United States Atomic Energy Commission* (University Park, Pa., 1969), 169, 521–5, 539; Millis, *The Forrestal Diaries*, 454–5, 457; Newhouse, *War and Peace*, 67; and Rearden, *The Formative Years*, 290–3.

129. *FRUS 1950*, 7: 713.
130. Rosemary Foot, *The Wrong War: American Policy and the Dimensions of the Korean Conflict, 1950–1953* (Ithaca, NY, 1985), 232–4. See, for example, NIE-3 of 15 Nov. 1950 [*FRUS 1950*, 1: 485].
131. *FRUS 1951*, 6: 35, 36, 37.
132. *FRUS 1951*, 7: 1382–99.
133. Truman, *Years of Trial and Hope*, 345.
134. Leffler, *A Preponderance of Power*, 18.
135. Foot, *The Wrong War*, 130.
136. *PPP 1951*, 267–8.
137. *FRUS 1950*, 7: 713.
138. See Mueller, *Retreat from Doomsday*, 4. For various explanations of the long peace, see Charles W. Kegley, Jr. (ed.), *The Long Postwar Peace: Contending Explanations and Projections* (New York, 1991).
139. Bundy, *Danger and Survival*, 197–8.
140. Rosenberg, 'American Atomic Strategy', 86. Also see Winkler, *Life Under A Cloud*, 68, and 73–5.
141. Newhouse, *War and Peace*, 74–5.
142. *FRUS 1949*, 1: 577, 579–81.
143. *FRUS 1950*, 1: 517.
144. R. Gordon Arneson, 'The H-Bomb Decision', *Foreign Service Journal*, 46 (May 1969), 27. Attending the meeting were Truman, Acheson, Lilienthal, Johnson, Executive Secretary of the National Security Council Admiral Sidney W. Souers, and Deputy Secretary of the National Security Council James S. Lay.
145. Lilienthal, *The Atomic Energy Years*, 632.
146. Truman, *Years of Trial and Hope*, 308.
147. *FRUS 1949*, 1: 481.
148. For estimates of the hydrogen bomb's relative explosive capacity, see Rearden, *The Formative Years*, 446; and the General Advisory Committee's report (*FRUS 1949*, 1: 571).
149. Michael Mandelbaum, *The Nuclear Revolution: International Politics Before and After Hiroshima* (Cambridge, 1981), 14.
150. *PPP 1945*, 365.
151. Joseph S. Nye, Jr., 'Nuclear Learning and U.S.–Soviet Security Regimes', *International Organization*, 41 (Summer 1987), 378–85.
152. See, for example, Alexander E. Wendt, 'The Agent-Structure Problem in International Relations Theory', *International Organization*, 41 (Summer 1987), 335–70.

153. International relations theorists, for example, have postulated that the international system is comprised of two overlapping but distinct subsystems or environments—an international security environment and an international economic environment. See George Modelski (ed.), *Exploring Long Cycles* (Boulder, Colo., 1987); and Simon Bromley, *American Hegemony and World Oil: The Industry, the State System and the World Economy* (University Park, Pa., 1991).

154. See Wittner, *One World Or None*, 329.

155. See n. 101. Also see Gaddis, 'Harry S. Truman and the Origins of Containment', 208.

156. Leffler argues that Truman 'had an abiding faith in America's moral superiority and ultimate righteousness' (Leffler, *A Preponderance of Power*, 26; also see page 49). A good example of this faith comes in remarks Truman made after hearing about the Hiroshima bombing: 'I believe [the atomic bomb] will turn out to be the greatest power for the good of mankind ever known because it is in the hands of two peaceful nations' (Ross notes 'Off the Atlantic Coast', 6 Aug. 1945, Atomic Bomb folder, Box 7, Ross Papers, HSTL). In a similar vein, Truman wrote the following entry in his diary on 25 July 1945: 'It is certainly a good thing for the world that Hitler's crowd or Stalin's did not discover this atomic bomb. It seems to be the most terrible thing ever discovered, but it can be made the mose [*sic*] useful' (Truman's Potsdam Diary (typed copy), 25 July 1945, Atomic Bomb folder, Box 7, Ross Papers, HSTL).

157. Commenting on the Baruch Plan in his memoirs, Dean Rusk suggests that 'a good test of an idea [i.e. a diplomatic proposal] is to examine whether it is reciprocal' (Dean Rusk, *As I Saw It* (New York, 1990), 139).

158. See n. 59.

159. Wittner contends that the Baruch Plan signalled the beginning of Truman's turn toward what is here labelled his fall-back position (Wittner, *One World Or None*, 251–2).

160. See, on this point, Winkler, *Life Under A Cloud*, 7.

161. For an interesting theoretical treatment of why Japan initiated a war with the United States from a position of strategic inferiority, see Arthur A. Stein, *Why Nations Cooperate: Circumstance and Choice in International Relations* (Ithaca, NY, 1990), 91–3.

162. International relations theorists refer to the dynamic of this system as the 'security dilemma'. According to Robert Jervis, the security dilemma applies to any situation in which 'an increase in one state's security will automatically and inadvertently decrease that of others' (Robert Jervis, *The Meaning of the Nuclear Revolution: Statecraft and the Prospects of Armageddon* (Ithaca, NY, 1989), 53). Also see Winkler, *Life Under A Cloud*, 53.

163. Ibid. 183.

Chapter 3

1. I would like to thank for support the US Institute of Peace and the Norwegian Nobel Institute in Oslo, whose grant and fellowship had been crucial at the earlier stages of working on this chapter. I also thank Yuri Smirnov of the Kurchatov Institute in Moscow and my colleagues at the National Security Archive, a non-government library and research center in Washington (particularly Malcolm Byrne, Thomas Blanton and William Burr) for assistance and friendly encouragement.

2. Yuli Khariton and Yuri Smirnov, 'The Khariton Version', *Bulletin of the Atomic Scientists*, 29/2 (May 1993), 20–31; by the same authors, *Mifi i realnost sovenskogo atomnogo proekta* [The myths and reality of the Soviet atomic project], Russian Federal Nuclear Centre: Arzamas-16, 1994; David Holloway, 'Soviet Scientists Speak Out', ibid. 18–19; *Andrei Sakharov: Facets of a Life* (Hong Kong: Editions Frontières, 1991).

3. David Holloway, *Stalin and the Bomb: The Soviet Union and Atomic Energy, 1939–1956* (New Haven: Yale University Press, 1994); Yuri Smirnov, 'Stalin i bomba' *Voprosi istorii iestestvoznaniia i tekhniki*, 2 (1994), 125–30; Steven J. Zaloga, *Target America: The Soviet Union and the Strategic Arms Race, 1945–1964* (Novato, Calif.: Presidio, 1993); Yuri Smirnov and Vladislav Zubok, 'The Soviet Leaders and the Nuclear Arms', *Cold War International History Project Bulletin*, 4 (1994); ibid., David Holloway, 'Sources for the Study of Soviet Nuclear History'.

4. E. Negin and L. Goleusova (eds.), *The Soviet Atomic Project: The End of the Atomic Monopoly: How it Happened* (Nizhni Novgorod: Arzamas-16, 1995); V. Mikhailov and A. Petrosiants (eds.), *The Creation of the First Soviet Nuclear Bomb* (Moscow: Energoatomizdat, 1995); German A. Goncharov, 'Thermonuclear Milestones', *Physics Today*, 49/11 (Nov. 1996), 44–61; Nikolai Simonov, *The Military-Industrial Complex of the USSR in the 1920s–1950s* (Moscow: Rosspen, 1996), 211–25.

5. A. O. Rzheshevsky, 'A visit by A. Eden to Moscow in December 1941: Negotiations with I. V. Stalin and V. M. Molotov', *Novaia i noveishaia istoriia*, 2 (1994), 90–5.

6. Dokumenti Komissii Litvinova po podgotovke mirnikh dogovorov i poslevoennogo ustroistva, Maisky to Molotov, 11 Jan. 1944, Archive of Foreign Policy of Russian Federation (hereafter AVP RF), *f.* 06, *op.* 6, *papka* 14, *d.* 145, p. 3.

7. Ibid. 9, 38–9.

8. On the comparison of Stalin's realism and the expectations of his diplomats see: Vladimir Pechatnov, 'The Big Three after World War II: New Documents on Soviet Thinking About Post-War Relations with the United States and Great Britain', Cold War International History Project, Working Paper, 13 (July 1991). A different interpretation of Stalin's 'realism' is in Vladislav Zubok and Constantin Pleshakov, *Inside the Kremlin's Cold War: From Stalin to Khrushchev* (Cambridge, Mass.: Harvard University Press, 1996), 32–5; and John Lewis Gaddis, *We Now Know: Rethinking Cold War History* (Oxford: Clarendon Press, 1997), 28–33.

9. As indicated by Stalin's instructions to his intelligence officer Alexandr Feklisov, *Za oreanom i na ostrove* [Overseas and on the island], *The Notes of an Intelligence Officer* (Moscow: DEM, 1994), 52–3; another testimony to this is Stalin's letter to Roosevelt in March 1945 about the contacts in Bern, Switzerland, between Allen Dulles and the emissaries of the Nazi top leadership. No doubt, more documents from the KGB archives will better document Stalin's mania on this point.

10. Vladimir Chikov, 'How the Soviet Intelligence Service "Split" the American Atom', *New Times*, 16 (1991), 39, cited in Steven J. Zaloga, *Target America: The Soviet Union and the Strategic Arms Race, 1945–1964* (Novato, Calif.: Presidio Press, 1993), 15.

11. Feklisov, *Za oreanom i na ostrove*, 53.

12. Recollections of S. Kaftanov, in *Khimia i zhizn* [Chemistry and life], 3 (1985), 6–10.

13. Efim Slavsky, head of the Ministry of Machine-Building Industry, alias the Soviet Atomic Ministry, recalled in 1991 that he was 'shocked to the extreme' by this discovery because he had been taught that atoms were the indivisible units of matter. E. P. Slavsky, 'When the Country Stood on the Shoulders of Nuclear Titans' (interview and comments by R. V. Kuznetsova, Director of the Kurchatov Museum), *Voenno-istorichesky zhurnal*, 9 (1993), 16.

14. *Izvestia*, 8 Dec. 1992; Khariton and Smirnov, *Mifi i realnost*, 5.

15. I. N. Golovin and Yu. N. Smirnov, *Eto nachinalos v Zamoskvorechie*, research paper, the Institute of Atomic Energy, no. 4926/3 (1989), 4–5.

16. On Stalin's suspicions of a Western 'set-up', see Zaloga, *Target America*, 11–12.

17. Conversation between Harriman and Stalin, 8 Aug. 1945, 'Far Eastern War and General Situation', W. Averell Harriman Papers, Box 181, Library of Congress; also cited in Holloway, *Stalin and the Bomb*, 128.

18. Pavel Sudoplatov, *Razvedka I Kreml* [Intelligence Service and the Kremlin] (Moscow: Gea, 1996), 203–4; Merkulov's report was reproduced in the American edition of this book: Pavel Sudoplatov and Anatoly Sudoplatov, with Jerrold and Leona Schecter, *Special Tasks: The Memoirs of an Unwanted Witness* (Boston: Little, Brown, and Co., 1994), 457.

19. A. O. Rzheshevsky, 'A visit by A. Eden to Moscow in December 1941 (conclusion)', *Novaia i noveishaia istoriia*, 3 (1994), 123.

20. Felix Chuev, *Sto sorok besed s Molotovym* [One hundred and forty conversations with Molotov] (Moscow: TERRA, 1991), 102–3; see also Vladislav Zubok and Contantine Pleshakov, 'The Soviet Union' in David Reynolds (ed.), *The Origins of the Cold War in Europe: International Perspective* (New Haven: Yale University Press, 1994), 57–64.

21. AVP RF, *f.* 06, *op.* 6, *papka* 14, *d.* 145, p. 15.

22. The wrong estimate is given in the letter from Merkulov to Beria on 28 February 1945 (*Special Tasks*, 457).

23. A report to Beria, published in *Kurier Sovetskoi Rzvedki* and reproduced in *Special Tasks*, 474–5.

24. Conversations of Stalin and Harriman, 8 Aug. 1945, Harriman Papers, Box 181, Library of Congress; A. A. Gromyko, *Pamyatnoye* [I remember] (Moscow: Progress Publishers, 1990), i.

25. Minutes of Dr Soong, Negotations with Stalin in Moscow, 7 Aug. 1945, Hoover Institution of War, Revolution and Peace, 47; Holloway, *Stalin and the Bomb*, 128–9; Khariton and Smirnov, *Mifi i realnost*, 63, 64; for Kuchatov's similar thinking see Mikhailov and Petrosiants (eds.), *The Creation*, 105–6.

26. *NWD 93–1. Russian/Soviet Nuclear Warhead Production*, 8 Sept. 1993, Natural Resources Defense Council, Working Paper, Washington, p. 14.

27. We will never know what went through Stalin's mind when he learned about this event. Svetlana, Stalin's daughter, recalled that she saw him at the moment when 'his usual visitors came and said that the Americans dropped the first atomic bomb in Japan . . . All were preoccupied by this news.' Svetlana Alliluyeva, *Dvadtsat pisem k drugu* [Twenty letters to a friend] (Moscow, 1990), 143–4. (I am thankful to Yuri Smirnov for bringing this fact to my attention.) Also Zhou Enlai recalled much later that 'many were frightened by the atomic bomb. At that time even Stalin was mentally shocked and was worried about the outbreak of World War III', quoted in Sergei N. Goncharov, John W. Lewis, and Xue Litai, *Uncertain Partners: Stalin, Mao, and the Korean War* (Stanford: Stanford University Press, 1994), 297. There is no way to check, however, if this can be said about Stalin in August 1945 or in the fall of 1950, when Zhou had talks with the Soviet leader about the Korean war.

28. G. K. Zhukov, *Vospominaniia i razmyshleniia* [Memories and reflections] (Moscow: Novosti, 1990), iii. 334; also see Andrei Gromyko, *Pamyatnoie*, i. 276.

29. Simonov, *The Military-Industrial Complex of the USSR*, 241–2.

30. Stalin's expertise in weapon technology impressed many; he liked to meet and talk with arms' designers and producers, see 'The Diary of Vyacheslav Alexandrovich Malyshev (1902–1955)', people's commissar of the tank industry during the war, after Stalin's death a chairman of the Atomic Ministry (Minsredmash), *Vestnik of the Archive of the President of the Russian Federation*, 5 (1997), 104–41.

31. In his book Zaloga reproduces a dubious story that in May 1942 Stalin 'expressed his outrage that a junior scientist like Flerov, and not one of the vaunted academicians, had foreseen the danger that would be posed if a foreign country developed a uranium bomb while the Soviet Union did nothing' (Target America, 13). First, there is no evidence that Stalin had actually read Flerov's letter. Second, in the light of what we know about atomic espionage, Stalin, had he ever said it, could have hardly been serious and sincere with his 'academicians'.

32. Igor Golovin, interview with the author, 20 Jan. 1993, Moscow.

33. On this side of Beria see Mikhailov and Petrosiants (eds.), *The Creation*, 43–4; also Zubok and Pleshakov, *Inside the Kremlin's Cold War*, 141–2.

34. I. N. Golovin, *Kurchatov—uchenii, gosudarstvennii deiatel, chelovek*, [Kurchatov—scientist, statesman, man] (Moscow: Russian Research Centre, or 'Kurchatov Institute', 1993), 24–5.

35. By 1950 the industrial production of the MVD (NKVD's successor) accounted for 28% of the total industrial output in the USSR, Simonov, *The Military–Industrial Complex of the USSR*, 208.

36. S. G. Kochariants and N. N. Gorin, *Stranitsi istorii iadernogo tsentra 'Arzamas-16'* (Pages from the history of the nuclear centre 'Arzamas-16') (Arzamas-16: VNIIEF, 1993), 13–14.

37. Khariton and Smirnov, *Mifi i realnost*, 31–2.

38. Mikhailov and Petrosiants (eds.), *The Creation*, 52–4.

39. Ibid. 69; Slavsky, op. cit., 20.

40. Another document from the abrogated publication of *Voprosi istorii estestvoznaniia i tekhniki*, 3 (1992), 126–9. The content of the report is described in David Holloway, *Stalin and the Bomb*, 138.

41. P. L. Kapitsa, *Pisma o nauke* [Letters on science] (Moscow: Moskovskii rabochii, 1989), 232–5, 237–47.

42. Ibid. 239.

43. Ibid. 248.

44. The discussion about Terletsky's mission was provoked by allegations in *Special Tasks*, 206–7, 212; for the memorandum from Terletsky, see the State Archive of the Russian Federation, The 'Special' Files for I. V. Stalin, From Materials of the Secretariat of the NKVD-MVD of the USSR, 1944–1953, file 102, pp. 78–93. Also see comments in Yuri Smirnov, 'The Truth About the Operation "Interrogation of Niels Bohr"', *Nezavisimaia gazeta*, Moscow, 22 June 1994.

45. The personal note by I. V. Kurchatov, Archive of the Russian Research Centre or 'Kurchatov Institute', f. 2, *op.* (collection) 1/c, *d.* (file) 16/4, cited in Yuri Smirnov, 'Stalin and the Atomic Bomb', *Voprosi istorii estestvoznaniia i tekhniki*, 2 (1994), 128–9.

46. Khariton in his interview in *Izvestia*, 8 Dec. 1992, repr. in Khariton and Smirnov, *Mifi i realnost*, 7.

47. Daniel Clery, 'The Once-Favored Discipline Has the Furthest to Fall', *Science*, 264 (27 May 1994), 1,268.

48. *New York Times*, 1 Jan. 1992.

49. Khariton and Smirnov, *Mifi i realnost*, 20.
50. A. Romanov, 'Father of the Soviet Hydrogen Bomb', *Priroda*, 20 (Aug. 1990).
51. At the Potsdam conference, the US leadership closed their eyes to the fact that Stalin unilaterally annexed Prussia and Silesia, and moved the borders of Poland two hundred kilometers to the east. But Stalin failed to pin down the size of German reparations to the Soviet Union and to obtain the Soviet share in the exploitation of the German steel and coal complex in the Ruhr.
52. Chuev, *Sto sorok besed s Molotovym*, 81.
53. Zhukov, *Vospominaniia i razmyshleniia*, 334.
54. AVP RF, *f. 06, op. 8, papka 125, por. 91*, p. 4.
55. Melvyn Leffler, *Preponderance of Power: National Security, the Truman Administration, and the Cold War* (Stanford: Stanford University Press, 1992), 38–9; AVP RF, *f. 059, op. 15, papka 76, por. 445*, 140–1; *por. 59*, 21–3, cited in Vladimir V. Shustov, 'A View on the Origins of the Cold War and Some Lessons Thereof', in Geir Lundestad and Odd Arne Westad (eds.), *Beyond the Cold War: New Dimensions in International Relations* (Oslo: Scandinavian University Press, 1993), 30, 31, 32
56. McGeorge Bundy, *Danger and Survival: Choices about the Bomb in the First Fifty Years* (New York: Random House, 1989), 151–2, 154–5.
57. Scott Parrish, 'A Diplomat's Report', *CWIHP Bulletin*, 1 (Spring 1992), 21.
58. The Acheson–Lilienthal Plan (March 1946), with its proposed 'carrot' in exchange for improvement in Russian behaviour, 'quite contradicted the prevailing winds in Washington'. James Hershberg, *James B. Conant: Harvard to Hiroshima and the Making of the Nuclear Age* (New York: Alfred A. Knopf, 1993), 268; John L. Gaddis, *Strategies of Containment: A Critical Appraisal of Post-war American National Security Policy* (Oxford: Oxford University Press, 1982), 18–24.
59. Charles Bohlen, *Witness to History, 1929–1969* (New York: Norton, 1973), 249.
60. James Hershberg, *James B. Conant*, 255.
61. The report of the panel on the control of atomic energy at the office of US Secretary of State was translated for Molotov's attention on 24 Dec. 1946, AVP RF, *f. 06, op. 8, papka 8, por. 107*, 64–5; Memorandum of 29 Mar. 1946 of A. Roschyn to A. Vyshinsky, AVP RF, *f. 06, op. 8, papka 7, d. 101*, 12–13, 30; Proposals on the American plan of control (Baruch Plan), AVP RF, *f. 06, op. 8, papka 7, por. 97.*
62. D. Skobeltsyn, 'On the Issue of Control of Atomic Energy', 12 Oct. 1946, AVP RF, *f. 06, op. 8, papka 7, por. 101*, 82–5. The document was published in *Vestnik Ministerstva Inostrannykh Del SSSR*, July 15, 1991, 39–40; also see Vladimir Batyuk, 'The Baruch Plan and the Soviet Union', a research paper presented at the Conference on the New Evidence about the Cold War, 12–15 Jan. 1993, Moscow, 6–7.
63. Alexandrov to Molotov, 9 Nov. 1946; Gromyko to Molotov (without a date), AVP RF, *f. 06, op. 8, papka 8, d. 107*, 25–31, 38–40; *d. 101*, 100–1.
64. Jonathan M. Weisgall, *Operation Crossroads: The Atomic Tests at Bikini Atoll* (Annapolis: Naval Institute Press, 1994), 143–4; about the debate on the Western side as to whether it was another example of 'atomic diplomacy' see John L. Graybar, 'Bikini Test of 1946', *Journal of American History*, 72 (Mar., 1986).
65. AVP RF, *f. 06, op. 8, papka 7, por. 101*, 65–6.
66. *Pravda*, 25 Sept. 1946.
67. Chuev, *Sto sorok besed s Molotovym*, 84–5.
68. Khariton and Smirnov, *Mifi i realnost*, 25–6.
69. Zubok and Pleshakov, *The Origins of the Cold War in Europe*, 60.

70. See this point in Zubok and Pleshakov, *Inside the Kremlin's Cold War*, 276.

71. Bruce Kuniholm, 'Evidence, Explanation and Judgement: The Origins of the Cold War in the Near East', paper prepared for the International Conference on Soviet Foreign Policy, 1917–1991, Moscow, 4–7 Feb. 1992; N. I. Yegorova, '"Iranian Crisis", 1945–1946: The Evidence From the Declassified Archival Documents', *Novaiia i noveishaia istoriia*, 3 (1994), 24–42, esp. 41.

72. Alexander Feklisov, *Za oreanom i na ostrove*, 149. See the calculations of David Alan Rosenberg, 'U.S. Nuclear Stockpile, 1945 to 1950', *Bulletin of the Atomic Scientists* (May 1982), 25–30; 'Nuclear Notebook: U.S. Secrets Revealed', *Bulletin of the Atomic Scientists* (Mar. 1993), 48.

73. AVP RF, *f.* 6, *op.* 8, *por.* 113, *papka* 8, 34–40, cited by V. L. Malkov, 'Intelligence and Counter-intelligence During the Cold War', a paper presented to the Conference on the New Evidence about the Cold War, Moscow, 12–15 Jan. 1993.

74. 'The Hiroshima and Nagasaki Tragedy in Documents', *International Affairs*, 8 (1990), Moscow.

75. The Ambassador in the Soviet Union (Harriman) to the Secretary of State, *Foreign Relations of the United States* (*FRUS*), *1945* (Washington: GPO, 1967), v. 923; British Ambassador in the Soviet Union (Clark-Kerr) to the British Secretary of State for Foreign Affairs, *FRUS*, *1945* (Washington, DC: GPO, 1967), ii. 83.

76. *Voenno-istoricheskii zhurnal*, 2 (1989), 24–5; see also Matthew Evangelista, 'Stalin's Post-war Army Reappraised', *International Security* (Winter 1982–3).

77. Gromyko to Dekanozov. On the proposals of Professor S. P. Alexandrov, AVP RF, *f.* 06, *op.* 8, *papka* 7, *por.* 101, 80–1.

78. 'Special Estimate: Soviet Capabilities for a Surprise Attack, on the Continental United States before July 1952', Central Intelligence Agency, 15 Sept. 1951, NARA, RG 263, Box 1 (National Intelligence Estimates, USSR), unit 17.

79. Slavsky in *Voenno-istoricheskii zhurnal*, 9 (1993); Mikhail Pervukhin, the head of Soviet uranium operation, related this episode in his confidential account prepared for the Party Politburo, 31 May 1967, 'In August of forty-nine . . .', *Rodina*, 33 (1992), 55.

80. 'Intelligence Memorandum no. 76, 19 Nov. 1948: Economic Trends in the USSR', released by CIA History Staff in October 1997; on the failure of US bombs as deterrent see Vojtech Mastny, *The Cold War and Soviet Insecurity: The Stalin Years* (New York: Oxford University Press, 1996), 49–53.

81. Negin and Goleusova (eds.), *The Soviet Atomic Project*, 160–73; Khariton, *Mifi i real-nost*, 14.

82. Ibid. 15.

83. Khariton and Smirnov, 'The Khariton Version', 27.

84. Igor Golovin, 'A Crucial Moment', *Science in the USSR* (Jan.–Feb. 1991), 21; cited in Zaloga, *Target America*, 62.

85. Pervukhin on the briefing of Stalin, *Rodina*, 58.

86. Steven Zaloga in his book describes Stalin's pre-test meeting with scientists, during which he asked Kurchatov if it was possible to make two bombs instead of one, from the same amount of uranium. Zaloga interprets this as evidence of Stalin's willingness to have one bomb extra 'to contain' the Americans if they decided to press on. The episode, in fact, took place between Stalin and Khariton, but, according to Khariton's recollections, Stalin did not share his strategic concerns with his scientists. (Zaloga, *Target America*, 58–9; Khariton and Smirnov, 'The Khariton Version', 28.

87. See Goncharov, Lewis, and Yue, *Uncertain Partners*, 130–69; Chen Jian, *China's Road to the Korean War: The Making of the Sino-American Confrontation* (New York: Columbia University Press, 1994); Kathryn Weathersby, 'To Attack, or Not to Attack? Stalin, Kim Il Sung, and the Prelude to War', *CWIHP Bulletin*, 5 (Spring 1995), 1–9; Zubok and Pleshakov, *Inside the Kremlin's Cold War*, 54–64; Mastny, *The Cold War and Soviet Insecurity* 90–7.

88. The text of this cable, among other documents, was declassified in December 1993. It is part of the collection that President Boris Yeltsin presented to the government of the Republic of Korea in June 1994.

89. Jerrold L. Schecter and Vyacheslv V. Luchkov (eds.), *Khrushchev Remembers: The Glasnost Tapes* (Boston: Little, Brown, and Co., 1991), 147.

90. Cable from Stalin to Kim Il Sung (with the text of Stalin's cable to Mao), 8 Oct. 1950, *CWIHP Bulletin*, 6–7 (Winter 1995/6), 116.

91. On the map of American intelligence that dealt with analysis of Soviet air defence in early 1955, only the area from Omsk to Irkutsk was beyond B-47 range. National Intelligence Estimate No. 11-5-55, 'Air Defense of the Sino-Soviet Bloc, 1955–1960', NARA, RG263, Box 3, Records of CIA, file NIE/Soviet Union 1950–61.

92. Grigory Kissunko, *A Secret Zone: The Confession of a Chief Designer* (Moscow: Sovremennik, 1996), 196–7; Simonov, *The Military-Industrial Complex of the USSR*, 235–6; Yu. V. Votintsev, 'The Unknown Forces of the Vanished Superpower', *Voenno-istoricheskii zhurnal*, 8 (1993), 58.

93. R. G. Bogdanov, *SShA: voennaia mashina i politika* [USA: Military machine and policies] (Moscow: Nauka, 1983), 58, 63, 69–70; Valentin Falin, a letter to the author, 11 Nov. 1993. Both were high-placed Soviet analysts, one in the KGB and another in the Committee of Information, Foreign Ministry and the Department of International Information of the Central Committee. On the secret 'Reaper' plan that Stalin might have obtained from Donald Maclean, see Mastny, *The Cold War*, 109–10.

94. Anatoly Dobrynin, *In Confidence* (New York: Random House, 1995), 525; also 'The Development of Soviet Military Strategy, Operational Art and Tactics After the Second World War', a chapter from an unpublished manuscript, the Institute of Military History, Moscow, 420–1.

95. Sudoplatov, *Special Tasks*, 334–5.

96. From an unpublished non-classified manuscript, provided to the author at the Institute of General History in June 1993.

97. 'On Some Issues of the Foreign Policy of the New U.S. Administration', the memorandum of the Committee of Information to I. V. Stalin, 31 Jan. 1953, AVP RF, *f. 595, op. 6, d. 769, tom 12*, 223.

Chapter 4

1. Ronald Pruessen, *John Foster Dulles: The Road to Power* (New York: Free Press, 1982); John Lewis Gaddis, 'The Unexpected John Foster Dulles', in Richard Immerman (ed.), *John Foster Dulles and the Diplomacy of the Cold War* (Princeton: Princeton University Press, 1990); and Mark Toulouse, *The Transformation of John Foster Dulles: From Prophet of Realism to Priest of Nationalism* (Macon, Ga.: Mercer University Press, 1985).

2. Letter, James P. Warburg to Dean Acheson, 31 Oct. 1945, Papers of Dean Acheson, Harry S. Truman Library, Independence, Mo. My thanks to Alonzo L. Hamby for bringing this document to my attention.

3. John Mueller, 'The Essential Irrelevance of Nuclear Weapons', *International Security* (Fall 1988), 56. It is not my intention to attempt to prove or disprove Mueller's general thesis that 'nuclear weapons neither crucially define a fundamental stability nor threaten seriously to disturb it' (p. 55). A response to this assertion would necessarily be speculative, and speculation is ordinarily not the historian's job. The question of whether nuclear weapons have been a crucial or even a necessary element of post-war international stability is ultimately academic; they are a fact of life and are indisputably a *sufficient* deterrent against bellicose actions which directly threaten a nuclear power's *clearly defined vital interests.*

What is historically demonstrable is that nuclear weapons have 'had a significant impact on the history of world affairs since World War II'. For example, an overview of the minutes of various NSC meetings during the Eisenhower administration provides a window into the agonized discussions of the President and his advisers as they wrestled with mind-numbing projections of 50 to 100 million American deaths in the event of a full US–Soviet nuclear exchange. Whatever other impact nuclear weapons have had on post-war world affairs, they consumed much of the psychic energy of America's policy formulators during the Cold War's early years. This paper illustrates in particular the anxiety the bomb, with its revolutionary threat of global annihilation and extraordinary moral ambiguities, inspired in John Foster Dulles and the difficulties this anxiety and ambiguity caused him in trying to formulate a coherent, credible foreign policy.

4. For a concise summation of the Mueller thesis test, see Ernest May's introduction to this volume.

5. John Foster Dulles, *War, Peace, and Change* (New York and London: Harper and Brothers, 1939), 90.

6. Press release from the Federal Council of the Churches of Christ in America, 9 Aug. 1945, in folder, 'Re Atomic Weapons, 1945', Box 26, John Foster Dulles Papers (JFDP), Seeley G. Mudd Library (SGML), Princeton University; Article offprint, 'The Atomic Bomb and Moral Law', 9 Jan. 1946, in folder, 'Re Atomic Weapons', Box 28, JFDP, SGML; 'Excerpt from address made by Mr. Dulles at Toronto, Canada, on March 8, 1948', in folder, 'Re Atomic Energy', Box 35, JFDP, SGML.

7. See, for example, Dulles' 8 Mar. 1948 speech in Toronto (cited *supra*).

8. *US News and World Report*, 8 July 1949, 30–1.

9. Dulles quoted in Toulouse, 236.

10. Dulles, *War, Peace and Change*, 89–90.

11. Ibid. 90.

12. Dulles, 'A Policy of Boldness', *Life*, 19 May 1952, 151–2; text of speech by Dulles, 'Evolution of Foreign Policy', before the Council on Foreign Relations, 12 Jan. 1954, in folder, 'Re [Dulles' article]: 'Policy for Security and Peace', Foreign Affairs, April 1954', JFDP, SGML.

13. Telegram from Richard M. Fagley and Dulles to Bishop G. Bromley Oxnam, 7 Aug. 1945, in folder, 'Federal Council of the Churches of Christ in America—Commission to Study the Basis of a Just and Durable Peace', Box 26, JFDP, SGML.

14. None of the standard works on Dulles contain any mention of his A-bomb statement, including Gaston Coblentz and Roscoe Drummond, *Duel at the Brink* (Garden City, NY: Doubleday, 1960); Michael A. Guhin, *John Foster Dulles: A Statesman and*

His Times (New York: Columbia University Press, 1972); Andrew H. Berding, *Dulles on Diplomacy* (Princeton: Princeton University Press, 1965); Louis L. Gerson, *John Foster Dulles* (New York: Cooper Square, 1968); Townsend Hoopes, *The Devil and John Foster Dulles* (Boston: Atlantic, Little, Brown,1973); and (particularly stunning, as he had full access to Dulles' papers, and the document furthers his thesis) Pruessen. Robert Divine, *Second Chance: The Triumph of Internationalism during World War II* (New York: Atheneum, 1967) and Anthony Clark Arend, *Pursuing a Just and Durable Peace: John Foster Dulles and International Organization* (New York: Greenwood Press, 1988) deal extensively with the Commission on a Just and Durable Peace but still fail to cite Dulles' statement. I have found only two citations, both brief. One is in Toulouse,who posits a sharp break in Dulles' thinking, with the Korean invasion as the watershed—I accept his watershed thesis but believe that there is a degree of ideological continuity in Dulles' thinking which Toulouse does not allow; the other citation is in an unpublished paper on the Eisenhower admin- istration and Dien Bien Phu by Frederick Marks III (my thanks to Mack Teasley of the Eisenhower Library for providing me with a copy of this paper).

15. Press release from the Federal Council of Churches of Christ in America, 9 Aug. 1945, in folder, 'Re Atomic Weapons', Box 26, JFDP, SGML.

16. However, it is clear from Truman's reply to one of Dulles' associates in the Federal Council of Churches that he was not particularly impressed at the time with the moralistic argument for restraint. The President wrote,

> Nobody is more disturbed over the use of Atomic bombs than I am but I was greatly disturbed over the unwarranted attack by the Japanese on Pearl Harbor and their murder of our prisoners of war. The only language they seem to understand is the one we have been using to bomb them.
>
> When you have to deal with a beast you have to treat him as a beast. It is most regrettable but nevertheless true. (Letter from Truman to Samuel McCrea Cavert, 11 Aug. 1945, in folder, 'Federal Council of the Churches of Christ in America—Commission to Study the Basis of a Just and Durable Peace', Box 26, JFDP, SGML.)

17. Letter from Dulles to Cavert, 14 Aug. 1945; Letter from Dulles to Dr A. J. Muste (of the Fellowship of Reconciliation), 21 Aug. 1945; Dulles and Oxnam wrote to Truman two weeks after they issued their statement:

> We express profound thankfulness, which we know is felt by millions of our fellow citizens, that the Japanese Government was brought to accept the Allied surrender terms without our continuing to the end to release the wholesale destructive force of atomic energy. As indicated by our statement of August ninth, it seemed to us that the way of Christian statesmanship was to use our newly discovered and awesome power as a potential for peace rather than an actual- ity of war. To the extent that our nation followed that way, it showed a capacity of self-restraint which greatly increases our moral authority in the world. Also, we have given a practical demonstration of the possibility of atomic energy bringing war to an end. If that precedent is constructively followed up, it may be of incalculable value to posterity. (All citations in folder, 'Federal Council of the Churches of Christ in America—Commission to Study the Basis of a Just and Durable Peace', Box 26, JFDP, SGML.)

Dulles later found out that his statement had not affected the decision to stop drop- ping A-bombs on the Japanese when, as Secretary of State, he examined the Department's records from 1945. (Toulouse, 110–11.)

18. Draft of article by Dulles for the *Dallas Morning News*, 13 Aug. 1945, in folder, 'Federal Council of the Churches of Christ in America—Commission to Study the Basis of a Just and Durable Peace', Box 26, JFDP, SGML.

19. Letter from Dulles to John C. Higgins, 4 Dec. 1945, in folder, 'Federal Council of the Churches of Christ in America—Commission to Study the Basis of a Just and Durable Peace', Box 26, JFDP, SGML.

20. Ibid.

21. Dulles, 'The Atomic Bomb and Moral Law'; Dulles' repeated calls for international control of nuclear weapons vividly illustrate the extent to which he perceived the atomic bomb as a diplomatic and military watershed: in his 1939 book *War, Peace, and Change*, Dulles had declared, in vintage realist fashion, 'It is highly doubtful that limitation of armament can serve as a *means* of obtaining peace. If limitation of armament comes, it will be as a result rather than a cause of peace. So long as the force system prevails, then armament has a utility' (p. 93). Dulles abandoned this view when he saw how the A-bomb represented a quantum leap in destructive power. When, during his tenure as Secretary of State, he expressed scepticism over arms control prospects in the aftermath of embracing massive retaliation, he was actually recalling his original, pre-nuclear argument. John Mueller, incidentally, expresses the similar belief that 'nuclear arms competition may eventually come under control not so much out of conscious design as out of atrophy born of boredom' ('The Essential Irrelevance of Nuclear Weapons', 56).

22. Dulles' speech in Toronto, 8 Mar. 1948.

23. There is no reason to believe that Dulles was privy to the information that the USA had taken no steps to introduce atomic bombs into the European theatre. Of course, this does not mean that it would have been impossible for a sufficiently motivated layperson to learn the 'secret' of the B-29s sent to England at the height of the Berlin blockade. The 2 Aug. 1948 *Aviation Week* explicitly declared that the B-29s were not carrying A-bombs; moreover, a reader knowledgeable about the unique physical configuration of atomic-capable B-29s would have discerned broad hints in the 16 July 1948 *New York Times* about the conventional nature of the bombers dispatched by President Truman—although, once again, there is no reason to believe Dulles would have possessed such knowledge. See Harry Borowski, *A Hollow Threat* (Westport, Conn.: Greenwood Press, 1982), *passim*, and Neal M. Rosendorf, 'Perceptions and Realities: The Deployment of B-29s to England during the Berlin Crisis of 1948' (Rutgers University Honors thesis, 1987 (unpub.)), 35.

24. Walter Millis (ed.), *The Forrestal Diaries* (New York: Viking, 1951), 488.

25. *US News and World Report*, 8 July 1949, 30–1. This is the most explicit quote by Dulles which would tend to support the Mueller thesis. There are several points which need to be taken into account, however. First, it should be remembered that Dulles had been campaigning in support of international control of atomic weapons for almost four years partly out of fear that the USSR might be recklessly adventuristic once it had developed an unregulated nuclear capability (see Dulles to Higgins, 4 Dec. 1945, cited *supra*). Second, Dulles had just participated in a top-secret State Department Council, code-named 'Fishing Party', convened to review the question of what information, if any, about nuclear weapons should be released to the public; he would have in all probability known that the USA had by 1949 built up a fairly substantial nuclear arsenal, and quite likely felt compelled to not even hint at his classified knowledge (Letter from Karl E. Compton to Dulles, with attached memorandum, 14 Mar. 1949, in folder, 'Re Atomic Weapons', Box 40, JFDP, SGML. Dulles reiterated his belief that the USSR did not want war with the West in an article in *Colliers* at about the same time; in this piece he first opined that

the Soviets might develop 'indigestion' from swallowing up so much territory. 'What I've Learned About the Russians', *Colliers*, 12 Mar. 1949, 25, 57.

26. *US News and World Report*, 8 July 1949, 30–1. Dulles originally expressed this opinion in his June 1946 *Life* magazine articles.
27. Dulles, *War or Peace* (New York: Macmillan Co., 1950), 111–19, 151–2, 175, 233–41.
28. Ibid.
29. Pruessen, 452.
30. Quoted in Toulouse, 236.
31. Ibid. 244.
32. Dulles, 'A Policy of Boldness', 146–50.
33. Dulles, *War, Peace and Change*, 89.
34. Ibid., 90.
35. Dulles argued for stringent control of military spending purely on the basis of not wanting the USA to seem like a garrison state in the eyes of the world. For example: 'It is always tempting to accede to military requests because they take a tangible, concrete form. You can see guns, battleships, airplanes, bases. They are material things that can be measured. On the other side are intangibles, things not seen. In reality, these are vitally important. To get an air base at the price of good will may be a very bad bargain.' Dulles, *War or Peace*, 238–9.
36. Dulles, *A Policy of Boldness*, 152.
37. Ibid.
38. Letter, Eisenhower to Dulles, 20 June 1952, in folder, 'John Foster Dulles, Prior Inauguration', Dulles-Herter series (DHS), Box 1, Dwight D. Eisenhower Papers, 1953–61 (DDEP), Dwight D. Eisenhower Library (DDEL), Abilene, Kan.
39. Robert Bowie, Dulles' chief adviser at the State Department, later said of Eisenhower, 'He would float ideas in meetings that didn't reflect settled judgment . . . or he would sometimes take contradictory positions in the same meeting. He wanted to promote discussion.' Quoted in John Newhouse, *War and Peace in the Nuclear Age* (New York: Alfred A. Knopf, 1989), 89.
40. Memorandum of 131st National Security Council (NSC) meeting, 11 Feb. 1953. NSC series, Box 4, DDEP, DDEL.
41. Memorandum of 132nd NSC meeting, 19 Feb. 1953, NSC series, Box 4, DDEP, DDEL.
42. Text of address by Dulles to UN General Assembly, 17 Sept. 1953, in folder, 'Re Atomic Energy and Disarmament', Box 67, JFDP, SGML.
43. Ibid.
44. Quoted in Gaddis, 'The Unexpected John Foster Dulles', 51 in reference to notes 51–2.
45. Ibid. 56.
46. Bundy, 291–2; Martin J. Medhurst, 'Eisenhower's Atoms for Peace Speech: A Case Study in the Strategic Use of Language', *Communication Monographs*, v. 54 (6/87), 216–18. C. D. Jackson, who as Eisenhower's Special Assistant for Cold War Strategy strongly supported the 'atoms for peace' proposal for its propaganda value, was among those who noticed Dulles' glaring inconsistencies on nuclear policy. The 'real problem' in reference to the proposed speech, Jackson wrote in his diary, 'is basic philosophy—are we or are we not prepared to embark on a course which may in fact lead to atomic disarmament? . . . Foster Dulles doesn't say yes or no, but says any atomic offer which does not recognize ultimate possibility is a phoney and should not be made. [Atomic Energy Commission Chairman Lewis] Strauss and I

say we won't be out of the trenches by Christmas, or next Christmas or the next one, but let's try to make a start and see what happens. Foster considers this mentally dishonest (he should talk!).' Unpublished log entry, 27 Nov. 1953, C. D. Jackson Papers, Box 56, DDEL, quoted in Medhurst, 217. My thanks to the author for bringing this article to my attention.

47. Memorandum of 173rd NSC meeting, 3 Dec. 1953, NSC series, Box 5, DDEP, DDEL.
48. Eisenhower, after flirting in early 1953 with the idea of using tactical nuclear weapons against Kaesong and other targets, backed away from the idea in May. 'His one great anxiety' about expanding the war outside Korea and using atomic weapons, 'was the possibility of attacks by the Soviet Air Force on the almost defenseless population centers of Japan. This, said the president, was always in the back of his mind.' Memorandum of 145th NSC meeting, 20 May 1953, NSC series, Box 4, DDEP, DDEL.
49. Dulles, 'A Policy of Boldness', 152.
50. Memorandum of 132nd NSC meeting, 18 Feb. 1953.
51. Text of speech by Dulles, 'Evolution of Foreign Policy', before the Council on Foreign Relations, 12 Jan. 1954, cited *supra*; for Eisenhower's view of the effect of the tacit nuclear threat against China, see Dwight David Eisenhower, *The White House Years: Mandate for Change*, 181. McGeorge Bundy argues that with Stalin gone the Chinese no longer felt constrained to display an unremittingly hard line (Bundy, 238–43); Burton Kaufman claims that new Soviet Premier Georgi Malenkov pressured China as part of his abortive programme of rapprochement with the West (Kaufman, *The Korean War: Challenges in Crisis, Credibility, and Command* (New York: Alfred A. Knopf, 1986), 305–7). Both authors cogently argue that Stalin's death was of significantly greater importance than any American sabre-rattling in bringing the war to a close.
52. Undated transcript, 'Probably shortly after a Speech by John Foster Dulles: "Evolution of Foreign Policy", Council on Foreign Relations, January 12, 1954', in folder, 'Re Atomic Energy, Atomic Weapons and Disarmament', Box 78, JFDP, SGML.
53. 'Proposed "Talking Paper" for Use in Clarifying United States Position Regarding Atomic and Hydrogen Weapons During Course of NATO Meeting in Paris on 23 April 1954', dated 22 Apr. 1954, in Ibid.
54. Ibid.
55. 'Impromptu Remarks of John Foster Dulles to the Republican Women's Centennial Conference', 7 Apr. 1954, in folder, 'Re Bipartisan Foreign Policy', Box 79, JFDP, SGML.
56. Letter, Dulles to Claire Booth Luce, 1 Sept. 1954, in folder, John Foster Dulles 9/54 (2), Box 3, DHS, DDEP.
57. See Gaddis, 'The Unexpected John Foster Dulles', 52.
58. Ibid. 53 (n. 23).
59. Draft outline of speech by Dulles, 14 June 1957, in folder, 'Re Speech by John Foster Dulles, "Political Importance of Flexible Military Strength"', Box 122, JFDP, SGML; Memorandum of 364th NSC meeting, 1 May 1958, 8–9, Box 10, NSC series, DDEP, DDEL.
60. Press and radio conference given by Dulles, 21 Dec. 1954, 3 p.m., in folder, 'Re Atomic Energy, Atomic Weapons, and Disarmament', Box 78, JFDP, SGML.
61. State Dept. press release: Strategic Concept', 21 Dec. 1954, in folder, 'Re Deterrent Strategy', Box 80, JFDP, SGML. This statement would seem to support Mueller's

thesis in that it intimates that Dulles considered nuclear weapons merely an intensified version of the strategic weapons used in World War II; however, it should be evident as the result of the many quotations, both private and public, cited in this chapter in which he described nuclear weapons as an awful watershed that Dulles did not believe a word of what he was saying here.

62. Joint State Dept.-US Information Agency message, 25 Feb. 1955, in folder, 'Re Atomic Energy, Atomic Weapons, and Disarmament', Box 89, JFDP, SGML.
63. Dulles' press and radio news conference, 15 Mar. 1955, 11.00 a.m., in folder, 'Re Quemoy and Matsu', Box 96, JFDP, SGML.
64. Hoopes, 277–8; Newhouse, 104.
65. Bundy, 296–7.
66. Ibid. 299–300.
67. See n. 21.
68. Memorandum of 253rd NSC meeting, 30 June 1955, Box 7, NSC series, DDEP, DDEL.
69. Memorandum of 256th NSC meeting, 28 July 1955, Box 7, NSC series, DDEP, DDEL.
70. Memorandum, Dulles to Eisenhower, 22 Jan. 1956, in folder, 'John Foster Dulles, January 1956', Box 5, DHS, DDEP, DDEL; Eisenhower perceived the inconsistent nature of Dulles' line of reasoning. He observed, in response to Dulles' memorandum,

> When flatly rejecting technical inspection as providing any practicable basis for disarmament, we thereby give to the Russians a great opportunity for hurting us politically. Yet another part of the program *assumes* that we can have a sufficient inspection or knowledge of productive capacity in both countries to insure that the amount of fissionable material in the hands of the international agency will be greater than that possessed by any particular country. In fact, we apparently assume that the proportion would be so great that any individual country would be foolish to challenge the international power.
>
> These conclusions seem to be somewhat contradictory between themselves.

However, Eisenhower believed for his part that 'if inspection were as thorough, as constant and as widespread as it could be made, and if such a proposal were accompanied by disarmament in easily discoverable means of delivery, it might be a very effective thing indeed.' Letter, Eisenhower to Dulles, 23 Jan. 1956, in folder 'John Foster Dulles, January 1956'.

71. See previous note.
72. State Dept. press release, Dulles' statement before Senate Foreign Relations Committee, 29 Feb. 1956, in folder, 'Re Atomic Energy', Box 100, JFDP, SGML. Dulles' use of the phrases 'potential power' and 'actual force in being' were drawn from his July 1950 reaction to the Korean invasion and its significance; it is possible that Dulles' invocation of these terms was an exercise in self-conscious symbolism—at the time of the Communist attack, Dulles had posited that 'since international Communism may not be deterred by moral principles backed by potential might, we must back these principles with military strength-in-being, and do so quickly' (see note 29). Now, Dulles seemed to be saying, at least tacitly, that his pre-Korean invasion perspectives had regained primacy. As this chapter subsequently documents, however, this mindset did not last; his attitude continued to oscillate.
73. Ibid.
74. State Dept. press release: Dulles' press conference, 18 July 1956, in folder 'Re Atomic Energy', Box 100, JFDP, SGML.

75. Memorandum of telephone conversation, Dulles and Hauge, 11 May 1957, 11.10 a.m, in folder, 'Telephone Conversation Series', Box 12, Memoranda of telephone conversations with the White House 3/57–8/30/57, JFDP, DDEL.

76. State Dept. press release, Dulles' 'Radio and Television Report to the World', 22 July 1957, in folder, 'Atomic Weapons', Box 113, JFDP, SGML.

77. State Dept. press release: 'Strategic Concept', 21 Dec. 1958 (cited *supra*).

78. Ibid.

79. Draft outline of Dulles' talk, 14 June 1957 (cited *supra*).

80. Memorandum of 326th NSC meeting, 13 June 1957, Box 9, NSC series, DDEP, DDEL.

81. Memorandum of telephone conversation, Eisenhower and Dulles, 25 June 1957, in folder, 'June 1957 Telephone Conversations', Box 25, Dwight D. Eisenhower Diaries series, DDEP, DDEL; 'Memorandum of Conference with the President', 24 June 1957, in folder, 'June 1957 Diary—Staff Memoranda', ibid.

82. Memorandum of 351st NSC meeting, 16 Jan. 1958, Box 9, NSC series, DDEP, DDEL; Nixon personally believed that the USA would be devastated beyond salvation by a nuclear war: 'There really wasn't much difference, in terms of national survival, between casualties of 30 million and 50 million Americans [the projected death tolls if the USA, variously, did or did not complete a shelter programme]. While it might matter to the 20 million who were not killed, the Vice-President believed that if 30 million Americans were killed in a nuclear exchange, there would be no hope of the United States surviving.' Eisenhower expressed a similar sentiment—he noted that the estimate of 30 million deaths in an attack on a sheltered population involved the initial exchange alone, whereas there might in fact be repeated attacks, perhaps at a time when people were just emerging from their shelters. 'So, said the President, he concluded that when we talk about a vast nuclear exchange between us and the enemy, we are in fact talking about something the results of which are almost impossible to conceive of.' Memorandum of 360th NSC meeting, 27 Mar. 1958, Box 10, ibid.

83. Ibid.

84. See n. 64.

85. Memorandum of 359th NSC meeting, 30 Mar. 1958, Box 9, NSC series, DDEP, DDEL.

86. Memorandum of 361st NSC meeting, 3 Apr. 1958, Box 10, NSC series, DDEP, DDEL.

87. Ibid.

88. Dulles' news conference, 1 Apr. 1958, in folder, 'Atomic Weapons and Disarmament' (1 of 2), Box 125, JFDP, SGML.

89. Memorandum from Dulles to Eisenhower, 30 Apr. 1958, with attached memorandum of conversation between Dulles and disarmament advisers, 26 Apr. 1958, in folder, 'John Foster Dulles, April 1958', Box 8, DHS, DDEP, DDEL.

90. Memorandum of 364th NSC meeting, 1 May 1958, Box 10, NSC series, DDEP, DDEL. Dulles went on to dismiss the present policy as a transparent farce: he derisively explained 'that he would presently go to Berlin. When he got there he would repeat what he had said in Berlin four years ago—namely, that an attack on Berlin would be considered by us to be an attack on the United States . . . he did not know whether he himself believed this or, indeed, whether his audience would believe it. But he was going to perform this ritual act.' Eisenhower, shocked at Dulles' cynicism, retorted heatedly 'that if we did not respond in this fashion to a Soviet attack on Berlin, we would first lose the city itself and, shortly thereafter, all of Western

Europe. If all of Western Europe fell into the hands of the Soviet Union and thus added its great industrial plant to the USSR's already great industrial might, the United States would indeed be reduced to the character of a garrison state if it was to survive at all.' (ibid.) It is evident that Eisenhower took credibility, and his Domino Theory, extremely seriously.

91. Quoted in Bundy, 279.
92. Ibid. 256.

Chapter 5

1. The author has acquired many debts during the development of this essay. The Nuclear History Program, the John M. Olin Institute for Strategic Studies, Harvard University, and the US Department of Education, Jacob K. Javits Fellowship Program financially supported its writing. For their critical comments and assistance in sharpening the argument, he would like to thank George Eliades, John Lewis Gaddis, Frank Gavin, Jeff Legro, Petra Anne Levin, Ernest May, James McAllister, Maureen O'Connor, Marc Trachtenberg, Stephen Peter Rosen, David Alan Rosenberg, Jon Rosenberg, and the late McGeorge Bundy. In August 1996 Robert Bowie, General Andrew J. Goodpaster, and General John S. D. Eisenhower generously shared with the author their unique recollections of President Eisenhower and his effort to come to grips with the thermonuclear revolution. David J. Haight of the Dwight D. Eisenhower Library provided invaluable guidance and advice during the author's visits to Abilene. Finally, a special debt of gratitude is owed to Fred Greene. Professor Greene patiently advised the undergraduate honors thesis at Williams College that provided the foundation for this essay. His influence unmistakably remains.

2. McGeorge Bundy, *Danger and Survival: Choices About the Bomb in the First Fifty Years* (New York: Random House, 1988), 516. The 'nuclear revisionists' are most closely associated with their advocacy of a nuclear declaratory policy of 'no-first-use'. In its strongest form, two basic premises inform the nuclear revisionist critique: first, *'nuclear weapons serve no military purpose whatsoever. They are totally useless—except only to deter one's opponent from using them'*; second, it is a 'myth' that 'nuclear weapons, even when militarily irrelevant, can serve political ends'. Robert S. McNamara, 'The Military Role of Nuclear Weapons: Perceptions and Misperceptions', *Foreign Affairs,* 62/1 (Fall 1983), 79, emphasis in original; McGeorge Bundy, *Blundering into Disaster: Surviving the First Century of the Nuclear Age* (New York: Pantheon Books, 1986), 74–5. See also, McGeorge Bundy, George F. Kennan, Robert S. McNamara, and Gerard Smith, 'Nuclear Weapons and the Atlantic Alliance', *Foreign Affairs*, 60/4 (Spring 1982), 753–68; McGeorge Bundy, 'The Unimpressive Record of Nuclear Diplomacy', in Gwyn Prins (ed.), *The Nuclear Crisis Reader* (New York: Vintage, 1984), 42–54; McGeorge Bundy *et al.*, 'Back from the Brink', *The Atlantic*, 258/2 (Aug. 1986), 35–41; Morton H. Halperin, *Nuclear Fallacy: Dispelling the Myth of Nuclear Strategy* (Cambridge, Mass.: Ballinger, 1987); George F. Kennan, *The Nuclear Delusion* (New York: Pantheon Books, 1983). For a valuable contemporary critique of the nuclear revisionists see Robert W. Tucker, *The Nuclear Debate: Deterrence and the Lapse of Faith* (New York: Holmes & Meier, 1985). Bundy, *Danger and Survival*, remains the best historical analysis of the key decisions shaping American nuclear policy from 1940 through the Cuban Missile Crisis.

3. John Mueller, *Retreat from Doomsday: The Obsolescence of Major War* (New York: Basic Books, 1989). See also id., 'The Essential Irrelevance of Nuclear Weapons: Stability in the Postwar World', *International Security*, 13/2 (Fall 1988), 55–79. For the most penetrating critiques of the 'essential irrelevance' argument, see John Lewis Gaddis, 'The Essential Relevance of Nuclear Weapons', in Gaddis, *The United States and the End of the Cold War: Implications, Reconsiderations, and Provocations* (New York: Oxford University Press, 1992), 105–18; Robert Jervis, *The Meaning of the Nuclear Revolution: Statecraft and the Prospect of Armageddon* (Ithaca, NY: Cornell University Press, 1989).

4. Jerome H. Kahan, *Security in the Nuclear Age: Developing US Strategic Arms Policy* (Washington: Brookings, 1975), 10.

5. David Alan Rosenberg, 'US Strategy: Theory vs. Practice', *Bulletin of the Atomic Scientists*, 43/2 (Mar. 1987), 22.

6. Out of thirteen nuclear crises of the Cold War era, seven occurred during the Eisenhower years. Eisenhower initiated nuclear signalling during six of these: the resolution of the Korean War, 1952–3; the Indo-China crisis, 1954; the first offshore island crisis, 1954–5; the American intervention in Lebanon, 1958; the second offshore islands crisis, 1958; and the Berlin Deadline crisis, 1958–9. The other seven crises included by Betts are: the Berlin Blockade, 1948; the Suez crisis, 1956; the Berlin Aide-Memoire crisis, 1961; the Middle East War, 1973; and the pronouncement of the Carter Doctrine, 1980. This assessment is based on the categorization of Richard Betts. For a discussion of his selection criteria, see Richard K. Betts, *Nuclear Blackmail and Nuclear Balance* (Washington: Brookings, 1987), 16–18.

7. The phrase is from Glenn H. Snyder and Paul Diesing, *Conflict Among Nations: Bargaining, Decision Making, and System Structure in International Crises* (Princeton: Princeton University Press, 1977), 8.

8. George W. Breslauer and Philip E. Tetlock (eds.), *Learning in US and Soviet Foreign Policy* (Boulder, Colo.: Westview, 1991); Willliam W. Jarosz with Joseph S. Nye, Jr., 'The Shadow of the Past: Learning from History in National Security Decision Making', in Philip E. Tetlock, Jo L. Husbands, Robert Jarvis, Paul C. Stern, and Charles Tilly (eds.), *Behavior, Society, and International Conflict* (New York: Oxford University Press, 1993), 126–89; Joseph S. Nye, Jr., 'Nuclear Learning and US–Soviet Security Regimes', *International Organization*, 41/3 (Summer 1987), 371–402. On the broader issue of the relationship between ideas and foreign policy, see Judith Goldstein and Robert O. Keohane (eds.), *Ideas and Foreign Policy: Beliefs, Institutions, and Political Change* (Ithaca, NY: Cornell University Press, 1993).

9. The literature on Eisenhower's military career is voluminous. For biographical information this section draws upon Stephen E. Ambrose, *Eisenhower*, i. *Soldier, General of the Army, President-Elect, 1890–1952* (New York: Simon & Schuster, 1983); Kenneth S. Davis, *Soldier of Democracy: A Biography of Dwight Eisenhower* (Garden City, NY: Doubleday, Doran & Co., 1945); Peter Lyon, *Eisenhower: Portrait of a Hero* (Boston: Little, Brown and Co., 1974); Merle Miller, *Ike the Soldier: As They Knew Him* (New York: G. P. Putnam's Sons, 1987). This section also exploits Eisenhower's own autobiographical reflections: Dwight D. Eisenhower, *At Ease: Stories I Tell to Friends* (Garden City, NY: Doubleday & Co.); id., Oral History no. 106, Dwight D. Eisenhower Library, Abilene, Kansas (hereafter DDEL); ibid., no. 501. Lastly, Maureen P. O'Connor's, 'General Eisenhower and the Use of Force in the Postwar Period', 1992 (an unpublished manuscript completed under the auspices of the Nuclear History Program) provides an excellent introduction to Eisenhower's professional development through the 1952 presidential campaign. Dr. O'Connor also generously

provided photocopies of public statements by Eisenhower from his pre-presidential papers and from the Ann Whitman File, Speech Series.

10. 1915 Efficiency Record of Dwight D. Eisenhower, 'Summary of Efficiency Reports', Dwight D. Eisenhower Personnel Records (a component of Records of the Office of the Adjutant General: Record Group 407), 1910–73 (hereafter DDE Personnel Records), Series III: Efficiency Reports, Box 4, Efficiency Reports (1911–20), DDEL. See also Eisenhower's foreword to Stephen E. Ambrose, *Duty, Honor, Country: A History of West Point* (Baltimore: Johns Hopkins University Press, 1966), pp. vii–ix.

11. Captain D. D. Eisenhower, 'A Tank Discussion', *Infantry Journal*, 17 (Nov. 1920), 453–8, repr. in Daniel D. Holt (ed.), *Eisenhower: The Prewar Diaries and Selected Papers, 1905–1941* (Baltimore: Johns Hopkins University Press, 1998) (hereafter *Prewar Diaries*), 28–35. Eisenhower, 'Tanks with Infantry' (May 1921), in Holt (ed.), *Prewar Diaries*, 35–42.

12. Memorandum for General Pershing, 11–16–21, Subject: Request of Fox Conner for Brigade Adjutant, DDE Personnel Records, Series I: General Historical, 1915–73, Box 1, General Historical (1922–25).

13. Decades later he reported that Clausewitz identified certain 'ageless' features of international conflict and that *On War* remained the single most important text he ever read on military affairs. Answers to questions originated by Dr Bela Kornitzer, asked the President by Dr Milton Eisenhower in 'interview' Thursday morning, 17 Mar. 1955, Dwight D. Eisenhower Papers as President of the United States, 1953–61 (Ann Whitman File) (hereafter AWF), Ann Whitman Diary Series, Box 4, ACW Diary Mar. 1955 (4), DDEL; Eisenhower to Olive Ann Tamberline, 2 Mar. 1966, Dwight D. Eisenhower Post-Presidential Papers, Convenience File, Box 1, DDE Personals, DDEL. On the later influence of Clausewitz upon Eisenhower's strategic outlook, see Andrew P. N. Erdmann, 'Explaining Massive Retaliation: Eisenhower as a Clausewitzian', Paper presented at the Twentieth Annual Society for Historians of American Foreign Relations Conference, Bentley College, Waltham, Mass., 24 June 1994; John Lewis Gaddis, *Strategies of Containment: A Critical Appraisal of Postwar American National Security Policy* (New York: Oxford University Press, 1982), 135, 188; John Lewis Gaddis, *We Now Know: Rethinking Cold War History* (New York: Oxford University Press, 1997), 233; William B. Pickett, 'Eisenhower as a Student of Clausewitz', *Military Review*, 65/7 (July 1987), 21–7; id., 'Eisenhower, Clausewitz, and American Power', *The SHAFR Newsletter*, 23/4 (Dec. 1991), 28–40; id., *Dwight D. Eisenhower and American Power* (Wheeling, Ill.: Harlan Davidson, 1995), 15–16, 18, 38, 52, 100–2, 182; Christopher Bassford, *Clausewitz in English: The Reception of Clausewitz in Britain and America, 1815–1945* (New York: Oxford University Press, 1994), 157–62.

14. Dwight D. Eisenhower, Oral History, no. 106, p. 9.

15. Eisenhower, *At Ease*, 187. On Eisenhower's time in Panama see n. 9 and Charles H. Brown, 'Fox Conner: A General's General', *Journal of Mississippi History*, 49/3 (Aug. 1987), 203–15; 15 June 1932 entry in Holt (ed.), *Prewar Diaries*, 226–7; Edward Hazlett to Eisenhower, 23 May 1944, with enclosure, Dwight D. Eisenhower Pre-Presidential Papers, 1916–52 (hereafter DDE-PPP), Name Series, Box 56, Hazlett, Edward E. ['Swede'] (5) (Oct. 1941–July 1945), DDEL.

16. Andrew J. Goodpaster, Jr., Oral History, no. 37, 14, DDEL. For further details on Eisenhower's time at Leavenworth see n. 9 and Mark C. Bender, *Watershed at Leavenworth: Dwight D. Eisenhower and the Command and General Staff School* (Fort Leavenworth, Kan.: US Army Command and General Staff College, 1990); Timothy

K. Nenninger, 'Leavenworth and Its Critics: The US Army Command and General Staff School, 1920–1940', *Journal of Military History*, 58/2 (Apr. 1994), 204, 223, 227–8; Eisenhower, 'On the Command and General Staff School', Aug. 1926, in Holt (ed.), *Prewar Diaries*, 43–58; 'A Young Graduate' [Eisenhower], 'The Leavenworth Course', *Infantry Journal*, 30 (June 1927), 589–600.

17. Colonel Jas. D. Taylor, ASW Course No. 1, Orientation, Outline of the Course, Committee Assignments, and Directives, 8–24 Dec. 1927, Record Group 165, Records of the War Department, General and Special Staffs, Entry 7, War College Division and War Plans Division, Army War College, Records of Instruction, 1912–40 (hereafter War College Records of Instruction), Box 29, Course at the Army War College, 1927–8, ASW, Docs. nos. 1–17, vol. V, National Archives and Records Administration I, Washington. On the curriculum of the Army War College during the late 1920s and its increased emphasis on inculcating the lessons of World War I and the cardinal importance of political, economic, and social factors in a future war, see Harry F. Ball, *Of Responsible Command: A History of the US Army War College* (Carlisle Barracks, Pa.: Alumni Association of the United States Army War College, 1983), 198–219; George S. Pappas, *Prudens Futuri: The US Army War College, 1901–1967* (Carlisle Barracks, Pa.: Alumni Association of the US Army War College, 1967), 119–27.

18. William D. Connor, WPD Course No. 1, 1927–8, Orientation Lecture, Outline of the Course and Committee Assignments, and Bibliography, 2–17 Sept. [1927], War College Records of Instruction, Box 29A, Course at the Army War College, 1927–8, WPD, Docs. nos. 1–10, vol. VIII, pt. I. For the lectures and course outlines for the Army War College Class of 1928 see War College Records of Instruction, Boxes 28–29A. Eisenhower's final Army War College assignment, which proposed a new enlisted reserve system, was judged so superior by Commandant Connor that he circulated it within the General Staff. Major D. D. Eisenhower, Memorandum for the Assistant Commandant, the Army War College, 1927–8, Command, 20 Mar. 1928, DDE-PPP, Miscellaneous File, Composite Series, Box 20, Army War College Course Papers, 1927–8 (1) portions of this memorandum are printed in Holt (ed.), *Prewar Diaries*, 62–79; William D. Connor to Eisenhower, 5 May 1928, DDE-PPP, Name Series, Box 27, Connor, William Durward. For further details on Eisenhower's time at the Army War College see n. 9 and Benjamin Franklin Cooling, 'Dwight D. Eisenhower at the Army War College, 1927–1928', *Parameters*, 5/1 (1975), 26–36.

19. Of the 431 Army graduates of the Industrial College by 1936, only 33 (under 8%) had also graduated from the Army War College. Harold W. Thatcher, *Planning for Industrial Mobilization, 1920–1940* (Washington: Historical Section, Office of the Quartermaster General, 1943), 40. Eisenhower was acutely conscious that he was unusual in that he resisted the prevailing ethos within the Army establishment that still held service as an industrial mobilization planner in low esteem. Eisenhower, 'Peace time Difficulties of Procurement Planning', Jan. 1930, quoted in Thatcher, *Planning for Industrial Mobilization*, 130–1. See also his Army Industrial College lecture Major Dwight D. Eisenhower, 'History of Planning for Procurement and Industrial Mobilization since World War', 2 Oct. 1931, DDE-PPP, Miscellaneous File, Composite Series, Box 20, War Department Study 1931 (A86–4).

20. US War Department, 'Plan for Industrial Mobilization', in US Congress, War Policies Commission, *Hearings before the Commission Appointed under the Authority of Public Resolution No. 98*, 71st Congress, Second Session, pt. 2 (Washington: GPO, 1931), 395–470; US War Department, *Industrial Mobilization Plan, Revised, 1933: A Revision*

of the plan for Industrial Mobilization Submitted by the War Department in 1931 to the War Policies Commission Appointed under the Authority of Public Resolution No. 98, Seventy-first Congress (Washington: GPO, 1935).

21. Bernard M. Baruch, *Baruch: The Public Years* (New York: Holt, Reinhart and Winston, 1960), 263–9; Jordan A. Schwartz, *The Speculator: Bernard M. Baruch in Washington, 1917–1965* (Chapel Hill: University of North Carolina Press, 1981), 331–49, 391; Thatcher, *Planning for Industrial Mobilization*, 19–20, 86–91, 246–53; Harold B. Yosphe, 'Bernard M. Baruch: Civilian Godfather of the Military M-Day Plan', *Military Affairs*, 29/1 (Spring 1965), 1–15.

22. Major Dwight D. Eisenhower, 'War Policies', *Infantry Journal* (Nov.–Dec. 1931), 489–93.

23. Dwight D. Eisenhower, *Crusade in Europe* (Garden City, NY: Doubleday & Co., 1948), 19. For the 1929–35 period of Eisenhower's career and the intellectual trends in American mobilization planning during this time, see n. 9 and Albert A. Blum, 'Birth and Death of the M-Day Plan', in Harold Stein (ed.), *American Civil-Military Decisions: A Book of Case Studies* (Birmingham, Ala.: University of Alabama Press, 1963), 63–70; Eisenhower, Oral History, no. 106, 5–7; Holt (ed.), *Prewar Diaries*, 110–282; Industrial College of the Armed Forces, *The Industrial College of the Armed Forces, 1924–1949: Twenty-Fifth Anniversary* (Washington: Industrial College of the Armed Forces, 1949), 8–12, 23, 31; D. Clayton James, *The Years of MacArthur*, i. *1880–1941* (Boston: Houghton Mifflin, 1970), 461–70, 674 n. 17, 687 n. 15; Paul A. C. Koistinen, 'The "Industrial-Military" Complex in Historical Perspective: The InterWar Years', *Journal of American History*, 56/4 (Mar. 1970), 819–39; Marvin A. Kreidberg and Merton G. Henry, *History of Military Mobilization in the United States Army, 1775–1945* (Washington: Department of the Army, 1955), 507–27; Kevin McCann, *Man From Abilene* (Garden City, NY: Doubleday & Co., 1952), 87–95; R. Elberton Smith, *The Army and Economic Mobilization* (Washington: Center of Military History, 1991), 39–40, 43–5, 73–97; Thatcher, *Planning for Industrial Mobilization*, 1–220; Harold B. Yoshpe, 'Economic Mobilization Planning Between the Two World Wars', pt. I, *Military Affairs*, 15/4 (Winter 1951), 199–204, and pt. II, *Military Affairs*, 16/2 (Summer 1952), 71–83.

24. 3 Sept. 1939 entry in Holt (ed.), *Prewar Diaries*, 445–7; Eisenhower to Leonard Gerow, 11 Oct. 1939, in ibid. 449–50; Eisenhower to George Patton, 17 Sept. 1940, in ibid. 491–2; 26 Sept. 1940 entry in ibid. 493–4; Eisenhower to Gerow, 25 Nov. 1940, in ibid. 505–8; Eisenhower to Everett Hughes, 26 Nov. 1940, in ibid. 508–9; Eisenhower to Douglas MacArthur, 11 Dec. 1940, in ibid. 513; Eisenhower, Draft Address to Graduates at Kelly Field, Texas, 12 Dec. 1941, in ibid. 561–3; Eisenhower, *Crusade in Europe*, 5.

25. Ray S. Cline, *Washington Command Post: The Operations Division* (Washington: Office of the Chief of Military History, US Army, 1951), 75–89, 107–42, 145–54; Maurice Matloff and Edwin M. Snell, *Strategic Planning for Coalition Warfare, 1941–1942* (Washington: Office of the Chief of Military History, US Army, 1953), 87–197; Alfred D. Chandler, Jr. (ed.), *The Papers of Dwight David Eisenhower: The War Years*, 5 vols. (Baltimore: Johns Hopkins University Press, 1970) (hereafter *The War Years*), i, 5–354. For Eisenhower's initial thoughts regarding these strategic priorities, see Eisenhower to Wade Haislip, 28 July 1941, in Holt (ed.), *Prewar Diaries*, 534; Eisenhower to Kenyon Joyce, 30 July 1941, in ibid. 536; Eisenhower to Mr & Mrs Edgar Eisenhower and Janis, 7 Oct. 1941, in ibid. 549.

26. Eisenhower, *Crusade in Europe*, 448–56.

27. Three seminal works establish the contours of contemporary Cold War historiography: John Lewis Gaddis, *We Now Know*; Melvyn P. Leffler, *A Preponderance of Power: National Security, the Truman Administration, and the Cold War* (Stanford: Stanford University Press, 1992); and, Marc Trachtenberg, *A Constructed Peace* (Princeton: Princeton University Press, forthcoming). For the integration of nuclear weapons into American national security policy in this era, see David Alan Rosenberg, *Toward Armageddon: The Foundations of United States Nuclear Strategy, 1945–1961* (Ph. D. diss., University of Chicago, 1983); David Alan Rosenberg, 'The Origins of Overkill: Nuclear Weapons and American Strategy, 1945–1960', in Steven E. Miller (ed.), *Strategy and Nuclear Deterrence* (Princeton: Princeton University Press, 1984), 113–81; Steven T. Ross, *American War Plans, 1945–1950* (New York: Garland, 1988); Samuel R. Williamson, Jr. and Steven L. Reardon, *The Origins of US Nuclear Strategy, 1945–1953* (New York: St. Martin's, 1993).

28. For Eisenhower's contemporaneous, public explication of his changing assessment of American–Soviet relations see Eisenhower, *Crusade in Europe*, 457–78. See also Eisenhower to George C. Marshall, 16 Aug. 1945, in Alfred D. Chandler, Jr. and Louis Galambos (eds.), *The Papers of Dwight David Eisenhower: Occupation, 1945*, 1 vol. (Baltimore: Johns Hopkins University Press, 1978), vi. 286–8; ibid. Eisenhower to Lucius Clay, 8 Nov. 1945, 521–7, esp. 525; Eisenhower to Henry Wilson, 30 Oct. 1947, in Louis Galambos (ed.), *The Papers of Dwight David Eisenhower: The Chief of Staff*, 3 vols. (Baltimore: Johns Hopkins University Press, 1978) (hereafter *The Chief of Staff*), ix. 2021–2. He later admitted—somewhat defensively—that the demands of his operational responsibilities during the war prevented him from giving sustained thought to the post-war world. Eisenhower to Al Wedemeyer, 2 May 1947, DDE-PPP, Name Series, Box 123, Wedemeyer, A. C. (3) (July 1943–May 1947).

29. Eisenhower to Joseph McNarney, 17 Apr. 1945, in *The Chief of Staff*, vii. 1010–13; S.W.D., Memorandum for record, 12 June 1946, Marshall Foundation National Archives Project, Xerox 3527, George C. Marshall Library, Lexington, Va.; 11 June 1946 and 21 Aug. 1946 entries in Walter Millis (ed.), *The Forrestal Diaries* (New York: Viking Press, 1951), 172, 195. On the JCS's initial war planning efforts, see Ross, *American War Plans*, 3–77; James F. Schnabel, *The History of the Joint Chiefs of Staff: The Joint Chiefs of Staff and National Policy*, i. *1945–1947* (Wilmington, Del.: Michael Glazier, 1979), 135–93.

30. Memorandum of Conversation, by the Counselor of the Department of State (Bohlen), 30 Aug. 1947, and Memorandum by the Counselor of the Department of State (Bohlen), 30 Aug. 1947, US Department of State, *Foreign Relations of the United States, 1947*, i. (Washington: GPO, 1973), 762–5.

31. 26 May 1946 and 16 Sept. 1947 entries in Robert H. Ferrell (ed.), *The Eisenhower Diaries* (New York: Norton, 1981), 136–7, 143–4; Eisenhower to Edward Everett Hazlett, Jr., 19 July 1947, in *The Chief of Staff*, viii. 1837; Eisenhower to Henry Wilson, 30 Oct. 1947, 2022; Eisenhower statement, 2 Apr. 1948, US Congress, Senate, *Hearings before the Committee on Armed Services on Universal Military Training*, 80th Congress, Second Session (hereafter *Universal Military Training, 1948*), 986–9; Eisenhower, Inaugural Address at Columbia University, DDE-PPP, Speech Series, Box 193, Speeches Aug. 48–June 49 (2). See also Eisenhower, Notes for Address before the American Bar Association, 5 Sept. 1949, DDE-PPP, Speech Series, Box 193, Speeches July 49–Dec. 49 (2); Eisenhower, Gabriel Silver Lecture on Peace: World Peace—A Balance Sheet, 30 Mar. 1950, DDE-PPP, Speech Series, Box 193, Speeches Jan. 1950–Dec. 1950 (2); The United States Delegation at the Eighth Session of the

North Atlantic Council to the Acting Secretary of State, 27 Nov. 1951, US Department of State, *Foreign Relations of the United States, 1951* (hereafter *FRUS*: 1951), iii (Washington: GPO, 1981), 733–5; Ira Chernus, 'Eisenhower's Ideology in World War II', *Armed Forces & Society*, 23/4 (Summer 1997), 595–613.

32. Eisenhower to Clay, 8 Nov. 1945, 524–5; S.W.D. Memorandum for record, 12 June 1946; 11 June 1946 and 21 Aug. 1946 entries in Millis (ed.), *The Forrestal Diaries*, 172, 195; Eisenhower to Bernard Law Montgomery, 20 Feb. 1947, in *The Chief of Staff*, viii. 1530–2; Eisenhower to Walter Bedell Smith, 28 Nov. 1947, in *ibid.* ix. 2084–5; Eisenhower statement, 29 Mar. 1950, US Congress, Senate, *Hearings before the Subcommittee of the Committee on Appropriations, Department of Defense Appropriations for 1951*, 81st Congress, Second Session (hereafter *Defense, 1951*), 687, 696–7; Eisenhower to Craig Campbell, 10 Oct. 1950, in Louis Galambos (ed.), *The Papers of Dwight David Eisenhower: Columbia University*, 2 vols. (Baltimore: Johns Hopkins University Press, 1984) (hereafter *Columbia*), xi. 1371; Eisenhower testimony, Executive Session, Hearings before the Committee on Armed Services and Foreign Affairs, House of Representatives, 2 Feb. 1951, 17–20, DDE-PPP, Subject Series, Box 145, Hearings 1951 (2); Diary, 3 Mar. 1951, in Louis Galambos (ed.), *The Papers of Dwight David Eisenhower: NATO and the Campaign of 1952*, 2 vols. (Baltimore: Johns Hopkins University Press, 1989) (hereafter *NATO*), xii. 90–1; Eisenhower statement, 9 July 1951, US Congress, Senate, *Hearings Before a Subcommittee of the Committee on Foreign Relations on United States Economic and Military Assistance to Free Europe*, 82nd Congress, First Session (hereafter *Foreign Aid Programs in Europe, 1951*), 12–13; Transcript of Briefing Held for Visiting Senate Foreign Relations Committee at SHAPE, 22 July 1951, 8–9 (including portions that were deleted from the public record for security reasons), DDE-PPP, Subject Series, Box 136, Congressional Visits: 1951 (2).

33. Eisenhower testimony, 15 Nov. 1945, US Congress, House, *Hearings Before the Committee on Military Affairs on H. R. 515 An Act to Provide Military or Naval Training for All Male Citizens who Attain the Age of 18 Years, and for Other Purposes*, 79th Congress, First Session (hereafter *Universal Military Training, 1945*), pt. I, 84; 16 Sept. 1947 and 27 Jan. 1949 entries in Ferrell (ed.), *The Eisenhower Diaries*, 143–4, 155–6.

34. Eisenhower to Arthur Eisenhower, 18 May 1943, in *The War Years*, ii. 1148–9; Eisenhower statement, 2 Apr. 1948, *Universal Military Training, 1948*, 999; Eisenhower to Andrew Wells Robertson, 11 Oct. 1950, in *Columbia*, xi. 1374; 30 May 1951 entry in Ferrell (ed.), *The Eisenhower Diaries*, 193; Transcript, Television Q & A Show, 1 Nov. 1952, AWF, Speech Series, Box 2, 10/23–12/52 (1); Eisenhower, *At Ease*, 250–1. On Eisenhower's visit to the Gotha concentration camp, see 18 Apr. 1945 entry in Harry C. Butcher, *My Three Years with Eisenhower: The Personal Diary of Captain Harry C. Butcher, USNR* (New York: Simon and Schuster, 1946), 803.

35. Eisenhower, Address before Bureau of Advertising of the American Newspaper Publishers' Association, New York, 25 Apr. 1946 in Rudolph L. Treuenfels (ed.), *Eisenhower Speaks: Dwight D. Eisenhower in his Messages and Speeches* (New York: Farrar, Strauss & Co., 1948), 84–91; Eisenhower, Gabriel Silver Lecture on Peace: World Peace—A Balance Sheet, 30 Mar. 1950, 1–2.

36. Eisenhower, handwritten notes, for 'Problems of Combined Command address to the National War College', 1949 address, DDE-PPP, Subject Series, Box 156, Problems of Combined Command (National War College), June 17 1949.

37. 15 Dec. 1945, 12 Nov. 1946, 27 Jan. 1949, 19 Feb. 1949, 6 Nov. 1950, and 22 Jan. 1952 entries in Ferrell (ed.), *The Eisenhower Diaries*, 136, 138, 156, 157–8, 181,

209–13; Eisenhower statement, 2 Apr. 1948, *Universal Military Training, 1948*, 993; Eisenhower, 'Problems of Combined Command' (corrected transcript), 17 June 1949, DDE-PPP, Subject Series, Box 156, Problems of Combined Command (National War College), June 17 1949. See also Eisenhower statement, 29 Mar. 1950, US Congress, Senate, *Defense, 1951*, 679–80, 703; Eisenhower to Lucius Clay, 9 Feb. 1952, in *NATO*, xiii. 962–5.

38. Eisenhower, *Crusade in Europe*, 443. See also Dwight D. Eisenhower, *The White House Years: Mandate for Change, 1953–1956* (Garden City, NY: Doubleday & Co., 1963), 312–13; John S. D. Eisenhower, *Strictly Personal* (Garden City, NY: Doubleday & Co., 1974), 97; Memorandum of Conference with the President (hereafter MCP followed by date of conversation), 11 Apr. 1960, AWF, DDE Diary Series, Box 49, Staff Notes Apr. 1960 (2); Gar Alperovitz, *The Decision to Use the Atomic Bomb and the Architecture of an American Myth* (New York: Knopf, 1995), 236–7, 276–7, 352–8. For an argument that questions whether Eisenhower expressed these concerns at Potsdam, see Barton J. Bernstein, 'Ike and Hiroshima: Did He Oppose It?' *Journal of Strategic Studies*, 10/3 (Sept. 1987), 377–403.

39. Eisenhower to Edward Everett Hazlett, Jr., 1 July 1946, in *The Chief of Staff*, vii. 1163; Chief of Staff of the United States Army (Eisenhower) to the United States Representative on the Atomic Energy Commission (Baruch), 14 June 1946, *Foreign Relations of the United States, 1946*, i. (Washington: GPO, 1972), 854–7; Millis (ed.), *The Forrestal Diaries*, 327; Eisenhower, Memorandum for the Director of Plans and Operations, 5 Feb. 1947, DDE-PPP, Subject Series, Box 140, Disarmament; Eisenhower, Broadcast on Bikini Atomic Bomb Test, NBC, 29 June 1946 in Treuenfels (ed.), *Eisenhower Speaks*, 115–16. See also Lloyd J. Graybar, 'The 1946 Atomic Bomb Tests: Atomic Diplomacy or Bureaucratic Infighting?' *Journal of American History*, 72/4 (Mar. 1986), 888–907; Larry G. Gerber, 'The Baruch Plan and the Origins and the Cold War', *Diplomatic History*, 6/1 (Winter 1981), 69–95.

40. Also it should be noted that Eisenhower was relatively free of the contentious, partisan debates over nuclear strategy between the Air Force and the Navy, and thus could situate his own appreciation within a broader strategic framework more easily than many of his peers. On the state of 'nuclear knowledge' within the military at this time see David Alan Rosenberg, 'American Atomic Strategy and the Hydrogen Bomb Decision', *Journal of American History*, 66/1 (June 1979), 62–87; Rosenberg, *Toward Armageddon*, 1–151; David Alan Rosenberg, 'US Nuclear Stockpile, 1945 to 1950', *Bulletin of the Atomic Scientists*, 38/5 (May 1982), 25–30. While Chief of Staff, Eisenhower ordered the formation of a small cell of young officers to 'look out as far as they could into the future to try to generate new ideas, new concepts' to cope with the new strategic environment. This Advanced Study Group was disbanded after Eisenhower's departure for Columbia University. Andrew J. Goodpaster, Senior Officers Debriefing Program, 29 Jan. 1976, 56–8, and 25 Feb. 1976, 6, US Army Military History Institute, Carlisle Barracks, Pa. Eisenhower also went beyond official analyses to study analyses of leading civilians like Bernard Brodie and James Conant. See Frederick S. Dunn to Eisenhower, 7 Mar. 1946; Eisenhower to Frederick S. Dunn, 14 Mar. 1946; James Stack, Memorandum for the Secretary of War *et al.*, 25 Mar. 1946 all in DDE-PPP, Subject Series, Box 127, Atomic Weapons (1); Advance draft of *The Absolute Weapon* (with Eisenhower marginalia); James B. Conant, The Atomic Age: A Preview, 1947 edn., 1947; Eisenhower to James B. Conant, 20 Oct. 1947, all in DDE-PPP, Subject Series, Box 127, Atomic Weapons and Energy (2); Eisenhower to Joseph Greene, 13 July 1946, in *The Chief of Staff*, vii. 1196–7.

41. 22 July 1949 entry in David E. Lilienthal, *The Journals of David E. Lilienthal: The Atomic Energy Years* (New York: Harper & Row, 1964), 549–50. On the limitations of the American nuclear arsenal, see Rosenberg, 'American Atomic Strategy and the Hydrogen Bomb Decision', 62–87; id., 'US Nuclear Stockpile, 1945 to 1950', 25–30; Ross, *American War Plans*, 313–15; Michael D. Yaffe, '"A Higher Priority than the Korean War!": The Crash Programmes to Modify the Bombers for the Bomb', *Diplomacy & Statecraft*, 5/2 (July 1994), 358–70.

42. Rosenberg, 'The Origins of Overkill', 121–4; Rosenberg, 'US Nuclear Stockpile, 1945 to 1950', 28.

43. Eisenhower statement, 15 Nov. 1946, *Universal Military Training, 1945*, 79; Eisenhower to Chester W. Nimitz, 6 Dec. 1946, in *The Chief of Staff*, viii. 1424–5; Eisenhower statement, 28 June 1947, US Congress, Senate, *Hearings for the Subcommittee of the Committee on Appropriations on H. R. 3678, A Bill Making Appropriations for the Military Establishment for the Fiscal Year Ending June 30, 1948, and for Other Purposes*, 80th Congress, First Session, 290–1, 295; Eisenhower statement, 2 Apr. 1948, *Universal Military Training, 1948*, 987.

44. Eisenhower statement, 15 Nov. 1946, *Universal Military Training, 1945*, 60–4, 78, 82; Eisenhower statement, 19 Feb. 1947, US Congress, House, *Hearings Before the Subcommittee of the Committee on Appropriations on the Military Establishment Appropriation Bill for 1948*, 80th Congress, First Session (hereafter *Appropriations, 1948*), 75–80; Eisenhower statement, US Congress, Senate, *Hearings Before the Committee on Armed Services on S. 758 a Bill to Promote the National Security by Providing for a National Defense Establishment*, 80th Congress, First Session, 89–91; Eisenhower, *Crusade in Europe*, 456. As Eisenhower later explained his relatively restrained assessment of the importance of nuclear weapons in a congressional hearing: 'Since we [the military] have always, or at least since World War I, believed that air power was achieving a more and more predominant position in warfare, we have looked at these vehicles as the means of delivering bombs—any kind of bomb—therefore, I do not think that the advent of the atomic bomb changed our thinking as much as it did the thinking of those who have previously been completely "land-minded".' Eisenhower statement, 29 Mar. 1950, *Defense, 1951*, 696. See also George A. Lincoln testimony, 17 Feb. 1947, *Appropriations, 1948*, 1–14. On the expansion of Americans' conceptions of 'national security' during this era, see Leffler, *A Preponderance of Power*; Ernest R. May, 'Cold War and Defense', in Keith Neilson and Ronald G. Haycock (eds.), *The Cold War and Defense* (New York: Praeger, 1990), 7–73.

45. JCS 1725/1, Memorandum by the Joint Staff Planners to the JCS, Strategic Guidance for Industrial Mobilization Planning, 13 Feb. 1947, and JCS 1725/2, Memorandum by the Chief of Staff, US Army, to the JCS, Strategic Guidance for Industrial Mobilization Planning, 12 Mar. 1947, in Steven T. Ross and David Alan Rosenberg, *America's Plans for War Against the Soviet Union, 1945–1950*, 15 vols. (New York: Garland, 1989), v. *The Limits of American Power*; Eisenhower to Robert Patterson, 17 Mar. 1947, in *The Chief of Staff*, viii. 1606; Rosenberg, *Toward Armageddon*, 90.

46. Eisenhower to Omar Bradley, Louis Denfield, and Hoyt Vandenberg, 28 Feb. 1949, in *Columbia*, x. 515–19; ibid. Eisenhower to Louis Johnson, 3 May 1949, x. 568–70; ibid. Eisenhower to Louis Johnson, 25 May 1949, x. 591–4; ibid. Eisenhower to Robert Carney, 21 June 1949, x. 651–7; ibid. Eisenhower to Louis Johnson, 14 July 1949, x. 699–704; JCS 1844/37, Preparation of a Joint Outline Emergency War Plan, 27 Apr. 1949, and JCS 1844/46, Report by the Joint Strategic Planning Committee

to the JCS, Joint Outline Emergency War Plan 'OFFTACKLE', 8 Nov. 1949, in Ross and Rosenberg, *American Plans for War Against the Soviet Union, 1945–1950*, xii. *Budgets and Strategy: The Road to OFFTACKLE*; Kenneth W. Condit, *The History of the Joint Chiefs of Staff and National Policy*, ii, *1947–1949* (Wilmington, Del.: Michael Glazer, 1979), 294–302; Leffler, *A Preponderance of Power*, 273–7; Steven L. Reardon, *History of the Office of the Secretary of Defense*, i, *The Formative Years, 1947–1950* (Washington: GPO, 1984), 364–79, 381–2; Ross, *American War Plans*, 110–19.

47. 27 Jan. 1949, 9 Feb. 1949, and 14 June 1949 entries in Ferrell (ed.), *The Eisenhower Diaries*, 154–6, 157, 195; 8 Apr. 1949 entry in Lilienthal, *The Journals of David E. Lilienthal*, 502–3; Eisenhower to William Stuart Symington, 29 Aug. 1949, in Galambos, *Columbia*, x. 738–40; Eisenhower statement, 29 Mar. 1950, *Defense, 1951*, 679–80, 682–5, 693–4.

48. Notes on a Meeting at the White House, 31 Jan. 1951, *FRUS*: 1951, iii. 449–58; Eisenhower testimony, Executive Session, Hearings before the Committee on Armed Services and Foreign Affairs, House of Representatives, 2 Feb. 1951; Eisenhower to Edward John Bermingham, 28 Feb. 1951, in *NATO*, xii. 74–8; ibid. Eisenhower to Joseph Lawton Collins, 28 Feb. 1951 xii. 79–82; ibid. Eisenhower to Bernard Law Montgomery, 6 Apr. 1951, xii. 196–7; The Ambassador in France (Bruce) to the Secretary of State, 18 July 1951, *FRUS*: 1951, iii. 838–9; Eisenhower statements, 9 July and 22 July 1951, US Congress, Senate, *Hearings Before a Subcommittee of the Committee on Foreign Relations on United States Economic and Military Assistance to Free Europe*, 82nd Congress, First Session, 11–22, 273–84; Transcript of Briefings Held for Visiting Senate Foreign Relations Committee at SHAPE, 22 July 1951 (which contains passages deleted from the Subcommittee's published hearings); Eisenhower to George C. Marshall, 3 Aug. 1951, in *NATO*, xii. 457–63; ibid. Eisenhower to Paul Hoffman, 28 Aug. 1951, xii. 500; ibid. Eisenhower to JCS, 3 Oct. 1951, xii. 592–5; George M. Elsey, Meeting of the President with General of the Army Dwight D. Eisenhower, 5 Nov. 1951, *President Harry S. Truman's Office Files, 1945–1953*, pt. 2: *Correspondence Files* (Bethesda, Mass.: University Publications of America, microfilm, 1989), Reel 6, General File, Eisenhower, Dwight D. (folder 1); Eisenhower to Joseph Lawton Collins, 20 Dec. 1951, in *NATO*, xii. 803–6; ibid. Eisenhower to Alphonse Pierre Juin, 19 May 1952, xiii. 1224–8. As examples of Eisenhower's hope for a conventional defence of Western Europe, see 11 June 1951 entry in Ferrell (ed.), *The Eisenhower Diaries*, 195; Colonel Walters, Memorandum of Conversation, 10 July 1951, DDE-PPP, Subject Series, Box 136, Conversations, Memos of (SHAPE) 1951–2; Eisenhower, Memorandum for Chief of Staff, 26 Sept. 1952, DDE-PPP, Name Series, Box 48, Gruenther, Alfred M. (1) (Aug 1950–Apr. 1952). The phrase the 'great deterrent' comes from Alfred M. Gruenther statement, 9 July 1951, *Foreign Aid Programs in Europe, 1951*, 10. For the development of strategic policy during Eisenhower's tenure as SACEUR and the efforts to integrate nuclear weapons into NATO defence plans, see John S. Duffield, *Power Rules: The Evolution of NATO's Conventional Force Posture* (Stanford: Stanford University Press, 1995), 49–69; David C. Elliot, 'Project Vista and Nuclear Weapons in Europe', *International Security*, 11/1 (Summer 1986), 163–83; Matthew Evangelista, *Innovation and the Arms Race: How the United States and the Soviet Union Develop New Military Technologies* (Ithaca, NY: Cornell University Press, 1988), 133–45, 152; Goodpaster, Senior Officer Debriefing Program, 25 Feb. 1976, 9–14; Leffler, *A Preponderance of Power*, 411, 415–16, 451; Ernest R. May, 'The American Commitment to Germany, 1949–55', *Diplomatic History*, 13/4 (Fall 1989), 431–60;

Lauris Norstad, Oral History, no. 385, DDEL, 7–22, 39–42; Walter S. Poole, *The History of the Joint Chiefs of Staff and National Policy*, iv. *1950–1952* (Wilmington, Del.: Michael Glazer, 1980), 179–330; Peter J. Roman, 'Curtis LeMay and the Origins of NATO Atomic Targeting', *Journal of Strategic Studies*, 16/1 (Mar. 1993), 46–74; Thomas M. Sisk, 'Forging the Weapon: Eisenhower as NATO's Supreme Allied Commander, Europe, 1950–1952', in Gunther Bischoff and Stephen E. Ambrose (eds.), *Eisenhower: A Centenary Assessment* (Baton Rouge, La.: Louisiana State University Press, 1995), 62–83; Robert A. Wampler, 'NATO Strategic Planning and Nuclear Weapons, 1950–1957', *Nuclear History Program Occasional Paper 6* (College Park, Md.: University of Maryland, 1990), 4–11; id., 'Conventional Goals and Nuclear Promises: The Truman Administration and the Roots of the NATO New Look', in Francis H. Heller and John R. Gillingham (eds.), *NATO: The Founding of the Atlantic Alliance and the Integration of Europe* (New York: St. Martin's, 1992), 353–80; Robert J. Wood, 'The First Years of SHAPE', *International Organization*, 6/2 (May 1952), 175–91.

49. For Eisenhower's views of national security leading up to and through the 1952 presidential campaign, see Robert R. Bowie and Richard H. Immerman, *Waging Peace: How Eisenhower Shaped an Enduring Cold War Strategy* (New York: Oxford University Press, 1998), 41–54, 70–80. For representative statements on strategy during the campaign, see Pentagon Press Conference excerpt re. Air power, 3 June 1952, AWF, Speech Series, Box 3, Eisenhower Quotes 1/1/52–8/22/52; Notes for Address by Dwight D. Eisenhower in Denver, 23 June 1952, AWF, Speech Series, Box 1, June 4, 1952 to July 11, 1952 (3); Text of Address by Dwight D. Eisenhower, American Legion Convention, 25 Aug. 1952, AWF, Speech Series, Box 1, July 12 1952 to Sept. 14, 1952 (1).

50. Eisenhower to John Foster Dulles, 15 Apr. 1952, in *NATO*, xiii. 1178–9; ibid. Eisenhower to Dulles, 20 June 1952, xiii. 1254–6.

51. 7 Nov. 1952 and 19 Nov. 1952 entries in Roger M. Anders (ed.), *Forging the Atomic Shield: Excerpts from the Office Diary of Gordon E. Dean* (Chapel Hill: University of North Carolina Press, 1987), 232, 233–5; Roy Snapp, memorandum to file re. 11 Nov. 1952 meeting with President-Elect Eisenhower, n.d., Author's Freedom of Information Act (FOIA) Request; Gordon Dean Office Diary, 19 Nov. 1952 entry with attachment of Dean, Opening with Eisenhower, 19 Nov. 1952, Author's FOIA Request; Thomas Murray, Notes on Discussion with President-Elect Eisenhower, 19 Nov. 1952, Author's FOIA Request; Gordon Dean Office Diary, 24 Nov. entry, Author's FOIA Request; Richard G. Hewlett and Jack M. Holl, *Atoms for Peace and War, 1953–1961: Eisenhower and the Atomic Energy Commission* (Berkeley: University of California Press, 1989), 1–16. On the 'Mike' test, see Richard Rhodes, *Dark Sun: The Making of the Hydrogen Bomb* (New York: Simon & Schuster, 1995), 482–512.

52. 21 Jan. 1953 entry in Ferrell (ed.), *The Eisenhower Diaries*, 225.

53. Detailed analyses of the Eisenhower's national security policies, ranging from the complimentary to the critical, are readily available in the secondary literature. For a recent survey see Stephen G. Rabe, 'Eisenhower Revisionism: A Decade of Scholarship', *Diplomatic History*, 17/1 (Winter 1993), 97–115. Bowie and Immerman, *Waging Peace* provides the most insightful and thorough analysis of the policy-making process that yielded the 'New Look'. The following works were also particularly helpful in framing the analysis that follows: H. W. Brands, Jr., 'The Age of Vulnerability: Eisenhower and the National Insecurity State', *American Historical Review*, 94/4 (Oct. 1989), 963–89; Bundy, *Danger and Survival*, 236–357; Saki Dockrill, *Eisenhower's New Look National Security Policy, 1953–61* (London:

Macmillan, 1996); Brian Duchin, *The New Look: President Eisenhower and the Political Economy of National Security* (Ph. D. diss., University of Texas, Austin, 1987); Gaddis, *Strategies of Containment*, 127–97; Gaddis, *We Now Know*, 107–12, 221–59, 281–95; Robert Griffith, 'Dwight D. Eisenhower and the Corporate Commonwealth', *American Historical Review*, 81/1 (Feb. 1982), 81–122; Richard H. Immerman, 'Confessions of an Eisenhower Revisionist: An Agonizing Reappraisal', *Diplomatic History*, 14/3 (Summer 1990), 319–342; Richard A. Melanson, 'The Foundations of Eisenhower's Foreign Policy: Continuity, Community, and Consensus', in Richard A. Melanson and David Mayers (eds.), *Reevaluating Eisenhower: American Foreign Policy in the 1950s* (Urbana, Ill.: University of Illinois Press, 1987), 31–66; Steven Metz, 'Eisenhower and the Planning of American Grand Strategy', *Journal of Strategic Studies*, 14/1 (Mar. 1991), 49–71; George Quester, 'Was Eisenhower a Genius?', *International Security*, 4/2 (Fall 1979), 159–79; Rosenberg, *Toward Armageddon*; id., 'The Origins of Overkill'; Richard M. Saunders, 'Military Force in the Foreign Policy of the Eisenhower Presidency', *Political Science Quarterly*, 100/1 (Spring 1985), 97–116; Glenn H. Snyder, 'The "New Look" of 1953', in Warner R. Schilling, Paul Hammond, and Glenn H. Snyder, *Strategy, Politics, and Defense Budgets* (New York: Columbia University Press, 1962), 379–524; Trachtenberg, *A Constructed Peace*, chs. 4–7; Marc Trachtenberg, *History & Strategy* (Princeton: Princeton University Press, 1991), 100–234, 261–86; Samuel F. Wells, 'The Origins of Massive Retaliation', *Political Science Quarterly*, 96/1 (Spring 1981), 31–52.

54. In 1952, the American stockpile consisted of 832 weapons; in 1956, 3,620 weapons; and in 1959, 12,305 weapons. In early 1954, the first thermonuclear weapon, the B14, entered the stockpile on an 'emergency' basis. By 1960, the stockpile approached approximately 20,000 megatons. Robert S. Norris, Thomas B. Cochran, and William M. Arkin, 'History of the Nuclear Stockpile', *Bulletin of the Atomic Scientists*, 41/7 (Aug. 1985), 107; Robert S. Norris, 'US Weapons Secrets Revealed', *Bulletin of the Atomic Scientists*, 49/2 (Mar. 1993), 48.

55. Memorandum of Discussion at the 187th NSC Meeting (hereafter Discussion at), 4 Mar. 1954, US Department of State, *Foreign Relations of the United States, 1952–1954*, 16 vols. (Washington: GPO, 1979–85) (hereafter *FRUS: 1952–4*), ii. 636.

56. Discussion at 203rd NSC Meeting, 23 June 1954, *FRUS: 1952–4*, ii. 1469. See also MCP, 22 Dec. 1954, AWF, Ann Whitman Diary Series, Box 3, ACW Diary Dec. 1954 (2), DDEL.

57. Eisenhower's comments to President Rhee of South Korea are often cited to demonstrate that Eisenhower had rejected the notion of war as 'unthinkable' by the middle of 1954. He stated that 'Atomic war will destroy civilization. . . . War today is unthinkable with the weapons which we have at our command. That is why we are opposed to war.' Eisenhower's words, however, were meant to reinforce the primary purpose of these talks from the American perspective: to convince Rhee that the United States would not sanction, nor participate in, efforts by South Korea to reunify the country by force. MCP, 27 July 1954, AWF, DDE Diary Series, Box 4, DDE Personal Diary Jan.–Nov. 1954 (1).

Eisenhower's comments before luncheon with senior American military officers in June 1954 are also cited in this regard. After describing the chaos that would result from the nuclear destruction of the Soviet Union, the president concluded with 'I repeat that there is no victory in any war except through our imaginations, through our dedication, and through our work to avoid it'. Again, however, the significance of these comments can only be fully appreciated by noting their proper, and usually neglected, context. Just before presenting this image of modern war, Eisenhower spoke out against irresponsible public statements by military officers. As James Hagerty recorded in his diary, 'while he did not say so, the President was speaking directly about recent statements by Admiral Carney [Chief of Naval operations] and some officers in the Army in presenting a "go to war" attitude'. 19 June 1954 entry in Robert H. Ferrell (ed.), *The Diary of James C. Hagerty: Eisenhower at Mid-Course, 1954–1955* (Bloomington: Indiana University Press, 1983), 69. In both cases, Eisenhower's words were chosen to restrain what he perceived to be irresponsible conduct on the part of others.

58. Discussion at 190th NSC Meeting, 25 Mar. 1954, *FRUS: 1952–4*, ii. 640–1.

59. Ibid. 638–43; ibid., NSC 5410/1, US Objectives in the Event of General War with the Soviet Bloc, 29 Mar. 1954, ii. 643–6.

60. Ibid., Discussion at 204th NSC Meeting, 24 June 1954, ii. 689.

61. Ibid., NSC 140/1, Summary Evaluation of the Net Capability of the USSR to Inflict Direct Injury on the United States Up to July 1955, 18 May 1953, ii. 328–49; ibid., Discussion at 148th NSC Meeting, 4 June 1953, ii. 369; ibid., Memorandum for the President by the Chairman of the United States Atomic Energy Commission, 17 Sept. 1953, ii. 1218–20; ibid., NSC 162/2, Basic National Security Policy, 30 Oct. 1953, ii. 579–81; ibid. Memorandum by the Acting Special Assistant to the Secretary of State for Intelligence (Howe) to the Acting Secretary of State, 1 Mar. 1954, ii. 634; ibid. Discussion at 209th NSC Meeting, 5 Aug. 1954, ii. 704–5; ibid. NSC 5422/2, Guidelines under NSC 162/2 for FY 1956, 7 Aug. 1954, ii. 716–17, 724–8; Time Chart of Relative Gross Capabilities to Deliver a Decisive Nuclear Attack, [nd], AWF, Ann Whitman Diary Series, Box 3, ACW Diary Nov. 1954 (1); Paper Presented by the Director of Central Intelligence (Dulles), 18 Nov. 1954, *FRUS: 1952–4*, ii. 776; NSC 5501, Basic National Security Policy, 7 Jan. 1955, US Department of State, *Foreign Relations of the United States, 1955–1957*, 27 vols. (Washington: GPO, 1985–93) (hereafter *FRUS: 1955–7*), xix. 25–6, 31; Trachtenberg, *History & Strategy*, 119–21, 130–3.

62. Discussion at 227th NSC Meeting, 3 Dec. 1954, *FRUS: 1952–4*, ii. 805.

63. MCP, 22 Dec. 1954, AWF, Ann Whitman Diary Series, Box 3, Dec. 1954 (2). See also Eisenhower to Winston Churchill, 25 Jan. 1955, in Peter G. Boyle (ed.), *The Churchill–Eisenhower Correspondence, 1953–1955* (Chapel Hill: University of North Carolina Press, 1990), 186–7. On the elements on pre-emption in American strategy at this time see Rosenberg, 'The Origins of Overkill', 143–60; David Alan Rosenberg, '"A Smoking Radiating Ruin at the End of Two Hours": Documents on American Plans for Nuclear War with the Soviet Union, 1954–1955', *International Security*, 6/3 (Winter 1981/2), 3–38; Rosenberg, *Toward Armageddon*, 197–201; Trachtenberg, *History & Strategy*, 134; id., *A Constructed Peace*, ch. 5.

64. Discussion at 190th NSC Meeting, 25 Mar. 1954, 641.

65. Discussion at 203rd NSC Meeting, 23 June 1954, 1469.

66. MCP, 22 Dec. 1954.

67. Although used originally in a slightly different context in the Technological Capabilities Panel report entitled 'Meeting the Threat of Surprise Attack', the phrase 'battered victor' none the less captures Eisenhower's views succinctly. Report by the Technological Capabilities Panel of the Science Advisory Committee, Meeting the Threat of Surprise Attack, 14 Feb. 1955, *FRUS: 1955–7*, xix. 43.

68. Discussion at 203rd NSC Meeting, 23 June 1954, 1469–70. For an early expression of these views, see Eisenhower, Memorandum for the Director of Plans and Operations, 5 Feb. 1947.

69. Discussion at 204th NSC Meeting, 24 June 1954, 688. Dulles later summarized Eisenhower's view as being that 'if we could insure that our industrial power could be kept intact, this would act both as a deterrent against general war and as a major aid in winning a war'. Memorandum of Conversation, 4 Jan. 1955, *FRUS*: 1955–7, xx. 6.

70. Quoted in Stephen E. Ambrose, *Eisenhower*, ii. *The President* (New York: Simon and Schuster, 1984), 89.

71. Discussion at 204th NSC Meeting, 24 June 1954, 689; Eisenhower to Wilson, 5 Jan. 1955, AWF, Administration Series, Box 40, Charles E. Wilson, 1955 (4). For an assessment of the relative coherence and credibility of these beliefs about future war in the early Eisenhower years, see Andreas Wenger, *Living with Peril: Eisenhower, Kennedy, and Nuclear Weapons* (Lanham, Del.: Rowman & Littlefield, 1997), 50–4, 118–20.

72. Andrew J. Goodpaster, Oral History, no. 37, 14–15.

73. For Dulles' assessment, see John Foster Dulles, 'Policy for Security and Peace', *Foreign Affairs*, 32/3 (Apr. 1954), 360; Lawrence Freedman, *The Evolution of Nuclear Strategy* (New York: St. Martin's, 1983), 84–5; James Shepley, 'How Dulles Averted War', *Life* (16 Jan. 1956), 77; Second Restricted Tripartite Meeting of the Heads of Government, 7 Dec. 1953, *FRUS*: 1952–4, v. 1811–13. When later asked what brought the Chinese to compromise at the armistice negotiations, Eisenhower replied, 'Danger of an atomic war'. Quoted in Betts, *Nuclear Blackmail*, 47. See also, Eisenhower, *Mandate for Change*, 181; Goodpaster, Memorandum of Meeting with the President, 17 Feb. 1965, Dwight D. Eisenhower Post-Presidential Papers, Augusta-Walter Reed Series, President-National Subseries, Box 1, Goodpaster Briefings (3).

74. Gaddis, *We Now Know*, 107–10; David Halloway, *Stalin and the Bomb* (New Haven: Yale University Press, 1994), 333–5; William Stueck, *The Korean War: An International History* (Princeton: Princeton University Press, 1995), 326–30; Vladislav Zubok and Constantine Pleshakov, *Inside the Kremlin's Cold War: From Stalin to Khrushchev* (Cambridge, Mass.: Harvard University Press, 1996), 154–5. Some recent interpretations still credit nuclear threats as a primary reason for the shift in the Communists' negotiating position. See Daniel Calingeart, 'Nuclear Weapons and the Korean War', *Journal of Strategic Studies*, 11/2 (June 1988), 195–8. Roger Dingman, on the other hand, has dismissed the role of nuclear diplomacy in the settlement. Roger Dingman, 'Atomic Diplomacy During the Korean War', *International Security*, 13/3 (Winter 1988/9), 81–91. Given the relative paucity of evidence regarding the Communist powers' deliberations, the most plausible conclusion remains not 'that nuclear threats played no role whatever in securing final agreement on the outstanding details of the POW issue', but rather 'that the centrality subsequently accorded to those threats by Eisenhower and Dulles was misplaced'. Rosemary Foot, *A Substitute for Victory: The Politics of Peacemaking at the Korean Armistice Talks* (Ithaca, NY: Cornell University Press, 1990), 176–83. See also, Rosemary Foot, 'Making Known the Unknown War: Policy Analysis of the Korean Conflict in the Last Decade', *Diplomatic History*, 15/3 (Summer 1991), 426–7; id., 'Nuclear Coercion and the Ending of the Korean War', *International Security*, 13/3 (Winter 1988/9), 99–112; Keefer, 'President Dwight D. Eisenhower', 279–82; Wenger, *Living with Peril*, 72–8.

75. See, for example, Robert A. Divine, *Eisenhower and the Cold War* (New York: Oxford University Press, 1981), 30.

76. Quoted in Ronald J. Caridi, *The Korean War and American Politics: The Republican Party as a Case Study* (Philadelphia: University of Pennsylvania Press, 1968), 253, emphasis in original. On Eisenhower's discussion with MacArthur, see Ambrose, *The President*, 31–4; Keefer, 'President Dwight D. Eisenhower', 270; MacArthur to Eisenhower, 12 Dec. 1952, AWF, Administration Series, Box 25, General Douglas MacArthur.

77. *Public Papers of the Presidents: Dwight D. Eisenhower, 1953–1961* (Washington: GPO, 1960–1) (hereafter *EPP*), *1953*, 16–17.

78. Barry M. Blechman and Robert Powell, 'What in the Name of God is Strategic Superiority?', *Political Science Quarterly*, 97/4 (Winter 1982), 591–2; Joseph C. Goulden, *Korea: The Untold Story of the War* (New York: Times Books, 1982), 632; Walter G. Hermes, *United States Army in the Korean War: Truce Tent to Fighting Front* (Washington: Office of Chief of Military History, United States Army, 1966), 461.

79. Second Restricted Meeting of the Heads of Government, Bermuda, 7 Dec. 1953, *FRUS: 1952–4*, v. 1811. For a discussion of the ambiguous record supporting the claim that the United States deployed tactical nuclear weapons in the Korean theatre, see Betts, *Nuclear Blackmail*, 43 n. 67.

80. On the signalling at the armistice talks, see Blechman and Powell, 'What in the Name of God is Strategic Superiority?', 594–5; Mark W. Clark, *From the Danube to the Yalu* (New York: Harper, 1954), 267–8; Commander in Chief, United Nations Command, to JCS, 14 May 1953, *FRUS: 1952–4*, xv. 1022–4; ibid., JCS to Commander in Chief, Far East, 22 May 1953, xv. 1082–6; Foot, *Substitute*, 165–6. Regarding the discussions between Bohlen and Molotov, see Charles E. Bohlen, *Witness to History, 1929–1969* (New York: Norton, 1973), 351; Secretary of State to the Embassy in the Soviet Union, 17 Apr. 1953, *FRUS: 1952–4*, xv. 915; ibid., Ambassador in the Soviet Union to the Department of State, 20 Apr. 1953, xv. 921; ibid., Acting Secretary of State to the Embassy in the Soviet Union, 26 May 1953, xv. 1103; ibid., Ambassador in the Soviet Union to the Department of State, 28 May 1953, xv. 1110–11; ibid., Ambassador in the Soviet Union to the Department of State, 3 June 1953, xv. 1133.

81. Ibid., Memorandum of Conversation, by Secretary of State, 21 May 1953, xv. 1068. See also ibid. 22 May 1953, xv. 1071.

82. John Foster Dulles, 'Korean Problems', *Department of State Bulletin*, 29/742 (14 Sept. 1953), 342. The next week Dulles explained that his comments were intended to deter the Chinese from 'overtly', as opposed to the covertly, intervening in Indo-China. Discussion at 161st NSC Meeting, 9 Sept. 1954, *FRUS: 1952–4*, xiii. 782.

83. John Foster Dulles, 'The Evolution of Foreign Policy', *Department of State Bulletin*, 30/761 (25 Jan. 1954), 108.

84. Leslie H. Gelb with Richard K. Betts, *The Irony of Vietnam: The System Worked* (Washington: Brookings, 1979), 52. For Dulles' clarifications of this speech, see John Foster Dulles, 'Foreign Policy and National Security', *Department of State Bulletin*, 30/770 (29 Mar. 1954), 464–5; id., 'Policy for Security and Peace', *Foreign Affairs*, 32/3 (Apr. 1954), 353–64.

85. As in the case of the Korean Armistice, recent scholarship indicates that Eisenhower erroneously assessed the efficacy of his deterrent signals in the 1954–5 Offshore Island crisis. New evidence of the Chinese Communist decision-making indicates that 'the Quemoy-Matsu crisis of 1954–1955 is not an example of successful deterrence, since there was not an immediate, specific threat to these two island groups.' Gordon H. Chang and He Di, 'The Absence of War in the US–China Confrontation

over Quemoy and Matsu in 1954–1955: Contingency, Luck, or Deterrence?', *American Historical Review*, 98/5 (Dec. 1993), 1500–24.

86. Quoted in Alexander George and Richard Smoke, *Deterrence in American Foreign Policy: Theory and Practice* (New York: Columbia University Press, 1974), 272.

87. Joint Resolution by the Congress, 29 Jan. 1955, *FRUS: 1955–7*, ii. 162–3.

88. *EPP, 1955*, 209–10.

89. Ambrose, *The President*, 245–6.

90. John Foster Dulles, 'Report from Asia', *Department of State Bulletin*, 32/821 (21 Mar. 1955), 459–64; Ambrose, *The President*, 239; H. W. Brands, Jr., 'Testing Massive Retaliation: Credibility and Crisis Management in the Taiwan Strait', *International Security*, 12/4 (Spring 1988), 142; Gordon H. Chang, *Friends and Enemies: The United States, China, and the Soviet Union, 1948–1972* (Stanford: Stanford University Press, 1990), 126.

91. *EPP, 1955*, 332.

92. Discussion at 131st NSC Meeting, 11 Feb. 1953, *FRUS: 1952–4*, xv. 769–70. The 'Kaesong sanctuary' was an area 28 miles square created to serve as a secure area for the first armistice negotiation sessions. On 25 Oct. 1951, the talks were moved to Panmunjom. Therefore, by 1953 Kaesong was no longer directly serving the negotiations but still retained its sanctuary status. William H. Vatcher, Jr., *Panmunjom: The Story of the Korea Military Armistice Negotiations* (New York: Praeger, 1958), 36–7, 74–5.

93. Discussion at NSC Special Meeting, 31 Mar. 1953, *FRUS: 1952–4*, xv. 826.

94. Ibid., Discussion at the 143rd NSC Meeting, 6 May 1953, xv. 977. See also ibid., Discussion at 144th NSC Meeting, 13 May 1953, xv. 1012–17. In Oct. 1953, this view was accepted as American policy in NSC 162/2. See Gaddis, *Strategies of Containment*, 149–50; NSC 162/2, 593.

95. Betts, *Nuclear Blackmail*, 41, emphasis in original; Dingman, 'Atomic Diplomacy', 81–5. For other interpretations stressing the earnestness of Eisenhower's plans to expand the war, see Rosemary Foot, *The Wrong War: American Policy and the Dimensions of the Korean Conflict, 1950–1953* (Ithaca, NY: Cornell University Press, 1985), 205–23; Keefer, 'President Dwight D. Eisenhower', 267–79. For Eisenhower's early willingness to consider the use of atomic weapons in Korea, see 30 June 1950 entry in Ferrell (ed.), *The Eisenhower Diaries*, 175–6.

96. Memorandum by the JCS to the Secretary of Defence, 19 May 1953, *FRUS: 1952–4*, xv. 1059–64.

97. Ibid., Discussion at 145th NSC Meeting, 20 May 1953, xv. 1065–8.

98. See n. 80.

99. Discussion at 179th NSC Meeting, 8 Jan. 1954, *FRUS: 1952–4*, xv. 1706–7. See also ibid., Discussion at 173rd NSC Meeting, 3 Dec. 1953, xv. 1637–42; 5 Jan. 1954 entry in Ferrell (ed.), *The Diary of James Hagerty*, 3.

100. Discussion at 179th NSC Meeting, 8 Jan. 1954, *FRUS: 1952–4*, viii. 949.

101. Betts, *Nuclear Blackmail*, 50; *The Pentagon Papers (Senator Gravel Edition): The Defense Department History of American Decisionmaking on Vietnam*, i. (Boston: Beacon Press, 1971), 100; Ronald H. Spector, *The United States Army in Vietnam, Advice and Support: The Early Years, 1941–1960* (Washington: Center of Military History, US Army, 1983), 199–201. For the dismissal of French Foreign Minister Bidault's claim that Dulles offered atomic weapons to the French for use at Dienbienphu, see Betts, *Nuclear Blackmail*, 52 n. 98; George C. Herring and Richard H. Immerman, 'Eisenhower, Dulles, and Dienbienphu: "The Day We Didn't Go to War"

Revisited', *Journal of American History*, 71/2 (Sept. 1984), 357–8; John Prados, *The Sky Would Fall, Operation Vulture: The US Bombing Mission in Indo-China, 1954* (New York: Dial Press 1983), 150–4.

102. Herring and Immerman, 'Eisenhower, Dulles, and Dienbienphu', 347–9; Richard H. Immerman, 'Between the Unattainable and the Unacceptable: Eisenhower and Dienbienphu', in Melanson and Mayers, *Reevaluating Eisenhower*, 130–4. See also Melanie Billings-Yun, *Decision Against War: Eisenhower and Dien Bien Phu, 1954* (New York: Columbia University Press, 1988); Laurent Ce'sari and Jacques de Folin, 'Military Necessity, Political Impossibility: The French Viewpoint on Operation *Vautour*', in Lawrence S. Kaplan, Denise Artaud, and Mark R. Rubin (eds.), *Dien Bien Phu and the Crisis of Franco-American Relations, 1954–1955* (Wilmington, Del.: SR Books, 1990), 105–20.

103. Spector, *Advice and Support*, 199; Discussion at 190th NSC Meeting, 25 Mar. 1954, *FRUS: 1952–4*, xiii. 1163–8.

104. Herring and Immerman, 'Eisenhower, Dulles, and Dienbienphu', 353; Immerman, 'Between the Unattainable and the Unacceptable', 135; *The Pentagon Papers*, i. 100–1.

105. Discussion at 204th NSC Meeting, 24 June 1954, 696; Herring and Immerman, 'Eisenhower, Dulles, and Dienbienphu', 363. For the American effort to enlist the British in a United Action front, see Geoffrey Warner, 'Britain and the Crisis over Dien Bien Phu, Apr. 1954: The Failure of United Action', in Kaplan, Artaud, and Rubin (eds.), *Dien Bien Phu and the Crisis of Franco-American Relations, 1954–1955*, 55–77.

106. Ambrose, *The President*, 463–4; Gordon H. Chang, 'To the Nuclear Brink: Eisenhower, Dulles, and the Quemoy-Matsu Crisis', *International Security*, 12/4 (Spring 1988), 99–101; Discussion at 213th NSC Meeting, 9 Sept. 1954, *FRUS: 1952–4*, xiv. 583–5; ibid., Memorandum by the Secretary of State, 12 Sept. 1954, xiv. 611–12; ibid., Discussion at 214th NSC Meeting, 12 Sept. 1954, xiv. 613–24; Eisenhower, *Mandate for Change*, 463–4; Bennett C. Rushkoff, 'Eisenhower, Dulles and the Quemoy-Matsu Crisis, 1954–1955', *Political Science Quarterly* 96/3 (Fall 1981), 465–80; Robert J. Watson, *History of the Joint Chiefs of Staff*, v. *The Joint Chiefs of Staff and National Policy, 1953–1954* (Washington: Historical Division, Joint Chiefs of Staff, 1986), 262. For the initial opinions of the JCS, see Memorandum by the Chairman of JCS to the Secretary of Defense, 11 Sept. 1954, *FRUS: 1952–4*, xiv. 598–610.

107. Chang, 'To the Nuclear Brink', 102; Discussion at 233rd NSC Meeting, 21 Jan. 1955, *FRUS: 1955–7*, ii. 89–96; Watson, *The Joint Chiefs*, 266.

108. Chang, 'To the Nuclear Brink', 104–5.

109. Id., *Friends and Enemies*, 131; id., 'To the Nuclear Brink', 105–8, 111; Discussion at the 240th NSC Meeting, 10 Mar. 1955, *FRUS: 1955–7*, ii. 346–7; Leonard H. D. Gordon, 'United States Opposition to Use of Force in the Taiwan Strait, 1954–1962', *Journal of American History*, 72/3 (Dec. 1985), 639; MCP, 15 Mar. 1955, AWF, Ann Whitman Diary Series, Box 4, ACW Diary Mar. 1955 (5). At this time, the JCS ordered the commander of SAC to begin target selection for an 'enlarged atomic offensive' against the People's Republic. Quoted in Brands, 'Testing Massive Retaliation', 141.

110. Chang, 'To the Nuclear Brink', 108.

111. Robert Accinelli, *Crisis and Commitment: United States Policy Toward Taiwan, 1950–1955* (Chapel Hill: University of North Carolina Press, 1996), 222–6; Chang,

Friends and Enemies, 134–7; id., 'To the Nuclear Brink', 114–17. The Eisenhower–
Dulles scheme was referred to as a 'maritime zone', not a blockade, for a variety of
legal and political reasons. MCP, 22 Apr. 1955, AWF, Ann Whitman Diary Series,
Box 5, ACW Diary Apr. 1955 (3); Goodpaster, Memorandum for the Record, 3 May
1955, AWF, Ann Whitman Diary Series, Box 5, ACW Diary May 1955 (7).

112. Phrase from Discussion at 194th NSC Meeting, 29 Apr. 1954, *FRUS*: 1952–4, xiii.
1440.

113. Foot, 'Nuclear Coercion', 102–4.

114. Hermes, *Truce Tent*, 409; Callum A. MacDonald, *Korea: The War Before Vietnam*
(New York: Free Press, 1987), 176–7; Watson, *The Joint Chiefs*, 256–7.

115. Eisenhower, *Mandate for Change*, 465–6; Watson, *The Joint Chiefs*, 263–4.

116. Ambrose, *The President*, 213–14, 229; Eisenhower, *Mandate*, 465; Eisenhower to
Wilson, 15 Dec. 1954, AWF, Administration Series, Box 40, Charles E.
Wilson–1955 (2).

117. See John Lewis Gaddis, 'The Origins of Self-Deterrence: The United States and the
Non-Use of Nuclear Weapons, 1945–1958', in Gaddis, *The Long Peace: Inquiries into
the History of the Cold War* (New York: Oxford University Press, 1987), 123–46.

118. SE 41, Probable Communist Reactions to Certain Possible US/UN Military Courses
of Action with Respect to Korean War, 8 Apr. 1953, *FRUS*: 1952–4, x. 886–92; ibid.,
Political Annex to NSC 147 Prepared in the Policy Planning Staff, 4 June 1953, xv.
1139–44; ibid., NIE 91, Probable Developments in Indochina through Mid-1954, 4
June 1953, xii. 602; ibid., Minutes of the First United States–French Meeting at the
Residence of the Secretary of State, 12 July 1953, xiii. 662–3; ibid., SE 53, Probable
Communist Reactions to Certain Possible US Courses of Action in Indochina
Through 1954, 18 Dec. 1953, xiii. 928–9; ibid., Discussion at 179th NSC Meeting,
8 Jan. 1954, xv. 1706; ibid., NSC 5405, United States Objectives and Courses of
Action with Respect to Southeast Asia, 16 Jan. 1954, xiii. 976; ibid., First Secretary
in France to the Department of State, 21 Apr. 1954, xiii. 1334; SNIE 100–3–55,
Communist Reactions to Certain Possible US Courses of Action With Respect to
the Islands Off the Coast of China, 25 Jan. 1955, *FRUS*: 1955–7, ii. 125–8; ibid.,
SNIE 11–4–55, Review of Current Communist Attitudes Toward General War, 15
Feb. 1955, ii. 273–6; ibid., NIE 100–4–55, Communist Capabilities and Intentions
With Respect to the Offshore Islands and Taiwan Through 1955, and Communist
and Non-Communist Reactions With Respect to the Defense of Taiwan, 15 Mar.
1955, ii. 376–80; and n. 61 above.

119. Ibid., Discussion at 243rd NSC Meeting, 31 Mar. 1955, ii. 433.

120. 26 Mar. 1955 entry in Ferrell (ed.), *The Eisenhower Diaries*, 296. See also Chang, 'To
the Nuclear Brink', 108–10; Discussion at 148th NSC Meeting, 4 June 1953, *FRUS*:
1952–4, ii. 369; Eisenhower to Gruenther, 1 Feb. 1955, *FRUS*: 1955–7, ii. 192; Foot,
The Wrong War, 223–29.

121. Discussion at 145th NSC Meeting, 1061–2.

122. See n. 61. The first Soviet test of a 'thermonuclear' device on 12 Aug. 1953, 'Joe-4',
had a yield of approximately 400 kilotons, or roughly twenty-five times smaller
than the 'Mike' test. Unlike the Teller–Ulam design of Mike, which offered almost
unconstrained destructive power, Joe-4's 'Layer Cake' design limited its explosive
potential. The physicist Hans Bethe led the American effort to evaluate this test.
The committee estimated the yield to be roughly 500 kilotons, and judged its
design to be more akin to a boosted fission device, not a 'true' thermonuclear
weapon. The committee also questioned whether the device tested could be used

as a weapon. 'It is, to some degree,' David Halloway notes, 'a matter of taste whether one calls it a thermonuclear bomb or a boosted weapon.' Confusion continued among American officials as to whether the USSR did indeed possess a 'true' thermonuclear ability into 1955. Halloway, *Stalin and the Bomb*, 306–9; Hewlett and Holl, *Atoms for Peace and War*, 57–9.

123. Discussion at 225th NSC Meeting, 24 Nov. 1954, *FRUS*: 1952–4, ii. 791–2. Eleven months later General Alfred Gruenther, the SACEUR, stated NATO could 'lick' the Soviets if they started a war, although he expressed concern about future power trends. Discussion at 262nd NSC Meeting, 20 Oct. 1955, *FRUS*: 1955–7, iv. 26.

124. NSC 5422/2, 7 Aug. 1954, 716–17.

125. NSC 5501, 7 Jan. 1955, 26.

126. The Technological Capabilities Panel report was also know as the 'Killian Report' after the committee's chairman, James Killian. Report by the Technological Capabilities Panel of the Science Advisory Committee, Meeting the Threat of Surprise Attack, 14 Feb. 1955, *FRUS*: 1955–7, xix. 41–56; ibid., Discussion at 258th NSC Meeting, 8 Sept. 1955, xix. 121; Freedman, *The Evolution of Nuclear Strategy*, 158–60; James R. Killian, Jr., *Sputnik, Scientists, and Eisenhower: A Memoir of the First Special Assistant to the President for Science and Technology* (Cambridge Mass.: MIT Press, 1977), 67–93; Rosenberg, 'The Origins of Overkill', 148–9. On the US missile programme following the Killian Report, see Robert J. Watson, *History of the Office of the Secretary of Defense*, iv. *Into the Missile Age, 1956–1960* (Washington: GPO, 1997), 157–201, 361–401.

127. Discussion at 257th NSC Meeting, 8 Aug. 1955, ibid. xix. 102–3. See also ibid., Supplementary Notes on the Legislative Leadership Meeting, 14 Feb. 1956, xix. 196–8.

128. Discussion at 263rd NSC Meeting, 27 Oct. 1955, *FRUS*: 1955–7, xix. 129. Throughout the discussions of the preceding year, doubts of whether the Soviets would discover the Teller–Ulam 'solution' persisted. See, for example, ibid., xix. 43, 96.

129. On 6 Nov. 1955 the Soviets tested another 'Layer Cake' design device. American intelligence considered it a boosted fission weapon and estimated its yield to be approximately 215 kilotons. The 22 Nov. weapon was of the new so-called 'Third Idea' design (i.e. the Soviet term for their Teller–Ulam solution). Four days later Nikita Khrushchev proudly announced to the world that Soviet 'scientists and engineers have succeeded, with a relatively small quantity of the nuclear materials used, in obtaining an explosion whose power is equal to the explosion of several million metric tons of conventional explosives'. Halloway, *Stalin and the Bomb*, 309–17.

130. Diary, 11 Jan. 1956, *FRUS*: 1955–7, xix. 177–8.

131. Ibid., Discussion at 272nd NSC Meeting, 12 Jan. 1956, x. 551–6.

132. In his diary, Eisenhower gives the dates for the scenarios as 1 July 1956. Ibid., Diary, 23 Jan. 1956, xix. 187–8. This is a mistake. Later in the diary entry, Eisenhower does give the correct year as "58'. Other relevant documents confirm that 1 July 1958 is the proper date. The directive for the Net Evaluation Subcommittee required the Subcommittee to prepare a report annually on the net capability of the Soviet Union to inflict damage upon the United States in a general war relating to a situation 'normally about three years in the future'. (NSC 5511, quoted in Editorial Note, ibid., xix. 56–7.) The Net Evaluation Subcommittee initially presented its report to the NSC (with Eisenhower not in attendance) on

27 Oct. 1955, when the discussion indicates the scenarios were set in 1958. (Discussion at 263rd NSC Meeting, 126–30.) Finally, the Memorandum for the Record by the President's Special Assistant for National Security Affairs (Anderson), 23 Jan. 1956 (ibid., xix. 189) gives the year as 1958. On the origins of the Net Evaluation Subcommittee, see Editorial Note, ibid., xix. 56–7; Watson, *The Joint Chiefs*, 139–41.

133. Memorandum for the Record by the President's Special Assistant for National Security Affairs (Anderson), 23 Jan. 1956, 189.

134. Eisenhower ruled out the option of a pre-emptive strike against the Soviet Union, arguing that it would contradict American 'traditions' and would be impossible to secure advance congressional approval in secret. Diary, 23 Jan. 1956, 187–8.

135. Memorandum for the Record by the President's Special Assistant for National Security Affairs (Anderson), 23 Jan. 1956, 190.

136. Discussion at 360th NSC Meeting, 27 Mar. 1958, AWF, NSC Series, Box 10. During this phase, Eisenhower spoke of nuclear war involving between 30 to 100 million total casualties (in the United States). Conversation between the President and Senator Styles Bridges, 21 May 1957, AWF, Ann Whitman Diary Series, Box 9, May 1957 Diary (1); Discussion at 351st NSC Meeting, 16 Jan. 1958, AWF, NSC Series, Box 9. See also Discussion at 306th NSC Meeting, 20 Dec. 1956, *FRUS: 1955–7*, xix. 379–81; ibid., Discussion at 344th NSC Meeting, 12 Nov. 1957, xix. 672–6; William F. Vandercook, 'Making the Very Best of the Very Worst: The "Human Effects of Nuclear Weapons" Report of 1956', *International Security*, 11/1 (Summer 1986), 190.

137. Memorandum of NSC Special Meeting, 7 Feb. 1956, AWF, Administration Series, Box 27, National Security Council (2).

138. Ibid. Later that month, Eisenhower expressed concern that SAC war plans might over-use thermonuclear weapons and therefore produce unnecessary population losses. He urged the JCS to review these plans to be sure that large yield weapons were only used when necessary. Rosenberg, *Toward Armageddon*, 221.

139. Eisenhower to Richard Simon, 4 Apr. 1956, AWF, DDE Diary Series, Box 14, Apr. 1956 Misc (5).

140. MCP, 29 Aug. 1956, AWF, DDE Diary Series, Box 17, May 56 Diary–Staff Memos.

141. Conversation between the President and Senator Styles Bridges, 21 May 1957. See also Notes on Expanded Cabinet Meeting, 25 July 1956, AWF, Cabinet Series, Box 7; Minutes of Cabinet Meeting, 19 July 1957, AWF, Cabinet Series, Box 9.

142. Route Slip, 6 Aug. 1957, Dwight D. Eisenhower, Records as President, White House Central Files, 1953–61, Confidential File, Box 104, World War III (2), DDEL.

143. MCP, 5 Apr. 1956, AWF, DDE Diary Series, Box 15, Apr. 1956 Goodpaster; Diary, 27 Apr. 1956, AWF, Ann Whitman Diary Series, Box 8, ACW Diary Apr. 1956 (1); Persons, Memorandum for the Record, 4 Apr. 1956, AWF, Ann Whitman Diary Series, Box 8, ACW Diary Apr. 1956 (2); MCP, 11 Nov. 1957, AWF, DDE Diary Series, Box 28, Nov. 57 Staff Notes; Discussion at 363rd NSC Meeting, 24 Apr. 1958, AWF, NSC Series, Box 10. Initially Eisenhower felt the advent of ICBMs would not revolutionize warfare in itself since the United States already possessed the ability to launch a serious and perhaps even 'decisive' blow to the Soviet industrial base by 1956. He did, however, presciently conclude that early development of ballistic missiles could produce a great 'world psychological reaction because people see [them] as the "ultimate" weapon'. 30 Mar. 1956 entry in Ferrell (ed.), *The Eisenhower Diaries*, 324. See also Supplementary Notes on the Legislative

Leadership Meeting, 14 Feb. 1956, 196; Rosenberg, 'The Origins of Overkill', 153–4.

144. Regarding Australia, see Discussion at 358th NSC Meeting, 13 Mar. 1958, AWF, NSC Series, Box 9. Eisenhower stressed the strategic importance of Australian bases in literally the first sentence of the first important strategic estimate he authored in the War Plans Division. Australia provided the strategic centre from which operations in the south-west Pacific emanated. Eisenhower to Marshall, 14 Dec. 1941, and Eisenhower to Marshall, 17 Dec. 1941, in *The War Years*, i. 5–6, 9. On the inability to deploy forces to Europe, see MCP, 17 Aug. 1956, AWF, DDE Diary Series, Box 17, Aug 56 Diary-Staff Notes; MCP, 11 Jan. 1958, AWF, DDE Diary Series, Box 30, Staff Notes Jan. 1958.

145. MCP, 10 Feb. 1956, quoted in Rosenberg, 'The Origins of Overkill', 151.

146. The Gaither Committee report advocated policies in five broad categories: first, improving the security of SAC bombers from surprise attack through reduction in reaction times, improved warning systems, better active and passive defence of airfields, and dispersal of the bomber fleet; second, increasing the nation's strategic nuclear striking power by expanding the number of IRBMs and ICBMs deployed, accelerating their deployment, and eventually hardening their bases; third, augmenting the limited warfare capabilities of the USA and its allies; fourth, and a lower priority, improving the active and passive defence of civilian population through enhanced air defence and a nation-wide fallout shelter programme; and fifth, achieving greater economy and efficiency through a reorganization of the Department of Defense. With a projected cost of roughly $8 billion per year for five years, the report proposed an increase of over 20% in annual defence expenditures. NSC 5724, Report to the President by the Security Resources Panel of the ODM Science Advisory Committee on Deterrence and Survival in the Nuclear Age, 7 Nov. 1957, *FRUS*: 1955–7, xix. 638–61. David Lindsey Snead, *Eisenhower and the Gaither Committee: The Influence of a Committee of Experts on National Security Policy in the Late 1950s* (Ph. D. diss., University of Virginia, 1997) provides the most thorough treatment of the origins, development and legacy of this report. See also Bundy, *Danger and Survival*, 334–49; Robert A. Divine, *The Sputnik Challenge* (New York: Oxford University Press, 1993), 35–41, 77–8, 125, 170; Dwight D. Eisenhower, *The White House Years: Waging Peace, 1957–1961* (Garden City, NY: Doubleday & Co., 1965), 219–23; Freedman, *Evolution of Nuclear Strategy*, 160–3; Rosenberg, 'The Origins of Overkill', 156–9.

147. MCP, 4 Nov. 1957, *FRUS*: 1955–7, xix. 621.

148. The combination of Eisenhower's emphasis on defending the retaliatory force with his rejection of widespread civil-defence measures implies that he desired to convince the Soviets that the US nuclear forces could eschew pre-emption, ride out a nuclear strike, and still deal a telling retaliatory blow. In other words, Eisenhower advocated insuring a secure second-strike capability.

149. Twining to Cutler, with attachment, 26 Mar. 1958, Office of the Special Assistant for National Security Affairs, Records, 1952–61 (hereafter SANSA), NSC Series, Briefing Notes Subseries, Box 14, Nuclear Policy, DDEL; Cutler to John Foster Dulles, with attachment, 7 Apr. 1958, SANSA, NSC Series, Briefing Notes Subseries, Box 14, Nuclear Policy.

150. Discussion at 277th NSC Meeting, 27 Feb. 1956, *FRUS*: 1955–7, xix. 204, 210–11.

151. MCP, 24 May 1956, AWF, DDE Diary Series, Box 15, May 56 Goodpaster. See also, MCP, 30 Mar. 1956, AWF, DDE Diary Series, Box 15, Goodpaster Apr. 56; MCP, 14 May 1956, AWF, DDE Diary Series, Box 15, May 56 Goodpaster.

152. NSC 5810/1, Basic National Security Policy, 5 May 1958, SANSA, NSC Series, Policy Papers Subseries, Box 25. See for comparison, NSC 5602/1, Basic National Security Policy, 15 Mar. 1956, *FRUS*: 1955–7, xix. 244, 258–9; ibid., NSC 5707/8, Basic National Security Policy, 3 June 1957, xix. 509.

153. For a critique of this paradox, see Robert Jervis, *The Illogic of American Nuclear Strategy* (Ithaca, NY: Cornell University Press, 1984), 31–3, 148–9; id., *Meaning of the Nuclear Revolution*, 19–22. The original statement of the 'stability–instability' paradox by Glenn Snyder actually presents a series of paradoxes. According to Snyder, the idea that strategic stability could breed lower level instabilities is the dominant view among civilian analysts. He notes, however, that the argument can cut the other way, namely that with strategic stability, gradual escalation of conflict at lower levels of violence becomes more likely and, in turn, may eventually destabilize the strategic level. Thus, leaders hesitate before taking lower level actions. He emphasizes that in the real world most people probably would fear the escalatory potential. Turning things on their head again, Snyder also suggests that efforts to improve conventional forces might be destabilizing. Glenn H. Snyder, 'The Balance of Power and the Balance of Terror', in Paul Seaburg (ed.), *The Balance of Power* (San Francisco: Chandler, 1965), 184–202, esp. 198–9. See also, Jervis, *Meaning of the Nuclear Revolution*, 141.

154. Discussion at 359th NSC Meeting, 20 Mar. 1958, AWF, NSC Series, Box 9. For Robert Cutler's efforts to stimulate a re-evaluation of massive retaliation in this period, see Peter J. Roman, *Eisenhower and the Missile Gap* (Ithaca, NY: Cornell University Press, 1995), 68–75, 78–9.

155. Discussion at 364th NSC Meeting, 1 May 1958, AWF, NSC Series, Box 10. On the evolution of Dulles' views of nuclear weapons, see John Lewis Gaddis, 'The Unexpected John Foster Dulles: Nuclear Weapons, Communism, and the Russians', in Richard H. Immerman (ed.), *John Foster Dulles and the Diplomacy of the Cold War* (Princeton: Princeton University Press, 1990), 47–77; Gaddis, *We Now Know*, 107–8, 222, 227–8, 233–4, 237, 239–40; Roman, *Eisenhower and the Missile Gap*, 68–71, 75–9; and Neal Rosendorf's contribution to this volume.

156. Discussion at 364th NSC Meeting, 1 May 1958.

157. Discussion at 309th NSC Meeting, 11 Jan. 1957, *FRUS*: 1955–7, xix. 409.

158. For development of the Eisenhower administration's national security policy in the wake of Sputnik, see Divine, *The Sputnik Challenge*; Ernest R. May, John D. Steinbruner, and Thomas W. Wolfe, *History of the Strategic Arms Competition, 1945–1972*, ed. Alfred Goldberg (Washington: Historical Office, Office of the Secretary of Defense, Mar. 1981), 421–54 (Frank Gavin generously provided the author with a copy of this declassified official study); and Roman, *Eisenhower and the Missile Gap*.

159. MCP, 5 Dec. 1957, *FRUS*: 1955–7, xix. 703. For an insightful analysis of the unanticipated consequences of one of Eisenhower's 'psychological' policy responses to Sputnik, see Philip Nash, *The Other Missiles of October: Eisenhower, Kennedy, and the Jupiters, 1957–1963* (Chapel Hill: University of North Carolina Press, 1997).

160. MCP, 30 Mar. 1956; MCP, 5 Apr. 1956; MCP, 18 May 1956, AWF, DDE Diary Series, Box 15, May 56 Goodpaster; MCP, 24 May 1956; Eisenhower to Frank Altschul, 25 Oct. 1957, AWF, DDE Diary Series, Box 27, DDE Diary Oct. 1957; MCP, 4 Nov. 1957, 621; Discussion at 359th NSC Meeting, 20 Mar. 1958; Discussion at 363rd NSC Meeting, 24 Apr. 1958; Discussion at 364th NSC Meeting, 1 May 1958.

161. MCP, 15 July 1958, AWF, DDE Diary Series, Box 35, Staff Memos-July 1958. See also Eisenhower, *Waging Peace*, 276.

162. Discussion at 368th NSC Meeting, 3 June 1958, AWF, NSC Series, Box 10; Discussion at 370th NSC Meeting, 26 June 1958, AWF, NSC Series, Box 10; MCP, 1 July 1958, AWF, DDE Diary Series, Box 35, Staff Memos-July 1958 (2); MCP, 14 July 1958 (dated 16 July 1958), AWF, DDE Diary Series, Box 35, Staff Memos-July 1958 (2); MCP, 14 July 1958 (dated 15 July 1958), AWF, DDE Diary Series, Box 35, Staff Memos-July 1958 (2); Staff Notes, 15 July 1958, AWF, DDE Diary Series, Box 35, Staff Memos-July 1958 (2); MCP, 16 July 1958, AWF, DDE Diary Series, Box 35, Staff Memos-July 1958 (2); Minutes of Cabinet Meeting, 16 July 1958, AWF, DDE Diary Series, Box 35, Staff Memos-July 1958 (1). On the broader strategic context of this crisis and the lack of concern about direct Soviet interference, see N. J. Ashton, '"A Great New Venture"?—Anglo-American Cooperation in the Middle East and the Response to the Iraqi Revolution, July 1958', *Diplomacy & Statecraft*, 4/1 (Mar. 1993), 59–89; Irene L. Gendzier, *Notes from the Minefield: United States Intervention in Lebanon and the Middle East, 1945–1958* (New York: Columbia University Press, 1997), 264–337; Douglas Little, 'Ike, Lebanon, and the 1958 Middle East Crisis', *Diplomatic History*, 20/1 (Winter 1996), 27–54.

163. Betts, *Nuclear Blackmail*, 71; Chang, *Friends and Enemies*, 184–90; Eisenhower, *Waging Peace*, 297; J. H. Kalicki, *The Pattern of Sino-American Crises: Political-Military Interactions in the 1950s* (New York: Cambridge University Press, 1975), 188–9.

164. Eisenhower, *Waging Peace*, 296.

165. MCP, 12 Aug. 1958, AWF, DDE Diary Series, Box 35, Aug 1958–Staff Notes (2). On the signalling of American commitment during the crisis, see also George C. Eliades, 'Once More unto the Breach: Eisenhower, Dulles, and Public Opinion during the Offshore Island Crisis of 1958', *Journal of American–East Asian Relations*, 2/4 (Winter 1993), 349, 355–6, 358–9; Appu K. Soman, '"Who's Daddy" in the Taiwan Strait? The Offshore Island Crisis of 1958', *Journal of American–East Asian Relations*, 3/4 (Winter 1994), 386–7.

166. Eisenhower and Dulles perceived the most likely source of escalation to be the Nationalist Chinese, not the Communists. In the later phases of the crisis, this became a dominant concern in shaping American policy. Eliades, 'Once More unto the Breach', 343, 346–50, 352–3, 357–65; Soman, '"Who's Daddy" in the Taiwan Strait', 379, 381, 391–3. Once the Chinese Nationalists seized air superiority over the Taiwan Strait with their F-86 Sabre jets armed with new Sidewinder missiles in a series of dogfights between 18 Sept. and 10 Oct., the risks of Communist invasion diminished further. Marc S. Gallicchio, 'The Best Defense is a Good Offense: The Evolution of American Strategy in East Asia, 1953–1960', in Warren I. Cohen and Akira Iriye (eds.), *The Great Powers in East Asia, 1953–1960* (New York: Columbia University Press, 1990), 77–9.

167. MCP, 14 Aug. 1958, AWF, DDE Diary Series, Box 35, Aug 1958–Staff Notes (2).

168. MCP, 29 Aug. 1958, AWF, DDE Diary Series, Box 35, Aug. 1958–Staff Notes (1); MCP, 4 Sept. 1958, AWF, DDE Diary Series, Box 36, Staff Notes-Sept 1958; Summary of Taiwan Straits Situation, 4 Sept. 1958, AWF, DDE Diary Series, Box 36, Staff Notes-Sept. 1958; Eliades, 'Once More unto the Breach', 350–2, 356–8; Eisenhower, *Waging Peace*, 295–6; Soman, '"Who's Daddy" in the Taiwan Strait', 381–3.

169. Brands, 'Testing Massive Retaliation', 141; Rushkoff, 'Eisenhower, Dulles and the Quemoy-Matsu Crisis', 472; Memorandum for Record, by the President, 29 Jan.

1955, *FRUS*: 1955–7, ii. 163–4; MCP, 6 Sept. 1958, AWF, DDE Diary Series, Box 36, Staff Notes Sept. 1958.

170. MCP, 29 Sept. 1958, AWF, DDE Diary Series, Box 36, Staff Notes-Sept. 1958. See also Diary, 7 Oct. 1958, AWF, Ann Whitman Diary Series, Box 10, ACW Diary Oct. 1958. Given that there was no sign of significant 'weakening on the continent', nor any suggestion of active American support for such operations, Eisenhower's offer of naval equipment for Chiang's withdrawal from the islands was not a provocative act. See also Eliades, 'Once More unto the Breach', 360.

171. MCP, 30 Nov. 1958, US Department of State, *Foreign Relations of the United States, 1958–1960*, 19 vols. (Washington: GPO, 1986–) (hereafter *FRUS*: 1958–60), viii. 143. For the development of American policy during the Berlin Deadline crisis, see William Burr, 'Avoiding the Slippery Slope: The Eisenhower Administration and the Berlin Crisis, Nov. 1958–Jan. 1959', *Diplomatic History*, 18/2 (Spring 1994), 177–205; Kori N. Schake, *The Case Against Flexible Response: Berlin Policy and Planning in the Eisenhower and Kennedy Administrations* (Ph. D. diss., University of Maryland, College Park, 1996), 58–223; Trachtenberg, *A Constructed Peace*, ch. 7; id., *History and Strategy*, 169–215; Watson, *Into the Missile Age*, 589–609.

172. Eisenhower to Dulles, Telephone Call, 27 Nov. 1958, AWF, DDE Diary Series, Box 37, Telephone Nov. 1958.

173. Telegram from the Mission at Berlin to the Department of State, 15 Nov. 1958, *FRUS*: 1958–60, viii. 69 n. 1. The mission in Berlin interpreted the interference with the convoy as 'carefully planned in advance' and constituting the 'most serious probe [of] our intentions in recent times'. Ibid., telegram from the Mission at Berlin to the Department of State, 15 Nov. 1958, viii. 71.

174. Quoted in Jack M. Schick, *The Berlin Crisis 1958–1962* (Philadelphia: University of Pennsylvania Press, 1971), 12–17.

175. This conversation did end with light humour. Memorandum of Telephone Conversation between President Eisenhower and Acting Secretary of State Herter, 22 Nov. 1958, *FRUS*: 1958–60, viii. 113–14.

176. See for example his press conference remarks on 4 and 11 Mar. 1959, *EPP, 1959*, 226–7, 243–4, 248.

177. Discussion at 386th NSC Meeting, 13 Nov. 1958, AWF, NSC Series, Box 10; Synopsis of Intelligence and State Material Reported to the President, 2 Jan. 1959 (reported 3 Jan. 1959), AWF, DDE Diary Series, Box 38, Goodpaster Briefings—Jan. 1959; Special National Intelligence Estimate, Berlin, 17 Mar. 1959, National Security Council Staff, Records, 1948–61 (hereafter NSC), Executive Secretary's Subject File, Box 7, Berlin (3), DDEL. In the first months of the crisis, CIA intelligence from Berlin indicated that the Soviets were preparing to evacuate Berlin and turn over authority to the GDR. In all likelihood, some of 'this information was deliberately planted by the Soviets to impress the West'. By late Apr., however, reports from Berlin indicated the opposite and by the end of June it was clear the Soviets would not leave in the near future. David E. Murphy, Sergei A. Kondrashev, and George Bailey, *Battleground Berlin: CIA vs. KGB in the Cold War* (New Haven: Yale University Press, 1997), 317–18, 327.

178. Special National Intelligence Estimate, Berlin, 17 Mar. 1959.

179. MCP, 17 Mar. 1959, AWF, DDE Diary Series, Box 40, Staff Notes 15–31 Mar. 1959.

180. MCP, 5 Mar. 1959, AWF, DDE Diary Series, Box 39, Staff Notes 1–15 Mar. 1959 (2).

181. MCP, Senator Johnson, *et al.*, 6 Mar. 1959, 10.30 a.m., AWF, DDE Diary Series, Box 39, Staff Notes 1–15 Mar. 1959 (2); MCP, Senator Wiley *et al.*, 6 Mar. 1959, 5.00

p.m., AWF, DDE Diary Series, Box 39, Staff Notes 1–15 Mar. 1959 (2); Eisenhower, *Strictly Personal*, 222–8.

182. Schake, *The Case Against Flexible Response*, 186–8; Eisenhower, *Waging Peace*, 331.

183. Burr argues that when Eisenhower 'approved' the State-Defense paper under discussion at this meeting 'he showed little concern about the military risks' ('Avoiding the Slippery Slope', 194). While Eisenhower favoured a firm stand to convince the Soviets of the West's resolve, it deserves emphasis, however, that he stressed repeatedly that the paper under consideration was acceptable for 'discussion purposes with our allies'. The paper did not tie the president's hands as his 29 Jan. 1959 decisions demonstrate. Moreover, Eisenhower underscored the main direction of his own thought by specifying 'that our main task should be to reach Khrushchev, ascertain what he wants, and proceed from there', as discussions with the allies proceeded. MCP, 11 Dec. 1958, *FRUS*: 1958–60, viii. 172–7; ibid., telegram from the Department of State to the Embassy in Germany, 11 Dec. 1958, viii. 177–80; Eisenhower, *Waging Peace*, 336–9; Eisenhower, *Strictly Personal*, 213–16.

184. The members of the JCS, for instance, believed in a forceful military response and opposed throughout the crisis Eisenhower's more moderate stance. General Twining argued: 'We must ignore the fear of general war. It is coming anyway. Therefore we should force the issue on a point we think is right and stand on it'. (Ibid., Memorandum of Conversation, 13 Dec. 1953, viii. 195). See MCP, 9 Mar. 1959, AWF, DDE Diary Series, Box 39, Staff Notes 1–15 Mar. 1959 (1); Memorandum from the Joint Chiefs of Staff to Secretary of Defense McElroy, 11 Mar. 1959, *FRUS*: 1958–60, viii. 454–5; Watson, *Into the Missile Age*, 603. On the greater willingness to risk escalation shared by many within the Eisenhower administration, see Burr, 'Avoiding the Slippery Slope', 185–6, 188–202.

185. Trachtenberg, *History and Strategy*, 197.

186. MCP, 29 Jan. 1959, *FRUS*: 1958–60, viii. 299–305; ibid., Memorandum Prepared by Secretary of State Dulles, 29 Jan. 1959, viii. 305–10; John Eisenhower, Comments on Memorandum of Conclusion of White House Conference on Berlin, 29 Jan. 1959, Office of the Staff Secretary, Records, 1952–61 (hereafter OSS), International Series, Box 6, Berlin-Vol. I(2), DDEL; Eisenhower, *Waging Peace*, 340–2; Eisenhower, *Strictly Personal*, 218–21.

187. MCP, 17 Mar. 1959.

188. The contingencies ranged from economic sanctions and taking the issue to the United Nations to naval blockades and sending probes into Berlin. For examples of the subsequent contingency planning, see Memorandum of Discussion at the First Meeting of the Berlin Contingency Planning Group, 9 Mar. 1959, *FRUS*: 1958–60, viii. 441–4; ibid., Memorandum of Discussion at the Second Meeting of the Berlin Contingency Planning Group, 14 Mar. 1959, viii. 471–8; contingency planning material in the Berlin files within NSC, Executive Secretary's Subject File, Boxes 7–9; assorted planning drafts and memoranda in Record Group 59, General Records of the Department of State, Records of the Policy Planning Staff, 1957–1961, Lot File 67D548, Box 179, G. A. Morgan Chron—1959, and Box 182, HO [Henry Owen] Chron Jan.–June 1959; Watson, *Into the Missile Age*, 601–7. On the graduated nature of the contemplated American responses, see also Schake, *The Case Against Flexible Response*, 191–206.

189. Merchant to Herter, 4 Mar. 1959, OSS, International Series, Box 6, Berlin-Vol. I(3).

190. In addition to the sources cited above, this assessment of President Eisenhower's deliberate approach to decision-making in this crisis, as well as his confidence that

a graduated response would prevent the crisis from escalating, has benefited considerably from the recollections of John S. D. Eisenhower and Andrew J. Goodpaster. Author's interviews with John S. D. Eisenhower (19 Aug. 1996) and Andrew J. Goodpaster (21 Aug. 1996).

191. Diary, 5 Mar. 1959, AWF, Ann Whitman Diary Series, Box 10, ACW Diary Mar. 1959 (2).

192. Eisenhower, *Waging Peace*, 354–5.

193. Ibid., 338–9; Schick, *The Berlin Crisis*, 20; Robert M. Slusser, 'The Berlin Crisis of 1958–59 and 1961', in Barry M. Blechman and Stephen Kaplan, *Force Without War: US Armed Forces as a Political Instrument* (Washington: Brookings, 1978), 351–2: Trachtenberg, *History and Strategy*, 191–8.

194. MCP (State), 17 Jan. 1959, AWF, DDE Diary Series, Box 38, Staff Notes, Jan. 1959 (2).

195. MCP, 29 Jan. 1959; Memorandum Prepared by Secretary of State Dulles, 29 Jan. 1959; Merchant to Herter, 4 Mar. 1959; MCP, Senator Wiley *et al.*, 6 Mar. 1959, 5.00 p.m.; Watson, *Into the Missile Age*, 608.

196. *EPP, 1959*, 229.

197. See the suggestive excerpt from David Bruce's diary quoted in *FRUS*: 1958–60, viii. 550 n 5.

198. *EPP, 1959*, 242–52.

199. *EPP, 1959*, 276.

200. Eisenhower had already repeatedly stated publicly that 'victory' in a thermonuclear war was impossible. For instance, during a press conference on 26 June 1957, he stated: 'I have told you this time and time again—I repeat it almost in my sleep: there will be no such thing as a victorious side in any global war of the future.' *EPP, 1957*, 504. To reiterate, the significance of his Mar. 1959 statements is that Eisenhower offered them after much consideration in a way that he knew would serve as a signal to the Soviets during the Berlin crisis.

201. Discussion at 445th NSC Meeting, 24 May 1960, AWF, NSC Series, Box 12.

202. Discussion at 460th NSC Meeting, 21 Sept. 1960, AWF, NSC Series, Box 13.

203. Discussion at 364th NSC Meeting, 2 May 1958.

204. Discussion at 391st NSC Meeting, 18 Dec. 1958, AWF, NSC Series, Box 10.

205. MCP, 4 Mar. 1959, AWF, DDE Diary Series, Box 39, Staff Notes 1–15 Mar. 1959 (2).

206. Discussion at 469th NSC Meeting, 8 Dec. 1960, AWF, NSC Series, Box 13.

207. Discussion at 391st NSC Meeting, 18 Dec. 1958.

208. MCP, 18 Nov. 1959, AWF, DDE Diary Series, Box 45, Staff Notes, Nov. 1959 (2); Discussion at 459th NSC Meeting, 15 Sept. 1960, AWF, NSC Series, Box 13.

209. Discussion at 425th NSC Meeting, 25 Nov. 1959, AWF, NSC Series, Box 11.

210. Discussion at 398th NSC Meeting, 5 Mar. 1959, AWF, NSC Series, Box 11. See Discussion at 233rd NSC Meeting, 18 Jan. 1956, *FRUS*: 1955–7, xix. 182–6.

211. Discussion at 433rd NSC Meeting, 21 Jan. 1960, AWF, NSC Series, Box 12; Discussion at 471st NSC Meeting, 22 Dec. 1960, AWF, NSC Series, Box 13. As late as July 1957 Eisenhower expressed his opinion that 'he was not so sure that stockpiling was a thing of the past'. Clearly, though, he was already reconsidering the coherence of the stockpiling effort. Discussion at 330th NSC Meeting, 11 July 1957, *FRUS*: 1955–7, x. 704.

212. Discussion at 471st NSC Meeting, 22 Dec. 1960.

213. MCP, 4 Mar. 1959; MCP, 25 Jan. 1960, AWF, DDE Diary Series, Box 47, Staff Notes, Jan. 1960 (1); MCP, 5 May 1960, AWF, DDE Diary Series, Box 50, Staff Notes, May

1960 (2); MCP, 6 July 1960, AWF, DDE Diary Series, Box 51, Staff Notes July 1960; MCP, 11 Aug. 1960, AWF, DDE Diary Series, Box 51, Staff Notes Aug 1960 (3). On the development of SIOP, see May, Steinbruner, and Wolfe, *History of the Strategic Arms Competition, 1945–1972*, 462–9; Roman, *Eisenhower and the Missile Gap*, 99–105; Rosenberg, 'The Origins of Overkill', 114–18, 174–81; Scott D. Sagan, 'SIOP-62: The Nuclear War Plan Briefing to President Kennedy', *International Security*, 12/1 (Summer 1987), 22–51; Watson, *Into the Missile Age*, 473–95. Despite its reputation as a pure pre-emptive war plan, SIOP embodied basic contradictions between the demands of a pre-emptive strategy and those of a retaliatory one. As Chief of Naval Operations Arleigh Burke observed at the time, in the first SIOP 'counterforce received higher precedence than is warranted for a retaliatory plan, and less precedence than is warranted for an initiative plan'. Burke concluded therefore that there needed to be a range of war plans, not just one SIOP. Burke quoted in Rosenberg, *Toward Armageddon*, 297. See also Roman, *Eisenhower and the Missile Gap*, 109, 111.

214. During Eisenhower's presidency the control over the nuclear stockpile shifted from the AEC to the Department of Defense (DOD) in order to facilitate rapid nuclear response. In 1953 only 9 weapons of the 1,161 stockpile were in DOD custody (< 1%); by 1959 the number had risen to 8,337 of 12,305 (67.8%). Norris, 'US Weapons Secrets Revealed', 48. Eisenhower struggled to devise a policy that would enable retaliation in case a Soviet attack disrupted communications between the president and military commands like SAC, yet would also maintain secure control over nuclear weapons and prevent their unauthorized use. See, for instance, Discussion at 277th NSC Meeting, 27 Feb. 1956, *FRUS: 1955–7*, xix. 204–5; MCP, 19 Dec. 1958, AWF, DDE Diary Series, Box 35, Staff Notes Dec. 1958. The latter document is available along with other recently declassified documents regarding predelegation of authority for nuclear weapons use at the National Security Archive's website: www. seas. gwu.edu/nsarchive/news/predelegation/predel.htm. On the dilemmas posed during this period by nuclear command and control, including the issue of predelegation, see May, Steinbruner and Wolfe, *History of the Strategic Arms Competition, 1945–1972*, 587–93, 604–8; Trachtenberg, *A Constructed Peace*, ch. 5.

215. Discussion at 389th NSC Meeting, 6 Dec. 1958, AWF, NSC Series, Box 10; MCP, 3 Nov. 1959, AWF, DDE Diary Series, Box 45, Staff Notes, Nov 1959 (3); MCP, 16 Nov. 1959, AWF, DDE Diary Series, Box 45, Staff Notes, Nov 1959 (3); MCP, 18 Nov. 1959; MCP, 21 Nov. 1959, AWF, DDE Diary Series, Box 45, Staff Notes, Nov. 1959 (2); Discussion at 453rd NSC Meeting, 25 July 1960, AWF, NSC Series, Box 12; Discussion at 459th NSC Meeting, 15 Sept. 1960.

216. Eisenhower quoted in Rosenberg, *Toward Armageddon*, 298. See also George B. Kistiakowsky, *A Scientist at the White House: The Private Diary of President Eisenhower's Special Assistant for Science and Technology* (Cambridge, Mass.: Harvard University Press, 1976), 379, 399–400, 405–6, 413–16, 421; Roman, *Eisenhower and the Missile Gap*, 103–5; Rosenberg, 'The Origins of Overkill', 174–5.

217. See ibid. 172–3, on Eisenhower's declining faith during the later years of his presidency in massive retaliation as an operatonal viable strategy. See also the critical assessment of Eisenhower's nuclear strategy during this period in Roman, *Eisenhower and the Missile Gap*, 195–200.

218. MCP, 21 Nov. 1959.

219. MCP, 5 Nov. 1959, AWF, DDE Diary Series, Box 45, Staff Notes, Nov 1959 (3);

Discussion at 453rd NSC Meeting, 25 July 1960; Discussion at 469th NSC Meeting, 8 Dec. 1960.

220. Before making this assertion, Eisenhower argued that Soviet 'Polaris' submarines would be invulnerable to American anti-submarine warfare. MCP, 6 Apr. 1960, AWF, DDE Diary Series, Box 49, Staff Notes, Apr. 1960 (2).

221. Discussion at 389th NSC Meeting, 6 Dec. 1958; Discussion at 425th NSC Meeting, 25 Nov. 1959; Discussion at 439th NSC Meeting, 1 Apr. 1960, AWF, NSC Series, Box 12.

222. Discussion at 469th NSC Meeting, 8 Dec. 1960. See also Andrew J. Goodpaster, Oral History no. 477, 21–2, 30, DDEL; MCP, 25 Jan. 1960.

223. As he explained to Robert Bowie, 'he did not see how there could be such a thing as a limited war in Europe, and thought we would be fooling ourselves and our European friends if we said we could fight such a war without recourse to nuclear weapons'. MCP, 16 Aug. 1960, *FRUS*: 1958–60, vii. 610. See also Discussion at 389th NSC Meeting, 6 Dec. 1958; Discussion at 412th NSC Meeting, 9 July 1959, AWF, NSC Series, Box 11; MCP, 14 July 1959, AWF, DDE Diary Series, Box 43, Staff Notes July 1959 (3); Discussion at 415th NSC Meeting, 30 July 1960, AWF, NSC Series, Box 11; Discussion at 424th NSC Meeting, 11 Nov. 1960, AWF, NSC Series, Box 11.

224. Discussion at 459th NSC Meeting, 15 Sept. 1960.

225. Discussion at 469th NSC Meeting, 8 Dec. 1960. A few months before this comment, Eisenhower made some 'general observations relating to the comparative emphasis on strategic and tactical weapons: the more the services depend on nuclear weapons the dimmer the President's hope gets to contain any limited war or to keep it from spreading into general war'. MCP, 24 Aug. 1960, AWF, DDE Diary Series, Box 51, Staff Notes Aug. 1960 (1). See also Discussion at 412th NSC Meeting, 9 July 1959.

226. Special Meeting of the NSC, 18 Feb. 1960, AWF, NSC Series, Box 12; MCP, 22 Apr. 1960, AWF, DDE Diary Series, Box 49, Staff Notes, Apr. 1960 (1).

227. Notes for the Files of John A. McCone, 10 Mar. 1960, Papers of John A. McCone, 1958–61, Sealed File Series, Box 5, Sealed File Number 5 (1), DDEL.

228. Labelling a war fought with missiles 'preposterous', Eisenhower thought that the advent of ICBMs posed an 'insoluble' problem for those who thought in traditional terms. Discussion at 309th NSC Meeting, 11 Jan. 1957, 409. Fittingly, on the day of Eisenhower's famous farewell address, the first National Intelligence Estimate of the year concluded that an American pre-emptive attack in the near future would most likely not prevent 'enormous damage' to the United States. NIE 1–61, Estimate of the World Situation, 17 Jan. 1961, US Department of State, *Foreign Relations of the United States, 1961–1963*, viii. (Washington: GPO, 1996), 3.

229. For a survey of Eisenhower's effort to rid the world of the threat posed by nuclear weapons through arms control, see Robert A. Strong, 'Eisenhower and Arms Control', in Melanson and Mayers (eds.), *Reevaluating Eisenhower*, 241–66. But also see the penetrating critique of the limitations of Eisenhower's approach to arms control in Jeremi Suri, 'America's Search for a Technological Solution to the Arms Race: The Surprise Attack Conference of 1958 and a Challenge for "Eisenhower Revisionism"', *Diplomatic History*, 21/3 (Summer 1997), 417–51.

230. 8 Feb. 1955 entry in Ferrell (ed.), *The Diary of James Hagerty*, 188.

231. Mueller, 'The Essential Irrelevance', 60.

232. This conclusion does not imply that Eisenhower sought to become engaged in peripheral military conflicts. Quite the contrary, Eisenhower had a host of reasons for avoiding involvement in such conflicts, including, but not limited to, concerns about alliance relations, American international prestige, defence expenditures, and distracting attention from the core concerns of the Cold War. None the less, in the early years of his presidency Eisenhower remained confident that the USA could, if necessary, intervene without prohibitive fear of direct Soviet escalation or counter-intervention.

233. Thomas C. Schelling, *The Strategy of Conflict* (Cambridge, Mass.: Harvard University Press, 1960), 187–203.

CHAPTER 6

1. Portions of this chapter were originally written for the Center for National Security Studies, Los Alamos National Laboratory, and have appeared in a different form as 'Nuclear Weapons in Kennedy's Foreign Policy,' *The Historian*, 56 (Winter 1994), 285–300. I gratefully acknowledge the comments of that journal's anonymous referee, Barton J. Bernstein, John Lewis Gaddis, Patrick J. Garrity, Lu Soo Chun, and Jonathan Rosenberg, as well as the generous support of CNSS and the Nuclear History Program.

2. JFK, 'Remarks at the High School Football Stadium, Los Alamos, New Mexico', 7 Dec. 1962, *Public Papers of the Presidents* (*PPP*), 1962 (Washington, 1963), 855–6.

3. JFK comment, 27 Nov. 1962, quoted in Benjamin C. Bradlee, *Conversations with Kennedy* (New York, paperback edn., 1976), 122.

4. On these issues, see Robert Jervis, 'The Military History of the Cold War', *Diplomatic History*, 15 (Winter 1991), 91–2, and Marc Trachtenberg, *History and Strategy* (Princeton, 1991), 261–86.

5. Kennedy was recovering from a grave illness at the time (see Nigel Hamilton, *JFK: Reckless Youth* (New York, 1992), 722), and probably devoted little attention to that or any other issue.

6. For good overviews, see Jean Edward Smith, 'Kennedy and Defense: The Formative Years', *Queen's Quarterly*, 74 (Winter 1967), 627–48, and especially Ronald J. Nurse, 'America Must Not Sleep: The Development of John F. Kennedy's Foreign Policy Attitudes, 1947–1960' (Ph.D. diss., Michigan State University, 1971).

7. See JFK, *Why England Slept* (New York, 2nd edn., 1961), esp. 229–30. The exception seems to have been an essay Kennedy wrote in February 1945 (but never published) entitled 'Let's Try An Experiment in Peace', in which he argued that a postwar arms buildup would cause rather than prevent another war. He returned to his earlier stance by the time of his 1946 Congressional bid. See Herbert S. Parmet, *Jack: The Struggles of John F. Kennedy* (New York, 1980), 129–30; Nurse, 'America Must Not Sleep', 20–1, 28.

8. JFK speech, 27 Mar. 1947, quoted in Joan and Clay Blair, Jr., *The Search for JFK* (New York, paperback edn., 1976), 558.

9. Parmet, *Jack*, 210–11; Nurse, 'America Must Not Sleep', 45–6, 49, 74, 91; *New York Times*, 10 Oct. 1949, 9.

10. JFK, extension of remarks, 3 May 1950, *Congressional Record*, 96, 81st Congress, 2nd Session, A3250–2; Nurse, 'America Must Not Sleep', 51–2. The study group

included future Kennedy appointees McGeorge Bundy, Arthur M. Schlesinger, Jr., and Jerome Wiesner.

11. The official discussion surrounding NSC-68 at the same time included similar views, but it is not known whether these influenced Kennedy or the study group.

12. JFK speech, 21 Jan. 1954, quoted in Parmet, *Jack*, 282–3.

13. JFK speech, 11 May 1954, quoted in Nurse, 'America Must Not Sleep', 110; see also 125–8.

14. Interestingly, it did include the following: 'Whereas the coming of the nuclear age reinforced the bipolar structure of world power, its secondary effects now stimulate a dispersion of strength and influence' (JFK, 'A Democrat Looks at Foreign Policy', *Foreign Affairs*, 36 (Oct. 1957), 44–59).

15. Fred Kaplan, *The Wizards of Armageddon* (Stanford, Calif., 1991), 248.

16. *New York Times*, 7 Nov. 1957, 16; 8 Dec. 1957, 81; 21 Jan. 1958, 19; Parmet, *Jack*, 443–5.

17. Analysts from the RAND Corporation secretly aided the Kennedy campaign (Kaplan, *Wizards of Armageddon*, 249–50). One particularly influential article was Wohlstetter's 'The Delicate Balance of Terror', *Foreign Affairs*, 37 (Jan. 1959), 211–34; see Desmond Ball, *Politics and Force Levels: The Strategic Missile Program of the Kennedy Administration* (Berkeley, 1980), 39–40.

18. Maxwell D. Taylor, *The Uncertain Trumpet* (New York, 1959), 6; JFK to Taylor, 9 Apr. 1960, Pre-Presidential Files (PPF): Senate—Legislation 1960, Books 4/60, Box 730, John F. Kennedy Library (JFKL); see also JFK to Evan Thomas, 17 Dec. 1959, ibid., Books 10/23/59–1/28/60, Box 730, JFKL. Gavin's book is *War and Peace in the Space Age* (New York, 1958); see JFK, 'General Gavin Sounds the Alarm', *The Reporter*, 19 (30 Oct. 1958), 35–6.

19. JFK, 'If the Soviets Control Space . . . they Can Control Earth', *Missiles and Rockets*, 7 (10 Oct. 1960), 13; see also his speech, 11 Dec. 1959, in *The Strategy of Peace* (New York, 1960), 28, and article, 'Disarmament *Can* Be Won', *Bulletin of the Atomic Scientists*, 16 (June 1960), 217. Signs of this belief had appeared as early as 1954; see JFK speech, 6 Apr. 1954, in *John Fitzgerald Kennedy: A Compilation of Statements and Speeches made during his Service in the United States Senate and House of Representatives* (Washington, 1964), 284.

20. JFK speech, 16 Oct. 1959, in *Strategy of Peace*, 185; see also JFK speeches, 2 Nov. 1959, ibid. 20, and 29 Feb. 1960, in *Compilation of Statements and Speeches*, 916.

21. On this subject, see Daniel Horner, 'Kennedy and the Missile Gap' (unpublished thesis paper, Fletcher School of Law and Diplomacy, 1987); Kaplan, *Wizards of Armageddon*, 155–73, 248–9, 286–90; Ball, *Politics and Force Levels*, 88–104; and Edgar M. Bottome, *The Missile Gap: A Study of the Formulation of Military and Political Policy* (Rutherford, NJ, 1971).

22. JFK speech, 14 Aug. 1958, in *Strategy of Peace*, 33, 36–8; JFK, interview by John Fischer, 9 Dec. 1959, ibid. 216; JFK, speech, 26 Aug. 1960, PPF: Speeches, Statements and Sections—Defense and Disarmament, V.F.W. Convention, Detroit, 8/26/60, Box 1029, JFKL, 1–3.

23. JFK to Col. John T. Carlton, 19 Oct. 1960, in 'Freedom of Communications', Final Report of the Committee on Commerce, US Senate, 87th Congress, 1st Session, Part I, 'The Speeches, Remarks, Press Conferences, and Statements of Senator John F. Kennedy, August 1 Through November 7, 1960' (Washington, 1961), 1172; speeches, 29 Feb. 1960, 918–19, and 26 Aug. 1960, 4–5.

24. Quotations from question and answer period, 17 Sept. 1960, and JFK speech, 4 Nov. 1960, in 'Freedom of Communications', 273, 897; see also his press conference, 4

Sept. 1960, and speech, 23 Oct. 1960, ibid. 106, 723; review of B. H. Liddell Hart's *Deterrent or Defense* in *Saturday Review*, 43 (3 Sept. 1960), 18; interview and letter to Thomas E. Murray, both in *Bulletin of the Atomic Scientists*, 16 (Nov. 1960), 346–8; and esp. 'Disarmament *Can* Be Won', 217–19. Kennedy apparently did not take a stand on the nuclear fallout issue until 1959.

25. JFK, 'Disarmament *Can* Be Won', 218.

26. 'Who ever believed in the missile gap?' he apparently would ask later in cabinet meetings (quoted in Taylor, *Swords and Plowshares* (New York, 1972), 205).

27. Perhaps the best, overarching statement of JFK's foreign policy plan is his speech, 14 June 1960, in *Strategy of Peace*, preface.

28. See John Lewis Gaddis, *Strategies of Containment: A Critical Appraisal of Postwar American National Security Policy* (New York, 1982), 214–16.

29. JFK, 'Special Message to the Congress on the Defense Budget', 28 Mar. 1961, *PPP*, 1961, 229–40; Ball, *Politics and Force Levels*, 43–6, 116, and *passim*; Cyrus Vance to Lyndon B. Johnson, 'Military Strength Increases Since Fiscal Year 1961', 3 Oct. 1964, *Declassified Documents Reference System* (*DDRS*) 1978, no. 350A, Schedule A. The total destructive force of the strategic weapons increased 34%, from about 7,420 to 9,960 megatons (equal to *three-quarters of a million* Hiroshima-sized explosions), in the same period; the missile buildup includes 18 fewer Titan II ICBMs but 352 more Polaris SLBMs (16 on each of 22 additional Polaris submarines) and 410 more Minuteman ICBMs, for a total of 744 additional strategic missiles. For different figures and a denial that Kennedy launched a large buildup, see Herbert F. York, *Making Weapons, Talking Peace: A Physicist's Odyssey from Hiroshima to Geneva* (New York, 1987), 193–7.

30. JFK, 'Radio and Television Report to the American People on the Berlin Crisis', 25 July 1961, *PPP*, 1961, 535; see also 'Annual Budget Message to the Congress, Fiscal Year 1963', 18 Jan. 1962, *PPP*, 1962, 28, and 'Commencement Address at American University in Washington', 10 June 1963, *PPP*, 1963, 462.

31. JFK, 'Address at the University of Maine', 19 Oct. 1963, *PPP*, 1963, 797; see also, for example, 'Address in New York City Before the General Assembly of the United Nations', 25 Sept. 1961, *PPP*, 1961, 385–7; 'Radio and Television Address to the American People on the Nuclear Test Ban Treaty', 26 July 1963, *PPP*, 1963, 603; 'Commencement Address at American University', 460.

32. Quotations from, respectively, Dean Rusk, as told to Richard Rusk, *As I Saw It* (New York, 1990), 246–7; JFK to Eleanor Roosevelt, 28 July 1961, quoted in Herbert Parmet, *JFK: The Presidency of John F. Kennedy* (New York, paperback edn., 1983), 198; David Halberstam, *The Best and the Brightest* (New York, 1972), 243; see also Taylor, interview by Elspeth Rostow, 26 Apr. 1964, Oral History Program (OHP), JFKL, 32–3.

33. Gaddis, *Strategies of Containment*, 208; Theodore C. Sorensen, *Kennedy* (New York, 1965), 634.

34. Quoted in Stewart Alsop, 'Kennedy's Grand Strategy', *Saturday Evening Post*, 31 Mar. 1962, 12; see also Michael R. Beschloss, *The Crisis Years: Kennedy and Khrushchev, 1960–1963* (New York, 1991), 60–1.

35. See Stewart Alsop, 'Kennedy's Grand Strategy', 12; Parmet, *JFK*, 154; Robert Komer, 'Memorandum for MCGB', 12 Jan. 1962, NSF: Meetings and Memoranda (M&M), Staff Memoranda, Robert Komer 1/62, Box 322, JFKL; McNamara Testimony, 'World Military Situation and Its Relation to United States Foreign Policy', 8 Feb. 1962, *Executive Sessions of the Senate Foreign Relations Committee* (Historical Series), 14, 87th Congress, 2nd Session (Washington, 1986), 162.

36. Significantly, where Truman had NSC 68 and Eisenhower had NSC 162/2, Kennedy approved no analogous policy design. But along with major speeches, which remain key indicators of administration thought, there are a few representative documents available that do serve as rough counterparts to those earlier papers.

37. JFK to Acheson, 24 Apr. 1961, Acheson Papers, Post Administration Files, State Dept. & White House Adviser, April–June 1961, Box 85, Harry S. Truman Library.

38. 'NATO and the Atlantic Nations', 20 Apr. 1961, *Foreign Relations of the United States (FR)* 1961–3, 13: 287.

39. McNamara, 'Memorandum for the Secretaries of the Military Departments (et al.)', 1 Mar. 1961, President's Office Files (POF): Departments and Agencies, Defense, 1/61–3/61, Box 77, JFKL, attachment, 1; Gregg Herken, *Counsels of War* (New York, 2nd edn., 1987), 147; Paul H. Nitze, with Ann M. Smith and Steven L. Rearden, *From Hiroshima to Glasnost: At the Center of Decision—A Memoir* (New York, 1989), 251; Ball, *Politics and Force Levels*, 189–90.

40. Gaddis, *Strategies of Containment*, 200; S/P draft, 'Basic National Security Policy', 26 Mar. 1962, Vice-Presidential Security, Box 7, Lyndon B. Johnson Library, 23–4, 35–7. The other BNSP, from Mar. 1963, is more or less a condensed version of the earlier one. One might expect to see reflected in it the impact of intervening events, most of all the Cuban missile crisis, but this is apparent only with regard to contingency planning, which 'should be reviewed . . . [to ensure] that a wide range of limited options—and especially non-nuclear options—for the application of force is available . . . Recent operations related to Cuba and contingency planning for a Berlin crisis should be taken as guides' (ISA, 'Basic National Security Policy', 25 Mar. 1963, *DDRS* 1983, no. 215, 15). See also 'Editorial Note', *FR*, 1961–3, 8: 243–7.

41. Nitze, *From Hiroshima to Glasnost*, 252. 41.

42. Walt Rostow, *The Diffusion of Power: An Essay in Recent History* (New York, 1972), 175–6; McGeorge Bundy, *Danger and Survival: Choices About the Bomb in the First Fifty Years* (New York, 1988), 354; Rusk, *As I Saw It*, 508; Ball, *Politics and Force Levels*, 190. Rostow says BNSP was used 'as a basis for speeches' (interview by Richard E. Neustadt, 25 Apr. 1964, OHP, JFKL, 66), which would only increase its historical importance.

43. Although one wonders to what extent Kennedy understood or helped to produce them. The quotation is the title of Part 6 of the excellent public television series *War and Peace in the Nuclear Age* (Boston, 1988).

44. 'Last conversation with the President before NATO meeting of December 1962', 10 Dec. 1962, NSF: M&M, Meetings with the President, General, 6/62–12/62, Box 317a, JFKL, 3.

45. JFK, 'Remarks Prepared for Delivery at the Trade Mart in Dallas', 22 Nov. 1963, *PPP*, 1963, 891–4.

46. JFK, 'Address on the Nuclear Test Ban Treaty', 603.

47. Regardless, the Soviet buildup began well *before* the Cuban missile crisis. See Raymond L. Garthoff, *Reflections on the Cuban Missile Crisis* (Washington, rev. edn. 1989), 133–4, 134 n. 241; Nitze, *From Hiroshima to Glasnost*, 235. We cannot know whether the Soviet buildup would have been any different had Kennedy reduced US strategic forces or maintained them at the Eisenhower levels.

48. Quoted in Harland B. Moulton, *From Superiority to Parity: The United States and the Strategic Arms Race, 1961–1971* (Westport, Conn., 1973), 62; see also Jerome H. Kahan, *Security in the Nuclear Age: Developing U.S. Strategic Arms Policy* (Washington, 1975), 88–90.

49. See 'Remarks by Secretary McNamara, NATO Ministerial Meeting, 5 May 1962', in Marc Trachtenberg (ed.), *The Development of American Strategic Thought: Basic Documents from the Eisenhower and Kennedy Periods, Including the Basic National Security Policy Papers from 1953 to 1959* (New York, 1988), 567, 571, 574; McNamara Testimony, 'World Military Situation', 151; McNamara speech, 'Major National Security Problems Confronting the United States', 18 Nov. 1963, *Department of State Bulletin*, 49 (16 Dec. 1963), 919; Gaddis, *Strategies of Containment*, 218; Ball, *Politics and Force Levels*, 181–3.

50. McNamara, *The Essence of Security: Reflections in Office* (New York, 1968), 58; see also JFK, 'Special Message to the Congress on the Defense Budget', 234; idem., 'The President's News Conference of February 7, 1962', *PPP*, 1962, 127; and Schlesinger, *A Thousand Days: John F. Kennedy in the White House* (Boston, 1965), 502.

51. Quoted in Beschloss, *Crisis Years*, 344–5 n.; see also Halberstam, *Best and the Brightest*, 91; Schlesinger, *A Thousand Days*, 500; Ball, *Politics and Force Levels*, 240–52; Kaplan, *Wizards of Armageddon*, 257; Bundy, 'Kennedy and the Nuclear Question', in Kenneth W. Thompson (ed.), *The Kennedy Presidency: Seventeen Intimate Perspectives of John F. Kennedy* (Lanham, Md, 1982), 205.

52. On this last point, see Ball, *Politics and Force Levels*, 257–63.

53. See 'Instructions for the Under Secretary of State for Political Affairs', 10 July 1963, *FR*, 1961–3, 7: 785–6. 'Nothing gave him greater satisfaction in the White House,' Sorensen wrote, 'than signing the Nuclear Test Ban Treaty' (*Kennedy*, 26).

54. See ibid. 617–24; Beschloss, *Crisis Years*, 306–7, 364; Edward Klein and Robert Littell, 'Shh! Let's Tell The Russians', *Newsweek*, 5 May 1969, 46–7; J. L. Gaddis, *The Long Peace: Inquiries Into the History of the Cold War* (New York, 1987), 201–6.

55. 'Don't you see?' one of McNamara's Assistant Secretaries griped to a British official. 'First we need enough Minutemen to be sure that we destroy all those Russian cities. Then we need Polaris missiles to follow in order to tear up the foundations to a depth of ten feet . . . Then, when all Russia is silent, and when no air defences are left, we want waves of aircraft to drop enough bombs to tear the whole place up down to a depth of forty feet to prevent the Martians recolonizing the country. And to hell with fallout' (quoted in Solly Zuckerman, *Nuclear Illusion and Reality* (New York, 1982), 46–7).

56. Quoted in Robert F. Futrell, *The United States Air Force in Southeast Asia: The Advisory Years to 1965* (Washington, 1981), 64–5; see also Charles A. Stevenson, *The End of Nowhere: American Policy Toward Laos Since 1954* (Boston, 1972), 136–7, 143, 151, 301–2 n. 60.

57. William P. Bundy and U. Alexis Johnson to JFK, 'Plan for Possible Intervention in Laos . . .,' 2nd rev. draft, 4 May 1961, NSF: Countries—Laos, General, 5/1/61–5/8/61, Box 130, JFKL, 6.

58. Rusk to JFK, 'Laos', 1 May 1961, *FR*, 1961–3, 24: 160.

59. Sorensen, *Kennedy*, 645; see also Stewart Alsop, 'Kennedy's Grand Strategy', 12.

60. RFK, memorandum, 1 June 1961, quoted in Schlesinger, *Robert Kennedy and His Times* (New York, paperback edn., 1978), 757–8; idem., interview by John B. Martin, 1 Mar. 1964, in Edwin Guthman and Jeffrey Shulman (eds.), *Robert Kennedy in His Own Words: The Unpublished Recollections of the Kennedy Years* (New York, 1988), 247–8; Bundy, 'Memorandum of Meeting With President Kennedy', 26 Apr. 1961, *FR*, 1961–3, 24: 142–4; Sorensen, *Kennedy*, 642–3; Schlesinger, *A Thousand Days*, 333–4; Stevenson, *End of Nowhere*, 152–4.

61. Sorensen, *Kennedy*, 645–6; the quotation is from JFK, 'Special Message to the Congress on Urgent National Needs', 25 May 1961, *PPP*, 1961, 397.

62. *To Move a Nation: The Politics of Foreign Policy in the Administration of John F. Kennedy* (New York, paperback edn., 1967), 147. Hilsman was then director of the State Department's Bureau of Intelligence and Research.

63. Hilsman, 'Memorandum to Hilsman', 11 May 1962, repr. in Stephen Pelz, '"When Do I Have Time to Think?" John F. Kennedy, Roger Hilsman, and the Laotian Crisis of 1962', *Diplomatic History*, 3 (Spring 1979): 224 (emphasis and exclamation points added, probably by Hilsman).

64. Pelz, ' "When Do I Have Time to Think?" ' 224 n. 19.

65. 'Memorandum of Conversation', 2 June 1962, *FR*, 1961–3, 24: 809–13; McNamara, Rusk, Taylor, Lemnitzer, and others attended the meeting. On the 1962 crisis, see Pelz, '"When Do I Have Time to Think?"'; Hilsman, *To Move a Nation*, 142–51; Beschloss, *Crisis Years*, 395–8; Stevenson, *End of Nowhere*, 174–8; and David K. Hall, 'The Laos Neutralization Agreement, 1962', in Alexander L. George, *et al.* (eds.), *U.S.–Soviet Security Cooperation: Achievements, Failures, Lessons* (New York, 1988), 435–65.

66. 'Every time I want to make the West scream, I squeeze on Berlin' (quoted in Rusk, *As I Saw It*, 227; see also C. L. Sulzberger, *The Last of the Giants* (New York, 1970), 860).

67. In 1959, Senator Kennedy had said that West Berlin should be held even if it meant nuclear war (Victor Lasky, *J.F.K.: The Man and the Myth* (New York, 1963), 361).

68. JFK, 'Report on Berlin', 534–8; Sorensen, *Kennedy*, 590–1; Jack M. Schick, *The Berlin Crisis, 1958–1962* (Philadelphia, 1971), 149–54.

69. See JFK to Rusk, 'Berlin Political Planning', 21 Aug. 1961, in Edward B. Claflin (ed.), *JFK Wants to Know: Memos from the President's Office, 1961–1963* (New York, 1991), 102–4; Bundy to JFK, '(1) Berlin Negotiations and (2) Possible Reprisals', 14 Aug. 1961, *FR*, 1961–3, 14: 330–1; and Trachtenberg, *History and Strategy*, 226.

70. Ibid. 218 (emphasis his). When asked in public, Kennedy dodged the $64,000-question as to whether he thought a war over Berlin would become a nuclear one ('The President's News Conference of August 10, 1961', *PPP*, 1961, 558).

71. JFK to McNamara, 14 Aug. 1961, and National Security Action Memorandum (NSAM) 70, 15 Aug. 1961, in *JFK Wants to Know*, 93, 96. On civil defence and Berlin, see Kaplan, *Wizards of Armageddon*, 307–14.

72. Bundy, 'Covering note on Henry Kissinger's memo on Berlin', 7 July 1961; see also Carl Kaysen to Bundy, 3 July 1961, both NSF: Countries—Germany, Berlin, General, respectively Kissinger Report 7/7/61 and 7/1/61–7/6/61, Box 81, JFKL. SIOP–62 was the Single Integrated Operational Plan for Fiscal Year 1962. Ongoing efforts to revise it, with which Kennedy and Bundy may not have been very familiar, had already begun as early as March (see Kaplan, *Wizards of Armageddon*, 270–9).

73. See ibid. 298–304; Herken, *Counsels of War*, 158–61; Trachtenberg, *History and Strategy*, 225–6, 226 n. 209; John Newhouse, *War and Peace in the Nuclear Age* (New York, 1989), 153–4.

74. JFK to Norstad, 20 Oct. 1961, and attachment, NSAM 109, 'U.S. Policy on Military Actions in a Berlin Conflict', *FR*, 1961–3, 14: 520–3; Nitze, *From Hiroshima to Glasnost*, 203. Nitze claims phase four was discussed in detail with only McNamara and two generals (*From Hiroshima to Glasnost*, 203–4), which may further reduce its importance.

75. Compare, however, Kenneth P. O'Donnell and David F. Powers, with Joe McCarthy, *'Johnny, We Hardly Knew Ye': Memories of John Fitzgerald Kennedy* (Boston, 1970), 299.

76. See Trachtenberg, *History and Strategy*, 282–3.
77. Newhouse, *War and Peace in the Nuclear Age*, 158–61; Beschloss, *Crisis Years*, 333–5; Vladislav Zubok and Constantine Pleshakov, *Inside the Kremlin's Cold War: From Stalin to Khrushchev* (Cambridge, Mass., 1996), 257; Garthoff, 'Berlin 1961: The Record Corrected', *Foreign Policy*, 84 (Fall 1991): 142–56; compare Sorensen, *Kennedy*, 595, and for Clay's perspective, see J. E. Smith, *Lucius D. Clay: An American Life* (New York, 1990), 658–65. A Soviet diplomat claims that Kennedy even offered to negotiate on Berlin as part of these secret October contacts (Beschloss, *Crisis Years*, 334).
78. See Beschloss, *Crisis Years*, 255; McNamara, 'Interview on "JFK Report" Television Program', 28 Sept. 1961, *Public Statements of Secretary of Defense Robert S. McNamara, 1961*, JFKL, 3: 1438; *New York Times*, 25 Sept. 1961, 3; and Nitze, Remarks to the Radio–TV Directors Association, 27 Sept. 1961, in Hearings, 'Nominations of Paul H. Nitze and William P. Bundy', US Senate, Committee on Armed Services, 88th Congress, 1st Session, 7 and 14 Nov. 1963 (Washington, 1963), 43.
79. Hilsman, *To Move a Nation*, 163; Ball, *Politics and Force Levels*, 97–8; Bundy, *Danger and Survival*, 381–2; Beschloss, *Crisis Years*, 328–9; McNamara Testimony, 'World Military Situation', 148; see also James Reston, *Deadline: A Memoir* (New York, 1991), 469–70.
80. Richard K. Betts, *Nuclear Blackmail and Nuclear Balance* (Washington, 1987), 106, but see also 102–4, where Betts has Kennedy relying more heavily on nuclear weapons in the Berlin crisis than I argue here.
81. Roswell Gilpatric, 'Present Defense Policies and Program', 21 Oct. 1961, *Vital Speeches of the Day*, 1 Dec. 1961, 98–101.
82. Over 3,500 strategic weapons to the Soviets' 250 (Vance to LBJ, 3 Oct. 1964, Schedule A; Garthoff, *Reflections on the Cuban Missile Crisis*, 208). 'ExCom' was the Executive Committee of the National Security Council.
83. George H. Quester, *Nuclear Diplomacy: The First Twenty-Five Years* (New York, 1970), 246–7; Gerard H. Clarfield and William M. Wiecek, *Nuclear America: Military and Civilian Nuclear Power in the United States, 1940–1980* (New York, 1984), 256–7; JFK, 'Radio and Television Report to the American People on the Soviet Arms Buildup in Cuba', 22 Oct. 1962, *PPP, 1962*, 808 (emphasis added). Kennedy implied months later that a Soviet attack on proposed MLF vessels would trigger massive retaliation ('The President's News Conference of March 6, 1963', *PPP, 1963*, 241–2).
84. Kaplan, *Wizards of Armageddon*, 305; see also 306, and Trachtenberg, *History and Strategy*, 245.
85. Taylor to McNamara, 'Nuclear-Free or Missile-Free Zones', 26 Oct. 1962, *DDRS* Retrospective Collection, no. 243C, 2 (Taylor did also point to 'tactical advantages of moral rightness, of boldness, of strength, of initiative, and of control of this situation'); *Presidential Recordings, Transcripts*, Cuban Missile Crisis Meetings, 'Off-the-Record-Meeting on Cuba', 16 Oct. 1962, 6.30–7.55 p.m., POF, JFKL, 10, also 27; see also Bromley Smith, 'Summary Record of NSC Executive Committee Meeting No. 24', 12 Nov. 1962, *FR, 1961–3*, 11: 432. Besides McNamara's comment, there is virtually no evidence that the extremely high state of alert on which US strategic forces were then placed was *deliberately intended* to exploit US superiority and intimidate the Soviets, although, again, the alert may have had that *effect*.
86. For such assertions, see D. Rusk, *et al.*, 'The Lessons of the Cuban Missile Crisis', *Time*, 27 Sept. 1982, 85, and Bundy, *Danger and Survival*, 445–53. Good counterarguments are found in Trachtenberg, *History and Strategy*, 235–60, and Betts, *Nuclear Blackmail*, 109–23.

87. *Recordings*, 16 Oct. 1962, evening, 15; *Presidential Recordings*, Cuban Missile Crisis Meetings, 27 Oct. 1962, POF, JFKL, 19, 24, 25, 27, 28.

88. Schlesinger, *A Thousand Days*, 841. Nor was Kennedy's initial response particularly cautious; see Mark J. White, *The Cuban Missile Crisis* (New York, 1995), ch. 5.

89. RFK, *Thirteen Days: A Memoir of the Cuban Missile Crisis* (New York, 1969), 98. It was also during the crisis that Kennedy remarked, 'the odds [are] somewhere near even that we shall see an H-bomb war within the next ten years' (quoted in Joseph W. Alsop, with Adam Platt, *'I've Seen the Best of It': Memoirs* (New York, 1992), 448).

90. Kennedy listed the increased 'danger of a worldwide nuclear war' as one of his reasons for rejecting an air strike ('Minutes of the 507th Meeting of the National Security Council on Monday, October 22, 1962, 3: 00 p.m., Cabinet Room', *FR*, 1961–3, 11: 156).

91. Herken, *Counsels of War*, 166; Philip Nash, *The Other Missiles of October: Eisenhower, Kennedy, and the Jupiters, 1957–1963* (Chapel Hill, NC, 1997), ch. 5.

92. Nash, *Other Missiles of October*, 141–3; Aleksandr Fursenko and Timothy Naftali, *'One Hell of a Gamble': Khrushchev, Castro, and Kennedy, 1958–1964* (New York, 1997), 282, 285. RFK's subsequent denial that he had issued an ultimatum is thus accurate (*Thirteen Days*, 108).

93. *Recordings*, 27 Oct. 1962, 26, 27, 28, 73; David A. Welch and James G. Blight, 'The Eleventh Hour of the Cuban Missile Crisis: An Introduction to the ExComm Transcripts', *International Security* 12 (Winter 1987/8): 21–2; Bundy, *Danger and Survival*, 437.

94. Stephen E. Ambrose, 'The Presidency and Foreign Policy,' *Foreign Affairs* 70 (Winter 1991/2): 129 (emphasis added).

95. 'Remarks of President Kennedy to the National Security Council', 22 Jan. 1963, *FR*, 1961–3, 8: 458. Immediately after the crisis, he did also argue that it had demonstrated the need for 'large conventional forces' (Sulzberger, *Last of the Giants*, 928), and publicly, as mentioned, he of course was at pains to attribute the success to all the resources of flexible response.

96. Rostow to JFK, 'The Problem We Face', 21 Apr. 1961, *DDRS*, 1985, no. 2889, 1; see also 'Basic National Security Policy', 26 Mar. 1962, 117–64; 'Basic National Security Policy', 25 Mar. 1963, 36.

97. Gaddis, *Strategies of Containment*, 220–3; Nash, *Other Missiles of October*, ch. 4. On the MLF, see David N. Schwartz, *NATO's Nuclear Dilemmas* (Washington, 1983), 82–135.

98. See Neustadt, *Alliance Politics* (New York, 1970), 30–55; Schwartz, *NATO's Nuclear Dilemmas*, 96–103; Timothy Maga, *John F. Kennedy and the New Pacific Community* (New York, 1990), 87–98; Knowlton Nash, *Kennedy and Diefenbaker: Fear and Loathing Across the Undefended Border* (Toronto, 1990), esp. 93–6, 116–20, 136–48, 207–15, 222–72, 291–6.

99. Frank Costigliola, 'The Pursuit of Atlantic Community: Nuclear Arms, Dollars, and Berlin', in T. G. Paterson (ed.), *Kennedy's Quest for Victory*, 27 and *passim*; JFK, 'Address Before the Canadian Parliament in Ottawa', 17 May 1961, *PPP*, 1961, 385.

100. Mordechai Gazit, *President Kennedy's Policy Toward the Arab States and Israel: Analysis and Documents* (Tel Aviv, 1983), 54–5, 116–20; Paterson, 'Fixation with Cuba: The Bay of Pigs, Missile Crisis, and Covert War Against Castro', in *Kennedy's Quest for Victory*, 151; Glenn T. Seaborg, with Benjamin S. Loeb, *Kennedy, Khrushchev, and the Test Ban* (Berkeley, 1981), 171, 193–4, 198–9.

101. Rostow, interview, 25 Apr. 1964, 63; Walter LaFeber, *America, Russia, and the Cold War, 1945–1996* (New York, 8th edn., 1997), 228; see also James Fetzer, 'Clinging to Containment: China Policy', in *Kennedy's Quest for Victory*, 182; Arthur Krock, *Memoirs: Sixty Years on the Firing Line* (New York, 1968), 370; Newhouse, *War and Peace in the Nuclear Age*, 197.

102. Gordon H. Chang, *Friends and Enemies: The United States, China, and the Soviet Union, 1948–1972* (Stanford, Calif., 1990), 229 (emphasis in original), and broadly 228–52; Bundy, *Danger and Survival*, 532.

103. Chang, *Friends and Enemies*, 224–7; Leonard H. D. Gordon, 'United States Opposition to the Use of Force in the Taiwan Strait, 1954–1962', *Journal of American History* 72 (Dec. 1985): 654–8; Fetzer, 'Clinging to Containment', 189–90. In June, Assistant Secretary of State Averell Harriman explicitly argued against using nuclear weapons to defend the Nationalist-held offshore islands, although McNamara did toy with the idea of letting Chiang retaliate if PRC aircraft attacked the offshore islands (Hilsman, 'Record of Meeting', 20 June 1962, *FR*, 1961–3, 22: 255).

104. In 1961, Kennedy did adopt a much more militant stance in South Vietnam than he did in neighbouring Laos, significantly expanding the aid and advisory effort. Several beliefs of Kennedy's made for the difference, including that the United States had a more serious commitment to Vietnam; that the chances for victory and applicability of flexible response were greater; that domestic repercussions could be serious otherwise; and that his decision to compromise over Laos now ruled out such an approach in Vietnam (see especially Stephen Pelz, 'John F. Kennedy's 1961 Vietnam War Decisions', *Journal of Strategic Studies*, 4 (Dec. 1981): 356–85).

105. (JCS Chair) Lyman Lemnitzer to McNamara, 'Concept of Use of SEATO Forces in South Vietnam', 9 Oct. 1961, NSF: Countries—Vietnam, 10/4/61–10/9/61, Box 194, JFKL, Appendix A, 7–8. Later the JCS were confident that further military aid to the region would not lead to Soviet nuclear use (McNamara, 'Notes by the Secretary of Defense', 6 Nov. 1961, *FR*, 1961–3, 1: 543–4).

106. William Bundy, cover memo, 5 Nov. 1961, quoted in *FR*, 1961–3, 1: 538 n. 1.

107. Ibid., draft paper, 'Reflections on the Possible Outcomes of US Intervention in South Vietnam', 7 Nov. 1961, 553–4 (emphasis added).

108. Ibid. 554 (emphasis added).

109. Ibid., Taylor to JFK, 3 Nov. 1961, Attachment 2, 'Evaluation and Conclusions', 502–3; see also 491.

110. See Joseph S. Nye, 'Nuclear Learning and U.S.–Soviet Security Regimes', *International Organization* 41 (Summer 1987): 371–402.

111. 'There was not a sentence in this speech,' Beschloss argues convincingly, 'with which [Kennedy] would have privately disagreed in 1960. The change was not in Kennedy but in what he perceived to be his political environment' (*Crisis Years*, 600; see also James N. Giglio, *The Presidency of John F. Kennedy* (Lawrence, Kan., 1991), 218–19).

112. John E. Mueller, *Retreat from Doomsday: The Obsolescence of Major War* (New York, 1989), 156.

113. For a similar argument, see J. L. Gaddis, *The United States and the End of the Cold War: Implications, Reconsiderations, Provocations* (New York, 1992), 108–12. Mueller erroneously states that Kennedy 'was intensely nervous about repeating the conventional war experience of 1914' (*Retreat from Doomsday*, 156). In fact, the

President feared getting into a war *in the same way* that Europe had in 1914, not getting into a war *of the same nature* as World War I.

114. O'Donnell and Powers, '*Johnny, We Hardly Knew Ye*', 299; Sorensen, *Kennedy*, 588; 'Television and Radio Interview: "After Two Years—a Conversation With the President"', 17 Dec. 1962, *PPP*, 1962, 898, see also 896, 897; 'Remarks of President Kennedy to the National Security Council', 1; JFK, 'Remarks to the Brazilian Ambassador and a Group of Brazilian Students', 31 July 1962, *PPP*, 1962, 586; JFK, 'Address on the Nuclear Test Ban Treaty', 603, also 604 (emphases added).

115. This argument meshes with that about 'nuclear danger' in Bundy, *Danger and Survival*.

116. In 1961, he said privately that when he wondered what he would have done had the missile gap actually materialized, he lost most of his night's sleep (Joseph Alsop, '*I've Seen the Best of It*', 415).

117. Krock, *Memoirs*, 358.

118. Beschloss' criticism of Kennedy for having 'provoked the adversary by exposing Soviet nuclear weakness to world' strikes me as unfair. Any US President in the fall of 1961 would have been hard-pressed not to act as Kennedy did to end Khrushchev's bluffing and reassure the West—including Eisenhower, whom Beschloss suggests would have been content to keep the strategic reality concealed (*Crisis Years*, 701–2, also 331, 350–1).

119. Quotes from, respectively, Beschloss, *Crisis Years*, 202 n.; Sulzberger, *Last of the Giants*, 811–12; see also Beschloss, *Crisis Years*, 202, and Stewart Alsop, 'Kennedy's Grand Strategy', 11.

120. For a good critique of the larger policy, see Paterson's introduction in *Kennedy's Quest for Victory*, 3–23; on Vietnam and Flexible Response, see Gaddis, *Strategies of Containment*, 237–73. McNamara has asserted a connection between Vietnam and the missile crisis; see J. G. Blight and D. A. Welch, *On the Brink: Americans and Soviets Reexamine the Cuban Missile Crisis* (New York, 1989), 193–4.

CHAPTER 7

1. Vladislav M. Zubok thanks for support the US Institute of Peace, whose grant had been crucial at the earlier stages of his work on the issue of the nuclear arms race on the Soviet side. He also would like to express appreciation to James G. Hershberg and Yuri Smirnov for their help and comments, and to his colleagues at the National Security Archive, non-government library and research centre in Washington (in particular William Burr, Malcolm Byrne, and Thomas Blanton) for sharing newly declassified American sources with him, and creating excellent conditions for his work on his part of this manuscript. Hope M. Harrison would like to thank the people at the Center for Science and International Affairs at the Kennedy School of Government at Harvard University, and also the Nuclear History Program for providing funding for her work on her part of this manuscript.

2. John Lewis Gaddis, 'The Long Peace: Elements of Stability in the Postwar International System', *International Security*, 10/4 (Spring 1986), 99–142; and id., 'Nuclear Weapons and International Systemic Stability: A Preliminary Methodological Inquiry', originally prepared for the Nuclear History Program Study and Review Conference, Wye Plantation, 5–8 July 1989.

3. The literature on this episode and on the evolution of Soviet military thinking after Stalin's death is extensive. The classic work remains Herbert Dinerstein, *War and the Soviet Union: Nuclear Weapons and the Revolution in Soviet Military and Political Thinking* (New York: Prager, 1959). For more recent books, see Raymond L. Garthoff, *Deterrence and the Revolution in Soviet Military Doctrine* (Washington: Brookings Institution, 1990); Honore M. Catudal, *Soviet Nuclear Strategy from Stalin to Gorbachev: A Revolution in Soviet Military and Political Thinking* (Atlantic Highlands, NJ: Humanities Press International, 1988); Thomas M. Nichols, *The Sacred Cause: Civil-Military Conflict over Soviet National Security, 1917–1992* (Ithaca, NY: Cornell University Press, 1993); and Christoph Bluth, *Soviet Strategic Arms Policy before SALT* (Cambridge: Cambridge University Press, 1992).

4. 'Zapis besedi t. G. K. Zhukova s Presidentom D. Eisenhauerom' [Memorandum of conversation between G.K. Zhurkov and President D. Eisenhower], 20 July 1955, Tsentr Khraneniia Sovremennoi Dokumentatsii (TsKhSD) [Centre for the Storage of Contemporary Documentation (the post-1952 archives of the Central Committee of the Communist Party of the Soviet Union)] *fond* [collection] 5, *opis* [series] 30, *delo* [file] 116, pp. 122–3; for the US record of this conversation, see *Foreign Relations of the United States, 1955–1957* (Washington: Government Printing Office, 1988), 408–18.

5. V. B. Adamsky in *Andrei Sakharov: Facets of a life* (Hong Kong: Editions Frontières, 1991), 31. A recent account on the Soviet side of the strategic arms race is in Steven J. Zaloga, *Target America: The Soviet Union and the Strategic Arms Race, 1945–1964* (Novato, Calif.: Presidio Press, 1993). Also, on the Soviet hydrogen project as taking a distinctly different route from the American one, see David Holloway, *Stalin and the Bomb: The Soviet Union and Atomic Energy, 1939–1956* (New Haven: Yale University Press, 1994), 294–319.

6. The 'New Look' strategy of the Eisenhower Administration was adopted in 1953. It put an emphasis on nuclear means of deterring the Soviet threat, which was reflected in the deployment of nuclear weapons of all kinds and ranges in Western Europe and a rhetoric of 'massive retaliation' to Soviet aggression. The strategy had the strong support of Eisenhower, who hoped it would help him reduce the costs of a conventional buildup, which had quadrupled during the years of the Korean War. MC-48 was a NATO document that summed up the fundamental strategy adopted by NATO at the end of 1954. It implied that if the Soviets launched an attack in Europe, the Alliance would respond by using nuclear weapons, both strategic and tactical. After May 1955 the Bundeswehr, the West German military force, became integrated into NATO military structures. At the end of 1957 Eisenhower, trying to soften the shock of the Soviet Sputnik in Western Europe, announced the deployment of IRBM missiles in those NATO countries who would be willing to host them. This led to IRBM deployments in Great Britain, Italy, Greece, and, finally in October 1959, in Turkey. See McGeorge Bundy, *Danger and Survival* (New York: Random House, 1988), 245–55; and Marc Trachtenberg, *History and Strategy* (Princeton: Princeton University Press, 1991), 138–9, 162, and 202.

7. Strobe Talbott (trans. and ed.), *Khrushchev Remembers: The Last Testament* (Boston: Little, Brown, and Co., 1971), 68.

8. Nikolai Simonov, *The Military-Industrial Complex of the USSR in the 1920s–1950s* (Moscow: Rosspen, 1996), 246.

9. Transcript of 3 July 1953 CC CPSU Plenum, *Izvestia TsK KPSS*, 2, 1991, pp. 166–70.

10. Sergei Khrushchev, *Nikita Khrushchev: krizisi i raketi* (Moscow: Novosti, 1994), i. 45.

11. Andrei Sakharov, *Vospominaniia* [Memories] (New York: Chekhov Publishing, 1990), 238–9; Holloway, *Stalin and the Bomb*, 324.

12. Sergei Khrushchev, *Nikita Khrushchev*, i. 45.

13. We saw the excerpts from this film in the documentary 'Scientific Director: The Life of Yuli B. Khariton', produced in Moscow.

14. N. A. Vlasov, 'Desiat' let riadom s Kurchatovym', in M. K. Romanovsky (ed.), *Vospominaniia ob akademike I. V. Kurchatove* (Moscow: Nauka, 1983), 42, cited in Holloway, *Stalin and the Bomb*, 307.

15. Holloway, *Stalin and the Bomb*, 337, writes about the enormous impact of that test on world's public opinion. Also see Jonathan M. Weisgall, *Operation Crossroads: The Atomic Tests at Bikini Atoll* (Annapolis, Md.: Naval Institute Press, 1994), 302–7; Herbert F. York, *The Advisors: Oppenheimer, Teller, and the Superbomb* (Stanford: Stanford University Press, 1989), 85–6; and Richard G. Hewlett and Jack M. Holl, *Atoms for Peace and War, 1953–1961: Eisenhower and the Atomic Energy Commission* (Berkeley: University of California Press, 1989), 168–82.

16. For Malenkov's speech, see *Pravda*, 13 Mar. 1954.

17. For Mikoyan's speech, see *Kommunist* (Yerevan), 12 Mar. 1954.

18. Memorandum of V. Malyshev to N. Khrushchev, 1 Apr. 1954, TsKhSD, *fond* 5, *opis* 30, *delo* 126, p. 38. This document is commented upon in David Holloway, *Stalin and the Bomb*, 336–9; and Yuri Smirnov and Vladislav Zubok, 'Moscow and Nuclear Weapons After Stalin's Death' in *Cold War International History Project (CWIHP) Bulletin*, 4 (Fall 1994), 14–15.

19. The best source on this and the Soviet H-programme is German A. Goncharov, 'Thermonuclear Milestones', *Physics Today*, 11 (Nov. 1996), 44–61, esp. pp. 57–9; also Y. B. Khariton, V. B. Adamskii, Yu. N. Smirnov, 'On the Creation of the Soviet Hydrogen (Thermonuclear) Bomb', *The Successes of Physical Sciences*, 166/2 (Feb. 1996).

20. Malyshev to Khrushchev, TsKhSd, *fond* 5, *opis* 30, *delo* 126, pp. 39, 40, There is some uncertainty whether the physicists had first communicated their concerns orally to the top leadership, at least to Malenkov.

21. *Pravda*, 27 Apr. 1954.

22. Mohammed Heikal, *Sphinx and Commissar: The Rise and Fall of Soviet Influence in the Arab World* (London: Collins, 1978), 129; cited in Holloway, *Stalin and the Bomb*, 339.

23. See the transcript of the June 1957 'anti-party group' Plenary Meeting of the CC CPSU, *Istoricheskii arkhiv*, 4 (1993), 4.

24. He remained loyal to this belief to the end of his days. See Felix Chuev, *Sto sorok besed s Molotovym* [One hundred and forty conversations with Molotov] (Moscow: TERRA, 1990).

25. Sergei Khrushchev, *Nikita Khrushchev*, i. 62–7.

26. See this point in Vladislav M. Zubok and Constantine Pleshakov's chapter in Reynolds (ed.), *The Origins of the Cold War in Europe*, 71.

27. 'Turnir dlinoi v tri desiatiletiia' [A tournament that lasted three decades], *Istoricheskii Arkhiv*, 2 (1993), 58–67.

28. Khrushchev's report to the CC CPSU Plenum, 31 Jan. 1955, quoted in Andrei Malenkov, *O moyem otse Georgii Malenkove* [On my father Georgy Malenkov] (Moscow: Tekhnoekos, 1992), 115; see Holloway, *Stalin and the Bomb*, pp. 338–9.

29. 'Zapis besedy . . .', 20 July 1955, TsKhSD, *fond* 5, *opis* 30, *delo* 116, pp. 122–3; and *FRUS, 1955–7* v. (Washington: GPO, 1988), 408–18; also Smirnov and Zubok, *CWIHP Bulletin*, 4: 16.

30. 'Memuari [Memoirs] Nikiti Sergeevicha Kruscheva', *Voprosi istorii*, 8–9 (Moscow, 1992), 76.
31. Yaroslav Golovanov, *Korolyov: Facts and Myths* (Moscow: Nauka, 1994), 464.
32. *Pravda*, 18 Nov. 1955; cited in Holloway, *Stalin and the Bomb*, 343.
33. *Pravda*, 15 Feb. 1956, 1–10; Sergei Khrushchev recollects an episode when he accompanied his father on a visit to the Korolev's firm on 27 Feb. 1956. Khrushchev asked Dmitry Ustinov, then head of the military-industrial commission of the Council of Ministers, how many bombs would suffice 'to knock out England'. When Ustinov said 'five', Khrushchev said, 'Well, terrible power. The last war was bloody, but with charges like this one it becomes simply impossible. Five charges—and a whole country is out. Terrible.' Sergei Khrushchev, *Nikita Khrushchev*, i. 103.
34. *Pravda*, 15 Feb. 1956, 10.
35. 'The Conference of First Secretaries of Central Committees of Communist and Workers Parties of Socialist Countries for the Exchange of Views on Questions Related to the Preparation and Conclusion of a German Peace Treaty, 3–5 August 1961' [translation by Zubok of the minutes, found in TsKhSD, Moscow], *CWIHP Bulletin*, 3 (Fall 1993), 60. On Khrushchev's 'duel' with the Dulles brothers, John Foster and Allen, see Zubok and Pleshakov, *Inside the Kremlin's Cold War* (Cambridge, Mass.: Harvard University Press, 1996), 190–1, 204 and Vladislav M. Zubok, 'Inside the Covert Cold War: The KGB vs. the CIA, 1960–1962', *CWIHP Bulletin*, 4 (Fall 1994), 25–7.
36. Transcript of the June 1957 CC CPSU Plenary Meeting, *Istoricheskii arkhiv*, 4, 1993, 36. Indeed, from 1957 on John F. Dulles began to have serious doubts in the practicability of his 'massive retaliation' doctrine, since, as he once put it himself, 'a nuclear exchange between the U.S. and the USSR could result not only in the destruction of the Soviet Union and the U.S. but could make all of the Northern Hemisphere uninhabitable or, in any event, risky to inhabit'. Memorandum of conversation at the National Security Council (NSC) meeting, 7 Apr. 1958, in the file at the National Security Archive. The authors thank William Burr for bringing this document to their attention; on Dulles' growing caution under the impact of nuclear weapons, see John Lewis Gaddis' chapter in Richard Immerman (ed.), *John Foster Dulles and the diplomacy of the Cold War: A Reappraisal* (Princeton: Princeton University Press, 1989).
37. *Pravda*, 14 May 1957.
38. Transcript of the June 1957 CC CPSU Plenum, *Istoricheskii arkhiv*, 4 (1993), 5.
39. Alexei Kosygin later remarked that he had backed Khrushchev without hesitation because had Molotov been victorious 'blood would have flowed again'. Oleg Troyanovsky, 'Nikita Khrushchev and the Making of Soviet Foreign Policy', a paper presented at the Khrushchev Centenary Conference, Brown University, 1–3 Dec. 1994, p. 10. See also, James Richter, *Khrushchev's Double Bind: International Pressures and Domestic Coalition Politics* (Baltimore: Johns Hopkins University Press, 1994); and James M. Goldgeier, *Leadership Style and Soviet Foreign Policy. Stalin, Khrushchev, Brezhnev, Gorbachev* (Baltimore: Johns Hopkins University Press, 1994).
40. Zaloga, *Target America*, 145. The cost of this obssession can be traced now. According to the Gosplan statistics, even in 1958 the missiles took up only 8.5% of the total purchase of equipment by the Ministry of Defence. In 1959 it was 21.5%, in 1960 31.9% and in 1962 43.8%. The missile industry became the leading branch of the Soviet military-industrial complex (Simonov, *The Military-Industrial Complex*, 247).

41. Cited in Robert Slusser, *The Berlin Crisis of 1961: Soviet-American Relations and the Struggle for Power in the Kremlin* (Baltimore: Johns Hopkins University Press, 1973), 44.

42. See Hope M. Harrison, 'Was Nikita S. Khrushchev a Student of Thomas Schelling? Khrushchev's Coercive Diplomacy in the 1958–1962 Berlin Crisis', unpub. MS, 1987; and Thomas Schelling, *Arms and Influence* (New Haven: Yale University Press, 1966).

43. Khrushchev's motivations and impulses are studied in Zubok and Pleshakov, *Inside the Kremlin's Cold War*. See also, James Richter, *Khrushchev's Double Bind*; and James Goldgeier, *Leadership Style*. William Taubman has also been researching this issue extensively for his biography of Nikita Khrushchev.

44. Arkhiv Vneshnei Politiki Russkoi Federatsii (AVP RF) [Russian Foreign Ministry archives] Moscow, Referentura po FRG, *opis* [series] 51, *papka* [folder] 17, *portfel'* [portfolio] 1, *delo* [file] 022. Adenauer and Defence Minister Franz-Joseph Strauss indeed sought the nuclearization of West Germany. See also, Daniel Kosthorst, *Brentano und die deutsche Einheit: Die Deutschland—und Ostpolitik des Aussenministers im Kabinett Adenauer 1955–1961* (Düsseldorf: Droste, 1993) 137–43. On the issue of West German nuclearization, see Catherine Kelleher, *Germany and the Politics of Nuclear Weapons* (New York, 1975), 43–9 and Marc Trachtenberg, *History and Strategy*, ch. 4, 'The Nuclearization of NATO and U.S.–West European Relations', and ch. 5, 'The Berlin Crisis', esp. 180–91. The most recent findings from the Soviet archives on this are in Hope M. Harrison, 'Ulbricht and the Concrete "Rose": New Archival Evidence on the Dynamics of Soviet–East German Relations and the Berlin Crisis, 1958–1961', working paper no. 5 of CWIHP (Woodrow Wilson International Center for International Scholars: Washington, May 1993), as well as Vladislav M. Zubok, 'Khrushchev and the Berlin Crisis, 1958–1962,' working paper no. 6 of the CWIHP, May 1993, 3–5.

45. Significantly, at the meeting of July–August 1958 between Khrushchev and Mao, the discussion revolved both around Khrushchev's methods of domination in the communist camp and the nuclear war, Zubok and Pleshakov, *Inside the Kremlin's Cold War*, 219–20 and Zubok, 'What a Chaos in the Beautiful Socialist Camp! Deng Xiao-Peng and the Sino-Soviet Split, 1956–1963', forthcoming in *CWIHP Bulletin*, 10; Thompson to Dulles, 11 Nov. 1958, *FRUS 1958–60*, viii. *Berlin Crisis 1958–1959* (Washington: GPO, 1993), 48; Troyanovsky, 'Nikita Khrushchev', 14.

46. The Soviet leader insisted that the three Western powers sign peace treaties with the FRG and the GDR and recognize West Berlin as a 'free city'. He warned that if these things did not happen within six months, the Soviet Union would conclude a separate peace treaty with the GDR and the access routes from West Germany to West Berlin would then pass under Ulbricht's jurisdiction. The Western powers feared that Ulbricht would close those routes, which would then put the West in a difficult quandary in which it would likely have to choose whether to withdraw from West Berlin or to fight. On the second Berlin crisis, see Hannes Adomeit, *Soviet Risk-Taking and Crisis Behavior: A Theoretical and Empirical Analysis* (Boston: George, Allen and Unwin, 1982); Jack Schick, *The Berlin Crisis, 1958–1962* (Philadelphia: University of Pennsylvania Press, 1971); and Robert Slusser, *The Berlin Crisis of 1961*; Honore Catudal, *Kennedy and the Berlin Wall Crisis: A Case Study of the U.S. Decision-Making* (Berlin: Berlin Verlag, 1980); Michael Beschloss, *The Crisis Years. Kennedy and Khrushchev, 1960–1963* (New York: Harper and Collins, 1991); McGeorge Bundy, *Danger and Survival*; and Trachtenberg, 'The Berlin Crisis', in *History and Strategy*, 169–234.

47. Harrison, 'Ulbricht and the Concrete "Rose" '; and Zubok 'Khrushchev and the Berlin Crisis'.

48. Troyanovsky, 'Nikita Khrushchev', 18–19; William Burr, 'Eisenhower's Search for Flexibility: Strategy and Diplomacy During the Berlin Crisis, 1958–1960', paper presented at the Conference on the Second Berlin Crisis, Woodrow Wilson Center for International Scholars, Washington, May 1993.

49. G. A. Mikhailov and A. S. Orlov, 'The Mysteries of the "Closed Skies" ', *Novaia I noveishaiia istoriia*, 6 (1992), 99–100.

50. Sergei Khrushchev, *Nikita Khrushchev*, i. 384.

51. Simonov, *The Military-Industrial Complex*, 249–50, 307.

52. Khrushchev's Memo to CC CPSU Presidium, 8 Dec. 1959, TsKhSD, *fond* 2, *opis* 1, *delo* 416, pp. 1–6, published in *CWIHP Bulletin*, 8–9: 416–20 in Vladislav Zubok's translation and with his comments; Nichols, *The Sacred Cause*, 71–83; and James Hansen, *Correlation of Forces: Four Decades of Soviet Military Development* (New York: Praeger, 1987), 67; also Matthew Evangelista, 'Why Keep Such an Army? Khrushchev's Troop Reductions', forthcoming working paper of the CWIHP.

53. The copies of *Military Thought* had been copied by Penkovsky and passed to the CIA. They were declassified and released in June 1992 and are available on file in the National Security Archive, Washington.

54. Lieut.-Gen. Valentin Larionov, his interview with V. M. Zubok, Moscow, Jan. 1990; V. Larionov, 'Tiazhkii put poznaniia (Iz istorii iadernoi strategii)' [The hard way of learning (From the history of nuclear strategy)], unpub. MS, pp. 9–10, courtesy of Valentin Larionov.

55. V. D. Sokolovskii (ed.), *Soviet Military Strategy*, trans. by Herbert S. Dinerstein, Leon Goure, and Thomas W. Wolfe (Englewood Cliffs, NJ: Prentice-Hall, 1963).

56. Dr Zhisui Li, *The Private Life of Chairman Mao: The Memoirs of Mao's Personal Physician* (New York: Random House, 1994), 118–20.

57. Sergei Khrushchev, *Nikita Khrushchev*, i. 347; Yuli Khariton and Yuri Smirnov, 'Otkuda vzialos i bilo li nam neobkhodimo iadernoie oruzhiie' [Where nuclear weapons came from and are they necessary for us], *Izvestiia*, 21 July 1994, 5.

58. Strobe Talbott (trans. and ed.), *Khrushchev Remembers* (Boston: Little, Brown and Co., 1970), 467–8; and Jerrold L. Schecter with Vyacheslav V. Luchkov (trans. and eds.), *Khrushchev Remembers: The Glasnost Tapes* (Boston: Little, Brown and Co., 1990), 147–50.

59. Li Zhisui, *Private Life of Chairman Mao*, 270–1.

60. Sergei Khrushchev, *Nikita Khrushchev*, i. 353.

61. Troyanovsky, 'Nikita Khrushchev and Foreign Policy', research paper presented at the Conference at Providence, Rhode Island, 2–3 Dec. 1994, 31.

62. CC CPSU to CC CCP, a letter of 27 Sept. 1958, translated and commented by Zubok in *CWIHP Bulletin*, 6–7: 219, 226–7.

63. Penkovsky's debriefings, 18–19 July 1961, p. 14, on the file in the National Security Archive; see also Jerrold L. Schecter and Peter S. Deriabin, *The Spy Who Saved the World: How a Soviet Colonel Changed the Course of the Cold War* (New York: Scribner's, 1992).

64. This decision is inferred from the document cited by retired Gen.-Maj. Vadim Makarevsky, 'O premiere N. S. Krushcheve, marshale G. K. Zhukove i generale I.A. Plieve', *Mirovaia ekonomika i mezhdunarodniie otnosheniia*, 8–9 (1994), 193.

65. Quoted in Beschloss, *The Crisis Years*, 330.

66. Sergei Khrushchev, *Nikita Khrushchev*, ii. 132.

67. See Vladislav Zubok, 'Khrushchev's Motives and Soviet Diplomacy in the Berlin Crisis, 1958–1962', paper presented at the Conference 'Soviet Union, Germany, and the Cold War, 1945–1962: New Evidence from Eastern Archives', Essen, Germany, 28–30 June 1994.

68. On the role of fear of nuclear war as a more important factor than US nuclear superiority during the Berlin crisis, see Bundy, *Danger and Survival*, 378–81.

69. 'Khrushchev: The Man, His Manner, His Outlook, and His View of the United States', background paper, 25 May 1961, John F. Kennedy Library, POF:CO:USSR, Vienna Meeting, Box 126, Folder 9.

70. The record of the Khrushchev–Ulbricht conversation, 30 Nov. 1960, AVP RF, *fond* 0742, *opis* 6, *papka* 43, *delo* 4, pp. 10–11, 12, English trans. Harrison, Appendix A, 'Ulbricht and the Concrete "Rose"'.

71. Anatoly Dobrynin, *In Confidence. Moscow's Ambassador to America's Six Cold War Presidents* (New York: Random House, 1995), 44; G. M. Kornienko, 'Upushchennaiia vozmozhnost. Vstrecha N. S. Kruscheva I Kennedi v Vene' [Missed opportunity. A meeting of Khrushchev and Kennedy in Vienna in 1961], *Novaiia i Noveishaia Istoriia*, 2 (1992), 102–3.

72. The Conference of First Secretaries of Central Committees, 3–5 Aug. 1961 (see n. 35), TsKhSD, 156, 157, 158, 159 and the translated excerpts in *CWIHP Bulletin*, 3 (1993), 60.

73. Shelepin's document is translated and commented in Zubok, 'Inside the Covert Cold War: The KGB vs. the CIA, 1960–1962', *CWIHP Bulletin*, 4 (Fall 1994), 26–7. On Penkovsky see Jerrold Schecter and Peter Deriabin, *The Spy who Saved the World*, 205–13. On 18 July 1961 Penkovsky said to his CIA handlers that 'if we consider today's situation, the Soviet Army is not ready for any widespread war'.

74. Andrei Sakharov, *Sakharov Speaks* (New York: Knopf, 1974), 33.

75. Yu. N. Smirnov, 'This Man Has Done More Than All of Us', in *Andrei Sakharov: Facets of a Life*, 602–3; Viktor Adamsky and Yuri Smirnov, 'Soviet 50-Megaton Test in 1961', *CWIHP Bulletin*, 4 (Fall 1994), 3, 19–20.

76. XXII Congress of the Communist Party of the Soviet Union, stenographic report, vol. 2, (Moscow: Gospolitizdat, 1992), 571–2.

77. The back-channel, i.e. communications outside of official diplomatic channels, came out of the efforts of both Khrushchev and Kennedy in the first months of the Kennedy administration to find out more about each other's positions. They exchanged 'personal' letters (the so-called 'pen-pal letters') through various intermediaries, among them Robert Kennedy, Georgi Bolshakov, and later Anatoly Dobrynin. On the Checkpoint Charlie episode, see Troyanovsky, 'Nikita Khrushchev', 37; for the opposite interpretation of the tank confrontation see Valentin Falin, *Politische Erinnerungen* (translated from Russian into German by Heddy Pross-Weerth) (Munich: Droemer Knaur, 1993), 345–6; and Raymond Garthoff, 'Berlin 1961: The Record Corrected', *Foreign Policy*, 84 (Fall 1991). On the importance of the 'back-channel' see Beschloss, *The Crisis Years*, 152–81.

78. Scholars continue to debate how close the two sides were to war. For recent polemics, see Mark Kramer, 'Tactical Nuclear Weapons, Soviet Command Authority, and the Cuban Missile Crisis', *CWIHP Bulletin*, 3 (Fall 1993), 40, 42–6; ibid., James G. Blight, Bruce J. Allyn, and David A. Welch, 'Kramer vs. Kramer,' 41, 47–50; and Richard Ned Lebow and Janice Gross Stein, *We All Lost the Cold War* (Princeton: Princeton University Press, 1994), 94–109.

79. Adam Ulam, *Expansion and Coexistence. The History of Soviet Foreign Policy, 1917–1967* (New York: Praeger, 1968), 668–72.

80. James G. Blight, Bruce J. Allyn, and David A. Welch, *Cuba on the Brink: Castro, The Missile Crisis, and the Soviet Collapse* (New York: Pantheon Books, 1993), 348.

81. Richter, *Khrushchev's Double Bind*, 147–9.

82. Troyanovsky, 'Nikita Khrushchev', 38–9.

83. On evidence based on research in US archives about US covert planning to invade Cuba and carry out other subversive actions against Cuba, see James G. Hershberg, 'Before "The Missiles of October": Did Kennedy Plan a Military Strike Against Cuba?', in James A. Nathan (ed.), *The Cuban Missile Crisis Revisited* (New York: St. Martin's Press, 1992).

84. Ibid. 38.

85. Aleksandr Fursenko and Timothy Naftali, *'One Hell of a Gamble': Khrushchev, Castro, and Kennedy, 1958–1964* (New York: Norton, 1997), 167–70.

86. Ibid.

87. On the meetings of the Soviet leadership to discuss this decision, see ibid. 179–81.

88. This miscalculation is recognized in Lebow and Stein, *We All Lost the Cold War*, 79–82; and Sergei Khrushchev, *Nikita Khrushchev*, ii. 174–5.

89. Fursenko and Naftali, *'One Hell of a Gamble'*, 212, 242.

90. Troyanovsky, 'The Caribbean Crisis: A View from the Kremlin', *International Affairs* (Moscow), 4–5 (1992), 147–57; and interview with Zubok, 2 Mar. 1993, Washington.

91. For the texts of Dobrynin's and others' accounts of the meeting, see Jim Hershberg, 'Anatomy of a Controversy: Anatoly F. Dobrynin's Meeting with Robert F. Kennedy, Saturday, 27 October 1962', *CWIHP Bulletin*, 5 (Spring 1995), 75, 77–80.

92. Blight, Allen, and Welch, *Cuba on the Brink*, 361–5.

93. Ibid. 360–1.

94. *Khrushchev Remembers: The Glasnost Tapes*, 177; the exchange of cables between Khrushchev and Castro is printed in *Cuba on the Brink*, 481–91.

95. Troyanovsky, 'Nikita Khrushchev', 44.

96. See, Zubok, 'The Missile Crisis and the Problem of Soviet Learning', and William Taubman, 'The Correspondence: Khrushchev's Motives and His Views of Kennedy', *Problems of Communism*, 41, special edn. (Spring 1992), 14–23; the text of the Khrushchev–Kennedy correspondence in Oct.–Dec. 1962 is also printed in this issue, pp. 30–120.

97. This found new support in the presentations by the military, veterans of the crisis three decades earlier, at the Conference on the Caribbean Crisis of 1962, Moscow, 27–9 Sept. 1994.

98. Bundy, *Danger and Survival*, 359.

99. Sergei Khrushchev, *Nikita Khrushchev*, ii. 208.

100. *Istoricheskii arkhiv*, 4 (1993), 36–7. In May 1957 Stassen, special assistant for disarmament to President Eisenhower, made an unauthorized approach to Soviet deputy foreign minister Zorin, during the talks in the subcommittee of the UN Disarmament Committee. Stassen gave Zorin his memorandum with a rough agenda of possible negotiations. Later, however, the White House, under pressure from John Foster Dulles and US Atomic Energy Commissioner Lewis Strauss, disavowed Stassen's 'initiative'.

101. Zubok, 'Soviet Approaches to Disarmament Negotiations in Late 1959–early 1960' and 'McCloy–Zorin Negotiations, May–September 1961', unpub. MSS, Moscow.

102. Yuri Smirnov in conversations with Zubok, Feb. 1994, Oslo. Smirnov worked in Sakharov's theoretical group in Arzamas-16 and recently has been writing extensively on the impact of nuclear weapons on the mentality of the Soviet leaders.

103. David Holloway, *Stalin and the Bomb*, 360–1; Yuri Smirnov and Zubok, 'Moscow and Nuclear Weapons After Stalin's Death', *CWIHP Bulletin*, 4 (Fall 1994), 16.

104. Sakharov, *Vospominaniia*, 271; on Kurchatov's 'enlightening' diplomacy see Yuri Smirnov and Vladislav Zubok, 'Moscow and Nuclear Weapons,' 16.

105. Matthew Evangelista, 'Soviet Scientists and Nuclear Testing, 1954–1963,' paper presented at the Conference on New Evidence on Cold War History, Moscow, 12–15 Jan. 1993.

106. Sakharov, *Vospominaniia*, 286–9; and Viktor Adamsky, 'Becoming a Citizen,' in *Andrei Sakharov: Facets of a Life*, 39.

107. On Khrushchev and the test-ban negotiations, see Christer Jonsson, *Soviet Bargaining Behavior: The Nuclear Test-Ban Case* (New York: Columbia University Press, 1979); Harold K. Jacobson and Eric Stein, *Diplomats, Scientists and Politicians: The United States and the Nuclear Test-Ban Negotiations* (Ann Arbor: University of Michigan Press, 1966); and Glenn Seaborg with Benjamin Loeb, *Kennedy, Khrushchev and the Test-Ban* (Berkeley: University of California Press, 1981).

108. Sakharov, *Vospominaniia*, 215–16; Sakharov reproduced this document from memory.

109. Yuri Smirnov, conversation with Zubok, Oslo, Norway, 20 Mar. 1994.

110. Sakharov, *Sakharov Speaks*, 31.

111. On the multiple levels and channels of the negotiations, see George Bunn, *Arms Control by Committee. Managing Negotiations with the Russians* (Stanford: Stanford University Press, 1992), 26–35.

112. Adamsky, 'Becoming a Citizen', in *Andrei Sakharov: Facets of a Life*, 38–9; see also Sakharov, *Vospominaniia*, 307–8. On the larger role of transnational scientific communities, see Matthew Evangelista, 'Soviet Scientists and Nuclear Testing, 1954–1963'.

113. The text of the documents was published for the first time by Yuri Smirnov in *Aftenposten*, 19 Apr. 1994.

114. This is acknowledged by Central Committee insiders Georgi Arbatov, *The System: An Insider's Life in Soviet Politics* (New York, 1992), 95; and Fedor Burlatsky, *Khrushchev and the First Russian Spring: The Era of Khrushchev Through the Eyes of His Advisor* (New York, 1991), 185–6.

115. N. S. Khrushchev, 'The Present International Situation and the Foreign Policy of the Soviet Union', Report to Session of USSR Supreme Soviet, 12 Dec. 1962, in *Current Digest of the Soviet Press*, 14/52 (23 Jan. 1963), 3; quoted in Peter Rodman, *More Precious than Peace: The United States, the Soviet Union, and the Third World* (New York: Scribner's, 1994), 111.

116. Quoted in Bunn, *Arms Control by Committee*, 37. On the Chinese nuclear programme, see John Lewis and Xue Litai, *China Builds a Bomb* (Stanford: Stanford University Press, 1988).

117. Sergei Khrushchev, *Nikita Khrushchev*, ii, 458.

118. Ibid. 488; and Garthoff, *Deterrence and Revolution*, 40.

119. Ibid. 40. On the evolution of the concept of 'victory' see Vadim Tsimburskii, *Voennaiia doctrina SSSR i Rossii: osmysleniia poniatii 'ugrozi' i 'pobedi' vo vtoroi polovine XX veka* [The military doctrine of the USSR and Russia: perceiving the notions of 'threat' and 'victory' in the second half of the twentieth century] (Moscow: Russian Science Foundation–Moscow Branch, 1994), 30–60.

120. On the 'restoration' of military policies and doctrine after Khrushchev's 'revolution' see Nichols, *The Sacred Cause*, 84–6.

Chapter 8

1. Martin Gilbert, *Winston S. Churchill, 1874–1965*, 8 vols. (London: Heinemann,
1966–88), v. 265 (hereafter *Churchill*). Note that Randolph Churchill authored
vols. 1 and 2.
2. A. G. Gardiner, *Pillars of Society* (London: Nisbet, 1915), 57–8.
3. Winston S. Churchill, *My Early Life: A Roving Commission* (New York: Scribner,
1958), 33.
4. *Churchill*, i. 132–3.
5. Ibid. 391–2.
6. Ibid. iii. 115.
7. Winston S. Churchill, *The Second World War*, 6 vols. (Boston: Houghton Mifflin,
1948–53), vi. 106–7. Field Marshal Alexander's recollection cited in *Churchill*, vii.
915.
8. Churchill, *The Second World War*, vi. 364–5. Simpson recollection cited in
Churchill, vii. 1,264.
9. Quoted in *Churchill*, vii. 697.
10. During World War I, Churchill strongly advocated the development of the tank
and consistently argued for an increase in tank production and in the number of
men assigned to the Tank Corps. His advocacy of innovative tactics is apparent in
a 1918 memorandum that argued in favour of developing a mechanically superior
army. Dominated by tanks and aircraft, such an army could initiate an offensive
that might win the war. Churchill sought 'to reduce reliance on infantry and
artillery, to increase the use of air power . . . of tanks, and to multiply the use of
poison gas five times'. Believing trench warfare could never produce victory,
Churchill argued, 'the resources are available, the knowledge is available, the time
is available . . . nothing is lacking except the will' (quoted in *Churchill*, iv. 144–5;
72). With respect to Churchill's predilection for aggressive war-fighting, the historical record is rife with examples. Some of the more striking are the Dardenelles
action of 1915, his advocacy of military action against Germany in Norway in
1940, and his plan to gain control of the Aegean and the accession of Turkey in
the Italian campaign of 1943. For a description of the Dardenelles campaign, see
Churchill, iii. chs. 6–15. On the Norway initiative, see Churchill's *Second World
War*, i. chs. 13–16; on the Aegean initiative, see ibid., v. ch. 12. For Churchill's
relationship with his defence chiefs during World War II, see Michael Carver,
'Churchill and the Defence Chiefs', in Robert Blake and Wm. Roger Louis (eds.),
Churchill (New York: Norton, 1993), ch. 20.

As a strategist, Churchill frequently expressed appreciation of the crucial role
naval power played in maintaining Great Britain's global position. Speaking in
1912, as the Anglo-German naval competition was unfolding, he declared: 'the
whole fortunes of our race and Empire, the whole treasure accumulated during so
many centuries of sacrifice and achievement would perish and be swept utterly
away if our naval supremacy were to be impaired.' (in Robert Rhodes James (ed.),
Winston S. Churchill: His Complete Speeches, 1897–1963, 8 vols. (London: Chelsea
House), ii. *1909–13* (hereafter *Complete Speeches*)). That same year he prepared a

thoughtful analysis of the naval situation in the Mediterranean, which sought to catalyse the government to move forward in its shipbuilding programme (reprinted in *Churchill*, ii. 572–5). Churchill expressed his support for a continued naval buildup in March 1914 when, as First Lord of the Admiralty, he introduced the Naval Estimates for 1914–15 to the House. The *Daily Telegraph* called the two and a-half hour speech 'the longest and perhaps also the most weighty and eloquent speech' the House had listened to 'during the present generation'. Churchill questioned why other powers needed to construct great ships and develop large navies: 'It is sport to them. It is life and death to us. Our diplomacy depends in great part . . . upon our naval position, and . . . our naval strength is the one great balancing force which we can contribute to our own safety and to the peace of the world.' (see *Complete Speeches*, iii. 2,233–62). This line of argument—that peace could best be preserved by maintaining a strong military force—was one Churchill would advance frequently in the future. For a sweeping discussion of Churchill's view of British seapower, see Jon Sumida, 'Churchill and British Seapower, 1908–1929', in R. A. C. Parker (ed.), *Winston Churchill: Studies in Statesmanship* (London: Brassey's, 1995), ch. 2.

For a highly critical view of Churchill the strategist, see Tuvia Ben-Moshe, *Churchill: Strategy and History* (Boulder, Colo.: Lynne Rienner, 1992). Ben-Moshe criticizes Churchill's 'debilitating weakness' as a strategist, claiming he was unable 'to harmonize and achieve a balance between the two basic dimensions of strategy . . . the military dimension . . . and the political dimension . . .' (p. 325). Ben-Moshe also criticizes Churchill's historical writing, claiming that in the memoirs of the world wars, Churchill is 'incorrect and misleading' and guilty in *The Second World War* of composing 'a false version of events . . .' (p. 333). For a quite different perspective on Churchill the historian, see J. H. Plumb, 'The Dominion of History', in R. Crosby Kemper (ed.), *Winston Churchill: Resolution, Defiance, Magnanimity, Good Will* (Columbia: University of Missouri Press, 1996), ch. 2.

Basil Liddell Hart is also critical of Churchill's strategic ability, writing that he had a tendency to concentrate on one problem and 'to forget the other problems which were bound up with its solution'. According to Liddell Hart, Churchill had difficulty in 'relating one part to another, and the parts to the whole'. Lacking the 'capacity for compassion', a man can be a successful tactician, but 'will be almost certain to go astray as a strategist and still more as a grand strategist'. See Hart's essay, 'The Military Strategist', in *Churchill Revised: A Critical Assessment* (New York: Dial, 1969), 221–2.

For other assessments of Churchill the strategist, see John Keegan, 'Churchill's Strategy', in Blake and Louis (eds.), *Churchill*, ch. 19; and David Jablonsky, *Churchill, the Great Game and Total War* (Portland: Frank Cass, 1991).

11. Quoted in *Churchill*, iii. 480.
12. Ibid. ii. 694; the remarks to Violet Asquith are quoted in Michael Howard, 'Churchill and the First World War', in Blake and Louis (eds.), *Churchill*, 129. On Churchill's reaction to the war, Howard writes that no Englishman could have greeted the coming of war 'more ecstatically' than Churchill (ibid.).
13. Quoted in *Churchill*, iii. 501.
14. Ibid. 481.
15. Ibid., vi. 860–1. For a suggestive essay on Churchill's attitude toward war, see Manfred Weidhorn, *A Harmony of Interests: Explorations in the Mind of Sir Winston Churchill* (Rutherford: Fairleigh Dickinson University Press, 1992), ch. 3. Weidhorn

writes that Churchill saw combat as the 'definitive altruistic gesture', but also possessed an 'undeniable love of combat for its own sake' (p. 61).

16. *Churchill*, i. 435.
17. *Complete Speeches*, iii. 2,328–34.
18. Ibid. 5,197–206.
19. *Complete Speeches*, v. 5,301–2. Quoted in *Churchill*, v. 494. On Churchill's critique of appeasement, see D. C. Watt, 'Churchill and Appeasement', in Blake and Louis (eds.), *Churchill*, ch. 12. See also Brian McKercher, 'Churchill, the European Balance of Power and the USA', in Parker (ed.), *Winston Churchill*, ch. 4.
20. *Complete Speeches*, v. 5,440–9.
21. Ibid. 5,433–6. Quoted in *Churchill*, v. 566–7.
22. *Complete Speeches*, v. 5,939–45.
23. Ibid., vi. 6,231–8.
24. One notable episode that saw Churchill take pause occurred in 1943 after the Royal Air Force had dumped 15,000 tons of bombs on Germany in twenty nights. Viewing a film showing the actual raids, Churchill 'sat bolt upright' and asked: 'Are we beasts? Are we taking this too far?' One of Churchill's guests answered that Britain 'hadn't started it, and that it was them or us.' Quoted in *Churchill*, vii. 437.

   The British government's decision to bomb German cities has been the focus of a great deal of scholarship. For the most comprehensive treatment of British policy, see Charles Webster and Noble Frankland, *The Strategic Air Offensive Against Germany, 1941–1945*, 4 vols. (London: HMSO, 1961). Of the many works that consider the subject, see Peter Calvocoressi and Guy Wint, *Total War: Causes and Courses of the Second World War* (New York: Penguin, 1972), ch. 23; George H. Quester, *Deterrence Before Hiroshima: The Airpower Background of Modern Strategy* (New York: John Wiley, 1966), see esp. ch. 9; Frederick M. Sallagar, *The Road to Total War* (New York: Van Nostrand, 1969), chs. 7–8; Max Hastings, *Bomber Command* (New York: Dial, 1979); and Thomas Wilson, *Churchill and the Prof* (London: Cassell, 1995), chs. 3–5. Also worth noting are the views of Bishop Bell of Chichester, one of the most outspoken critics of the British government's strategic bombing policy against German cities (see Ronald C. D. Jasper, *George Bell: Bishop of Chichester* (London: Oxford University Press, 1967), 275–9). See also Christopher C. Harmon, '"Are We Beasts?": Churchill and the Moral Question of World War II "Area Bombing"', Newport Paper, no. 1 (Newport: Center for Naval Warfare Studies, Dec. 1991). Harmon argues that for much, but not all, of the war, 'area bombing' was necessary, and Churchill accepted the bombing of civilian targets as a 'grim necessity of a just war' (p. 3). During a 1949 speaking tour of the United States, Churchill was reminded of the bombings over Germany and tearfully recalled: 'Tens of thousands of lives were extinguished in one night. Old men, old women, little children, yes, yes—children about to be born' (quoted in Harmon, p. 4). Michael Walzer explores the ethical dimension of the British decision to bomb German civilian targets during World War II in *Just and Unjust Wars: A Moral Argument with Historical Illustrations* (New York: Basic, 1977), 255–63, 323–7.

25. Quoted in *Churchill*, vi. 472–3; Prem 3/76A/12 War Cabinet Paper no. 373 (dated 23 Aug. 1942), Public Records Office, Kew (hereafter PRO).
26. Quoted in *Churchill*, vii. 251.
27. Prem 3/88/3 Folio 321 (27 Feb. 1943), PRO. During World War I, Churchill advocated using gas against the Turks at Gallipoli in 1915. In 1918, Churchill supported using gas against the Germans, desiring 'the fullest utilisation of the winds, which

favour us so much more than the enemy.' On the use of gas against the Turks, see *Churchill*, iii. 555–6. On the 1918 episode, see ibid., iv. 105.

28. Ibid., vii. 776–7.

29. Ibid. 840–1.

30. The best study of Britain's role in this sphere is Margaret Gowing's *Britain and Atomic Energy, 1939–1945* (New York: St. Martin's Press, 1964) (hereafter Gowing). Professor Gowing, the official historian of Britain's atomic energy programme, had (to that time) unprecedented access to archival material and produced an exhaustive study of the subject. Superbly weaving together the scientific, bureaucratic, and political strands of this complex period, Gowing has written a work that is fundamental for understanding the British side of the matter. The American counterpart to Gowing's study, *The New World, 1939–1946* (University Park, Pa.: Penn State University Press, 1962), by Richard G. Hewlett and Oscar E. Anderson, Jr. is the first volume in the history of the US Atomic Energy Commission. For a brief overview of the British role in the development of the bomb, see A. J. R. Groom's *British Thinking About Nuclear Weapons* (London: Frances Pinter, 1974) (hereafter Groom), which covers the period from 1939 to the 1960s. Also interesting, though somewhat thin on the early period, is Peter Malone's study, *The British Nuclear Deterrent* (New York: St. Martin's Press, 1984). Malone's thematic account covers the story through the 1980s.

31. Gowing, 33.

32. Margaret Gowing, 'The Origins of Britain's Status as a Nuclear Power' (Oxford: Oxford Project for Peace Studies, 1988) (hereafter Gowing Lecture), 1–2.

33. Churchill, *Second World War*, i. 301.

34. Gowing, 41–2.

35. Memo reprinted in Gowing, 389–93.

36. Quoted in Groom, 1.

37. The Maud Reports are reprinted in Gowing, 394–412.

38. Gowing Lecture, 2–3. Churchill was kept abreast of the Committee's work by Professor Lindemann (Lord Cherwell), his scientific adviser, who was in contact with Committee members. Briefed by Lindemann on the Report, Churchill minuted the Chiefs of Staff Committee on 30 Aug. 1941: 'Although personally I am quite content with the existing explosives, I feel we must not stand in the path of improvement, and I therefore think that action should be taken in the sense proposed by Lord Cherwell.' Reprinted in Churchill, *Second World War*, iv. 378–9. For an examination of Churchill's relationship with Lindemann, see the Earl of Birkenhead, *The Professor and the Prime Minister* (Boston: Houghton Mifflin, 1962). R. F. Harrod's *The Prof* (London: Macmillan, 1959) treats the same topic. Also illuminating is Thomas Wilson, *Churchill and the Prof* (London: Cassell, 1995).

39. Quoted in Gowing, 97.

40. Ibid. 168.

41. Even Clement Attlee, deputy Prime Minister during the war (and later prime minister), saw no alternative. Looking back on Britain's decision to play an active part in the bomb's development, he said, 'I do not believe that we could have afforded to neglect so revolutionary a development . . . At whatever cost we should have been bound to make the attempt to develop it . . .' (quoted in Francis Williams (ed.), *A Prime Minister Remembers* (London: Heinemann, 1961), 113 (hereafter Williams (ed.)).

42. Groom describes an 'almost complete breakdown in the exchange of information and cooperation', which 'brought a sharp reaction from Churchill' at Casablanca in

early 1943 (see Groom, 7–8). Gowing treats the difficulties fully, see ch. 5. Hewlett and Anderson also examine the Anglo-American discord in detail (see Hewlett and Anderson, ch. 8). See also John W. Wheeler-Bennett, *John Anderson Viscount Waverly* (London: Macmillan, 1962), 291–2.

43. Gowing Lecture, 3. Gowing, Groom, and Hewlett and Anderson all examine the Quebec Agreement fully. In particular, note Gowing's discussion of its qualifications and ambiguities (pp. 164–77, 233–4). Groom's assessment is also of interest (pp. 11–12). Attlee's comments are worth noting: 'It was really a rather loose Agreement.' (Williams (ed.), 108). On the 1943 agreement, see also Warren F. Kimball, *Forged in War: Roosevelt, Churchill, and the Second World War* (New York: William Morrow, 1997), 220–1; and Leslie Groves, *Now It Can Be Told: The Story of the Manhattan Project* (New York: Harper, 1962), ch. 9.

44. Reprinted in Gowing, 447.

45. It is worth noting that the Hyde Park Agreement was informal and non-binding, which made it irrelevant in practical terms. Indeed, the atomic energy personnel in Washington were unaware of the Agreement, a transcript of which could not be found for some time.

46. Cited in Groves, *Now It Can Be Told*, 132.

47. J. W. Pickersgill, *The Mackenzie-King Record 1939–1944* (Chicago: University of Chicago Press), 532.

48. Quoted in *Churchill*, vii. 761.

49. Churchill, *Second World War*, vi. 391.

50. Prem 3/356/4 Folios 114–15 (24 Feb. 1945), PRO; cited in *Churchill*, vii. 1232–3. Churchill's animosity toward the Soviet Union was long standing. As early as the Bolshevik Revolution he had strongly criticized the system and its followers. See *Churchill*, iv. 305, 308–9, 374–5; vii. 768.

51. Ibid., vii. 1233.

52. Ibid. 1,332.

53. Charles Moran, *Churchill: The Struggle for Survival, 1940–1965* (Boston: Houghton Mifflin, 1966), 301–2.

54. Churchill, *Second World War*, vi. 545.

55. Cited in *Churchill*, viii. 90.

56. Much of the criticism concerning the American decision to use the atomic bomb originated in the scholarly literature. The most celebrated revisionist critique is Gar Alperovitz, *Atomic Diplomacy* (New York: Penguin, 1985). Alperovitz raises several questions about the American decision, the most controversial of which is his suggestion that 'a major reason the bomb was used' was to rein in the Soviet Union after the war (p. 1). Although many have criticized his conclusions, Alperovitz raises important questions about America's motives for using the bomb against Japan.

　　A second work on the subject is Martin Sherwin, *A World Destroyed* (New York: Vintage, 1977). Sherwin argues that while the principal reason for the atomic attack was to win the war, policy-makers did not question the assumption that the bomb would be used against Japan. Their disinclination to question this assumption was attributable to their belief in the bomb's potential for restraining the Soviets after the war.

　　On this issue, note Churchill's view on 23 July 1945 in discussing America's possession of the bomb: Russia need not enter the war against Japan because the new explosive would settle the matter. Further the bomb would 'redress the balance with the Russians . . . and would completely alter the diplomatic equilibrium which was adrift since the defeat of Germany . . . now we could say, "If you insist on doing this or that, well . . ." And then where are the Russians!' Quoted in Sir Arthur Bryant, *Triumph in the West: A History of the War Years Based on the Diaries of Field-Marshal Lord Alanbrooke* (Garden City, NY: Doubleday, 1959), 363–4.

    On the American decision to use the bomb against Japan, see two pieces by Barton Bernstein: 'Understanding the Atomic Bomb and the Japanese Surrender', *Diplomatic History* (Spring 1995), 227–73; and 'Seizing the Contested Terrain of Early Nuclear History: Stimson, Conant, and Their Allies Explain the Decision to Use the Atomic Bomb', *Diplomatic History* (Winter 1993), 35–72.

57. Churchill, *Second World War*, vi. 553. Attlee's view on the decision is worth noting since he headed the government when the bombs were used against Japan. He supported the decision completely, claiming, 'we knew nothing . . . about the consequences of dropping the bomb except that it was larger than an ordinary bomb and had a much greater explosive force. . . . We knew nothing whatever at that time about the genetic effects of an atomic explosion. I knew nothing about fall-out and all the rest of what emerged after Hiroshima' (quoted in Williams (ed.), 73–4).

58. Gowing examines this issue in detail (see Gowing, ch. 14). She notes that Britain played virtually no role in the decision to use the bomb, writing, 'whether and where the bombs should be used was . . . left largely to the Americans' (p. 370).

59. *Complete Speeches*, vii. 7,206–8. Also note John Anderson's broadcast to the British people on 7 Aug. 1945, in which he describes for the layman the meaning of the new age (reprinted in Wheeler-Bennett, *John Anderson*, 297–9).

60. Margaret Gowing's two-volume work, *Independence and Deterrence: Britain and Atomic Energy, 1945–1952* (New York: St. Martin's Press, 1974), is fundamental for understanding Britain's atomic energy policy during this period. Groom is also helpful, as are the following: Ian Clark and Nicholas Wheeler, *British Origins of Nuclear Strategy, 1945–1955* (Oxford: Clarendon Press, 1989); Michael Dockrill and John Young (eds.), *British Foreign Policy, 1945–56* (Basingstoke: Macmillan, 1989), see esp. Gowing's essay; and Kenneth O. Morgan, *Labour in Power, 1945–1951* (Oxford: Clarendon Press, 1984), ch. 6. Richard Hewlett and Oscar Anderson's, *The Atomic Shield 1947–1952* (University Park, Pa: Penn State University Press, 1962) outlines Anglo-American relations during the Attlee years; see esp. chs. 9–10.

61. Groom, 22.

62. Ibid. 23. Gowing argues similarly in Dockrill and Young, *British Foreign Policy, 1945–56*, 38–44. She writes that Britain decided to develop an independent nuclear deterrent for three reasons: strategy, status, and the nature of Anglo-American relations. The strategic reason was based on what became known as deterrence doctrine: one needed to possess a retaliatory capability to deter potential foes. Second was the belief that to maintain her status as a major player Britain needed the bomb. As Lord Cherwell said: 'If we are unable to make the bomb ourselves and have to rely entirely on the United States for this vital weapon, we shall sink to the rank of a second-class nation . . .' Finally, the nature of Anglo-American relations (strained and stressful) led Britain to conclude that an independent deterrent was necessary.

63. Williams (ed.), 118–19.

64. Gowing, *Independence and Deterrence*, i. ch. 2.

65. Cited in Clark and Wheeler, *British Origins of Nuclear Strategy, 1945–1955*, 17.

66. Reprinted in Gowing, i. 78.

67. See letter quoted in n. 66.

68. Williams (ed.), 119.
69. Quoted in Denis Richards, *Portal of Hungerford: The Life of Marshal of the Royal Air Force Viscount Portal of Hungerford* (London: Heinemann, 1977), 362.
70. Quoted in Alan Bullock, *Ernest Bevin: Foreign Secretary 1945–1951* (London: Heinemann, 1983), 352.
71. Quoted in *Churchill*, viii. 277.
72. Ibid. 119.
73. Ibid. 422.
74. *Complete Speeches*, vii. 7,795–801.
75. Ibid. 7,379–82.
76. Ibid., viii. 8,065–9. On Churchill's view of Britain's relationship with Europe, particularly after 1945, see Max Beloff, 'Churchill and Europe', in Blake and Louis (eds.), *Churchill*, ch. 25. Several essays in Parker (ed.), *Winston Churchill* also shed light on Churchill's views on Europe in the post-war period. See also the following: Maurice Vaisse, 'Churchill and France, 1951–55' (ch. 12); Hans-Peter Schwarz, 'Churchill and Adenauer' (ch. 13); Wolfgang Krieger, 'Churchill and the Defence of the West, 1951–55' (ch. 14); Martin Gilbert, 'Churchill and the European Idea' (ch. 15).
77. *Complete Speeches*, viii. 8,056–65.
78. Ibid. 8,289–97.
79. Moran, *Churchill*, 337–8.
80. Cited in *Churchill*, viii. 362–3.
81. *Foreign Relations of the United States* (hereafter *FRUS*) 1948, iii. (Washington: GPO), 90.
82. *Churchill*, viii. 464.
83. Moran, *Churchill*, 577.
84. *Complete Speeches*, viii. 7,979–87.
85. Ibid. 8,281–6. For an illuminating discussion of the role foreign affairs played in the 1951 electoral campaign, see John W. Young, *Winston Churchill's Last Campaign: Britain and the Cold War, 1951–5* (Oxford: Oxford University Press, 1996), 38–40.
86. *Complete Speeches*, viii. 8,323–9.
87. Ibid. 8,418–19.
88. Cited in *Churchill*, viii. 837–8.
89. Gowing, i. 405–6.
90. *Complete Speeches*, viii. 8,342–55.
91. Anthony Seldon, *Churchill's Indian Summer: The Conservative Government, 1951–1955* (London: Hodder, 1981), 330.
92. Ibid. 333. According to N. J. Wheeler, the 1952 Global Strategy Paper was also quite important, given its emphasis on the value of nuclear weapons, rather than conventional forces, where the West was at a disadvantage (see N. J. Wheeler, 'British Nuclear Weapons and Anglo-American Relations 1945–1954', *International Affairs*, 62/1 (Winter 1985/6), 71–86). For a comprehensive analysis of the 1952 Global Strategy Paper, see John Baylis, *Ambiguity and Deterrence: British Nuclear Strategy, 1945–1964* (Oxford: Oxford University Press, 1995), ch. 4.
93. Quoted in Groom, 100. For a discussion of British strategic developments in 1954–5, see Baylis, *Ambiguity and Deterrence*, ch. 6. To understand the course of British atomic policy during these years, one must also consider the ideas of its chief formulator, Marshal of the Royal Air Force Sir John Slessor. A. J. R. Groom has examined Slessor's influence on British and American policy-making and described as

'seminal' his impact on the public debate concerning atomic matters (see Groom, 61–2). According to Slessor, 'war had abolished itself because the atomic and hydrogen bombs have found their way into the armouries of the world. So the greatest disservice that anyone could possibly do the cause of peace would be to abolish nuclear arms on either side . . .' In Slessor's view, atomic weapons had a dual purpose: they had to be maintained in order to prevent war and also—in the event of war—they served 'as the primary agent for the defeat of the enemy if the deterrent fails . . .' This principle would become a key tenet of nuclear strategy in the 1950s (Sir John Slessor, *Strategy for the West* (New York: William Morrow, 1954), 15, 49; see also Slessor's *Great Deterrent* (London: Cassell, 1957), in which he outlines his view of strategy from World War I to the nuclear age).

94. *Complete Speeches*, viii. 7,936–44.
95. Ibid. 8,289–97.
96. Moran, *Churchill*, 598.
97. Seldon contains a good, brief discussion of this tension (pp. 396–408). Martin Gilbert explores the subject more closely in *Churchill*, viii. M. Steven Fish has examined Anglo-American relations after Stalin's death and argues that nuclear fears, belief in a new Soviet flexibility, and concern about personal and national prestige were all factors in Churchill's desire to hold a summit (see Steven Fish, 'After Stalin's Death: The Anglo-American Debate Over a New Cold War', *Diplomatic History*, 10/4 (Fall 1986), 333–55). While Churchill undoubtedly considered these factors, his comments on summitry as early as 1950 suggest that nuclear concerns were pre-eminent. See also Martin Gilbert, 'From Yalta to Bermuda and Beyond: In Search of Peace with the Soviet Union', in James W. Muller (ed.), *Churchill as Peacemaker* (Cambridge: Cambridge University Press, 1997), ch. 10.
98. *Complete Speeches*, viii. 8,475–85.
99. Cabinet Papers, 128/27 (July 7, 1954), PRO.
100. Cabinet Papers, 128/27 (July 26, 1954), PRO.
101. *Complete Speeches*, viii. 8,576–85.
102. Ibid. 8,531–8. Churchill's policy, which combined a willingness to negotiate with the Soviets along with a determination to maintain a powerful defensive capability, is explored in Steven James Lambakis, *Winston Churchill: Architect of Peace* (Westport: Greenwood Press, 1993). See ch. 6, in which Lambakis writes that 'there is no contradiction between defensive preparations on the one hand and reconciliation on the other' (p. 136).
103. The question of Churchill's attitude toward using the bomb in the Korean conflict remains elusive. Churchill supported American intervention in 1950. In 1952 he told Truman that Truman's 'decision to resist in Korea had done more than anything else to reverse the tide in our relations with the Soviets in the postwar period'. Indeed 25 June 1950 'marked the turning point in the danger to the free world of Communist aggression . . .' (quoted in *Churchill*, viii. 680).

The question of whether to use the bomb arose at the Bermuda Conference in December 1953. Eisenhower told Churchill that a communist breach of the Armistice would lead the United States to strike with atomic weapons at military targets. Churchill responded that he 'quite accepted this', saying Eisenhower's statement 'put him in a position to say to Parliament that he had been consulted in advance and had agreed' (*FRUS*, 1952–4, v. 1,739). On 5 Dec. Eisenhower expressed 'his belief that atomic weapons were now coming to be regarded as a proper part of the conventional armament and that he thought this a sound concept'. Churchill concurred with this view (ibid. 1,768). But later that evening, Churchill, apparently at Eden's insistence, expressed reservations about the American position. The British felt the use of the bomb in Korea 'would be morally repellent to most of the world' (ibid. 1,786). Eden was 'particularly disturbed' by Eisenhower's plan, and worried about its 'effect on public opinion in England' (see *Churchill*, viii. 928–9). Eden's memoirs are silent on the matter (see *Full Circle: The Memoirs of Anthony Eden* (Boston: Houghton Mifflin, 1960)). Eisenhower hardly mentions it in his memoirs (see *Mandate for Change 1953–1956* (New York: Doubleday, 1963), 248). In *The Churchillians* (London: Weidenfeld and Nicolson, 1981), John Colville recalls taking a message from Eisenhower to Churchill at Bermuda. Eisenhower spoke of the difference between himself and Churchill: 'Winston looked on the atomic bomb as something entirely new and terrible [while I saw it as] just the latest improvement in military weapons . . . all weapons in due course became conventional' (pp. 106–7). See also Evelyn Shuckburgh's diary recollection, which records the distress felt by Churchill and Eden over the American position (quoted in David Carlton, *Anthony Eden* (London: Allen and Unwin, 1986), 335–6). *FRUS*, 1952–4, xv., provides a brief overview of the Bermuda Conference (pp. 1,654–5). In sum, it is difficult to ascertain precisely why Churchill changed his position on the matter. On the discussion of atomic matters at the conference, see Young, *Winston Churchill's Last Campaign*, 130–7. See also Henry Pelling, *Churchill's Peacetime Ministry, 1951–55* (New York: St. Martin's Press, 1997), 109–12.

104. *Complete Speeches*, viii. 8,497–505.
105. Ibid. 8,551–8.
106. Peter Boyle (ed.), *The Churchill–Eisenhower Correspondence, 1953–1955* (Chapel Hill: University of North Carolina Press, 1990), 122–4.
107. Moran, *Churchill*, 672–3.
108. *Complete Speeches*, viii. 8,625–33. In his memoirs, Defence Minister Harold Macmillan called the speech 'noble in tone and temper'. It made 'a deep impression' as Churchill 'moved his audience with the depth of his conviction' (see Harold Macmillan, *Tides of Fortune, 1945–1955* (New York: Harper and Row, 1969), 578). Macmillan agreed with the view that nuclear weapons enhanced the prospect for peace (see ibid. 569–72). Foreign Minister Anthony Eden, who would soon become premier, also believed the bomb kept the peace in Europe. See his comments in *Full Circle*, 123–4, 367–80. On the 1 Mar. speech, see also Young, *Winston Churchill's Last Campaign*, 309–10; and Pelling, *Churchill's Peacetime Ministry, 1951–55*, 166–7.

Chapter 9

1. John Wilson Lewis and Xue Litai, *China Builds the Bomb* (Stanford, Calif.: Stanford University Press, 1988). In developing their account of how China acquired nuclear weapons, Lewis and Xue had access to a great deal of information previously held secret by the Chinese government.
2. Division of War Theories, Chinese Academy of Military Science (ed.), *Sun Tzu Bingfa Xinzhu* [A New Interpretation of Sun Tzu's *Art of War*] (Beijing: Zhonghua shuju, 1977), 3–5.

3. Mao Zedong, 'On Protracted War' (May 1938), in *Selected Military Writings of Mao Tse-tung* (Beijing: Foreign Languages Press, 1963), 217–18.
4. Ibid. 225–6.
5. Ibid. 230.
6. Mao Zedong, 'Talk with American Correspondent Anna Louise Strong, August 1946', *Selected Works of Mao Tse-tung* (Beijing: Foreign Languages Press, 1961), iv. 100–1.
7. Mao's speech at the 9th session of the Central Chinese Government Council, 5 Sept. 1950, cited in Division of Military History, Chinese Academy of Military Science (ed.), *Zhongguo Renmin Zhiyuanjun Kangmei Yuanchao Zhanshi* [Combat History of the Chinese People's Volunteers in the War to Resist US Aggression and Aid Korea] (Beijing: Military Science Press, internal edition, 1988), 6–7.
8. *Pan Jijiong, Meidi Hewaijiao de Buochan* [World Affairs Study Materials Series, no. 2: The Bankruptcy of US Nuclear Diplomacy] (Beijing: World Knowledge Press, Dec. 1950), 5–6.
9. Wen Qizhe, 'Questions and Answers with Regard to Atomic Weapons', originally in *Shishi Souce* [Handbook on Current Affairs], 2 (1950), 33–7, repr. in *Xinhua Yuebao* [New China Monthly], 3/2 (25 Dec. 1950), 429–30.
10. *Renmin Ribao*, editorial, 'The Greatest Gospel for World Peace: On Stalin's Statement on Nuclear Weapons', 7 Oct. 1951, repr. in *Xinhua Yuebao*, 4/6 (25 Oct. 1951), 1,271–2.
11. Wen Qizhe, 'Questions and Answers with Regard to Atomic Weapons'.
12. Mao's speech at the meeting of regional officials, 12 Dec. 1958, 'Mao Zedong Sixiang Wansui' [Long Live Thought of Mao Zedong] (Beijing: an unofficial collection of Mao's speeches, Aug. 1969), 256.
13. Mao's outline of a speech at the 24th Session of the Central People's Government Council, Sept. (undated) 1953, *Jianguo yilai Mao Zedong Wengao* [Mao Zedong Manuscripts since the Founding of the People's Republic of China] (Beijing: internal edition, 1990), iv. 330.
14. Peng Dehuai's speech at the 24th Session of the Central People's Government Council, 12 Sept. 1953, 'Peng Dehuai Junshi Wenxuan' [Selected Military Writings of Peng Dehuai] (Beijing: Central Archives and Manuscripts, 1988), 446–7.
15. Peng Dehuai's speech at the meeting of high-ranking military commanders, 2 Dec. 1953, ibid. 466–7.
16. Deng Hua's speech at the meeting of high-ranking military commanders, Jan. [undated] 1954, 'Deng Hua, Lun Kangmei Yuanchao Zhanzheng de Zuozhan Zhidao' [On Combat Guidelines of the War to Resist US Aggression and Aid Korea] (Beijing: internal document collection, undated), 189.
17. Ibid. 190–1.
18. In October 1988, I interviewed a group of senior Chinese officials in Beijing. Yao Xu, who has worked as a military intelligence analyst for a long time, particularly confirmed that Mao did not take into serious account the threat of US use of the nuclear bomb in Korea and Indo-China. For detailed discussion, see Shu Guang Zhang, *Deterrence and Strategic Culture: Chinese-American Confrontations,1949–1958* (Ithaca, NY: Cornell University Press, 1992), chs. 4–6.
19. Xu Yan, 'Diyici Jiaoliang' [The First Encounter] (Beijing: Chinese Radio and TV Press, 1990), 326; also see CCP Central Foreign Liaison Department's report to the CCP Central Committee, 29 June 1962, *Wang Jiaxiang Xuanji* [Selected Works of Wang Jiaxiang] (Beijing: People's Press, 1989), 447–50, 452–4.

20. Contemporary China Institute (ed.), *Dangdai Zhongguo Jundui de Junshi Gongzuo* [China Today: Military Affairs] (Beijing: Chinese Social Sciences Press, 1989), i. 53–4.

21. Bo Yibo, *Ruogan Zhongda Juece yu Shijian de Huigu* [My Recollections of Decision-Making on Several Important Policies and Events] (Beijing: CCP Central Archives Press, 1991), i. 297–9.

22. Zhou's statement is cited in Tan Wenrui, 'Oppose the US Preparation for Atomic War', *Renmin Ribao*, 16 Jan. 1955; Zhou Enlai, 'Speech at the Asian-African Convention', 19 Apr. 1955, *Zhou Enlai Xuanji* [Selected Works of Zhou Enlai], ii (Beijing: People's Press, 1988), 148; 'The United States Are Bluffing Us', *Shijie Zhishi* [Semi-Monthly Commentary], 7 (5 Apr.1955), 2.

23. Mao Zedong, 'The Atomic Bomb Cannot Scare the Chinese People', 28 Jan. 1955, Michael Y. M. Kao and John K. Leung (eds.), *The Writings of Mao Zedong, 1949–1976*, i. *September 1949–October 1955* (Armonk, NY: M. E. Sharpe, 1986), 516.

24. Lewis and Xue, *China Builds the Bomb*, 37.

25. Guo Moruo, 'To Strengthen Peaceful Force and To Crack Down on the Threat of Nuclear War', *Xinhua Yuebao*, 3 (22 Feb. 1955), 1–5.

26. Mao Zedong, 'Concluding Remarks at the National Conference of the CCP', 31 Mar. 1955, Kao and Leung, *The Writings of Mao Zedong*, 540.

27. Gi Nong, 'The US Military Strategy is At Stake', *Shijie Zhishi*, 23 (5 Dec. 1957), 12–13.

28. Id., 'The Power Politics Is Facing a Dead-End: Current US Military Strategy', *Shijie Zhishi*, 2 (20 Jan. 1958), 10–11.

29. *Renmin Ribao*, editorial, 'Where Is the United States Heading?' 19 Jan. 1958, repr. in *Xinhua Yuebao*, 4 (1968), 178–9.

30. Zhou Enlai, 'Report on My Visit of Eleven Countries', 5 Mar. 1957, *Zhou Enlai Waijiao Wenxuan* [Selected Works of Zhou Enlai on Diplomacy] (Beijing: Central Archives and Manuscripts Press, 1990), 222.

31. 'The Announcement of the Ministry of Foreign Affairs to Protest Against US Deployment of Nuclear Weapons on Taiwan', *Xinhua Yuebao*, 11 (12 May 1957), 89.

32. Xiao Yuan, 'To Understand US Conspiracy of Invading Taiwan Through the Sino-American Talks', *Xinhua Yuebao*, 14 (15 July 1958), 34–6.

33. *Renmin Ribao*, commentary, 'To Watch For US War Preparations', *Xinhua Yuebao*, 5 (31 Jan. 1958), 176.

34. Mao Zedong, 'The Second Speech at the Second Session of the Eighth Party Congress', 5–23 May 1958, cited in Lewis and Xue, *China Builds The Bomb*, 69.

35. Li Jie, Lei Rongtian, and Li Yi (eds.), *Dangdai Zhongguo Hegongyie* [China Today: Nuclear Industry] (Beijing: Chinese Social Science Press, 1987), 4.

36. Ibid. 5–11.

37. Ibid. 11–12.

38. Ibid. 13.

39. Ibid. 13–14.

40. Ibid. 14.

41. Ibid. 14–15.

42. Shiyouchi Sakata, 'A Dialogue Concerning New Views of Elementary Particles', *Hongqi* [Red Flag], 6 (June 1965). For Mao's understanding of Sakata's work, see Stuart Schram (ed.), *Chairman Mao Talks to the People* (New York: 1974), 251.

43. Guo Fuwen, 'China's Sun', *Zuoping Yu Zhengming* [Literature and Commentary], 2 (1988), 3. Also see Li Mingsheng, 'Flying to the Outer Space', *Dangdai* [Contemporary], 1 (1991), 24.

44. Mao Zedong, 'On Ten Relationships', 25 Apr. 1956, 'Mao Zedong Sixiang Wansui', 45–6.
45. See Lewis and Xue, *China Builds the Bomb*, 42 (US dollar figures are used).
46. Ibid. 65.
47. Liu Xiao, *Chushi Sulian Banian* [My Eight-year Ambassadorship in the Soviet Union] (Beijing: 1986), 10–13. China's proposal on Sino-Soviet strategic co-operation, presented by Peng Dehuai, has yet to be declassified.
48. Ibid. 13.
49. Mao's speech at the meeting with the Chinese students in the University of Moscow, 17 Nov. 1957, *Xinhua Banyuekan* [New China Semimonthly], 24 (1957) 14.
50. *China Today: Nuclear Industry*, 20–1.
51. Ibid. 19–22.
52. Ibid. 32; Li Mingsheng, 'Flying to the Outer Space', 24.
53. Malinovskii's letter to Peng Dehuai, 19 Apr. 1958, cited in Xue Mouhong and Pei Jianzhang (eds.), *Dangdai Zhongguo Waijiao* [China Today: Diplomacy] (Beijing: Chinese Social Science Press, 1987), 112.
54. Minutes, Mao–Iudin meeting, 21 July 1958, ibid. 113. Mao clearly stated that 'first of all we ought to establish a principle, that is, we will be mainly responsible to the programme only with your assistance.' Newly declassified Soviet documents on this issue contradict the Chinese material. See the chapter by Zubok and Harrison in this volume.
55. Peng to Soviet Ministry of National Defence, 12 June 1958, ibid. 113.
56. Minutes, Mao–Iudin meeting, 21 July 1958, *Mao Zedong, Mao Zedong Waijiao Wenxuan* [Selected Works of Mao Zedong on Foreign Affairs] (Beijing: Zhongyang Wenxuan Press, 1994), 322–33. For English version of this minute, see Shu Guang Zhang and Chen Jian, 'The Emerging Dispute between Beijing and Moscow: Ten Newly Available Chinese Documents, 1956–1958', *CWIHP Bulletin* 6–7 (Winter 1995/6), 155–9.
57. Minutes of Mao–Khrushchev talks, 31 July 1958, Xue and Pei, *China Today: Diplomacy*, 114.
58. Andrei A. Gromyko, *Memoirs* (New York: Doubleday, 1989), 251–2; Minutes, Mao–Gromyko talks (undated) Sept. 1958, cited in Xue and Pei, *China Today: Diplomacy*, 115. After reading Gromyko's memoirs, Chinese officials have denied that Mao made the proposal as Gromyko described it in his memoirs (Division of Diplomatic History, Ministry of Foreign Affairs (ed.), *Xinzhongguo Waijiao Fengyun* [Winds and Clouds in New China's Diplomacy] (Beijing: World Knowledge Press, 1990), 136–8).
59. Khrushchev's letter to Eisenhower, 7 Sept. 1958, Xue and Pei, *China Today: Diplomacy*, 115–16.
60. Liu, *My Eight-year Ambassadorship in the Soviet Union*, 62–3.
61. Ibid. 63–5.
62. Nikita Khrushchev, *Khrushchev Remembers: The Last Testament* (Boston: Little, Brown, and Co., 1974), 268–9.
63. Li, Lei, and Li (eds.), *China Today: Nuclear Industry*, 32.
64. Xue and Pei, *China Today: Diplomacy*, 115–21.
65. Allen S. Whiting, 'Quemoy 1958: Mao's Miscalculations', *China Quarterly*, 62 (June 1975), 263–70.
66. Mao's speech at a meeting of the Politburo of the CCP Central Committee held at Wuchang, 1 Dec. 1958, see *Selected Works of Mao Tse-tung*, iv. 98–9.

67. Mao Zedong, 'On the Ten Major Relations', ibid. v. 288.
68. Cited from Lewis and Xue, *China Builds the Bomb*, 71.
69. Ibid. 70 for quotation.
70. Li, Lei, and Li (eds.), *China Today: Nuclear Industry*, 36.
71. Ibid. 36.
72. Ibid. 36; and also see Zhang Jun *et al.*, *Dangdai Zhongguo de Hangtian Shiye* [China Today: Space Cause] (Beijing: Chinese Social Science Press, 1986), 16.
73. Huang Chaihong and Zeng Guoqiang, 'How China's Nuclear Submarines Came into Being', *Renmin Ribao*, 28 Sept. 1989, 3.
74. Yang Mingwei, 'The Decision-Making on Building and Developing Chinese Atomic Programs', *Dang de Wenxian* [The Party's Documents and Materials], 3 (1994), 30.
75. Liu Shuqing and Zhang Jifu, 'A Loud Crash of Thunder—Report on the Detonation of Our Country's First Atomic Bomb', in Ministry of Nuclear Industry (ed.), *Mimi Licheng* [A Secret Course] (Beijing: 1985), 3–5. Also see Lewis and Xue, *China Builds the Bomb*, 142.
76. Ibid. 142.
77. CCP Central Committee to the Soviet Government, 6 June 1963, Xue and Pei, *China Today: Diplomacy*, 121.
78. 'Statement of the Government of the People's Republic of China', *Renmin Ribao*, 16 Oct. 1964, 1. For the English version, see Appendix A, in Lewis and Xue, *China Builds the Bomb*, 241–3.
79. Li, Lei and Li (eds.), *China Today: Nuclear Industry*, 59.
80. Ibid.
81. Ibid. 61.
82. Ibid. 64.
83. Hu Sisheng, 'One Word to Shock the World: Comrade Chen Yi at a Press Conference', in *Huiyi Chen Yi* [Recollections of Chen Yi] (Beijing: People's Press, 1980), 215.
84. Sun Tzu, 'On Strategy [*mou gong bian*]', *Sun Tzu Bingfa Xinzhu*, 22.
85. Xue Litai, 'Chinese Nuclear Strategy', paper presented at the 'Workshop on Strategic Culture and China's Conflict Resolution Behavior',13 May 1992, Athens, Oh., 2.
86. Ibid. for citation. Also see John Wilson Lewis and Xue Litai, *China's Strategic Seapower: The Politics of Force Modernization in the Nuclear Age* (Stanford, Calif.: Stanford University Press, 1994), 231–4.
87. *China Today: Military Affairs*, i. 66.

Chapter 10

1. From the conclusion to de Gaulle's book *Le Fil de l'épée* (Paris: Berger-Levrault, 1932). This quote taken from the 1944 paperback edition (Paris: Berger-Levrault), 157. Throughout this essay, translations will be mine unless otherwise noted.
2. The account of the scientists' meeting with de Gaulle is found in Bertrand Goldschmidt, *The Atomic Complex* (LaGrange Park: American Nuclear Society, 1982), 60–1 (translated from *Le complexe atomique* (Paris: Fayard, 1980)). The phrase 'apocalyptic work' [travail d'apocalypse] is also de Gaulle's and can be found on p. 61 of *Atomic Complex*.
3. Interview with Goldschmidt, May 1991.

4. Curiously, de Gaulle appears to have made no public comment about Hiroshima on the day of the first bomb, and even failed to allude to it in a speech three days later. Indeed, looking back at de Gaulle's press conferences and speeches of late 1945 what stands out where the atomic bomb is concerned is simply the dearth of references to it. With the country devastated by war and facing problems of justice, hunger, security, diplomacy, and government, the new American weapon was apparently not what interested de Gaulle or the French press corps most. The only evidence of de Gaulle's immediate reaction we have are reports by his 'close collaborators' that the General was 'profoundly moved' by this event, and his own account published in his memoirs:

> I must say that the revelation of these frightful devices moved me to the very depths of my soul. To be sure, I had long since been aware that the Americans were in the process of realizing irresistible explosives by splitting the atom. But if not surprised, I was none the less tempted by despair upon seeing the means appear that would, perhaps, permit man to destroy mankind.

For the assertion (albeit unattributed) that de Gaulle's collaborators found him 'profoundly moved', see Aline Coutrot, 'La création du Commissariat à l'Energie Atomique', in Institut d'Histoire du Temps Présent and Institut Charles-de-Gaulle, *De Gaulle et la nation face aux problèmes de défense: 1945–1946* (Paris: Plon, 1983), 130. For the General's account, see Charles de Gaulle, *Mémoires de guerre: Le salut* (Paris: Plon, 1959), iii. 227.

5. See the speech given in Béthune on 11 Aug. 1945, whose text is reprinted in de Gaulle, *Mémoires de guerre*, iii. 596.

6. See the press conference of 12 Oct. 1945 in Charles de Gaulle, *Discours et messages* (Paris: Plon, 1970), i. 637–8. In a version of the statement transcribed by Bertrand Goldschmidt, the last line is: 'We or our descendants will see whether such merit is to be recognized in the future.' See Bertrand Goldschmidt, 'La genèse et l'héritage', in Université de Franche-Comté and Institut Charles de Gaulle, *L'aventure de la bombe: De Gaulle et la dissuasion nucléaire, 1958–1969*, Colloque organisé à Arc-et-Senans par l'Université de Franche-Comté et l'Institut Charles-de-Gaulle les 27, 28 et 29 septembre 1984 (Paris: Plon, 1985), 23.

7. Another one of de Gaulle's own admitted first reflections about the Hiroshima bomb was seen in terms of how it might benefit France: 'However, these bitter thoughts [about nuclear cataclysm] could not prevent me from exploiting the situation created by the effect of the bombs. For the capitulation [of Japan] removes all at once both Japanese defences and the American veto that kept us from the Pacific. Indo-China becomes accessible overnight.' See de Gaulle, *Mémoires de guerre*, iii. 227.

8. The quote, of course, is from the opening to de Gaulle's War Memoirs. See the English version as Charles de Gaulle, *War Memoirs: The Call to Honor, 1940–1942* 1 (New York: Viking Press, 1955), 9. De Gaulle's history of the French army is *La France et son armée* (Paris: Plon, 1938).

9. On the beginnings of the CEA, see Goldschmidt, *Atomic Complex*, 121–7.

10. The statute gives the CEA 'financial and administrative authority . . . under the direction of the President of the Provisional Government' (later the prime minister), and refers to 'the uses of atomic energy in various fields of science, industry and national defence'. See *France's First Atomic Explosion*, French White Paper (New York: Ambassade de France, Service de Presse et d'Information, 1960); Coutrot, *La création du Commissariat*, 131–2; and Goldschmidt, *Atomic Complex*, 122.

11. See Coutrot, *La création du Commissariat*, 132.

12. Admittedly well after the fact, de Gaulle confirmed in 1954 that this was the case: 'France needs a system of defence to be sure in proportion to her resources, and associated with that of her allies, but autonomous and balanced. That is why I created the High Commission (CEA) in 1945. Thanks to its accomplishments, it depends entirely upon us to endow ourselves with nuclear arms.' See the press conference of 7 May 1954 in *Discours et messages*, ii. 606.

13. In Jean Lacouture's felicitous phrase, de Gaulle was not about to 'play Gamelin and Pétain'. See Lacouture, *De Gaulle: Le Souverain* (Paris: Seuil, 1986), iii. 456.

14. In the United States, Admiral William Leahy doubted the effectiveness of the new weapon, General George Marshall saw it as primarily useful as 'preparation for landings' on Japan, General Dwight Eisenhower—publicly, at least—stated by 1953 that atomic weapons had 'virtually acquired conventional status within our armed services', and Admiral Arthur Radford and General Curtis Le May argued for years that the bomb was 'usable' in conventional situations. In France, the first published analysis of nuclear weapons by a military leader—Admiral Raoul Castex—recognized that it was 'a completely new device', but went on to compare it at length to the nerve gas used in World War I. De Gaulle, as far as I could tell, never referred to the bomb in such ways, either publicly or privately. On Leahy and Marshall see John Mueller, *Retreat from Doomsday: The Obsolescence of Major War* (New York: Basic Books, 1988), 87. On Eisenhower and Radford, see John Lewis Gaddis, *The Long Peace: Inquiries Into the History of the Cold War* (New York: Oxford University Press, 1987), 124 (for Eisenhower) and 130 (for Radford.) For Le May, see McGeorge Bundy, *Danger and Survival: Choices About the Bomb in the First Fifty Years* (New York: Vintage, 1988), 541–2. And for Castex, see 'Aperçus sur la bombe atomique', *Revue de défense nationale* (Oct. 1945), repr. in Dominique David (ed.), *La politique de défense de la France: Textes et documents* (Paris: Fondation pour les Études de Défense Nationale, 1989), 65–70. Castex also argued that 'Strategically, atomic bombing takes its place in the bombing we already know, amplifying its effects, but conserving the same character' (David, *Politique de défense*, 66).

15. This point is particularly important in the debate about John Mueller's thesis because if de Gaulle revised his view of war only in 1954—and not in 1945—then this revision would have more to do with the development of nuclear weapons than with the shock of World War II, as Mueller's argument would suggest.

16. See the press conference of 23 July 1964 in *Discours et messages*, iv. 231.

17. On de Gaulle's 'obsession with national defence' (Jean Touchard's words) and pessimism about a coming war in Europe, see Jean Touchard, *Le gaullisme: 1940–1969* (Paris: Seuil, 1978), 106–7; and Jean Lacouture, *De Gaulle: le Politique* (Paris: Seuil, 1985), ii. 286–375. Also see the foreboding speeches and press conferences of the years 1947–54 in *Discours et messages*, ii.

18. See de Gaulle's speech in Rennes on 27 July 1947 in *Discours et messages*, ii. 102.

19. See Claude Mauriac, *Aimer de Gaulle* (Paris: Grasset, 1978), 48, as cited in Lacouture, *De Gaulle: le Politique*, ii. 286.

20. See de Gaulle's declaration of 17 Aug. 1950 in *Discours et messages*, ii. 379.

21. See Georges Pompidou, *Pour rétablir une verité* (Paris: Flammarion, 1982), 129–30, as cited in Lacouture, *De Gaulle*, ii. 357.

22. That de Gaulle's private comments seem just as pessimistic about war as his public rhetoric suggests that the latter was not merely anti-communist domestic politics. Interviews conducted in the spring of 1991 with men close to the General—

including Pierre Messmer, Etienne Burin des Roziers, and Pierre Lefranc—suggest that de Gaulle's concerns about a coming war were genuinely felt.

23. See de Gaulle's 17 Aug. 1950 speech, *Discours et messages*, ii. 380.

24. See Pompidou, *Pour rétablir une verité*, 130.

25. The concept of 'nuclear danger' is emphasized by Bundy in *Danger and Survival*.

26. This conclusion only applied, of course, to confrontations between two nuclear powers. That non-nuclear states—or even a nuclear and a non-nuclear state—could still fight conventional wars was, alas, all too obvious.

27. See de Gaulle's hard-line statement on Berlin at the beginning of his March 1959 press conference in *Discours et messages*, iii. 82–96. On de Gaulle and the Berlin crisis, see Cyril Buffet: 'La politique nucléaire de la France durant la seconde crise de Berlin (1958–1962)', *Relations internationales*, 59 (Fall 1989), 347–58.

28. See Charles de Gaulle, *Lettres, notes et carnets* (Paris: Plon, 1980–6), Jan. 1958–Dec. 1960, viii. 204. De Gaulle tells how he used the same logic with a sceptical Eisenhower and Macmillan in December 1959: 'You don't want to die for Berlin,' said de Gaulle to his two guests at Rambouillet, 'but rest assured that the Russians don't want to either.' See de Gaulle, *Mémoires d'espoir: Le renouveau, 1958–1962* (Paris: Plon, 1970), 236.

29. See the press conference of 25 Mar. 1959, in *Discours et messages*, iii. 86.

30. See Arthur M. Schlesinger, Jr., *A Thousand Days: John F. Kennedy in the White House* (Boston: Houghton Mifflin, 1965), 812. The Cuban missile crisis indeed seems an important step towards de Gaulle's conviction that the superpowers would refrain from war; the two giants had approached the nuclear chasm in October 1962 and they did not like the view. De Gaulle would surely have shared the retrospective conclusion of his foreign minister, Maurice Couve de Murville: 'this demonstrated, this time decisively, that the Soviet Union did not want war'. See Maurice Couve de Murville, *Une politique étrangère* (Paris: Plon, 1971), 189.

31. 'Les Russes n'oseront pas' [The Russians will not dare] is Jean Lacouture's apt paraphrase of de Gaulle's thinking. See Lacouture, *De Gaulle*, iii. 387. Like Eisenhower, de Gaulle thus seemed convinced that Soviet leaders were not risk-takers, particularly when the risk was so great.

32. See Charles de Gaulle, *Mémoires d'espoir* (Paris: Plon, 1970), 212–13.

33. See the press conference of 10 Nov. 1959 in *Discours et messages*, iii. 129–30. On another occasion (in 1960), after noting that in both East and West people were realizing that nuclear war would be a 'disaster for everyone', de Gaulle argued that 'it was then that in Soviet Russia one heard a new song. A statesman [Khrushchev], having reached the highest authority, proclaimed the necessity of peaceful coexistence . . .' According to de Gaulle, then, Khrushchev's nuclear learning process had also taken place. See the televised speech of 31 May 1960 in *Discours et messages*, iii. 218. When nearly ten years later de Gaulle recounted his reasons for believing in détente, the first was once again the 'certainty, on the Russian side, that a conflict would result in general annihilation'. See de Gaulle, *Mémoires d'espoir*, i. 233.

34. See the broadcast of 26 Mar. 1962 in *Discours et messages*, iii. 396. The Soviet Empire was also 'the most terribly imperialist and colonialist power that had ever been known . . .' See the broadcast of 4 Nov. 1960 in *Discours et messages*, iii. 260.

35. It is plausible—although not known for sure—that de Gaulle was kept informed about progress on French nuclear military research throughout the mid-1950s by 'insiders' such as Gaston Palewski, minister delegate to the President of the Council in charge of atomic energy; Pierre Koenig, minister of armed forces under Premier

Edgar Faure; and Olivier Guichard, director of external relations of the CEA (and de Gaulle's chef de cabinet from 1951–8). Others sympathetic to de Gaulle and closely involved in the French nuclear adventure included Generals Pierre Billotte, Albert Buchalet, Pierre Gallois, and Charles Ailleret.

36. Gallois recounts this entertaining episode in Université de Franche-Comté, *L'aventure de la bombe*, 199–200. Also see Lacouture, *De Gaulle*, iii. 455.

37. See de Gaulle's press conference of 23 July 1964, in *Discours et messages*, iv. 223; translation 'President de Gaulle Holds Tense Press Conference', *Speeches and Press Conferences* (New York: Ambassade de France, Service de Press et d'Information, 1964), no. 208, p. 9.

38. See de Gaulle's press conference of 14 Jan. 1963, in *Discours et messages*, iv. 74; translation from Charles de Gaulle, *Major Addresses, Statements and Press Conferences of General Charles de Gaulle: May 1958–January 31, 1964* (New York: Ambassade de France, Service de presse et d'information, 1964), 218.

39. On the weakness of French conventional forces in the context of nuclear spending, see Michael M. Harrison, *The Reluctant Ally: France and Atlantic Security* (Baltimore and London: The Johns Hopkins University Press, 1981), 122–3.

40. This was de Gaulle's conclusion put forth in a 27 Jan. 1968 speech to the Centre des Hautes Etudes Militaires. See the text of the speech—unrecorded but re-established by General Lucien Bourgue from the notes of several listeners—in Université de Franche-Comté, *L'aventure de la bombe*, 210–11. De Gaulle would surely have subscribed to the 1984 formula of French Defence Minister Charles Hernu, who said that 'those who would prefer an infantry division to a nuclear submarine have got their eras all mixed up'. (And he would doubtless have revelled in the fact that it was a Socialist who said it!) Hernu's comment was quoted in *L'Express*, 15 Oct. 1982, p. 100.

41. 'Notre temps et notre monde sont dominés par un fait immense qui tient en suspens le destin de chaque peuple et de chaque individu'. From a 15 May 1962 press conference at the Elysée, see *Discours et messages*, iii. 402–3.

42. Radio and television speech, 31 May 1960, *Discours et messages*, iii. 218.

43. From de Gaulle's press conference of 14 Jan. 1963, see *Major Addresses*, 217.

44. From a press conference of 23 July 1964, in *Discours et messages*, iv. 231 (emphasis added).

45. For Dulles, the hypothetical city would perhaps be divided between an unscrupulous mafia (the USSR) and a virtuous police force (the United States). But one suspects de Gaulle would have preferred the analogy to rival gangs . . .

46. From a press conference of 28 Oct. 1966, see *Discours et messages*, v. 105; translation from General Charles de Gaulle, *Speeches and Press Conferences*, no. 253A, 6.

47. Professor Alfred Grosser has put a similar conclusion this way: 'Nuclear weapons,' he suggests, 'did not change de Gaulle's vision of international relations. De Gaulle's view of international relations changed France's view of nuclear weapons'. Discussion with Grosser, May 1991.

48. The literature on the motivations behind the French nuclear force is, of course, enormous. For just a few good sources, see Kohl, *French Nuclear Diplomacy*; Harrison, *The Reluctant Ally*; David S. Yost, *France's Deterrent Posture and Security in Europe*, Adelphi Papers No. 194 and 195 (London: IISS, 1984), and Philip H. Gordon, *A Certain Idea of France: French Security Policy and the Gaullist Legacy* (Princeton: Princeton University Press, 1993).

49. The domestic political justification of the *force de frappe* was de Gaulle's argument that a nuclear country needed the sort of strong executive constitution and

authoritative leader (that he wanted for France). Who else but a strong popular leader could take responsibility for initiating nuclear war? There is thus a clear link between the French referendum on a directly elected president in 1962 and France's joining of the nuclear club less than two years before. See de Gaulle's own public justifications for a strong president as including the 'renovation of [French] defence'. Televised speech of 4 Oct. 1962 in *Discours et messages*, iii. 30. Technological justifications were also often used, if sometimes hyperbolically: 'A nuclear armament programme provides technical know-how that in a thousand ways makes one competitive on world markets . . .', de Gaulle asserted to Eisenhower in 1960. See the account of the Rambouillet meeting in Vernon A. Walters, *Services discrets* (Paris: Plon, 1979), 254, cited in Lacouture, *De Gaulle*, iii. 352.

50. From de Gaulle's public telegram to Armed Forces Minister Pierre Guillaumat: 'Hurrah for France! Since this morning she is stronger and prouder. From the bottom of my heart, my thanks to you and to those who have obtained for her this magnificent success.' Cited in *Le Monde*, 14–15 Feb. 1960. See Wilfred L. Kohl, *French Nuclear Diplomacy* (Princeton: Princeton University Press, 1971), 103.

51. See the letter to Philippe de Gaulle of 14 Feb. 1960 in Charles de Gaulle, *Lettres, notes et carnets*, June 1958–Dec. 1960, viii. 330–1.

52. From the preface to Université de Franche-Compté, *L'aventure de la bombe*, 16. I have used the translation found in Bundy, *Danger and Survival*, 481.

53. See General Albert Buchalet, 'Les premières étapes (1955–1960) in Université de Franche-Comté, *L'aventure de la bombe*, 52.

54. It was not only necessary for France to *join* the United States, Soviet Union, and United Kingdom, but also important to distinguish itself from the non-nuclear countries, most notably the Federal Republic of Germany. For de Gaulle, French nuclear status would always be a compensatory factor for superior German economic strength. Bertrand Goldschmidt tells how de Gaulle asked him repeatedly during the 1950s and 1960s whether the Germans could build the bomb and how long it would take, suggesting a preoccupation with this distinction. That de Gaulle cut off French nuclear co-operation with the Germans immediately upon returning to power, and never resumed it, also suggests he was content to see this difference maintained. Interview with Goldschmidt, May 1991; and Kohl, *French Nuclear Diplomacy*, 54–64.

55. See de Gaulle's speech in Strasbourg of 23 Nov. 1961 in André Passeron, *De Gaulle parle: des institutions, de l'Algérie, de l'armée, des affaires étrangères, de la Communauté, de l'économie et des questions sociales* (Paris: Plon, 1962), 360–1.

56. See Kohl, *French Nuclear Diplomacy*, 103.

57. See the press conference of 21 Feb. 1966, in *Discours et messages*, v. 18. This comment by Daniel Colard is also indicative of the Gaullist argument: 'In short, . . . the strategic nuclear force was a "multiplier" of influence, providing General de Gaulle's initiatives on the international scene with unmatched weight and credibility. [The nuclear force] emerges as the jewel of Gaullist diplomacy and as a completely unreplaceable trump card with which to earn the respect of others in the world'. See Université de Franche-Comté, *L'aventure de la bombe*, 350.

58. See the 13 June 1961 note written by de Gaulle to Prime Minister Michel Debré and Foreign Minister Maurice Couve de Murville in de Gaulle, *Lettres, notes et carnets*, Jan. 1961–Dec. 1963, ix. 96. The note was written in the context of France's attempts to organize tripartite consultations with the United States and Great Britain that de Gaulle believed the Americans were not taking seriously.

59. See the 15 Feb. 1963 statement in *Discours et messages*, iii. 85.
60. See de Gaulle, *Mémoires d'espoir*, i. 221.
61. Ibid. 228.
62. For Debré ('les états privés de la bombe sont des satellites'), see Lacouture, *De Gaulle*, iii. 298; and for Sanguinetti, see his *La France et l'arme atomique* (Paris: René Julliard, 1964), 32.
63. From a speech to the 24 Sept. 1958 United Nations General Assembly, in Couve de Murville, *Une politique étrangère*, 31. The title of a Pierre Messmer article is also indicative: 'The Atom: Cause and Means of an Autonomous Military Policy', *The Atlantic Community Quarterly* (Summer 1968), 270–7, repr. from *Revue de défense nationale* (March 1968), 395–402.
64. 'Independence implies obviously that [France] possess . . . modern means of deterrence', De Gaulle, *Mémoires d'espoir*, i. 214.
65. The introduction to the 1965–70 military programme law states that 'Whatever our fidelity to our alliances and our confidence in our allies, to depend on some of them to set off a nuclear response would be . . . to make ourselves dependent upon them.' See the text in Alfred Grosser, *Affaires extérieures: La politique de la France, 1944–1984* (Paris: Flammarion, 1984), 195.
66. See de Gaulle's speech in Strasbourg of 23 Nov. 1961, in *Discours et messages*, iii. 369.
67. See Mueller, *Retreat from Doomsday*, 226.
68. What is important here, though, is the caveat 'as long as the present conjuncture lasts . . .' See Raymond Aron, *Penser la Guerre: Clausewitz, L'âge planétaire* (Paris: Gallimard, 1976), ii. 179.
69. See Bundy, *Danger and Survival*, 499–500.
70. That our assessment of the French *force de frappe* must be based on deduction does not undermine its conclusions. The same is true, after all, in explaining the functioning of deterrence in preventing war between the United States and the Soviet Union: it is nearly impossible, without using deduction, to demonstrate why something did *not* happen.
71. Vernon Walters recalls de Gaulle telling President Eisenhower as early as 1956 that 'When I come back to power [when, not if!], I will have to shake up the French, give them the feeling of participation in their future. To do this, I will whip them with words. I will say things which will seem disagreeable to you. But remember the goal in which I will do this: to give back to the French the taste of excellence, the taste of grandeur.' See the collection of reflections on de Gaulle in Jean Lacouture et Roland Mehl, *De Gaulle ou l'éternel défi* (Paris: Seuil, 1988), 140.
72. Several Gaullists with whom I spoke assert specifically, for example, that the withdrawal from NATO commands in 1966 would have been impossible before France had its own bombs. How could it have claimed—before public opinion—to have been 'independent' without the possession of a nuclear deterrent?
73. In fact, it might have worked the other way around. De Gaulle explained his wartime stubbornness to Churchill by the fact that he was 'too poor to bend'. See Charles de Gaulle, *Mémoires de guerre: l'Appel, 1940–1942* paperback edn. (Paris: Plon, 1954), i. 70.
74. For strategic reasons, the Americans in late 1944 nearly pulled their forces out of Strasbourg, leaving the city open to a brutal Nazi reoccupation. De Gaulle, who finally managed to persuade Eisenhower not to pull back, understood the larger American aims but saw this as a case in which particular French interests might be sacrificed if France did not control its own defence.

75. In this sense, the French deterrent has been more like a seat-belt in a car with airbags installed. It is 'useless' so long as there are no accidents or if the airbags work. But the relevance of the seat-belt would become quickly clear should either of these conditions not hold.
76. See the 27 Jan. 1968 speech at the Centre des Hautes Etudes Militaires, in Université de Franche-Comté, *L'aventure de la bombe*, 210.
77. On the *vastes entreprises*, de Gaulle wrote in his memoirs that 'only great enterprises are able to compensate for the ferment of dispersion that [the French] people carry within themselves.' See de Gaulle, *Mémoires de guerre*, 5. The reference to NATO's recognition of the contribution of the French deterrent refers to the Ottawa declaration of 1974.

Chapter 11

1. Letter to Efferoth, 16 Apr. 1946, *Adenauer: Briefe 1945–1947* (Rhöndorfer edn.), ed. Rudolf Morsey and Hans-Peter Schwarz (Berlin: Siedler Verlag, 1984), 223. To compensate for missing material see also the overview of Adenauer's daily schedule in 1945, which was compiled by the Stiftung Bundeskanzler-Adenauer-Haus [Chancellor Adenauer Memorial Foundation] in Rhöndorf. The letters provide the best reference for Adenauer's thinking in the immediate aftermath of World War II. The Foundation also hosts the Adenauer papers.

   Adenauer's letters during the period of National Socialism prove his neglect of issues on warfare. For details see *Adenauer im Dritten Reich* (Rhöndorfer edn.), ed. Rudolf Morsey and Hans-Peter Schwarz (Berlin: Siedler, 1991). The edition also provides an excellent biographical sketch of Adenauer's career up to 1945 (pp. 7–22).

   Concerning the archival material on Adenauer's political career, I would like to offer the following thoughts. The first reference for any Adenauer scholar are his papers as well as the material covering his career in the Christian Democratic Party, which are located in the party archives at the Konrad Adenauer Foundation in St Augustin outside Bonn. The primary published sources are the four volumes of Adenauer's letters (1945–1953) and the four volumes of Adenauer's so-called 'tea-talks' with journalists during the years 1950–63. The three volume memoirs also provide excellent reference because Adenauer simply copied extracts of (classified) material. However, like other politicians or diplomats, the pensioner also considered his memoirs as a political instrument. Compare Hans-Peter Schwarz, 'Das Aussenpolitische Konzept Konrad Adenauers', in: *Adenauer-Studien I.*, ed. Rudolf Morsey and Konrad Repgen (Mainz: Matthias-Grünewald-Verlag, 1971), 71–108, at pp. 73–6. Hans-Peter Schwarz also offers the most recent assessment of the memoirs in the second volume of his Adenauer biography, *Adenauer: Der Staatsmann: 1952–1967* (Stuttgart: Deutsche Verlags-Anstalt, 1991), 937–61. The archives of the German Foreign Ministry and those of the Ministry of Defence hold the material covering the setting of Adenauer's nuclear policy. Hans-Peter Schwarz, the foremost Adenauer expert, in his capacity as the editor of both Documents on the Foreign Relations of the Federal Republic of Germany and as editor of selected material of the above-mentioned foundations definitely has the best access to all of these holdings. The last part of this essay draws on the archival material quoted in the second volume of Schwarz's biography, which is otherwise not yet available: *Adenauer: Der Staatsmann, 1952–1967* (Stuttgart: Deutsche Verlags-Anstalt, 1991).

2. See Peter Weilmann, *Die Anfänge der Europäischen Atomgemeinschaft: Zur Gründungs-geschichte von EURATOM, 1955–1957* (Baden-Baden: Nomos Verlagsgesellschaft, 1983), 49–57.

3. *Adenauer und die Hohen Kommissare 1952: Akten zur Auswärtigen Politik der Bundesrepublik Deutschland, 1952*, ed. Hans-Peter Schwarz (München: R. Oldenbourg Verlag, 1990), 135–40.

4. See *Anfänge westdeutscher Sicherheitspolitik, 1945–1956*, ed. Militärgeschichtliches Forschungsamt (München: Oldenbourg, 1990).

5. Report delivered in the Council meeting of the Christian Democratic Party, 14 June 1952, in *Konrad Adenauer: Reden, 1917–1967. Eine Auswahl*, ed. Hans-Peter Schwarz (Stuttgart: Deutsche Verlags-Anstalt, 1975), 246.

6. The biographical focus of the overall project of which this article is a part implies the neglect of strategic issues for nuclear policy of and in Germany. For further details see the following NHP working papers: Robert A. Wampler, *NATO Strategic Planning and Nuclear Weapons, 1950–1957*, Nuclear History Program Occasional Paper 6 (School of Public Affairs, University of Maryland: Center for International Security Studies, 1990); Christian Tuschhoff, *Die MC 70 und die Einführung Nuklearer Trägersysteme in die Bundeswehr, 1956–1959* (Ebenhausen: Stiftung Wissenschaft und Politik, 1990); idem, *In Search for Influence: Germany's Policy of Nuclear Developments in the Late 1950s and Early 1960s*, Working paper prepared for the Third Study and Review Conference of the Nuclear History Program, 26–9 June 1991; Gregory W. Pedlow, *Multinational Contingency Planning During the Second Berlin Crisis: The Live Oak Organization, 1959–1963*, Draft for the Third Study and Review Conference, Ebenhausen 26–9 June 1991; Peter Fischer, *Zwischen Abschreckung und Verteidigung: Die Anfänge Bundesdeutscher Nuklearpolitik (1952–1957)*, paper presented at Conference, 'Das Nordatlantische Bündnis [The North Atlantic Alliance], 1949–1956', Militärgeschichtliches Forschungsamt in Freiburg, 11–13. Sept. 1990.

7. General Graf Johann Adolf von Kielmansegg's testimony in a German NHP-Oral History project (*Die Nuklearpolitik der Bundesrepublik Deutschland*, testimony of: General a.D. Graf Johann Adolf Kielmansegg; Dr. Ulrich Sahm; General a.D. Johannes Steinhoff; General a.D. Heinz Trettner; Dr. Hans-Georg Wieck; General a.D. Harald Wust; 13 July 1987, MS, p. 5).

8. See, for example, General Kielmansegg's laconic response to Uwe Nerlich's question, whether the willingness in principle of the United States to equip non-American forces with tactical nuclear weapons in the aftermath of the fall meeting of the NATO-council had been discussed in the 'Office Blank': 'No, not intensively at all' (ibid. 15).

9. Konrad Adenauer, *Erinnerungen, 1945–1953* (Stuttgart: Deutsche Verlags-Anstalt, 1965), 348. The determining factor of Soviet expansionism is a constant theme in all of Adenauer's writings.

10. *Adenauer: Der Aufstieg, 1876–1952*, 728.

11. Marc Cioc, *Pax Atomica: The Nuclear Defence Debate in West Germany During the Adenauer Era* (New York: Columbia University Press, 1988), 38.

12. Paul Adenauer's contribution in *Konrad Adenauer's Regierungsstil*, ed. Hans-Peter Schwarz, Rhöndorfer Conversations, vol. 11, Stiftung Bundeskanzler-Adenauer-Haus (Bonn: Bouvier Verlag, 1991), 131–2.

13. Hans-Peter Schwarz, 'Adenauer und die Kernwaffen', *Vierteljahrshefte für Zeitgeschichte*, 37 (Oct. 1989), 567–93, at p. 586. The article is based on a presenta-tion Hans-Peter Schwarz gave on a panel 'The Nuclear Age: Origins and

Development, 1945–1967' at the annual meeting of the German Historical Society in 1988.

14. John Mueller, 'The Essential Irrelevance of Nuclear Weapons', *International Stability*, 13. (Fall 1988), 55–79, at p. 59. Compare also *Retreat from Doomsday: The Obsolescence of Major War* (New York: Basic Books, 1988).

15. *Die Nuklearpolitik der Bundesrepublik*, 17.

16. *Zwischen Abschreckung und Verteidigung: Die Anfänge bundesdeutscher Nuklearpolitik (1952–1957)*, 10.

17. General a.D. Johannes Steinhoff's testimony in *Die Nuklearpolitik der Bundesrepublik*, 45–7 and 49.

18. See Christian Greiner, 'General Adolf Heusinger (1897–1982): Operatives Denken und Planen 1948–1956', in *Operatives Denken und Handeln in deutschen Streitkräften im 19. und 20. Jahrhundert*, ed. Militärgeschichtliches Forschungsamt (Herford/Bonn, 1988), 225–61.

19. Catherine McArdle Kelleher, *Germany and the Politics of Nuclear Weapons* (New York/London: Columbia Press, 1975), 282. Marc Cioc for example concludes that 'Heusinger had added the bomb to his mental arsenal without integrating its fallout into his logic' (*Pax Atomica*, 36).

20. Compare 'Beurteilung der strategischen Weltlage', Memorandum by Heusinger (26 June 1954), in Heusinger Papers (MGFA Freiburg). Quoted in *Zwischen Abschreckung und Verteidigung*, 14. Heusinger's conclusion reflects one of Adenauer's early statements on nuclear weapons. Like the Chancellor he warned of 'the partial overevaluation of nuclear weapons' and the current trend to base the overall defence of the West exclusively on them, because he too expected an eventual nuclear stalemate, which would consequently accord conventional weapons the crucial role in Western defence.

21. *Pax Atomica*, 38.

22. Ibid. 14.

23. Adenauer's biographer Hans-Peter Schwarz asserts on one hand that the Chancellor realized 'already relatively early' the horrendous character of the weapons (*Adenauer und die Kernwaffen*, 586), but on the other hand emphasized in his presentation 'Adenauer and the Berlin Crisis' at the Third Study and Review Conference of the Nuclear History Program that 'in Adenauer's perspective everything started with Sputnik.' Peter Fischer, who over the last years has examined some other relevant papers like those of Heusinger, Speidel, de Maizière and Blankenhorn, argues that West Germany had already lost its nuclear 'innocence' in the aftermath of the reassessment of the American nuclear policy in the early 1950s (*Zwischen Abschreckung und Verteidigung*, 2), whereas he argued in his presentation 'Prohibition or Abstention? The German Case' at the same NHP conference that it was the Radford crisis which 'turned Adenauer's policy around'.

24. Speech delivered before the Association de la Presse Diplomatique Française and the Association de la Presse Etrangère in Paris, 11 Dec. 1953, quoted in *Adenauer und die Kernwaffen*, 586.

25. *Adenauer: 'Wir haben wirklich etwas geschaffen.' Die Protokolle des CDU-Bundesvorstandes, 1953–1957* (Droste: Düsseldorf, 1990), 1,081.

26. Ibid.

27. Derek Fred and S. David Broscious, *Nuclear Weapons, Nuclear War and Statecraft: A Review of the Debate* (NHP Working Paper, 1990), 1.

28. *Adenauer: 'Wir haben wirklich etwas geschaffen'*, 1,226.

29. *Adenauer: 'Wir haben wirklich etwas geschaffen'*, 1,227.
30. Ibid.
31. Adenauer, *Erinnerungen, 1955–1959* (Stuttgart: Deutsche Verlags Anstalt, 1967), 296.
32. Compare Hans-Peter Schwarz, *Die Ära Adenauer, 1957–1963* (Stuttgart/Wiesbaden: Deutsche Verlags-Anstalt, 1983), 356–63.
33. A favourable account of Adenauer's reaction to the public debate provoked by his 'artillery statement' is provided in *Adenauer: Der Staatsmann, 1952–1967*, 333–42.
34. Adenauer: *Erinnerungen, 1955–1959*, 297.
35. 'Bericht zur Politischen Lage vor dem Bundesparteivorstand der CDU in Hamburg', in *Konrad Adenauer: Reden 1917–1967*, 353–60, at p. 358.
36. *Adenauer: 'Wir haben wirklich etwas geschaffen'*, 1,234.
37. Ibid. 1,229.
38. Ibid. 1,231.
39. Letter to Blumenfeld, 4 Aug. 1953, in *Adenauer: Briefe, 1951–1953*, 416–17.
40. Quoted in *Adenauer: Der Staatsmann, 1952–1967*, 302.
41. Adenauer: *Erinnerungen, 1959–1963* (Stuttgart: Deutsche Verlags-Anstalt, 1968), 240.
42. *Adenauer: 'Es musste alles neu gemacht werden'*, 1,029.
43. Speech before the *Grandes Conférences Catholiques*, 25 Sept. 1956, in *Adenauer: Reden, 1917–1967*, 327–32, at p. 329.
44. Adenauer's reactions are described in François Seydoux, *Beiderseits des Rheins: Erinnerungen eines französischen Diplomaten* (Frankfurt/Main: Camopus, 1975), 244–5. See also *Adenauer: Der Staatsmann, 1952–1967*, 564–5.
45. Blankenhorn Papers (Bundesarchiv-Koblenz), no. 33b, p. 131, quoted in *Zwischen Abschreckung und Verteidigung*, 10.
46. *Zeitzeugenbeitrag zum 'ABC-Waffenverzicht'*, 1–2 July 1988, Ebenhausen, General a.D. Graf Johann Adolf von Kielmansegg, German NHP-Oral History Project, MS. See also *Adenauer: Der Staatsmann, 1952–1967*, 154–9.
47. Adenauer's report in the Council meeting of the Christian Democratic Party on 11 Oct. 1954, in *Adenauer: 'Wir haben wirklich etwas geschaffen'*, 255).
48. Adenauer: *Erinnerungen, 1953–1955* (Stuttgart: Deutsche Verlags-Anstalt, 1966), 347.
49. *Adenauer: Der Staatsmann, 1952–1967*, 157.
50. Adenauer: *Erinnerungen, 1953–1955*, 347.
51. *Zeitzeugenbefragung zum ABC-Waffenverzicht*.
52. Ibid. 299.
53. Ibid.
54. Note by von Merkatz, 19 Sept. 1956, Archives of the Konrad Adenauer Foundation, von Merkatz papers, quoted ibid. 299.
55. Meeting of Adenauer with Kennedy, 20 Nov. 1961, Adenauer Papers, iii. 89 [top secret], quoted ibid. 707.
56. Ibid.
57. *Adenauer: Der Staatsmann, 1952–1967*, 319–20.
58. This term is widespread in the Western literature and has different connotations in the various countries. Henry Kissinger, for example, defines the 'nuclear dilemma' of the United States primarily as the challenge to resist the refusal to run any risks, and so giving the Soviet rulers a blank cheque: 'we have had to learn that power which is not clearly related to the objectives for which it is to be employed may merely paralyze the will.' (Henry Kissinger, *Nuclear Weapons and Foreign Policy* (New York: Norton and Company, 1969), 4). Uwe Nerlich, reflecting the German perspective, concludes that Germany, on the one hand was heavily dependent on the

Western allies, who alone could guarantee its security, but at the same time had a particular status in the Alliance (Uwe Nerlich, 'Die nuklearen Dilemmas der Bundesrepublik Deutschland', *Europa-Archiv* (Folge 16, 1965), 637–52, at p. 638).

59. For details see *Adenauer: Der Staatsmann, 1952–1967*, 291–5.
60. McGeorge Bundy, *Danger and Survival: Choices About the Bomb in the First Fifty Years* (New York: Random House, 1988), 599–600, at p. 600.
61. Adenauer distrusted the rising star from Bavaria for the latter's controversial standing in public opinion as well as for being a challenger in party politics. Adenauer, for example knew of Strauß's negative remarks about the Chancellor's own political future. Party pressure left Adenauer no other choice than to go ahead with a cabinet reshuffling. For details see *Adenauer: Der Staatsmann, 1952–1967*, 272–3.
62. Blankenhorn an Adenauer, 9.10.1956, Materialien zum Tagebuch, quoted ibid., p. 273.
63. For details see Franz-Josef Strauß, *Die Erinnerungen* (Berlin: Siedler, 1989), 301–8.
64. *Adenauer: 'Wir haben wirlich etwas geschaffen'*, 120.
65. Compare his speech on the Bavarian radio on 3 July 1957, in *Adenauer: Reden, 1917–1967*, 361–4, at pp. 361–2.
66. Notes by von Eckart, Sept. 1956, Konrad Adenauer Foundation, Eckart papers (i-010–019/4), quoted in *Adenauer: Der Staatsmann, 1952–1967*, 321.
67. *Adenauer: Der Staatsmann, 1952–1967*, 14–15.
68. Ibid. 321.
69. Ibid. 321–8.
70. Compare Eckart Conze, 'La cōopération franco-germano-italienne dans le domaine nucléaire dans les anneés 1957–1958: un point de vue allemand', *Revue d'histoire diplomatique,* 1–2 (1990), 115–32, at pp. 120–3.
71. Compare ibid. 118–20 and Collete Barbier: 'Les négociations franco-germano-italiennes en vue de l'établissement d'une coopération militaire nucleaire au cours des années 1956–1958', *Revue d'histoire diplomatique*, 1–2 (1990), 81–113, at pp. 81–5.

   Although the French archives are still closed to researchers, a group of French military historians ('Group d'Etudes français d'Histoire de l'Armement nucléaire' = GREFHAN) have gathered the currently available evidence for the beginning of French nuclear policy, in particular the trilateral co-operation. See for example François Puaux, 'La France, L'Allemagne et L'Atome', *Revue de Défense nationale* (Dec. 1985), 9–18; Maurice Vaísse, 'Aux origines du mémorandum de septembre 1958', *Rélations internationales* (Summer 1989), 256; Georges-Henri Soutou, 'Die Nuklearpolitik der IV Republik', *Vierteljahrshefte für Zeitgeschichte* (Oct. 1989), 605–10.

   German scholarship lags behind. The only studies are those already mentioned by Hans-Peter Schwarz and Eckart Conze. The best first-hand account is provided by Franz-Josef Strauß (*Erinnerungen*, 312–19), of which Conze writes that 'in general they come close to describing correctly the centre points of the bilateral and trilateral aspects of the co-operation' (*La coopération franco-germano-italienne*, 132).

   For the Italian point of view see Leopold Nuti's article ('Le rôle de l'Italie dans les négotiations trilaterales 1957–1958, *Revue d'histoire diplomatique*, 1–2 (1990), 133–56.
72. *Adenauer: Der Staatsmann, 1952–1967*, 394–5; see also Georges-Henri Soutou, 'Les Problèmes de securité dans les rapports franco-allemands de 1956 à 1963', *Relations Internationales*, 58 (Summer 1989), 228–31.
73. For details, see *Les négociations franco-germano-italiennes*, 84–97.

74. *Adenauer: Der Staatsmann, 1952–1967*, 395–6; *Les négociations franc-germano-itali-ennes*, 97–8; *La coopération franco-germano-italienne*, 123–4.

75. For details of the negotiations see *Les négociations franco-germano-italiennes*, 97–111; Franz-Josef Strauß, *Erinnerungen*, 313–19; *Adenauer: Der Staatsmann, 1952–1967*, 397–401.

76. *Adenauer: Der Staatsmann, 1952–1967*, 398–9.

77. *Les négociations franco-germano-italiennes*, 94–7; *Adenauer: Der Staatsmann, 1952–1967*, 399.

78. *La coopération-germano-italienne*, 130–1; *Adenauer: Der Staatsmann, 1952–1967*, 399–400.

79. *Aux origines du mémorandum de 1958*, 256.

80. See the chapter 'Berlin Crisis' in Mark Trachtenberg: *History and Strategy* (Princeton: Princeton University Press, 1991), 188–91.

81. For details compare *Adenauer: Der Staatsmann, 1952–1967*, 576–81.

82. For details see *'Berlin Crisis'*, 169–234 and Michael Beschloss, *The Crisis Years: Kennedy and Khrushchev 1960–1963* (New York: Harper Collins, 1991).

83. For details on 'Live Oak' see Pedlow, *Multinational Contingency Planning During the Second Berlin Crisis: The Live Oak Organization, 1959–1963*.

84. *Adenauer: Der Staatsmann, 1952–1967*, 491–4.

85. For details see Beschloss, *The Crisis Years*, 174–7, 256–61.

86. Ibid. 340–1, *Adenauer: Der Staatsmann, 1952–1967*, 706–7.

87. Ibid. 382–5.

88. Adenauer: *Erinnerungen, 1959–1963*, 243.

Chapter 12

1. For Mueller's own assessment of these events, see his *Quiet Cataclysm: Reflections on the Recent Transformation of World Politics* (New York: HarperCollins, 1995).

2. Rosenberg, Ch. 8 this vol., 177–87.

3. Zubok, Ch. 3 this vol., 39–56.

4. Erdmann, Ch. 5 this vol., 95–6.

5. Rosendorf, Ch. 4 this vol., 64–70.

6. Zhang, Ch. 9 this vol., 194–7.

7. Gordon, Ch. 10 this vol., 218–21.

8. Messemer, Ch. 11 this vol., 236–41. Khrushchev and Kennedy were, at the time, too far from power for them to have recorded any particular views, one way or another, on the atomic bomb 'revolution'.

9. David Holloway, *Stalin and the Bomb: The Soviet Union and Atomic Energy, 1939–1954* (New Haven: Yale University Press, 1994), 295–9.

10. Broscious, Ch. 2 this vol., 15–28.

11. Rosenberg, Ch. 8 this vol., 188.

12. Ibid. 191.

13. Rosendorf, Ch. 4 this vol., 70–5.

14. Zubok and Harrison, Ch. 7 this vol., 141–8.

15. Zhang, Ch. 9 this vol., 197–203.

16. Gordon, Ch. 10 this vol., 223–5.

17. Messemer, Ch. 11 this vol., 241–56.

18. Erdmann, Ch. 5 this vol., 107–8, 115–16.

19. Nash, Ch. 6 this vol., 124–5.
20. John Lewis Gaddis, *We Now Know: Rethinking Cold War History* (New York: Oxford University Press, 1997), 262.
21. Nash, Ch. 6 this vol., 132–3.
22. For an interesting discussion on this subject, see Scott D. Sagan and Kenneth N. Waltz, *The Spread of Nuclear Weapons: A Debate* (New York: Norton, 1995).
23. See Scott D. Sagan, *The Limits of Safety: Organizations, Accidents, and Nuclear Weapons* (Princeton: Princeton University Press, 1993).

Epilogue

1. Winston S. Churchill, *In the Balance: Speeches 1949 and 1950* (Boston: Houghton Mifflin, 1951), 356. For other similar statements by Churchill, see the essay by Jonathan Rosenberg, Ch. 8 this vol.
2. Elsewhere, Gaddis has put it this way: nuclear weapons 'forced . . . the emergence of a new kind of rationality capable of transcending . . . antagonisms that had always, in the past, given rise to great power wars'. John Lewis Gaddis, *We Now Know: Rethinking Cold War History* (New York: Oxford University Press, 1997), 86.
3. Kenneth N. Waltz, Presidential Address, Annual Meeting, American Political Science Association, Washington, Sept. 1988; Rostow quoted in Ernest May, Ch. 1 this vol.
4. John Foster Dulles, *War, Peace and Change* (New York: Harper, 1939), 3–5.
5. In 1953 Ambassador Averell Harriman, certainly no admirer of Stalin, observed to a *Newsweek* interviewer that the Soviet dictator 'was determined, if he could avoid it, never again to go through the horrors of another protracted world war' (16 Mar. 1953, 31). The Soviets presumably gained some special conclusions from their World War I experience as well. In particular, as William Taubman notes, they learned the 'crucial lesson . . . that world war . . . can destroy the Russian regime'. *Stalin's American Policy* (New York: Norton, 1982), 11.
6. Nikita Khrushchev, *Khrushchev Remembers: The Last Testament* (Boston: Little, Brown, 1974), 511, 533, 531, emphasis in the original.
7. Frederic S. Burin, 'The Communist Doctrine of the Inevitability of War', *American Political Science Review*, 57/2 (June 1963), 339. For the argument that the Soviets, contrary to Churchill's confident claims, never contemplated, much less planned for, an offensive against the West, see Stephen E. Ambrose, 'Secrets of the Cold War', *New York Times*, 27 Dec. 1990, A19. Taubman concludes that Stalin sought 'to avert war by playing off one set of capitalist powers against another and to use the same tactic to expand Soviet power and influence without war' (*Stalin's American Policy*, 12).
8. Winston S. Churchill, *The Story of the Malakand Field Force: An Episode of Frontier War* (New York: Norton, 1989), 117.
9. Thus the following exchange, which takes place between two characters in Bernard Shaw's play, *Major Barbara*, is a *non sequitur*: 'Well, the more destructive war becomes, the sooner it will be abolished, eh?' 'Not at all, the more destructive war becomes the more fascinating we find it.' For a further discussion of this phenomenon, concluding that war is natural but not necessary, see John Mueller, *Quiet Cataclysm: Reflections on the Recent Transformation of World Politics* (New York: HarperCollins, 1995), ch. 8.

10. Winston S. Churchill, *A Roving Commission: My Early Life* (New York: Scribner's, 1930), 64–5.

11. Winston S. Churchill, *Amid These Storms: Thoughts and Adventures* (New York: Scribner's, 1932), 246, 248. Churchill reprinted major sections of this essay in *The Gathering Storm* (Boston: Houghton Mifflin, 1948), ch. 3. In a 1932 interview he predicted, cheerily if inaccurately, that 'I do not believe that we shall see another great war in our time,' explaining that 'War, today, is bare—bare of profit and stripped of all its glamour. The old pomp and circumstance are gone. War now is nothing but toil, blood, death, squalor, and lying propaganda.' Martin Gilbert, *Winston Churchill: The Wilderness Years* (Boston: Houghton Mifflin, 1982), 45.

12. Churchill, *Amid These Storms*, 252. It should be pointed out that Adolf Hitler made similar statements in every foreign policy speech of the 1930s. For examples, see Mueller, *Retreat from Doomsday*, 69; for the full panoply, see Adolf Hitler, *The Speeches of Adolf Hitler, April 1922–August 1939* (London: Oxford University Press, 1942), 1,003, 1,016, 1,017, 1,046, 1,047, 1,056, 1,057, 1,061, 1,079, 1,085, 1,090, 1,091, 1,099, 1,105, 1,135, 1,168, 1,177, 1,178, 1,181, 1,184, 1,185, 1,186, 1,187, 1,193, 1,198, 1,199, 1,205, 1,208, 1,211, 1,212, 1,213, 1,214, 1,215, 1,216, 1,218, 1,219, 1,220, 1,229, 1,231, 1,234, 1,235, 1,247, 1,251, 1,254, 1,257, 1,258, 1,260, 1,263, 1,307, 1,308, 1,310, 1,311, 1,314, 1,317, 1,321, 1,328, 1,347, 1,348, 1,351, 1,409, 1,459, 1,502, 1,509, 1,510, 1,511, 1,513, 1,514, 1,526, 1,535, 1,536, 1,545, 1,546, 1,555, 1,561, 1,575, 1,586, 1,587, 1,597, 1,598, 1,602, 1,625, 1,638, 1,640, 1,660, 1,661, 1,667, 1,669, 1,693, 1,697, 1,698, 1,744, 1,745. The difference, of course, was that Hitler was lying—it was, in fact, the biggest lie.

13. William Manchester, *The Last Lion, Winston Spencer Churchill: Alone, 1932–1940* (Boston: Little, Brown, 1989), 29.

14. *Roving Commission*, 65.

15. Kenneth W. Thompson, *Winston Churchill's World View: Statesmanship and Power* (Baton Rouge, La: Louisiana State University Press, 1983), 180.

16. For similar or related conclusions about the essential irrelevance of nuclear weapons, see McGeorge Bundy, 'World Without War, Amen', *Washington Post Book World*, 12 Mar. 1988, 1; Robert L. Holmes, *On War and Morality* (Princeton: Princeton University Press, 1989), 238–48; John A. Vasquez, 'The Deterrence Myth: Nuclear Weapons and the Prevention of Nuclear War', in Charles W. Kegley, Jr. (ed.), *The Long Postwar Peace: Contending Explanations and Projections* (New York: HarperCollins, 1991), 205–23; Evan Luard, *War in International Society* (New Haven: Yale University Press, 1986), 396. Michael Mandelbaum has argued, 'The tanks and artillery of the Second World War, and especially the aircraft that reduced Dresden and Tokyo to rubble might have been terrifying enough by themselves to keep the peace between the United States and the Soviet Union' (*The Nuclear Revolution* (Cambridge: Cambridge University Press, 1981), 21). And George Kennan: 'The atom has simply served to make unavoidably clear what has been true all along since the day of the introduction of the machine-gun and the internal combustion engine into the techniques of warfare—what should have been clear to people during World War I and was not: namely, that modern warfare in the grand manner, pursued by all available means and aimed at the total destruction of the enemy's capacity to resist, is, unless it proceeds very rapidly and successfully, of such general destructiveness that it ceases to be useful as an instrument for the achievement of any coherent political purpose' (*Russia and the West Under Lenin and Stalin* (Boston: Little, Brown, 1961), 391).

17. John Mueller, 'The Bomb's Pretense as Peacemaker', *Wall Street Journal*, 4 June 1985, 32; id., *Retreat from Doomsday: The Obsolescence of Major War* (New York: Basic Books, 1989), 116; id., 'The Essential Irrelevance of Nuclear Weapons: Stability in the Postwar World', *International Security*, 13/2 (Fall 1988), 66–7; id., *Quiet Cataclysm*, 63. At the risk of getting into a contest of duelling metaphors, I should suggest I find misdirection in the proposition of John Gaddis that the distance between conventional and nuclear weapons 'was roughly that between getting a new kind of shoe allowing better traction in tackling the other team's players' and 'developing a device capable of instantly destroying not only the other team but also one's own, to say nothing of the playing field, the spectators, that stadium, the parking lot, and the television rights' (*We Now Know*, 86). Even war enthusiasts like Churchill found that the conventional developments of World War I (much less World War II) had already destroyed the game not to mention the spectators, the stadium, and the parking lot. And, of course, without a game, television will look elsewhere for material.

18. Some essays in this book argue not so much that nuclear weapons necessarily prevented war, but that they inspired Cold War statesmen to be more cautious than they would have been otherwise. Thus, Philip Nash stresses that the Soviet nuclear arsenal 'made Kennedy *additionally* reluctant to risk war' and caused him 'to take war *even more* seriously and made him fear "escalation" *even more* deeply than he would have otherwise'. But, again, it is important as well to consider what those levels were before they were changed. Nuclear weapons may well have 'reinforced an already declining propensity on the part of great powers to fight one another', as John Gaddis puts it (*The United States and the End of the Cold War: Implications, Reconsiderations, Provocations* (New York: Oxford University Press, 1992), 108). Or, as Nash stresses, leaders like Kennedy who were *already* extremely cautious about war, doubtlessly found that nuclear weapons '*reinforced* . . . existing restraint'. But a $10,000 gift also reinforces a millionaire's wealth and a straitjacket reinforces a Quaker's propensity to shun violence. The Churchill counterfactual can only be confirmed if it can be established that any caution increment provided by nuclear weapons was crucial or, to use Gaddis' expression, determining. In my view, it was merely confirming or, to use Nash's word, reinforcing.

Actually, it does not seem that the impact of the bomb was always to enhance caution. In his essay, Vladislav Zubok seems to suggest that, if the atomic bomb had any impact on Stalin, it was to make his foreign policy behaviour, if anything, more belligerent because he was concerned that apparent timorousness about the bomb might tempt the United States dangerously to exploit his 'underdog' status in the atomic arms race. On this point, see also David Holloway, *Stalin and the Bomb: The Soviet Union and Atomic Energy 1939–1956* (New Haven: Yale University Press, 1994), 169. Moreover, Jonathan Rosenberg indicates that Churchill, under the hugely heroic assumption that another world war would inevitably erupt before 1950, suggested in a conversation in 1946 that Russia be attacked with the atomic bomb before it attained a nuclear capacity, a proposition a handful of other people also advocated at the time—inconsequentially, of course. And, as Rosenberg also notes, Churchill was among those who advocated that the Americans rattle their bombs more noisily in their era of atomic monopoly to gain major concessions from the Soviets. However, as Zubok suggests, the US atomic monopoly does not seem to have done much to cramp Stalin's style. Or, as Gaddis has concluded, 'The American monopoly over nuclear weapons, while it lasted, yielded unimpressive results' (*We Now Know*, 111).

19. The official US estimate was that it would have taken 210 bombers loaded with conventional loads to equal the destruction done at Hiroshima by the atomic bomb and 120 bombers at Nagasaki (*Retreat from Doomsday*, 90). Elsewhere, however, Gaddis has argued that 'the vision of future war that Hiroshima burned into *everyone's* mind was *vastly more frightening* than any that had existed before' (*United States and the End of the Cold War*, 109, emphasis added).

20. Gaddis suggests that Georgii Malenkov 'may well have been the first leader anywhere to raise the possibility in public that a war fought with thermonuclear weapons might end world civilization'. But when Malenkov uttered this thought in March 1954 that notion was already quite commonplace in the West as applied to atomic weapons. David Broscious observes that, beginning at least as early as October 1945 Harry Truman repeatedly 'envisioned nuclear weapons as the gateway to Armageddon'. And, according to Neal Rosendorf, two days after Nagasaki, John Foster Dulles had issued and co-authored a public statement asserting that 'the atomic bomb places mankind in deadly peril'. Actually, the same sentiment was quite popular (though certainly not universal) in the 1920s and 1930s when the fear was of gas and aerial bombardment. As noted above, Churchill voiced it. And British Prime Minister Stanley Baldwin was one of many who concurred: 'When the next war comes . . . European civilization [will be] wiped out'; while Sigmund Freud concluded his 1930 book, *Civilization and Its Discontents*, by dramatically expressing his own discontent with the way civilization had developed: 'Men have brought their powers of subduing nature to such a pitch that by using them they could now very easily exterminate one another to the last man' (*Retreat from Doomsday*, p. 59). In some respects, such apocalyptic talk was not so much the cause of anti-war sentiment as its result (on this point, see Mueller, *Quiet Cataclysm*, 146–7), something that may also be true in the atomic age. Hitler, of course, did not accept this proposition though he often voiced agreement with it in public speeches.

21. Of course, in some important respects nuclear weapons continued to be included in what were presumably 'rational' policy considerations. Philip Nash discusses their incorporation into the Kennedy administration's flexible response policies, and he notes that, although 'Kennedy and his advisers never seriously considered nuclear use' during the Berlin crisis of 1961, they did at least 'consider how they would use nuclear weapons should it come to that'. Later administrations, including those of Nixon, Carter, and Reagan, all continued to consider nuclear weapons in developing policy options. According to Annette Messemer, Adenauer was in favour of using nuclear weapons under some circumstances in 1961. And, as Erdmann notes, Eisenhower continued in the thermonuclear age to consider the use of tactical nuclear weapons.

22. Gaddis, *We Now Know*, 86.

23. See Gaddis, *We Now Know*, ch. 9.

24. See, for example, Hartmut Pogge von Strandmann, 'Germany and the Coming of War', in R. J. W. Evans and Hartmut Pogge von Strandmann (eds.), *The Coming of the First World War* (Oxford: Clarendon Press, 1988), 87–123. Indeed, military historian Michael Howard concludes after a lifelong study of the subject that 'The conflicts between states which have usually led to war have normally arisen, not from any irrational and emotive drives, but from almost a superabundance of analytic rationality . . . men have fought during the past two hundred years neither because they are aggressive nor because they are acquisitive animals, but because they are reasoning ones.' And: 'Wars begin by conscious and reasoned decisions based on the

calculation, made by *both* parties, that they can achieve more by going to war than by remaining at peace' (Howard, *The Causes of Wars and Other Essays*, 2nd edn. (Cambridge, Mass.: Harvard University Press, 1984), 14–15, 22). On this issue, see also Geoffrey Blainey, *The Causes of Wars* (New York: Free Press, 1973), 127, ch. 9; Bruce Bueno de Mesquita, *The War Trap* (New Haven: Yale University Press, 1981), ch. 2; Luard, *War in International Society*, ch. 5.

25. Henry Kissinger, *White House Years* (Boston: Little, Brown, 1979), 885. In his extensive study of actual and potential nuclear accidents, cited by Gaddis, Scott Sagan finds the 'probability of a serious nuclear weapons accident' to be 'extremely low' and 'escalation from a single accident to an accidental nuclear war' to be 'even more unlikely'. And when he tries to discover cases in history in which it might be said consequential accidents happened, he comes up with an extremely short list, and one dominated not by a true accident, but by an unauthorized deliberate act—the Japanese invasion of Manchuria in 1931. Sagan does assess a large number of 'dangerous incidents with nuclear weapons and command and control systems', several occurring during the Cuban missile crisis no less. But the overall effect of the study can be to generate support for the validity of Kissinger's observation. Wars are not caused by glitches, kinks, machines, or organizational clutter; they are caused by real decisions made by real people (Scott D. Sagan, *The Limits of Safety: Organizations, Accidents, and Nuclear Weapons* (Princeton: Princeton University Press, 1993), 3, 163, 251). Indeed in its way, Sagan's study seems to support the notion suggested in *Retreat from Doomsday* (152–6) that the Cuban missile crisis was far from war.

26. Indeed, many of the anxieties would have substantially been there regardless: after all, concerns about a non-nuclear World War III would have consumed a great deal of energy and anxiety and planning as well—as did concerns about World War II in many quarters in the 1920s and 1930s.

27. *Retreat from Doomsday*, 116.

28. However, the US demand was that *offensive* arms, whether nuclear or not, should not be implanted in Cuba. Therefore, it is still possible that Khrushchev could have created a crisis by putting offensive conventional arms on the island as a potential deterrent. As Gaddis notes, historians are giving increasing credence to the notion that Khrushchev was primarily seeking to defend Cuba with his move, as opposed to attempting to redress the strategic nuclear imbalance (*We Now Know*, ch. 9).

29. 'Essential Irrelevance', 69; *Retreat from Doomsday*, 218–19; *Quiet Cataclysm*, 75.

30. See John Mueller, *Policy and Opinion in the Gulf War* (Chicago: University of Chicago Press, 1994), 142–3.

31. In a book on the issue Zhang notes that those arguing against Mao cited the country's economic weakness, the danger that the Chinese people would quickly become disenchanted, the lack of heavy industry in China, and the military difficulties of fighting in a long, narrow peninsula without air or naval support. Fear of the American bomb does not figure in the discussion in this source (Shu Guang Zhang, *Mao's Military Romanticism: China and the Korean War, 1950–1953* (Lawrence, Kan.: University Press of Kansas, 1995), 80).

32. See also *Retreat from Doomsday*, 114.

33. See also *Retreat from Doomsday*, 127; Gaddis, *We Now Know*, 107–10.

34. Gaddis, *We Now Know*, p. 92.

35. Some lesser, more atmospheric impacts might also be explored. Zubok and Harrison amass some evidence to suggest that nuclear weapons speeded up Khrushchev's abandonment of certain ideological dogmas. I do not find their case

fully convincing (and, of course, it hardly confirms the Churchill counterfactual even if it were), but it does show that systematic historical research can potentially enlighten us on the validity of counterfactuals. Similarly, Zhang notes that Mao used the American atomic threat to help push forward his disastrous Great Leap Forward. However, I strongly suspect that he would have been able to put the programme across even without that threat, or that he could have used a threat of conventional (that is, non-nuclear) invasion by the USA almost as productively. He also suggests that Mao's atomic programme, and perhaps even more his atomic rhetoric, speeded up the Sino-Soviet split, though, of course, there were many other contributing factors as well. And David Holloway notes that the Soviet tactic of trying to demonstrate that it could not be intimidated by the atomic bomb 'appears to have led to a quicker breakdown of cooperation than Stalin might have envisaged' before Hiroshima (*Stalin and the Bomb*, 169).

36. *Causes of Wars*, p. 9.
37. Thomas Jefferson, *Democracy* (New York: Appleton-Century, 1939), 262–3.
38. Roland Stromberg, *Redemption by War: The Intellectuals and 1914* (Lawrence, Kan.: Regents Press of Kansas, 1982), 1–2. For example, Oliver Wendell Holmes told the Harvard graduating class in 1895 that war's message was 'divine', John Ruskin found war to be the 'foundation of all the higher virtues and faculties of men'; Alexis de Tocqueville concluded that 'war almost always enlarges the mind of a people and raises their character'; Emile Zola considered war to be 'life itself'; Igor Stravinsky believed that war was 'necessary for human progress'. For a discussion, see Mueller, *Retreat from Doomsday*, ch. 2.
39. Norman Angell was one of the important idea entrepreneurs in this movement. In books like *The Great Illusion* Angell did not so much argue that major war was 'obsolete' but rather that it had become futile from an economic standpoint. To be successful in his anti-war agitation, therefore, he needed to get people not only to accept that notion, but also to accept the proposition that economic improvement should be a primary value—more important, for example, than heroism, religious purity, honour, nationalism, etc. Other idea entrepreneurs in the pre-1914 anti-war movement opposed war on moral, aesthetic, or class-conflict grounds. For references and a discussion, see Mueller, *Retreat from Doomsday*, ch. 1. On the rise of the highly consequential notion that economic development should be a primary value, see John Mueller, *Democracy, Capitalism and Ralph's Pretty Good Grocery* (Princeton: Princeton University Press, forthcoming).
40. As Nathan Rosenberg and L. E. Birdzell stress: 'If we take the long view of human history and judge the economic lives of our ancestors by modern standards, it is a story of almost unrelieved wretchedness. The typical human society has given only a small number of people a humane existence, while the great majority have lived in abysmal squalor. We are led to forget the dominating misery of other times in part by the grace of literature, poetry, romance, and legend, which celebrate those who lived well and forget those who lived in the silence of poverty. The eras of misery have been mythologized and may even be remembered as golden ages of pastoral simplicity. They were not' (*How the West Grew Rich* (New York: Basic Books, 1986), 3). In the nineteenth century for the first time in history, this ancient pattern substantially and unambiguously improved for what we now call the developed world.

The experience of the peaceful nineteenth century in Europe suggests that, while trade and interdependence may not lead inexorably to peace, peace leads to, or at any rate facilitates, trade and economic growth. That is, peace ought to be seen not as a dependent, but rather as an independent, variable in such considerations. Thus the growing economic unity of Europe is a consequence of continental peace, not its cause.

41. For an extended discussion of this change, see *Quiet Cataclysm*, ch. 9. Ernest May applies the concept, or metaphor, of 'learning' when discussing such changes as the rise of war aversion. While that metaphor has some valuable resonances, it seems to me that it is more promising to stress promotion and persuasion when trying to account for what Robert Dahl has called the 'historical movement of ideas' (*Polyarchy* (New Haven: Yale University Press, 1971), 182). The learning metaphor can be misleading because it often seems to imply betterment and gradualness, and because it may suggest that an idea, once ingested, cannot be undone. It is not so much, I think, that people 'learn' ideas like war aversion; rather they become persuaded to accept them. At any given time there are always a huge array of ideas around, and only a few of these catch on. Some may be of lengthy pedigree while others may be quite new and original. People sort through this market of ideas and prove receptive to some while remaining immune to others. Their receptivity may not be very predictable, but it is surely not random. Like the writers of the essays in this book, I find the specific actions of individuals often to be historically significant, and I think idea entrepreneurs have been extremely important in the historical movement of ideas. However, the process by which an idea becomes accepted can be quite complicated, and it does not follow that the growth in acceptance of an idea derives simply from the manipulative cleverness of its advocates: if concentrated efforts at promotion and persuasion alone could assure the success of a product, we'd all be driving Edsels. Moreover, success need not be permanent: even a great triumph of promotion and persuasion may prove short-lived as tastes change or competing ideas gain favour. On these issues, see Mueller, *Quiet Cataclysm*, chs. 9, 10; id., *Democracy, Capitalism*; Ethan A. Nadelmann, 'Global Prohibition Regimes: The Evolution of Norms in International Society', *International Organization*, 44/4 (Autumn 1990), 479–526; Neta C. Crawford, 'Decolonization as an International Norm: The Evolution of Practices, Arguments, and Beliefs', in Laura W. Reed and Carl Kaysen (eds.), *Emerging Norms of Justified Intervention* (Cambridge, Mass.: American Academy of Arts and Sciences, 1993), 37–61.

42. The point is developed more fully in John Mueller, 'Is War Still Becoming Obsolete?', paper delivered at American Political Science Association Convention, Washington, 30 Oct. 1991. John Mearsheimer argues that 'if any war could have convinced Europeans to forswear conventional war, it should have been World War I, with its vast casualties' ('Back to the Future: Instability in Europe After the Cold War', *International Security*, 15/1 (Summer 1990), 30. Although, as suggested, I do not think the casualty count alone caused the change, a consequence of World War I was that the vast majority of Europeans *did* forswear war—at least war of that sort. Indeed, one of the reasons Hitler was so successful for so long was that his opponents assumed that, since it was so obvious that no one could want another war, he must be serious when he continuously professed his yearning for peace.

43. For a discussion that does not seem to consider these distinctions, see Marc Trachtenberg, 'The Future of War', *Diplomatic History*, 15/2 (Spring 1991), 287–90.

44. Michael Howard, *The Lessons of History* (New Haven: Yale University Press, 1991), 175. In reviewing *Retreat from Doomsday*, Howard suggested to prudent readers that they check that their 'air-raid shelter is in good repair' (*New York Times Sunday Book Review*, 30 Apr. 1989, 14). In his 1991 book, however, he essentially suggested that

readers need not, perhaps, overdo their repair efforts, concluding that it is 'quite possible that war in the sense of major, organised armed conflict between highly developed societies may not recur, and that a stable framework for international order will become firmly established' (p. 176). And he chiefly derives this conclusion from a set of observations about ideas—about the way people in the developed world have changed their attitudes toward war. See also John Keegan, *A History of Warfare* (New York: Knopf, 1993), 59.

45. See also 'Containment and the Decline of the Soviet Empire: Some Tentative Reflections on the End of the World as We Know It', paper given at the National Convention of the International Studies Association, Anaheim, Calif., 25–9 Mar. 1986. In 1985 and 1986 I tried to get this paper published, in various versions, in *Foreign Policy*, *National Interest*, *Washington Post*, *New York Times*, *Wall Street Journal*, *Los Angeles Times*, and *New Republic* to no avail. I then gave up and blended the argument into *Retreat from Doomsday*—even as Gorbachev dismembered the Cold War as fast as I could write about it.

46. In his concluding essay, John Gaddis contends that when *Retreat from Doomsday* was published its thesis about the obsolescence of major war 'was relatively uncontroversial'. That is not the way I remember it. The book came out at the end of a decade in which fears of major war reached huge proportions. For years, the media was filled with detailed and doom-laden stories about the imminence and the horrors of nuclear war, and there were massive anti-war protests in Europe and the United States. As late as 1987, the American public volunteered 'the fear of war' in polls as the single most important problem facing the country (for data, see Mueller, *Policy and Opinion*, 212).

47. Paul Schroeder, 'Does Murphy's Law Apply to History?', *Wilson Quarterly* (New Year's, 1985), 88. Jack Levy calculates that 'the probability of no war occurring between the handful of leading states' for such a long time to be about .005. 'Long Cycles, Hegemonic Transitions, and the Long Peace', in Charles W. Kegley, Jr. (ed.), *The Long Postwar Peace: Contending Explanations and Projections* (New York: HarperCollins, 1991), 147.

48. For the argument that nuclear weapons were irrelevant to the ending of the Cold War, see John Mueller, 'The Escalating Irrelevance of Nuclear Weapons', in T. V. Paul, Richard J. Harknett, and James J. Wirtz (eds.), *The Absolute Weapon Revisited: Nuclear Arms and the Emerging International Order* (Ann Arbor: University of Michigan Press, 1998), 78–9.

49. See Mueller, *Retreat from Doomsday*, 236–40.

INDEX